Contents

	Acknowledgements	iv
	Introduction	v
1	The molecules of life	1
2	Enzymes	33
3	Cells	49
4	Cell division	81
5	DNA and protein synthesis	97
6	Genetics	127
7	Evolution	147
8	Photosynthesis and plant nutrition	271
9	Respiration	191
10	Transport in mammals	205
11	Transport in plants	235
12	Gas exchange	249
13	Heterotrophic nutrition	271
14	The mammalian nervous system	297
15	Regulation and control	323
16	Support and movement	359
17	Reproduction in animals	377
18	Reproduction in plants	397
19	Ecology	419
20	Human effects on the environments	447
21	Infectious disease and immunity	477
22	Classification	497
Appendix 1	Some basic chemistry	528
Appendix 2	Units	540
	Index	542

Photo acknowledgements

t, top; m, middle; b, bottom; l, left; r, right

1.7 t, 1.13, 3.2, 3.6, 3.8, 3.12, 3.17 l, 3.21, 3.22, 3.23, 5.11, 8.2 (p.172), 8.2 (p.173), 10.2, 10.14 b, 11.1, 11.3 r, 14.10, 16.4, 16.9 l, 16.10, 18.14, 22.18 l Biophoto Associates; 1.7 b, 3.15 tr, 3.20 Dr Don Fawcett/Science Photo Library (SPL); 1.16 J.C. Revy/SPL; 3.5 Geoff Tompkinson/SPL; 3.7 Dr Tom Ford, Royal Holloway College; 3.15 ml, 5.9 Dr Gopal Murti/SPL; 3.15 mr, 4.3 Biophoto Associates/SPL; 3.16 Fawcett, Hirokawa, Heuser/SPL; 3.17 r Francis Leroy/SPL; 3.18 K.R. Porter/SPL; 3.19 Dr David Patterson/SPL; 4.5, 4.10 Dr Peter Brandham, Royal Botanic Gardens, Kew; 5.10, 6.2 CNRI/SPL; 5.14 l James Holmes/Cellmark Diagnostics/SPL; 5.14 m Dr John Olds, National Haemoglobinopathy Reference Service, Oxford; 5.14 r David Parker/SPL; 5.18 Professor Stefan Buczacki; 5.20 Philippe Plailly/Eurelios/SPL; 5.21 Cellmark Diagnostics; 5.22, 8.2 (p.173) inset, 18.8, 18.12 Dr Jeremy Burgess/SPL; 5.23 tl, 19.10tr Garden/Wildlife Matters; 5.23 br Deni Bown/Oxford Scientific Films; 6.1 t G.I. Bernard/NHPA; 6.1 b Steve Hopkin/Planet Earth Pictures; 6.6 Michael Leach/NHPA; 7.1 National Library of Medicine/SPL; 7.6 Mary Evans Picture Library; 7.7 t David Jesse Chesney/Planet Earth Pictures; 7.7 b Pete Oxford/Natural Science Photos; 7.9 John Durham/SPL; 7.12 l, 7.15 r, 7.19, 11.4 bl, 11.4 mr, 11.4 br, 13.14, 22.11 (p.509) l Heather Angel; 7.12 r John Mason/Ardea; 7.13, 7.14 l Philippe Plailly/SPL; 7.14 r Dr Zosimo Huaman, Genetic Resources, International Potato Center, Peru; 7.15 l Nigel J. Dennis/NHPA; 8.3 Dr Kenneth R. Miller/SPL; 10.11, 22.7 Simon Fraser/SPL; 10.14 t, 13.5, 14.2 b, 16.7, 17.3 Prof. P. Motta/ Dept. of Anatomy, 'La Sapienza' University Rome/SPL; 11.3 l Andrew Syred (1993) Microscopix; 11.4 tl Martin Land/Natural Science Photos; 11.4 tr R.P.B Erasmus/Natural Science Photos; 12.8, 14.1, 16.8 r CNRI/SPL; 12.9 Mike Wyndham Picture Collection; 12.14, 14.2 t Manfred Kage/SPL; 13.3 Alfred Pasieka/SPL; 13.6, 22.6 David Scharf/SPL; 13.12, 22.4 t Andrew Syred/SPL; 15.5 Astrid & Hans-Frieder Michler/SPL; 16.5 Larry Mulvehill/SPL; 16.8 l Eric Grave/SPL; 16.9 r SPL; 16.12 Don Fawcett/SPL; 17.1, 22.17 l, 22.22 br Sinclair Stammers/SPL; 17.5 Prof. P. Motta et al./SPL; 18.7 t Stephen Dalton/NHPA; 18.7 b Anthony Bannister/NHPA; 18.10 t Alan Weaving/Ardea; 18.10 b David Thompson/Oxford Scientific Films; 19.3 l John Mead/SPL; 19.3 r, 20.19 tr Jorgen Schytte/Still Pictures; 19.10 tl J. Birks/ICCE; 19.10 bl David Woodfall/NHPA; 19.10 mr, 19.10 br P. Morris; 19.15 tl GSF Picture Library; 19.15 tr S.R.J. Woodell; 19.15 bl Ecoscene/Corbett; 19.15 br David Middleton/NHPA; 19.17 Alan Watson/Still Pictures; 20.3 Crown copyright; 20.5 t, 20.5 b NASA GSFC/SPL; 20.7 Geoff Tompkinson/SPL; 20.13 Vanessa Vick/SPL; 20.15 Telegraph Colour Library; 20.17 David Barron/Earthwatch Europe; 20.18 John R. Bracegirdle/Planet Earth; 20.19 tl Still Pictures; 20.19 bl Hartmut Schwarzbach/Still Pictures; 20.19 br Mark Edwards/Still Pictures; 20.20 Dustin Becker; 20.22 David Whitaker/Crown copyright; 20.23, 20.24 BBONT; 21.5 Prof. P. Motta, G Machiarelli, S.A. Nottola/SPL; 21.6 Alastair MacEwen/Oxford Scientific Films; 22.2 t Secchi-Lecaque/Roussel-Uclaf/CNRI/SPL; 22.2 bl Dr Tony Brain/SPL; 22.2 br, 22.19 Georgette Douwma/Planet Earth; 22.3, 22.4 b Peter Parks/Oxford Scientific Films; 22.5 John Lythgoe/Planet Earth; 22.8 l Mark Mattock/Planet Earth; 22.8 r G. Jones; 22.10 t Laurie Campbell/NHPA; 22.10 b Scott McKinley/ Planet Earth; 22.11 (p.508) Niall Benvie/BBC Natural History Unit Picture Library; 22.11 (p.509) r N.A. Callow/NHPA; 22.12 Tsuneo Nakamura/Oxford Scientific Films; 22.16 Jeff Rotman/BBC Natural History Unit Picture Library; 22.17 r Ken Lucas/Planet Earth; 22.18 r James D. Watt/Planet Earth; 22.20 tl Sinclair Stammers/BBC Natural History Unit Picture Library; 22.20 tr Kurt Amsler/Planet Earth; 22.20 bl Martin Dohrn/SPL; 22.21 Ken Lucas/Planet Earth; 22.22 tl Adam Powell/Footprints; 22.22 tr Steve Hopkins/Planet Earth; 22.23 l, 22.24 (p.524) tl Claude Nuridsany & Marie Perennou/SPL; 22.23 r Dr Morley Read/SPL; 22.24 (p.523) tl Doug Perrine/SPL; 22.24 (p.523) mr Mike Laverack/Planet Earth; 22.24 (p.523) bl Pete Atkinson/Planet Earth; 22.24 (p.524) br Jonathan Scott/Planet Earth; 22.24 (p.524) mr Mary Clay/SPL; A1.2 Driscoll, Youngquist & Baldeschweiler, Caltech/SPL.

Examination questions

The examination questions have been reproduced by kind permission of the Associated Examining Board, London Examinations (a division of Edexcel Foundation), the Northern Examinations and Assessment Board and the University of Cambridge Local Examinations Syndicate.

Introduction

This book is for any student of Biology at advanced level, for example A level, AS level, IB or AICE. We have assumed that you have already studied Biology or Science to a standard equivalent to GCSE, IGCSE or O level.

Anyone studying Biology at advanced level needs an understanding of basic Chemistry. If you are not sure about your knowledge of Chemistry then you may find Appendix 1 (pages 528 to 539) helpful.

There are many different advanced level Biology syllabuses. All of them, however, contain the same core material, and you will find all of this in this book. Many syllabuses also have a choice of options, which differ in their content and their titles. Do not think that, just because you cannot find a Chapter with the same heading as the option that you are studying, there is nothing in this book about that option. For example, you may be studying an option which covers microbiology and biotechnology. You will find relevant material in various parts of the book, such as Chapter 5 (about genetic engineering, for example) and Chapter 2 (about the use of enzymes in industry). So do make use of the index to look for topics which you need for your particular option.

Some of the text and illustrations in the book are in Boxes. The material in the Boxes is there either because it is a little more difficult than the rest of that topic, or because it is quite likely that you do not really need it for your particular syllabus – perhaps because it is only specified by one syllabus, or because it is not on any syllabus at all (we have just included it because we thought you might find it interesting!). So, on first reading through a topic, you may choose to miss out the Boxes, perhaps going back to them later. If you find a topic difficult to understand, then it may be best for you to avoid the 'difficult' Boxes completely; you may be better off putting all your efforts into understanding the basics as thoroughly as you can, rather than making yourself confused by attempting too much.

We hope that you will enjoy using the illustrations to help you to understand particular topics. Quite often, there are explanations and pieces of information on the illustrations which do not appear in the text, so do look carefully at them as you read. In many of the illustrations, the colours are 'coded' – that is , we have used a particular colour to represent a type of object or material consistently throughout the book.

Authors' acknowledgements

We owe considerable thanks to very many people for help in writing and producing this book, and we can only name just a few of them here, Several people have provided us with information about their own particular research. In particular, Peter Grant of Princetown University gave us help with information about his research into beak depth in Darwin's finches; Denis Murphy of Cambridge Laboratory, Norwich, gave us information about the development of genetically modified oilseed rape varieties; Dr Dustin Becker of Indiana University provided us with much information, and some photographs, of the forest conservation project in Ecuador with which she is involved; and Yvonne Boyd gave us up-to-date information about loci on the human X chromosome. A number of people have gone to particular trouble to provide us with photographs, especially Dr John Olds of the National Haemoglobinopathy Reference Service, Oxford; Dr Peter Brandham, of the Royal Botanic Gardens, Kew, for photographs and information about mitosis in *Aloe*; and the staff at BBONT in Oxford, who not only provided photographs but also a great deal of information about the history of, and management plan for, the conservation area at Asham Meads.

Especial thanks are also due to Dr Roger Sayle of Glaxo Research and Development for help in using the excellent molecular modelling program, RasMol, which he was instrumental in developing and which is available free from the Internet. Dr Jonathan Goodman of the Department of Chemistry at Cambridge University also provided useful RasMol files.

We would also like to thank the many people who read and provided detailed comments on early drafts of each chapter. These included teachers and also specialists in each academic field we have attempted to cover.

But our greatest thanks of all must go to Sue Kearsey for her tireless, always patient, knowledgeable work on the text and illustrations, and to Barbara Ellis for her thoughtful proofreading.

1 The molecules of life

As biology has advanced through the twentieth century, we have increased our knowledge of the structure and functions of the molecules from which living things are made. Most branches of biology – especially biochemistry and physiology – now look in detail at these molecules and how they interact, to explain what happens inside living organisms.

In this chapter you will learn about the structure and functions of five of the most important classes of molecules which make up the bodies of living organisms: water, carbohydrates, proteins, lipids and nucleic acids.

WATER

1.1 Dipoles

Fig. 1.1 shows the structure of a water molecule. It is formed from two hydrogen atoms and one oxygen atom which are covalently bonded together.

A covalent bond is a shared pair of electrons. In a water molecule the electrons are shared unevenly. The oxygen atom tends to attract the electrons away from the hydrogen atoms. As electrons have a negative charge, this gives the oxygen part of the molecule a small negative charge, written δ^-. The hydrogen atoms, on the other hand, have a small positive charge, which is written as δ^+. (δ is the Greek letter delta.)

This uneven distribution of charge on the molecule is called a **dipole**. The dipolar nature of water molecules gives water many properties that are very unusual and which are extremely important for living things. If there were no dipoles on water molecules there would be no life on Earth! The next four sections explain why this is so.

1.2 Thermal properties of water

'Thermal' means to do with heat. The dipoles of water molecules affect the way in which water responds to the gain or loss of heat.

Molecules in a liquid move around quite freely, but there are attractive forces between the molecules which stop them escaping completely from each other. They stay together, forming a substance which fills its container and

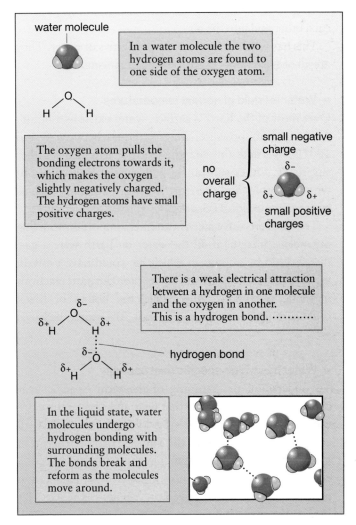

Fig. 1.1 The structure of water molecules.

can flow but does not escape into the air. If you heat the liquid, you increase the energy of the molecules. Once this energy is high enough, the molecules can escape from each other and move rapidly in random directions. The liquid becomes a gas.

The forces attracting water molecules to each other are especially strong. These attractive forces arise because of the dipoles on the water molecules. The oxygen atoms, with their small negative charge, are attracted to the hydrogen atoms, with their small positive charge, on other water molecules. The attractive force is called a **dipole–dipole interaction**, or a **hydrogen bond**.

Compared with a covalent bond, a hydrogen bond is a very weak bond. However, it is strong enough that water molecules need to be given a lot of energy before they can escape from one another. To change liquid water into water vapour, you have to transfer a lot of heat energy into it, to give the molecules sufficient energy to escape from each other and into the air.

This has several effects on the properties of water. They are all of great importance to living organisms.

● **Water is liquid at normal temperatures**

Over most of the Earth's surface, water exists as a liquid. At normal air pressure, water is liquid between 0 and 100 °C. We take this for granted, but it is really rather surprising. Other substances with similar molecules but without dipoles and therefore hydrogen bonding, such as hydrogen sulphide, H_2S, are gases at these temperatures.

This property of water is extremely important to living organisms. Imagine if all the water on Earth were a gas: there would be no seas in which life could have evolved; water could not be used as a solvent for chemical reactions in living organisms; what could the bodies of living organisms, which are usually at least 70% water, be based on?

● **Water has a high specific heat capacity**

To understand the meaning of the term 'specific heat capacity' you must realise that heat and temperature are not the same thing. 'Heat' is a kind of energy; like all energy, you can measure the amount of heat energy in joules. When you heat something, you are transferring energy into it. 'Temperature', on the other hand, is a measure of the kinetic (movement) energy of the particles in a substance. (If you are studying physics, you will discover that temperature cannot really be defined that simply – but this is a reasonable working explanation for now.)

When you heat water the attractive forces between the water molecules mean that you have to transfer in, or out, a lot of heat energy to have much effect on their kinetic energy. You have to transfer in a lot of heat to raise the temperature significantly. In fact, you will need to put in 4.2×10^3 joules of heat energy to raise the temperature of one kilogram of water by one degree Celsius. We say that the **specific heat capacity** of water is $4.2 \times 10^3 \mathrm{~J\,kg^{-1}\,°C^{-1}}$. This is a high value. For example, ethanol (alcohol) has a specific heat capacity of $2.4 \times 10^3 \mathrm{~J\,kg^{-1}\,°C^{-1}}$, while the specific heat capacity of benzene is $1.5 \times 10^3 \mathrm{~J\,kg^{-1}\,°C^{-1}}$.

What does this mean to living organisms? Firstly, it is important because the bodies of living organisms are largely made of water, and therefore do not change temperature readily. You, for example, have a specific heat capacity of about $4.0 \times 10^3 \mathrm{~J\,kg^{-1}\,°C^{-1}}$. Your body temperature is probably about 37 °C. If you stand in the middle of a desert on a hot day, where the air temperature is 42 °C, then heat energy will transfer into your body. It *will* raise your temperature – but nowhere near as quickly as if you were made of alcohol.

Secondly, the high specific heat capacity of water is very important to aquatic organisms (those which live in water). Large bodies of water, such as the sea and lakes, do not readily change their temperature when heat transfers into or out of them. Their temperature stays quite stable. In a climate such as that of Britain, the temperature of the sea will increase in summer and decrease in winter, but the resulting temperature changes are relatively slow and small. For example, air temperatures in south-west Britain in a particular year may range between about –10 °C and 30 °C, with quite rapid ups and downs. Sea temperatures off the coast of south-west Britain, however, will probably only vary between 7 °C in winter and 16 °C in summer, and the changes will take place very gradually. This means that water is a very stable environment for living organisms – much more so than on land.

● **Water has a high latent heat of vaporisation**

When liquid pure water is heated to 100 °C, it boils because the water molecules gain sufficient kinetic energy to escape into the air as water vapour. While this is happening, the temperature of the water does not rise – all the heat energy that is going into it is being used to provide the energy for the liquid to become a gas rather than raising the temperature. The heat energy that is being used to produce this change is called the **latent heat of vaporisation**. ('Latent' means 'hidden' – it was given this name because the heat seems to disappear without causing a change in temperature.) Water does not have to be at 100 °C, of course, to evaporate – think of what happens to a puddle on a sunny day! Even at lower temperatures, individual water molecules will gain sufficient energy to escape as water vapour, but they need a lot of heat energy to do this.

Water has a particularly high latent heat of evaporation, once again because a lot of energy is needed to break the hydrogen bonds between the molecules. Many living organisms use this feature of water as a cooling mechanism. For example, humans sweat. The liquid water in sweat absorbs heat energy from the skin, providing enough energy to turn the water into water vapour. The evaporation of liquid water from the cell walls of mesophyll cells in plant leaves has the same effect, and is important in stopping the leaves' temperature from rising too high on a hot day.

1.3 Density

Water is a fairly dense liquid. Density is a measure of the mass of a certain volume of a substance and is usually measured in grams per cubic centimetre, $g\,cm^{-3}$. The density of pure water is $1.0\,g\,cm^{-3}$, and the density of sea water is a little more than this at about $1.026\,g\,cm^{-3}$. This compares with a density of $0.79\,g\,cm^{-3}$ for ethanol.

The body tissues of most living organisms have average densities which are very slightly more than the density of water, so living organisms tend to sink in water. There are two solutions to this problem for aquatic organisms which do not live on the bottom. Many fish and plankton (tiny organisms which float in the upper layers of the sea or lakes) make swimming movements which keep them afloat. Others use 'buoyancy aids', such as a gas-filled swim bladder in some fish or a pocket of gas in a *Nautilus*'s shell, which reduce their average density to below that of water.

If the density of water was much lower, then it would become even more difficult for living organisms to stay afloat in it. It is not suggested that you try swimming in ethanol, but you would find it extremely difficult.

There is another way in which the density of water is unusual. In most substances, the density decreases as they are heated. This is because heating causes expansion so that there are fewer particles – and therefore less mass – in a given space. Water does this too, between temperatures of 4 °C and 100 °C. However, it behaves very oddly between 0 °C and 4 °C, where its density *increases* as the temperature rises.

How is this important to living organisms? It is extremely important to aquatic organisms that live in lakes or ponds which tend to freeze in winter (Fig. 1.2).

First, imagine what would happen if water behaved like everything else, with its maximum density at 0 °C. As the air above the pond gets colder it causes the temperature of the water to drop. The coldest water is nearest the surface where it is directly in contact with the cold air. As it cools it gets more dense, so it sinks. This brings slightly warmer water to the surface where it cools, gets more dense and sinks. This process would continue, with the water getting colder and colder. Eventually, some of it would get to 0 °C, and sink to the bottom. The pond would freeze from the bottom up.

As you have probably noticed, this is not what happens! It would be very awkward for fish and other aquatic organisms if it did. Instead, ponds freeze from the top down. This is because the maximum density of water is not at 0 °C, but at 4 °C. The process described above does take place to start with, as the coldest water drops to the bottom of the pond. But once the surface layers start to get colder than 4 °C, they are actually less dense than the water below them, so they stay on the surface rather than sinking. They get colder and colder and eventually freeze. The ice forms on top of the water, not at the bottom.

This leaves liquid water – albeit rather cold –

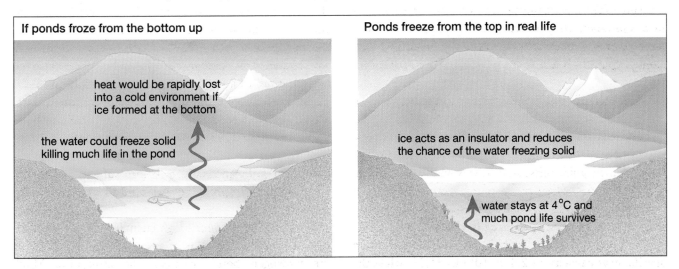

Fig. 1.2 Why ponds freeze from the top downwards.

underneath a layer of ice, in which organisms can live. Moreover, the layer of ice slows down the rate at which heat is lost from the water underneath it because ice is a good insulator.

1.4 Viscosity

Viscosity is a measure of how resistant a liquid is to flowing. The lower the viscosity, the more easily the liquid flows. Water is not really unusual here – it has a viscosity that is a little lower than that of ethanol, for example.

The ease with which water flows is important in the transport systems of living organisms. Blood, for example, is mostly water, and it is important that it can flow easily through vessels. If too much water is lost from the body then the viscosity of blood increases, it flows more slowly and transport becomes less efficient. Plants, too, rely on the flow of water in xylem and phloem vessels to transport substances around their bodies.

Aquatic organisms swimming in water have to push through it. The force they have to use is related to the water's viscosity. If water were more viscous, much more energy would have to be used. Imagine swimming through treacle, which has a very high viscosity.

1.5 Solvent properties

Water is an excellent solvent for ionic substances (such as sodium chloride) and many covalent compounds (such as many of the organic substances in living organisms). It is sometimes called the 'universal solvent', although this is not quite true as some substances, such as fats, do not dissolve in water. It is the dipoles of water molecules that make it such a good solvent.

Fig. 1.3 shows how an ionic compound dissolves in water. The small positive charges on the hydrogen atoms in the water molecule attract negatively charged ions, while the small negative charge on the oxygen atom

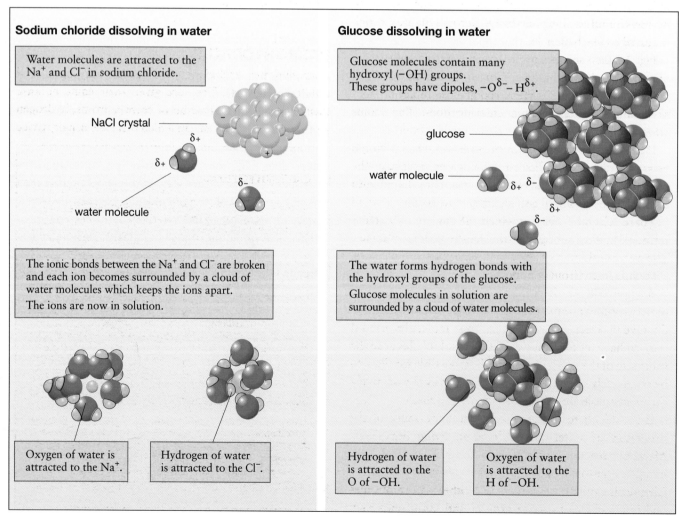

Sodium chloride dissolving in water

Water molecules are attracted to the Na$^+$ and Cl$^-$ in sodium chloride.

NaCl crystal

$\delta+$

$\delta+$

$\delta-$

water molecule

The ionic bonds between the Na$^+$ and Cl$^-$ are broken and each ion becomes surrounded by a cloud of water molecules which keeps the ions apart.
The ions are now in solution.

Oxygen of water is attracted to the Na$^+$.

Hydrogen of water is attracted to the Cl$^-$.

Glucose dissolving in water

Glucose molecules contain many hydroxyl (−OH) groups.
These groups have dipoles, $-O^{\delta-}-H^{\delta+}$.

glucose

water molecule

$\delta+$ $\delta-$

$\delta+$

$\delta-$

The water forms hydrogen bonds with the hydroxyl groups of the glucose.
Glucose molecules in solution are surrounded by a cloud of water molecules.

Hydrogen of water is attracted to the O of −OH.

Oxygen of water is attracted to the H of −OH.

Fig. 1.3 Water as a solvent.

attracts positively charged ions. The positive and negative ions in the ionic compound are therefore separated from each other. If you stir sodium chloride (common salt) into water, it seems to disappear – the ions become spread out amongst the water molecules.

So, when sodium chloride dissolves in water, it is effectively no longer sodium chloride, but a mixture of sodium ions, chloride ions and water molecules. (It is very important that you understand this, because it is vital for understanding many topics that you will meet in your Advanced Biology course.) The sodium ions and chloride ions are free to move independently – for example to react with other substances or to diffuse across membranes. In most of our body fluids we have many different ions dissolved in water, including sodium, chloride, potassium, calcium, carbonate and many others. You will meet many instances where the freedom of these ions to move around independently of one another is extremely important to living processes, for example in the transmission of nervous impulses along nerves and across synapses, which is described in Chapter 14.

Fig. 1.3 also shows how a covalent compound such as glucose dissolves in water. (You will read more about glucose in section 1.7.) Here, the glucose molecule does not come apart as sodium chloride does. The atoms remain firmly held together by their covalent bonds.

However, glucose molecules have —OH (hydroxyl) groups with dipoles. Just as in a water molecule, the oxygen atom attracts the electrons which are shared with the hydrogen atoms more strongly and so has a small negative charge. These oxygen atoms are therefore attracted to the hydrogen atoms on the water molecules. The water molecules cluster around the glucose molecules, separating them from one another.

As you will see later in this chapter, many organic molecules have groups with dipoles and therefore they will dissolve in water. However, very large molecules, even if they do have dipoles, may not be very soluble because the sheer size of the molecules makes it impossible for them to be completely separated from each other by the relatively tiny water molecules which cluster around them.

It is difficult to overemphasise the importance of the properties of water as a solvent in living organisms. Metabolic reactions (chemical reactions that take place in living organisms) normally take place in solution. Chemicals can only react with each other if the molecules and ions are free to move around and bump into each other. If they were in solid form, they could not do this.

Thus all metabolic reactions, and therefore all of life, is dependent on the solvent properties of water.

These solvent properties also mean that water can be used to transport substances within organisms. Blood plasma, which is mostly water, transports a wide range of substances in solution, as does phloem sap in plants. Urea, which is the main nitrogenous excretory product of mammals, is transported out of the body in urine, in solution in water.

1.6 Reactions involving water

As well as providing an environment in which metabolic reactions can happen, water itself takes part as a reactant in many reactions. You will meet several of these throughout your Biology course. Two important ones are **photosynthesis**, where water is involved in the light-dependent reaction (described in Section 8.3), and **digestion**, where water takes part in hydrolysis reactions in the alimentary canal.

CARBOHYDRATES

Carbohydrates include sugars, starch, glycogen and cellulose (Fig. 1.4). They are given their name because their molecules are made up of carbon atoms, hydrogen atoms and oxygen atoms, in which there are usually twice

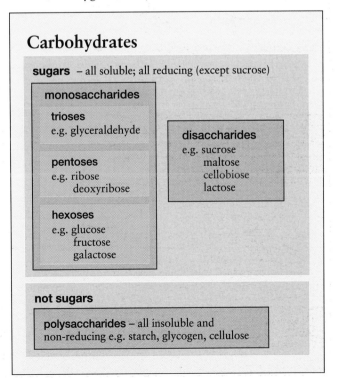

Carbohydrates

sugars – all soluble; all reducing (except sucrose)

monosaccharides

trioses
e.g. glyceraldehyde

pentoses
e.g. ribose
deoxyribose

hexoses
e.g. glucose
fructose
galactose

disaccharides
e.g. sucrose
maltose
cellobiose
lactose

not sugars

polysaccharides – all insoluble and non-reducing e.g. starch, glycogen, cellulose

Fig. 1.4 Carbohydrates.

as many hydrogen atoms as oxygen atoms – just as in water. The ratio of these atoms is 1C : 2H : 1O, or very close to this.

1.7 Sugars – monosaccharides

Sugars are carbohydrates with relatively small molecules. They taste sweet and are soluble in water. Sugars include **monosaccharides**, which are made of a single 'sugar unit', and **disaccharides**, which are made of two units bonded together.

Fig. 1.5 shows the structure of the monosaccharide sugar **glucose**. Glucose has six carbon atoms and has the formula $C_6H_{12}O_6$. Because it has six carbon atoms, it is a **hexose** sugar. Table 1.1 lists the most important monosaccharides in living organisms.

The glucose molecules in Fig. 1.5 are shown in their ring form, with the carbon atoms numbered in a clockwise direction. This ring can break apart between carbon atom 1 and the oxygen atom in the ring to form a straight chain

molecule. In solution, glucose exists in a mixture of ring and chain forms, with individual molecules flipping back and forth between the two shapes but spending most of the time in the ring form.

The ring form itself can exist in two varieties, depending on the way the hydrogen and hydroxyl groups attached to carbon 1 are orientated. The two forms are called α **glucose** and β **glucose**. This tiny difference might seem insignificant, but it has great importance when many glucose molecules link together to form starch or cellulose.

Glucose has many functions in living organisms. Its main use is as a fuel. Glucose molecules are oxidised to release energy in the process of respiration. This process is described in detail in Chapter 9. In mammals, glucose is the form in which carbohydrates are transported around the body, and blood normally contains about 80 mg of glucose per 100 cm³. Glucose molecules are also important building blocks for making larger carbohydrate molecules, such as starch, glycogen and cellulose.

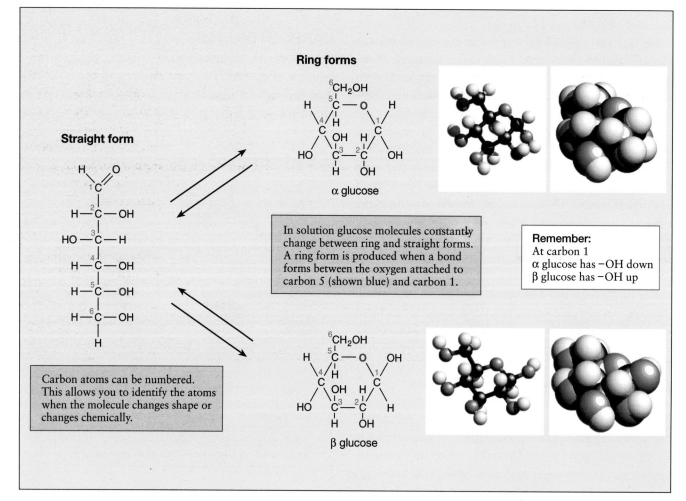

Fig. 1.5 The structure of glucose.

Type of sugar	Name	Molecular formula	Displayed formula	Functions
triose	glyceraldehyde	$C_3H_6O_3$		an intermediate compound in respiration (page 192) and photosynthesis (page 183)
pentose	ribose	$C_5H_{10}O_5$		a component of RNA (page 27), of ATP (page 30) and of NAD (page 30)
	deoxyribose	$C_5H_{10}O_4$		a component of DNA (page 29)
hexose	glucose	$C_6H_{12}O_6$		an energy source, which is broken down in respiration (page 192); the monomer from which starch and cellulose are made (page 9)
	fructose	$C_6H_{12}O_6$		an energy source, like glucose; with glucose a component of sucrose

Table 1.1 Some biologically important monosaccharides.

Box 1.1 Aldehydes and ketones

All sugars contain the **C=O** group. This is called a **carbonyl group.**

The carbonyl group may be part of either an **aldehyde** (when it is joined to at least one hydrogen atom):

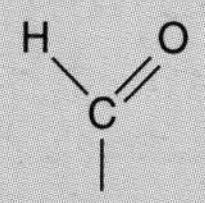

or a **ketone** (when it is between carbon atoms):

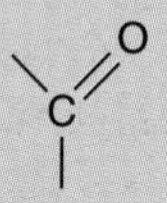

Sugars that are aldehydes are called **aldose** sugars. Sugars that are ketones are called **ketose** sugars.

Glucose is an aldose sugar:

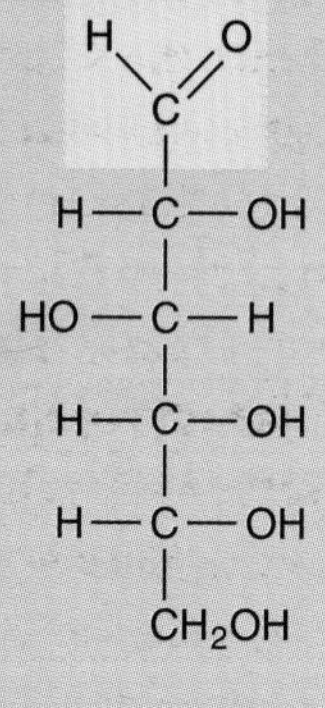

Fructose is a ketose sugar:

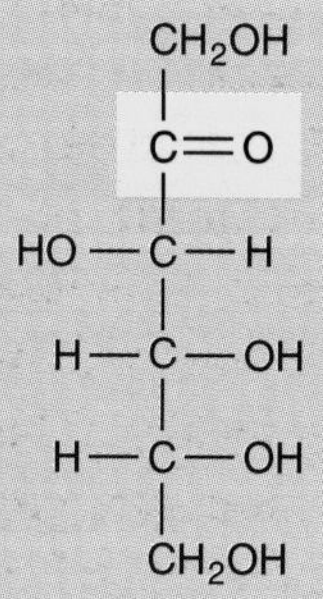

Aldehydes are **reducing agents**. This means that aldose sugars are reducing agents, and are called **reducing sugars**. When a reducing agent reduces another compound, the reducing agent is oxidised. Ketose sugars are not reducing agents but they react to form reducing agents in the alkaline conditions used to test for reducing sugars. Hence ketoses, such as fructose, are not as strong reducing agents as aldoses, such as glucose.

The test which you will use for reducing sugars, the **Benedict's test**, relies on this property. Benedict's reagent contains copper(II) ions, which give a blue colour to the Benedict's solution. When heated with a reducing sugar, the copper(II) ions are reduced to copper(I) ions, and an orange-red precipitate of copper(I) oxide is formed:

$$\text{reducing sugar (oxidised)} + Cu^{2+} \rightarrow \text{oxidised sugar} + Cu^{+} \text{(reduced)}$$

As all monosaccharides are either aldoses or ketoses, they all give a positive test with Benedict's solution. Most disaccharides, too, are reducing sugars. Sucrose, however, is an exception; it is a **non-reducing sugar**. This is because the reducing groups on the glucose and fructose molecules are involved in the glycosidic bond and so are not free to react. To use the Benedict's test to test for sucrose, you first have to break it apart into glucose and fructose, which you can do by heating it with hydrochloric acid. Having freed the carbonyl groups, you can then test for these by boiling with Benedict's solution.

1.8 Sugars – disaccharides

Disaccharides are carbohydrates whose molecules are made of two monosaccharides linked together. Fig. 1.6 shows the structure of the disaccharide **maltose**, which is formed from two α glucose molecules.

The bond that links the two glucoses is called a **glycosidic bond**. It is a covalent bond and therefore strong. The reaction between the two glucose molecules to form maltose is a **condensation reaction**. (It is given this name because water is released as the reaction takes place. The name originated because, when this kind of reaction takes place in glass containers, water may condense on the sides of the glassware. However, the name 'condensation reaction' is now also used by chemists to describe similar reactions in which small molecules other than water are released.)

If the reaction happens in reverse, that is when a disaccharide breaks into two monosaccharide molecules, it is called a **hydrolysis reaction**. 'Hydro' means 'water' and 'lysis' means 'splitting'. In this reaction water provides hydrogen and a hydroxyl group, which allows the glycosidic bond to break.

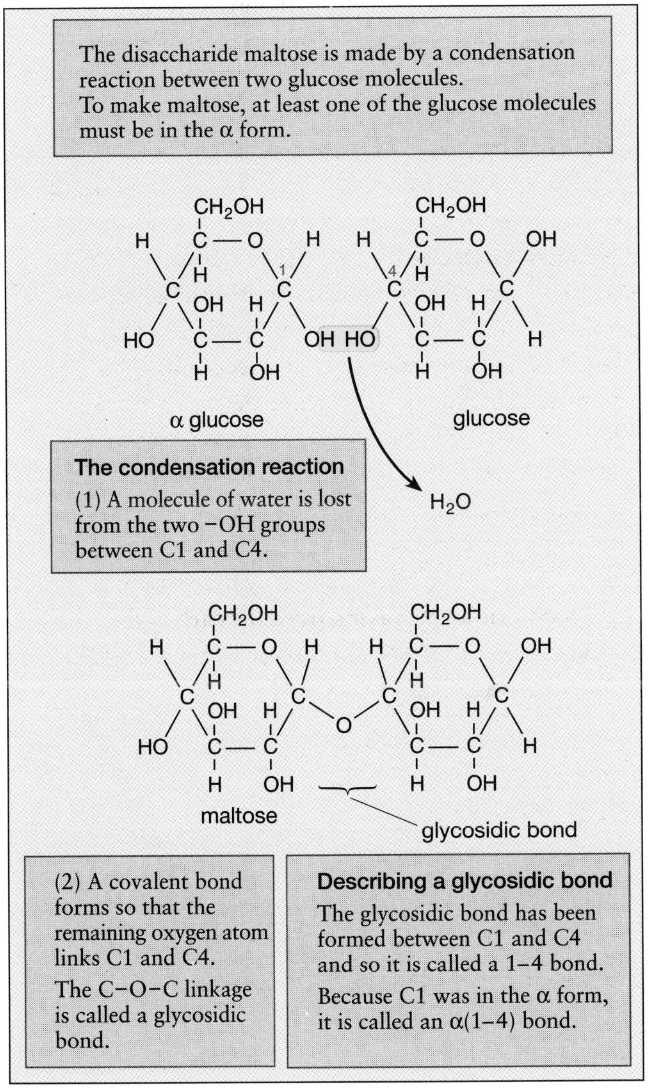

Many different disaccharides exist. There are many possible different pairings of monosaccharides, each pairing producing a different disaccharide. It even matters whether the monosaccharides are in their α or β forms. Two β glucoses linked together, for example, do not form maltose but a sugar called **cellobiose**. Table 1.2 lists some of the more important disaccharides in living organisms.

1.9 Polysaccharides

Polysaccharides are substances whose molecules are polymers made of many sugar units linked together. The sugar units are the monomers from which the polymer is built up. 'Poly' simply means 'many', and polysaccharide molecules can contain thousands of sugar units. The sugars are linked by glycosidic bonds.

A polysaccharide found in the human body is **glycogen**. Plants contain a similar polysaccharide, **starch**. Both glycogen and starch are made of many α glucose molecules linked together. Fig. 1.7 shows the structure of glycogen and starch molecules. Both glycogen and starch are used as energy stores. As they are such large molecules, they are not soluble. ('Soluble starch' is starch whose molecules have been broken into short lengths so that it becomes partly soluble in water.) The glycogen or starch forms solid grains inside cells. In this form it does not interfere with metabolic reactions taking place in the cell, nor does it affect the water potential (Section 3.26) of the cell. Starch tends to form large grains which you can see easily with a light microscope; they are often inside chloroplasts. Glycogen forms smaller grains that are visible in electron micrographs of liver cells.

The commonest polysaccharide in the world is **cellulose** (Fig. 1.8). Its molecules are made of long chains of β glucose units linked together. Cellulose is a structural material. Molecules of cellulose are straight and lie side by side, each molecule forming hydrogen bonds with those around it. Many cellulose molecules group together to form microfibrils, which form the cell walls of plants. Cellulose is not as easy to digest as starch, because the links between β glucose units are less easy to break than those between α glucose units. This, together with its great tensile strength, makes cellulose an excellent material for protecting and supporting plant cells.

The disaccharide maltose is made by a condensation reaction between two glucose molecules.
To make maltose, at least one of the glucose molecules must be in the α form.

α glucose   glucose

The condensation reaction

(1) A molecule of water is lost from the two −OH groups between C1 and C4.

H_2O

maltose

glycosidic bond

(2) A covalent bond forms so that the remaining oxygen atom links C1 and C4.
The C−O−C linkage is called a glycosidic bond.

Describing a glycosidic bond

The glycosidic bond has been formed between C1 and C4 and so it is called a 1–4 bond.
Because C1 was in the α form, it is called an α(1–4) bond.

Fig. 1.6 A glycosidic bond.

Name	Units from which it is made	Displayed formula	Functions
maltose	α glucose and glucose	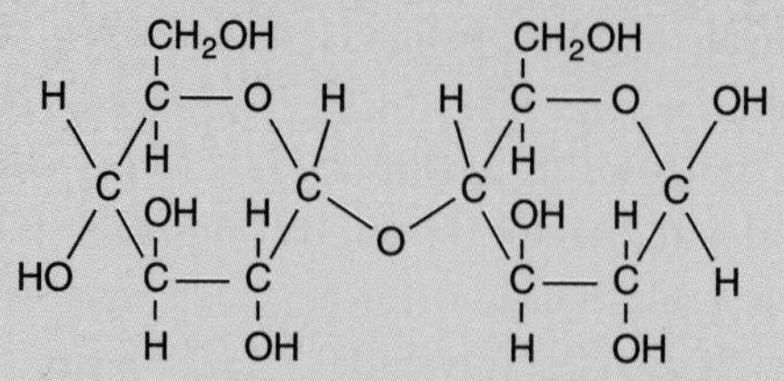	an intermediate in the digestion of starch to glucose; the sugar which gives malt its characteristic taste
sucrose	α glucose and fructose	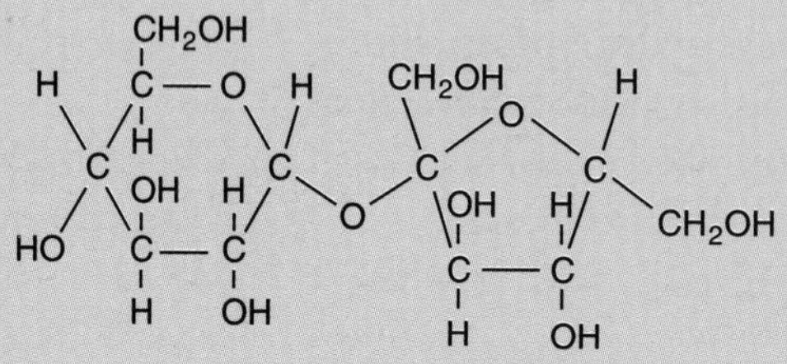	the form in which carbohydrates are transported in the phloem tubes of plants; a storage carbohydrate in many plants, including sugar cane and sugar beet, from which we obtain sugar
lactose	β galactose and glucose	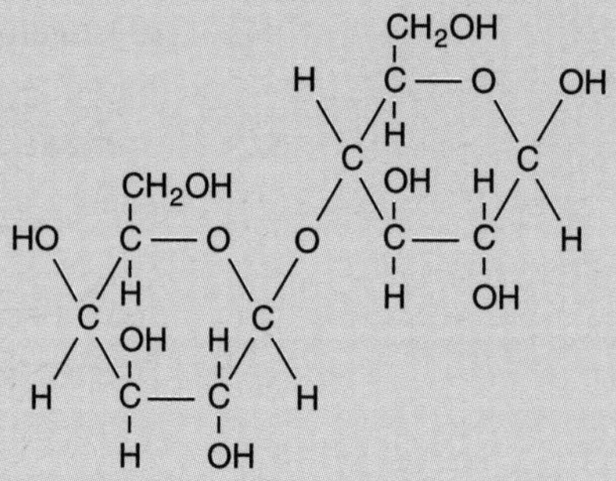	the sugar in milk, where it provides an energy source for young mammals

Table 1.2 Some biologically important disaccharides.

Q1 Copy and complete the table below, giving the chemical nature and one function of the carbohydrates, glycogen, ribose and sucrose. The information for starch has been given for you as an example.

Carbohydrate	Chemical nature	One function
starch	polysaccharide	carbohydrate storage in plants
glycogen		
ribose		
sucrose		

London 1995

(*Total 6 marks*)

Starch, which is found in plants, is a mixture of two polysaccharides, amylose and amylopectin. Both of them are polymers of α glucose. Both have a basic spiral shape, part of which is shown below. Amylopectin is only different from amylose in being a branched molecule.

Glycogen, which is found in animals, is similar to amylopectin, though it has less tendency to spiral.

Light micrograph of isolated starch grains (×1000)

Part of a starch molecule

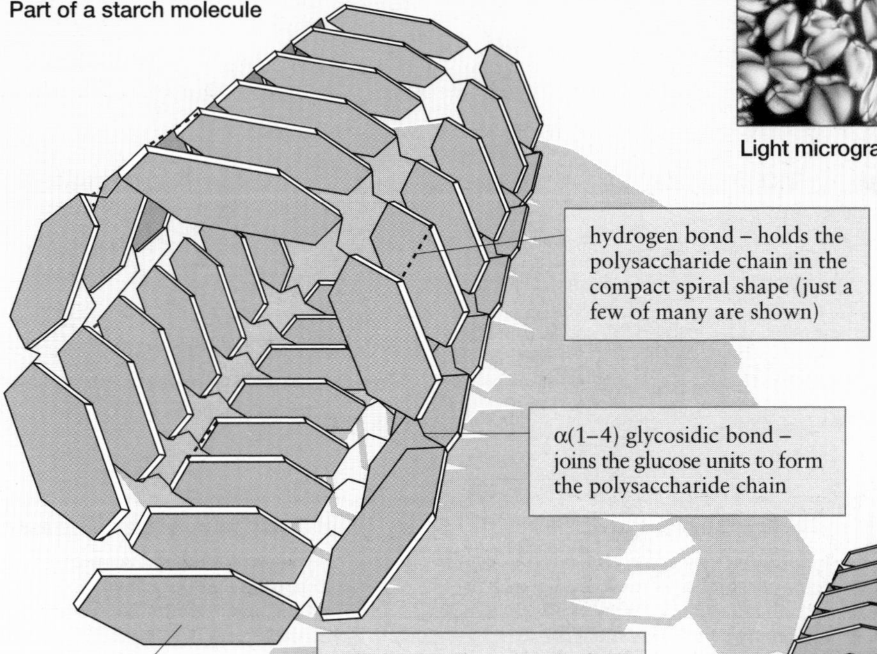

hydrogen bond – holds the polysaccharide chain in the compact spiral shape (just a few of many are shown)

α(1–4) glycosidic bond – joins the glucose units to form the polysaccharide chain

one glucose unit

The basic polysaccharide chain of starch consists of thousands of glucose molecules joined by glycosidic bonds.

Starch test

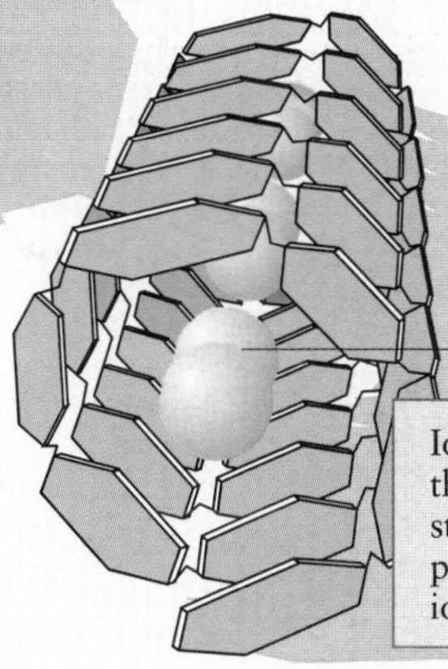

iodine molecule

Iodine molecules can fit into the hole in the middle of a starch molecule and this produces the blue colour of iodine–starch mixtures.

Part of a glycogen molecule

Glycogen and amylopectin are branched molecules. Branching reduces the tendency for spiralling. Glycogen is particularly rich in branches.

Amylopectin and glycogen molecules contain a few thousand glucose units.

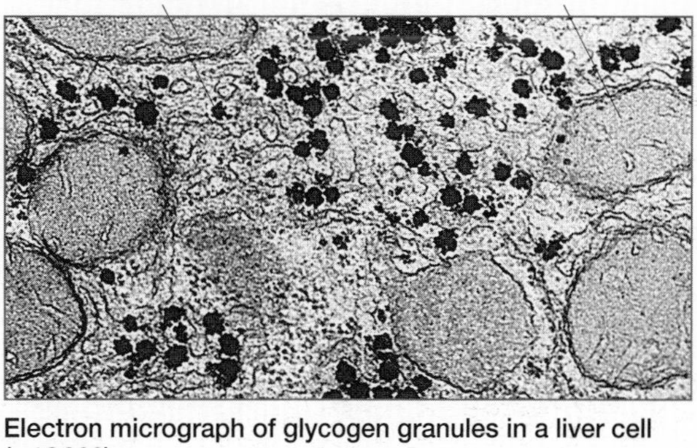

glycogen granule   mitochondrion

Electron micrograph of glycogen granules in a liver cell (×18 000)

Fig. 1.7 Starch and glycogen.

Part of two cellulose molecules

shown as simplified structural formulae

glucose rotated in relation to neighbours

stabilising and strengthening H bond within the molecule

stabilising and strengthening H bond between molecules

Glucose rotation

Every other glucose unit is rotated. This rotation and the β(1–4) link makes the molecule straight and not wound into a helix like glycogen and starch.

H bonds inside the molecule

Hydrogen bonding between rotated glucose units stabilises the chain, keeping the cellulose molecules straight and stopping them twisting. This strengthens the molecule.

H bonds between the molecules

Hydrogen bonding between molecules stabilises their arrangement within microfibrils, further strengthening them.

Part of two cellulose molecules

shown as ball-and-stick and as space-filling molecular models

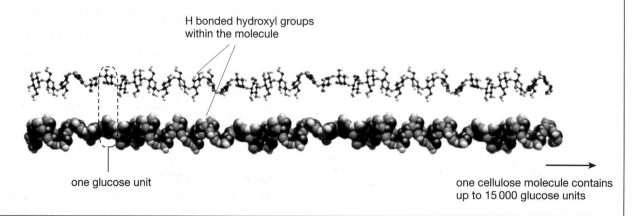

H bonded hydroxyl groups within the molecule

one glucose unit

one cellulose molecule contains up to 15 000 glucose units

Fig. 1.8 The structure of cellulose molecules.

PROTEINS

1.10 Amino acids

Proteins are polymers whose molecules are made from many amino acid molecules linked together. Proteins have a very wide range of different functions in living organisms, and you will meet proteins in many different areas of your biology course. Some examples are haemoglobin, enzymes, antibodies – all of which are involved in metabolic reactions – and also structural proteins such as collagen and keratin.

Fig. 1.9 shows the structure of an amino acid. There are 20 different amino acids naturally incorporated into proteins, plus others which can be made in the laboratory. All amino acids have an **amino group**, —NH_2, and a **carboxyl group**, —COOH. They differ in their R groups. You do not need to learn these, but you should recognise the name of an amino acid when you see it (not too difficult, because they usually end in 'ine'), and you may like to look at Fig. 1.11 to get an idea of just how much these R groups can vary.

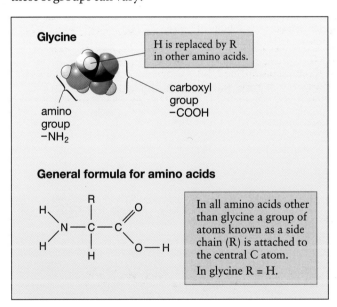

Fig. 1.9 Amino acid structure.

1.11 Polypeptides

Amino acids can link together to form polypeptides or proteins. There is no sharp dividing line between a polypeptide and a protein, and the two words are often used interchangeably. However, the term 'polypeptide' is usually used to describe just a single chain of amino acids, whereas a 'protein' *may* be made up of several polypeptide molecules.

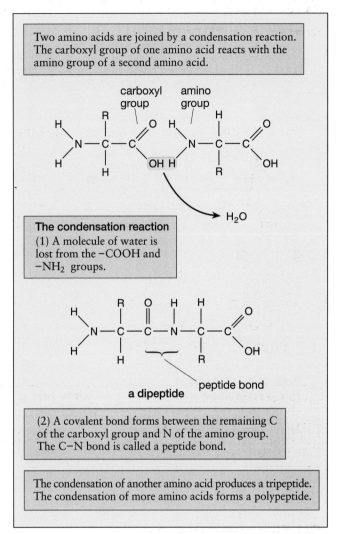

Fig. 1.10 A peptide bond.

Fig. 1.10 shows how a **peptide bond** forms between two amino acids. As in the formation of a glycosidic bond between two sugars, this reaction involves the removal of water and so is a condensation reaction. In reverse it is a hydrolysis reaction. The new molecule which is formed, containing two amino acids, is a **dipeptide**. If more and more amino acids are added to the chain, then a **polypeptide** molecule is formed.

1.12 Primary structure

You will remember that there are 20 different amino acids used for making polypeptides. These can be linked together in any order to make a protein. However, this order is of tremendous importance – just changing one amino acid in the sequence can completely change the behaviour of the protein. You can read about an example of this on page 109. The number and sequence of amino

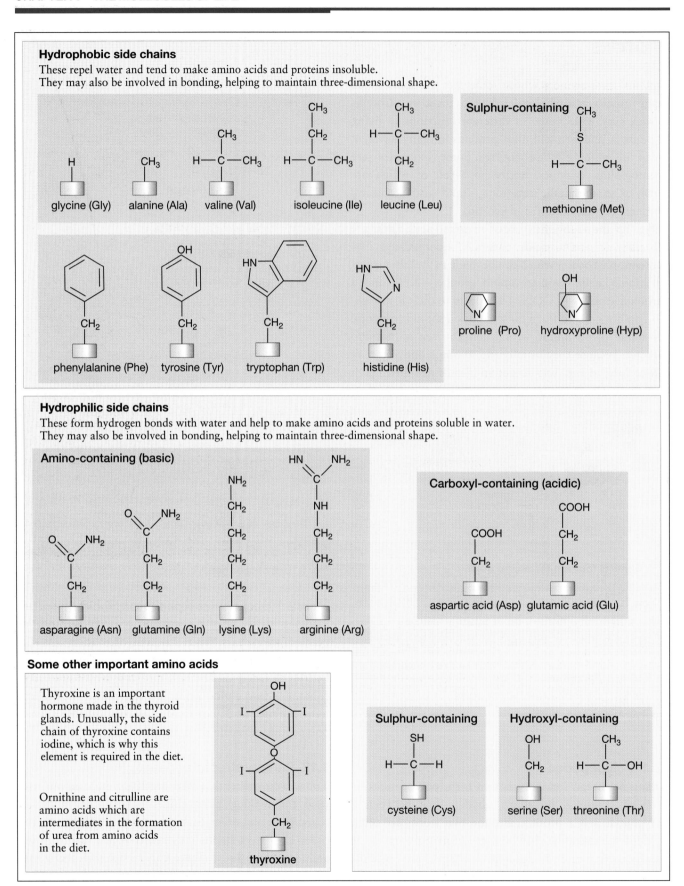

Fig. 1.11 Side chains of amino acids commonly found in proteins.

Box 1.2 Amino acids in solution

In solution amino acids ionise. Both the amino group and the carboxyl group can ionise:

$$-NH_2 + H^+ \rightleftharpoons -NH_3^+$$

$$-COOH \rightleftharpoons -COO^- + H^+$$

You can see that the carboxyl group can produce hydrogen ions and so act as an acid. The amino group can remove hydrogen ions from the solution and so act as a base. An amino acid molecule therefore has both acidic and basic properties. It is said to be **amphoteric**.

In a solution of pH 7, most amino acids carry both ionised amino groups and ionised carboxyl groups. In a solution with a pH below 7, in which there are many H^+ ions, it becomes more difficult for the carboxyl group to lose a H^+ ion. In a solution with a pH above 7, in which there are few H^+ ions, it becomes more difficult for the amine group to pick up an H^+ ion. The degree of ionisation of these two groups therefore varies with pH.

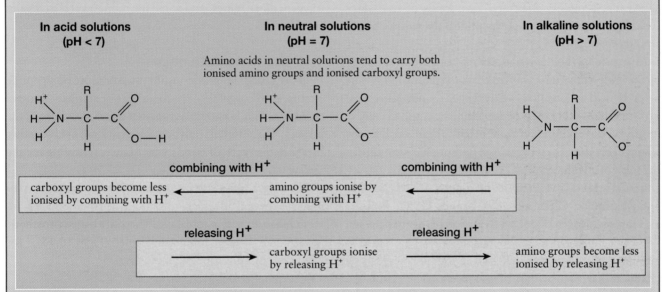

In a protein containing hundreds of amino acids, only one amino acid at one end of the chain has an exposed amino group and one at the other end an exposed carboxyl group. So these groups may not have a very significant effect on the molecule. However, if you look at Fig. 1.11, you will see that many R groups also contain amino and carboxyl groups, which behave in just the same way as those on isolated amino acids. They, too, are affected by pH, and you will see in Section 1.16 that this can affect the whole shape and function of the protein.

acids in a polypeptide or protein is called its **primary structure.** The primary structure of a protein determines its overall shape and therefore its function. The primary structure of insulin is shown in Fig. 1.12.

Proteins are made on the ribosomes (Section 3.8) of a cell. There the amino acids are linked by peptide bonds one by one and gradually build up a complete polypeptide molecule. The sequence in which the amino acids are linked together is determined by the DNA in the nucleus of a cell. This is described in Sections 5.2 and 5.3.

1.13 Secondary structure

The chain of amino acids which makes up a polypeptide does not remain perfectly straight – it twists into a shape called the **secondary structure.** Two kinds of secondary structure are common in polypeptides: the α helix and β strand (Fig. 1.12).

In an α **helix,** the chain twists into a regular spiral, rather like a curly cable on a hairdryer or telephone cord. The helix is held in position by hydrogen bonds (Box 1.3) between the —NH group of one amino acid and the —CO group of the amino acid four places ahead of it in the chain. Most proteins have at least part of their structure in the form of an α helix.

In a β **strand,** the chain is not tightly coiled, but lies almost straight. Often, several β strands lie side by side, and form hydrogen bonds with each other, again between —NH groups of one amino acid and —CO groups of another, but this time between *different* polypeptide chains rather than within the same one. The result is a group of polypeptide chains lying side by side, called a β **sheet.** Once again, this can form part of the structure of many proteins. It is the main secondary structure in the protein called **fibroin,** which forms **silk.**

1.14 Tertiary structure

The tertiary structure is the overall three-dimensional structure of a polypeptide or protein. The amino acid chain, perhaps already in the form of an α helix or β strand, coils again to form a very precise shape which is characteristic of that protein. The shape is held firmly in position by bonds between amino acids that lie close to each other in the three-dimensional structure. These bonds include **hydrogen bonds, ionic bonds, disulphide bonds, van der Waals forces** and **hydrophobic interactions.** These are all described in Box 1.3.

In some proteins the tertiary structure forms a long supercoiled chain, usually with a very regular repeating pattern. These proteins are called **fibrous proteins.** They are used for producing various structures in organisms. Some examples include **keratin** (Fig. 1.13) which forms hair, horn, nails and part of the upper layers of skin; **collagen,** also found in skin, which is an important component of bone, and forms tendons; and **fibrin,** whose fibres trap red blood cells and so form blood clots. Fibrous proteins are insoluble and are usually metabolically inactive.

In other proteins, the tertiary structure is more spherical, forming a **globular protein.** Globular proteins are usually soluble, and are involved in metabolic reactions inside and outside cells. Some examples include **haemoglobin,** the red pigment in blood which transports oxygen; all **enzymes;** and some hormones, such as **insulin** (Fig. 1.12).

1.15 Quaternary structure

In many proteins, such as insulin, two or more polypeptide chains curl together to form the complete protein molecule. This is known as the **quaternary structure** of the protein. The different polypeptide chains are held together by the same types of bonds which are responsible for the tertiary structure.

The term quaternary structure is also sometimes used to describe the way in which non-amino acid components are included in a protein molecule. These are called **prosthetic groups.** A haemoglobin molecule (Fig. 10.15), for example, contains four haem groups.

Q2 'Globular proteins tend to be metabolically active, whilst fibrous proteins usually have structural roles.' With reference to at least two globular proteins and two fibrous proteins, discuss this statement. (You will need to use the index to obtain information from later chapters in this book.)

Protein structure

Primary structure

Primary structure is the sequence of amino acids in a polypeptide chain.
Insulin is made of two polypeptide chains, the A chain and the B chain.
Two lists of amino acids, therefore, describe the primary structure of insulin.
The A chain starts with glycine joined to isoleucine then valine, as shown below.

Primary structure of A chain

Gly Ile Val Glu Gln Cys Cys Thr Ser Ile Cys Ser Leu Tyr Gln Leu Glu Asn Tyr Cys Asn

Primary structure of B chain

Phe Val Asn Gln His Leu Cys Gly Ser His Leu Val Glu Ala Leu Tyr Leu Val Cys Gly Glu Arg Gly Phe Phe Tyr Thr Pro Lys Thr

Secondary structure

Secondary structure is a repeating three-dimensional structure of the polypeptide backbone.

There are two common repeating structures, the α helix and β strand. However, parts of polypeptides may have neither α helix nor β strand secondary structure.

The A chain of insulin starts with an α helix secondary structure. Near the end of the B chain is a section of β strand.

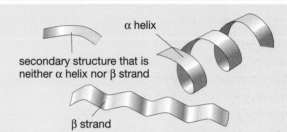

α helix

secondary structure that is neither α helix nor β strand

β strand

Tertiary structure

Tertiary structure is the next level of folding of the chain. It is the three-dimensional shape of a polypeptide chain.

Ribbon models of proteins show both secondary and tertiary structure of proteins.

tertiary and secondary structure of the A chain of insulin

tertiary and secondary structure of the B chain of insulin

Quaternary structure

In many proteins two or more polypeptide chains are bonded to make a complete molecule.

Quaternary structure is the arrangement of the polypeptide chains making up the complete protein.

The roughly spherical shape of insulin is characteristic of soluble proteins.
Many soluble proteins are very active chemicals like hormones, enzymes and transport proteins.

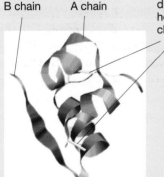

B chain   A chain

disulphide links holding the A and B chains together

This face of the insulin molecule is the part that binds to the insulin receptor.
Binding involves some of the hydrophobic side chains found on the surface of insulin here.

ribbon model of insulin showing quaternary, tertiary and secondary structure

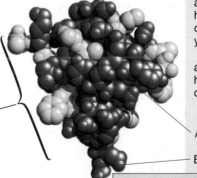

amino acids with hydrophobic side chains shown yellow

amino acids with hydrophilic side chains shown blue

A chain

B chain

space-filling model of insulin (same view as left)

The amino acids with hydrophilic side chains are very common on the surface of the molecule. This makes insulin soluble.

Fig. 1.12 The structure of proteins using insulin as an example.

Box 1.3 Bonds which hold protein molecules in shape

The secondary, tertiary and quaternary structures of protein molecules are held in shape by a number of different bonds between amino acids in different parts of the polypeptide chains.

Hydrogen bonds

Hydrogen bonds form between groups with dipoles, which are:

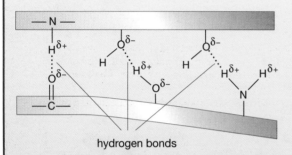

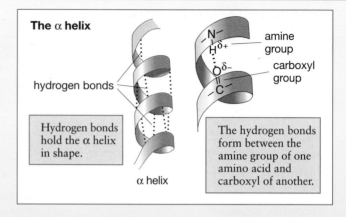

The α helix

Hydrogen bonds hold the α helix in shape.

α helix

The hydrogen bonds form between the amine group of one amino acid and carboxyl of another.

hydrogen bonds

Hydrogen bonds form between any groups with dipoles, where a group containing a hydrogen atom with a δ^+ charge is attracted to the part of another group with a δ^- charge. In protein molecules, the α helix is held in shape entirely by hydrogen bonds between the amine group of one amino acid, and the carboxyl group of another.

Hydrogen bonds also form between R groups, and help to hold the tertiary and quaternary structures of proteins in shape. Hydrogen bonds are relatively weak bonds, but are stronger than van der Waals forces.

Ionic bonds

Ionic bonds form between groups with opposite charges:

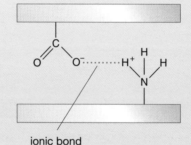

ionic bond

Ionic bonds (sometimes called electrostatic bonds or salt links) form between R groups which can ionise. These are the R groups containing carboxyl or amino groups (Fig 1.10).

Carboxyl groups ionise to form a negatively charged group, while amino groups ionise to form a positively charged group. These are strongly attracted together.

Ionic bonds are stronger than hydrogen bonds.

1.16 Denaturation

The structure of a protein molecule can be changed if the bonds which hold it in shape are broken. This process is called **denaturation**.

High temperatures break hydrogen bonds and van der Waals forces. In a globular protein this may mean that the whole molecule unfolds, becoming a long chain instead of a curled-up ball. The molecule will no longer be soluble. Egg white contains the globular protein albumin which is dispersed amongst water molecules. When albumin is heated, hydrogen bonds holding the molecules in shape are broken. So the molecules uncurl and become insoluble, forming a solid white substance.

Extremes of pH break ionic bonds, because they alter the charges on R groups. Most globular proteins are very sensitive to pH and only remain in their correct shape over a narrow pH range.

Reducing agents break disulphide bonds. This is made use of when perming hair. Keratin, from which hair is made (Fig. 1.13), contains many disulphide bonds that hold the hair in shape. During perming the hair is first treated with a reducing agent to break the bonds. The hair is then formed and held in a new shape, the reducing agent washed off, and an oxidising agent applied. This allows the disulphide bonds to reform, but in new positions.

In general, globular proteins tend to be more susceptible to denaturation than fibrous proteins. This is partly because fibrous proteins often have many disulphide bonds holding them in shape, which are not easily damaged even by quite extreme temperatures and pH. Perhaps this situation has evolved because fibrous proteins are often found *outside* cells (think of hair, for example). Here temperature and pH cannot be regulated so fully as *inside* cells, which is where many globular proteins exist.

Van der Waals forces and hydrophobic interactions

Water, excluded from the hydrophobic side chains, helps to keep the side chains together.

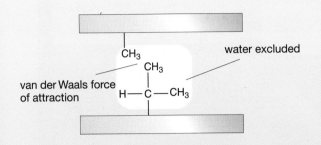

van der Waals force of attraction

CH₃

CH₃

water excluded

H — C — CH₃

Hydrophobic interactions, sometimes called hydrophobic attractions, are the result of hydrophobic hydrocarbon R groups of certain amino acids gathering in the centre of the folded polypeptide to keep away from the surrounding water. Most protein molecules, of course, are in watery liquids all the time, so hydrophobic interactions can be very important in maintaining their shape.

Van der Waals forces act between any two atoms which are quite close together. They are weak forces, but they become important if many of them all act in the same direction at the same time. This happens in the interiors of many protein molecules, where the three-dimensional shape may allow a large number of atoms to be attracted to each other by van der Waals forces, so helping to maintain the shape of the molecule.

Disulphide links

Disulphide links form between cysteine side chains:

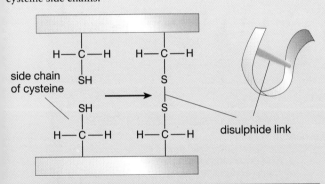

side chain of cysteine

disulphide link

Disulphide links, sometimes called sulphur bridges, are formed between the R groups of cysteine molecules. They are strong covalent bonds between two sulphur atoms.

Denaturation

Some bonds holding protein molecules in shape are broken by heat, high or low pH and concentrated salt solutions. The bonds affected are hydrogen bonds, ionic bonds, van der Waals forces and hydrophobic interactions.

If the protein is soluble, denaturation makes it insoluble and the protein is inactivated.

denaturation

If the protein is an insoluble fibrous protein, it loses its structural strength.

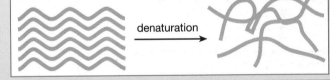

denaturation

Q3 The diagram below shows part of the primary structure of the enzyme ribonuclease. The amino acids that make up the first and the last parts of the molecule have been named with their standard abbreviations.

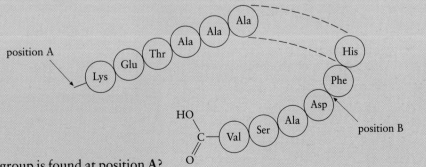

position A

Lys Glu Thr Ala Ala Ala

His

Phe

Asp

HO

C

O

Val Ser Ala

position B

(a) Which chemical group is found at position **A**? *(1)*

(b) What name is given to the chemical bond between the amino acids Asp and Phe at position **B**? *(1)*

(c) Describe **two** differences between the secondary structure and the tertiary structure of a protein like a ribonuclease molecule. *(2)*

AEB 1994 (modified)   *(Total 4 marks)*

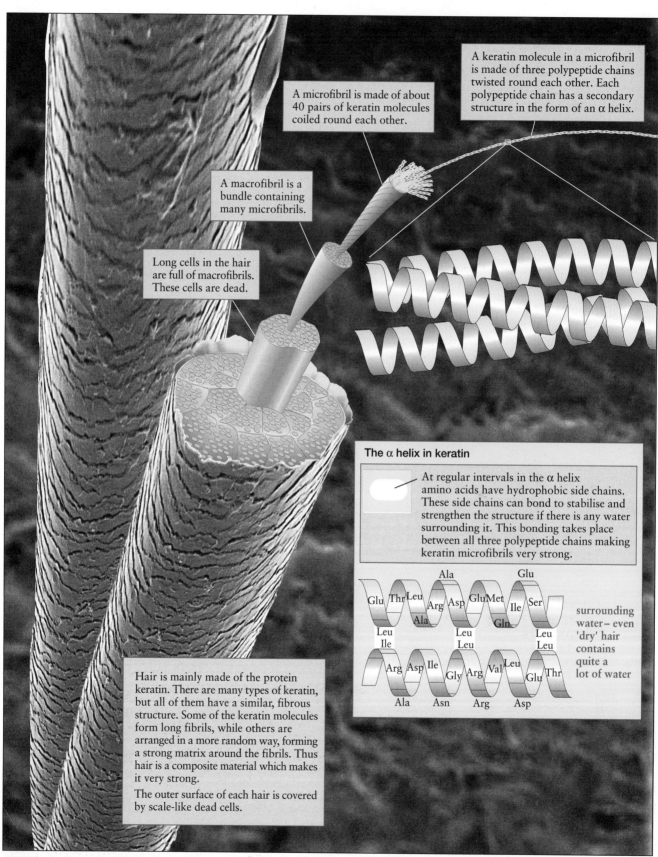

A microfibril is made of about 40 pairs of keratin molecules coiled round each other.

A keratin molecule in a microfibril is made of three polypeptide chains twisted round each other. Each polypeptide chain has a secondary structure in the form of an α helix.

A macrofibril is a bundle containing many microfibrils.

Long cells in the hair are full of macrofibrils. These cells are dead.

The α helix in keratin

At regular intervals in the α helix amino acids have hydrophobic side chains. These side chains can bond to stabilise and strengthen the structure if there is any water surrounding it. This bonding takes place between all three polypeptide chains making keratin microfibrils very strong.

surrounding water – even 'dry' hair contains quite a lot of water

Hair is mainly made of the protein keratin. There are many types of keratin, but all of them have a similar, fibrous structure. Some of the keratin molecules form long fibrils, while others are arranged in a more random way, forming a strong matrix around the fibrils. Thus hair is a composite material which makes it very strong.

The outer surface of each hair is covered by scale-like dead cells.

Fig. 1.13 The structure of keratin.

Box 1.4 Gel electrophoresis

Gel electrophoresis is a technique that is used to separate different molecules from a mixture. It is frequently used with fragments of DNA and RNA – genetic fingerprinting uses this technique (see Section 5.15). Gel electrophoresis can be used to separate proteins according to their size or to the relative amounts of acidic and basic R groups which they contain. Gel electrophoresis is also used to separate the different amino acids in a protein once the polypeptide chains have been split apart. Here we will concentrate on the way in which different protein molecules may be separated in a mixture.

Separating according to size

The protein mixture is first dissolved in a solution of the detergent sodium dodecyl sulphate (SDS) which attaches negatively charged ions to the protein molecules. The mixture is then placed onto a gel

(Fig.1.14). A potential difference of about 200 V is then applied. The negatively charged protein molecules move through the gel towards the anode (positively charged electrode).

The protein molecules can move only quite slowly through the gel. The gel contains tiny pores which act rather like molecular sieves. Small protein molecules can move through quite rapidly but large protein molecules move much more slowly. Thus gel electrophoresis separates the protein molecules according to their size.

The process takes an hour or two. After this time the proteins will be spread through the gel, largest ones nearest to the starting point and smaller ones furthest away. They are invisible at this stage, and have to be stained so that they can be seen.

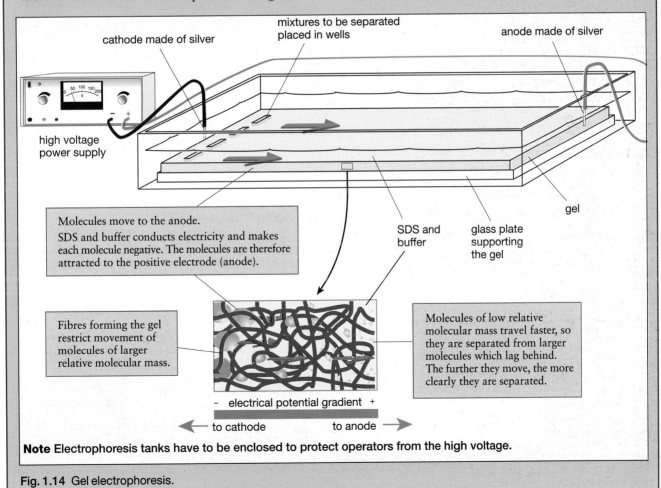

cathode made of silver

mixtures to be separated placed in wells

anode made of silver

0 50 100 150 200
V

high voltage power supply

Molecules move to the anode.
SDS and buffer conducts electricity and makes each molecule negative. The molecules are therefore attracted to the positive electrode (anode).

SDS and buffer

glass plate supporting the gel

gel

Fibres forming the gel restrict movement of molecules of larger relative molecular mass.

Molecules of low relative molecular mass travel faster, so they are separated from larger molecules which lag behind. The further they move, the more clearly they are separated.

- electrical potential gradient +

← to cathode   to anode →

Note Electrophoresis tanks have to be enclosed to protect operators from the high voltage.

Fig. 1.14 Gel electrophoresis.

Box 1.4 Gel electrophoresis (cont.)

Separating according to relative amounts of acidic and basic groups

You have seen that pH affects the ionisation of —NH$_2$ and —COOH groups (Box 1.2). For any particular protein molecule, there will be a particular pH at which these two groups are exactly equally ionised, so that the molecule as a whole has a net charge of zero. This pH is called the **isoelectric point** of the protein. Electrophoresis can be used to separate proteins according to their isoelectric points.

First, a gel is made containing a pH gradient (Fig. 1.15). The mixture of protein molecules is then applied to the gel and a potential difference set up across the gel. Each protein molecule moves through the gel until it reaches the pH of its isoelectric point.

Combining the two methods

Both of the methods of electrophoresis described above are good at separating protein molecules. But you can get an even better result if you use first one and then the other.

The protein mixture is first subjected to the method which separates it according to isoelectric points in a vertical direction. The resulting gel is placed onto another gel, this time impregnated with SDS, and the potential difference applied in a horizontal direction. So the proteins are first spread out vertically according to their isolectric points, and then horizontally according to their sizes. This is called *two-dimensional* electrophoresis.

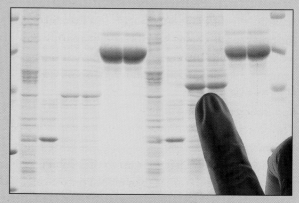

Fig. 1.16 Electrophoresis gel. The four bands on the left show proteins from a normal cell, and the group of four bands just right of centre show proteins from a similar cell which has been infected by a virus. The gloved finger is pointing to two proteins found in the infected cell, but not the normal cell.

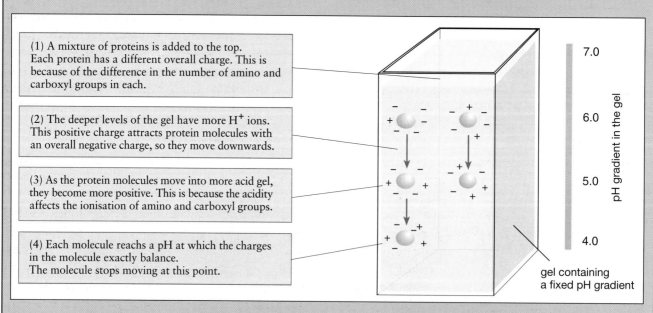

(1) A mixture of proteins is added to the top. Each protein has a different overall charge. This is because of the difference in the number of amino and carboxyl groups in each.

(2) The deeper levels of the gel have more H$^+$ ions. This positive charge attracts protein molecules with an overall negative charge, so they move downwards.

(3) As the protein molecules move into more acid gel, they become more positive. This is because the acidity affects the ionisation of amino and carboxyl groups.

(4) Each molecule reaches a pH at which the charges in the molecule exactly balance. The molecule stops moving at this point.

7.0

6.0

5.0

4.0

pH gradient in the gel

gel containing a fixed pH gradient

Fig. 1.15 Gel electotrophoresis using a pH gradient.

LIPIDS

1.17 Lipids include fats and oils

Lipids are not as easy to define as carbohydrates or proteins. They include a wide variety of molecules. However, they all have the following in common:

- they contain carbon, hydrogen and oxygen, with far more hydrogen and carbon compared with oxygen than in carbohydrates;
- they are insoluble in water.

The three most important groups of lipids in living organisms are **triglycerides, phospholipids** and **steroids.** Here, we will look at the first two of these groups. (Fig. 15.3 shows the structure of a steroid.)

1.18 Triglycerides

Fig. 1.17 shows a triglyceride molecule. The 'tri' part of its name refers to the three **fatty acid chains.** The 'glyceride' part refers to the **glycerol** molecule.

Glycerol is an alcohol containing three carbon atoms. (An alcohol is an organic compound with an —OH group – glycerol has three such groups.) A fatty acid is a molecule containing a long chain of hydrogen and carbon atoms, called a **hydrocarbon chain,** with a —COOH group at one end. You have met this group, called a carboxyl group, before in amino acids. The —COOH group has a tendency to ionise to produce hydrogen ions:

$$—COOH \rightleftharpoons —COO^- + H^+$$

which is why fatty acids are acids.

When fatty acids react with glycerol, a condensation reaction occurs and **ester linkages** are formed between them (Fig. 1.17). This involves the —COOH groups of the fatty acids, so they no longer have any acidic properties.

Fatty acids may be **saturated** or **unsaturated.** A saturated fatty acid is one in which there are no double bonds in the hydrocarbon chain – each carbon atom is bonded to a carbon atom on either side of it, and also to two hydrogen atoms. An unsaturated fatty acid contains one or more double bonds between carbon atoms in the hydrocarbon chain (Fig. 1.18). A 'polyunsaturated' fatty acid, as its name suggests, has two or more double bonds, while a 'monounsaturated' fatty acid has only one double bond. You will have seen these terms on food labels; this information is provided because there is some evidence that a high proportion of saturated fatty acids in the diet may increase the risk of heart disease.

Triglycerides with relatively short fatty acid chains, or with unsaturated fatty acids, tend to be liquid at normal temperatures and are called **oils.** Triglycerides with longer fatty acid chains, or with saturated fatty acids, are more likely to be solid and are called **fats.** There is a tendency for plants to produce oils (for example olive oil and corn oil), and animals to produce fats (for example butter and lard), but there are many exceptions to the rule.

Triglycerides, like all lipids, are insoluble in water. This is because they have no dipoles and so no charges which can attract water molecules.

The main use of triglycerides in the body is as an **energy source.** Triglycerides can be broken down and oxidised in respiration (Chapter 9) and the energy from them used to make ATP.

Triglycerides are especially useful as **energy stores,** because they contain much more energy per gram than either carbohydrates or proteins. One gram of fat can be respired to produce twice as much ATP as one gram of carbohydrate or protein.

Triglycerides can be stored as droplets inside cells where their insolubility is very useful as they do not disperse into the cytoplasm. Mammals have cells specialised for storing fat in this way under their skin; the cells are grouped together to form **adipose tissue.** This has two other useful functions. Firstly, it is an excellent **heat insulator,** preventing the loss of heat from deeper regions of the body to the outside. Secondly, it has a relatively low density and so provides **buoyancy** for aquatic animals. Large mammals that live in cold seas, such as whales and seals, often have very thick layers of adipose tissue called blubber. Both the heat insulation and buoyancy help them to survive in this environment.

1.19 Phospholipids

A phospholipid molecule has a structure very like a triglyceride but one of the fatty acids is replaced by a phosphate group (Fig. 1.19).

The phosphate group ionises, ending up with a negative charge making it **polar.** This attracts water molecules to it, and so it is **hydrophilic** ('water-loving'). As you have seen, however, the fatty acid chains carry no charges. Water molecules are not attracted to them, so they are **hydrophobic** ('water-hating'). Phospholipid molecules therefore have one end which is attracted to water and another end which is repelled by it.

This property of phospholipids enables them to form **cell membranes.** Cells contain cytoplasm, which is mostly

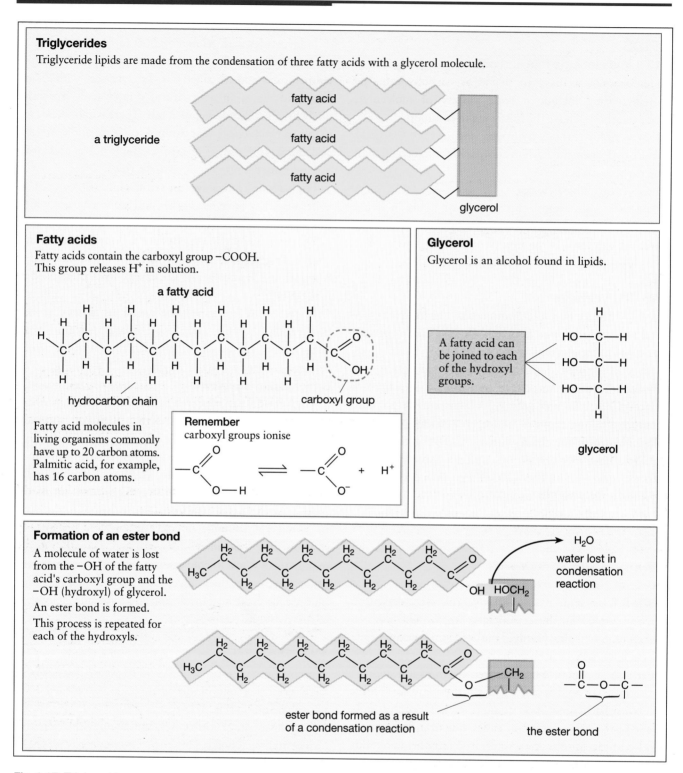

Fig. 1.17 Triglycerides.

Q4 (a) Make a list of similarities and differences between the molecular structures of carbohydrates and triglycerides.

(b) How do the differences explain their different physical and chemical properties?

Types of fatty acids

Two important types are saturated and unsaturated fatty acids.
Saturated fatty acids contain only single bonds between the carbon atoms of the hydrocarbon chain.

Unsaturated fatty acids contain one or more double bonds between the carbon atoms.
A polyunsaturated fatty acid contains two or more double bonds.

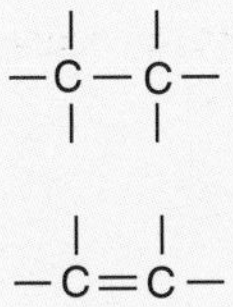

Saturated fatty acids

These are often used in animals to make triglyceride lipids.
Lipids made of them are usually solid at room temperature (fats).

a saturated fatty acid

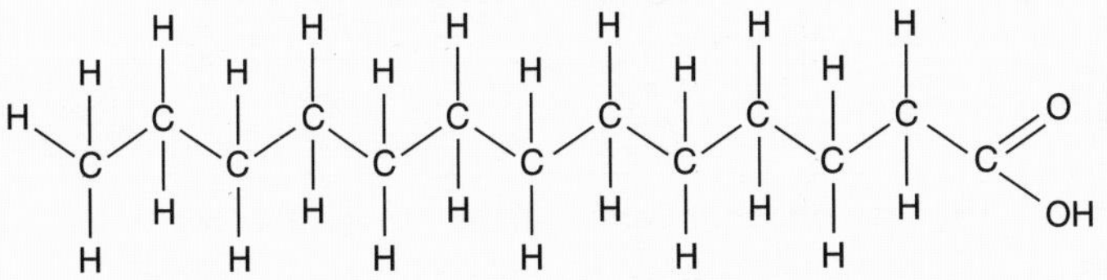

An example of a saturated fatty acid found in living organisms is palmitic acid which contains 16 carbon atoms.
It is common in human lipids.

Unsaturated fatty acids

These are often used to make triglyceride lipids in plants.
Lipids made from them are usually liquid (oils).

an unsaturated fatty acid

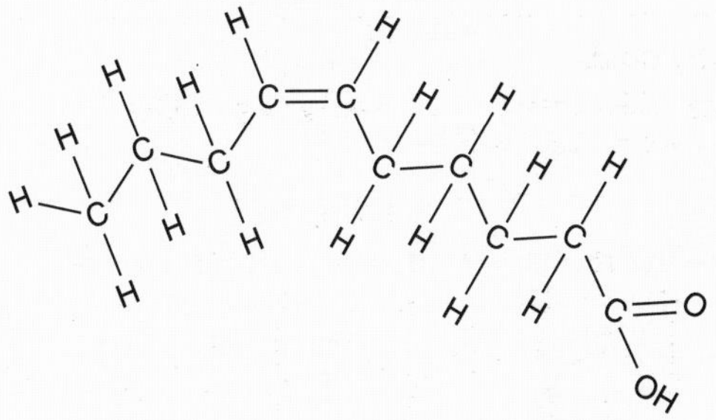

An example of an unsaturated fatty acid found in living organisms is oleic acid which contains 18 carbon atoms and a single double bond. It is common in human lipids.

Fig. 1.18 Types of fatty acid.

water with various other substances dissolved in it. Cells are usually surrounded by liquids containing water too. The cell surface membrane is made up of a double layer of phospholipid molecules, each molecule lying with its hydrophilic head in the watery liquid either inside or outside the cell, and its tail pointing away, towards the centre of the membrane (Fig. 1.19). The arrangement is called a **bimolecular sheet**, or a **phospholipid bilayer**.

The individual phospholipid molecules in the bilayer are free to move around in their particular layer, so it is fluid – rather like the skin on a soap bubble. However, the bilayer is also quite strong because the phospholipid molecules will not readily move into a position that exposes their tails to water, or moves their heads away from it. The tails are also attracted to each other by hydrophobic forces. So cell membranes have both flexibility and strength.

The hydrophobic nature of the phospholipids' tails confers another important property on cell membranes – they will not allow polar molecules, or ions, to pass easily through them. As you will see in Chapter 3, these substances *can* pass through membranes, but only through purpose-built pores which the cell can control. Thus the phospholipid bilayer that surrounds every living cell helps

to keep the cell's contents inside and the outside world outside. Without it, no cell can exist.

There are other molecules in cell membranes, especially proteins. You can read about these and their roles in the membrane in Section 3.6.

Q5
(a) Write down the molecular formula for
(i) palmitic acid and (ii) oleic acid.

(b) Write the general formula for saturated fatty acids.

(c) Explain why it is not possible to write a general formula for unsaturated fatty acids.

Phospholipids

Phospholipids are made of two fatty acid chains joined to a polar head. This head always contains a phosphate group and usually glycerol and another polar group.

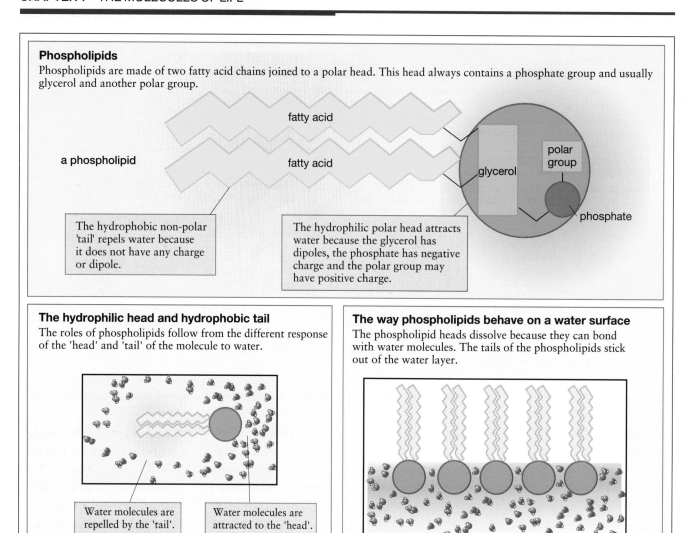

a phospholipid

fatty acid

fatty acid

glycerol

polar group

phosphate

The hydrophobic non-polar 'tail' repels water because it does not have any charge or dipole.

The hydrophilic polar head attracts water because the glycerol has dipoles, the phosphate has negative charge and the polar group may have positive charge.

The hydrophilic head and hydrophobic tail

The roles of phospholipids follow from the different response of the 'head' and 'tail' of the molecule to water.

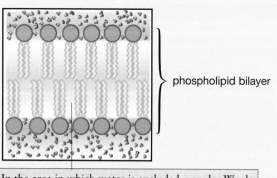

Water molecules are repelled by the 'tail'.

Water molecules are attracted to the 'head'.

The way phospholipids behave on a water surface

The phospholipid heads dissolve because they can bond with water molecules. The tails of the phospholipids stick out of the water layer.

Phospholipid bilayer

When phospholipid is mixed into water it can produce sheets made up of a double layer of molecules.

Each sheet is a phospholipid bilayer.

phospholipid bilayer

In the area in which water is excluded, van der Waals forces and hydrophobic interactions hold the phospholipid tails together.

The fluidity of the lipid bilayer

Van der Waals forces are not very strong and so the phospholipids move around.

The structure acts rather like a fluid.

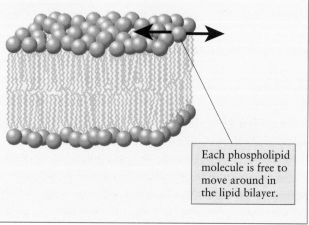

Each phospholipid molecule is free to move around in the lipid bilayer.

Fig. 1.19 Phospholipids.

NUCLEIC ACIDS

1.20 Polynucleotides

Almost all living cells contain two very important substances – **DNA** and **RNA**. These molecules carry instructions for making proteins; they specify the sequence in which amino acids are to be linked together and thus which proteins will be made. The way in which these instructions are provided and interpreted by the cell is described in Chapter 5. Here we will concentrate on the structure of DNA and RNA, and give only a brief outline of their functions. You may like to read this section first and then go straight on to Chapter 5 where you can read about the functions of these fundamentally important molecules.

Both DNA and RNA are **nucleic acids**, or **polynucleotides**. As you can guess from this second name, they are polymers, made up of many smaller units called **nucleotides** linked together.

Fig. 1.21 shows the structure of a nucleotide. A nucleotide is made up of three smaller molecules. These are:

● a phosphate group;
● a pentose (5-carbon) sugar, either deoxyribose or ribose;
● a nitrogenous base, either thymine, adenine, guanine, cytosine or uracil.

(Note that the base *thymine* is a very different substance from the *thiamine* which you may see on the side of your breakfast cereal packet and is a vitamin.)

Nucleotides can link together by condensation reactions, to form a polynucleotide (Fig. 1.20).

If the nucleotides contain ribose, then the resulting polynucleotide is **ribonucleic acid**, or **RNA**. RNA molecules may contain several thousand nucleotides, but are often much shorter than this. They never contain thymine, the four possible bases being adenine, guanine, cytosine and uracil. RNA molecules are always just a single strand, although this may loop back on itself to form complex three-dimensional shapes.

If the nucleotides contain deoxyribose, then the resulting polynucleotide is **deoxyribonucleic acid**, or **DNA** (Fig. 1.22). DNA molecules tend to be much longer than RNA molecules, and are frequently enormous. One DNA molecule from the fruit fly *Drosophila*, for example, contains 6.2×10^7 nucleotides and is 2.1 cm long! DNA molecules never contain uracil; the four possible bases are adenine, guanine, cytosine and thymine. DNA molecules contain two polynucleotide strands. The strands are held together by hydrogen bonds between the bases. Hydrogen

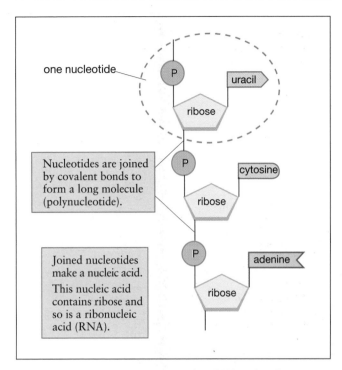

Fig. 1.20 A polynucleotide – part of an RNA molecule.

bonds can form between cytosine and guanine, or between thymine and adenine. The bases can only fit together in these pairs – always A with T, and C with G. This **complementary base pairing** is the basis of the way in which information on DNA can be copied, either to be passed on to a new generation or to be used for building proteins. This is described in Chapter 5.

1.21 The genetic code and protein synthesis

The sequence of bases on one strand of a DNA molecule – the 'sense strand' – is a code telling the cell in which order to string together amino acids to make polypeptides or proteins. A length of DNA specifying the amino acid sequence for one polypeptide is called a **gene**.

A row of three bases, called a **codon**, specifies one amino acid. If you do a quick calculation, you can work out that, as there are three bases, there are 64 possible arrangements of them in a codon. This means that the code could specify 64 different amino acids. However, as there are only 20 amino acids, this leaves a lot of 'code words' spare. Some of these are used as full stops, while others 'double up' with two or more different codons specifying the same amino acid. You can see just what each arrangement of bases means in Table 5.1.

When a polypeptide is to be made, the two strands of the DNA making up the gene for that polypeptide separate and a RNA molecule is built against the sense strand.

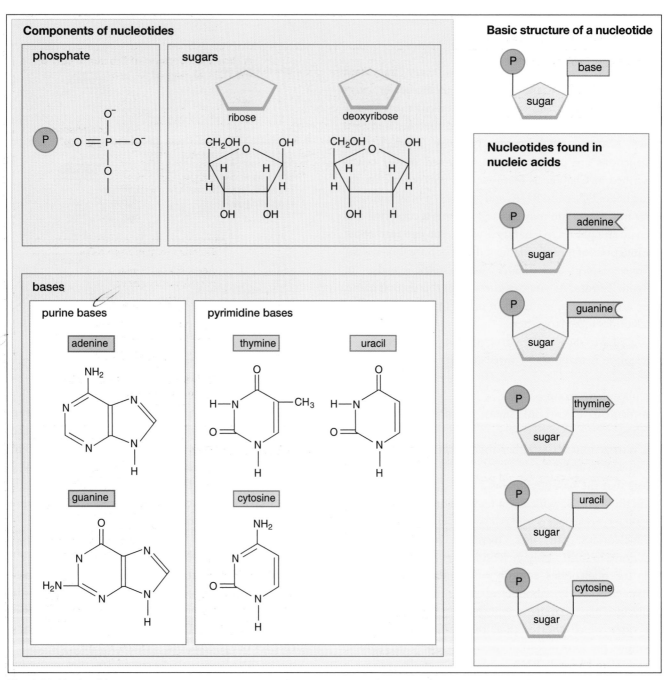

Fig. 1.21 Nucleotides.

Because each base can only pair with a particular partner, the sequence of bases on the RNA molecule must be exactly complementary to that on the DNA molecule. The completed RNA molecule then peels away from the DNA and travels to the place in the cell where the polypeptide will be made. This process is described in detail in Sections 5.2 and 5.3.

The genetic code in Table 5.1 is virtually identical in all living organisms. In other words, a particular sequence of bases on a DNA molecule means exactly the same, no matter whether it is in a bacterium, a seaweed or a human. This may mean that the genetic code evolved right at the beginning of the history of life on Earth. So it is possible to take a piece of DNA from a human cell and put it into a bacterium, where the bacterium will follow the instructions on the DNA to make the human protein. This is the basis of genetic engineering, which is described in Sections 5.10 to 5.13. ∎

The structure of DNA

Part of a DNA molecule

DNA is made up of two polynucleotides.

The polynucleotides are held together by H bonds between adjacent complementary bases.

A links with T through two hydrogen bonds; C links with G through three hydrogen bonds.

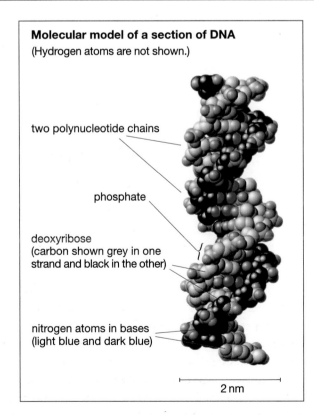

P

thymine ⟩ adenine

deoxyribose

P

cytosine ⟩ guanine

P

adenine ⟨ thymine

P

P

P

A simplified version of the same part of the DNA shown to the left

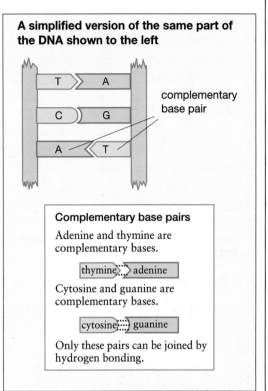

T A

C G

A T

complementary base pair

Complementary base pairs

Adenine and thymine are complementary bases.

thymine ⟩ adenine

Cytosine and guanine are complementary bases.

cytosine ⟩ guanine

Only these pairs can be joined by hydrogen bonding.

Molecular model of a section of DNA
(Hydrogen atoms are not shown.)

two polynucleotide chains

phosphate

deoxyribose
(carbon shown grey in one strand and black in the other)

nitrogen atoms in bases
(light blue and dark blue)

2 nm

The double helix of DNA

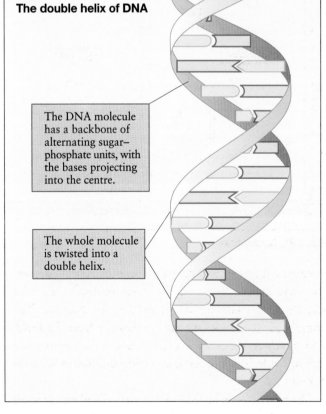

The DNA molecule has a backbone of alternating sugar–phosphate units, with the bases projecting into the centre.

The whole molecule is twisted into a double helix.

Fig. 1.22 DNA.

Box 1.5 Other nucleotides

A slightly different version of one of the nucleotides which makes up RNA also has a vitally important role to play on its own. This nucleotide is **adenosine triphosphate**, or **ATP**.

The structure of ATP is shown in Fig. 1.23. An ATP molecule contains the sugar ribose, the base adenine and three phosphate groups. Thus it only differs from the adenine-containing nucleotide in RNA in that it contains three phosphate groups instead of one. Two of these phosphate groups can be lost, usually one at a time, to form adenosine diphosphate, **ADP**, and adenosine monophosphate, **AMP**.

All living cells make ATP. It is essential to them because it is the **energy currency** of a cell. Every cell must make its own supply of ATP, which it does by photosynthesis, respiration or both. ATP is made almost continuously and an ATP molecule is unlikely to last for more than a minute before it is broken down again. You probably make at least 40 kg of ATP in your cells every day and use it all almost immediately. If you are doing something very energetic, you may be making and using 0.5 kg of ATP a minute. However, at any one moment, you probably have only about 5 g of ATP in total in your body.

When a cell requires energy, it hydrolyses ATP molecules. This can be done easily and quickly, and releases energy in relatively small 'packets'.

The way in which ATP is used as energy currency in a cell is described in Section 8.1 and in Appendix 1, Section 1.11.

Another nucleotide which is found in all cells, and is also involved in energy transfers, is **nicotinamide adenine dinucleotide**, or **NAD**. Its structure is shown in Fig. 1.24. Here, as in ATP, the molecule contains the sugar ribose and the base adenine. However, a NAD molecule contains *two* nucleotides, one of which does not contain any one of the five bases found in DNA or RNA, but a group called a nicotinamide ring. This group can

accept hydrogen, when the whole molecule becomes **reduced NAD** or **NADH**. NAD is therefore a hydrogen acceptor, and it has a central role accepting and passing on hydrogen during the reactions of respiration (pages 192 to 194). In photosynthesis, a slightly different version of this molecule, which carries an extra phosphate group and is called **NADP**, performs the same function.

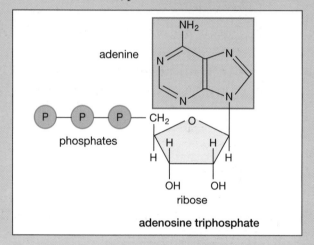

adenine

phosphates

ribose

adenosine triphosphate

Fig. 1.23 ATP.

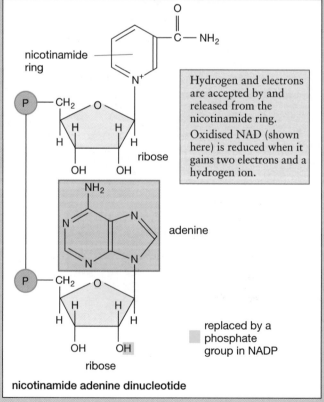

nicotinamide ring

ribose

Hydrogen and electrons are accepted by and released from the nicotinamide ring.

Oxidised NAD (shown here) is reduced when it gains two electrons and a hydrogen ion.

adenine

ribose

replaced by a phosphate group in NADP

nicotinamide adenine dinucleotide

Fig. 1.24 NAD.

Q6 The table below shows two physical properties of water and ethanol.

Property	Water	Ethanol
boiling point/ °C	100	78
latent heat of evaporation/ $10^4\,kJ\,kg^{-1}$	226.1	83.9

(a) Briefly explain how the structure and behaviour of the water molecule are responsible for the relatively high values of these two physical properties of water compared with ethanol. (2)

(b) Describe **one** way in which the relatively high latent heat of evaporation of water is important to mammals. (3)

(c) Water has a relatively high specific heat capacity, which means that a large amount of heat energy is required to change its temperature significantly. Outline how this property of water is of importance in the environment of aquatic organisms. (2)

(d) Human blood contains a high percentage of water. State two properties of water, not included in the table, which make it suitable as a transport medium in the mammalian blood system. (2)

UCLES 1995 *(Total 9 marks)*

Q7 The diagram below is an example of a key for the identification of some organic molecules found in living organisms.

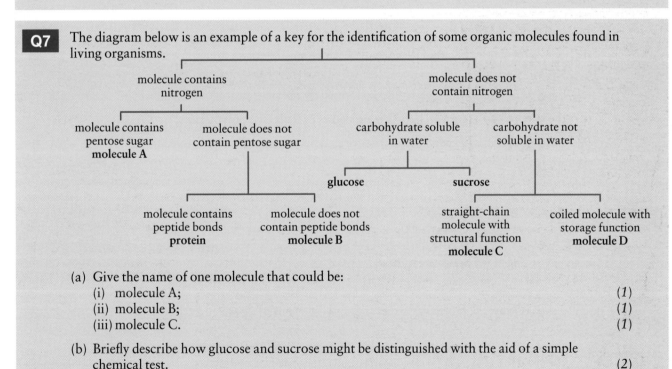

(a) Give the name of one molecule that could be:
(i) molecule A; (1)
(ii) molecule B; (1)
(iii) molecule C. (1)

(b) Briefly describe how glucose and sucrose might be distinguished with the aid of a simple chemical test. (2)

AEB 1994 *(Total 5 marks)*

Q8 The diagram below shows three molecules which are important components of living organisms.

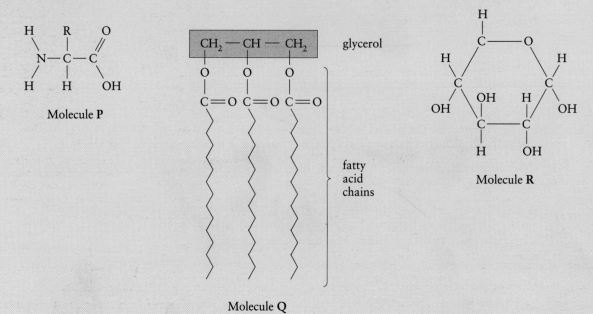

Molecule P

glycerol

fatty
acid
chains

Molecule Q

Molecule R

Name:
(a) molecules **P**, **Q** and **R**; (3)

(b) one element always found in molecule **P** which would **not** be found in a carbohydrate molecule; (1)

(c) the type of molecule which would be formed by polymerisation of molecule **P**; (1)

(d) the bond which is formed between molecules of **P** when it polymerises; (1)

(e) the type of molecule which would be formed by polymerisation of molecule **R**. (1)

UCLES 1995 *(Total 7 marks)*

Q9 Discuss the importance of water

(a) as a component of living organisms, and

(b) as an environment for living organisms.

Q10 Compare and contrast the molecular structures and functions of starch and cellulose.

Q11 Briefly explain each of the following.

(a) There is an infinite number of possible proteins.

(b) Globular proteins tend to be soluble, while fibrous proteins tend to be insoluble.

(c) Proteins frequently lose their function when exposed to high temperature.

Q12 Compare and contrast the molecular structure and functions of DNA and proteins.

2 Enzymes

Enzymes are proteins which are responsible for catalysing almost every metabolic reaction which occurs in living organisms. Most enzymes catalyse only one reaction or type of reaction, so each living organism requires thousands of different enzymes. A cell can control which metabolic reactions go on inside it by controlling the synthesis or activity of the enzymes it contains. Enzymes are now being widely used in industry, where the fact that they are left unchanged after each reaction means that a small amount of enzyme can catalyse the formation of a large amount of product. This makes their use very economical and profitable.

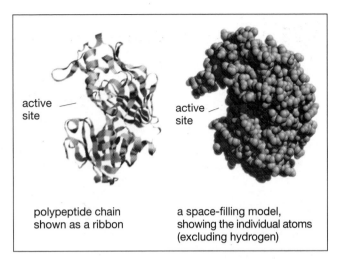

active site —   active site —

polypeptide chain shown as a ribbon   a space-filling model, showing the individual atoms (excluding hydrogen)

Fig. 2.1 The structure of a pepsin molecule.

HOW ENZYMES WORK

2.1 Active sites

Enzymes are biological catalysts; they increase the rate of a reaction without being permanently changed. Almost all enzymes are proteins. Enzymes which work in solutions, such as in the cytoplasm of a cell, in tissue fluid (Section 10.14) or in the alimentary canal, are globular proteins and are soluble. Other enzymes are held in position in cell membranes, and these are often *not* soluble. An example of a membrane-bound enzyme is ATP synthase (Box 8.4).

Fig. 2.1 shows the structure of the enzyme **pepsin**. Pepsin is an enzyme which catalyses the breakdown of proteins and so is a **protease**. It is a globular, soluble enzyme.

The pepsin molecule is made of a single polypeptide chain curled into a very precise shape. On the left-hand side of the molecule as it appears in Fig. 2.1, there is a depression or cleft. This is the enzyme's **active site**.

The shape of the active site is designed to allow unfolded polypeptide chains of denatured proteins to fit into it precisely. Protein (polypeptide) molecules are the **substrate** for pepsin. The R groups of the amino acids lining the enzyme's active site form temporary bonds with the protein molecule, and distort it so that its peptide bonds break. A hydrolysis reaction occurs. The enzyme then releases the broken protein molecule and is ready to accept another. The enzyme is unchanged by the reaction. A very small amount of enzyme can therefore catalyse the conversion of a large amount of substrate.

All enzymes have active sites. In most enzymes, when the substrate slots into the active site, the shape of the whole enzyme changes slightly so that it can accommodate the substrate better. This is called **induced fit**; the arrival of the substrate molecules causes, or induces, a change in the shape of the enzyme which makes the substrate fit perfectly into the active site. The substrate, too, changes shape, thus becoming more likely to react chemically and form a product.

2.2 Enzyme specificity

The active site of an enzyme is just the right shape for a particular substrate molecule to fit into. Pepsin, for example, can only accept straight polypeptide chains into its active site. In humans, pepsin works in the stomach where the acid conditions denature any proteins in the food, unwinding their polypeptide chains and allowing them to fit into pepsin's active site. Complete, undenatured globular protein molecules, or any other kind of molecule such as starch, will not fit into the active site.

This is true of almost all enzymes – they each have just one kind of substrate on which they can act. Most are even more specific than pepsin. While pepsin will catalyse the breakage of peptide bonds between quite a wide range of amino acids, the protease **trypsin** will only act on peptide bonds involving lysine or arginine. Another protease, **thrombin** (which is not a digestive enzyme but is involved in blood clotting) will only act on peptide bonds between arginine and glycine, and then only when they are part of a particular sequence of amino acids.

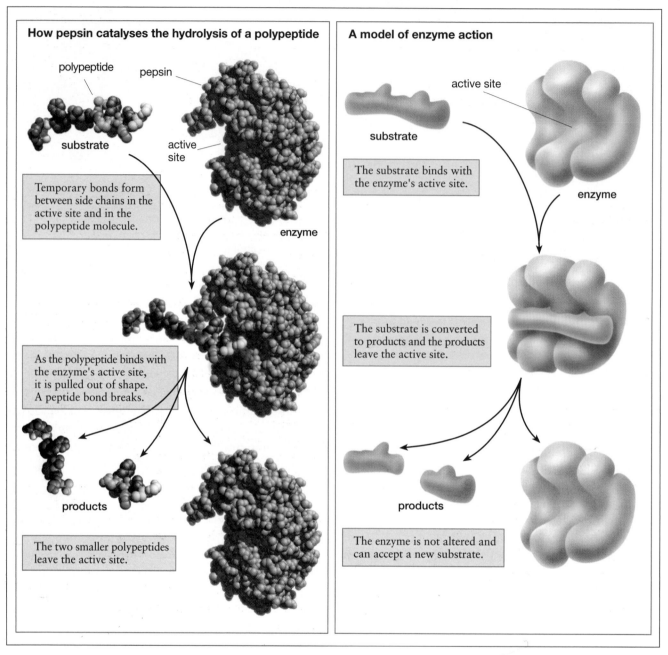

How pepsin catalyses the hydrolysis of a polypeptide

polypeptide

pepsin

substrate

active site

Temporary bonds form between side chains in the active site and in the polypeptide molecule.

enzyme

As the polypeptide binds with the enzyme's active site, it is pulled out of shape. A peptide bond breaks.

products

The two smaller polypeptides leave the active site.

A model of enzyme action

active site

substrate

The substrate binds with the enzyme's active site.

enzyme

The substrate is converted to products and the products leave the active site.

products

The enzyme is not altered and can accept a new substrate.

Fig. 2.2 How enzymes work.

2.3 Activation energy

In most metabolic reactions, the substrate must temporarily be provided with energy before it can change into a product. This is true for both endothermic and exothermic reactions (Section A1.10). This energy is called **activation energy** (Fig. 2.3).

If you want to make a reaction happen in a test tube, you can often provide the necessary activation energy by heating the contents of the tube. You do this, for example, when you are doing the Benedict's test for reducing sugars

(Box 1.1). Up to a point we do this in our bodies too, because we maintain our body temperature at about 37 °C. This is higher than the external temperature and helps to provide energy to drive chemical reactions. But the vast majority of metabolic reactions need much more help than this, and we cannot have higher body temperatures because this would denature protein molecules.

Enzymes solve this problem because they reduce the activation energy needed to change a substrate into a product. They do this by holding the substrate in a

Type of enzyme	Type of reaction it catalyses	Examples	Where you can read more
protease (a hydrolase)	hydrolysis of proteins or polypeptides into shorter chains of amino acids	In humans, they are involved in the digestion of proteins in the alimentary canal. In addition, many proteases have the function of catalysing the conversion of one protein into another - for example the protease thrombin converts fibrinogen to fibrin.	pages 33, 42, 279 281, 483
carbohydrase (a hydrolase)	hydrolysis of polysaccharides or disaccharides into shorter chains of, or single, monosaccharides	In humans, they are involved in the digestion of carbohydrates in the alimentary canal. Amylase and sucrase are two examples.	pages 278, 281, 289, 413
lipase (a hydrolase)	hydrolysis of fats into fatty acids and glycerol	In humans, they are involved in the digestion of fats in the alimentary canal. Lipases also break down fat in adipose tissue, when it is to be used in respiration.	pages 279, 281
transferases	remove part of one molecule and add it to another	Liver cells contain aminotransferases. These transfer amino groups from one molecule to another, and so can convert one amino acid into another.	
oxidoreductases	oxidation and/or reduction reactions	A very wide range of reactions involve oxidation and reduction, so oxidoreductases are found in every cell. For example catalase (or peroxidase) catalyses the reduction of hydrogen peroxide to water and oxygen. Oxidoreductases are involved in many of the steps of glycolysis and the Krebs cycle.	pages 41, 194
ligases	link two molecules together	DNA ligase links together the ends of DNA molecules, which happens when DNA is being made or mended, so it is found in all cells. DNA ligase is used in genetic engineering.	pages 116, 117

Enzymes are usually named according to the substrate on which they act, or the type of reaction which they catalyse. Their names almost always end in -ase.

Table 2.1 Some examples of enzymes.

Box 2.1   Why is enzyme specificity useful?

Enzyme specificity allows precise control over which reactions happen where and when.

Consider the specificity of two of the proteases mentioned in Section 2.2 which are both found in humans. Pepsin is a digestive enzyme found in the human stomach which breaks down proteins that are ingested in food. These proteins will be of a very wide variety, and it is obviously of benefit if just one enzyme can attack a very wide variety of protein molecules. In fact, there are several slightly different pepsins secreted by the human stomach wall which, between them, can break peptide bonds between many different amino acids within protein molecules.

Thrombin, on the other hand, is an enzyme found in blood. It is much more specific than pepsin in the peptide bonds which it will break. This specificity means that, in effect, it acts only on one protein – fibrinogen. Moreover, it always breaks the same

four arginine–lysine peptide bonds in fibrinogen, so always converts it to the same product – fibrin. You may already know that fibrinogen is a soluble globular protein which is always present in human blood plasma, and that fibrin is an insoluble fibrous protein which forms the basis of blood clots.

It would certainly be very inconvenient if thrombin was not so specific. Imagine the chaos if it could break peptide bonds at random in any protein in the blood.

In fact, even the precise specificity of thrombin is not enough to prevent chaos – if it was allowed to act all the time, the blood would clot permanently. To prevent this, active thrombin is only produced when clotting is required. Moreover, blood contains thrombin inhibitors which further regulate its action. You can read more about inhibitors in Box 2.2, and more about the blood clotting mechanism in Section 21.6.

particular way, inside the active site, pulling it slightly out of shape and making it easier for bonds to be broken or made within the substrate or with other molecules.

2.4   The time-course of an enzyme-catalysed reaction

Fig. 2.4 shows what happens as a reaction catalysed by an enzyme takes place. Imagine that you have a test tube containing a fairly large amount of substrate in solution in water and that the enzyme is added at time 0. The substrate and enzyme molecules will both be moving around freely in the solution. They will bump into each other and, quite often, a substrate molecule will bump into an enzyme molecule in such as way that it fits into the enzyme's active site. The enzyme molecule will convert the substrate molecule into product, release it, and continue moving around until it hits another substrate molecule.

If you measure the amount of product which is formed, you will see a pattern like that in the left-hand graph in Fig. 2.4. To begin with there are many substrate molecules, so most of the enzyme molecules will collide with a substrate molecule as soon as they have released the product. Product will be made very rapidly, as shown by the steep

rise of the curve. However, as time goes on, fewer and fewer substrate molecules are left, so there are less of them to bump into the enzyme molecules and the rate at which product forms slows down. Eventually all of the substrate molecules are changed into product molecules and the graph becomes horizontal.

In some reactions, it is easier to measure the disappearance of the substrate, rather than the appearance of the product. In this case you would obtain a graph like the one on the right in Fig. 2.4.

2.5   Measuring rate of reaction

Biologists are often interested in the rate at which a reaction happens. Enzymes speed up reactions. As you will see, the degree to which they can do this is affected by many other things, such as temperature, pH, the amount of enzyme and the amount of substrate. You may want to compare the rate of an enzyme-catalysed reaction under different conditions, but how can you make an accurate measurement of the rate of a reaction?

The rate of a reaction is **the amount of substrate which is converted to product per unit time**. The best way of measuring this will depend on the particular reaction

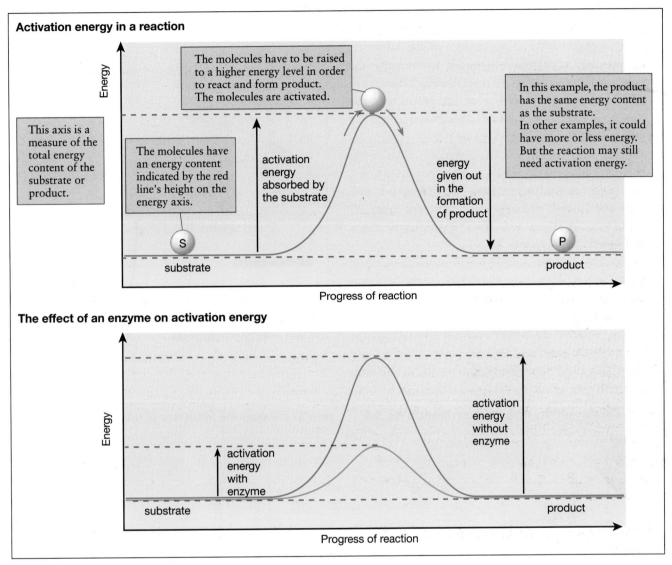

Activation energy in a reaction

Energy

This axis is a measure of the total energy content of the substrate or product.

The molecules have to be raised to a higher energy level in order to react and form product. The molecules are activated.

The molecules have an energy content indicated by the red line's height on the energy axis.

activation energy absorbed by the substrate

energy given out in the formation of product

In this example, the product has the same energy content as the substrate. In other examples, it could have more or less energy. But the reaction may still need activation energy.

S

substrate

P

product

Progress of reaction

The effect of an enzyme on activation energy

Energy

activation energy with enzyme

activation energy without enzyme

substrate

product

Progress of reaction

Fig. 2.3 Activation energy in a reaction.

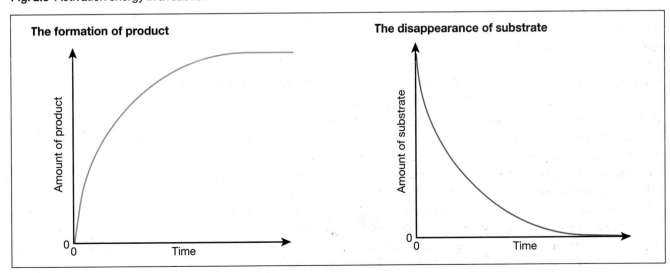

The formation of product

Amount of product

0

0   Time

The disappearance of substrate

Amount of substrate

0

0   Time

Fig. 2.4 The rate of the formation of a product and disappearance of substrate during an enzyme-catalysed reaction.

which you are interested in, and you will probably meet several different ones in your practical work. Sometimes it is easier to measure the disappearance of the substrate, while in other reactions it is easier to measure the appearance of the product. One reaction where it is easy to measure the appearance of one of the products is the conversion of hydrogen peroxide to water and oxygen by the enzyme catalase:

$$2H_2O_2 \quad \rightarrow \quad 2H_2O \quad + \quad O_2$$

You could use the apparatus shown in Fig. 2.5, and measure the amount of oxygen gas produced every 20 seconds. Fig. 2.6 shows some results which you might obtain from such an experiment.

It is obvious that the rate at which substrate is being converted into product is changing as the reaction proceeds. At first, the rate is very rapid, but it then slows down and would eventually stop.

Usually, we are most interested in the rate right at the start of the reaction, when the rate is fastest and the curve steepest. If the enzyme has plenty of substrate, so that each

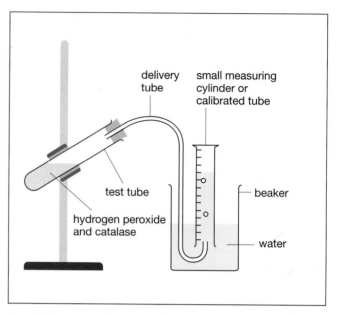

Fig. 2.5 Apparatus for measuring oxygen production by catalase on hydogen peroxide.

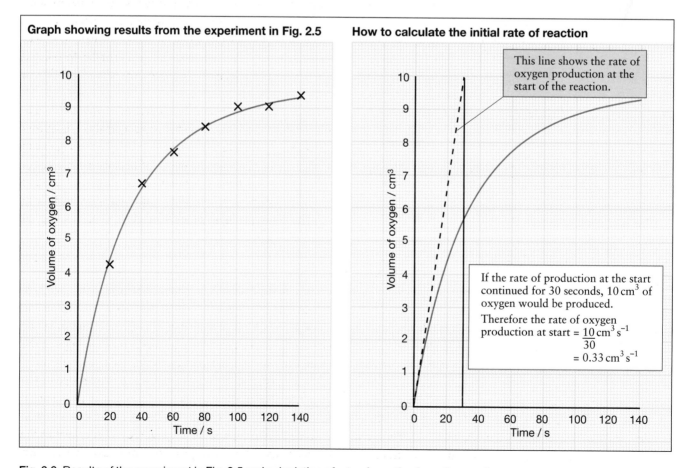

Fig. 2.6 Results of the experiment in Fig. 2.5 and calculation of rate of reaction from the results.

enzyme molecule is working as fast as it can and is not waiting for substrate molecules to bump into it, then this *initial* rate is the enzyme's maximum possible working rate under the conditions of the experiment.

To calculate this initial rate from the graph, we need to work out how much product is being made per unit time. A sensible unit time to use here would be a minute. We therefore want to know how much product is made in a minute.

You *could* do this just by looking at your results table. However, if you look at the graph, you will see that the points obtained in the experiment do not lie exactly on the curve. There has been some experimental error, as there usually is. Because we have a lot of points we can feel confident in drawing the curve, but we may not have perfect confidence in each individual point. This means that the *line* of the graph may be more reliable than the individual points. It is therefore better to calculate the rate of the reaction from the line rather than looking at one individual point.

If you use the graph to read off how much oxygen was made in one minute you get a value of $7.75 \, cm^3$, so the rate would be $7.75 \, cm^3 \, min^{-1}$. But is this really the *initial* rate? A better way would be to see how much oxygen was made in half a minute – in this case $5.65 \, cm^3$ – which would give us a rate of $11.30 \, cm^3 \, min^{-1}$. But even by 30 seconds the number of substrate molecules is less than it was to start with, so the rate of the reaction will already have begun to slow down. We really want to know the rate right at the start of the reaction.

To do this, you first draw a line which continues at the same angle as the very beginning of the curve, because we want to know the rate as near the beginning of the reaction as possible. You continue this line until you reach 30 seconds. You can then read off how much product would be made if this initial rate of reaction had continued for 30 seconds. In this case, $10 \, cm^3$ of oxygen would have been made in 30 seconds. This gives us a rate of $0.33 \, cm^3 \, s^{-1}$, or $19.80 \, cm^3 \, min^{-1}$.

In the section which follows, which is about factors which affect rate of reaction, it is important that you remember that we are always talking about this *initial* rate of reaction. If you want to compare rates of reaction under different conditions, it would not be sensible to compare the rates of the reactions after the reaction has been running for several minutes because, by then, you have introduced another variable – the amount of substrate the enzyme still has left to work on. Comparing initial rates of reaction is the only fair way to compare rates of reaction under different conditions.

FACTORS AFFECTING RATE OF REACTION
2.6 Temperature
Raising the temperature often increases the rate of a reaction. This is because molecules have more energy and so move faster at higher temperatures than they do at lower ones. They are therefore more likely to bump into each other and react. Moreover, because they have more energy, when they do collide they are more likely to be able to overcome the activation energy barrier and form a product. In many cases a temperature rise of $10 \, °C$ approximately doubles the rate of reaction.

This is just as true of enzyme-catalysed reactions as any other – up to a point. As you raise the temperature, you increase the rate at which enzyme–substrate collisions occur and so increase the rate of the reaction. However, because enzymes are proteins they can be denatured by high temperatures. High temperatures cause hydrogen bonds and hydrophobic interactions to break in the enzyme molecule so that it begins to lose its shape. As soon as the shape of the active site is altered, the enzyme can no longer hold its substrate molecule and so it can no longer act as a catalyst. As the temperature continues to rise, all the enzyme molecules become denatured and the reaction stops (Fig. 2.7).

The temperature at which the rate of reaction can take place fastest is called the **optimum temperature**. Enzymes which act in the human body normally have optimum temperatures of about $37–40 \, °C$. Enzymes which act in plants normally have optimum temperatures of around $25 \, °C$. Some enzymes made by some bacteria and fungi may have much higher optimum temperatures, up to about $80 \, °C$ in some cases.

2.7 pH
pH changes can affect the structure of an enzyme molecule and so affect its ability to bind and act on its substrate. Changes in pH affect ionic bonds that are holding the enzyme in shape, and also may affect the R groups in the active site which form temporary bonds with the substrate.

Most enzymes act over only a very narrow range of pH (Fig. 2.8). The optimum pH is normally around 7. Pepsin is unusual in that it has an optimum of pH 2 – it is well adapted for working in the very acidic environment of the stomach, as most other proteins are denatured in such strong acids.

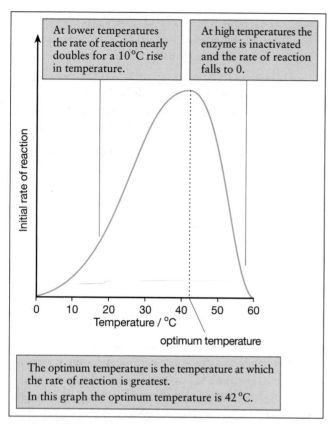

At lower temperatures the rate of reaction nearly doubles for a 10 °C rise in temperature.

At high temperatures the enzyme is inactivated and the rate of reaction falls to 0.

optimum temperature

The optimum temperature is the temperature at which the rate of reaction is greatest.
In this graph the optimum temperature is 42 °C.

Fig. 2.7 How temperature affects the rate of an enzyme-catalysed reaction.

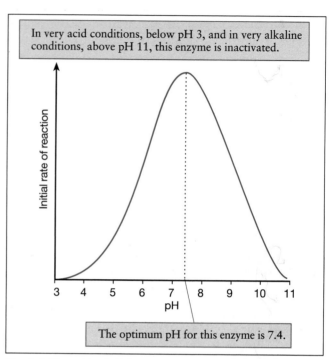

In very acid conditions, below pH 3, and in very alkaline conditions, above pH 11, this enzyme is inactivated.

The optimum pH for this enzyme is 7.4.

Fig. 2.8 How pH affects the rate of an enzyme-catalysed reaction.

2.8 Enzyme concentration

Provided that there is plenty of substrate available, it is obvious that the more enzyme there is available, the faster will be the rate of reaction (Fig. 2.9). The more enzyme molecules present, the more likely it is that a substrate molecule will bump into an empty active site.

However, if there is only a small amount of substrate then, even if you add more enzyme molecules, there is no more substrate to go round. Therefore, the line on the graph does not go upwards for ever but levels off, although in practice you would need very large amounts of enzyme compared to substrate to reach this point.

2.9 Substrate concentration

The more substrate molecules there are available, the more often one will bump into an enzyme, so the more rapidly they will be converted to product. Therefore, increasing substrate concentration increases the rate of a reaction (Fig. 2.10).

However, if you only have a limited amount of enzyme available, this pattern will not continue for ever. At high

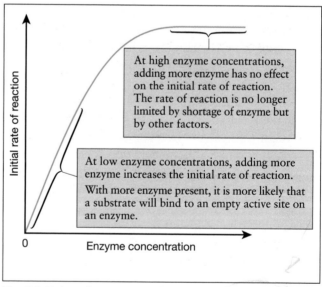

At high enzyme concentrations, adding more enzyme has no effect on the initial rate of reaction.
The rate of reaction is no longer limited by shortage of enzyme but by other factors.

At low enzyme concentrations, adding more enzyme increases the initial rate of reaction.
With more enzyme present, it is more likely that a substrate will bind to an empty active site on an enzyme.

Fig. 2.9 Rates of enzyme-catalysed reactions at different enzyme concentrations.

substrate concentrations each enzyme will be working as fast as it can, with substrate molecules virtually 'queuing up' for empty active sites. The curve of the graph of the reaction therefore flattens out at very high substrate concentrations.

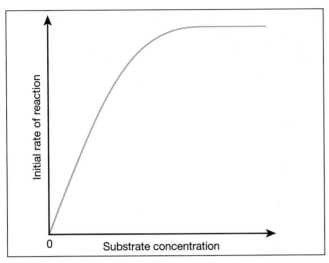

Fig. 2.10 Rates of enzyme-catalysed reactions at different substrate concentrations.

Q1 (a) What is an enzyme? With reference to **one** named example, outline the way in which an enzyme functions. (8)

(b) Explain how (i) temperature, (ii) enzyme concentration and (iii) substrate concentration affect the rate of an enzyme-controlled reaction. (16)

UCLES 1993   (*Total 24 marks*)

Box 2.2 Using enzymes in industry

The specificity of enzymes for their particular substrate, and the fact that they can be reused, means that they have a wide variety of uses in industry.

Sometimes, the enzymes are used in solution. They are simply mixed with their substrate, kept at a suitable temperature and pH, and allowed to catalyse the reaction in which substrate is converted to product. In many cases, however, the enzymes are **immobilised**. This involves attaching the enzyme molecules to an insoluble support. There are several methods by which this can be done. For example, the enzymes may be trapped in little beads of the jelly-like substance sodium alginate. The beads can be packed into a container, and a solution of the substrate allowed to flow over them. The enzymes convert the substrate into product as it flows by, so the solution leaving the container contains the product.

There are several advantages of using immobilised enzymes, rather than enzymes in solution:

- the enzymes are easy to recover, so that they can be used over and over again;
- the product does not contain enzymes, so it does not need expensive purification;
- the immobilisation of the enzymes often makes them more stable if temperature or pH changes,

probably because it is more difficult for their molecules to change shape.

However, there can also be problems with immobilisation:

- if enzymes are encapsulated in beads of a substance such as sodium alginate, then the substrate has to penetrate the beads in order to come into contact with enzymes; if it cannot, then only the enzymes on the surface of the beads can catalyse its conversion to product.
- immobilised enzymes often work more slowly than enzymes in free solution.

Using enzymes as analytical reagents

The enzymes **glucose oxidase** and **peroxidase** are used in dipsticks to estimate the concentration of glucose in blood or urine. The dipstick has a little pad of cellulose fibre at one end, onto which glucose oxidase and peroxidase are adsorbed. The pad also contains a colourless substance which changes to a coloured substance when it is oxidised. The pad is covered with a partially permeable membrane, allowing small molecules such as glucose to pass through, but not proteins.

When the dipstick comes into contact with glucose in solution, the glucose oxidase converts it to glucono–δ–lactone and hydrogen peroxide.

Box 2.2 Using enzymes in industry (cont.)

Peroxidase then catalyses a reaction between the hydrogen peroxide and the colourless substance, converting it to a coloured compound. The more glucose there is, the darker the colour obtained.

Making fructose from starch

Fructose is widely used in food manufacture because it is sweeter than glucose. It is made from starch, usually obtained from maize. First, the starch is converted to glucose using the enzyme **amylase**. Amylase is cheap and easy to obtain (it usually comes from fungi), so this reaction takes place with the enzymes in free solution because this gives the fastest rate of reaction.

Next, the glucose is converted to fructose using the enzyme **glucose isomerase**. This enzyme is more expensive to produce, so it is used in immobilised form. The reaction is quite slow, but it is more economical to do it this way because it is easier to recover and reuse the relatively expensive enzymes.

Proteases in biological detergents

Proteases are enzymes which hydrolyse proteins to polypeptides or amino acids. They are used in biological detergents to remove stains such as blood and sweat.

It was not easy to find suitable proteases, because they have to work alongside bleaches and other substances in the detergent which can change their shapes. One protease which is now frequently used is **subtilisin**, which is obtained from a bacterium. Subtilisin and other proteases have been engineered (Section 5.10) by replacing particular amino acids in their structure. These engineered proteases can resist oxidation by bleaches, but still retain good activity against proteins. They have also been made more thermostable (able to work at a wide range of temperatures). This can be done by changing amino acids in such a way that more bonds form between them. For example, replacing an amino acid which lies opposite a cysteine inside the enzyme molecule by another cysteine means that the two cysteines can form a disulphide bond. However, care has to be taken that these changes do not change the overall shape of the enzyme or it will lose its catalytic activity.

Q2 The graph shows the effect of increasing substrate concentration on the rate of an enzyme-catalysed reaction at a temperature of 35 °C and a constant pH.

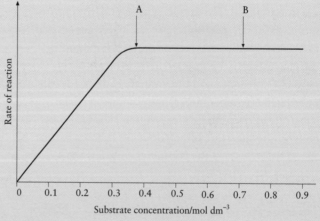

(a) Explain the shape of the curve between points **A** and **B**. (2)

(b) Copy the graph and sketch on it a curve to illustrate the effect of increasing substrate concentration on the rate of reaction at a temperature of 25 °C. (2)

AEB 1993 (modified)

(*Total 4 marks*)

2.10 Inhibitors

An inhibitor is a substance which prevents an enzyme from catalysing its reaction. By definition, inhibitors reduce the rate of enzyme-catalysed reactions.

There are several ways in which inhibitors work. Some inhibitors have shapes which are similar to those of the substrate molecule. They fit into the active site of the enzyme and stop the substrate fitting in. These inhibitors are called **competitive inhibitors** because they *compete* with the substrate for the active site. The degree to which they reduce the rate of the reaction will depend on the relative concentration of inhibitor and substrate. If there is lots of substrate and only a little inhibitor, then it will be more likely that substrate will get into the active site than the inhibitor, so the inhibitor will not have much effect. If, on the other hand, there is a lot of inhibitor and not much substrate, then the rate of reaction may be greatly reduced.

Other inhibitors act by combining with a different part of the enzyme, not its active site. They cause the shape of the enzyme to change, changing the shape of its active site and so making it less likely that the enzyme can catalyse its reaction. These are called **non-competitive inhibitors**. Unlike competitive inhibition, the relative concentrations of inhibitor and substrate do not affect the degree of inhibition, because the inhibitor can successfully bind with the enzyme even if there are very large amounts of substrate present. ■

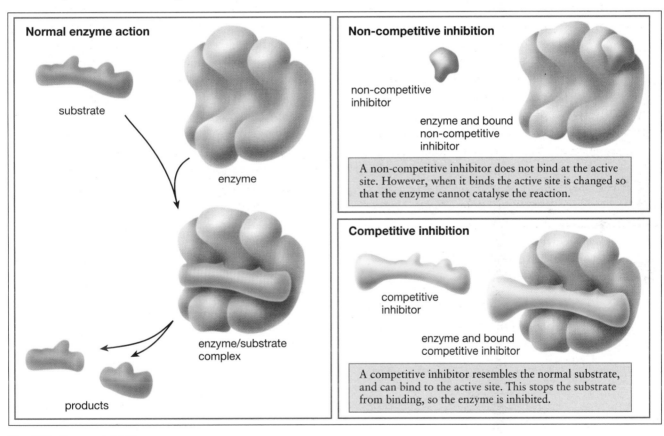

Normal enzyme action

substrate

enzyme

enzyme/substrate complex

products

Non-competitive inhibition

non-competitive inhibitor

enzyme and bound non-competitive inhibitor

A non-competitive inhibitor does not bind at the active site. However, when it binds the active site is changed so that the enzyme cannot catalyse the reaction.

Competitive inhibition

competitive inhibitor

enzyme and bound competitive inhibitor

A competitive inhibitor resembles the normal substrate, and can bind to the active site. This stops the substrate from binding, so the enzyme is inhibited.

Fig. 2.11 Enzyme inhibition.

Q3 Read through the following passage about enzymes, then copy out the passage filling in the gaps with the most appropriate word or words to complete the account.

Enzymes are catalysts which increase the rate of chemical reactions by reducing the _____ energy needed to cause the reaction to take place. Chemically, enzymes are globular _____ . They possess a particular region known as the _____ which binds temporarily to the substrate(s). The weak chemical bonds which hold the enzyme together can be disrupted by _____ and _____, thus affecting catalytic activity.

London 1994 (modified)   (*Total 5 marks*)

Box 2.3 Other ways of classifying enzyme inhibition

In Section 2.10 we classified inhibitors into competitive inhibitors (which compete with the substrate to bind with the active site) and non-competitive inhibitors (which bind elsewhere on the enzyme). However, if an inhibitor binds *permanently* with the active site of the enzyme, then it is not, strictly speaking, competitive. Even a relatively small amount of inhibitor compared with the amount of genuine substrate will eventually stop the enzymes working because all the active sites will be blocked by the inhibitor. For this reason it is often better to describe inhibitors which bind with the active site as **active site directed inhibitors**. These may be **reversible**, if they just pop in and out, or **irreversible**, if they stay tightly bound. There are, of course, active site directed inhibitors of all grades in between reversible and irreversible, depending on how tightly they are bound with the active site.

For example, we have seen that the enzyme **thrombin** catalyses the conversion of fibrin to fibrinogen in the blood and so causes blood clotting. Thrombin is normally only produced when a blood vessel is broken and the blood needs to clot (Fig. 21.5). Even then, its activity is strictly controlled, so that blood does not clot everywhere or for too long. To achieve this control, there is an active site directed inhibitor of thrombin, called **antithrombin**, in the blood, which binds with the active site of thrombin and stops it catalysing the conversion of fibrin to fibrinogen. The amounts of thrombin and antithrombin in the blood are balanced to achieve just the right amount of clotting, in the right place at the right time. Once antithrombin has bound with thrombin, it stays firmly bound, so its inhibition is **irreversible**.

Leeches produce an active site directed inhibitor of thrombin called **hirudin**. The leech injects hirudin into a person when it bites – the hirudin stops the blood clotting so that it flows easily into the leech as it feeds. Hirudin works by binding to thrombin and inhibiting it.

Another example of an active site directed inhibitor is the drug **sulphanilamide**, which is used to treat bacterial infections. This drug mimics pAB, which is one of the two substrates of an enzyme that catalyses one of the steps in the production of folic acid in bacteria (Fig. 2.12). Folic acid is essential for growth. (However, the drug does not cause harm to a person who takes it because we do not *make* folic acid – we have to eat it.)

The sulphanilamide fits into the enzyme's active site along with pteridine, and binds with the pteridine. The sulphanilamide–pteridine product then leaves the active site. So, sulphanilamide is a

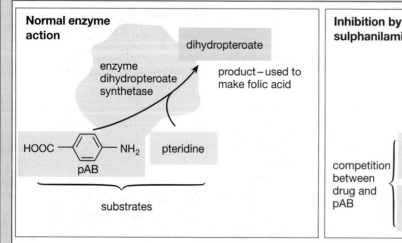
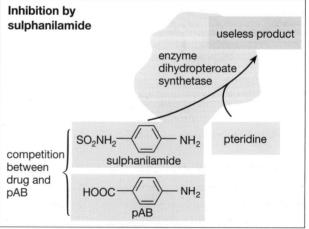

Fig. 2.12 How sulphanilamide kills bacteria.

Box 2.3 Other ways of classifying enzyme inhibition (cont.)

reversible inhibitor. However, because it actually uses up the pteridine, there is eventually none left for the pAB to bind with. So the sulphanilamide effectively stops the reaction completely even if there is a lot of the real substrate – the pAB – present. So you could say that sulphanilamide is partly a reversible inhibitor, and partly an irreversible one!

Non-active site directed inhibitors bind with the enzyme at a position other than its active site. The drug **digitalis** is a non-active site directed inhibitor of the ATP synthase in cell surface membranes that catalyses the hydrolysis of ATP to provide energy for the sodium–potassium pump (Section 3.27). This increases the force of contraction of heart muscle, so digitalis is widely used to treat people with heart failure.

Box 2.4 Controlling enzyme activity

Do not think that enzyme inhibitors are 'bad'! If all your enzymes were allowed to work all of the time, you would be in trouble. Inhibitors are very useful because they can help to control the time and place in which particular enzymes work. Some examples are described in Box 2.3. We have many natural inhibitors in our body, and many medicinal drugs work by inhibiting enzymes.

Imagine that three enzymes are catalysing a chain of reactions – a **metabolic pathway** – in which substrate A is being changed into product D:

$$A \xrightarrow{\text{enzyme 1}} B \xrightarrow{\text{enzyme 2}} C \xrightarrow{\text{enzyme 3}} D$$

You may have a lot of substrate A in your body, but you only need a little product D. If the enzymes were able to go on catalysing this reaction all the time, you would become swamped with unwanted D. An excellent way of stopping this from happening is if D acts as an inhibitor of one of the enzymes involved in these reactions – let us say enzyme 1 (although it could be any of them). As the amount of D builds up, it switches off the activity of enzyme 1, so stopping the production of more B. As B runs out, so C runs out, and no more D will be produced.

This is called **end product inhibition**, and it is a very common way of regulating the amount of products which are made by enzyme-catalysed reactions. For example, the bacterium *Brevibacterium flavi* converts aspartate to the amino acid lysine using a

pathway with a number of enzyme-catalysed steps. Normally, lysine inhibits the enzyme catalysing the first step:

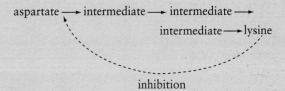

There is a mutant form of this bacterium in which the enzyme is not sensitive to lysine, so the end product inhibition does not work and the bacterium produces large quantities of lysine. This bacterium is used to make lysine commercially, producing up to 30 g of lysine per dm^3 of culture medium. The lysine is used as a food supplement for humans.

Another way of ensuring that an enzyme only works when you want it to is to produce it in an **inactive form** and only switch it on when it is needed. For example, the digestive protease enzyme **trypsin** is produced by the pancreas as a protein called **trypsinogen**. If trypsin was secreted in an active form, it would hydrolyse the proteins in the cell which made it! The trypsinogen passes along the pancreatic duct and into the duodenum (Section 13.9). Here, cells in the walls of the duodenum secrete a protein called **enterokinase** which hydrolyses a bond in the trypsinogen, removing a length of polypeptide chain from it and converting it into active trypsin.

Box 2.5 Cofactors and coenzymes

Many enzymes require the presence of another, non-protein and non-catalyst, substance in order to function. These substances are called **cofactors** or **coenzymes.**

There is no clear-cut distinction between a cofactor and a coenzyme. However, most biologists use the term 'cofactor' for simple molecules or inorganic ions, and the term 'coenzyme' for larger molecules. Both cofactors and coenzymes usually work by binding briefly with the enzyme. They sometimes alter its shape so that it can bind more effectively with its substrate, and sometimes help the enzyme to transfer a particular group of atoms from one molecule to another.

For example, **chloride ions** act as cofactors for salivary amylase. They bind with the amylase, slightly changing its shape and making it easier for starch molecules to fit into its active site. This change of shape is called **allostery** ('other shape'). **CoenzymeA**, often known as coA, is a coenzyme which is needed in many different metabolic pathways. You will meet it when you study respiration (Chapter 9). It can bind with a group called an acyl group, to form **acetylcoA**, which it can then pass on to other molecules. It is therefore needed to help enzymes which catalyse the transfer of these groups from one molecule to another. Another coenzyme involved in respiration is **nicotinamide adenine dinucleotide** (**NAD**), which helps dehydrogenase enzymes by accepting hydrogen atoms from the enzyme's substrate.

Many coenzymes, and some cofactors, are made from vitamins, which is why we need these vitamins in our diet. You can read more about this in Box 9.2.

Q4 The enzyme phenol oxidase is often released when plant cells are disrupted and leads to the oxidation of colourless phenols into coloured products. Samples of an extract containing phenol oxidase were subjected to various treatments, then mixed with a solution of phenols buffered at pH 7 and incubated at 35 °C for 10 minutes. The pre-treatment and results are shown in the table below.

Tube	Pre-treatment of enzyme extract	Colour of extract after incubation with phenol
A	none	intense brown
B	incubated with protease for 10 minutes	colourless
C	mixed with trichloroacetic acid for 5 minutes	colourless
D	mixed with mercuric chloride for 5 minutes	very light yellow

(a) Assuming these experiments were all appropriately standardised, what do you conclude from the results of each experiment? (4)

(b) How would you have discovered
   (i) if any **non-enzymic** oxidation of phenols occurs in tube A?
   (ii) if **enzymic** oxidation of phenols occurs in tube D? (3)

In some further experiments, samples of the enzyme extract were mixed with different substrate concentrations, with or without the presence of a standard amount of chemical, PTU (phenylthiourea). The results are shown in the table below.

Concentration of substrate/mmol dm^{-3}	Initial rate with PTU present/units	Initial rate without PTU present/units
0.5	2.4	4.2
1.0	4.1	6.3
1.5	5.1	7.1
2.0	5.5	7.6
2.5	5.5	7.6

(c) Plot these results. (3)

(d) Phenylthiourea (PTU) binds to copper atoms.
   (i) Suggest a hypothesis which might reasonably explain how PTU inhibits the action of phenol oxidase.
   (ii) Explain how, from the information provided, it is possible to determine that the inhibition caused by PTU is non-competitive rather than competitive. (3)

NEAB 1994   (*Total 13 marks*)

Q5 Living cells contain the enzyme catalase, which catalyses the breakdown of hydrogen peroxide to water:

$$2H_2O_2 \xrightarrow{\text{catalase}} 2H_2O + O_2$$

An experiment was carried out to investigate the effects of enzyme concentration and substrate concentration on rate of reaction. Some cabbage leaves were ground up with distilled water. The resulting liquid was filtered to produce 'cabbage extract', and the residue on the filter paper discarded.

(a) Suggest why the processes of grinding the cabbage leaves with water, and filtration, were carried out. (3)

Cabbage extract was then added to hydrogen peroxide solution. This was done three times, using the following quantities.

Experiment	Volume of cabbage extract/cm^3	Volume of hydrogen peroxide/cm^3	Volume of distilled water/cm^3
A	5	5	0
B	2	5	3
C	5	2	3

(b) Explain why water was added in experiments **B** and **C**. (2)

The volume of gas evolved was recorded over time for each experiment. The results for experiments **A** and **B** are shown in the graph below.

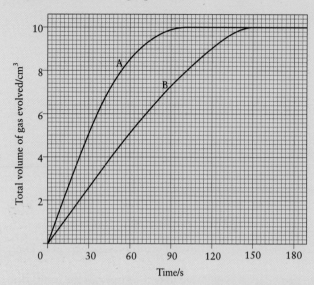

(c) (i) Explain the shape of the curve obtained for experiment **A**. (4)

(ii) Copy the graph and calculate the rate of reaction in the first 15 seconds for experiments **A** and **B**. Show your working. (2)

(iii) Explain why this initial rate is different in experiments **A** and **B**. (2)

(iv) Explain why the total volume of gas released from 150 seconds onwards is the same in both experiments. (1)

(v) On your copy of the graph, sketch the curve you would expect to obtain for experiment **C**. (2)

(d) A chemical **X** is thought to be a competitive inhibitor of catalase. Suggest how you could investigate this hypothesis. (5)

UCLES 1994 (*Total 21 marks*)

Q6 Give an account of the structure and function of enzymes in living organisms.

London 1995 (*Total 10 marks*)

3 Cells

All living organisms (except viruses which do not show all of the characteristics of living things) are made of one or more cells. A cell is always surrounded by a cell surface membrane, and contains a solution of proteins and other substances in water. This solution is called cytoplasm. Within the cytoplasm there are many structures called organelles.

3.1 What is a cell?

A cell is the basic unit from which living organisms are made. Some organisms, such as bacteria and many protoctists (page 500), are made from just one cell, and these are known as **unicellular** organisms. Others, including all plants and animals, are made from many cells, and these are called **multicellular** organisms.

Most cells are very small, although some are big enough to be seen with the naked eye. Bacteria tend to have particularly small cells, often around 0.5 μm across. These are so small that you can only just see them with a good light microscope. Human cells range between about 10 μm and 30 μm in diameter, while those of plants tend to be a little larger, with diameters from 10 μm to several hundred μm. A few very unusual cells can be quite enormous. For example, the yolk of a hen's egg is a single cell, and there is a tropical seaweed called *Caulerpa* which is made of a single cell, yet can grow up to 1 m long!

Despite this wide variation in size, all cells have certain features in common. Figs. 3.1 and 3.2 show an animal and a plant cell as they appear if viewed through a light microscope. Like all cells, these are both surrounded by a **cell surface membrane** which is made of phospholipids and proteins. This membrane serves to keep the contents of the cell separate from its surroundings, but still allows substances to enter and leave in a controlled way. Every cell contains **cytoplasm**. This is a colloidal solution of many substances, mainly proteins, in water and in which many metabolic reactions take place. Every cell contains various **organelles** within its cytoplasm, but the types and numbers of these organelles vary from cell to cell.

Most biologists consider that there are two basic types of cell. Bacteria are made of cells without true nuclei, and

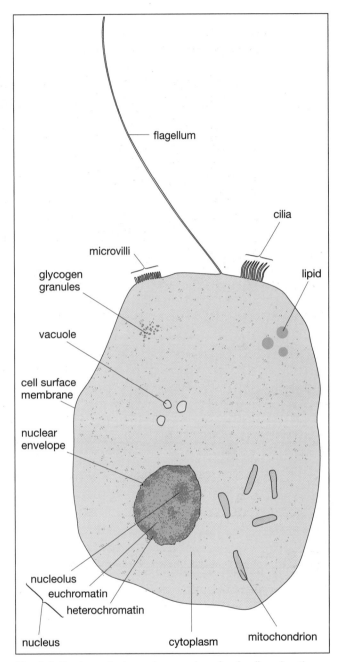

Fig. 3.1 Features that may be seen in animal cells using the light microscope and appropriate staining. No cell will have all these features. The colour will depend on the stain used.

contain no organelles that are surrounded by membranes. These are called **prokaryotic** ('before a nucleus') cells. Plants, animals, fungi and proctoctists are made of cells which usually have true nuclei enclosed in membranes, and contain various organelles surrounded by membranes. These are called **eukaryotic** ('true nucleus') cells. The cells in Figs. 3.1 and 3.2 are eukaryotic cells. Most of this chapter concentrates on eukaryotic cells. Prokaryotic cells are described in Section 3.22.

Light micrograph of plant cells (×800)

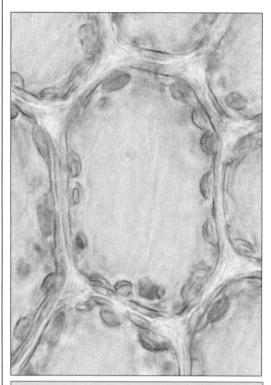

In living, unstained tissue it is often difficult to see the difference between cytoplasm and vacuole using a light microscope.

Drawing of a plant cell showing features visible using a light microscope

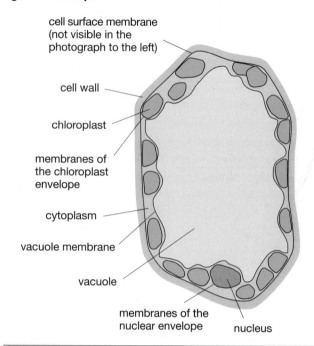

cell surface membrane (not visible in the photograph to the left)

cell wall

chloroplast

membranes of the chloroplast envelope

cytoplasm

vacuole membrane

vacuole

membranes of the nuclear envelope

nucleus

No membranes can be seen using the light microscope because they are too thin. However the *positions* of the cell surface membrane, vacuole membrane and membranes of the nuclear and chloroplast envelopes can often be identified.

Mitochondria are also usually not visible using the light microscope in unstained cells. Mitochondria are large enough to be seen, but they just look like the surrounding cytoplasm.

Fig. 3.2 Structure of a plant cell as seen by light microscopy.

3.2 Cells, tissues and organs

Although all eukaryotic cells have the same basic structure, there are almost infinite variations on this basic design. You can probably pick out several differences, for example, between the plant and animal cells in Figs. 3.1 and 3.2. Even within a single organism such as yourself, there are considerable differences between cells in different areas of your body. Each type of cell is specialised to carry out particular functions especially well, leaving other cells to carry out different functions. In a unicellular organism, on the other hand, the one cell has to be able to do everything well.

Within a multicellular organism, cells are usually arranged in groups to form **tissues.** A tissue is a structure made of many similar cells which are adapted to perform a particular function. Several different kinds of tissues may be grouped together to form an **organ.** An organ is a structure in an organism which carries out a particular function, such as the leaf of a plant or the eye of an animal. You will meet many different tissues (such as xylem tissue in plants and blood in mammals) and organs (such as a plant leaf and the mammalian heart) in your biology course and will learn about some of them in detail.

MICROSCOPY

3.3 Light microscopes

Fig. 3.3 shows how a light microscope, such as the ones you may use in your laboratory, works. Light rays are focused on to a transparent specimen by a condenser lens. The rays pass through the specimen and are focused again by two more lenses – the objective lens and the eyepiece lens. These two lenses produce a magnified image.

As many biological specimens are colourless and nearly transparent, stains are often used to make different parts show up clearly. Stains usually colour just a particular part of a cell; iodine solution, for example, colours starch grains blue-black. Some stains, such as methylene blue or iodine solution, can be added to living cells. In other cases, the specimen is 'fixed' by adding a chemical such as acetic acid or alcohol, known as a fixative. These chemicals react with substances such as proteins or nucleic acids in the structures in the cell, making them insoluble and so anchoring them in position. The cells are killed when the fixative is added. Stains may be added either before or after the fixing process.

So long as the specimen is thin enough to allow light to pass through, there are no limitations on what you can look at using a light microscope. Living, moving organisms such as protoctists can be watched, or you can look at a permanent stained preparation of a thin section through a piece of a human tissue.

3.4 Electron microscopes

Fig. 3.4 shows how a transmission electron microscope works. The principle is the same as that of a light microscope except that beams of electrons are used instead of beams of light. They are focused using electromagnets rather than glass lenses. As electrons are easily stopped by air molecules, the space inside an electron microscope must be a vacuum. As our eyes do not respond to electrons, the electrons are allowed to hit a fluorescent screen which emits visible light where the electrons hit.

Electrons cannot penetrate materials as well as light rays can, so specimens for viewing in an electron microscope must be much thinner than those used in a light microscope. This, and the fact that the specimen has to be placed in a vacuum, places great limitations on what can be viewed using an electron microscope. In particular, it is not usually possible to look at living material.

As in a light microscope, specimens are stained. Heavy metal ions, such as lead or osmium, are added to the specimen and are taken up by particular parts of the cells.

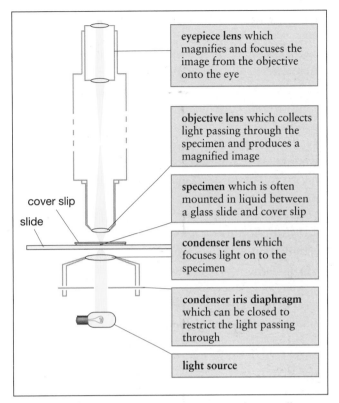

eyepiece lens which magnifies and focuses the image from the objective onto the eye

objective lens which collects light passing through the specimen and produces a magnified image

specimen which is often mounted in liquid between a glass slide and cover slip

cover slip
slide

condenser lens which focuses light on to the specimen

condenser iris diaphragm which can be closed to restrict the light passing through

light source

Fig. 3.3 How a light microscope works.

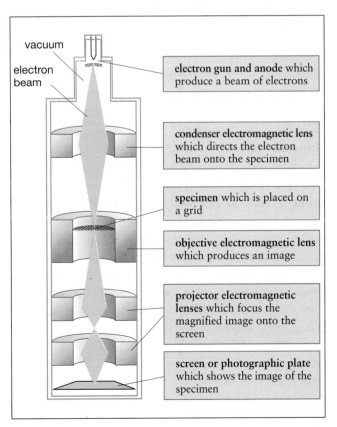

vacuum
electron beam

electron gun and anode which produce a beam of electrons

condenser electromagnetic lens which directs the electron beam onto the specimen

specimen which is placed on a grid

objective electromagnetic lens which produces an image

projector electromagnetic lenses which focus the magnified image onto the screen

screen or photographic plate which shows the image of the specimen

Fig. 3.4 How an electron microscope works.

Atoms of these metals have large, positively charged nuclei which scatter electrons rather than letting them pass straight through. These electrons therefore do not arrive on the screen, so leaving a dark area in the image. The structures in a cell which have taken up these heavy metal stains therefore appear dark.

Scanning electron microscopes work in a very different way. The electrons do not pass through the specimen but are reflected off its surface. Scanning electron microscopes are used to provide three-dimensional images of surfaces (Fig. 12.14 for example).

3.5 Magnification and resolution

Magnification is the number of times larger an image is than the specimen. For example, if a cell is $10\,\mu m$ in diameter, and a microscope produces an image of it which is $1\,mm$ ($1000\,\mu m$) in diameter, then the microscope has magnified the specimen 100 times.

$$\text{magnification} \quad = \quad \frac{\text{size of image}}{\text{size of specimen}}$$

The magnification produced by a light microscope depends on the strengths of the objective lens and the eyepiece lens. If you are using a $\times 40$ objective lens and a $\times 10$ eyepiece lens, then your specimen is being magnified 400 times.

There is no limit to the amount a light microscope can magnify. By putting in stronger lenses, or more lenses, you could produce a huge image several metres across. But the image would not be at all clear, and you would not be able to see any more detail than before. This is because the **resolution** of a light microscope is limited.

Resolution is the degree of detail which can be seen (Fig. 3.6). The limit of resolution of a microscope is the minimum distance by which two points can be separated and still be seen as two separate points and not one fuzzy one. Newspaper photographs, for example, have a rather poor resolution, being made up of quite large dots which you can see with the naked eye. This limits the amount of detail which you can see. Compare this with a good quality photograph with a higher resolution (smaller dots).

The limit of resolution depends on the wavelength of light. The resolution limit is about 0.45 times the wavelength. Shorter wavelengths give the best (smallest) resolution. The shortest wavelength light which we can see is blue light, which has a wavelength of about $450\,nm$. This gives a resolution of about $0.45 \times 450\,nm$, which is

close to $200\,nm$. Any objects smaller than this, or any points less than $200\,nm$ apart, will either be invisible or appear as blurs.

Electron beams, however, have a much shorter wavelength than light, so much better resolutions can be achieved. Electron microscopes have a maximum resolution around 400 times better than that of light microscopes, being able to separate objects as little as $0.5\,nm$ apart.

Fig. 3.5 A transmission electron microscope in use. The various knobs can be used to alter the magnification, the focus and the brightness of the image. The specimen is inside the white column. The beam of electrons passes down inside the column and through the specimen, before hitting the fluorescent screen where the image is produced.

Q1 (a) Using your own words as much as possible, explain the differences between magnification, resolution and limit of resolution.

(b) What is the significance of magnification, resolution and limit of resolution to the study of cells by microscopes?

The effects of magnification and increase in resolution

Magnification with no change in resolution

This is a photograph of a chloroplast in a plant cell taken with an electron microscope.

> The photograph has been magnified 5×. But there is no extra detail in the photograph. There has been no increase in resolution.

Increase in resolution with no change in magnification

> The resolution of the image has been increased 10×, by having 10 dots of visual information in each one of the dots (squares) shown above.
> Much more detail of the internal structure of the chloroplast is now shown.

What is the limit of resolution in this photograph?

This is a photograph of RER (Section 3.9) in an animal cell, taken with an electron microscope.

> To estimate the limit of resolution of the microscope, as it was used to take this photograph, we need to look at some small objects that are close together.

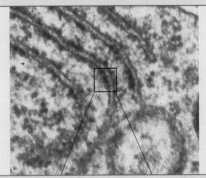

> The line of ribosomes here are very close together. Some are so close that is not clear if they are separate objects.
>
> To help you see the limit of resolution, look at the image below, which is larger but has the same resolution.

possible positions of two ribosomes

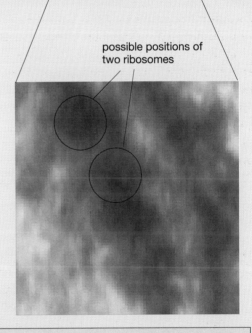

> You can now see that the top two ribosomes are about as close as they can be and still be clearly seen as separate. The distance between them is near the limit of resolution. The actual distance is about 4 nm. So the limit of resolution here is 4 nm.

Fig. 3.6 Magnification and resolution.

Electron micrograph of an animal cell (×9600)

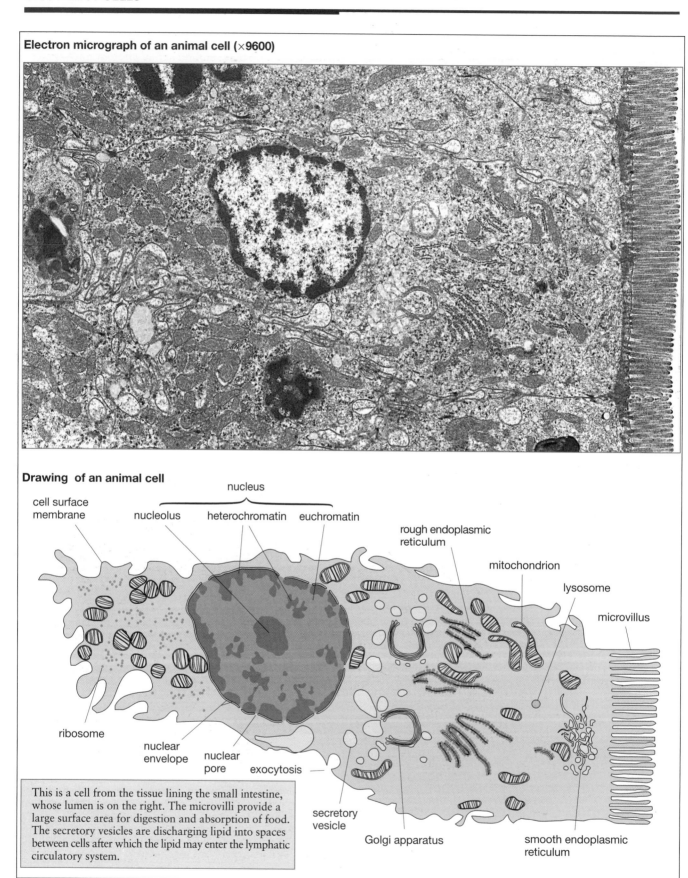

Drawing of an animal cell

This is a cell from the tissue lining the small intestine, whose lumen is on the right. The microvilli provide a large surface area for digestion and absorption of food. The secretory vesicles are discharging lipid into spaces between cells after which the lipid may enter the lymphatic circulatory system.

Fig. 3.7 Some features of animal cells visible using an electron microscope.

Electron micrograph of young plant cells (×7000)

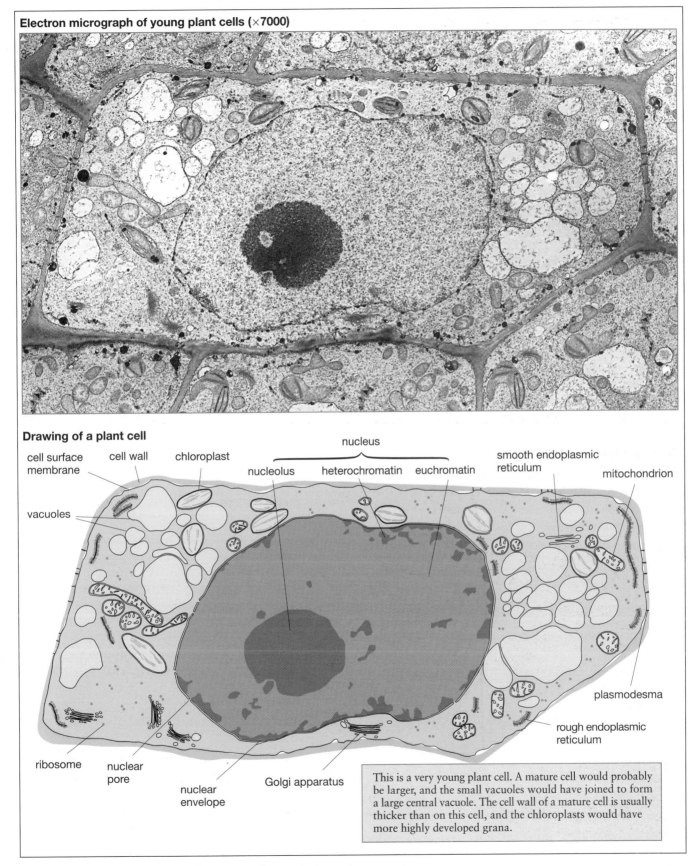

Drawing of a plant cell

cell surface membrane cell wall chloroplast

nucleus

nucleolus heterochromatin euchromatin

smooth endoplasmic reticulum

mitochondrion

vacuoles

plasmodesma

rough endoplasmic reticulum

ribosome nuclear pore

nuclear envelope

Golgi apparatus

This is a very young plant cell. A mature cell would probably be larger, and the small vacuoles would have joined to form a large central vacuole. The cell wall of a mature cell is usually thicker than on this cell, and the chloroplasts would have more highly developed grana.

Fig. 3.8 Some features of plant cells as seen using an electron microscope.

Box 3.1 Cell fractionation using centrifugation

Electron microscopy is an excellent technique for obtaining information about the structures of organelles. To find out how these organelles function, it is often useful to be able to separate one kind of organelle from all the rest.

First, a quantity of cells is taken from a suitable tissue. The cells are put into a buffered solution which has the same pH as the cell, so that enzymes (whose activity might be investigated later) are not damaged. The cell surface membranes are then broken, either by high frequency vibrations, immersion in a dilute solution, exposure to detergents or mechanical disruption by being forced through a narrow opening or grinding with an abrasive. This produces a liquid containing all the cell organelles in suspension.

This suspension is then spun in a centrifuge to separate cell organelles and fragments. In one method, called zonal centrifugation, the suspension is centrifuged at high speed in a tube containing a sucrose solution. Larger and denser particles move towards the bottom of the tube faster than smaller and less dense particles. This separates small objects such as ribosomes from larger ones such as mitochondria.

By removing a particular layer in the tube, you can obtain a suspension containing just nuclei,

for example, or just ribosomes. The biochemical activity of these structures can then be investigated without interference from other components of the cells.

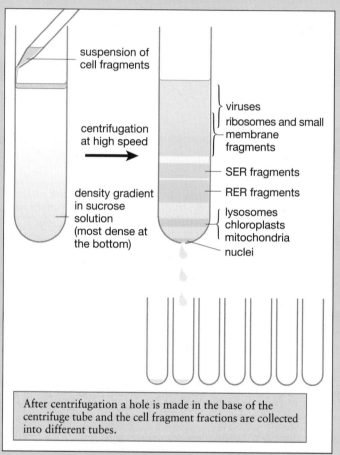

suspension of cell fragments

centrifugation at high speed

density gradient in sucrose solution (most dense at the bottom)

viruses
ribosomes and small membrane fragments

SER fragments

RER fragments

lysosomes
chloroplasts
mitochondria
nuclei

After centrifugation a hole is made in the base of the centrifuge tube and the cell fragment fractions are collected into different tubes.

Fig. 3.9 Cell fractionation using zonal centrifugation in a sucrose density gradient.

Q2 Liver cells were ground to produce a homogenate. The flow chart below shows how centrifugation was used to separate endoplasmic reticulum, mitochondria and nuclei.

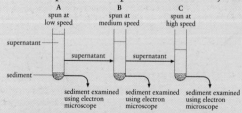

A
spun at low speed

B
spun at medium speed

C
spun at high speed

supernatant

supernatant

supernatant

sediment

sediment examined using electron microscope

sediment examined using electron microscope

sediment examined using electron microscope

(a) In which sediment, **A**, **B** or **C** would each of these organelles be found?
(i) endoplasmic reticulum, (ii) nuclei, (iii) mitochondria (2)

(b) Explain why it is possible to separate organelles in this way. (2)

NEAB 1995 (modified) (*Total 4 marks*)

CELL STRUCTURE

The sections which follow describe the structures and functions of each type of organelle which is found inside cells. There are many organelles, and therefore many of these descriptions have to be quite brief. You will also find many references to how the organelles are involved in functions which you may know little or nothing about at the moment, but you will be studying them later in your course. You may find it helpful to look back at this chapter again at a later stage, when you understand a little more about topics such as cell division, protein synthesis and respiration, for example.

3.6 Cell membranes

There is no living cell that is not surrounded by a cell membrane, and most cells have membranes inside them too. The membrane around the outside of a cell is called the **cell surface membrane.** Fig. 3.10 shows the structure of a cell surface membrane. This representation of its structure is called the **fluid mosaic model.**

A cell membrane is formed from a **phospholipid bilayer** whose structure is described and explained in Fig. 1.19. Interspersed amongst the phospholipid molecules are **cholesterol** molecules. Cell surface membranes of animal cells may contain almost as many cholesterol molecules as phospholipid molecules, while plant cell surface membranes contain other molecules similar to cholesterol.

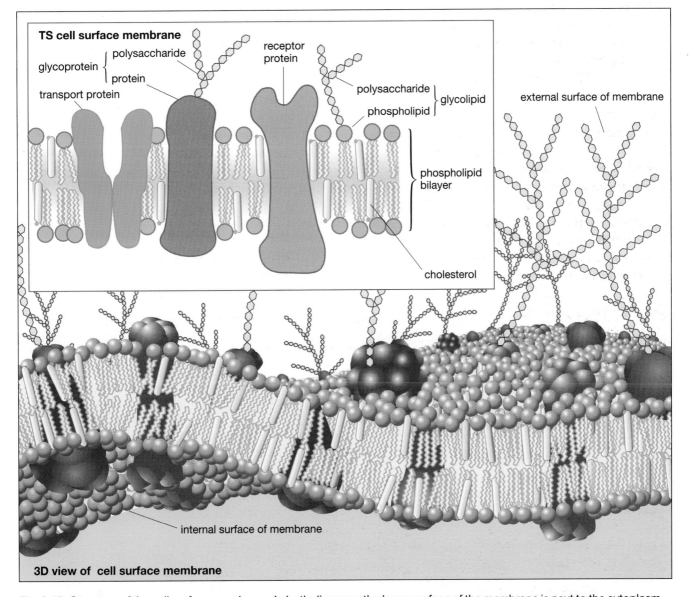

TS cell surface membrane

glycoprotein { polysaccharide / protein }

transport protein

receptor protein

polysaccharide } glycolipid
phospholipid

external surface of membrane

phospholipid bilayer

cholesterol

internal surface of membrane

3D view of cell surface membrane

Fig. 3.10 Structure of the cell surface membrane. In both diagrams the lower surface of the membrane is next to the cytoplasm.

Cholesterol molecules help to make the membrane more fluid at low temperatures and less fluid at high temperatures.

Floating amongst the phospholipid and cholesterol molecules are many globular **protein** molecules, many of which span from one side to the other. These proteins tend to be arranged with hydrophilic parts of their chains (that is parts containing amino acids with hydrophilic R groups) on the outer surfaces of the membrane, and hydrophobic parts within the membrane amongst the hydrophobic tails of the lipids. Many of these proteins act as pores or transporters, allowing substances to pass from one side of the membrane to the other (Sections 3.25 and 3.27).

Most of the protein molecules and many of the lipid molecules have short **carbohydrate** chains attached to them. These molecules are called **glycoproteins** and **glycolipids**. The carbohydrate chains are all on the outer surface of the membrane.

Glycolipids and glycoproteins help to stabilise membrane structure by forming hydrogen bonds with water molecules outside the membrane. They are found in especially high concentrations in membranes which have to survive in difficult conditions, such as those of cells lining the duodenum where the membranes might be disrupted by bile salts. Another, quite different function of glycolipids and glycoproteins in membranes is in recognition. Human A, B, AB and O blood groups are the result of small differences in the carbohydrate chains of glycolipids in the cell surface membrane of red blood cells, while many receptors for hormones and neurotransmitters (Section 14.10) are glycoproteins.

Why is this structure called a *fluid mosaic*? All of these molecules are in constant motion, vibrating and bumping into each other and changing place within their layer. So the membrane behaves rather like a **fluid** – although it does not flow away into its surroundings! The **mosaic** part of the name refers to the mosaic pattern of protein molecules which you would see if you looked down on the surface of the membrane.

Membranes *inside* cells have a very similar structure to cell surface membranes. However, the relative proportions of the different kinds of molecules can vary considerably. For example, the membranes around mitochondria have hardly any carbohydrate attached to their lipids and proteins.

The most important functions of cell membranes are

Function	Where you can read more about it
At the cell surface	
Controlling the passage of substances into and out of a cell	pages 74 to 78
Receiving information from outside the cell, in the form of chemicals such as neurotransmitters and hormones	pages 308 to 310, 312, 326
Cell recognition	pages 484 to 485
Transmitting nervous impulses	pages 303 to 306
Inside the cell	
Providing attachment sites for molecules involved in, for example: • capturing light energy • transferring electrons in photosynthesis and respiration • ATP synthesis	page 178 pages 180, 195, 197 pages 180, 197
Providing separate compartments inside a cell, within which different processes can take place in isolation from each other	pages 61, 191

Table 3.1 Functions of cell membranes.

listed in Table 3.1, together with references to the pages where you can find out more about them.

3.7 Cytoplasm

The term cytoplasm is often used to refer to the 'background material' inside a cell, within which all the organelles such as mitochondria and ribosomes are found. This is how the term is used throughout this book. Alternatively, the term cytoplasm can be used to refer to the entire contents of the cell, including the organelles, except for the nucleus. In this case, the background material is called cytosol.

Cytoplasm is mostly water, with a variety of other molecules dissolved or suspended in it. Many of these are proteins, especially enzymes.

3.8 Ribosomes

Ribosomes appear in electron micrographs as small black dots. They are usually in clusters called **polyribosomes.** Some ribosomes are found free in the cytoplasm, while others are attached to the outer surfaces of the membranes of the rough endoplasmic reticulum (Section 3.9). Ribosomes are also found inside mitochondria and chloroplasts.

A ribosome is about 30 nm in diameter and is made of protein and ribosomal RNA (rRNA). The structure of a ribosome is shown in Fig. 3.11. Each ribosome has a small subunit and a large subunit.

The function of ribosomes is to provide a platform on which protein synthesis takes place and to help with several stages of this process. Protein synthesis, including the roles of ribosomes, is described in Section 5.3.

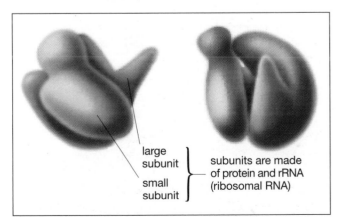

Fig. 3.11 Ribosome structure. Two views of a ribosome are shown.

3.9 Endoplasmic reticulum

'Endoplasmic' means 'inside the cytoplasm', and 'reticulum' means 'network'. The endoplasmic reticulum (often abbreviated to ER) is a network of membranes running through the cytoplasm of every cell. The membranes enclose spaces called **cisternae** (Fig. 3.12) which form an interconnecting channel throughout the cytoplasm.

Some parts of the endoplasmic reticulum have ribosomes attached to the cytoplasmic side of the membranes. This is called **rough endoplasmic reticulum** (or RER). These ribosomes synthesise proteins which are to be secreted from the cell, to form lysosomes (Section 3.11) or to become part of the cell surface membrane. As these proteins are being made, some of them are passed through pores in the endoplasmic reticulum membrane into the cisternae, while others become part of the membrane itself. The cisternae then break into small vesicles and carry these proteins to the Golgi apparatus (also sometimes called the Golgi body) (Fig. 3.12).

Other parts of the endoplasmic reticulum have no ribosomes attached. These are called **smooth endoplasmic reticulum** (or SER). The cisternae of SER tend to be more tubular, in contrast to the flattened sacs of RER. SER has many different functions, including the synthesis of cholesterol and of steroid hormones such as testosterone, and the breaking down of toxins such as drugs.

3.10 Golgi apparatus

The Golgi apparatus (or Golgi body) is a stack of curved cisternae with several smaller vesicles entering and leaving it (Fig. 3.12). Vesicles containing newly synthesised proteins break off from the rough endoplasmic reticulum, and travel towards the Golgi apparatus where they fuse with its convex face. Here the proteins are 'finished off' and packaged before being exported from the cell. They may, for example, have carbohydrates added to them to form glycoproteins. The proteins are concentrated within the Golgi cisternae; in pancreatic cells secreting insulin, for example, the insulin is concentrated so much in the Golgi that it crystallises.

When the protein is ready, small vesicles break away from the concave face of the Golgi apparatus and move towards the surface of the cell. They fuse with the cell surface membrane and release their contents to the outside. The membranes of the vesicles, which were originally part of the rough endoplasmic reticulum membrane, become incorporated in the cell surface membrane.

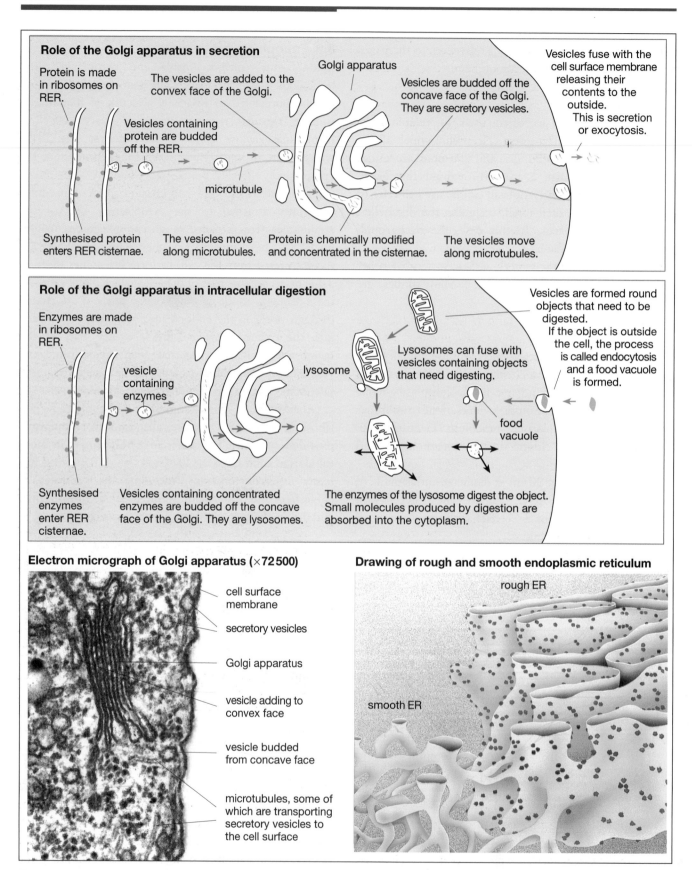

Role of the Golgi apparatus in secretion

Protein is made in ribosomes on RER.

The vesicles are added to the convex face of the Golgi.

Golgi apparatus

Vesicles are budded off the concave face of the Golgi. They are secretory vesicles.

Vesicles fuse with the cell surface membrane releasing their contents to the outside.
This is secretion or exocytosis.

Vesicles containing protein are budded off the RER.

microtubule

Synthesised protein enters RER cisternae.

The vesicles move along microtubules.

Protein is chemically modified and concentrated in the cisternae.

The vesicles move along microtubules.

Role of the Golgi apparatus in intracellular digestion

Enzymes are made in ribosomes on RER.

vesicle containing enzymes

lysosome

Lysosomes can fuse with vesicles containing objects that need digesting.

Vesicles are formed round objects that need to be digested.
If the object is outside the cell, the process is called endocytosis and a food vacuole is formed.

food vacuole

Synthesised enzymes enter RER cisternae.

Vesicles containing concentrated enzymes are budded off the concave face of the Golgi. They are lysosomes.

The enzymes of the lysosome digest the object. Small molecules produced by digestion are absorbed into the cytoplasm.

Electron micrograph of Golgi apparatus (×72 500)

cell surface membrane

secretory vesicles

Golgi apparatus

vesicle adding to convex face

vesicle budded from concave face

microtubules, some of which are transporting secretory vesicles to the cell surface

Drawing of rough and smooth endoplasmic reticulum

rough ER

smooth ER

Fig. 3.12 The roles of the Golgi apparatus.

Not all the proteins dealt with in the Golgi are destined for export. In animal cells some of the vesicles released from the convex face become **lysosomes** (Section 3.11). Plant cells do not have lysosomes. In plant cells, some of the Golgi vesicles take proteins to the large vacuole where they are released into the cell sap (Section 3.20).

In plant cells the Golgi is also involved in processing carbohydrates. The polysaccharides which will make up the matrix (background material) of the cell wall are first made in the endoplasmic reticulum, then assembled in the Golgi apparatus, then carried to the cell surface inside secretory vesicles. The whole process, from endoplasmic reticulum to cell surface, can take as little as 20 minutes.

3.11 Lysosomes

Lysosomes are tiny vesicles found in most animal cells but not in plant cells. They are usually about 0.5 µm in diameter and are surrounded by a single membrane. They have no structure inside them, but simply contain a variety of hydrolytic (digestive) enzymes in solution.

Lysosomes are formed as buds which break away from the Golgi apparatus. Their main function is to fuse with other vesicles in the cell which contain something which needs to be digested, for example a bacterium which has been brought into the cell by phagocytosis (Section 3.28) or a worn-out mitochondrion which needs to be destroyed. The enzymes in the lysosome then digest the contents of this vesicle, producing soluble substances which can be absorbed into the cytoplasm. In plant cells these functions are carried out by enzymes in the vacuole.

3.12 Microtubules

In the previous sections there have been many examples of structures *moving* inside the cell. Microtubules are structures which help to direct this movement.

Fig. 3.13 shows the structure of a microtubule. They are hollow cylinders that are made of many **tubulin** molecules. Tubulin is a globular protein. A microtubule is about 25 nm in diameter, and may be several millimetres long.

Microtubules are found throughout the cytoplasm of all eukaryotic cells. They are also found inside cilia and flagella (Fig. 3.15). Also, the spindle fibres which appear during mitosis and meiosis are microtubules.

Fig. 3.14 shows how microtubules are involved in moving structures around in the cytoplasm. The microtubules themselves have no way of moving, but they act as anchors for a protein which provides a driving force. Two proteins which commonly do this are **dynein** and

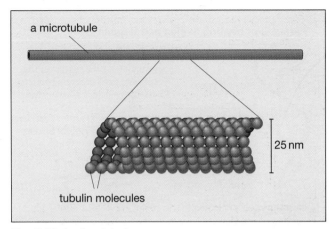

Fig. 3.13 A microtubule.

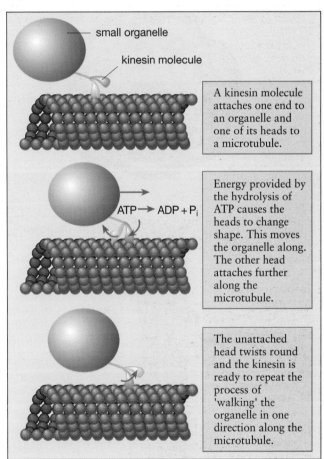

A kinesin molecule attaches one end to an organelle and one of its heads to a microtubule.

$ATP \rightarrow ADP + P_i$

Energy provided by the hydrolysis of ATP causes the heads to change shape. This moves the organelle along. The other head attaches further along the microtubule.

The unattached head twists round and the kinesin is ready to repeat the process of 'walking' the organelle in one direction along the microtubule.

Fig. 3.14 How microtubules may direct the movement of organelles.

kinesin. Kinesin, for example, can attach one end of itself to a microtubule and its other end to an organelle, perhaps a small vesicle. The kinesin molecule swivels its head, which pushes the organelle along relative to the microtubule. The head then attaches further along the microtubule, and the kinesin molecule returns to its original shape and repeats the process. The organelle is

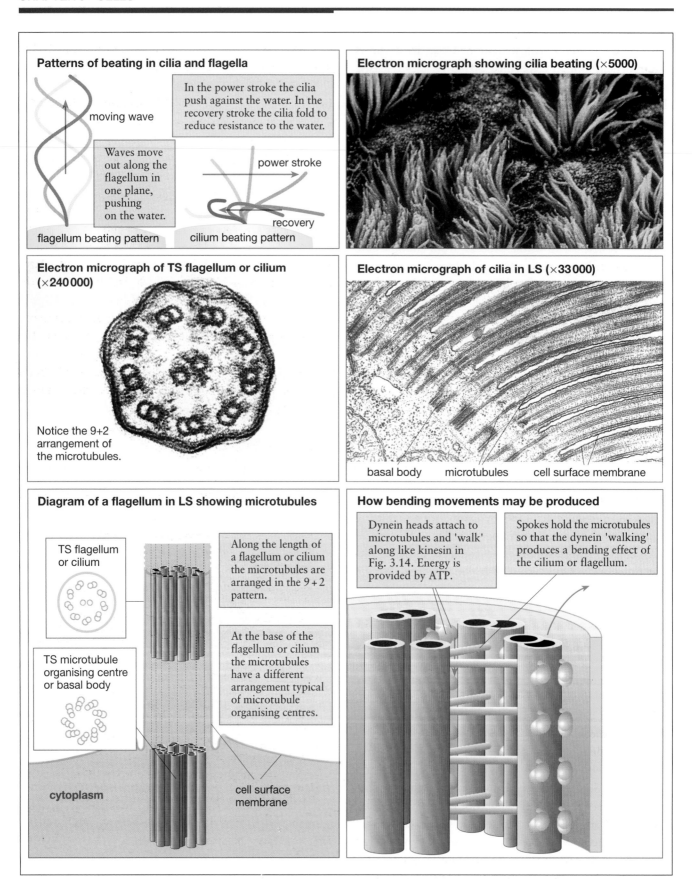

Patterns of beating in cilia and flagella

moving wave

In the power stroke the cilia push against the water. In the recovery stroke the cilia fold to reduce resistance to the water.

Waves move out along the flagellum in one plane, pushing on the water.

power stroke

recovery

flagellum beating pattern

cilium beating pattern

Electron micrograph showing cilia beating (×5000)

Electron micrograph of TS flagellum or cilium (×240 000)

Notice the 9+2 arrangement of the microtubules.

Electron micrograph of cilia in LS (×33 000)

basal body   microtubules   cell surface membrane

Diagram of a flagellum in LS showing microtubules

TS flagellum or cilium

TS microtubule organising centre or basal body

Along the length of a flagellum or cilium the microtubules are arranged in the 9 + 2 pattern.

At the base of the flagellum or cilium the microtubules have a different arrangement typical of microtubule organising centres.

cytoplasm

cell surface membrane

How bending movements may be produced

Dynein heads attach to microtubules and 'walk' along like kinesin in Fig. 3.14. Energy is provided by ATP.

Spokes hold the microtubules so that the dynein 'walking' produces a bending effect of the cilium or flagellum.

Fig. 3.15 How microtubules cause movement in cilia and flagella.

thus moved along beside the microtubule. The process requires energy which is obtained from ATP.

Microtubules are thought to cause the movement of chromosomes in a different way. This movement probably occurs by growth of the microtubules. One end of a microtubule becomes attached to the centromere of a chromosome. At this end, tubulin molecules are added or subtracted, lengthening or shortening the microtubule and so causing movement of the chromosome. This is probably how microtubules arrange the chromosomes on the equator of the cell during division of the nucleus (Section 4.2).

In many cells, the formation of microtubules may be coordinated by structures called **microtubule organising centres**. For example, in animal cells two paired structures called **centrioles** (Fig. 3.7) are present, and the microtubules which make up the spindle are organised by these organelles (Section 4.2).

3.13 Cilia and flagella

Cilia and flagella are long, thin extensions from the cell surface which can produce movement. They have the same structure; the term cilia is used for relatively short structures, which usually occur in large numbers on a particular cell, while a flagellum is longer, only one or two usually occurring on any one cell. Plant cells do not usually have cilia or flagella, but they are found, for example, in the male gametes of ferns, liverworts and mosses.

Fig. 3.15 shows the structure of cilia and flagella. Most cilia are about 3–4 μm long. As they are extensions of the cell, they are covered with cell surface membrane. Running along their length are microtubules. These are very precisely arranged. In a cross-section of a cilium, you can see two microtubules in the centre surrounded by a ring of nine pairs or doublets. At the base of each cilium is a microtubule organising centre, called a **basal body**, from which the cilium has developed.

Movement is caused by the action of a protein called **dynein**, which projects as a pair of arms from each doublet. The heads of these dynein arms can latch on to the next-door microtubule. The head swivels, pulling one microtubule along with respect to the other. This causes bending of the cilium. These actions can be superbly coordinated not only within a cilium, causing rhythmic bending and straightening, but also amongst all the cilia in a cell and all its neighbours. The cilia move slightly out of phase with one another so that the overall effect is like a field of grass blowing gently in the wind. These movements can either cause the cell to which the cilia are attached to move, or they can move liquids surrounding the cell.

3.14 Actin filaments and intermediate filaments

All cells contain a network of protein filaments, which act as a 'skeleton' supporting the cell, and help to determine its shape. Together with microtubules, these protein filaments are known as the **cytoskeleton**.

Actin filaments are made from many globular protein molecules linked into a long chain, with two chains twisted together (Fig. 3.16). The filaments are very small, about 7 nm in diameter, and so are often known as **microfilaments.** Muscle cells contain especially large amounts of actin filaments which are involved in the contraction of the muscle (Section 16.11).

Intermediate filaments are wider than actin filaments, being about 10 nm in diameter. Several different, but similar, proteins form intermediate filaments of which one is keratin (Fig. 1.13). Keratin is found in many cells, but is present in especially large amounts in cells in the epidermis of the skin.

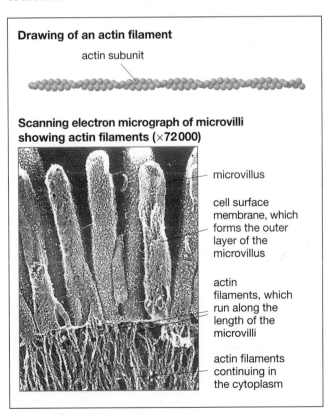

Drawing of an actin filament

actin subunit

Scanning electron micrograph of microvilli showing actin filaments (×72 000)

microvillus

cell surface membrane, which forms the outer layer of the microvillus

actin filaments, which run along the length of the microvilli

actin filaments continuing in the cytoplasm

Fig. 3.16 Actin filaments.

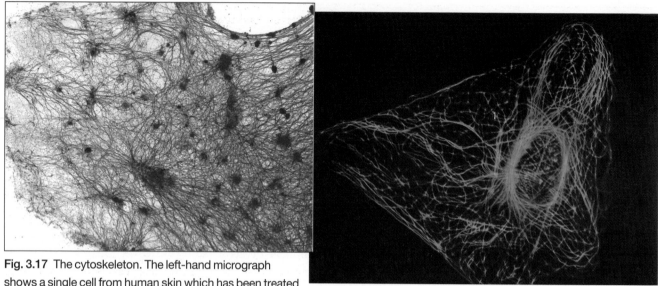

Fig. 3.17 The cytoskeleton. The left-hand micrograph shows a single cell from human skin which has been treated to show the keratin (intermediate) filaments. The right-hand micrograph shows a cell treated to show the network of microtubules.

3.15 Mitochondria

Mitochondria are quite large organelles which can be seen with a good light microscope, especially if stained with a chemical which colours them specifically and no other part of the cell. However, to see detail in their structure, an electron microscope is needed. Mitochondria are very variable in size and shape, with large ones up to 10 μm in length and several micrometres in diameter. Indeed, mitochondria can move around, divide, fuse and change shape.

Fig. 3.18 shows the structure of a mitochondrion. It has two membranes, separated by an **intermembrane space**. The **outer membrane** is relatively smooth, but the **inner membrane** is folded to form projections called **cristae**.

Between the cristae is the **matrix** which fills the rest of the space inside the mitochondrion. The matrix also contains ribosomes and DNA which are used to make some of the mitochondrion's own proteins.

Mitochondria are the site of the aerobic stages of respiration, **Krebs cycle** and **oxidative phosphorylation.** You can read about these in detail on pages 192 to 196.

3.16 Nucleus

The nucleus is the part of the cell which contains DNA. Here, the DNA is isolated from the reactions occurring in other parts of the cell, decreasing the likelihood that it will be damaged.

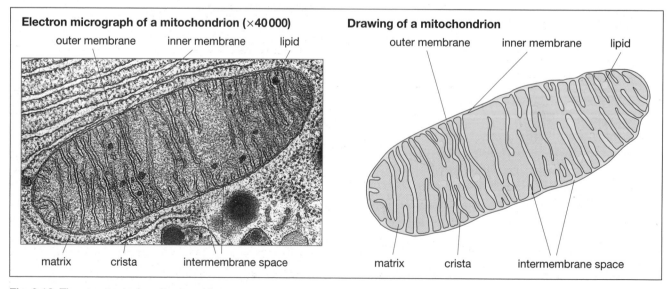

Electron micrograph of a mitochondrion (×40 000)

outer membrane   inner membrane   lipid

matrix   crista   intermembrane space

Drawing of a mitochondrion

outer membrane   inner membrane   lipid

matrix   crista   intermembrane space

Fig. 3.18 The structure of a mitochondrion.

Box 3.2 Were chloroplasts and mitochondria once bacteria?

Several features of chloroplasts and mitochondria are very similar to features of bacteria. In particular, chloroplasts and mitochondria are self-replicating. They contain circular DNA molecules. (All the other DNA in a plant or animal cell is inside the nucleus.) They contain ribosomes which are smaller than those found elsewhere in the cell. They use the DNA and ribosomes to make some of the proteins which they need. They have two membranes around them – the outer one is similar in structure and composition to other membranes in the cell, but the inner membrane has similarities with bacterial membranes.

It is believed that, several thousand million years ago, bacteria which could photosynthesise or respire aerobically took up residence in other cells. A mutualistic relationship – one which benefits both organisms – evolved. The bacteria which could photosynthesise became chloroplasts – they could provide the cell with an organic energy source, while the cell provided them with nutrients. The bacteria which could respire aerobically became mitochondria – they could provide the cell with more ATP than could be produced by anaerobic respiration while the cell provided glucose and other nutrients. Eventually, these bacteria became permanent inhabitants of eukaryotic cells.

There is an intriguing piece of evidence for this hypothesis. Behind the University Museum in Oxford, there is a pond into which the carcasses of elephants were thrown after taxidermists had prepared their skins for exhibition. In the mud at the bottom of this pond lives a kind of amoeba called *Pelomyxa palustris* (Fig. 3.19).

Pelomyxa is a very unusual organism. Although it has a nucleus and so is classified as a eukaryotic organism, it has several strange features. One is that it does not contain mitochondria. However, it does contain two sorts of bacteria living mutualistically in its cytoplasm. If these bacteria are killed, then *Pelomyxa* dies. It seems that the bacteria remove lactic acid from *Pelomyxa*'s cytoplasm and metabolise it. Might this represent an early stage of the mutualistic relationship between bacteria and eukaryotic cells which gave rise to today's plant and animal cells?

Fig. 3.19 *Pelomyxa*.

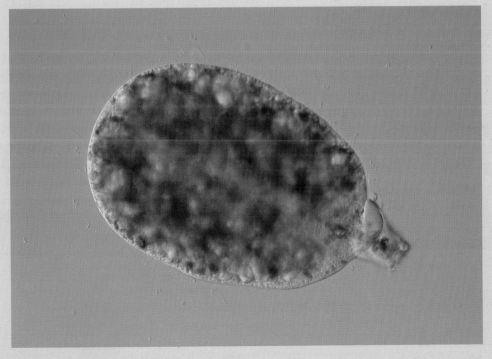

DNA is contained in **chromosomes**. A chromosome is made of a DNA molecule, associated with proteins called **histones** (Fig. 4.3). In a cell which is not dividing – that is in interphase – the chromosomes are not visible as threads but appear as a rather disorganised material called **chromatin**. In some parts of the nucleus, the chromatin is densely packed and looks dark in an electron micrograph. This is known as **heterochromatin**. In other parts, it is less densely packed, looks lighter in colour and is called **euchromatin**. The DNA in the heterochromatin is not active, but the DNA in the euchromatin can be used for transcription (page 104), the first stage of protein synthesis.

Within the nucleus (Fig. 3.20) there is often a particularly darkly staining region called the **nucleolus**. Here, ribosomal RNA is made by transcription from DNA. The small and large subunits of ribosomes are assembled in the nucleolus. They leave the nucleus through pores (Fig. 3.20) before being assembled into complete ribosomes in the cytoplasm.

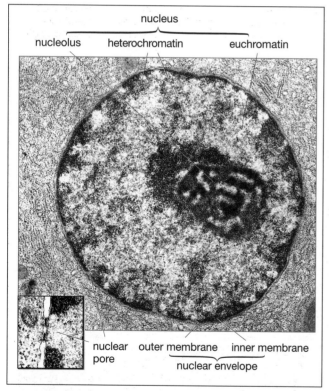

Fig. 3.20 The nucleus of a cell as seen in the electron microscope.

3.17 Nuclear envelope

The nuclear envelope is made up of two membranes, with a narrow space between them. The outer of these two membranes links up with the endoplasmic reticulum. Indeed, in some cells it is exactly like a piece of rough

endoplasmic reticulum complete with attached ribosomes.

These two membranes have many gaps in them which are called **nuclear pores**. The gaps are relatively large – much bigger than the protein pores in the cell surface membrane which are discussed in Section 3.6. They are large enough to allow partially assembled ribosomes from the nucleolus to pass through, as well as messenger RNA on its way out of the nucleus and enzymes such as DNA polymerase on their way in.

3.18 Cell wall

All plant cells are surrounded by a cell wall. Animal cells never have cell walls. The cell wall is outside the cell surface membrane, so it is actually an extracellular structure. Cell walls are usually about 1 µm thick. They are made of glycoproteins and several different polysaccharides, the most important of which is **cellulose** (Section 1.9).

The polysaccharides making up the cell wall are assembled at the cell surface membrane, so that those parts of the wall which are made first end up further away from the membrane than those which are made later. In most cell walls three layers can be seen (Fig. 3.21). The layer which is laid down first, and therefore is furthest from the cell, is called the **middle lamella**. It is called the middle lamella because, when two plant cells are next to each other, it is this layer which forms the dividing line between their two cell walls. The middle lamella is made of polysaccharides called **pectins**. Pectins are very large branched molecules, with many electrical charges on them. This allows them to trap water molecules and form **gels**. (Pectin is used to make jam set.) Pectin molecules do not form fibres like cellulose but are arranged quite randomly.

The other two layers of the cell wall are the **primary cell wall**, which lies next to the middle lamella, and the **secondary cell wall**, which is closest to the cell surface membrane. Both of these contain pectins, but this time mixed with other polysaccharides called **hemicelluloses** and also with **lignin**. The pectins and hemicelluloses, together with smaller amounts of glycoproteins, form a gel-like matrix in which fibres of **cellulose** are embedded (Fig. 3.21). In the primary cell wall the cellulose fibres are arranged more or less randomly, but in the secondary cell wall they lie in neatly ordered parallel rows. In some cell walls, there are many layers of cellulose fibres in the secondary cell wall, each layer lying in a different direction.

The various molecules forming the matrix, and the cellulose molecules forming the fibres, are bonded to each other by hydrogen bonds. Thus the cell wall is immensely

Electron micrograph of part of a plant cell which has recently divided

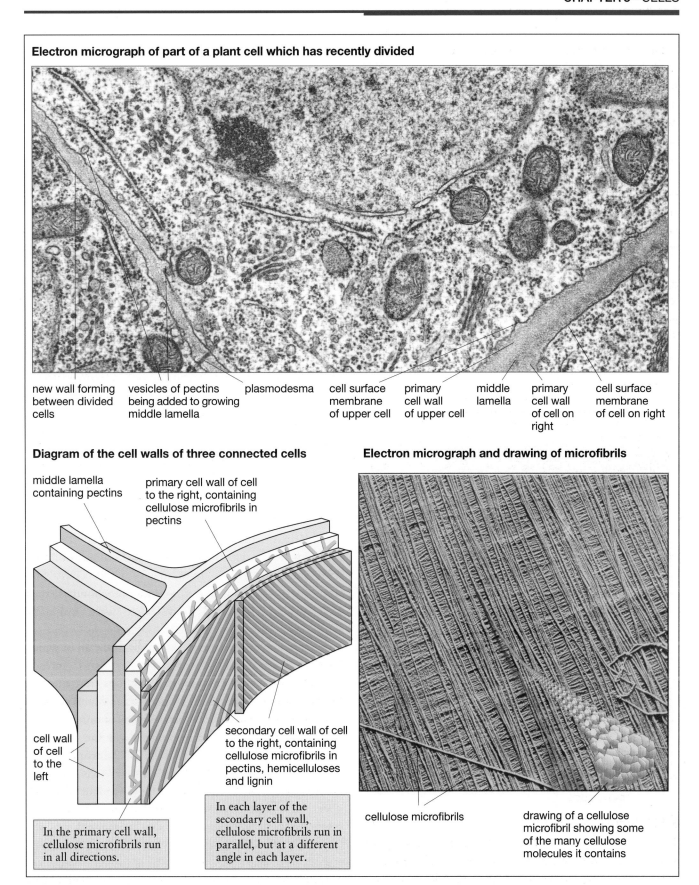

new wall forming between divided cells

vesicles of pectins being added to growing middle lamella

plasmodesma

cell surface membrane of upper cell

primary cell wall of upper cell

middle lamella

primary cell wall of cell on right

cell surface membrane of cell on right

Diagram of the cell walls of three connected cells

middle lamella containing pectins

primary cell wall of cell to the right, containing cellulose microfibrils in pectins

cell wall of cell to the left

secondary cell wall of cell to the right, containing cellulose microfibrils in pectins, hemicelluloses and lignin

In the primary cell wall, cellulose microfibrils run in all directions.

In each layer of the secondary cell wall, cellulose microfibrils run in parallel, but at a different angle in each layer.

Electron micrograph and drawing of microfibrils

cellulose microfibrils

drawing of a cellulose microfibril showing some of the many cellulose molecules it contains

Fig. 3.21 The plant cell wall.

strong and has tremendous resistance to extension and compression. It is also very difficult to digest because few organisms produce enzymes which can successfully break the β(1-4) linkages in the cellulose molecules, let alone all the other many different linkages in the polysaccharides in the matrix. The cell wall therefore forms a strong supportive and protective structure enclosing the entire plant cell. It also holds adjacent plant cells firmly together because the middle lamellae of adjacent cells are continuous. However, because the wall is made up of a network of large molecules with many gaps between them, small molecules such as water and ions can diffuse through the wall without difficulty. The cell wall plays virtually no part in regulating what enters or leaves the cell.

3.19 Plasmodesmata

Although small molecules and ions can pass easily through cell walls, plant cells need a faster and more reliable way of allowing larger substances to move between adjacent cells. This is done through **plasmodesmata**. Most plant cells have many plasmodesmata, with typical numbers ranging between about 100 to 100 000.

A plasmodesma is a gap in the cell wall, running right through the walls of two adjacent cells (Fig. 3.22). This gap is about 25 nm wide at its narrowest point. The cell surface membranes of the two cells run right through the gap and are continuous with each other – the cells are actually joined. Cytoplasm and endoplasmic reticulum fill the plasmodesma leaving about 3 nm space for molecules to pass through. This makes it possible for many

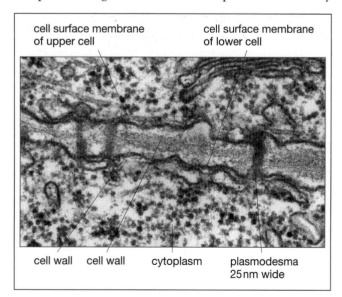

Fig. 3.22 Plasmodesmata between two plant cells.

different kinds of molecules to pass easily from one cell to the next, although this passage does appear to be regulated by the cells.

3.20 Vacuole

A vacuole is a membrane-bound organelle that usually contains liquid. All cells have vacuoles, but plant cells differ from animal cells in that their vacuoles are very large, permanent, and usually occupy a position fairly near the centre of the cell. In a mature plant cell, up to 90% of its volume may be taken up by the vacuole. The membrane surrounding a plant cell vacuole is often known as the **tonoplast**.

Plant cell vacuoles contain many different substances in solution in water. These include sugars, storage proteins, pigments (coloured substances) and enzymes.

Vacuoles have a wide variety of functions. For example, the colours of some flower petals are caused by pigments held inside vacuoles in their cells. Some plants store sucrose in their vacuoles, either temporarily or for much longer periods; the sugar which we obtain from sugar beet, sugar cane and many fruits comes from vacuoles. In many plants the vacuoles perform the same functions as lysosomes in animal cells (Section 3.11) and contain digestive enzymes.

3.21 Plastids

Plastids are found only in plant cells, not in animal cells. Plastids are organelles surrounded by two membranes. In this they are similar to mitochondria. Another similarity with mitochondria is that they contain DNA and ribosomes, which suggests that, like mitochondria, they have probably evolved from what were originally symbiotic prokaryotes (Box 3.2).

There are many different kinds of plastids, all of which develop from small 'proplastids'. Plastids include **amyloplasts,** which contain starch grains and may be found in large quantities in storage organs such as roots and potato tubers, **chromoplasts**, which contain pigments such as carotene and are responsible for the colour of carrot roots and many flower petals, and **chloroplasts.**

Chloroplasts are not found in all plant cells, but only those which need to photosynthesise. The plant cells with most chloroplasts are the palisade cells in leaves; spongy mesophyll cells and guard cells also contain chloroplasts (Fig. 8.2). Chloroplasts may also be found in cells near the surface of stems. They are never found in cells which are not exposed to light, such as those in parts of the plant which are underground.

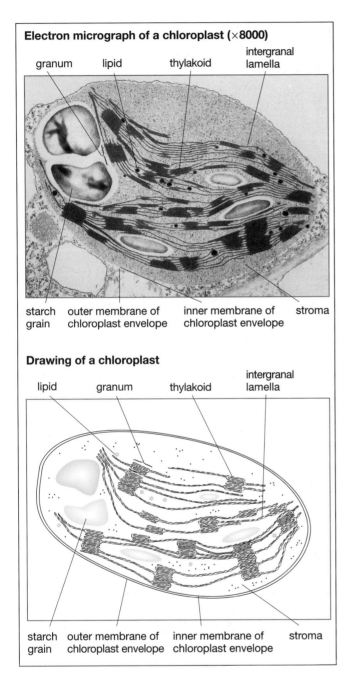

Electron micrograph of a chloroplast (×8000)

granum   lipid   thylakoid   intergranal lamella

starch grain   outer membrane of chloroplast envelope   inner membrane of chloroplast envelope   stroma

Drawing of a chloroplast

lipid   granum   thylakoid   intergranal lamella

starch grain   outer membrane of chloroplast envelope   inner membrane of chloroplast envelope   stroma

Fig. 3.23 The structure of a chloroplast.

Fig. 3.23 shows the structure of a chloroplast. They are large organelles, often about 10 µm in length. Within any one cell the chloroplasts are usually larger than the mitochondria, and there are fewer of them.

Inside the chloroplast is a third system of membranes, forming many tiny flattened sacs called **thylakoids**. In places these thylakoids are stacked on top of each other to form **grana**. Grana are linked by extensions of some of the thylakoids, forming long membrane-bound tubes called **intergranal lamellae**. All of these membranes lie in a matrix called the **stroma**.

The thylakoid membranes contain **chlorophyll** molecules, which give the whole chloroplast – and the whole leaf – its green colour. Also in these membranes are the molecules involved in the light-dependent reactions of photosynthesis, including photophosphorylation (Section 8.4). These reactions involve the ejection of electrons from some of the chlorophyll molecules when light hits them; the electrons are then passed along a chain of carrier molecules in the thylakoid membrane. This process provides energy for synthesising ATP. You can read much more about these processes on pages 171 to 185.

The stroma contains the enzymes required for the Calvin cycle, in which carbohydrates are made from carbon dioxide and water. The most abundant of these enzymes is ribulose bisphosphate carboxylase, usually known as Rubisco. It is not only the most abundant enzyme in the world, but actually the most abundant *protein*. Up to one-quarter of the total protein in a leaf is Rubisco. In 1993, it was estimated that there were 10 kg of Rubisco in the world for every person on Earth.

If the plant makes more carbohydrate in photosynthesis than it needs, then some may be temporarily stored as starch inside the chloroplasts. The starch forms granules which may take up a large amount of space in the stroma. The stroma also contains lipid droplets, DNA and ribosomes.

Q3 (a) Explain the difference between resolution and magnification in microscopy. (4)

(b) How, and to what extent, has the use of the electron microscope increased our knowledge of the structure of cells? (15)

(c) In what types of investigation would it be necessary to use a light microscope, rather than an electron microscope? (4)

UCLES 1993   (*Total 23 marks*)

PROKARYOTIC CELLS
3.22 Structure of a prokaryotic cell

Fig 3.24 shows the structure of a bacterium. Like all bacteria it is single-celled and has no nucleus. Such cells are called **prokaryotic cells**. All bacteria, including blue greens, are prokaryotes. Plant, animal and fungal cells, which do have nuclei, are **eukaryotic cells**.

Prokaryotic cells are usually smaller than eukaryotic cells, typically with volumes about 1000 or 10 000 times less than a typical plant or animal cell. They are similar in size to a mitochondrion or a chloroplast. Indeed, mitochondria and chloroplasts probably were prokaryotic cells which came to live inside the larger eukaryotic ones (Box 3.2) many millions of years ago.

All prokaryotic cells are surrounded by a **cell wall** which gives support and protection to the cell and is made of a variety of polysaccharides. These polysaccharides, however, are very different from those in plant cell walls; prokaryote cell walls do not contain cellulose, for example. Bacterial cell walls contain large amounts of substances known as **peptidoglycans**, which, as their name suggests, are made up of molecules in which peptides and sugars are combined. These form long, branched, cross-linked chains and make the wall very strong. Cell walls are very important to bacteria. They stop them from bursting when they absorb water (Fig. 3.30) and help to protect them from invasion by viruses (Section 21.1). If you can damage the cell wall you can kill the bacterium. The antibiotic penicillin inhibits the enzymes which help to form the cross-links between the peptidoglycans.

Many bacteria have a thick layer of jelly-like material surrounding them called a **capsule**. The capsule is made of polysaccharides which absorb water to form a slimy material. (Bacterial capsules make up a high proportion of the plaque which can collect on your teeth.) The capsule protects the bacterium from attack by viruses, and from antibodies (Section 21.9). For example, the bacterium *Pneumococcus* exists in two forms, one with a capsule and one without. The one with a capsule is a dangerous pathogenic (disease-causing) organism, able to infect a person's lungs and cause severe pneumonia. The one without a capsule is easily destroyed by the immune system, and does not cause disease at all.

Beneath the cell wall is a **cell surface membrane**. This has a very similar structure to that of eukaryotic cells, being made up of a phospholipid bilayer in which protein molecules float. (Some bacteria, known as Gram-negative bacteria, have another membrane which is described in

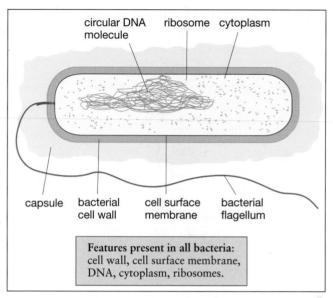

Fig. 3.24 Structure of a typical bacterium.

circular DNA molecule   ribosome   cytoplasm

capsule   bacterial cell wall   cell surface membrane   bacterial flagellum

Features present in all bacteria: cell wall, cell surface membrane, DNA, cytoplasm, ribosomes.

Box 3.3.) In photosynthetic bacteria, there may be extensive membrane systems inside the cell, sometimes closely associated with the cell surface membrane. These membrane systems hold the molecules which are involved in capturing light energy.

The cytoplasm often contains large numbers of **ribosomes**. Like the slightly larger ribosomes of eukaryotic cells, these are made of ribosomal RNA and protein and are the sites of protein synthesis.

The DNA of bacteria is a single, large, circular molecule. This is unlike the DNA of eukaryotes, which is linear rather than circular and is usually made up of several molecules each of which forms a chromosome. The chromosomes of eukaryotic cells are complex structures involving proteins called histones as well as DNA. Prokaryotic DNA does not form chromosomes, and although it does have proteins associated with it, these are not histones. There is no nuclear envelope in a prokaryotic cell so the DNA lies free in the cytoplasm.

Prokaryotic cells do not have a **cytoskeleton**, that is they do not have microtubules or intermediate filaments supporting the structure of the cell.

Some prokaryotic cells have a **flagellum** which is used for movement. These flagella have no similarity in structure with those of eukaryotic cells (Fig. 3.15) and are unique to prokaryotes both in their structure and the way they work. While eukaryotic flagella throw waves along themselves, bacterial flagella actually rotate like the propellor of a boat. At the base of the flagellum is a true motor with a rotating bearing – the smallest motor known.

Structure	Prokaryotic cells	Eukaryotic cells	
		plant cells	animal cells
cell surface membrane	yes	yes	yes
cell wall	yes, containing peptidoglycans and other polysaccharides	yes, containing pectin, hemicellulose and cellulose	no
ribosomes	yes, about 20 nm in diameter	yes, about 30 nm in diameter	yes, about 30 nm in diameter
endoplasmic reticulum	no	yes	yes
Golgi apparatus	no	yes	yes
microtubules	no	yes	yes
intermediate filaments	no	yes	yes
mitochondria	no	yes	yes
true nucleus with envelope	no	yes	yes
DNA	single circular molecule, with no histones	several linear molecules, with histones	several linear molecules, with histones
plasmodesmata	no	yes	no
plastids	no	yes	no
cilia and flagella	yes – may have flagella, but different from those of animal cells	rarely	frequently
lysosomes	no	no, but large vacuole carries out the same function	yes

Table 3.2 A comparison of prokaryotic, plant and animal cells.

Box 3.3 Bacterial walls and membranes

Bacteria are often grouped according to the way in which they react to a staining technique invented last century by a Danish scientist, Hans Christian Gram. The technique involves fixing the bacteria, usually by heating, and then adding a stain called crystal violet followed by iodine. An organic solvent such as alcohol is then added which removes some of the stain. Some bacteria lose most of their colour quickly during this process and are known as **Gram-negative**, while others lose it more slowly and look deep blue. These are known as **Gram-positive** bacteria. A red stain is then added, to make Gram-negative bacteria visible. The red stain does not change the blue colour already taken up by Gram-positive bacteria.

The different reactions to the Gram staining technique reflect different structures that surround the cell (Fig. 3.25). Both Gram-positive and Gram-negative bacteria have a cell wall containing **peptidoglycans** (sometimes called mureins). These are molecules that have a backbone of repeating two-sugar units with short peptide chains attached. Gram-positive bacteria have a thick cell wall made up of a single layer of peptidoglycans. This, as you would expect, lies next to the cell surface membrane.

Gram-negative bacteria, however, have *two* membranes. There is a standard cell surface membrane, with a thin peptidoglycan layer lying

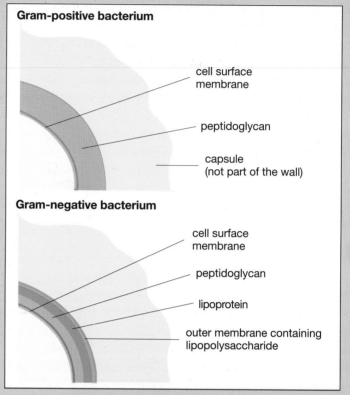

Fig. 3.25 Structure of bacterial cell walls.

just outside it. Outside this is a thin layer of lipoprotein, and then a second, outer, membrane. This has a rather unusual structure, as its outer surface is made up of molecules called **lipopolysaccharides** rather than phospholipids. Lipopolysaccharides appear to be peculiar to bacteria – so far, they have not been found in any other living organism.

Q4 (a) Describe how you would carry out Gram's staining technique on a sample of bacteria. (3)

(b) What result would you expect to see if the bacteria were Gram negative? (1)

(c) Suggest why penicillin is active against bacteria, but has no effect on animal cells. (2)

NEAB 1995 (modified) (*Total 6 marks*)

HOW SUBSTANCES GET INTO AND OUT OF CELLS

3.23 Movement across cell surface membranes

Cell surface membranes separate the living contents of a cell from its surroundings. This allows metabolic reactions to take place in isolation inside the cell – without the cell surface membrane the cell contents would mix with everything outside it and the cell would cease to exist.

However, cell contents cannot remain totally isolated from the outside world. Every cell needs a constant supply of building materials and energy sources, to carry out all the processes of life. These materials must enter through the cell surface membrane, while waste products of the reactions taking place inside the cell must be allowed to leave. The cell surface membrane allows these substances into and out of the cell, in quantities appropriate to the cell's needs, without allowing unwanted substances in or wanted ones out.

The different ways in which substances can pass across cell surface membranes are described in the following four sections. Some of these ways – **diffusion** (including **osmosis**) and **facilitated diffusion** – do not require any energy input from the cell, and are called passive methods of movement. The other ways – **active transport** and **cytosis** – need the cell to use energy to move the substances into or out of the cell, and are called active methods.

3.24 Diffusion

The solutions on either side of a cell surface membrane are mixtures of water molecules and a wide variety of other molecules and ions. All of these molecules and ions are constantly moving around randomly, bumping into each other and rebounding in different directions. Over a period of time such random movement tends to result in a fairly even distribution of each kind of molecule or ion.

To some kinds of molecules, the cell surface membrane presents very little in the way of a barrier. These include **lipid-soluble** molecules of all sizes, such as glycerol and steroid hormones (Section 15.2). If these happen to bump into the phospholipid bilayer, they can easily move through between the waving fatty acid tails to the other side of the membrane. Small uncharged molecules such as oxygen and carbon dioxide can also pass through in this way (Fig. 3.26).

Imagine a cell surface membrane where there is a relatively high concentration of oxygen molecules on the outside and a low concentration on the inside. We say there is a **concentration gradient** for oxygen. Oxygen molecules on both sides of the membrane are randomly moving around. These molecules – on both sides – will sometimes hit the membrane and pass through to the other side. As there are more oxygen molecules on the outside, more of them will hit the membrane than on the inside. Overall, there will be a net movement of oxygen molecules from the outside to the inside of the membrane. So, the oxygen **diffuses** through the membrane, down its concentration gradient.

It is very important to realise that the oxygen molecules are not doing this purposefully. It is a purely random process, a result of completely random movements of the oxygen molecules. Some of these molecules are actually moving *out* of the cell. Nor is the cell doing anything to make this happen. The energy for the movement is simply the kinetic energy of the oxygen molecules.

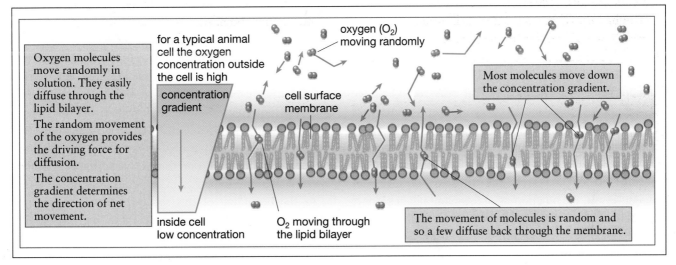

Fig. 3.26 Diffusion of oxygen across a cell surface membrane.

3.25 Facilitated diffusion

Most large or polar molecules such as glucose, or ions such as sodium ions, cannot pass easily through the lipid bilayer. In order to enter or leave a cell, these molecules move through **protein pores** (Fig. 3.27).

Cell surface membranes contain a wide variety of protein pores, each of just the right size and structure to allow particular substances to pass through. The rate at which a substance can diffuse into or out of a cell will depend on how many of its particular pores are present, and whether they are open or not. It also, of course, depends on the difference in concentration of that substance on the two sides of the membrane – that is, the steepness of the concentration gradient.

Diffusion which takes place through these protein pores is called **facilitated diffusion**. 'Facilitated' means 'made easy', which refers to the fact that the pores make it easy for these substances to pass through the membrane. In all other ways, this type of diffusion is just like that described in Section 3.24. The cell does nothing actively to move the substances through the pores, so the process is entirely passive.

3.26 Osmosis

The solutions on either side of cell surface membranes always contain water molecules. Water molecules are very small (Section 1.1) and always present in large amounts both inside and outside a cell. So, despite being polar, they have little difficulty in passing through the membrane as they can move through tiny temporary gaps which appear between the waving phospholipid tails. Just like any other molecule, they will diffuse through the membrane down their concentration gradient.

This diffusion of water is of tremendous importance to cells. There are always far more water molecules than any other kind of molecule, both in the cytoplasm and in the solution surrounding a living cell. If a lot of water diffuses from one side of the membrane to the other, this can have very significant effects on the concentration, volumes and pressures of the liquids inside and outside the cell. These effects are involved in many processes in living organisms, including the absorption of water into plants and its transport up xylem vessels, the transport of sugars in phloem vessels, the functioning of the mammalian kidney, and the exchange of materials between blood and body tissues.

The diffusion of water molecules across cell surface membranes is so important that it is given a special name –

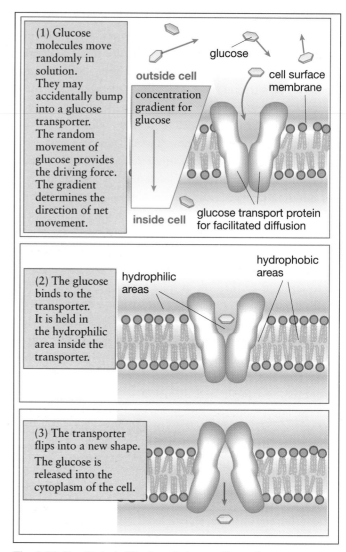

Fig. 3.27 Facilitated diffusion of glucose through a membrane.

osmosis. The term applies to the diffusion of water across any **partially permeable** membrane – that is a membrane which will allow some molecules or ions to pass across but not others. As you have seen in Section 3.25, cell surface membranes are indeed partially permeable, allowing some ions and molecules to move across freely, but not others. There are also several kinds of artificial partially permeable membranes. You will probably use one called visking tubing when carrying out osmosis experiments. Similar types of membrane are used in kidney dialysis machines.

At the beginning of this section, we said that water molecules diffuse down their concentration gradient. This is true, but it is not usual to talk about the 'concentration' of water molecules because, if we say that a solution is concentrated, we mean that it contains a lot of solute rather than a lot of water. There are other factors which also affect the tendency of water molecules to diffuse across a membrane, the most important of which is the pressure on each side of the membrane. So a special term is used to describe the combined effect of 'concentration' and pressure in a solution, which will affect the tendency of water molecules to diffuse into or out of it across a membrane. This term is **water potential**, often written as the Greek letter Ψ, psi. Water potential is measured in units of pressure, usually kilopascals (kPa). You can think of the water potential of a solution as the *tendency for water to diffuse out of it*. **Water diffuses from a high water potential to a low water potential, down its water potential gradient.**

By definition, **pure water at atmospheric pressure has a water potential of 0.** If you add a solute, such as sugar, to this water, you are effectively *decreasing* the concentration of water molecules because there are less of them in any given space. Moreover, they will be attracted to the solute molecules (Fig. 1.3) and so move around less freely. This decreases the tendency for the water molecules to diffuse out of the solution. So, by adding solute to the pure water, you have *decreased* its water potential (Fig. 3.28).

If pure water has a water potential of 0, and if this water potential is decreased when solute is added, then a solution must have a negative water potential. The more solute you add, the more you lower the water potential. For example, a solution containing 17 g of sucrose in 1 dm³ of water has a water potential of −130 kPa, whereas if this solution contained 35 g of sucrose its water potential would be −260 kPa.

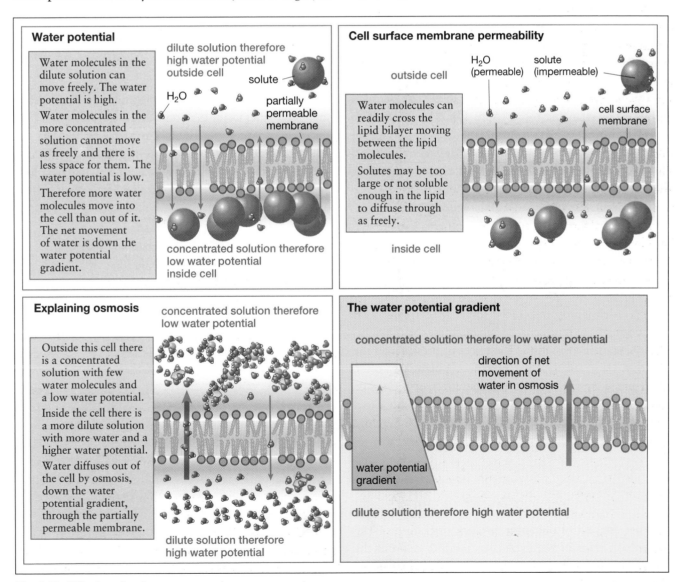

Fig. 3.28 Diffusion of water across membranes – osmosis.

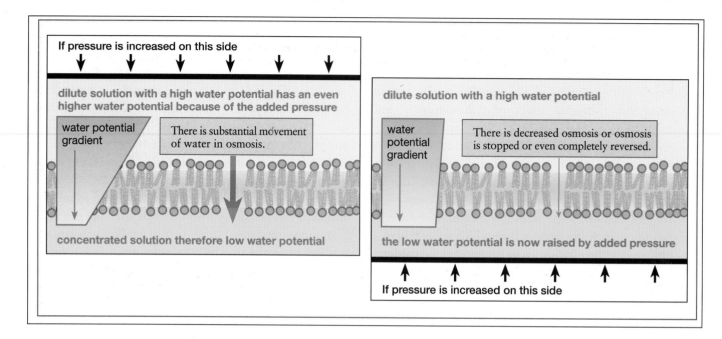

If pressure is increased on this side

dilute solution with a high water potential has an even higher water potential because of the added pressure

water potential gradient

There is substantial movement of water in osmosis.

concentrated solution therefore low water potential

dilute solution with a high water potential

water potential gradient

There is decreased osmosis or osmosis is stopped or even completely reversed.

the low water potential is now raised by added pressure

If pressure is increased on this side

Fig. 3.29 The effect of pressure on osmosis and water potential.

You could also change the water potential of these solutions by changing the pressure applied to them (Fig. 3.29). If you *increased* the pressure, perhaps by putting the solution into a syringe and pressing down the plunger, you would *increase* the tendency of the water to diffuse through the membrane. You would therefore be *increasing* the water potential of the solution.

We can therefore say that:

| water potential of a solution | = | effect of pressure on that solution | + | effect of the solute concentration of that solution |

This is rather wordy and cumbersome. We can simplify it by using terms to represent the two quantities on the right-hand side of the equation. The effect of pressure on the solution is called the **pressure potential**, often represented by the symbol Ψ_P. The effect of the solute concentration is called the **solute potential**, often represented by the symbol Ψ_s. The equation therefore becomes:

water potential = pressure potential + solute potential of a solution

$$\Psi = \Psi_P + \Psi_s$$

What does all of this mean for living organisms? The water potentials of the cytoplasm inside a cell and the solution bathing the cell will determine whether water diffuses into the cell or out of it. If the water potential is higher outside the cell than inside, then water will diffuse in; if it is higher inside than outside, then water will diffuse out. These water potentials are affected both by the relative solute concentrations inside and outside the cell, and also by the relative pressures. Figs. 3.30 and 3.31 look at some possible scenarios for animal and plant cells in different circumstances.

Q5 A, B and C represent three adjoining cells from a leaf. The cells have water potentials of –2.1, –2.4 and –2.7 MPa respectively.

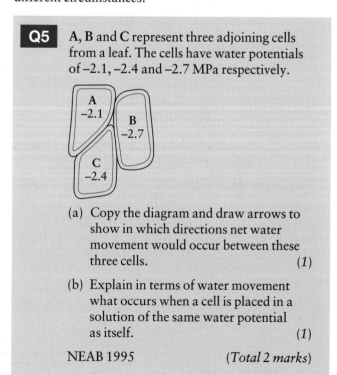

A –2.1

B –2.7

C –2.4

(a) Copy the diagram and draw arrows to show in which directions net water movement would occur between these three cells. *(1)*

(b) Explain in terms of water movement what occurs when a cell is placed in a solution of the same water potential as itself. *(1)*

NEAB 1995 *(Total 2 marks)*

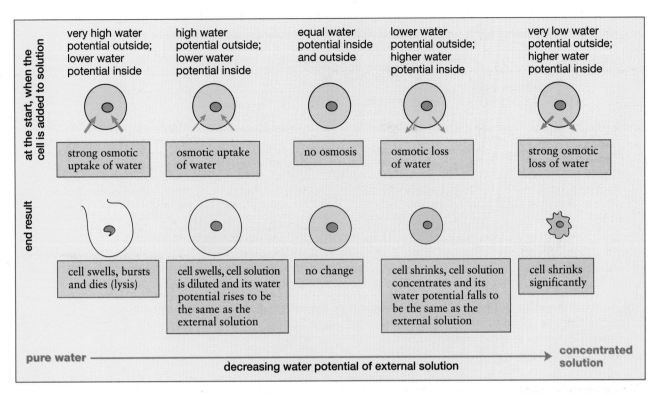

Fig. 3.30 Osmosis and animal cells. The diagram shows what happens to animal cells in solutions of different concentrations.

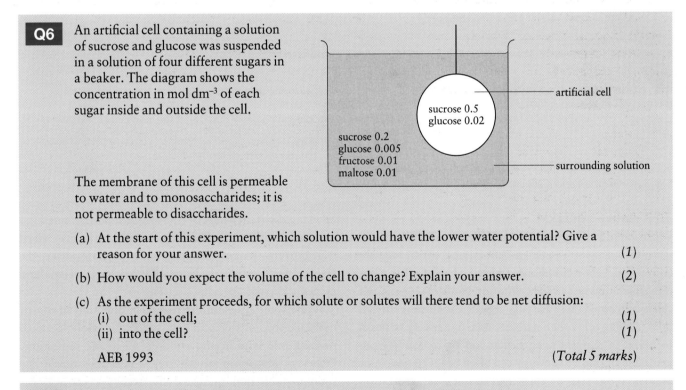

Q6 An artificial cell containing a solution of sucrose and glucose was suspended in a solution of four different sugars in a beaker. The diagram shows the concentration in mol dm⁻³ of each sugar inside and outside the cell.

The membrane of this cell is permeable to water and to monosaccharides; it is not permeable to disaccharides.

(a) At the start of this experiment, which solution would have the lower water potential? Give a reason for your answer. *(1)*

(b) How would you expect the volume of the cell to change? Explain your answer. *(2)*

(c) As the experiment proceeds, for which solute or solutes will there tend to be net diffusion:
   (i) out of the cell; *(1)*
   (ii) into the cell? *(1)*

AEB 1993 *(Total 5 marks)*

Q7 (a) Explain the terms diffusion, osmosis, facilitated diffusion and active transport.

(b) Name one substance, appropriate to each term in (a), which crosses the cell membrane.

(c) How does the structure and composition of the cell surface membrane help to explain why some substances pass across it whereas others tend not to?

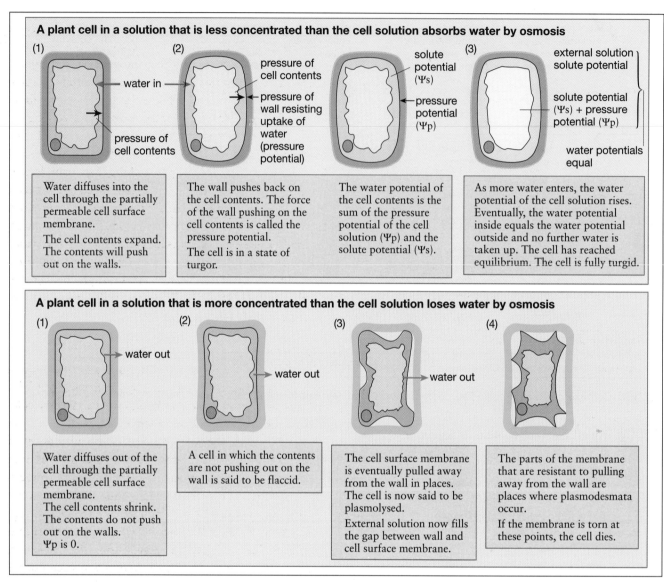

Fig. 3.31 Osmosis and plant cells.

3.27 Active transport

Diffusion (including osmosis) and facilitated diffusion are net movements of ions and molecules which depend entirely on their random movements. They result in a net movement down their concentration gradients. As far as a cell is concerned these are **passive** processes, where the cell does nothing other than perhaps open or close some pores to allow or prevent a particular ion or molecule from getting in or out. However, a cell often needs to take in or remove molecules or ions *against* their concentration gradients. To do this, it has to use energy. So this process is called **active transport.**

Fig 3.32 shows how an ion can be actively transported into a cell. The cell surface membrane contains protein molecules which act as transporters for this ion; there will

be many different kinds of transporters, at least one kind for each kind of ion or molecule which may need transporting. As an ion bumps into its transporter, the transporter uses energy from ATP to change shape and push the ion into the cell.

While some transporters just push one kind of ion or molecule into or out of a cell, others give double value, pushing one kind in and another out at the same time. One very important transporter which does this is the **sodium–potassium pump.** Cells usually need a lower concentration of sodium ions, and a higher concentration of potassium ions, in their cytoplasm than there is outside the cell. Fig. 3.32 also shows how this pump pushes three sodium ions out of the cell for every two potassium ions that it pulls in. Sodium–potassium transporters are present

Active transport of a single substance

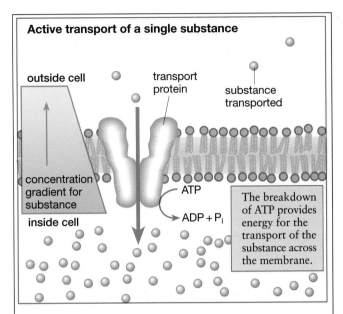

The breakdown of ATP provides energy for the transport of the substance across the membrane.

The sodium–potassium pump

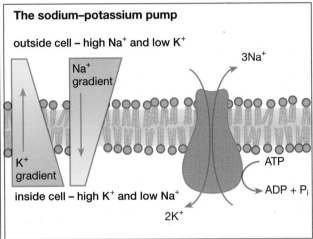

Glucose and sodium cotransport

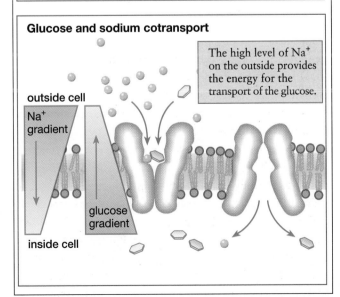

The high level of Na^+ on the outside provides the energy for the transport of the glucose.

Fig. 3.32 Active transport.

in many kinds of cell, but they are particularly important in nerves and the transmission of nervous impulses.

Another type of transporter, called a **cotransporter**, moves two substances across the membrane in the same direction at the same time. Fig. 3.32 shows a particularly important example of this kind of transport involving the cotransport of glucose and sodium ions into a cell. The sodium ions move down their concentration gradient, and this provides enough energy to pull the glucose molecules into the cell even if they are actually moving *against* their concentration gradient. No ATP is needed, so in some ways this is not really active transport. However, it only works because the cell has used ATP to pump sodium ions *out* of the cell in the first place, so providing the sodium ion concentration gradient which 'drives' the glucose uptake. So this kind of transport is sometimes called **indirect active transport.**

3.28 Cytosis

Cytosis is a method of moving substances into or out of a cell using vesicles. (A vesicle is a small vacuole.) This method moves substances in bulk, rather than molecule-by-molecule, as in diffusion or active transport.

Moving substances out of a cell in this way is called **exocytosis** (Fig. 3.12). A vesicle containing the substance to be removed from the cell is moved towards the cell surface membrane with the help of microtubules, using energy from ATP. The vesicle fuses with the cell surface membrane releasing its contents to the outside. Most cells perform this activity. In plant cells, for example, exocytosis is used to secrete some of the components of the cell wall, and cells on the stigma secrete the glycoproteins which prevent self-fertilisation in flowers (Box 18.1). In animal cells, exocytosis is used for secreting mucus into the digestive and respiratory systems and for secreting hormones and enzymes.

Bringing substances into a cell is called **endocytosis** (Fig. 3.12). When the substance being brought in is solid, such as a bacterium, the process can also be called **phagocytosis.** The cell surface membrane surrounds the material to be taken in and fuses around it, forming a vacuole. Little is known about endocytosis in plant cells except that it does occur; the presence of the cell wall obviously limits the possibilities! Animal cells, such as those of mammals, take up a very wide variety of substances by endocytosis. For example, a blood protein called transferrin which carries iron is taken up by most cells in the body in this way; the cells need the iron for the manufacture of proteins such as cytochromes. White blood cells use phagocytosis to take up bacteria or damaged body cells, in order to destroy them.

Exo- and endocytosis not only move substances into and out of cells, but also add or subtract membrane from the cell surface membrane. The balance between these two mechanisms determines the surface area of the membrane around the cell. ■

Q8 Copy the table below and, for each structure in the table, indicate whether it is present (✔) or absent (✕) in plant and animal cells and state the main chemical components from which it is made.

Structure	Plant cells	Animal cells	Main chemical components
cell surface membrane			1 2
cell wall			1 2
ribosome			1 2
chromosome			1 2

UCLES 1994

(Total 8 marks)

Q9 Copy the following passage on the water relations of plant cells, and fill in the gaps with the most appropriate word or words to complete the account.

The water potential of a cell (Ψ_{cell}) is determined by its solute potential (Ψ_s) and its pressure potential (Ψ_p). The relationship can be summarised in the following equation.

$$\Psi_{cell} = \Psi_s + \Psi_p$$

When a cell is plasmolysed, Ψ_p is _____, Ψ_{cell} is equal to _____ and the cell is said to be _____ . If this cell is placed in pure water, its water potential is _____ than that of the external solution so water _____ by osmosis. The Ψ_p _____ until the cell becomes _____ .

London 1995

(Total 7 marks)

Q10 (a) Describe the structure of a generalised plant cell, as it appears in an electron micrograph. *(12)*

(b) Describe how plant cells respond to immersion in solutions with water potentials above and below the water potential of the cell contents. *(6)*

UCLES 1995

(Total 18 marks)

4 Cell division

Multicellular organisms begin life as a single cell, which grows and divides repeatedly to form an adult organism. The cycle of growth, division, growth, division and so on is called the cell cycle. Usually, the division is mitosis, which produces new cells genetically identical to the old. In sexual cycles, however, a different kind of division called meiosis takes place, which produces genetically different daughter cells.

4.1 The cell cycle

You began life as a single cell, a **zygote**, which was formed by the fusion of a sperm and an egg. This cell divided many times, and the cells which were produced became specialised to form all the different types of cells which make up your tissues and organs. Many of these cells are programmed to carry out a repetitive sequence of growing and dividing, growing and dividing. At a certain point in its life, perhaps when it has grown to a certain size, a cell divides to form two smaller cells, which in turn grow before dividing once more. This is the **cell cycle** (Fig. 4.1).

In humans, normal cells are not able to continue dividing for ever. Many cells can undergo about 50 divisions, after which they stop dividing and begin to die. In your body in your lifetime, about 10^{16} cell divisions will take place.

Some cells do not divide at all once they have become specialised. For example, once a nerve cell has been formed it spends the rest of its life carrying out the functions of a nerve cell, and never enters the cell cycle again.

The cell cycle has two main stages, **interphase** and **cell division**. There are two types of cell division, called **mitosis** and **meiosis**. Mitosis is by far the commoner of the two types of cell division, so we will begin by looking at a cell cycle in which division is by mitosis.

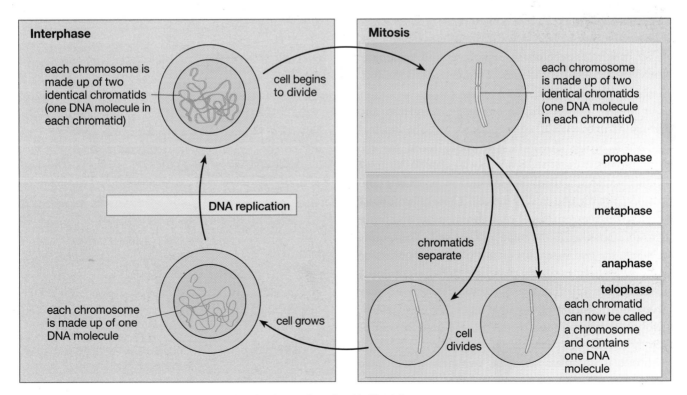

Fig. 4.1 The mitotic cell cycle. The stages in mitosis are described in Fig 4.4.

MITOSIS

4.2 The mitotic cell cycle

Mitosis takes place when cells divide to produce new cells for growth, for repair of damaged tissues, or for the production of new organisms by asexual reproduction. Cell division by mitosis produces two new, 'daughter', cells from one parent cell. The daughter cells have the same number of chromosomes as the parent cell, and these chromosomes carry exactly the same genes as the parent cell. The daughter cells are therefore genetically identical to their parent and to each other.

Interphase is by far the longest phase of the mitotic cell cycle. In a cell in a human embryo, it lasts for about 24 hours (Fig. 4.2). During interphase, the nucleus of the cell looks like Fig. 3.20. Individual chromosomes are not visible. Each chromosome (there are 46 of them in a human cell) is made of a single molecule of DNA, associated with proteins (Fig. 3.20 and Fig. 4.3). About halfway through interphase the DNA of the cell replicates (Section 5.1), producing two identical molecules of DNA which form sister chromatids. The two identical chromatids remain attached to each other at several points, including a region called the centromere. This all takes between 6–10 hours, after which another 4–6 hours is needed before the cell is ready to divide.

The division stage – mitosis – takes about 30 minutes. The events which take place during this process are shown in Figs. 4.4 and 4.5. They are divided into four stages, called prophase, metaphase, anaphase and telophase. However, the whole process is continuous, and the four phases blend smoothly into each other.

As mitosis begins, the chromosomes condense and become visible with a light microscope. The nuclear membrane breaks down to give more room for the chromosomes to be moved around inside the cell. An array of microtubules, called the spindle, is produced and radiates from the two ends of the cell. These microtubules attach to the centromeres of each chromosome and move them to a position in the middle of the cell. Then, quite suddenly, the two sister chromatids of each chromosome break away from each other, and are pulled to opposite sides of the cell by the microtubules. Here, they 'decondense', becoming invisible again, as new nuclear membranes form around them. Fig. 4.4 describes all of these processes in more detail.

Mitosis is complete once the two new nuclei have formed; the term mitosis actually refers to the division of the *nucleus*, rather than the division of the cell. However, the cell itself now usually divides into two, in a process called cytokinesis. This does not always happen, and sometimes the two new nuclei remain in a single cell.

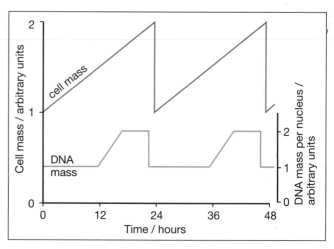

Fig. 4.2 Time scale of the events in a mitotic cell cycle in cells in a human embryo.

Q1 Explain the shapes of the curves in Fig. 4.2.

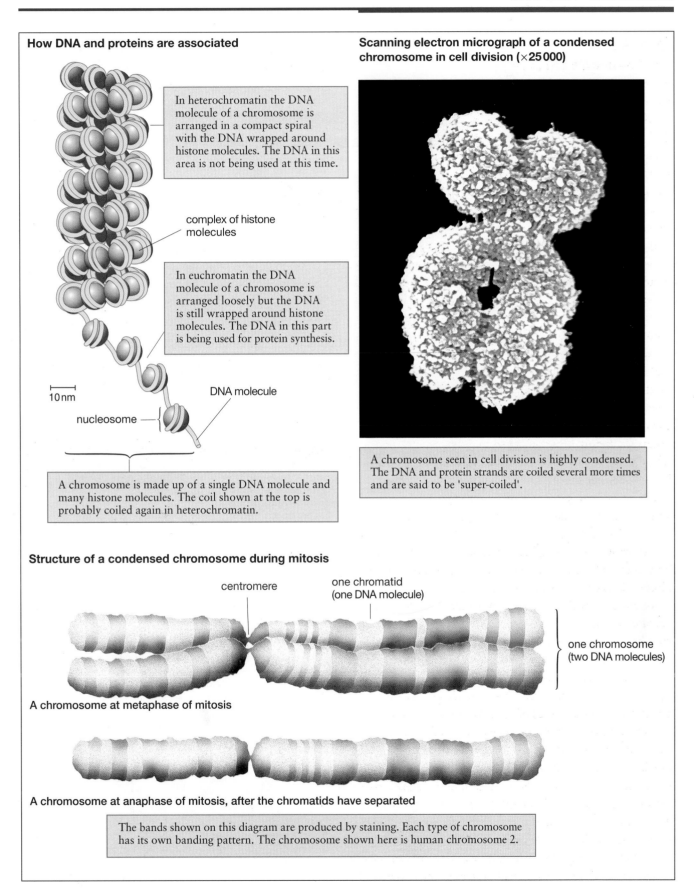

How DNA and proteins are associated

In heterochromatin the DNA molecule of a chromosome is arranged in a compact spiral with the DNA wrapped around histone molecules. The DNA in this area is not being used at this time.

complex of histone molecules

In euchromatin the DNA molecule of a chromosome is arranged loosely but the DNA is still wrapped around histone molecules. The DNA in this part is being used for protein synthesis.

10 nm

nucleosome

DNA molecule

A chromosome is made up of a single DNA molecule and many histone molecules. The coil shown at the top is probably coiled again in heterochromatin.

Scanning electron micrograph of a condensed chromosome in cell division (×25 000)

A chromosome seen in cell division is highly condensed. The DNA and protein strands are coiled several more times and are said to be 'super-coiled'.

Structure of a condensed chromosome during mitosis

centromere

one chromatid (one DNA molecule)

one chromosome (two DNA molecules)

A chromosome at metaphase of mitosis

A chromosome at anaphase of mitosis, after the chromatids have separated

The bands shown on this diagram are produced by staining. Each type of chromosome has its own banding pattern. The chromosome shown here is human chromosome 2.

Fig. 4.3 The structure of a chromosome.

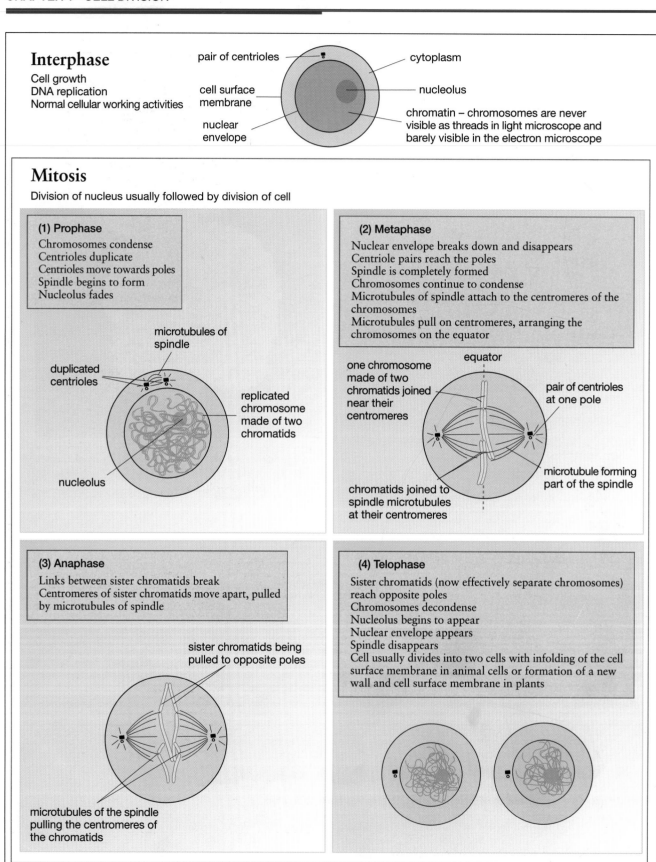

Interphase

Cell growth
DNA replication
Normal cellular working activities

pair of centrioles

cell surface membrane

nuclear envelope

cytoplasm

nucleolus

chromatin – chromosomes are never visible as threads in light microscope and barely visible in the electron microscope

Mitosis

Division of nucleus usually followed by division of cell

(1) Prophase

Chromosomes condense
Centrioles duplicate
Centrioles move towards poles
Spindle begins to form
Nucleolus fades

microtubules of spindle

duplicated centrioles

replicated chromosome made of two chromatids

nucleolus

(2) Metaphase

Nuclear envelope breaks down and disappears
Centriole pairs reach the poles
Spindle is completely formed
Chromosomes continue to condense
Microtubules of spindle attach to the centromeres of the chromosomes
Microtubules pull on centromeres, arranging the chromosomes on the equator

one chromosome made of two chromatids joined near their centromeres

equator

pair of centrioles at one pole

microtubule forming part of the spindle

chromatids joined to spindle microtubules at their centromeres

(3) Anaphase

Links between sister chromatids break
Centromeres of sister chromatids move apart, pulled by microtubules of spindle

sister chromatids being pulled to opposite poles

microtubules of the spindle pulling the centromeres of the chromatids

(4) Telophase

Sister chromatids (now effectively separate chromosomes) reach opposite poles
Chromosomes decondense
Nucleolus begins to appear
Nuclear envelope appears
Spindle disappears
Cell usually divides into two cells with infolding of the cell surface membrane in animal cells or formation of a new wall and cell surface membrane in plants

Fig. 4.4 Mitosis in an animal cell.

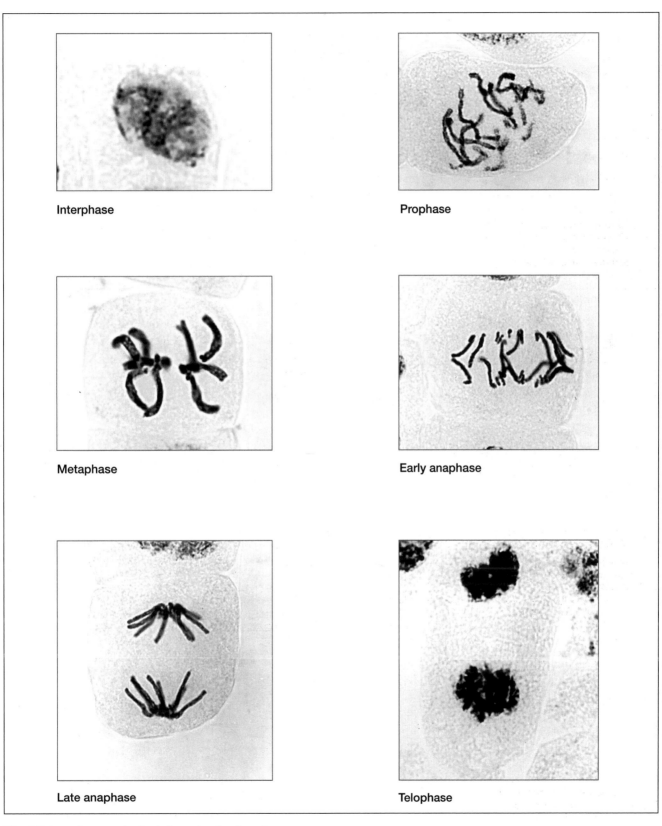

Interphase

Prophase

Metaphase

Early anaphase

Late anaphase

Telophase

Fig. 4.5 Interphase and mitosis in root cells of an aloe.

Box 4.1 Differences between mitosis in plant and animal cells

The events shown in Fig. 4.4 describe the way in which mitosis occurs in an animal cell. There are some small differences in these events in plant cells.

In animal cells, the formation of the spindle is controlled from two microtubule organising centres, the **centrosomes**. Each centrosome contains two structures containing nine triplets of microtubules (as in the basal body of a cilium, Fig. 3.15), called **centrioles**. In an interphase animal cell there is usually a single centrosome which divides to form two just before the cell enters mitosis. The two centrosomes then move apart and the microtubules begin to assemble to form the spindle. The centrosomes eventually form the poles of the spindle. There is considerable evidence that the centrosomes control the assembly of the spindle microtubules and also their behaviour during mitosis, but the mechanism by which this occurs is not yet known.

In plant cells, however, there are no visible centrioles. Spindle formation occurs with no obvious microtubule organising centre being involved, but the net result is the same. A spindle is formed made up from microtubules radiating from the poles of the cell, and the microtubules attach to the centromeres of the chromatids and pull them to opposite sides of the cell just as occurs in an animal cell.

A second difference between animal and plant cells occurs during the cell division, cytokinesis, stage. This results from the fact that plant cells have cell walls, whereas animal cells do not. Cytokinesis in an animal cell is a relatively straightforward affair, requiring no more than a folding in, then breaking and rejoining of the cell surface membrane. In a plant cell, vesicles from the Golgi apparatus move towards the area where the equator of the spindle used to be, guided by microtubules. These vesicles contain chemicals which will be converted into pectin, hemicellulose and cellulose. The vesicles fuse together, forming a layer of material that stretches right across the cell (Fig. 4.6). The contents of the vesicles become a new cell wall, while their membranes fuse to form new cell surface membranes on either side of it. The whole structure, made up of the two new cell surface membranes and the cell wall between them, is called the **cell plate**. Where endoplasmic reticulum is caught up in between the fusing vesicles, gaps remain. These form the plasmodesmata that link the two cells.

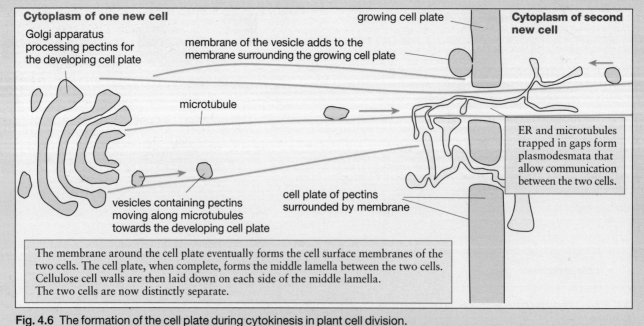

Cytoplasm of one new cell

Golgi apparatus processing pectins for the developing cell plate

membrane of the vesicle adds to the membrane surrounding the growing cell plate

growing cell plate

Cytoplasm of second new cell

microtubule

ER and microtubules trapped in gaps form plasmodesmata that allow communication between the two cells.

vesicles containing pectins moving along microtubules towards the developing cell plate

cell plate of pectins surrounded by membrane

The membrane around the cell plate eventually forms the cell surface membranes of the two cells. The cell plate, when complete, forms the middle lamella between the two cells. Cellulose cell walls are then laid down on each side of the middle lamella. The two cells are now distinctly separate.

Fig. 4.6 The formation of the cell plate during cytokinesis in plant cell division.

Box 4.2 The control of the mitotic cell cycle

What controls when a cell divides? Within a single organism, cells in different tissues have cell cycles of very different durations. For example, the cells lining the small intestine have very short lives and need to be replaced constantly. The cells which divide to replace them may do so every ten hours. Liver cells do not divide at all, unless tissue around them is damaged, in which case they may enter a cell cycle and divide rapidly. Neurones never divide. In plants, the majority of cells in roots, stems and leaves never divide, and cell division is only carried out by groups of cells in regions known as meristems.

A large number of factors appear to influence whether or not a cell divides, and how rapidly it does so. The most important of these factors is the cell's own genes. Many different genes are known to interact to determine when the cell divides. However, the effects of these genes are modified by what is happening in the environment of the cell. Some cells, for example, are prevented from dividing if they are in close contact with other cells; this is called **contact inhibition**. Chemicals which come into contact with the cells may cause them to divide. For example, platelets release a chemical called **platelet-derived growth factor** (PDGF) when they come into contact with a damaged blood vessel wall. PDGF stimulates the cells in the area of the wound to divide repeatedly, so causing the wound to heal.

There is considerable interest in the control of the cell cycle because, when it goes wrong in animals, **cancer** may result. Cancer occurs when cells divide uncontrollably; cells which should not be dividing at all begin to go through repetitive and very rapid cell cycles. The cells form a **tumour**, which may just grow in one place or may shed cells which travel to other parts of the body and begin to form secondary tumours. Many cancers can be cured, especially if discovered at a relatively early stage, but cancer is still a major cause of death all over the world.

Cancer is caused by changes in the genes which control division. There are two types of genes which are involved. The first type, called **proto-oncogenes**, stimulate cell division in a normal cell, while the second type, called **tumour suppressor genes**, inhibit cell division. In a healthy cell, the activity of these two types of genes is balanced, and controlled by external factors, so that cell division only takes place when required. If, however, the genes mutate so that the proto-oncogenes become more active (they are then called **oncogenes**) and the tumour suppressor genes less active, then the cell may divide uncontrollably.

Most tumours in humans appear to be caused by these mutations. Mutations in many different genes are usually required in order for cancer to develop. The mutations may occur randomly, or because DNA is damaged by ionising radiation or chemicals (Section 5.6). In a few cases **viruses** may be the cause, as some viruses carry oncogenes which may be introduced into cells. In humans, infection with some forms of the papilloma virus can lead to cervical cancer, for example, while the hepatitis B virus may cause liver cancer to develop.

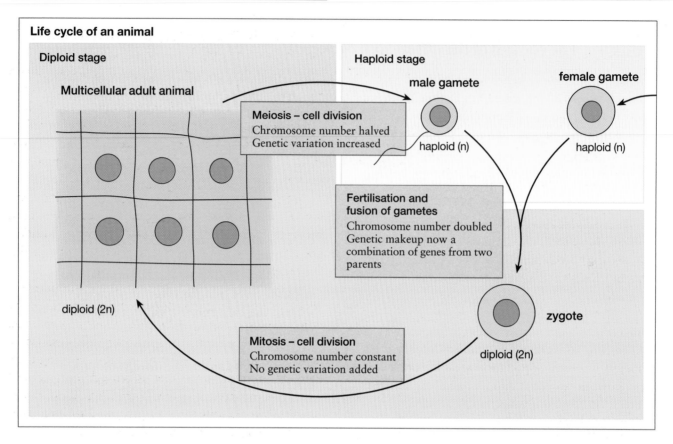

Fig. 4.7 The life cycle of an animal.

MEIOSIS

4.3 Chromosome number and sexual reproduction

Many organisms, including humans, use sexual reproduction. Gametes (sex cells) are produced, which fuse together to form a single cell called a **zygote**. The zygote grows into an embryo, which eventually develops into an adult organism.

In order to ensure that the new adult organism has the same number of chromosomes as its parent, the two gametes must each have only half of that number. In humans, for example, each cell contains 46 chromosomes. The gametes (eggs and sperm) each contain only 23 chromosomes, so that when they fuse together they form a zygote which has 46.

The 46 chromosomes in a human cell are made up of two complete sets of 23 different chromosomes. (You can read more about these in Chapter 5.) Cells with two complete sets of chromosomes are **diploid** cells. The gametes contain only one complete set, and so are called **haploid** cells.

In humans, gametes are produced by cell division of cells in the ovaries and testes. This division must be different from mitosis, because it must produce daughter cells with only half the number of chromosomes of the parent cell. This type of cell division is called **meiosis**.

Meiosis occurs in the life cycle of all organisms which reproduce sexually. In animals, the cells produced by meiosis always form gametes (Fig. 4.7). In other organisms, meiosis may not produce gametes but other haploid cells which play different roles in the life cycle. The timing of meiosis in some different life cycles is shown in Figs. 18.3 and 18.5.

4.4 The stages of meiosis

Fig. 4.8 shows the events which occur during meiosis in an animal cell. You will see that there are many similarities with mitosis, but also several very significant differences.

While mitosis involves a single division, meiosis involves two. During the first division, called **meiosis I**, the chromosomes are separated into two sets, one set going into each daughter cell. During the second division, called **meiosis II**, the chromosomes behave just as in mitosis, splitting into two chromatids which separate into two

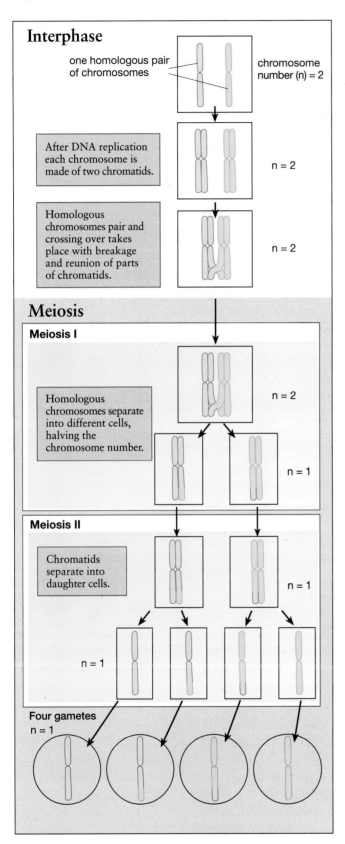

Interphase

one homologous pair of chromosomes

chromosome number (n) = 2

After DNA replication each chromosome is made of two chromatids.

n = 2

Homologous chromosomes pair and crossing over takes place with breakage and reunion of parts of chromatids.

n = 2

Meiosis

Meiosis I

Homologous chromosomes separate into different cells, halving the chromosome number.

n = 2

n = 1

Meiosis II

Chromatids separate into daughter cells.

n = 1

n = 1

Four gametes
n = 1

Fig. 4.8 A summary of chromosome behaviour during interphase and meiosis.

daughter cells. Thus four daughter cells are formed, rather than the two which result from mitosis.

In Section 4.3, you saw that diploid cells contain two complete sets of chromosomes. This means that there are two copies of each kind of chromosome, one of which came from the organism's mother and one from its father. These two similar chromosomes are called **homologous chromosomes**. Human cells have 23 pairs of homologous chromosomes.

During interphase, before meiosis begins, the homologous chromosomes pair up. The pairs are called **bivalents**. Each chromosome is made up of two identical sister chromatids, so a bivalent contains four chromatids lying side by side.

Frequently, a chromatid from one chromosome will break, and exchange a portion with a chromatid of the other chromosome (Fig. 4.11). The points at which you can see this happening in prophase are called **chiasmata** (singular chiasma), and the event is called **crossing over**. Pairs of chromosomes whose chromatids have formed chiasmata produce interesting shapes (Fig. 4.10). If you see chromosomes with these shapes, you can be sure that you are looking at meiosis, not mitosis.

During metaphase I, the pairs of homologous chromosomes, still joined together, become arranged on the equator of the spindle. They are then pulled apart from each other, during anaphase I, by the microtubules of the spindle and are dragged to opposite sides of the cell. This event differs from what happens in mitosis, where the *chromatids* of a single chromosome are pulled apart at this stage. In meiosis I, the two chromatids of a chromosome remain firmly attached together at this stage.

This first division of meiosis produces two cells, each containing a single set of chromosomes. Usually, the cell does not go into interphase now, but continues into the second division. This takes place at right angles to the division in meiosis I, and is just like mitosis.

4.5 How meiosis produces genetic variation

You have seen how meiosis results in daughter cells which have only one set of chromosomes rather than the two sets in the original diploid cell. Meiosis halves chromosome number. However, meiosis does more than this; it produces daughter cells which differ genetically from each other.

Each chromosome in a cell contains a DNA molecule, and that DNA molecule is made up of many genes. A gene is a length of DNA which provides instructions for making

Interphase

Cell growth
DNA replication
Normal cellular working activities
Homologous chromosomes pair
Chromatids cross over producing gene recombination

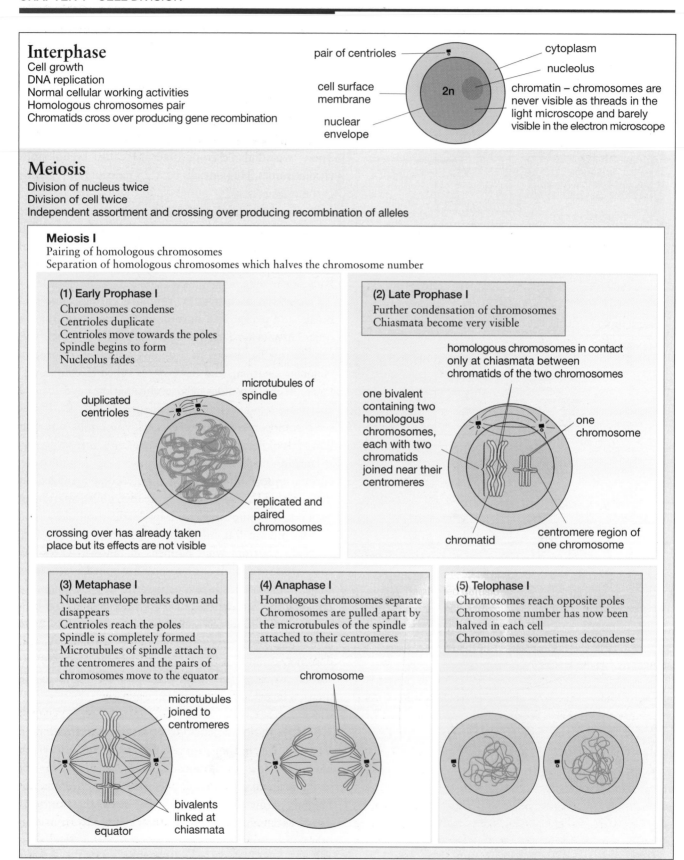

Meiosis

Division of nucleus twice
Division of cell twice
Independent assortment and crossing over producing recombination of alleles

Meiosis I
Pairing of homologous chromosomes
Separation of homologous chromosomes which halves the chromosome number

(1) Early Prophase I
Chromosomes condense
Centrioles duplicate
Centrioles move towards the poles
Spindle begins to form
Nucleolus fades

(2) Late Prophase I
Further condensation of chromosomes
Chiasmata become very visible

(3) Metaphase I
Nuclear envelope breaks down and disappears
Centrioles reach the poles
Spindle is completely formed
Microtubules of spindle attach to the centromeres and the pairs of chromosomes move to the equator

(4) Anaphase I
Homologous chromosomes separate
Chromosomes are pulled apart by the microtubules of the spindle attached to their centromeres

(5) Telophase I
Chromosomes reach opposite poles
Chromosome number has now been halved in each cell
Chromosomes sometimes decondense

Fig. 4.9 Meiosis in an animal cell.

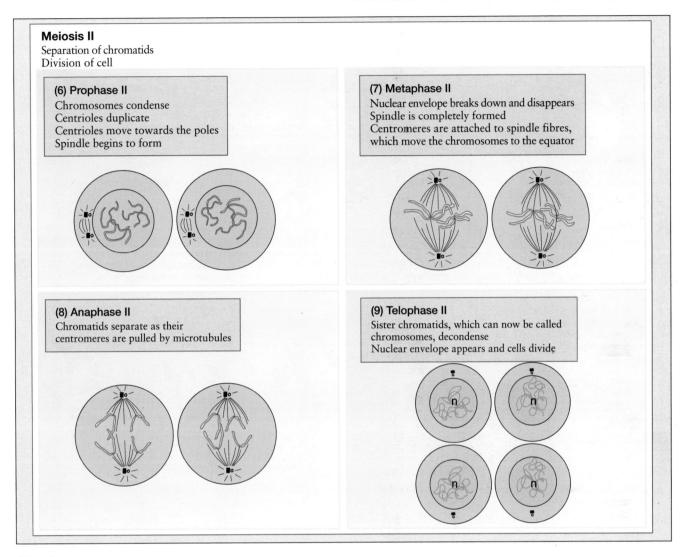

Meiosis II
Separation of chromatids
Division of cell

(6) Prophase II
Chromosomes condense
Centrioles duplicate
Centrioles move towards the poles
Spindle begins to form

(7) Metaphase II
Nuclear envelope breaks down and disappears
Spindle is completely formed
Centromeres are attached to spindle fibres, which move the chromosomes to the equator

(8) Anaphase II
Chromatids separate as their centromeres are pulled by microtubules

(9) Telophase II
Sister chromatids, which can now be called chromosomes, decondense
Nuclear envelope appears and cells divide

Fig. 4.9 *cont.*

a certain protein molecule (Section 5.2). Many genes have several different forms, or **alleles**, which provide slightly different instructions that produce slightly different protein molecules.

Before meiosis begins, each chromosome duplicates its DNA, so that by the time the chromosomes appear they are made up of two identical sister chromatids. Sister chromatids therefore carry identical alleles.

Homologous chromosomes carry genes for the same proteins in the same positions. Therefore, in a diploid cell, there are two copies of each gene, one on each chromosome. The two copies may be identical, or they may be different alleles. Fig. 4.11 shows a cell containing just two pairs of chromosomes, on each of which we are interested in just two genes. Each pair of chromosomes carries different alleles for these genes.

Two events which occur during meiosis may result in the daughter cells carrying different combinations of these alleles. The first is called **independent assortment**, and depends on the fact that each pair of homologous chromosomes may line up either way up on the equator of the spindle at metaphase, quite independently of what the other pairs are doing. The second is **crossing over,** in which portions of one chromatid swap over with the matching portion of a chromatid from the other chromosome in the pair. Fig. 4.11 shows how each of these two processes may result in different combinations of alleles in the daughter cells produced. In a human cell, with 46 chromosomes, these two processes make it virtually impossible for two cells produced by meiosis to be genetically identical. You can read about the potential importance of this genetic variation in Chapter 7. ■

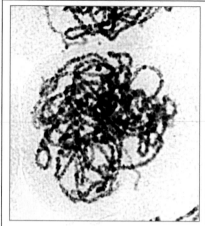

Prophase I. The 14 chromosomes have already associated into bivalents, although this is not yet clearly visible.

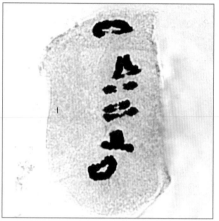

Metaphase I. There are 4 large bivalents, each with 2 chiasmata, and 3 small bivalents each with 1 chiasma.

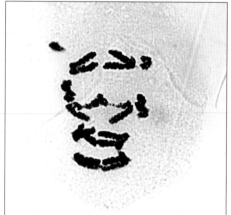

Early anaphase I. The chromosomes of the small bivalents have separated before those in the large ones.

Late anaphase I. All the chromosomes have now separated from their homologous partners. Each chromosome still contains two chromatids (looking like spirals) joined together at a centromere.

Prophase II. The two chromatids of each chromosome are still joined, but only at the centromeres - along the rest of their lengths they are spreading apart.

Metaphase II. The photograph has been taken looking down onto the two equators.

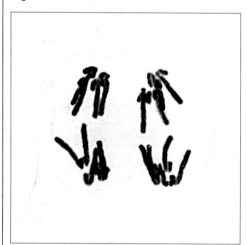

Anaphase II. The chromatids have each separated from their partner.

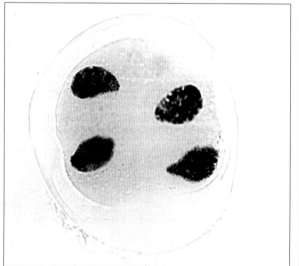

Telophase II. Notice that, although four nuclei (all haploid) have formed, the cytoplasm has not yet begun to divide.

Fig. 4.10 Meiosis in cells of an aloe.

Independent assortment

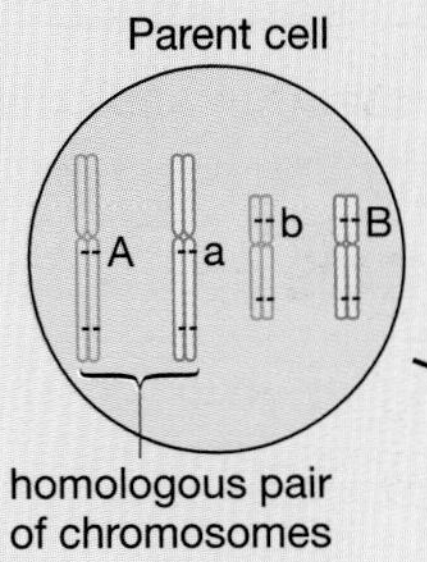

– A – a

pair of alleles for a genetic characteristic e.g. allele 'A' could be for normal height and 'a' for tallness

– b – B

pair of alleles for a different genetic characteristic e.g. allele 'B' could be for brown hair and 'b' for fair hair

How alternative gene combinations occur

It is due to the randomness of the bivalents' move to the equator in meiosis I. When homologous chromosomes separate in anaphase I they move to the pole that they happen to be nearest, as shown below.

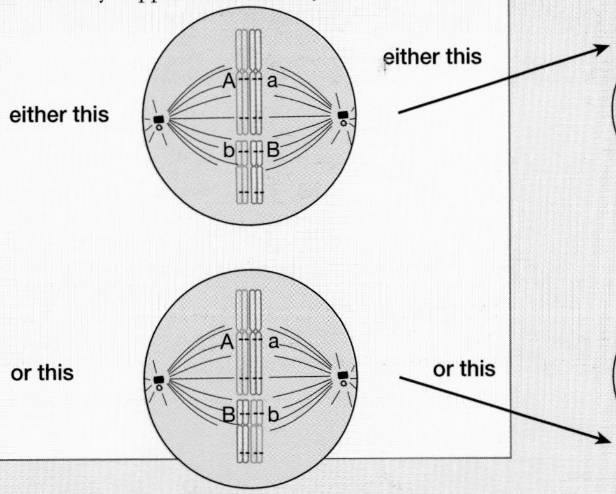

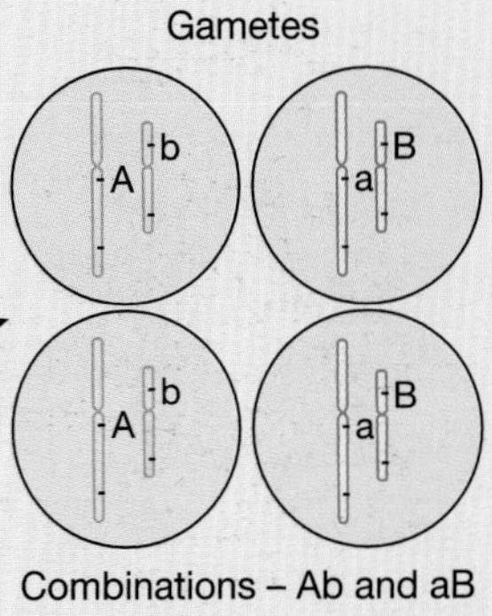

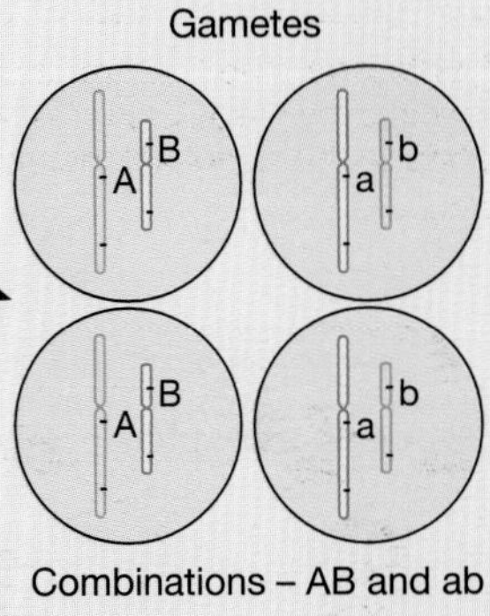

Remember – The two chromatids within a chromosome contain the same alleles – they are exact copies of each other. Each gamete always contains one chromatid from each homologous pair of chromosomes. This ensures that each gamete contains one gene for each genetic characteristic.

Crossing over

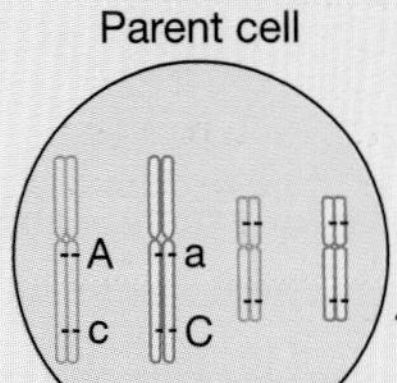

Homologous chromosomes pair and crossing over takes place in interphase.

The genes A and c are linked because they are found on the same chromosome. Similarly, a and C are linked.

How alternative gene combinations occur

Crossing over occurs randomly. Any two chromatids in a homologous pair can break at the same point and rejoin resulting in the exchange of sections of chromatid. Often there is one crossover in each homologous pair and sometimes more.

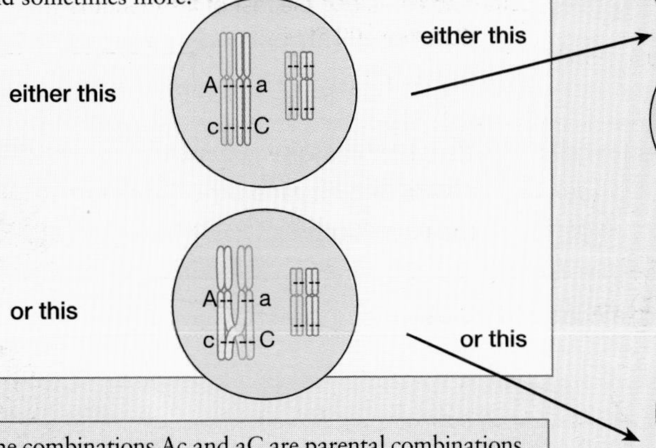

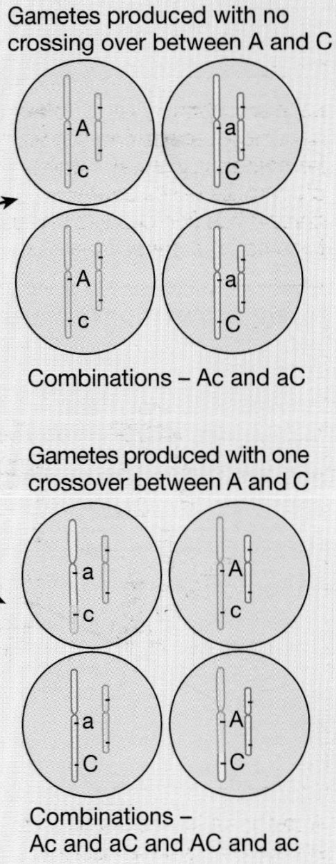

The combinations Ac and aC are parental combinations because they are the same as on the parental cell's chromosomes. But AC and ac are recombinants.

Question

Draw your own labelled diagrams to show how (a) there would be independent assortment between alleles c C and d D, and (b) how recombination would occur if there was a crossover between b and D.

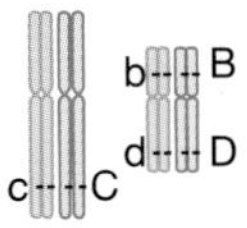

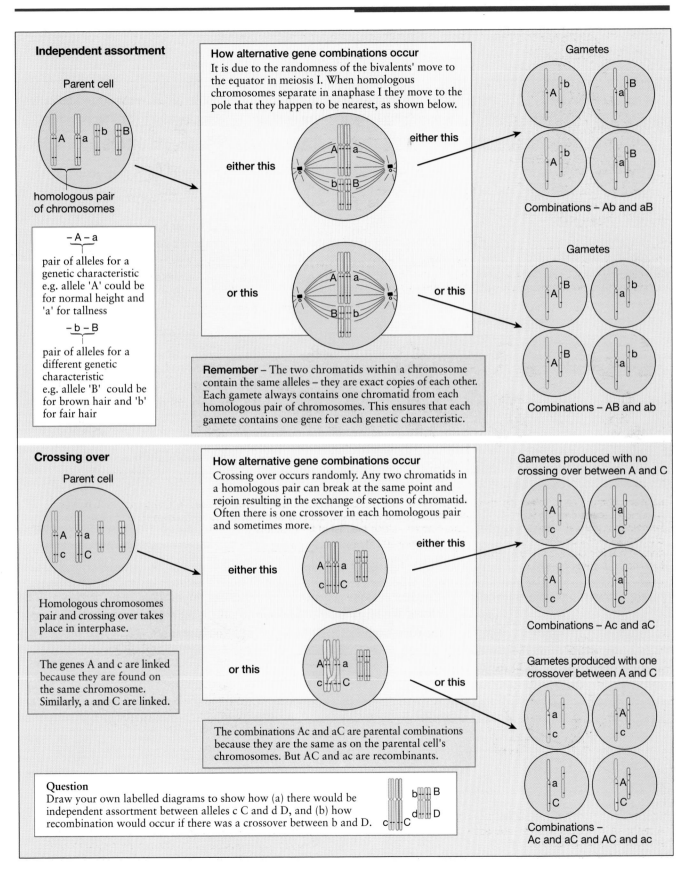

Fig. 4.11 How meiosis produces genetic variation.

	Mitosis	Meiosis
number of divisions	a single division, resulting in two cells being formed from a single parent cell	two divisions, resulting in four cells being formed from a single parent cell
ploidy of parent cell	haploid and diploid cells may divide by mitosis	only diploid cells may divide by meiosis
events in prophase	chromosomes (each made of two chromatids) do not associate with each other	in meiosis I, chromosomes (each made of two chromatids) pair up with their homologous partner
	no chiasmata formed	in meiosis I, chiasmata form between chromatids of homologous chromosomes
events in metaphase	individual chromosomes are arranged on the equator of the spindle	in meiosis I, pairs of homologous chromosomes are arranged on the equator of the spindle
events in anaphase	centromere splits, and chromatids separate	in meiosis I, the chromatids stay joined, and the homologous chromosomes separate
chromosome number in daughter cells	daughter cells have the same number of chromosomes as the parent cell	daughter cells have half the number of chromosomes as the parent cell
genetic variation in daughter cells	daughter cells are genetically identical with each other, and with the parent cell	daughter cells are genetically different from each other, and from the parent cell

Table 4.1 Differences between mitosis and meiosis.

Q2 (a) What is:

    (i) a bivalent *(1)*

    (ii) a chiasma? *(1)*

Diagrams **A**, **B** and **C** show the same stage in mitosis, meiosis I and meiosis II in a plant cell.

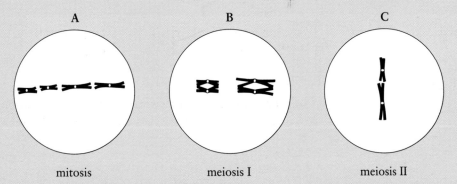

A	B	C
mitosis	meiosis I	meiosis II

(b) Identify the stage shown giving your reason. *(1)*

(c) The cell in diagram **A** has 20 units of DNA. How many units of DNA would there be in a cell from this plant at the end of:

    (i) mitosis; *(1)*

    (ii) meiosis? *(1)*

AEB 1994 *(Total 5 marks)*

Q3 The diagram below shows the metaphase stage of mitosis in an animal cell.

X

(a) What is the diploid number (2n) for the species shown? *(1)*

(b) The part labelled X is a region of a chromosome.

    (i) Name the region labelled X. *(1)*

    (ii) State two functions of X. *(2)*

(c) How would the appearance of the chromosomes in this animal cell differ at metaphase I of meiosis? *(2)*

London 1994 *(Total 6 marks)*

Q4 Diagram **A** below shows the different phases during the cell cycle of an animal cell. Diagram **B** shows the quantity of DNA present during these different phases. G_1 and G_2 represent growth phases, separated by an intermediate phase S, in the cell cycle.

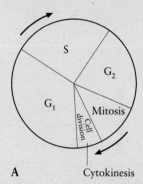

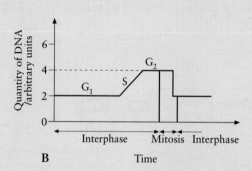

A

B

(a) Describe how the quantity of DNA in cells is increased during phase S, between growth phase G_1 and growth phase G_2, leading up to mitosis. (2)

(b) (i) What would be the quantity of DNA in arbitrary units in a cell at the end of mitosis? (1)

　　 (ii) Describe how the quantity of DNA is returned to this level. (2)

(c) Name one metabolic process of a cell which stops when a nucleus divides. (1)

(d) Indicate the importance of mitosis in the cell cycle. (2)

London 1993　　　　　　　　　　　　　　　　　　　　　　　　　(*Total 8 marks*)

5 DNA and protein synthesis

Every living organism contains DNA. The sequence of nucleotides on the DNA molecules is a code which provides instructions for the sequences of amino acids which are used to build protein molecules. In this Chapter you will see how this code works and how protein molecules are made.

DNA AS THE GENETIC MATERIAL

A molecule which is to act as the genetic material in a living organism must have certain properties. Firstly, it must be able to **replicate**, being copied perfectly so it can pass unchanged into the new cells that are produced when an old cell divides. Secondly, it must be able to **store information** which provides the instructions used by the cell to determine the characteristics of the cell and the organism of which it is a part. DNA does this by giving instructions for the making of proteins.

5.1 DNA replication

With only a very few exceptions, every living cell contains DNA. (Red blood cells are one such exception.) In prokaryotic cells there may be just one DNA molecule. In eukaryotic cells there are usually several. For example, humans have 46 DNA molecules in their cells (when they are not dividing), because each of our 46 chromosomes contains one DNA molecule.

The DNA molecules carry coded instructions for the kinds of proteins which will be made by the cell. A human begins life as a single cell that contains 23 DNA molecules from its father and 23 from its mother. Each of these DNA molecules is essential to the proper development of that single cell into a complete adult organism. Therefore, before the cell divides by mitosis, each DNA molecule is copied so that one copy can be distributed to each of the two daughter cells. Fig. 4.4 shows how this distribution takes place during mitosis. At the start of mitosis each chromosome contains two identical copies of its DNA molecule. Each copy is called a **chromatid**.

DNA replication takes place during interphase in the nucleus of the cell. Fig. 5.1 shows how it is done. It requires a supply of free nucleotides (that is nucleotides which exist singly, in solution, not joined into long chains as they are in DNA) to which extra phosphate groups are added to activate them. The DNA molecule unwinds and the two strands are separated by the breakage of the hydrogen bonds between the bases. Nucleotides with the appropriate complementary bases then slot into place opposite the exposed bases on each strand, that is A with T and C with G. Hydrogen bonds between the complementary bases hold them in place. The sugar of one nucleotide is then joined to the phosphate of the next nucleotide to form a new polynucleotide chain. These processes are dependent on a number of enzymes, including DNA polymerase.

The result is that two new DNA molecules are formed from one old one. Each new molecule contains one old polynucleotide strand and one new one, so this method of replication is known as **semi-conservative** replication because half of the old molecule is conserved.

Very few errors are made during DNA replication, because DNA polymerase effectively 'proof-reads' the new molecules it is making. This enzyme will only link a new nucleotide into the growing chain if the previous one is paired correctly. If it is not, then the enzyme removes the wrong nucleotide and replaces it with the correct one before it continues along the chain.

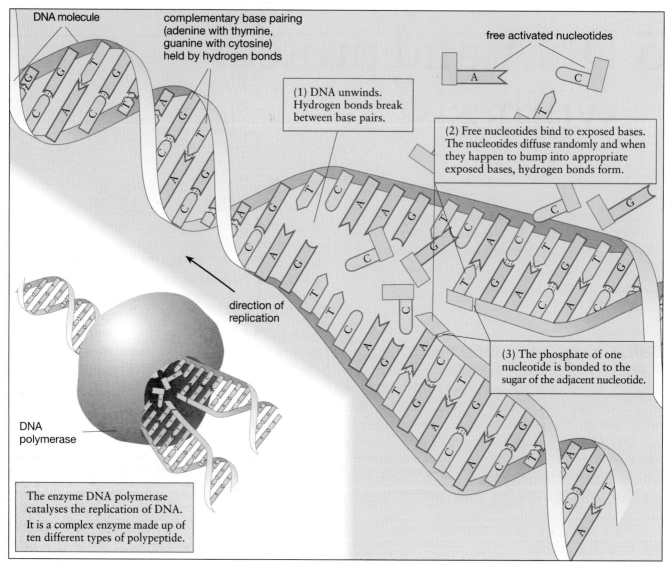

DNA molecule

complementary base pairing (adenine with thymine, guanine with cytosine) held by hydrogen bonds

free activated nucleotides

(1) DNA unwinds. Hydrogen bonds break between base pairs.

(2) Free nucleotides bind to exposed bases. The nucleotides diffuse randomly and when they happen to bump into appropriate exposed bases, hydrogen bonds form.

direction of replication

(3) The phosphate of one nucleotide is bonded to the sugar of the adjacent nucleotide.

DNA polymerase

The enzyme DNA polymerase catalyses the replication of DNA.

It is a complex enzyme made up of ten different types of polypeptide.

Fig. 5.1 Semi-conservative replication of DNA.

PROTEIN SYNTHESIS

5.2 How DNA codes for protein synthesis

The function of DNA is to provide instructions for protein synthesis. One DNA molecule contains enough instructions for making many proteins. A length of DNA which contains the instructions for making a single protein or polypeptide is called a **gene**.

DNA contains a code which dictates the sequence in which amino acids are to be linked together to make a protein. *The sequence of bases in a gene is a code for the sequence of amino acids in a protein.*

The code in a DNA molecule is carried in the sequence of the four bases, adenine (A), thymine (T), guanine (G) and cytosine (C), in one of its two strands, the 'reference' strand. This base sequence is always 'read' in the same direction.

A group of three bases, called a **triplet**, codes for one amino acid (Fig. 5.2). As there are four bases, there are 64 possible different triplets. There, are however, only 20 different amino acids which need to be coded for. This means that, if only one triplet coded for one amino acid, there would be 44 left-over triplets which coded for nothing. This does not happen. Most amino acids have two or more similar triplets which code for them. There are still some 'spare' triplets and these are used as 'punctuation marks', indicating starting and stopping points for beginning and ending an amino acid chain. Table 5.1 shows the triplets of bases on the reference strand of a DNA molecule which code for each of the 20 amino acids used to make proteins in cells.

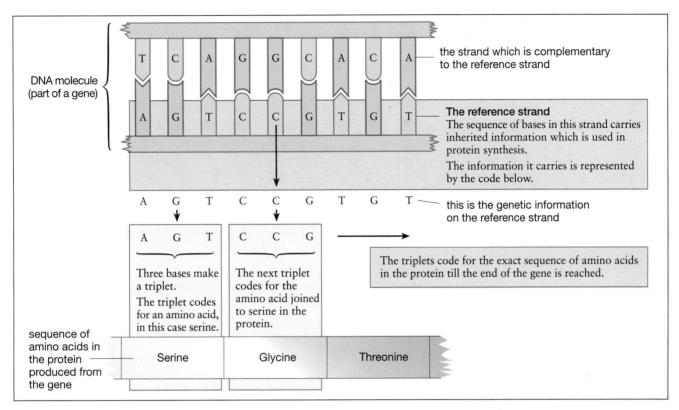

Fig. 5.2 How DNA codes for the sequence of amino acids in a protein. A very small part of one gene is shown.

The first column shows the triplet of bases on the reference strand of DNA. The second column shows the abbreviation for the amino acid which this triplet codes for. Check back to Fig. 1.11 if you need the full names of the amino acids.

base triplet in DNA	amino acid it codes for	base triplet in DNA	amino acid it codes for	base triplet in DNA	amino acid it codes for	base triplet in DNA	amino acid it codes for
AAA	Phe	GAA	Leu	TAA	Ile	CAA	Val
AAG	Phe	GAG	Leu	TAG	Ile	CAG	Val
AAT	Leu	GAT	Leu	TAT	Ile	CAT	Val
AAC	Leu	GAC	Leu	TAC	Met	CAC	Val
AGA	Ser	GGA	Pro	TGA	Thr	CGA	Ala
AGG	Ser	GGG	Pro	TGG	Thr	CGG	Ala
AGT	Ser	GGT	Pro	TGT	Thr	CGT	Ala
AGC	Ser	GGC	Pro	TGC	Thr	CGC	Ala
ATA	Tyr	GTA	His	TTA	Asn	CTA	Asp
ATG	Tyr	GTG	His	TTG	Asn	CTG	Asp
ATT	stop	GTT	Gln	TTT	Lys	CTT	Glu
ATC	stop	GTC	Gln	TTC	Lys	CTC	Glu
ACA	Cys	GCA	Arg	TCA	Ser	CCA	Gly
ACG	Cys	GCG	Arg	TCG	Ser	CCG	Gly
ACT	stop	GCT	Arg	TCT	Arg	CCT	Gly
ACC	Trp	GCC	Arg	TCC	Arg	CCC	Gly

Table 5.1 The genetic code.

Box 5.1 The evidence that DNA replication is semi-conservative

The structure of a DNA molecule was worked out in 1953 by James Watson and Francis Crick, working in Cambridge. They also suggested how it replicated: the two strands could unwind and split apart. New strands would then be built up against each of the two old ones, following the rules of complementary base pairing. We now know that this method, called **semi-conservative replication**, is what happens. However, at that time, there were two other theories about the method of DNA replication.

One theory was that a completely new DNA molecule, with two new strands, might be made from the original one. This was called **conservative replication**. Another possibility, called **dispersive replication**, involved parts, but not all, of each strand of the old DNA molecule becoming part of the new ones, with new bits scattered in between (Fig. 5.3).

In 1958 Mathew Meselson and Franklin Stahl, two American scientists, carried out an experiment to see if DNA is copied semi-conservatively. They chose to use bacteria rather than eukaryotic cells because bacterial cells divide quickly and are easy to culture in large quantities.

The bacterium they used was *Escherichia coli*, a common and usually harmless rod-shaped bacterium found in the human gut. First, they grew *E. coli* in a medium (food source) whose only nitrogen-containing substance was ammonium chloride (NH_4Cl) containing the heavy nitrogen isotope, ^{15}N. The bacteria used this nitrogen to make new DNA. The *E. coli* were grown in this medium for so many generations that it was certain that all the bases in the DNA molecules must contain virtually 100% ^{15}N. Their DNA was therefore heavy, because of the quantity of the heavy N atoms it contained.

Then the bacteria were transferred into a medium containing only the lighter isotope of nitrogen, ^{14}N. Some of them were left in this medium for just 50 minutes – just long enough for each cell, and therefore each molecule of DNA, to reproduce once. Others were left for two, three or more generation times. The DNA from each group of bacteria was then extracted, put into a caesium chloride solution and spun at 40 000 g in a centrifuge.

The DNA molecules came to lie in the part of the caesium chloride solution which had a density the same as theirs. DNA molecules containing ^{15}N are heavier than those containing ^{14}N, so they ended up nearer the base of the tubes. Fig. 5.4 shows the results which Meselson and Stahl obtained.

newly synthesised parts of
DNA shown dark blue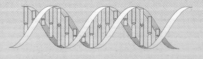

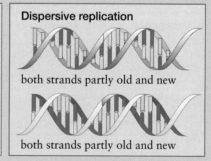 parent DNA molecule, used as a source of information for the synthesis of two molecules

The two new DNA molecules produced by replication by each method would be like this:

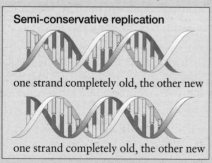

Semi-conservative replication

one strand completely old, the other new

one strand completely old, the other new

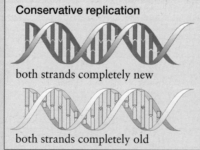

Conservative replication

both strands completely new

both strands completely old

Dispersive replication

both strands partly old and new

both strands partly old and new

Fig. 5.3 Three theoretically possible methods of DNA replication.

Box 5.1 The evidence that DNA replication is semi-conservative (cont.)

Density gradient centrifugation of DNA

less dense

dense

As a result of centrifugation a density gradient is set up. In this gradient the density of CsCl gets greater the nearer the base of the tube.

DNA is extracted from many bacteria and added to the tube

tube centrifuged

at high speed

DNA rests where its density matches the density of the CsCl around it. The lower the resting point the more dense (heavier) the DNA.

The broader the band, the more DNA is present.

Meselson and Stahl's experiment

DNA is extracted from bacteria grown in $^{15}NH_4Cl$ for many generations. The DNA is centrifuged:

Bacteria grown in $^{15}NH_4Cl$ for many generations are moved to $^{14}NH_4Cl$ for one, two, three or four generations. Their DNA is extracted and centrifuged.

after one generation in ^{14}N

after two generations in ^{14}N

after three generations in ^{14}N

after four generations in ^{14}N

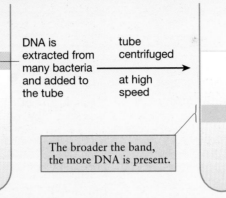

How the experiment is interpreted

Key

parts of DNA made using heavy nitrogen (^{15}N)

parts of DNA made using normal nitrogen (^{14}N)

DNA synthesised after many generations of growth in $^{15}NH_4Cl$ will have all its N atoms as ^{15}N.

Because ^{15}N is heavier than the normal ^{14}N, DNA containing ^{15}N is heavier and therefore more dense than normal DNA. A single density band is expected whatever the mode of replication.

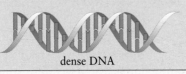

dense DNA

DNA produced after one generation in ^{14}N will show the consequences of one DNA replication. A single band of DNA, of a single density, is produced.

This rules out conservative replication, which would produce two bands. In the diagram below you can see the result of one replication by semi-conservative means.

intermediate density DNA

After two generations and two DNA replications the results rule out dispersive replication. Dispersive replication would result in one density band getting gradually less dense after each generation.

The two bands produced fit in with semi-conservative replication as shown below:

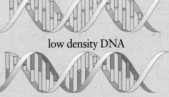

low density DNA

intermediate density DNA

Q1　(a) Why would you expect two density bands if DNA replicates once by conservative replication?
　　(b) Explain why dispersive replication cannot be expected to produce DNA of more than one density.

Fig. 5.4 Meselson and Stahl's experiment.

Box 5.2 The earliest evidence that DNA is the genetic material

Griffith's experiment

In the 1920s and 1930s it was known that genes contained DNA and protein, and that genes contained inherited information. Most scientists up to the 1940s would probably have put their money on the protein component of genes being the genetic material. It was not until 1944 that an experiment was done which showed without doubt that the genetic material is DNA.

The 1944 experiment was based on an earlier one performed in 1928 by an English microbiologist, Frederick Griffith. He had used two strains of

Pneumococcus bacterium. One strain has a capsule and can cause pneumonia, while the other has no capsule and is harmless (Section 3.22). The strain with the capsule is called **smooth**, because the capsules around the bacteria make colonies growing on agar look smooth and shiny. The harmless strain is **rough**. Smooth bacteria can be killed, and therefore made harmless, by exposing them to heat. Griffith injected mice with each of these types of bacteria, and also a mixture of live rough and heat-killed smooth. His experiment and results are shown in Fig. 5.5.

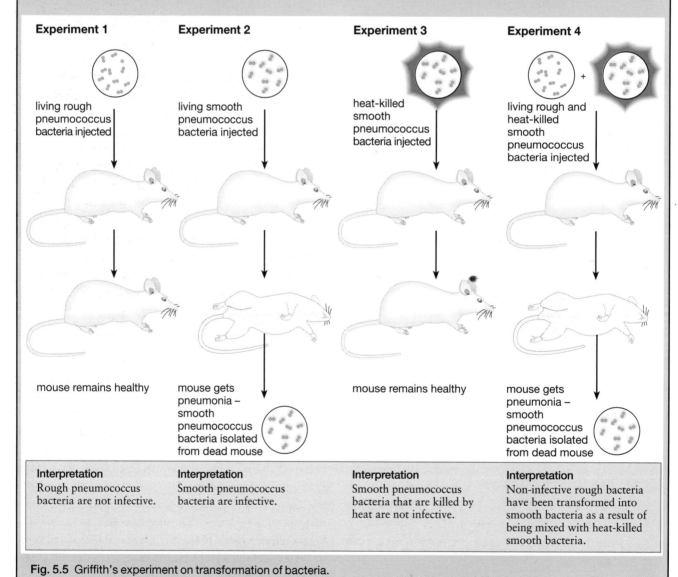

Experiment 1

living rough pneumococcus bacteria injected

mouse remains healthy

Interpretation
Rough pneumococcus bacteria are not infective.

Experiment 2

living smooth pneumococcus bacteria injected

mouse gets pneumonia – smooth pneumococcus bacteria isolated from dead mouse

Interpretation
Smooth pneumococcus bacteria are infective.

Experiment 3

heat-killed smooth pneumococcus bacteria injected

mouse remains healthy

Interpretation
Smooth pneumococcus bacteria that are killed by heat are not infective.

Experiment 4

living rough and heat-killed smooth pneumococcus bacteria injected

mouse gets pneumonia – smooth pneumococcus bacteria isolated from dead mouse

Interpretation
Non-infective rough bacteria have been transformed into smooth bacteria as a result of being mixed with heat-killed smooth bacteria.

Fig. 5.5 Griffith's experiment on transformation of bacteria.

Box 5.2 The earliest evidence that DNA is the genetic material (cont.)

Griffith concluded that something in the dead smooth bacteria had been taken up by the living, normally harmless, rough bacteria and enabled them to cause disease in the mice. The heat-killed smooth bacteria had **transformed** the capsule-free rough bacteria into capsule-covered smooth bacteria.

But Griffith did not know what this 'transforming principle' was. Was it protein, or was it DNA? The proof that it was DNA was obtained in 1944 by Oswald Avery, Colin Macleod and Maclyn McCarty in America. They purified preparations of the 'transforming principle'. They showed that it contained no protein. Moreover, when they incubated it with proteases, the transforming principle still worked – if it had been protein it would have been destroyed by these enzymes. However, if it was incubated with DNAase (an enzyme which digests DNA), it was destroyed.

The Hershey and Chase experiment
Further evidence that DNA, not protein, is the genetic material was supplied in 1952 by Alfred Hershey and Martha Chase. They used a type of virus which infects bacteria called a **bacteriophage**, or 'phage' for short. The phage has a coat made of protein and contains a strand of DNA.

Hershey and Chase made use of the fact that protein contains sulphur but not phosphorus, while DNA contains phosphorus but not sulphur. They grew some phages in the presence of radioactive sulphur, which was taken up by their protein coats, and so 'labelled' the protein. Other phages were grown in the presence of radioactive phosphorus, which labelled the DNA.

Each of these groups of phages were then allowed to infect bacteria, which they do by injecting their DNA into the bacterium and leaving their protein coat outside. When the phage had had time to attach to the outside of the bacterial cells, the culture was vigorously mixed in a blender so that the virus coats were broken away from the bacteria. The mixture was then centrifuged, which produced a pellet containing the infected bacteria and a supernatant fluid containing the virus coats.

Hershey and Chase found that the bacteria which had been infected with phosphorus-labelled phage contained most of the labelled phosphorus. Those which had been infected with sulphur-labelled phage contained virtually no labelled sulphur. Moreover, when they looked at the phage which had multiplied inside the bacterial cells, they found that the new phage contained a lot of labelled phosphorus but only a very small amount of sulphur. This can be explained if the phage were passing on DNA from generation to generation, but not protein. It must be the phage's DNA which, when it has entered the bacterium, provides instructions for making the next generation of phage.

5.3 An outline of protein synthesis
Protein molecules are made by linking together amino acids. This is done on the ribosomes in the cytoplasm of a cell. The sequence of amino acids, the **primary structure** (Section 1.12), determines the overall shape and function of the protein (Fig. 5.6).

DNA, in the chromosomes in the nucleus of the cell, contains the codes laying down the sequence in which the amino acids are joined together. In a eukaryotic cell, the DNA molecules remain inside the nucleus. The code is carried from the nucleus to the ribosomes by a messenger molecule, **messenger RNA (mRNA)**.

When a particular kind of protein is required, the length of DNA which carries the instructions for making that protein – the gene – unwinds and unzips (Fig. 5.6). This exposes the bases on the two strands. Free mRNA nucleotides (Fig. 1.21) slot into place opposite the exposed bases on the DNA reference strand, following the rules of complementary base pairing. The sugars and phosphates of the mRNA nucleotides are then linked together to form a long mRNA molecule. *The sequence of bases on the mRNA molecule is a complementary copy of the sequence of bases on the reference strand of the DNA molecule.* The formation of the mRNA molecule is called **transcription**. Enzymes, including RNA polymerase, are required for this process.

Transcription

The transcription (copying) of a gene occurs inside the nucleus.
It involves the synthesis of messenger RNA (mRNA) using the code on the reference strand of part of the DNA.

Step 1
DNA unwinds.

Step 2
Hydrogen bonds between the DNA bases break (DNA unzips).

Step 3
When a free nucleotide moves randomly next to an exposed base complementary to it, hydrogen bonding occurs.

Step 4
The newly bonded nucleotide is joined to the growing mRNA.

Step 5
The mRNA is released and the DNA returns to a double helix.

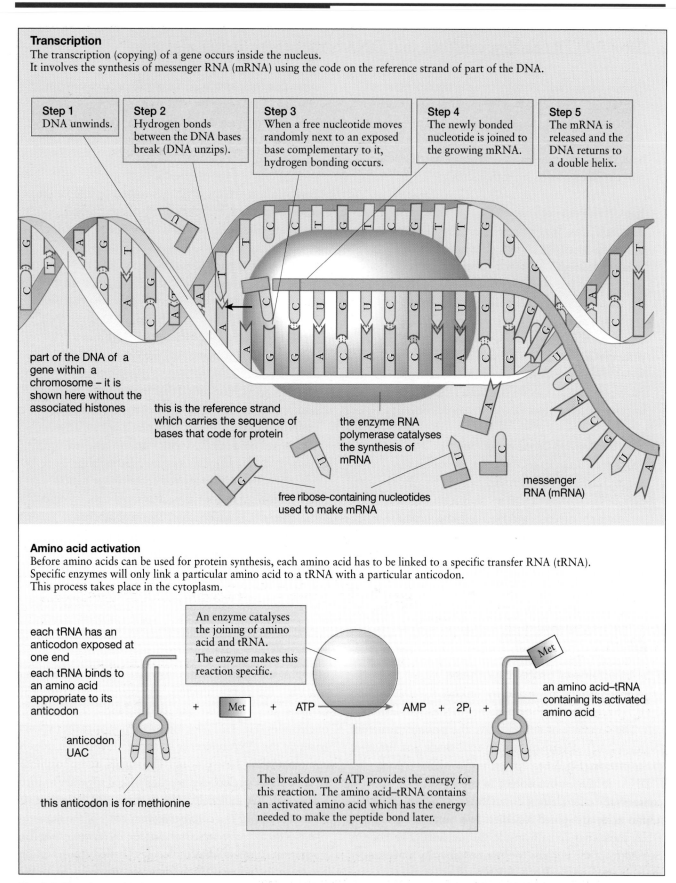

part of the DNA of a gene within a chromosome – it is shown here without the associated histones

this is the reference strand which carries the sequence of bases that code for protein

the enzyme RNA polymerase catalyses the synthesis of mRNA

free ribose-containing nucleotides used to make mRNA

messenger RNA (mRNA)

Amino acid activation

Before amino acids can be used for protein synthesis, each amino acid has to be linked to a specific transfer RNA (tRNA).
Specific enzymes will only link a particular amino acid to a tRNA with a particular anticodon.
This process takes place in the cytoplasm.

each tRNA has an anticodon exposed at one end

each tRNA binds to an amino acid appropriate to its anticodon

anticodon UAC

this anticodon is for methionine

An enzyme catalyses the joining of amino acid and tRNA.
The enzyme makes this reaction specific.

+ Met + ATP ⟶ AMP + 2P$_i$ +

an amino acid–tRNA containing its activated amino acid

The breakdown of ATP provides the energy for this reaction. The amino acid–tRNA contains an activated amino acid which has the energy needed to make the peptide bond later.

Fig. 5.6 Protein synthesis.

Translation   In translation the code on the mRNA describing a sequence of amino acids is used to make the protein containing that sequence. This process occurs in the cytoplasm after the mRNA has left the nucleus through a nuclear pore.

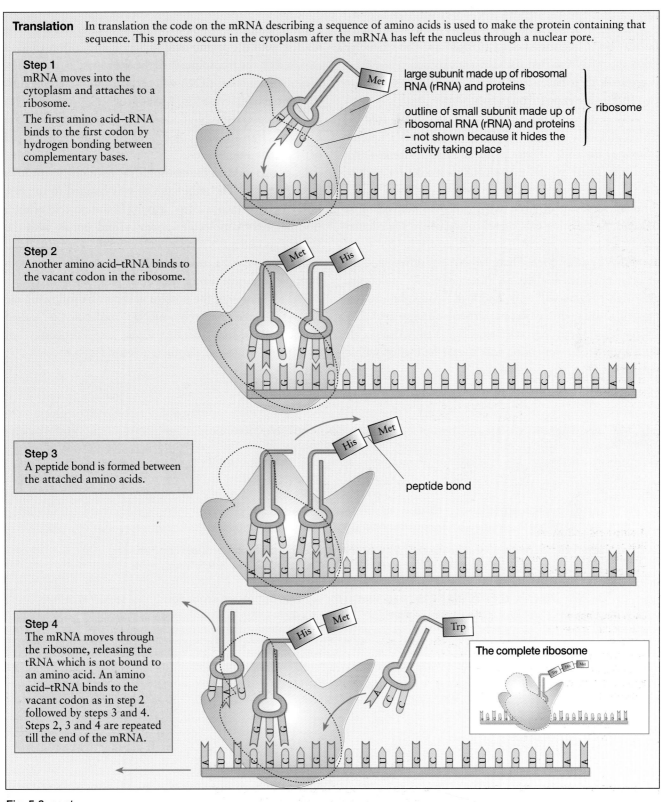

Step 1
mRNA moves into the cytoplasm and attaches to a ribosome.

The first amino acid–tRNA binds to the first codon by hydrogen bonding between complementary bases.

large subunit made up of ribosomal RNA (rRNA) and proteins

outline of small subunit made up of ribosomal RNA (rRNA) and proteins – not shown because it hides the activity taking place

ribosome

Step 2
Another amino acid–tRNA binds to the vacant codon in the ribosome.

Step 3
A peptide bond is formed between the attached amino acids.

peptide bond

Step 4
The mRNA moves through the ribosome, releasing the tRNA which is not bound to an amino acid. An amino acid–tRNA binds to the vacant codon as in step 2 followed by steps 3 and 4. Steps 2, 3 and 4 are repeated till the end of the mRNA.

The complete ribosome

Fig. 5.6 *cont.*

Q2   (a) Draw diagrams to show how the next two amino acids are joined to the growing amino acid chain.

(b) What is the primary structure of the protein being made here?

The mRNA molecule then leaves the nucleus through a nuclear pore, and attaches to a ribosome. The ribosome holds the mRNA so that six bases are exposed at one time. A group of three bases on the mRNA is called a **codon**, so two codons are exposed on the ribosome.

Another type of RNA, called **transfer RNA (tRNA)** brings amino acids to the ribosome. *It is the tRNA which translates the code of base sequences into an amino acid sequence.* There are different tRNA molecules for each of the 20 amino acids, and each of these tRNAs has a different sequence of three bases, called an **anticodon**, at one end. At the other end, there is a site where a particular amino acid can be joined. The amino acid is loaded on to the tRNA by an enzyme. There are as many different kinds of these enzymes as there are different tRNA molecules, and each enzyme will only load a tRNA containing one particular anticodon with one particular amino acid. The specificity of these enzymes means that a tRNA molecule with a particular anticodon will always be loaded with a particular, 'matching', amino acid.

For example, a tRNA with the anticodon AGG will be loaded with the amino acid serine. If the codon UCC is exposed on the ribosome, then the tRNA will bond with it. Next to it, another tRNA will then slot into place against its complementary codon. As these two tRNAs bond with the two exposed mRNA codons, their two amino acids are brought close together. A peptide bond is then formed between the amino acids.

Once this is done, the ribosome moves along to the next mRNA codon. The tRNA which was bonded to the first mRNA codon moves away, leaving its amino acid behind. Another tRNA molecule moves in and bonds with the newly exposed mRNA codon. Once again, a peptide bond forms between the amino acids. The process continues until the ribosome reaches a codon signifying 'stop'.

The formation of the protein molecule by following the base sequence on the mRNA molecule is called **translation**. More detail about the processes of transcription and translation is given in Fig. 5.6.

Q3 The diagram below shows part of a messenger RNA (mRNA) molecule.

> U A C C G A C C U U A A

(a) (i) How many codons are shown in this section of mRNA? *(1)*

(ii) What is specified by a sequence of codons in an mRNA molecule? *(1)*

(b) A tRNA molecule carries a complementary base sequence for a particular codon.

(i) Write the complementary sequence for the first codon in the mRNA sequence given above. *(1)*

(ii) Describe the role of tRNA molecules in the process of protein synthesis. *(3)*

London 1996 *(Total 6 marks)*

MUTATION

5.4 Maintaining the structure of DNA

The ability of a cell to survive depends on the instructions carried by its DNA. If the DNA is damaged, then the cell may not be able to make the correct proteins. Cells have evolved many ways of ensuring that any damage done to their DNA molecules is kept to a minimum.

One of the most dangerous times for a DNA molecule is when it is replicating. You have already seen (Section 5.1) that one of the enzymes responsible for the control of this process, DNA polymerase, effectively proof-reads the DNA copies it is making, to ensure that most errors in base-pairing are corrected immediately. If, for example, an A nucleotide incorrectly slots into place against another exposed A nucleotide, then DNA polymerase will remove it and replace it with a correct T nucleotide before it moves on. This helps to keep errors occurring during replication down to less than one in a million base pairs.

Nevertheless, errors do slip through. Most of these are recognised and repaired. Cells are able to repair DNA because, even if there is a mistake in a base in one of the two strands, the correct base is probably still in position in the other strand; the information about which base should be there is therefore not lost. There are several different mechanisms in a cell which can remove the incorrect nucleotide and replace it with the correct one.

5.5 Different types of mutations

A **mutation** is an unpredictable change in the genetic material of an organism.

This change may be on a very small scale, involving just one or two bases in a DNA molecule. Such changes are sometimes known as **point mutations**. Point mutations can happen at any time, but are most likely to occur when DNA is being replicated during interphase. They affect the *sequence* of the bases in the DNA molecule (Fig. 5.7), and so may affect the *sequence* of amino acids in the protein for which that gene codes. Often, this affects the three-dimensional structure of the protein and its function. An example of such an effect is described in Section 5.7.

All of the different alleles of a gene must once have been produced by this type of mutation. The mutation which produced a particular allele may have occurred many generations ago, and the allele has been passed on from generation to generation. This is only likely to happen, however, if the new allele codes for a protein which is useful to the organism. If the new allele codes for a useless or harmful protein, then the organism possessing this allele might not survive, and the new allele would not be passed on. You can read more about this process, called natural selection, in Chapter 7.

Other mutations may be on a larger scale, affecting large sections of chromosomes, or chromosome number. These are sometimes called **chromosome mutations**. Chromosome mutations are most likely to occur during mitosis or meiosis. Quite large pieces of chromosomes may break off and be lost, or re-attach themselves in the wrong place. They may join to other chromosomes, a process called **chromosome translocation**. Unequal division of chromosomes between daughter cells may occur; whole chromosomes may fail to move into the daughter cells, so that one cell ends up with too many and one with too few. This is called **non-disjunction**. Examples of this kind of mutation are described in Sections 5.8 and 5.9.

5.6 The causes of mutations

Mutations may occur spontaneously – that is, for no apparent reason. However, there are several factors which are known to increase the chances of mutations occurring. These factors are known as **mutagens**.

Many different **chemicals** are mutagens. These chemicals can react with bases, changing their characteristics so that they pair wrongly. For example, hydroxylamine (NH_2OH) acts as a mutagen by reacting with cytosine, changing the cytosine to a substance which pairs with adenine rather than with guanine. Other chemical mutagens may actually become incorporated into a DNA molecule, taking the place of a base which is already there, or slipping in between two adjacent nucleotides and so leading to the insertion or deletion of a base pair.

Some forms of **radiation** can also damage DNA. It does this by directly altering the structure of bases, or the sugar–phosphate backbone, in DNA molecules which it hits. Mutagenic radiation includes ultraviolet radiation, most of which we receive from the Sun; and also the three types of ionising radiation emitted by radioactive substances. Of these three types, α radiation can only penetrate very short distances into cells, so is not harmful unless it is breathed in or swallowed. However, once it is inside the body it is very likely to damage DNA, because it consists of relatively large particles which can do considerable damage to any DNA molecules which they do hit. β radiation can penetrate further than α, so can act as a mutagen even if it remains outside the body. **Gamma** radiation is even more penetrating than β radiation. **X rays** can also damage DNA.

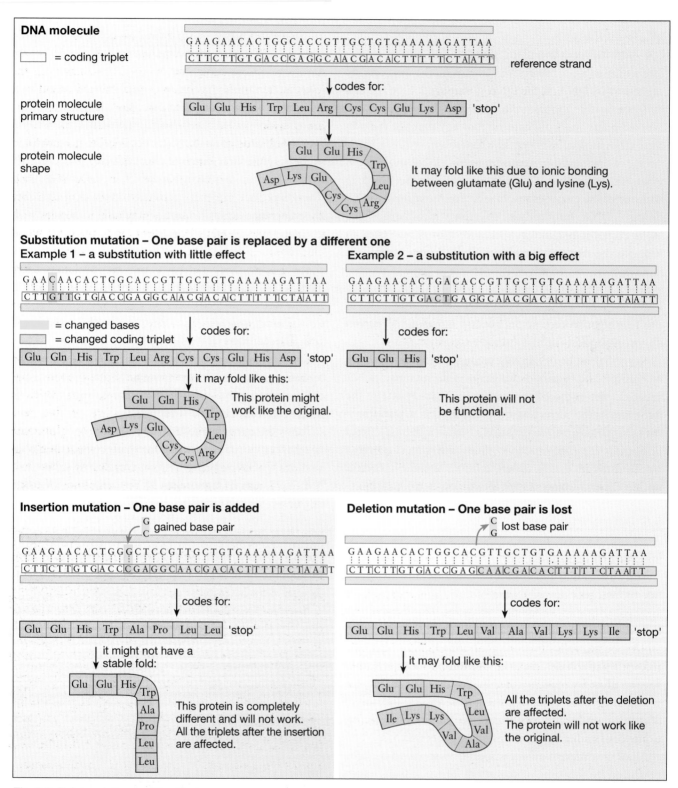

Fig. 5.7 Point mutation and its effects.

Q4 (a) What would be the consequence of the deletion of the third base pair of the original DNA?

(b) What would be the consequence of the substitution of T–A by A–T at the 24th base pair?

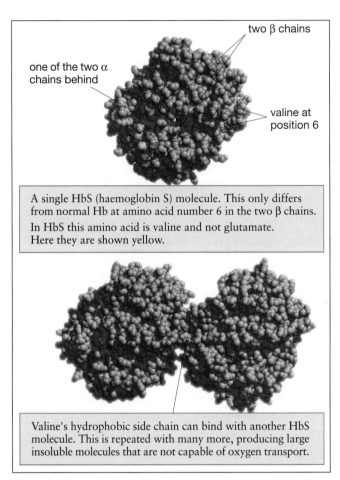

two β chains

one of the two α
chains behind

valine at
position 6

A single HbS (haemoglobin S) molecule. This only differs
from normal Hb at amino acid number 6 in the two β chains.
In HbS this amino acid is valine and not glutamate.
Here they are shown yellow.

Valine's hydrophobic side chain can bind with another HbS
molecule. This is repeated with many more, producing large
insoluble molecules that are not capable of oxygen transport.

Fig. 5.8 Sickle haemoglobin: a mutant form of haemoglobin.

5.7 An example of a point mutation – sickle cell haemoglobin

One human gene in which we know of many mutations is the gene which codes for two of the polypeptides in the haemoglobin molecule. Haemoglobin is a globular protein, made from four polypeptide chains (Fig. 5.8). Two of these chains are α chains, and two are β chains. The mutation we are interested in is in the gene coding for the amino acid sequence of the β chains.

The β polypeptide chains each start with the following sequence of amino acids:

Val–His–Leu–Thr–Pro–Glu–Glu–Lys

However, in some people, the β polypeptide chains contain a slightly different amino acid sequence:

Val–His–Leu–Thr–Pro–Val–Glu–Lys

There is just one difference: the amino acid valine has been substituted for the amino acid glutamate. This small change

has a very large effect on the behaviour of the haemoglobin molecule. This part of the polypeptide chain is on the surface of the haemoglobin, where it interacts with the water molecules in the cytoplasm of the red blood cell. Glutamate has a hydrophilic side chain. Valine, however, has a hydrophobic side chain. This can bind with a hydrophobic 'dent' on the surface of another haemoglobin molecule when it is not combined with oxygen. In people with this sort of haemoglobin, problems arise when their blood does not contain much oxygen – for example, if they do strenuous exercise. Their haemoglobin molecules stick to each other, forming long fibres inside their red blood cells. These fibres pull the cell out of shape, into a 'sickle' shape (Fig. 5.9). The red blood cells can no longer carry oxygen, and they have a strong tendency to get stuck in narrow blood capillaries. The person suffers from a severe lack of oxygen in their body tissues. They have **sickle cell anaemia**.

The haemoglobin of people with sickle cell anaemia contains valine instead of glutamate because their genes coding for the β polypeptide have one base which is different from normal. The usual allele of this gene contains the base triplet CTT, which codes for glutamate (Table 5.1), whereas the allele for sickle cell haemoglobin contains the base triplet CAT, which codes for valine. Just this single base change causes all the symptoms of sickle cell anaemia.

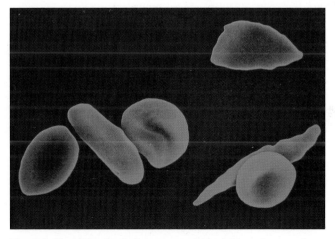

Fig. 5.9 Red blood cells in a person with sickle cell anaemia. Some cells are normal, while others are sickled.

Box 5.3   Another example of a point mutation – acute intermittent porphyria

Cells and organisms function by changing one substance into another, and then that substance into something else… These chemical reactions are called metabolic reactions, and a chain of such reactions is called a **metabolic pathway**. Each step in the pathway is catalysed by a particular enzyme.

Enzymes are proteins, and therefore their structure is coded for by DNA. A mutation in the gene coding for a particular enzyme may mean that a faulty enzyme is manufactured which cannot catalyse the reaction as it should. This may disrupt the entire metabolic pathway.

The inherited disease **acute intermittent porphyria** is caused by a gene mutation which affects an enzyme called **porphobilinogen deaminase** – or, rather more comfortably, **PBGD**. This enzyme is responsible for one of the steps in making haem (see pathway below), which is a vital component of haemoglobin (page 223), myoglobin and cytochromes.

In people with acute intermittent porphyria, PBGD does not catalyse the conversion of compound C to compound D as effectively as it should. These people therefore accumulate compounds A, B and C, and these are excreted in their urine. They feel well for most of the time, but every now and then suffer from bouts of intense abdominal pain and neurological problems. (It is thought that King George III's

madness may possibly have been due to this disease, but the evidence is very sketchy.) However, many people with the faulty enzyme have no symptoms at all.

Acute intermittent porphyria is especially common in Scandinavia, and a recent study has shown that the disease in Finland is caused by at least 19 different mutations of the PBGD gene. The base sequence of the 'correct' version of the gene was worked out in the 1980s, and in 1995 the base sequences of this gene in 81 Finnish people with the disease were investigated. It was found that virtually all of the many different mutations involve a change in a single base in the gene, most being base substitutions. Most of them result in a 'wrong' amino acid in the primary structure of PBGD, which affects its folding and solubility. Some of them, however, result in there being a 'stop' codon in the wrong place, so that an incomplete version of PBGD is synthesised.

This information is useful, because it can help to diagnose the disease. A person who knows that acute intermittent porphyria runs in his or her family may want to know whether they have a normal or a mutant gene. Because the disease does not always produce clear symptoms, it can often be difficult to diagnose. Now their DNA can be tested to see what base sequence is present in their PBGD gene.

glycine ⟶ compound A → compound B → compound C $\xrightarrow{\text{PBGD}}$ compound D → compound E → compound F → haem

succinyl coenzyme A   coenzyme A

5.8 An example of a chromosome mutation – Down's syndrome

Down's syndrome is caused by the possession of an extra chromosome 21.

Chromosome 21 is one of the smallest chromosomes. People with Down's syndrome therefore usually have 47 chromosomes in their cells, rather than the usual 46 (Fig. 5.10). The possession of extra chromosomes is known as **polysomy**. Sometimes, however, the extra chromosome 21 attaches itself to the end of another chromosome, so the person has the normal number of 46 chromosomes in their cells.

The extra chromosome 21 usually comes from the mother's egg. This happens because of an error during meiosis in her ovary in which the two chromosome 21s fail to separate, both of them going into one daughter cell and none into the other. This error is called **non-disjunction**. It probably happens quite often, involving any of the 23 pairs of chromosomes, but in most cases the cells produced will simply die. Indeed, it is thought that even when it involves chromosome 21, 70% of the zygotes produced if an egg with two chromosome 21s is fertilised fail to develop.

Down's syndrome is quite a common disorder. One in every 2000 children born to mothers of 25 years of age has Down's syndrome, and the frequency rises sharply with the age of the mother, reaching one in 50 for mothers who are 45 years old or more. Children with Down's syndrome are very happy and friendly. They have characteristic facial features and often have some degree of mental handicap. Their biggest problem, however, is that they have a greater risk than normal of suffering from infections, and many have some kind of heart disease.

5.9 Another example of chromosome mutation – polyploidy

Non-disjunction during meiosis, such as that which produces eggs with three chromosome 21s, may sometimes affect all of the chromosomes. If this happens, then two of the gametes end up with two of each chromosome and the other two gametes with none (Fig. 5.12). Diploid gametes have been produced.

A diploid gamete may then fuse with a normal, haploid gamete. The resulting zygote will have three sets of chromosomes which is called **triploid**. It can divide by mitosis, to produce a triploid organism. However, this organism will not be able to make gametes, because its cells will not be able to divide by meiosis. This is because the chromosomes will not be able to pair up successfully; they do try, but there are three of each of them. So, the organism will be sterile.

If, however, *two* diploid gametes fuse, then the resulting zygote will have four complete chromosome sets; it will be **tetraploid**. Tetraploid cells are often able to divide by meiosis, because each chromosome will be able to find a homologous partner. Thus tetraploid organisms may be able to produce gametes; if so, they are fertile.

The possession of three or more complete sets of chromosomes is called **polyploidy**. Polyploidy is common in plants, and has been an important mechanism by which new species of plants have evolved (Section 7.19).

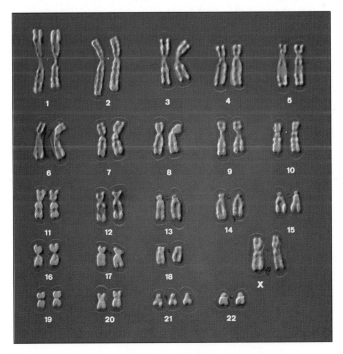

Fig. 5.10 Karyotype of person with Down's syndrome.

Fig. 5.11 The flower on the right is from the diploid wild primrose, *Primula vulgaris*. The much larger flower on the left is from a tetraploid hybrid between *P. vulgaris* and *P. veris*. Tetraploid plants are often larger then diploid ones.

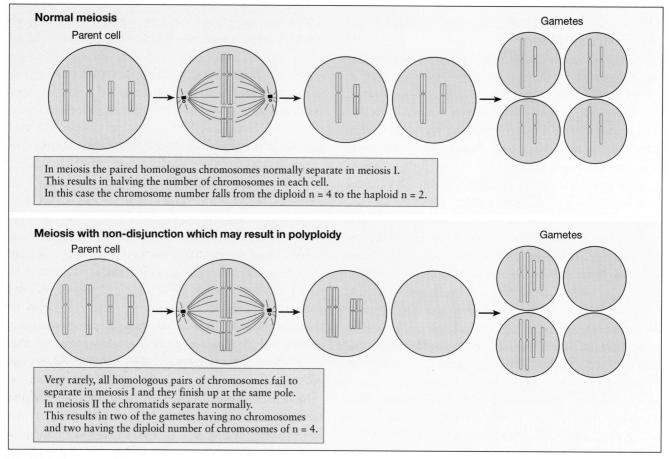

Fig. 5.12 How non-disjunction can lead to polyploidy.

Q5 Show, by means of diagrams, what happens when

(a) a gamete with no chromosomes is fertilised by a normal gamete and

(b) a gamete with the diploid number of chromosomes is fertilised by a normal gamete.

(c) What term would be used to describe the zygote formed in (b)?

Q6 The base sequences from two strands of DNA are shown in the diagram below. The two sequences are from the same section of a chromosome: the first is the normal sequence and the second is a mutant form.

    normal DNA   AATCAGGTTA

    mutant DNA   ATACCAGTTA

(a) Describe and name *two* point mutations in the mutant DNA. (2)

(b) After transcription, a strand of mRNA is produced. Write the mRNA sequence which would be produced from the mutant DNA. (1)

(c) (i) Describe how the polypeptide chain produced from this mRNA sequence may differ from the normal polypeptide. (1)

    (ii) Suggest how this might affect the activity of the polypeptide. (2)

London 1995   *(Total 6 marks)*

GENE TECHNOLOGY

5.10 Genetic engineering

Genetic engineering is the transfer of a gene from one organism, the **donor**, into another, the **recipient**. For example, the gene coding for human insulin may be removed from a human cell and inserted into a bacterium. The bacterium multiplies, producing many bacteria all containing this gene. The bacteria use the instructions on the gene to make human insulin, which can be extracted and purified.

Genetic engineering is a relatively new and very rapidly developing technology, which has opened up almost limitless possibilities for influencing the genetic makeup of living organisms. While this may lead to many useful and exciting developments in industry, conservation and medicine, it also has the potential for producing considerable ecological or human problems. These are discussed in Section 5.16.

The process of genetic engineering involves three basic stages (Fig. 5.13), each of which has several smaller steps. Firstly, the desired gene in the donor organism must be isolated and identified. At this stage it is cloned, that is multiple identical copies are made. When this has been successfully achieved, copies of the gene are inserted into **vectors**, usually a virus or a bacterial plasmid (Section 5.12). The vector is also cloned so that many new vectors

containing the required gene are produced. Lastly, the vector inserts the gene into the recipient organism.

5.11 Identifying and isolating the gene

Task: identify and remove the gene coding for protein X from a human cell. *Problem*: the gene for protein X is a piece of DNA about 10 000 base pairs long. The total DNA in the cell is about 10 000 000 000 base pairs long. How do you track down and extract the particular 0.001% of all this DNA that you want?

There are two basic approaches which can be taken.

● Making a genomic library of DNA

This is done by extracting all the DNA from a cell and chopping it up into many small fragments. Enzymes called **restriction endonucleases** are used to do this. (Restriction endonucleases are enzymes found in bacteria, which the bacteria produce to defend themselves against invasion by foreign DNA from viruses.) These fragments are then inserted into a vector (Section 5.12), which produces many copies of each fragment. Such sets of DNA fragments, or **genomic libraries**, have been produced for many different species.

To identify the fragment of DNA containing the gene which is wanted, a **probe** is used. One way of doing this is described in Box 5.4.

● Making cDNA from mRNA

Alternatively, it may be possible to *make* the DNA which is wanted. One way of doing this is to work backwards from mRNA.

Within a plant or animal, each type of cell only makes some of the proteins coded for by the DNA it contains. For example, certain cells in the pancreas specialise in making insulin. These cells therefore contain large amounts of mRNA transcribed from the insulin gene.

The mRNA in a pancreas cell can be extracted and purified. This mRNA can then be used to make DNA (Fig. 5.16). This is not a process which usually happens in eukaryotic cells, but there is a group of viruses, called retroviruses ('retro' means 'backwards', and these viruses perform transcription backwards; HIV is a retrovirus) which do this, using enzymes called **reverse transcriptases**. The mRNA from the pancreas cell is incubated with reverse transcriptase and all the necessary DNA nucleotides, and a complementary DNA molecule is built up using the mRNA as a template. This DNA is called **cDNA**. If the mRNA used as a template was originally

---

Stage 1

Isolate – Purify the DNA from the donor organism and isolate fragments, one of which will contain the required gene.
Alternatively, make a gene from isolated mRNA.

Clone – Make multiple copies of the gene.

Identify gene –
Identify the gene of interest using a gene probe.

Stage 2

Insert gene into vector –
Isolated gene is introduced into a vector, usually either a bacterial plasmid or a virus.

Clone – Multiple copies of the gene in its vector are produced.

Stage 3

Vector inserts gene into organism –
The vector inserts the gene into a recipient organism where the gene is expressed.

Fig. 5.13 Genetic engineering.

Box 5.4 Identifying a required gene

Even the simplest cell contains many genes. There are many instances when it is necessary to pick out a particular gene from amongst all the rest of the cell's DNA. For example, a genetic engineer may want to extract a gene for making a particular protein from a human cell so that it can be transferred into a bacterium. Or a sample of cells may have been taken from a fetus to check whether or not it contains a particular gene which would cause an inherited disease.

To be able to pick out a particular gene, you first need to know its base sequence. Then a **gene probe** can be made which will seek out this particular gene. A gene probe is a length of single-stranded DNA containing the complementary base sequence to the gene you are interested in. The DNA of the probe is 'labelled' in some way, often by using a radioactive isotope of phosphorus, ^{32}P, as a component of its phosphate groups.

If the DNA in the cell is cut into pieces, using restriction endonucleases, the pieces can be separated using gel electrophoresis (Box 1.4). The gel, containing the DNA fragments, is then soaked in sodium hydroxide solution, which breaks the double-stranded DNA apart so that it now consists of single strands. A nitrocellulose sheet is then placed on the gel, and the single-stranded DNA fragments stick to it, in the same pattern as on the gel (Fig. 5.14). This technique is called **Southern blotting** after E.M. Southern who invented it in 1975.

Now the nitrocellulose sheet, containing the single-stranded DNA molecules, is incubated with the probe. The single-stranded probe will base-pair with the gene you are looking for, because it has a complementary base sequence.

X-ray film is then laid over the nitrocellulose sheet. It will darken where the radioactivity from the probe affects it, so you can tell exactly where your required gene is.

Loading the gel with a solution containing DNA fragments.

Peeling off the nitrocellulose sheet from the gel.

Examining the X-ray film.

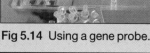

Fig 5.14 Using a gene probe.

Box 5.5 Switching on genes: promoters

In bacteria and other prokaryotes, genes coding for proteins are situated next to lengths of DNA which control the use of that gene for protein synthesis. A stretch of DNA called a **promoter** (Fig. 5.15), which is often about 40 bases long, identifies the point at which transcription should begin. There is also another, usually shorter, length of DNA which determines when the gene is transcribed. This is called an **operator**. The whole length of DNA, made up of the gene, its promoter and operator, is called an **operon**.

In eukaryotes, the situation is a little more complicated. This is necessary because a eukaryote cell contains many more genes than a prokaryote. Any one cell in a multicellular organism such as yourself contains all of these genes, but only a small proportion of them will be **expressed**, that is be used to make proteins. Sophisticated control mechanisms are needed to make sure that, for example, the gene for making the enzyme pepsin is expressed in a cell lining the stomach but not in a skin cell.

Eukaryote genes do, like prokaryotes, have promoters which indicate where transcription should begin. They also have other regulatory elements which determine when the gene should be transcribed. However, although the promoter is usually situated next to the protein-coding part of the gene, other lengths of DNA which control when the gene is expressed may be thousands of nucleotides away from it. There may be many such regulatory elements for any one gene.

The regulation of gene expression has to be considered carefully when genetic engineering is carried out. There is absolutely no point in inserting a human insulin gene into a bacterium if you do not also insert the gene's promoter, and possibly some of its regulatory sequences as well. If the promoter is not there, then the bacterium will not use the gene to make mRNA and hence insulin.

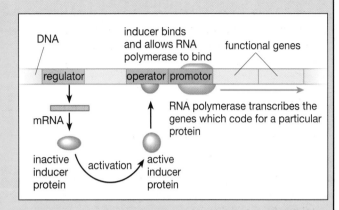

Fig. 5.15 How transcription of a gene can be controlled.

Knowledge of promoters and regulators can be used in another way. For example, Box 5.6 describes how a gene for the enzyme thioesterase has been transferred from the California bay tree into rapeseed plants. The enzyme catalyses the formation of a type of oil called lauric oil, which can be extracted from the rape seeds and used as an industrial surfactant. It is important that the oil is made *only* in the seeds, and not in other parts of the plant such as the leaves where it could kill the plant.

To achieve this, a gene in the California bay tree which is only expressed in the seeds is identified. The regulatory sequences for this gene, which are seed-specific promoters, are identified and extracted, and inserted into the rapeseed plants along with the gene for thioesterase. These regulatory sequences should ensure that the thioesterase gene is only switched on in the seeds.

This sounds easy in theory, but is very difficult in practice. One of the main problems is identifying the appropriate regulatory sequences, most of which are very poorly understood.

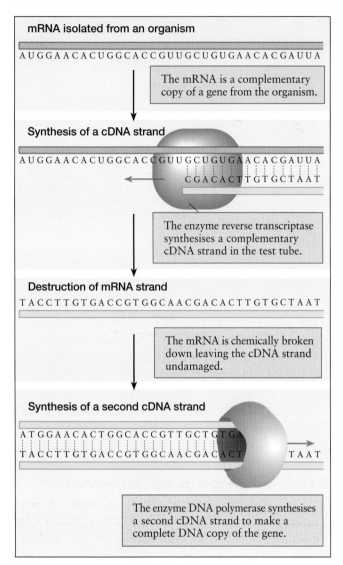

mRNA isolated from an organism

AUGGAACACUGGCACCGUUGCUGUGAACACGAUUA

The mRNA is a complementary copy of a gene from the organism.

Synthesis of a cDNA strand

AUGGAACACUGGCACCGUUGCUGUGAACACGAUUA
CGACACTTGTGCTAAT

The enzyme reverse transcriptase synthesises a complementary cDNA strand in the test tube.

Destruction of mRNA strand

TACCTTGTGACCGTGGCAACGACACTTGTGCTAAT

The mRNA is chemically broken down leaving the cDNA strand undamaged.

Synthesis of a second cDNA strand

ATGGAACACTGGCACCGTTGCTGTGA
TACCTTGTGACCGTGGCAACGACACT   TAAT

The enzyme DNA polymerase synthesises a second cDNA strand to make a complete DNA copy of the gene.

Fig. 5.16 Making cDNA from mRNA.

transcribed from the insulin gene, then this cDNA will also be an insulin gene.

There were probably many different mRNAs in the pancreas cell, so there will be many different cDNAs. They can be identified with a probe in the same way as DNA in genomic libraries. However, a much bigger proportion of the cDNA is likely to be the required gene than is the case in the genomic library, because the mRNA was taken from a cell making a lot of the required protein.

5.12 Inserting the gene into a vector

In biology, the term 'vector' is used for an agent which can carry something from one organism to another. In genetic engineering, a vector transfers DNA from one organism into another.

One type of vector which is often used to transfer genes is a **plasmid**. Plasmids are small circular DNA molecules which are found in bacteria, quite separate from the bacterium's main DNA. Most bacteria contain plasmids. Plasmids often contain lengths of DNA which are useful to the bacterium in particular circumstances. Many plasmids, for example, contain genes which make the bacterium resistant to a particular antibiotic.

To insert a piece of DNA – for example the human insulin gene – into a plasmid, the plasmid is cut open, using a restriction endonuclease. Restriction endonucleases make staggered cuts in the DNA, leaving a short length of unpaired bases at each end (Fig. 5.17). These are called **sticky ends**. If the length of DNA to be inserted was produced using the same restriction endonuclease, then it too will have sticky ends, and they will have the same base sequences as those on the plasmid. If the broken plasmid and the required DNA are mixed, the sticky ends will stick together, as complementary bases pair. Another enzyme, called **DNA ligase**, is used to join the sugar–phosphate backbones of the plasmid and the inserted DNA together. This new DNA molecule – part plasmid DNA and part human DNA – is called **recombinant DNA**.

5.13 Inserting the vector into the required organism

The plasmids can now be inserted into bacteria. This can be done by mixing them together, often after treating the bacteria with a solution which makes their cells more likely to take up the plasmids. To sort out the bacteria which have taken up a plasmid from those which have not, the bacteria can be grown with an antibiotic whose resistance gene is known to be carried on the plasmid (Fig. 5.19). The bacteria which survive are the ones which have taken up the plasmid. These bacteria, containing genes from another organism (in this case human DNA), are said to be **transformed**.

The transformed bacteria are now grown on a large scale. Each time a bacterial cell divides, the plasmid inside it also divides and replicates the human gene. A large population of bacteria, all containing the human gene, is produced. If the engineering has been a success, the bacteria will use the code on the gene to make the human protein. They can be grown on a large scale and the protein extracted and purified. For example, the bacterium *Escherichia coli* is being used in this way to produce human insulin.

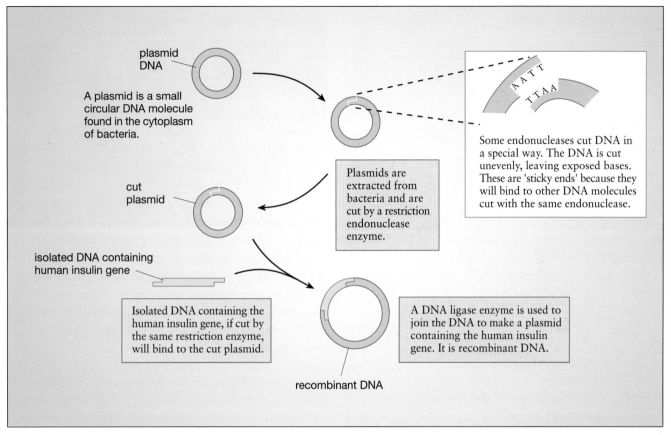

plasmid DNA

A plasmid is a small circular DNA molecule found in the cytoplasm of bacteria.

cut plasmid

isolated DNA containing human insulin gene

Plasmids are extracted from bacteria and are cut by a restriction endonuclease enzyme.

Some endonucleases cut DNA in a special way. The DNA is cut unevenly, leaving exposed bases. These are 'sticky ends' because they will bind to other DNA molecules cut with the same endonuclease.

Isolated DNA containing the human insulin gene, if cut by the same restriction enzyme, will bind to the cut plasmid.

A DNA ligase enzyme is used to join the DNA to make a plasmid containing the human insulin gene. It is recombinant DNA.

recombinant DNA

Fig. 5.17 Inserting a gene into a plasmid.

Genes can, of course, be inserted into organisms other than bacteria. To insert genes into plants, for example, the required gene may first be inserted into a plasmid which is then inserted into a bacterium called *Agrobacterium tumefaciens*. This bacterium naturally infects many plants where it transfers the plasmids into their cells. An example of the production of a genetically engineered plant is described in Box 5.6.

Fig. 5.18 Galls on a garden shrub, caused by infection with *Agrobacterium tumefaciens*.

5.14 Applications of genetic engineering

The first artificial recombinant DNA molecules were produced in the early 1970s. As the techniques for identifying, extracting and copying DNA, and for inserting it into particular cells, have become faster and more sophisticated, tremendous possibilities have emerged for altering living organisms so that they perform in a desired way.

One of the first applications of genetic engineering was the production of transformed bacteria containing genes for human proteins which are needed to treat disease. These bacteria could be cultured on a large scale in fermenters to synthesise the protein. This has been done for several proteins such as human insulin, growth hormone and the blood clotting factor that is missing in haemophiliacs, Factor VIII.

Transformed bacteria are also used to manufacture other proteins which are useful in industry. The enzymes in biological washing powders are produced in this way, as are many of those used in the food industry.

Genetic engineering is also used to produce pest-resistant varieties of crops. Genes producing chemicals which confer resistance to attack by fungi or insects can

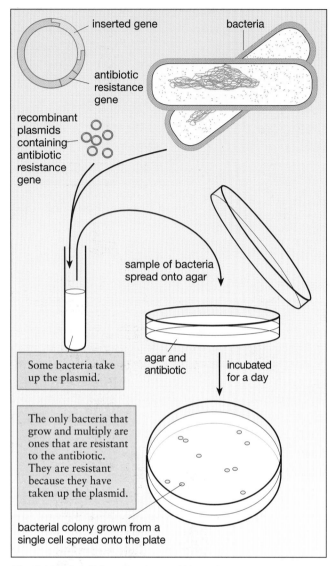

Fig. 5.19 Identifying transformed bacteria.

inserted gene

bacteria

antibiotic resistance gene

recombinant plasmids containing antibiotic resistance gene

sample of bacteria spread onto agar

Some bacteria take up the plasmid.

agar and antibiotic

incubated for a day

The only bacteria that grow and multiply are ones that are resistant to the antibiotic. They are resistant because they have taken up the plasmid.

bacterial colony grown from a single cell spread onto the plate

Fig. 5.20 The cells of these sheep contain a human gene which codes for the production of a protein called α-1-antitrypsin. Some people do not have a working copy of this gene, and they suffer from lung problems. The sheep make the protein, and secrete it in their milk. It is hoped that it may be used to treat people who do not make the protein themselves.

be extracted from a wild, naturally resistant plant or other organism, and inserted into the crop plant. This can greatly increase yields and reduce the amount of pesticide which needs to be used, resulting in less environmental pollution.

Tomatoes have been produced containing genes which result in them remaining fresh for much longer than usual after picking. This makes it much easier, and therefore cheaper, to transport them from grower to sale point, and they have a much longer shelf life.

Domestic animals have also had foreign genes inserted into them. For example, a transgenic cow has been produced by inserting the gene for human interferon (a protein which helps to destroy viruses) into an egg. The cow has the gene in all of her cells, and produces human interferon which is secreted in her milk.

Q7 Restriction endonucleases occur naturally in bacteria and cut DNA between specific base sequences.

(a) Suggest how the presence of restriction endonucleases may help to protect bacteria from viruses. (2)

(b) Many different restriction endonucleases have been purified and are widely used in genetic engineering.

Suggest why:

(i) incubating DNA with a particular restriction endonuclease cuts the DNA into fragments of different lengths; (1)

(ii) restriction endonucleases that produce staggered cuts are more useful in genetic engineering than those that do not. (2)

AEB 1995 (modified) *(Total 5 marks)*

For humans, considerable advances in genetic engineering are making **gene therapy** possible. Gene therapy is intended to correct inherited disorders, such as cystic fibrosis (Box 5.7), which are caused by a defective gene. If the 'correct' gene could be inserted into the affected person's cells, then they should be free of the disease. In practice, it is proving very difficult to deliver enough genes into enough cells, although some success has been achieved with clinical trials.

5.15 DNA fingerprinting

Because humans reproduce sexually, there is considerable variation in their genetic make-up. Unless they are identical twins, no two people have identical sequences of bases in their DNA. This fact can be used to identify a person from a sample of their DNA. It is especially useful in helping to settle cases of disputed paternity, or to identify a person who has left body fluids such as semen or blood, or tissues such as skin cells, at the scene of a crime.

There is a huge amount of DNA in a human cell, and it would be quite impossible to analyse it all. So particular areas of DNA are chosen which are known to vary a lot between different people. Sometimes, four or five different areas of DNA are tested. In other instances, just one area may be analysed.

In a rape case, for example, DNA can be extracted from a semen stain on clothing. Only a small amount is needed, because many copies of the chosen areas of the DNA can be made using a technique called the **polymerase chain reaction**, or PCR.

DNA probes and the Southern blotting technique (Box 5.4) are then used to produce a DNA profile from the semen sample. At the same time, on the same gel, DNA profiles are produced from DNA samples taken from suspects, and also from a person who is known *not* to have any involvement in the crime. This person's DNA acts as a control. The banding patterns produced on the gel (Fig. 5.21) are then compared. An identical match between the DNA from the semen sample and the DNA of a suspect is very strong (but not incontrovertible) evidence that the suspect was responsible for the rape. Just as importantly, any differences between the DNA profiles can eliminate individuals as suspects.

5.16 Ethical, moral and legal issues raised by gene technology

Advances in genetic engineering have opened up all sorts of possibilities which have not previously had to be

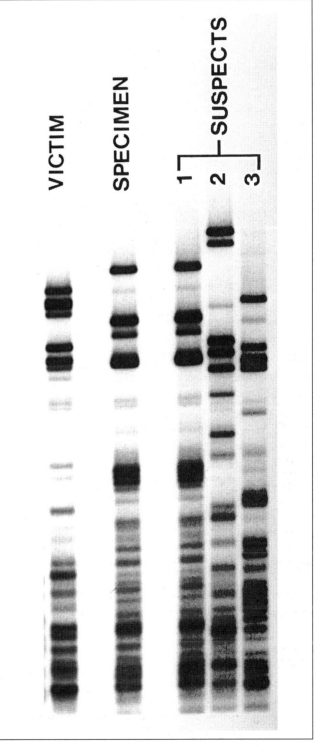

Fig. 5.21 These DNA profiles were made to help to provide evidence in a rape case. The banding pattern from the victim's DNA is shown on the far left, with the DNA from a specimen of semen taken from her clothing to the right of it. The other three DNA samples are from possible suspects. The first one is a very close match for the specimen, and this could be used as evidence against him.

considered by society. The ethics of which of these possibilities should be pursued and which should not are having to be sorted out very rapidly. This is proving quite difficult, partly because it is having to be done so quickly, and partly because most people do not have any real scientific understanding of the issues involved. Even scientists working in the field may not be able to predict just what possibilities their research may open up.

Only some of the most important issues are discussed here.

● Legal implications of DNA fingerprinting

The use of DNA fingerprinting to convict a suspect of a crime has proved not to be quite as straightforward as was originally expected. It depends on an assumption that there is virtually no possibility of two people producing identical DNA profiles. In general, this is true. However, in small communities where there is a lot of intermarrying, so that genetic variability between individuals is much less than in the general population, the possibility becomes much greater. This must be taken into account when deciding how much weight to give to evidence from DNA profiling.

Another problem with DNA fingerprinting is that the tiny amounts of DNA taken from body fluid samples may possibly become contaminated with tiny amounts of DNA taken from somewhere else – perhaps from the forensic scientists performing the investigation, for example. The polymerase chain reaction could then produce multiple copies of this contaminating DNA, and this – rather than the DNA from the sample – could be analysed by mistake. Laboratories must take great care to reduce this possibility to a minimum.

For example, in the O. J. Simpson trial, a blood sample taken from the scene of the crime was found to have the same DNA profile as the defendant's blood. But the defence argued that the sample of O. J. Simpson's blood had been carelessly handled, and droplets of it could easily have gone into the air of the laboratory. It was perfectly possible that a few DNA molecules from this blood could have got into the samples taken from the scene of the crime. The DNA evidence was discredited.

● Concerns about release of genetically engineered organisms into the environment

Genetic engineering has often involved the alteration of DNA in microorganisms. One microorganism in particular, *Escherichia coli*, has been used over and over again. This microorganism normally lives in the human gut, where it is usually harmless. However, some strains of *E. coli* can cause illness. There has been some concern that genetically altered strains of *E. coli* might 'escape' from laboratories, especially where they are cultured on a large scale, and infect people. Although this remains a theoretical possibility, it so far appears not to be a problem. The recombinant *E. coli* strains which are being used for such processes as manufacturing human insulin (Section 5.14) do not appear to colonise the human gut. Moreover, it is relatively straightforward to use precautions to ensure that these organisms do not escape from the industrial plant in which they are being cultured.

However, some applications of genetic engineering involve the *deliberate* release of recombinant organisms. For example, genetically altered bacteria might be released onto an oil spill, to digest the oil and reduce the effects of pollution. Genetically modified viruses have been released into a small area near Oxford, in an experiment to determine if they can successfully control infestation by caterpillars. Great care must be taken over such programmes, because, once released, it would be impossible to 'recall' these organisms. No-one can be sure just what effect they might have on other organisms in the environment. In the UK, strict legislation exists to control these kinds of experiments and applications, and anyone who wants to release genetically modified organisms into the environment cannot do so until rigorous checks have been made.

Genetically modified crop plants have also caused concern. For example, potatoes have been produced containing a gene which makes them resistant to a herbicide. This herbicide can then be sprayed onto the crop and will kill the weeds but not the potatoes. Might this gene somehow spread into wild plants, and affect the balance of the ecosystem in some way? So far, there is no indication that this does happen. A different concern is that the production of herbicide-resistant crop plants will increase the use of herbicides, which themselves are 'environmentally unfriendly'. Whether this is so has yet to be seen.

● Potential for biological warfare

The techniques of genetic engineering could be used deliberately to create new organisms which could infect and kill humans. There are, of course, already many organisms which can do this (which have not been created by genetic engineering), but little use has been made of biological warfare. Many countries currently do research at least on defence against such biological weapons, if not openly on the production of them. About half of the nations of the world signed a treaty in 1972 pledging not to produce biological weapons of any kind. However, the concern remains, and it is certainly possible that new, highly dangerous forms of infectious organisms could be produced deliberately.

● **Gene therapy**

Few people would argue against the use of gene therapy (Box 5.7) to relieve the symptoms of someone suffering from a genetic disease. But the possibility of inserting 'correct' genes into a person's cells opens all sorts of possibilities.

For example, in theory any desired genes could be inserted into a human egg, either before or after fertilisation. The child resulting from that egg would have those genes in all of its cells. Should this be allowed at all? And, if so, what kind of genes should be allowed to be inserted? Where should any line be drawn? For example, it might be thought allowable to insert a 'correct' copy of the cystic fibrosis gene into an egg which would otherwise grow into a person with cystic fibrosis. But what about inserting genes to produce extra height or blonde hair? At the moment, there is a complete ban on performing any genetic engineering on eggs and sperm, and this is likely to continue for the foreseeable future. ■

Q8 The diagram below shows a bacterial plasmid before and after a required DNA sequence has been spliced into it.

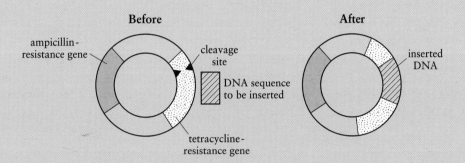

(a) Briefly describe the part played by enzymes in this process. (2)

Only a small percentage of plasmids accept the foreign DNA. Additionally, only a small percentage of bacteria take up a plasmid of any kind. A genetic engineer needs to know which bacterial cells contain plasmids with the required DNA sequence before cloning them. This is done by growing colonies on suitable media.

First, all the bacteria are spread onto a medium containing ampicillin, an antibiotic that only allows the growth of resistant bacteria.
Second, samples of these resistant bacteria are transferred to a medium containing the antibiotic tetracycline, which allows only bacteria with an intact resistance gene to grow.

(b) Explain why bacteria are unsuitable for cloning if:

    (i) they fail to grow on a medium containing ampicillin; (1)

    (ii) they can grow on a medium containing both ampicillin and tetracycline. (1)

(c) Explain why bacteria which grow on a medium containing ampicillin but do not grow on tetracycline are kept for cloning. (1)

AEB 1995   (*Total 5 marks*)

Box 5.6 Designer oilseed rape

Oils have many uses. We use oils in food, as fuels and as lubricants. Oils are important components or raw materials in the manufacture of cosmetics, detergents, leather goods, paper, paints, textiles and many other materials.

Petroleum has been the major source of oils for industrial uses for many years. However, there are growing concerns about the non-renewability of this resource and the need to look for renewable sources of oils. The extraction and refining of petrochemicals also produces environmental problems. Moreover, most petroleum products are not biodegradable (able to be broken down by microorganisms), so they can cause long-lasting and damaging effects if they are accidentally released into the environment as spillages.

There has therefore been an increasing interest in using plants to produce oils. Many plants naturally produce oils, usually as a food source for the embryo in the seed. Oils from plants are renewable resources and biodegradable. Some of these oils, such as olive, palm and sunflower oils have been used for centuries. While their major use has been as food, many are used in industrial processes to produce surfactants (detergents) and cosmetics.

Rape, with its bright yellow flowers, is a familiar crop in much of Europe. Most of it is currently grown as a source of rapeseed oil, which is used to make animal feed, and also as an ingredient in some foods for people, but some is used to produce oil for industrial applications. Worldwide, rape is the third most important oil crop. 90% of the natural oil produced by rape contains very long fatty acid chains (Section 1.18), with 22 or more carbon atoms. This produces quite heavy oils which are useful for making lubricants or cosmetics. Genetic engineering is now making it possible to produce rape varieties which synthesise other oils suitable for other purposes.

For example, oils containing fatty acids with short hydrocarbon chains, with 10 to 14 carbon atoms, can be used to make detergents. A plant called California bay naturally makes such an oil, which is called lauric oil. The enzyme responsible for the production of this oil, thioesterase, has been identified, and the gene coding for it identified and cloned. In 1993, a new variety of genetically engineered rapeseed that contained this gene was produced.

The thioesterase gene from California bay was inserted into a plasmid vector which inserted it into *Agrobacterium tumefaciens* (Fig. 5.23). This bacterium was allowed to infect cells of rapeseed, so inserting the thioesterase gene. These transformed rapeseed cells were then grown using tissue culture into whole rapeseed plants. Every cell in the plant contained the thioesterase gene. Large numbers of these plants were grown, and field trials carried out to check the oil content and composition of their seeds. Risk assessments were also carried out, to ensure that the transferred genes would not 'escape' and become incorporated into other plants growing nearby. When it has passed all of these tests, the new rapeseed variety can be made available to farmers.

The entire process of developing a new genetically engineered variety of a crop in this way takes between 5 and 10 years.

Fig. 5.22 Oilseed rape in flower.

Box 5.6 Designer oilseed rape (cont.)

Stage 1

Isolate – Purify the DNA from the organism.

Identify – Identify the gene of interest.

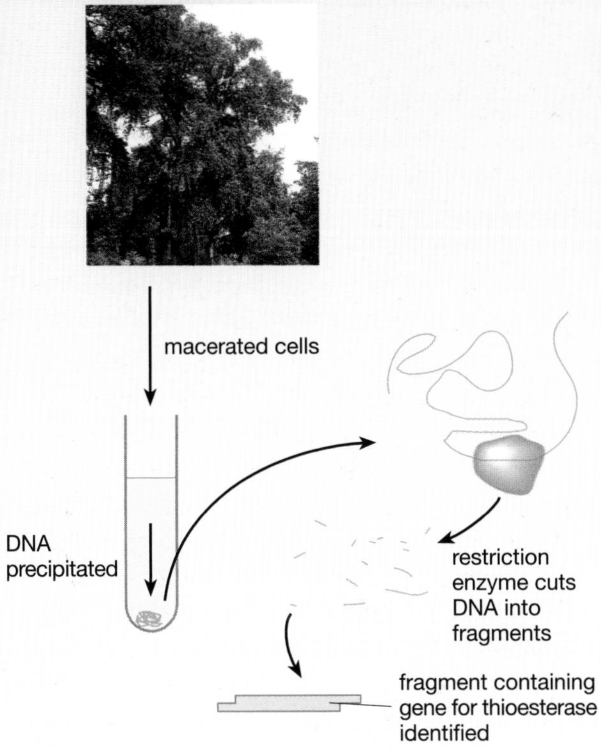

macerated cells

DNA
precipitated

restriction
enzyme cuts
DNA into
fragments

fragment containing
gene for thioesterase
identified

Stage 2

Insert gene into vector –
Isolated gene is introduced into a bacterial plasmid.

Clone – Transformed plasmid is introduced into *Agrobacterium tumefaciens* bacterium and is multiplied.

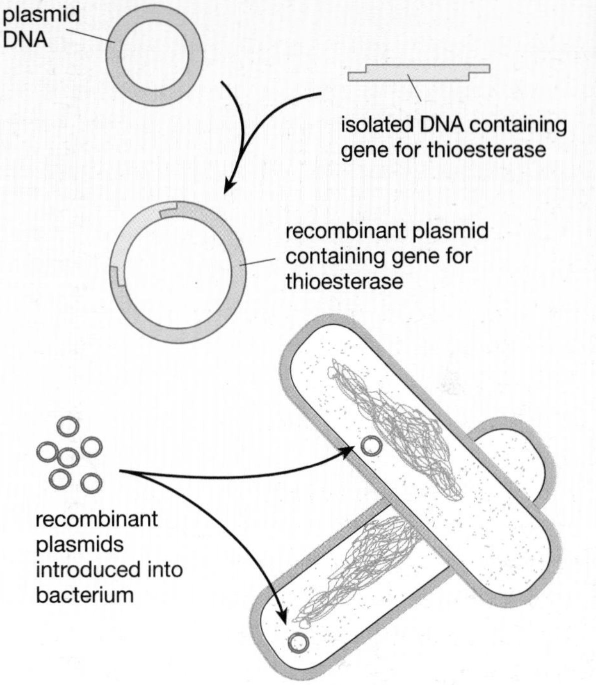

plasmid
DNA

isolated DNA containing
gene for thioesterase

recombinant plasmid
containing gene for
thioesterase

recombinant
plasmids
introduced into
bacterium

Stage 3

Vector inserts gene into organism –
The bacterium and plasmid act as a vector
and they insert the gene into rapeseed cells
grown in tissue culture.

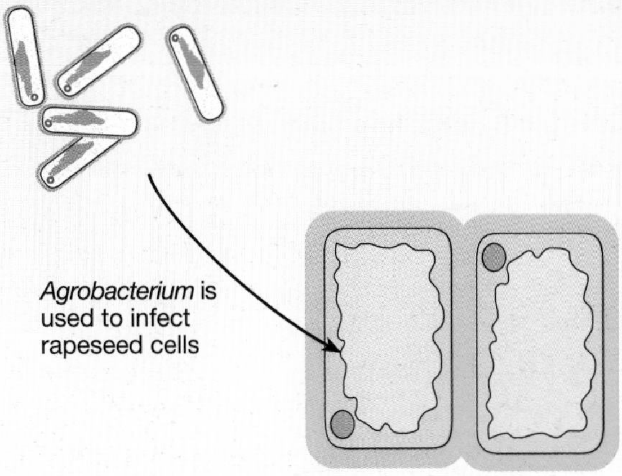

Agrobacterium is
used to infect
rapeseed cells

Stage 4

Risk assessment and production –
Transgenic rapeseed tissue is grown and many
new plants are produced by micropropagation.

Field trials of plants.

Seed tested for oil content.

Perform risk assessment according to government
regulations.

Release new rapeseed variety to farmers.

Fig. 5.23 Production of a new rapeseed plant by genetic engineering.

Box 5.7 Gene therapy for cystic fibrosis

Cystic fibrosis is an inherited disease caused by a recessive allele (Section 6.2) of a gene which codes for the production of a membrane protein called CFTR. This protein, which is present in the cell surface membrane, acts as a chloride ion transporter and allows chloride ions to move out of cells (Fig. 5.24). In the cells lining the lungs, this movement of chloride ions causes water also to move out of the cell. The water keeps the linings of the airways wet and smooth.

In cystic fibrosis, the gene coding for this protein has an incorrect base sequence. There are several faulty alleles; some code for no protein at all, some code for the protein but it is not delivered to the cell surface membrane; and some code for a protein which *is* delivered correctly to the cell surface membrane but does not produce an open channel. In each case, the result is the same – chloride ions cannot pass out of the cells and this greatly reduces the amount of water which passes out. The linings of the airways remain dry. Excessively sticky mucus builds up. The lungs are very likely to become infected.

People with cystic fibrosis have to undergo daily therapy to move the mucus from their lungs, to try to reduce the severity of infections. Despite this, repeated infections will eventually damage the lungs, and many people with cystic fibrosis die before they are 30.

The gene for the CFTR protein was tracked down to a particular position on a chromosome in 1985, and isolated and cloned in 1989. If copies of the 'correct' gene could somehow be introduced into the cells in the lungs of people with cystic fibrosis, they should be able to make the correct CFTR protein and become well. Introducing correct copies of a gene in this way is called **gene therapy**.

Several methods have been tried. In the USA, viruses have been used to deliver the gene. The chosen virus was an adenovirus which naturally infects the target cells. The viruses were first treated to damage them and so stop them causing disease. The CFTR gene was then inserted into them and the viruses introduced into the nostrils of volunteers. The virus delivered the gene into significant numbers of the cells lining the lungs and airways and did indeed reduce their symptoms. However, one volunteer was made ill by the viruses, and it seems that this may be a real problem with this method.

UK teams are testing a different method of delivering the genes into cells. They are using tiny spheres made of lipid molecules, called **liposomes**. Liposomes can easily pass through cell surface membranes. The gene is combined with liposomes, and the liposomes sprayed into the nostrils of volunteers. Other volunteers are given liposomes with no gene. To check whether the genes have been taken up, samples are taken from the cells in the nostrils. The trial is being done under 'double-blind' conditions, so that neither the volunteers nor the experimenters know whether the liposomes being sprayed contain the gene or not.

Even if the trial is successful, the volunteers will still not be cured. The method of delivery being tested only gets the genes into cells in the upper respiratory passages, not deep into the lungs. The researchers are doing it this way because it is relatively easy for them to test these cells for the presence of the gene, so they can find out whether the liposomes are delivering the gene or not. It would be much more difficult for them to find out if the gene has successfully entered cells deep in the lungs.

However, if the liposomes do turn out to be able to deliver the gene to enough cells, and if the gene is expressed and results in working chloride channels, then further developments may enable genes to be delivered to where they are really needed, inside the lungs. The genes would need to be reapplied regularly, because the cells lining the respiratory passages are regularly shed and replaced by new ones. Liposomes containing the gene could be manufactured on a large scale by a pharmaceutical company.

Box 5.7 Gene therapy for cystic fibrosis (cont.)

The problem

Cystic fibrosis is caused by defective Cl^- channels in the cell surface membrane. These channels should transport Cl^- ions out of the cell. Water follows by osmosis and this keeps the lungs well lubricated. In cystic fibrosis, the Cl^- ions are not transported, so water does not leave by osmosis. Therefore, the lung secretions are thick and block the airways.

outside cell

cell surface membrane

inside cell

Cl^-

CFTR protein forming a Cl^- channel.
This protein is defective or not in place in cystic fibrosis.

A genetic engineering solution

Stage 1

Identify – Identify the normal cystic fibrosis gene.
Isolate and clone –
    Isolate the gene and make copies of the gene.

healthy CF gene, which allows
normal CFTR functioning

Stage 2

Insert gene into vector –
    Normal cystic fibrosis gene (CF gene) inserted into
    a bacterial plasmid.
Clone – Insert recombinant plasmid into bacteria and grow
    the bacteria to make multiple copies of the plasmid.

cloned copies of the
recombinant plasmid
produced by bacteria

bacterial

Stage 3

Vector inserts gene into humans –
    The plasmid vector is inserted into
    human cells using liposomes.

recombinant plasmid
containing a healthy CF gene

liposome - made of lipids so that
it can penetrate the cell surface
membrane

liposomes absorbed
by cells lining
respiratory passages

liposomes taken as

liposomes combined
with plasmids

healthy CF gene expressed

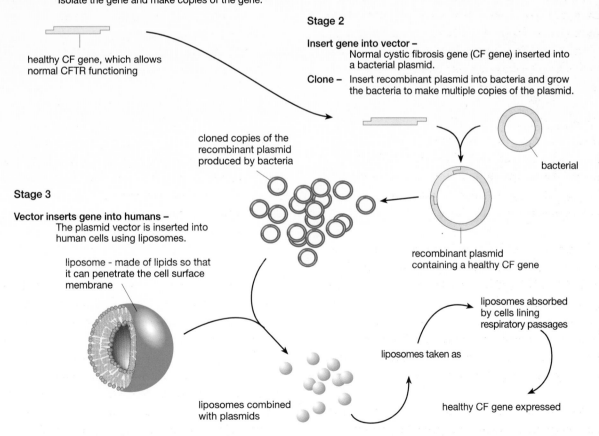

Fig. 5.24 Treating cystic fibrosis using genetic engineering.

Q8 The diagram below shows the sequence of bases along part of the coding strand of a DNA molecule and three possible mutants of this.

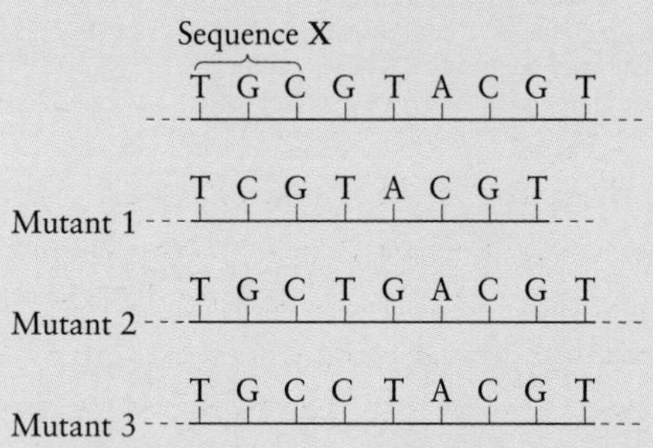

Sequence **X**

T G C G T A C G T

Mutant 1 —— T C G T A C G T

Mutant 2 —— T G C T G A C G T

Mutant 3 —— T G C C T A C G T

(a) Give the anticodon corresponding to sequence **X**.   (1)

(b) Name the type of mutation in:
    (i) mutant 1;   (1)
    (ii) mutant 2.   (1)

(c) Which of the three mutants shown would you expect to have the greatest effect on the phenotype of the organism? Explain your answer.   (2)

AEB 1994   (*Total 5 marks*)

Q9 Australian scientists have recently produced genetically engineered clover containing a protein high in sulphur-containing amino acids. As proteins in wool are also rich in these amino acids, it is thought that feeding sheep on this new strain of clover will produce an increase in the yield of wool. A length of DNA was prepared from the sequences shown in the diagram for insertion into the clover.

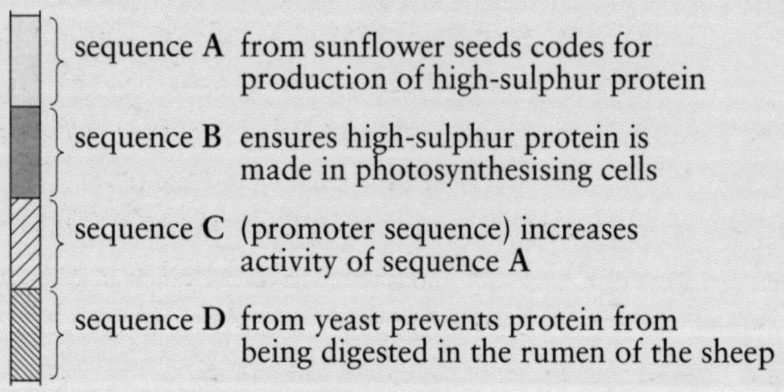

sequence **A** from sunflower seeds codes for production of high-sulphur protein

sequence **B** ensures high-sulphur protein is made in photosynthesising cells

sequence **C** (promoter sequence) increases activity of sequence **A**

sequence **D** from yeast prevents protein from being digested in the rumen of the sheep

(a) Describe how each of the following enzymes might be used in preparing this sequence of DNA:

    (i) ligase;   (1)

    (ii) restriction enzyme.   (1)

(b) Briefly explain why it is necessary to:

    (i) ensure that the protein is made in photosynthesising cells;   (1)

    (ii) prevent the protein from being digested in the rumen of the sheep.   (2)

AEB 1994   (*Total 5 marks*)

6 Genetics

Genetics is the study of inheritance. Many characteristics of an organism are controlled by its genes. Most genes have more than one form, and these different forms are called alleles. Some characteristics are controlled by a single gene, but many are influenced by two or more genes which interact with each other.

6.1 Genes and alleles

The instructions for the synthesis of proteins in a cell are carried in the cell's DNA. The sequence of bases in the DNA determines the sequence of amino acids in the protein (Section 5.2). A length of DNA which codes for one polypeptide, or for one protein, is called a **gene**.

A gene coding for a specific protein may have several forms, or **alleles**. Each allele has a different base sequence, and so produces a different sequence of amino acids and therefore a different form of the protein.

By coding for the kinds of proteins made in a cell, genes influence virtually everything which takes place in the cell, and in the organism as a whole. Some of the proteins made are structural proteins, such as keratin or collagen. Differences in alleles of genes coding for these proteins may produce differences in the structures, such as skin and hair, which contain them. Other proteins may have roles in transporting substances within the body, such as haemoglobin; Section 5.7 describes how a tiny difference in the base sequence of the gene for one of the polypeptides in haemoglobin can have a very great effect on the physiology of a person.

But most of the proteins which a cell makes are enzymes. These control nearly all of the metabolic reactions which take place in an organism. A slight difference in the base sequence of a gene coding for an enzyme can totally disrupt a metabolic pathway, and so have large effects on more than one feature of an organism (Box 5.3).

In some cases, we know quite a bit about how different alleles of a gene produce different characteristics, and you have probably read about some of these in Chapter 5. However, we still do not know very much about how most genes affect particular characteristics. For example, although we know that genes determine the shape of a person's ears, or the length of a dog's legs, very little is known about how they do this. In this chapter, we will not worry about how a particular allele has its effect, but will just look at how different combinations of alleles may influence an organism's characteristics, and how these characteristics can be inherited.

6.2 Genotype and phenotype

The **genotype** of an organism is its genetic makeup. Usually, we are interested in just one or two genes and use the term 'genotype' to describe which alleles of these genes the organism possesses.

In diploid organisms, such as almost all animals and many plants, there are **two** of each kind of chromosome in each cell. Two similar chromosomes are called **homologous chromosomes**, and they each carry the same genes in the same position or **locus** on the chromosome. Each cell of an organism therefore contains **two** copies of each gene. If that gene has two alleles, then there are three possible genotypes that the organism may have.

For example, the fruit fly *Drosophila melanogaster* has four pairs of homologous chromosomes. The gene for wing size is found on one of these pairs. This gene has an allele which produces normal-sized wings, and another allele which produces very tiny wings, called vestigial wings (Fig. 6.1). We can use the symbol **A** to represent the allele for normal wings and **a** to represent the allele for vestigial wings. (V and v, or W and w are not a good choice, because they are difficult to tell apart if you are writing quickly.) Any one fruit fly will have two copies of the gene for wing size. It might have two **A** alleles, two **a** alleles, or one of each (Fig. 6.1). The three possible genotypes are therefore **AA, Aa** or **aa**.

Organisms in which the two alleles of a gene are the same are said to be **homozygous**. If the two alleles are different, then the organism is **heterozygous.** Thus a fruit fly with the genotype **AA** or **aa** is homozygous, while one with the genotype **Aa** is heterozygous.

The observable characteristics of an organism are its **phenotype**; in this case, the phenotype we are interested in

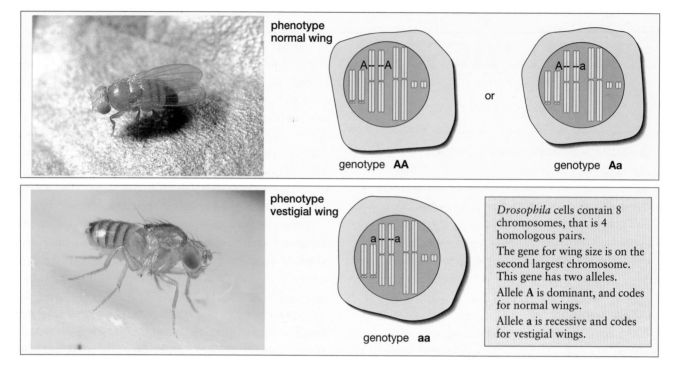

phenotype
normal wing

or

genotype **AA**

genotype **Aa**

phenotype
vestigial wing

genotype **aa**

Drosophila cells contain 8 chromosomes, that is 4 homologous pairs.

The gene for wing size is on the second largest chromosome. This gene has two alleles.

Allele **A** is dominant, and codes for normal wings.

Allele **a** is recessive and codes for vestigial wings.

Fig. 6.1 Genotype and phenotype.

is 'wing size'. The genotype of the fruit fly controls its wing size. Fruit flies with the genotype **AA** have normal wings, while flies with the genotype **aa** have vestigial wings and cannot fly. Flies with the genotype **Aa** also have normal wings, exactly the same as flies with the genotype **AA**.

genotype	phenotype
AA	normal wings
Aa	normal wings
aa	vestigial wings

The allele **A** is therefore said to be **dominant**, while allele **a** is **recessive**. A dominant allele is one which has its full effect in a heterozygous organism. A recessive allele only has an effect when there is no dominant allele present.

MONOHYBRID CROSSES
6.3 A simple monohybrid cross

A monohybrid cross is one in which you look at the way in which the alleles of just one gene are passed on from parents to offspring. We will look at the way in which the wing-size gene can be inherited in fruit flies. What offspring would you expect to get from a cross between a homozygous normal-winged, female fruit fly, and a vestigial-winged, male fruit fly?

Within the fruit flies' ovaries and testes, cells will divide by meiosis to produce gametes (eggs and sperms). Gametes are haploid cells (Section 4.3), containing only *one* copy of each gene. The normal-winged fly will have the genotype **AA** and so it will produce eggs containing one **A** allele each. The vestigial-winged fly will have the genotype **aa**, and its sperm will each contain one **a** allele. This can be written like this:

parents' phenotypes	normal	vestigial
parents' genotypes	AA	aa
gametes' genotypes	Ⓐ	ⓐ

Notice that a circle has been drawn around the genotype of the gametes. This is a standard convention and helps other people to understand what you are writing when you summarise a cross such as this one. (You will find that it will also help *you* to sort out the cross when you are working with much more complicated ones later on.)

When the two flies mate, the gametes of the male will fuse with gametes of the female. New cells, called **zygotes**, will be formed. Each zygote will have two copies of each gene, just like its parents. Every zygote which is produced will have an **A** allele from its mother, and an **a** allele from its father, so all the zygotes will have the genotype **Aa**. They will all develop into flies with normal wings. We can show this by continuing the cross like this:

offspring genotypes and phenotypes

female gametes

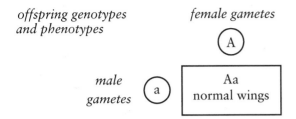

This method of writing out a genetic cross is called a **genetic diagram**.

6.4 A more complex monohybrid cross

Things become slightly more complicated if the two parents are heterozygous, with the genotype **Aa**.

When their cells divide by meiosis to form gametes, half of the gametes will receive an **A** allele and half will receive an **a** allele. When the flies mate, there may be 10 000 **A** sperm and 10 000 **a** sperm swimming towards 25 **A** eggs and 25 **a** eggs. There is an equal chance that either an **A** sperm or an **a** sperm will fertilise either an **A** egg or an **a** egg.

parents' phenotypes   normal   normal

parents' genotypes   Aa   Aa

gametes' genotypes   (A) and (a)   (A) and (a)

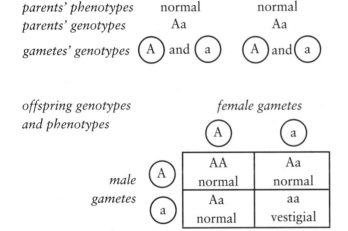

You can see that this cross produces three different possible genotypes in the offspring; any one offspring could have the genotype **AA**, **Aa** or **aa**. But the genetic diagram tells us more than this. It tells us the probabilities of each of these genotypes occurring in the offspring.

The diagram shows that there are four different possibilities that can happen at fertilisation. An **A** sperm might join with an **A** egg, giving the genotype **AA**. It is just as likely that an **A** sperm will join with an **a** egg, giving the genotype **Aa**. Equally likely is that an **a** sperm will join with an **A** egg (genotype **Aa**) or with an **a** egg (**aa**). There are therefore four different combinations which can occur, each of them equally likely.

Each time, therefore, that a zygote is formed, there is a 1 in 4 chance that it will have the genotype **AA**, a 2 in 4 chance that it will be **Aa**, and a 1 in 4 chance that it will be **aa**. Another way of stating this is to say that the probability of **AA** occurring is 0.25, for **Aa** it is 0.5, and for **aa** it is 0.25. If the flies produce 40 offspring, we would expect about 10 of them to be **AA**, 20 to be **Aa** and 10 **aa**. However, because this is all to do with chance and probabilities, it is unlikely that it will turn out exactly as we predict. It is quite possible that, of the 40 offspring, 12 could be **AA**, 19 **Aa** and 9 **aa** for instance.

Although there are three different *genotypes* in the offspring, there are, of course, only two different *phenotypes*. Each fly will either have normal wings or vestigial wings. Looking at the genetic diagram again, you can see that there is a 3 in 4 chance that any particular offspring will have normal wings, and a 1 in 4 chance that it will have vestigial wings. We would therefore expect a ratio of 3 normal-winged offspring to 1 vestigial-winged offspring.

This 3:1 ratio is typical of the results of a monohybrid cross between two heterozygous organisms, where one of the alleles of the gene concerned is dominant and the other recessive.

6.5 Test crosses

You will have realised by now that, if an organism shows a recessive characteristic in its phenotype, then you know its genotype – it must be homozygous for the recessive allele. But if the organism shows the dominant characteristic, you do not know if it is homozygous for the dominant allele or heterozygous.

Animal and plant breeders often need to know the genotypes of the animals and plants with which they are working. In a few cases it is now possible to use DNA probes to detect the presence or absence of a particular allele (Box 5.4), but the techniques involved are expensive and 'hi-tec', and so are not suitable for many breeders to use.

Take, for example, a cat breeder who has a short-haired cat. The breeder knows that the allele for short hair, **H**, is dominant to the allele for long hair, **h**. The cat could therefore be homozygous for the allele for short hair, or it could be heterozygous. The breeder can find out which of these is the case by breeding her cat with a long-haired cat, who she knows must have the genotype **hh**. This is called a **test cross**.

If the female cat is homozygous, then all of her eggs will have the genotype **H**, and so all the kittens from the test cross will have the genotype **Hh**. They will all have short hair. If, on the other hand, the cat is heterozygous, then the kittens would be expected to be in a 1:1 ratio of short:long hair, as explained in the following genetic diagram.

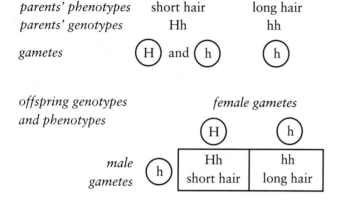

However, the breeder must take care not to jump to early conclusions if the first litter of kittens all have short hair. If there is only a small number of kittens – say four or five – then it is perfectly possible that the female cat is heterozygous, but that, just by chance, only her eggs with the genotype **H** were fertilised by the long-haired male's sperm. The breeder will need to repeat the test cross several times to make absolutely sure. Of course, if even only one long-haired kitten appears, then there is no doubt – the female cat is heterozygous.

6.6 Codominance

In many instances, two alleles of a gene may both have an effect when they are present together. In this case, a heterozygous organism has characteristics which are part-way between the characteristics of the homozygous ones. Alleles which behave like this are said to be **codominant**.

When choosing symbols to represent codominant alleles, it would be misleading to use a capital and small letter, because this would suggest that the one with the capital letter was dominant. Instead, a capital letter is chosen to represent the *gene*, and then two different superscripts to represent the two codominant alleles of the gene. (This is quite a nuisance when you are drawing genetic diagrams because it means extra writing, but it is extremely important that you do take the trouble to do it!)

For example, in some breeds of cattle two of the alleles for coat colour are codominant. We could use the symbol **C** to represent the gene for coat colour, and the symbols C^R

and C^W for the alleles for red and white coat respectively. The possible genotypes and phenotypes are:

genotype	phenotype
C^RC^R	red coat
C^RC^W	roan coat
C^WC^W	white coat

Roan is a pinkish colour, produced by a mixture of red and white hairs.

If sperm from a roan bull were used to fertilise a roan cow, what are the possible colours of the calf which she has? We can show the cross in a genetic diagram:

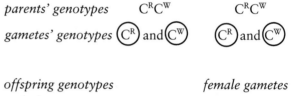

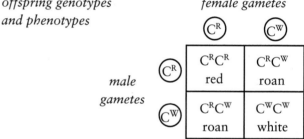

There is therefore a 1 in 4 chance that the calf will be red, a 2 in 4 chance that it will be roan and a 1 in 4 chance that it will be white.

6.7 Multiple alleles

So far, we have assumed that each gene has just two alleles. However, there are very many cases where there are three or more alleles of a gene. These are known as **multiple alleles**. A classic example is the gene which determines a person's ABO blood group.

The gene for blood group has the symbol **I**. Two of the alleles – those which give the blood groups A and B – are codominant, while the third, which gives the blood group O, is recessive to the other two. The alleles for groups A and B are therefore given capital letter superscripts, and the allele for blood group O is given a small letter superscript:

I^A	allele for blood group A
I^B	allele for blood group B
I^o	allele for blood group O

Locus	The position of a gene on a chromosome. Different genes have different loci.
Allele	A variety of a gene. Many genes have multiple alleles, that is they have more than two varieties.
Genotype	The alleles contained in an organism's cells.
Phenotype	The characteristics of an organism, determined by its genotype and also by its environment.
Homozygous	Possessing two identical alleles of the same gene.
Heterozygous	Possessing two different alleles of the same gene.
Dominant allele	An allele which affects the phenotype of a heterozygous organism just as much as when the organism is homozygous for this allele.
Recessive allele	An allele which only affects the phenotype of an organism when the dominant allele is not present.
Codominance	Both alleles affect the phenotype of a heterozygous organism.
Pure breeding or true breeding	An organism which, when crossed with itself or others like itself, always produces offspring like itself. In other words, it is homozygous.
Selfing	Crossing an organism with itself, or with others like itself.
F_1	The first filial generation; the offspring of two pure breeding parents.
F_2	The second filial generation – the offspring resulting from selfing the F_1.

Table 6.1 Terms used in genetics.

Box 6.1 Population genetics – the Hardy–Weinberg equations

Cystic fibrosis is a disease caused by a recessive allele, f, of a gene which codes for a transporter protein in the cell surface membrane. The effects of this allele are described in Box 5.7 on page 124.

We know that about 1 in every 2000 babies born in England has cystic fibrosis, and so is homozygous for the recessive allele f. From this figure, we can work out the chance that any one person is heterozygous, with the genotype Ff, and so is a carrier for the cystic fibrosis allele. The equations which we can use were worked out by two people called Hardy and Weinberg, so they are now known as the Hardy–Weinberg equations.

Let us say that the **frequency** of the recessive allele f in the population of England is represented by the letter q. This could be any number between 0 and 1. If q is 0, then it means there are no f alleles in the population. If q is 1, then it means that all the alleles in the population are f and none of them is F. If q is 0.5, then half of the alleles for the membrane protein are f and half are F.

We can use the letter p to represent the frequency of the dominant allele F. Because every allele for the membrane protein must be either F or f, the total frequency for the two alleles is 1. So we can write the first equation:

Equation 1 $p + q = 1$

Now let us consider what are the chances of any one person having a particular combination of the F and f alleles. A person may have the genotype FF, or Ff, or ff. Assuming we have no idea of the genotypes of a baby's parents, we can consider that the chances of two particular alleles coming together at fertilisation are influenced by the relative frequency of those alleles in the population. If the frequency of allele F is very high, for example, and the frequency of allele f is very low, then there is a very high chance of a baby receiving two F alleles, a lower chance that it will receive one F allele and one f allele, and a very low chance that it will receive two f alleles.

If we know the values of p and q (the frequencies of alleles f and F in the population), then we can work out the chances of each of the three possible combinations occurring. (If you have done much maths, you will understand how to do this already.) The chances are as follows:

chance of F from father and F from mother coming together $= p \times p = p^2$

chance of f from father and f from mother coming together $= q \times q = q^2$

chance of F from father and f from mother coming together $= p \times q = pq$

chance of F from mother and f from father coming together $= p \times q = pq$

Thus, in the population as a whole, we would expect the frequency of the genotype FF to be p^2, the frequency of the genotype ff to be q^2, and the frequency of the genotype Ff to be $pq + pq$, which is $2pq$. Because everyone must have one of these three genotypes, the total frequencies add up to 1. So we can now write a second equation:

Equation 2 $p^2 + q^2 + 2pq = 1$

Now to get back to our original question. If 1 in 2000 births in England are of babies with cystic fibrosis, what is the chance that any one person is heterozygous for this disease?

A baby with cystic fibrosis has the genotype ff. We know that the frequency of this genotype is 1 in 2000. 1/2000 represents a frequency of 0.0005. (Use your calculator to check this.) We are using the symbol q to represent the frequency of the f allele, so we know that the frequency of genotype ff is q^2. We therefore know that:

$q^2 = 0.0005$

From this, we can work out q.

$q = \sqrt{0.0005} = 0.0224$

Box 6.1 Population genetics – the Hardy–Weinberg equations (cont.)

Using the first equation above, we can then work out the frequency of the **F** allele, which is represented by the letter p.

$p + q = 1$

so $p = 1 - 0.0224 = 0.9776$

Now that we know p and q, we can work out the frequency of the genotype Ff in the population. This frequency is represented by the value $2pq$, so it is:

$2 \times 0.9776 \times 0.0224 = 0.0438$

So, according to the Hardy–Weinberg equations, the chance of anyone being a carrier for cystic fibrosis is 0.0438, or 4.38%. About 4 people in every 100 in England would be expected to be carriers for cystic fibrosis.

Do the Hardy–Weinberg equations always work? The answer is yes – provided certain conditions apply to the population we are working with. The population must be **large**, because otherwise probabilities tend not to work out very well. There must be **random mating**, with individuals of any genotype being equally likely to mate with individuals of any other genotype. There must be no significant **selection pressures** on any particular genotype, as this would change the allele frequencies from one generation to another. And there must be no significant introduction of new alleles into the population, either by **mutation**, or by **immigration** of individuals from a different population.

In practice, all of these conditions are extremely unlikely to be true for any alleles at all, in any population. They are certainly not true for the cystic fibrosis allele, where there is selection against the **f** allele, as people with cystic fibrosis only rarely have children. However, the equations are useful in providing an approximate idea of allele frequencies, as long as the conditions listed above come reasonably close to being met.

With three alleles, there are six possible genotypes:

genotype	phenotype
$I^A I^A$	group A
$I^A I^B$	group AB
$I^A I^o$	group A
$I^B I^B$	group B
$I^B I^o$	group B
$I^o I^o$	group O

Once you have sorted out the possible genotypes and phenotypes in this way, you can draw genetic diagrams to explain crosses in exactly the same way as before.

For example, a mother may be puzzled that her baby has the blood group O, although the mother's blood group is A and the father's is B. If you look at the list of genotypes and phenotypes, you can see that the only possible genotype for the baby is $I^o I^o$. So it must have received an I^o allele from each parent. And you can also see that that is possible, because you can have blood group A or B and carry an I^o allele.

parents' phenotypes	group A	group B
parents' genotypes	$I^A I^o$	$I^B I^o$

gametes: I^A and I^o I^B and I^o

offspring genotypes and phenotypes

		female gametes	
		I^A	I^o
male gametes	I^B	$I^A I^B$ group AB	$I^B I^o$ group B
	I^o	$I^A I^o$ group A	$I^o I^o$ group O

So these parents should not be at all surprised, whatever the blood group of their baby. Anything is possible, and there are equal chances of any of the four blood groups turning up.

When dealing with anything the least bit complicated in genetics, it is always really useful to begin by drawing up a list of all the possible genotypes and phenotypes as we did here, even if you cannot complete it to begin with. It can

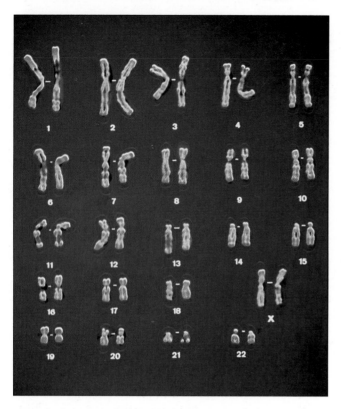

Fig. 6.2 Karyotypes for human female and male.

help you to sort out the various possibilities, and is very useful to refer back to if you are working through a long problem.

6.8 Sex inheritance

In many animals, sex is determined by a pair of **sex chromosomes**. All the rest of the chromosomes are called **autosomes** (Fig. 6.2).

In humans, there are two types of sex chromosome, called **X** and **Y** chromosomes (Fig. 6.3). A person with two X chromosomes is female, and a person with one X and one Y is male. During meiosis, the sex chromosomes pair up and segregate into the daughter cells. All of a woman's eggs therefore contain one X chromosome. A man's sperm, however, may contain either an X or a Y chromosome. If a baby inherits a Y chromosome from its father, it is a boy; if it inherits an X chromosome from its father, it is a girl. It is therefore the father's sperm which determines a child's sex.

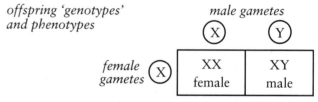

It is really the Y chromosome which determines sex. A gene on the Y chromosome codes for the production of a substance called sex determining factor (Fig. 6.3). This causes testes to develop, and to secrete hormones called androgens which stimulate the development of male genital organs. Without this gene, ovaries and female genital organs develop. Apart from this gene, however, the Y chromosome appears to carry very few active genes.

6.9 Sex linkage

The X chromosome is much larger than the Y, and carries many genes which are not present on the Y chromosome (Fig. 6.3). A gene which is found on one of the sex chromosomes and not on the other is called a **sex-linked gene**.

One such gene, present on the X chromosome but not the Y, determines the ability to see red and green as separate colours. The normal dominant allele allows full

parents' phenotypes	male	female
parents' 'genotypes'	XY	XX
gametes	Ⓧ and Ⓨ	Ⓧ

Box 6.2 Sex determination in other organisms

The XX = female, XY = male system of sex determination is found not only in humans but also in many other animals. For example the fruit fly, *Drosophila*, has this system, as do many other insects and most vertebrates.

In birds, however, it is the *female* which is XY and the male XX. Some fish also have this arrangement, and so do moths and butterflies. In these animals, it is the female gamete which determines the sex of the offspring.

Some insects have yet another system. Here, the female has two X chromosomes and the male just one X and no other sex chromosome. This occurs in grasshoppers. The female is XX and the male XO.

Some insects can reproduce parthenogenetically, that is eggs can develop into embryos without being fertilised. Honey bees and aphids can do this. In honey bees, either queens or workers (which are all female) develop from fertilised eggs which receive an X chromosome from both their parents. Drones (which are male) develop from unfertilised eggs and receive only one set of chromosomes, including a single X chromosome from their mother.

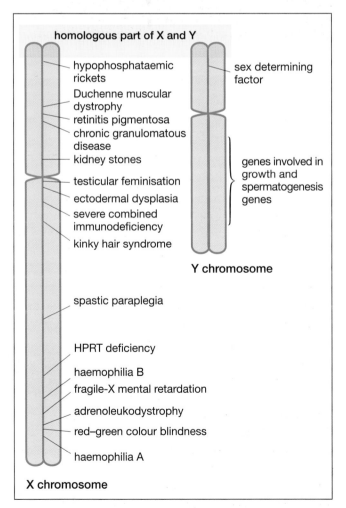

Fig. 6.3 Human X and Y chromosomes.

colour vision, but the less common recessive allele produces red–green colour blindness.

When choosing symbols for sex-linked genes, it is essential always to include the letter of the chromosome on which the gene is found. The symbol for the allele of the gene is then written as a superscript. In this case, we will use the symbol X^N for the allele which gives normal vision, and X^n for the recessive allele which gives red–green colour blindness. The possible genotypes and phenotypes are:

genotype	phenotype
$X^N X^N$	female with normal vision
$X^N X^n$	female with normal vision
$X^n X^n$	female with red–green colour blindness
$X^N Y$	male with normal vision
$X^n Y$	male with red–green colour blindness

You will see that, while there are three possible genotypes for a woman, there are only two for man. If a man has a recessive, **n**, allele, then he is red–green colour blind. However if a woman has this allele on one of her X chromosomes, there is a strong chance that she will have a normal, **N**, allele on her other X chromosome. If this is the case, she has normal vision but is a **carrier** of the recessive allele. Sex-linked conditions such as red–green colour blindness are therefore much commoner in men than in women. In Britain, about 8% of men are red–green colour blind, while only 0.7% of women have this condition.

The following genetic diagram shows how a red–green colour blind son may be born to two parents with normal vision where the woman is a carrier of the recessive allele.

parents' phenotypes	woman with normal vision	man with normal vision
parents' genotypes	$X^N X^n$	$X^N Y$
gametes	X^N and X^n	X^N and Y

offspring genotypes and phenotypes

	female gametes	
	X^N	X^n
X^N (male gametes)	$X^N X^N$ normal female	$X^N X^n$ normal female
Y	$X^N Y$ normal male	$X^n Y$ colour blind male

Each time this couple have a child, there is a 1 in 4 chance that it will be a boy with red–green colour blindness.

Although red–green colour blindness can be a nuisance (sufferers report problems not only with traffic lights, but also with picking raspberries and strawberries), it is of no significance at all compared with some other sex-linked inherited characteristics. **Haemophilia** is probably the most well-known sex-linked disease, occurring in about 0.1% of males in Britain. It is caused by a recessive allele of the gene which codes for the production of one of the proteins involved in blood clotting, Factor VIII. Females

with haemophilia are almost unknown. Less well known but even more common is the disease **Duchenne muscular dystrophy**, which occurs in about 0.25% of boys. Here the problem is with a recessive allele of a gene which produces a protein called dystrophin that affects muscle development. Once again, it is virtually unknown in females.

Even though a boy needs only one recessive allele from one parent to inherit a sex-linked condition, a man who suffers from such a condition cannot pass it on to *any* of his children unless his partner is a carrier. This is because the allele concerned is on his X chromosome, and his sons of course, each inherit a Y chromosome from him. He will, however, pass on the allele to his daughters, but none of them will show the condition unless they also inherit this allele from their mother. His daughters will be carriers – that is they will be heterozygous. It is then quite possible that a daughter will pass on the affected X chromosome to her son who will suffer from the condition (as shown in the genetic diagram above). It is as though a generation has been 'jumped'; the condition cannot be passed from a father to his son, but it can be passed on to his grandson, via his daughter.

6.10 Pedigrees

Fig. 6.4 is a pedigree showing the occurrence of haemophilia in a family. In a pedigree such as this, circles are used to represent females and squares to represent males. A shaded circle or square represents a person with the condition you are interested in – in this case haemophilia. Horizontal lines running directly between a circle and a square link two parents, and vertical lines run down from them to their children. The children of one family are linked by a horizontal line which runs above them.

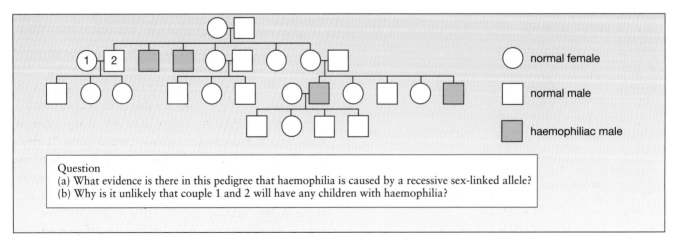

Question
(a) What evidence is there in this pedigree that haemophilia is caused by a recessive sex-linked allele?
(b) Why is it unlikely that couple 1 and 2 will have any children with haemophilia?

Fig. 6.4 A pedigree of a family in which haemophilia has occurred.

DIHYBRID CROSSES

6.11 A simple dihybrid cross

So far, all the crosses we have looked at involve just a single gene. These are monohybrid crosses. We are now going to consider the inheritance of *two* genes. Such crosses are called dihybrid crosses.

In peas, the seeds may be either wrinkled or smooth, and either yellow or green. Two genes are involved, one for the shape of the seed, and one for the colour. These two genes are found on different chromosomes.

The two alleles for seed shape can be given the symbols **B** for the allele for smooth seeds, and **b** for the allele for wrinkled seeds. (Neither S/s or W/w are good choices, because the capital and small letters are so similar.) The allele **B** is dominant, while **b** is recessive. The possible genotypes and phenotypes for seed shape are therefore:

genotype	phenotype
BB	smooth
Bb	smooth
bb	wrinkled

The two alleles for seed colour can be given the symbols **Y** for the allele for yellow seeds, and **y** for the allele for green seeds, where the allele **Y** is dominant and allele **y** recessive. The possible genotypes and phenotypes for seed colour are:

genotype	phenotype
YY	yellow
Yy	yellow
yy	green

If we consider both of these characteristics together, we can see that there are nine possible genotypes and four possible phenotypes:

genotype	phenotype
BBYY	smooth yellow
BBYy	smooth yellow
BByy	smooth green
BbYY	smooth yellow
BbYy	smooth yellow
Bbyy	smooth green
bbYY	wrinkled yellow
bbYy	wrinkled yellow
bbyy	wrinkled green

Notice that the two alleles for one gene are always written together. You must always write **BBYY**, not **BYBY**. This makes it much easier when you are working out crosses, both for yourself and for anyone reading what you have written.

What offspring would you expect from a cross between a plant with the genotype **BBYY** and one with the genotype **bbyy**?

First, think about the gametes which these plants can produce. You should remember that a gamete receives *one* copy of each gene (Section 6.3). A plant with the genotype **BB** for the seed shape gene will produce gametes with one **B** allele. A plant with the genotype **YY** for the seed colour gene will produce gametes with one **Y** allele. So a plant with genotype **BBYY** will produce gametes with one **B** allele and one **Y** allele. The gametes will all have the genotype **BY**. Similarly, the plant with the genotype **bbyy** will produce gametes with the genotype **by**.

parents' phenotypes	smooth yellow	wrinkled green
parents' genotypes	BBYY	bbyy
gametes	(BY)	(by)

offspring genotypes and phenotypes

gametes from one parent
(BY)

gametes from the other parent (by)	BbYy smooth yellow

All of the offspring will have the genotype **BbYy**. They will have smooth yellow seeds.

6.12 A more complex dihybrid cross

What offspring would you expect if two of the plants produced from the cross above were crossed together?

Fig. 6.5 shows what happens during meiosis in a pea plant which is heterozygous for both of these genes. In the first division of meiosis, the chromosomes line up, in their homologous pairs, on the equator, before separating to opposite poles. Each pair of chromosomes may lie either way round. So the gametes which are formed may have any of four combinations of alleles. Either allele of the seed shape gene may find itself in a gamete with either allele of the seed colour gene.

Because each parent can produce four different kinds of gametes, the chart looks much more complicated than

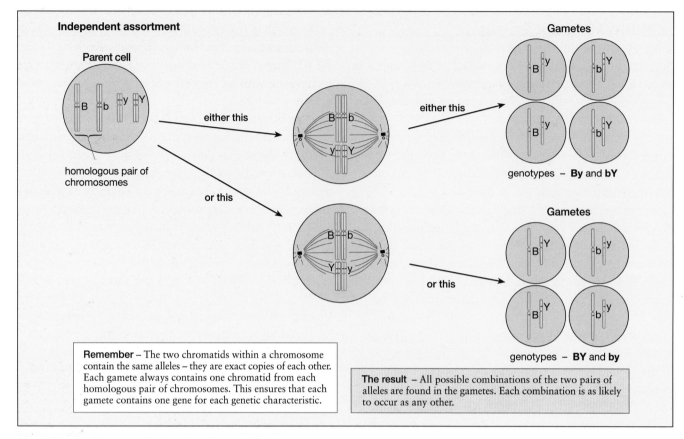

Fig. 6.5 Independent assortment in dihybrid inheritance.

anything you have met so far. But you deal with it in exactly the same way as you have done before. Do remember to keep the alleles of one gene together when you write the genotypes of the offspring – don't mix **B**s and **Y**s.

parents' phenotypes	smooth yellow	smooth yellow
parents' genotypes	BbYy	BbYy
gametes	BY and By and bY and by	BY and By and bY and by

Count up the numbers of times that each of the four possible phenotypes turns up. The commonest is smooth yellow, which arises 9 out of 16 times. Smooth green and wrinkled yellow each occur 3 out of 16 times, while the wrinkled green arises just one out of 16 times. We would therefore expect the following ratio of phenotypes in the offspring:

9 smooth yellow : 3 smooth green :
3 wrinkled yellow : 1 wrinkled green

offspring genotypes and phenotypes	gametes from one parent			
	BY	By	bY	by
BY	BBYY smooth yellow	BBYy smooth yellow	BbYY smooth yellow	BbYy smooth yellow
By	BBYy smooth yellow	BByy smooth green	BbYy smooth yellow	Bbyy smooth green
bY	BbYY smooth yellow	BbYy smooth yellow	bbYY wrinkled yellow	bbYy wrinkled yellow
by	BbYy smooth yellow	Bbyy smooth green	bbYy wrinkled yellow	bbyy wrinkled green

gametes from the other parent

This 9:3:3:1 ratio of phenotypes is typical of a dihybrid cross between two organisms who are both heterozygous for both the genes involved.

Box 6.3 Epistasis

Quite frequently two different genes both affect the same characteristic. This is often because the two genes code for two enzymes in the same metabolic pathway.

For example, a particular plant might produce the pigments which colour its petals in a two-step pathway:

colourless   enzyme 1   yellow   enzyme 2   orange
substance $\longrightarrow$ pigment $\longrightarrow$ pigment

The gene which codes for enzyme 1 may have two alleles. **A** is the normal, dominant allele, while **a** does not produce a functioning enzyme. Similarly, **B** is the normal dominant allele for enzyme 2, while **b** does not produce any enzyme 2.

So, before the plant can produce any colour at all, it must have at least one **A** allele. If not, then its flowers will have no pigment and will remain white. It does not matter what alleles it has for the **B/b** gene; if it has no enzyme 1, there is no yellow pigment being made, and so nothing for enzyme 2 to work on. The possible genotypes and phenotypes are therefore:

genotype	phenotype
AABB	orange
AABb	orange
AAbb	yellow
AaBB	orange
AaBb	orange
Aabb	yellow
aaBB	white
aaBb	white
aabb	white

Thus, the genotype for one gene (the **A/a** one) affects the expression of another quite separate gene (the **B/b** one). This situation is called **epistasis**.

Coat colour in many animals is determined by epistatic genes (Fig. 6.6). Quite frequently, one gene determines whether there is any pigment produced at all, while another determines its pattern. Obviously, the 'pattern' gene cannot have any effect unless there is some pigment there. In fact, the situation is usually even more complicated than this, with many different genes all interacting to determine coat colour. You only have to look at all the possible coat colours in cats and dogs to appreciate this!

For example, the colours of 'wild' and black mice are determined by a gene **A/a**, which codes for the distribution of the pigment melanin in the hairs. The coat of a 'wild' mouse is made up of banded hairs, which produce a grey-brown colour called agouti. Allele **A** determines the presence of this banding. Allele **a** determines the uniform black colour of the hair of a black mouse.

A second gene, **C/c**, determines the production of melanin. The dominant allele **C** allows colour to develop, while a mouse with the genotype **cc** does not make melanin and so is albino.

Fig. 6.6 Coat colour in mice as an example of epistasis.

Q1
(a) List the possible genotypes of each of the three mice in Fig. 6.6.

(b) What would be the expected result of a cross between two agouti mice with genotypes **AaCc**?

(c) How would you determine if an agouti mouse was heterozygous **Cc**?

6.13 Dihybrid test crosses

Try for yourself a cross between parents with the genotypes **BbYy** and **bbyy**. You should find that you get a 1:1:1:1 ratio of smooth yellow : smooth green : wrinkled yellow : wrinkled green in the offspring. It is worth remembering these ratios, as they can often help you quickly to see the solution to a genetics problem.

An organism which is homozygous recessive for the two genes, for example a plant with the genotype **bbyy**, can be used to carry out test crosses in the same way as described in Section 6.5. Plants with the genotype **BBYY**, **BBYy**, **BbYY** and **BbYy** all have the same phenotype – they all grew from smooth yellow seeds. You could find out the genotype of a plant with this phenotype by breeding it with a plant which grew from a wrinkled green seed, which you know has the genotype **bbyy**. Try each of these crosses for yourself (you have probably just done the one for **BbYy** crossed with **bbyy**). You will find that, if any wrinkled offspring turn up, then the unknown parent must be **Bb**. Similarly, if there are any green offspring, then the unknown parent has the genotype **Yy**. So, no green or wrinkled offspring probably means the parent is **BBYY**; some wrinkled but no green means that it is **BbYY**; some green but no wrinkled that it is **BBYy**; and some of everything that it is **BbYy**.

6.14 Polygenic inheritance

When a characteristic is influenced by the combined effect of many different genes, this is known as polygenic inheritance. Polygenic characteristics tend to show continuous variation and a normal distribution (Fig. 7.4).

To illustrate how polygenes can produce continuous variation, we will look at the variation which can be produced with just *two* genes, **A** and **B**, each with *two* codominant alleles. This, of course is not really polygenic inheritance, which requires at least three genes to be involved, but it will give you the idea without getting too complicated. Imagine that these genes are responsible for the systolic blood pressure (Box 10.2) of a person. (In practice, blood pressure is probably influenced by many more genes than this, and also by environment.) Let's say that allele A^M contributes 4 units to blood pressure, while allele A^N contributes 1. Allele B^R contributes 6 units, while allele B^S contributes 2. If the 'basic' blood pressure is 100 units, then the possible blood pressures are:

genotype	phenotype
$A^M A^M B^R B^R$	$100 + 4 + 4 + 6 + 6 = 120$ units
$A^M A^M B^R B^S$	$100 + 4 + 4 + 6 + 2 = 116$ units
$A^M A^M B^S B^S$	$100 + 4 + 4 + 2 + 2 = 112$ units
$A^M A^N B^R B^R$	$100 + 4 + 1 + 6 + 6 = 117$ units
$A^M A^N B^R B^S$	$100 + 4 + 1 + 6 + 2 = 113$ units
$A^M A^N B^S B^S$	$100 + 4 + 1 + 2 + 2 = 109$ units
$A^N A^N B^R B^R$	$100 + 1 + 1 + 6 + 6 = 114$ units
$A^N A^N B^R B^S$	$100 + 1 + 1 + 6 + 2 = 110$ units
$A^N A^N B^S B^S$	$100 + 1 + 1 + 2 + 2 = 106$ units

If this amount of variation can be produced with just two genes, each with just two alleles, it is not difficult to see that more genes with more alleles can produce an immense range. You might like to work out for yourself what variation you could obtain with a truly polygenic example, if you imagine there is a third gene, **C**, with alleles C^T and C^U contributing 3 and 0 units respectively. ■

Box 6.4 Linkage

In the examples of dihybrid crosses we have looked at so far the two genes have been on *different* chromosomes. Because these different chromosomes behave independently of each other during meiosis, the gametes can inherit any combination. The genes are said to assort independently.

This is not the case if two genes are on the *same* chromosome. Such genes are said to be **linked**. Linked genes, for obvious reasons, tend to be inherited together.

Fig. 6.7 shows the possible genotypes of gametes produced by a single cell from an organism which is heterozygous for both of two linked genes, **F/f** and **G/g**. In this organism, one chromosome carries the two dominant alleles, **F** and **G**, while the other carries the two recessive alleles, **f** and **g**. Its genotype is **FfGg**. However, rather than producing four different kinds of gametes, it produces only two, because the **F** allele is inherited with the **G** allele, and the **f** allele is inherited with the **g** allele.

This actually makes life much easier when dealing with crosses, because there are far fewer possibilities to consider. If **F** and **f** produce long fur and short fur, and **G** and **g** produce grey fur and white fur respectively, then the offspring from a cross between a heterozygous parent and one with short white fur would be as follows.

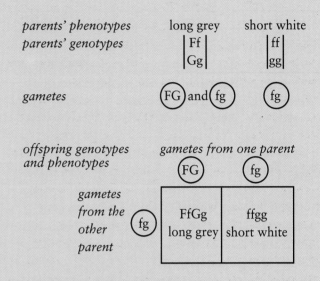

This cross would therefore give a 1:1 ratio of long grey : short white. The offspring would all have the same combinations of characteristics as their parents and no new combinations will occur.

Notice how the genotypes of the parents were written. You can, if you like, just write them in the normal way, for example **FfGg**. But by writing this as $\begin{vmatrix} Ff \\ Gg \end{vmatrix}$ you have a reminder of which alleles are on the same chromosome, and so will be inherited together. You can think of the vertical lines as representing the two chromosomes.

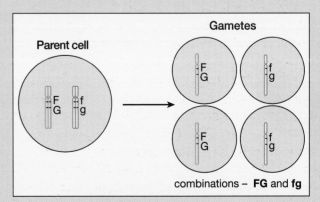

Fig. 6.7 Gametes produced by a cell with two linked genes.

Box 6.5 Crossing over

Quite frequently, in a cross involving linked genes, you do find that a few of the offspring have combinations of characteristics which are not found in either of their parents. These offspring are called **recombinants**, and they are caused by crossing over taking place during meiosis (Fig. 6.8).

In primulas, a gene for the length of the style is found on the same chromosome as a gene for the colour of the stigma. The style length gene has two alleles, **L** which is dominant and produces a long style, and **l** which is recessive and gives a short style. The stigma colour alleles are **G** and **g**, giving green and red stigmas respectively.

In a cross between a heterozygous primula and one homozygous for both recessive alleles, you would expect the following results assuming that the alleles are completely linked (that is, if no crossing over occurs):

parents' phenotypes	long style green stigma	short style red stigma
parents' genotypes	|Ll| |Gg|	|ll| |gg|
gametes	(LG) and (lg)	(lg)

offspring genotypes and phenotypes

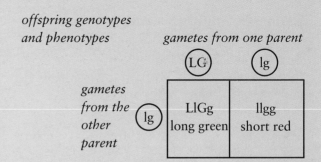

gametes from one parent

	(LG)	(lg)
gametes from the other parent (lg)	LlGg long green	llgg short red

However, when this cross was carried out, the results were as follows:

phenotype	*number of offspring*
long green	610
long red	341
short green	349
short red	607

This is a sort of 'half-way house' between what you would expect if there was linkage, and if there was no linkage. With linkage you would expect a result of 1:1 long green : short red. With no linkage, you would expect a result of 1:1:1:1 long green : long red : short green : short red.

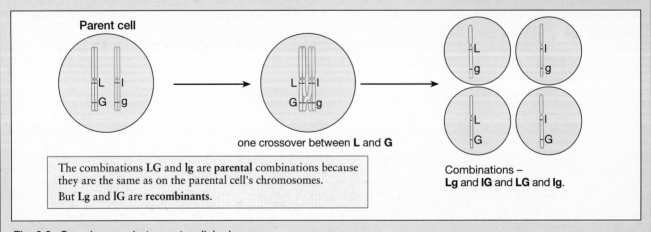

The combinations **LG** and **lg** are **parental** combinations because they are the same as on the parental cell's chromosomes.
But **Lg** and **lG** are **recombinants**.

Combinations –
Lg and **lG** and **LG** and **lg**.

Fig. 6.8 Crossing over between two linked genes.

Box 6.5 Crossing over (cont.)

If you look at Fig. 6.8, you should be able to see what has happened. In some of the cells of the **LlGg** parent which divided to produce the gametes, crossing over took place between two chromatids of the pair of homologous chromosomes on which these two genes are found. Pieces of chromatid containing the alleles swapped places, so that an **l** allele was now on the same chromatid as a **G** allele, and an **L** allele on the same chromatid as a **g** allele. The resulting gametes therefore contained new combinations of alleles – **lG** and **Lg**. When these fused with the **lg** gamete from the other parent, they produced offspring with the genotypes **llGg** and **Llgg**:

parents' phenotypes	long style, green stigma	short style red stigma
parents' genotypes	Ll Gg	ll gg
gametes	LG or lg	lg
	lG or Lg	

offspring genotypes and phenotypes

gametes from one parent

	LG	lg	lG	Lg
gametes from the other parent lg	LlGg long green	llgg short red	llGg short green	Llgg long red

The shaded gametes and offspring are the ones resulting from crossing over – the **recombinants**.

How many recombinants there are will depend on how often crossing over takes place between the two genes. This will partly depend on how far away they are from each other on the chromosome. If the style length and stigma colour genes were very close together, then there is less chance that crossing over would take place between them, and you would expect very few recombinant offspring. Because a lot of recombinants appeared in this cross, we can assume that the genes are quite a long way apart.

Q2 (a) Distinguish between the following terms:

    (i) *genotype* and *phenotype;*

    (ii) *gene* and *allele.* (4)

Two mice, a male with black eyes and a long tail and a female with black eyes and a short tail, were bred together several times producing the following offspring.

black eyes, long tail	9
black eyes, short tail	10
red eyes, long tail	4
red eyes, short tail	3

(b) Assuming that the allele for black eyes **B** is dominant to the allele for red eyes **b**, and that the allele for long tail **T** is dominant to the allele for short tail **t**, draw a genetic diagram to explain these results. (6)

(c) A breeding pair which always produced mice with black eyes and short tails was required. How might this be achieved using these offspring? (3)

UCLES 1992   *(Total 13 marks)*

Q3 Familial hypophosphataemia is a sex-linked condition caused by a dominant allele on the X chromosome. The pedigree of a family with this condition is shown in the diagram below.

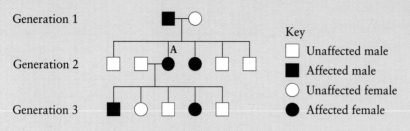

(a) What is meant by the term *sex linkage*? (2)

(b) Explain why none of the males in generation 2 suffers from hypophosphataemia. (2)

(c) If person A were to have another son, what is the probability that this son would suffer from hypophosphataemia? Give a reason for your answer. (2)

London 1994 *(Total 6 marks)*

Q4 In a species of bird, the allele for green feathers, **G**, is dominant to the allele for blue feathers, **g**. A second gene locus on another chromosome controls the intensity of the colouring with the heterozygote ($C^P C^P$) intermediate between the two homozygotes ($C^P C^P$ and $C^D C^D$). The complete range of colours is shown in the table.

Colour of feathers	Intensity of colouring		
	Pale	Intermediate	Dark
green blue	light green sky blue	dark green cobalt	olive mauve

(a) What name describes the condition in which the heterozygote is intermediate in appearance between the homozygotes? (1)

(b) Copy and complete the following scheme to show the expected results of a cross between cobalt and homozygous light green birds.

Parental phenotypes: Cobalt   ×   Homozygous light green

Parental genotypes:

Gamete genotypes:

Offspring genotypes:

Offspring phenotypes:

Expected ratio: (3)

(c) Explain why the ratio of the different offspring phenotypes obtained from this cross may not be exactly equal to the expected ratio. (1)

AEB 1993 *(Total 5 marks)*

Q5 In the fruit fly (*Drosophila*), males are the heterogametic sex (**XY**). Two different crosses using these flies gave the following results.

	CROSS A		CROSS B
Parents	normal × 'cut' wing ♀ wing ♂	*Parents*	'cut' × normal wing ♀ wing ♂
F_1	all normal wing	F_1	normal wing ♀ 'cut' wing ♂
F_2	789 normal wing ♀	F_2	356 normal wing ♀
	391 normal wing ♀		339 'cut' wing ♀
	376 'cut' wing ♂		342 normal wing ♂
			333 'cut' wing ♂

N.B. ♂ = male
   ♀ = female

(a) Given that the 'cut' wing characteristic is controlled by a single gene, explain how these results show that the 'cut' wing allele
   (i) is recessive;
   (ii) is carried on the X chromosome, rather than on an autosome.   (2)

(b) Using **N** as the normal wing allele, and **n** as the allele for 'cut' wing, give the genotypes for all the flies represented in cross B.   (2)

Another fruit fly mutant, caused by a change in a single gene, is known as bar-eye. Normal, round-eyed flies have nearly one thousand facets in their compound eyes. This number is greatly reduced in a bar-eyed individual, in which the eye appears as a narrow vertical strip.

In another investigation, a virgin female from a homozygous stock with normal, round eyes was crossed with a bar-eyed male. All the female offspring had bar-eyes, and all the males had round eyes.

(c) What may be concluded about the nature of the bar-eyed allele from this information?   (2)

An F_2 generation was obtained from the previous investigation, but the eggs were separated into two batches immediately after laying, with each batch being maintained at a different temperature. Once the F_2 adults had emerged, the mean number of facets per eye for each phenotypic class was recorded. The results are shown in the table.

Phenotypic class in F_2 offspring		Mean number of facets per eye at the development temperature	
		15 °C	30 °C
Males	round-eyed	996	997
	bar-eyed	270	74
Females	round-eyed	997	996
	bar-eyed	214	40

(d) (i) Using this information, give **two** conclusions about the expression of the bar-eye allele.
   (ii) Suggest a hypothesis which might reasonably account for one of the conclusions given in (d)(i).   (4)

NEAB 1994   (*Total 10 marks*)

Q6 A queen honey bee can lay both fertilised and unfertilised eggs. Fertilised eggs develop into diploid females and unfertilised eggs develop into haploid males. The diagram shows the formation of gametes in male and female bees.

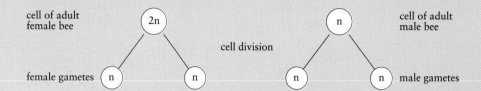

(a) Giving a reason for your choice in each case, give the type of cell division in the bee that produces:
   (i) female gametes;
   (ii) male gametes.   (1)

(b) The table shows some features which contribute to variation in the offspring of bees. Copy and complete the table with a tick if the feature may contribute or a cross if it does not.

	Female offspring	Male offspring
Crossing over		
Independent segregation		
Random fusion		

                                                                                           (2)

(c) Body colour is determined by a single gene with the allele **B** for yellow body dominant to **b** for black body.

Explain why, in the offspring of a mating between a pure-breeding black female and a yellow male:
   (i) all the females will be yellow;   (1)
   (ii) all the males will be black.   (2)

AEB 1993   (*Total 6 marks*)

Q7 (a) Assume that an organism is heterozygous for two different genes, **D** and **E**, and that these genes are present on the same chromosome. With the aid of diagrams, describe the movements of the genes and chromosomes during meiosis that would lead to the formation of four different gametes. (8)

(b) (i) What genotypes are possible if this organism is crossed with another of the same species which has a genotype of **ddee**?
     (ii) Would you expect the possible genotypes (A) to be phenotypically distinct from each other and (B) to occur in equal numbers? Explain your answers.   (6)

NEAB 1993   (*Total 14 marks*)

7 Evolution

Evolution is a change, over time, in the characteristics of a population or of a species. It is caused by changes in the gene pool of the population, usually as a result of natural selection. Sometimes, evolution results in the production of a new species. Humans can also change the characteristics of a species, using a process called artificial selection or selective breeding.

7.1 Charles Darwin's theory of natural selection

When, in 1859, Charles Darwin first published his ideas suggesting that the species of organisms on Earth might not always have been there but had evolved from different organisms which lived in the past, his book was met with horror by many people. The idea that species might *change* was not only against people's religious beliefs, but also against their instinctive beliefs. People knew that hedgehogs for example, generation after generation, continued to be hedgehogs; they did not turn into anything different. Worst of all was the suggestion that humans might not have been created as humans, but evolved from something similar to a monkey or ape. It is not surprising that these views provoked controversy and impassioned argument. Indeed, in some communities and religious groups they still do so today.

Darwin proposed a mechanism called **natural selection** to explain what might bring about such changes. He recognised that organisms belonging to a particular species were not all identical, but *varied* in many of their characteristics. He also recognised that there is a high death rate in many wild populations, so that only some individuals live long lives and produce large numbers of offspring. There is a *struggle for existence*, in which those individuals with characteristics which give them a better chance of survival are more likely to reproduce and pass on these characters to their offspring, while those without them are more likely to die young. Over time, therefore, more and more of the population will come to possess these advantageous characteristics. If this continues over many generations, there may be a change, or *evolution*, in the characteristics of the species as a whole.

Darwin's theory was based mostly on logic, plus evidence of how *artificial* selection, carried out by humans, could produce changes in the characteristics of domestic animals such as pigeons. There was also indirect evidence, such as the existence of fossils, which indicated that different species had existed in the past than exist today. But Darwin had no real scientific evidence or data to support his hypothesis of *natural* selection. Nor did he understand anything about the causes of the variations which are the essential basis on which natural selection can act, because at that time nothing was known about genes. Of course, this also meant that nothing was known about how these variations could be passed on from parents to offspring. Nor, despite the words in the title of his book *On the Origin of Species*, did Darwin attempt to explain how a new species could arise.

Despite all of this, the essential ideas behind Darwin's theory of evolution by natural selection still hold firm

Fig. 7.1 A portrait of Charles Darwin, made around 1859 when he was 50 years old.

today. Indeed, most biologists would say that evolution by natural selection is no longer a theory, but fact. We now know what produces heritable variation in living organisms. Several experiments and investigations have shown clearly that natural selection does happen in the wild, and produces evolution. And we are beginning to get a clearer understanding of several different ways in which new species may be produced. Nevertheless, there are still very many unanswered questions, and much research is currently being done on the processes of natural selection, evolution and speciation.

VARIATION
7.2 Genetic and environmental variation

It is easy to see, if you look around, that individual organisms within the same species vary from one another. We are especially aware of this in our own species, but you can pick out variations in almost any kind of organism you look at.

● Genetic variation

Some of the variation between individuals is caused by **genes**. Most genes have several different forms, called alleles. In sexually reproducing organisms, these alleles are reshuffled each time a new organism is produced. Reshuffling happens because of events in meiosis: **crossing over** in interphase before meiosis I, and **independent assortment** at metaphase of meiosis I (Fig. 4.9).

The **random fusion of gametes** from two parents also produces new combinations of alleles in the offspring. Sections 6.11 and 6.13 show how many different combinations of alleles and different phenotypes you can get if you look at just two alleles of two genes. Imagine how many you can get if you consider all the alleles of all the thousands of genes in a human!

While crossing over, independent assortment and random fusion of gametes all produce new *combinations* of alleles, **mutation** (Section 5.5) can produce completely *new* alleles.

When organisms reproduce, they pass on some of their genes to their offspring. *Genetic variation can be inherited.* Genetic variation is due to differences in base sequences in DNA, and this DNA is passed on from generation to generation.

● Environmental variation

Some of the variation which you can see between individuals is not caused by their genes. For example, two people with naturally fair skin may have very different skin colours, because one has been sunbathing and the other has not. Two people with genes which would allow them to grow tall may be very different heights, because they ate very different diets when they were young. Two plants may have very different sizes and colours of leaves, because one is growing in shade, or in poor soil, while the other is growing in the sun, or in rich soil.

These differences are ones which arise during an organism's lifetime, as a result of the environment in which it lives. They are not caused by differences in their DNA, and they do not affect the DNA. They cannot, therefore, be passed on to an organism's offspring. So *environmental variation cannot be inherited.*

Of course, if you consider a particular characteristic, both genetic and environmental variation may be involved. For example, people's height is influenced both by their genes and by their environment. So when two short people reproduce, they might be expected to produce short children – unless the parents' short stature was caused by them both having a poor diet when they were young. As you will see, an understanding of the degree to which genes and the environment affect a characteristic is important for plant and animal breeders, as well as helping us to understand the process of natural selection. Only characteristics with a relatively high genetic influence are really important in natural selection, or can be improved by selective breeding.

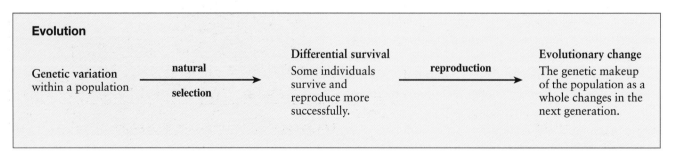

Fig. 7.2 How evolution happens.

7.3 Discontinuous and continuous variation

● Discontinuous variation

Variation in some characteristics is very 'cut and dried'. For example, a person belongs to one of four blood groups in the ABO system – A, B, AB or O. There are no 'in-betweens'. This kind of variation, where there are relatively few, clearly defined groups to which an individual belongs, is called **discontinuous variation** (Fig. 7.3).

Discontinuous variation is always caused by genes. Usually, just one or two genes are involved, each of them with only a few alleles. Human ABO blood groups, for example, are controlled by a single gene, with three alleles (Section 6.7).

● Continuous variation

However, in most characteristics variation is not so clear-cut. For example, human skin or eye colour is impossible to categorise into clearly defined colours. Leaf length on an Oxford ragwort plant can range between around 2 mm to 180 mm, with any length possible between these two extreme values. This kind of variation is called **continuous variation** (Fig. 7.4). The classes into which the leaves have been divided in order to produce the graph are artificial. They have been decided by a person, for convenience.

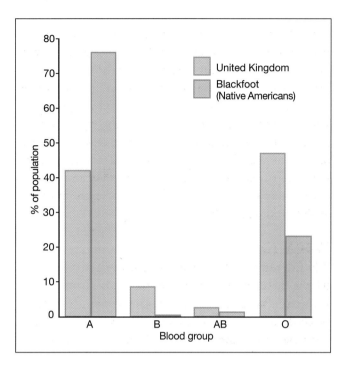

Fig. 7.3 An example of discontinuous variation. In the ABO blood grouping system, each person belongs to one of four discrete groups.

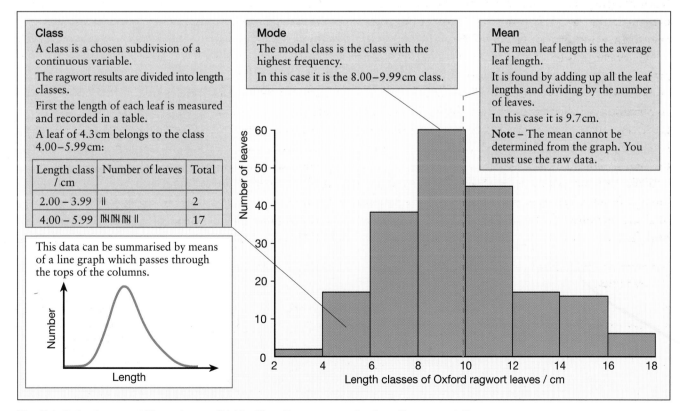

Fig. 7.4 Oxford ragwort (*Senecio squalida*) leaf lengths; an example of continuous variation.

Continuous variation may be caused by genes, or by the environment, or both. One example is human eye colour which is caused entirely by genes, but so many different genes, each with many different alleles, that there are hundreds of possible combinations producing all sorts of different colours which grade almost imperceptibly into each other. This is typical of polygenic characters (Section 6.13). Variations in skin colour, on the other hand, are caused partly by genes (again there are many of these with many different alleles) and partly by environment, in particular the degree of exposure to the sun. Variations in leaf length on a single Oxford ragwort plant, however, must be caused entirely by the environment (for example, the degree of shading on the leaf, or its age), because all the cells in the plant were produced by mitosis from a single zygote and so contain exactly the same genes.

NATURAL SELECTION
7.4 Darwin's finches

The Galapagos islands are a group of about 24 islands in the Pacific Ocean (Fig. 7.5). They are the tips of volcanoes which erupted deep under the sea about 5 million years ago. They are famous for the many unique species of animals and plants which live on them and are not found anywhere else in the world. Charles Darwin visited the islands on the *Beagle* in 1835 and what he saw there helped him to formulate his theory of natural selection.

There are 13 species of finch on the Galapagos islands. Because Darwin was the first scientist to observe and collect them, they are known as Darwin's finches. There are no other finches quite like them anywhere else. It is thought that, a long time ago, a few individuals of a species of finch from the mainland of South America arrived on the islands and began to breed. Over time, the birds adapted to life on the islands by developing beaks which allowed them to specialise in feeding on different things (Figs. 7.7 and 7.8). From one original type of finch, the thirteen species have all arisen. Darwin was fascinated by the fact that different islands in the Galapagos group had different species of finches living on them, of different sizes and with different shapes of beak. He wrote: 'I never dreamed that islands, about fifty or sixty miles apart, and most of them in sight of each other, formed of precisely the same rocks, placed under a quite similar climate, rising to a nearly equal height, would have been differently tenanted'. This set him thinking about *how* and *why* the finches on the different islands were different from each other.

However, Darwin only visited the Galapagos islands briefly, and he did no experiments there. Indeed, he did not realise the significance of the finches until he arrived back home in England, and he never returned to the Galapagos.

To try to find out how the different species of Darwin's finches might have arisen, and to provide insight into how natural selection might cause evolution, two researchers,

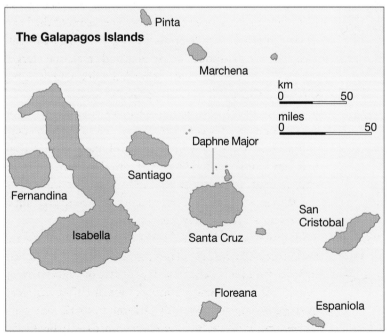

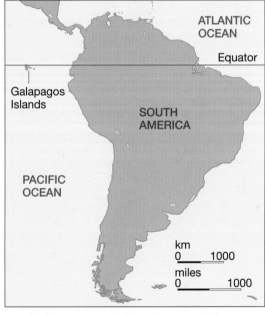

Fig. 7.5 The Galapagos Islands.

Fig. 7.6 The *Beagle* in the Straits of Magellan, off Tierra del Fuego, in 1831.

The large cactus finch, *Geospiza conirostris*.

The large ground finch, *Geospiza magnirostris*.

Fig. 7.7 Two species of Darwin's finches. Notice the different shapes of their beaks.

Peter and Rosemary Grant, have been investigating Darwin's finches since 1973. Their investigations, and those of other researchers working on the islands, have provided clear evidence of natural selection and evolution at work, but – like most good scientific investigations – have also produced many more questions to be answered.

7.5 The effects of the 1977 drought on Daphne Major

Much of the Grants' research has taken place on an island called Daphne Major. It is a small island, with only a few different species of plants and animals living on it, which makes it relatively easy to understand how these species interact with each other. The Grants have studied six species of finches which feed on the ground, called ground finches (Fig. 7.8). These finches all belong to the same genus, *Geospiza*. (The term 'genus' is explained in Section 22.1.)

Since 1973, each bird has been captured (they are very tame), ringed and measured. One measurement which has proved to be very interesting is the depth of the bird's beak, which is the measurement from top to bottom at its widest point. Beak depth appears to be caused almost entirely by a bird's genes and does not change once the bird is fully grown. Birds with big beaks tend to have offspring with big beaks; beak size has a strong genetic component. Although nothing is yet known about the genes which control beak size, it is probably a polygenic characteristic.

The ground finches feed on seeds, and use their beaks like pliers to crack open seed cases. The depth of the beak is very important in determining what the bird can eat. Deep beaks can produce more force and crack open larger seeds. Very small differences in beak depth can make a big difference to the ability to eat particular foods.

When there is plenty of rain the plants on Daphne Major produce plenty of seeds. The Grants found that, in these conditions, all the six kinds of ground finches tend to eat the same kind of seeds. When seeds are abundant, the birds tend to eat the softer, smaller seeds no matter what beak size they have. Because there is plenty of food to go round, there is no competition for food.

However, in 1977 it did not rain. The drought meant that most of the plants did not flower or set seed. Whereas in 1976 there had been an average of 10 g of seeds on every square metre of ground surface, in June of 1977 there were only 6 g per square metre. By December, there were only 3 g per square metre, and these were mostly very big seeds, the most difficult to crack open and eat.

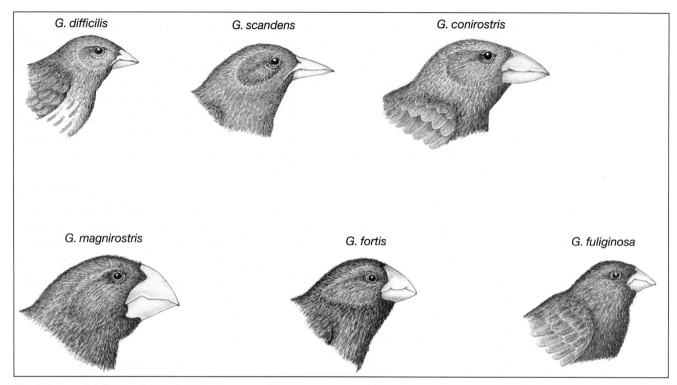

Fig. 7.8 Darwin's finches. All belong to the genus *Geospiza*.

Now there was great competition between the birds. There was not enough food to go around, and many birds died of starvation. The Grants knew every individual finch (they had all been ringed), and had records of their beak depths. They knew every kind of seed, and could watch the birds feeding and identify the seeds they were feeding on. They were therefore able to see whether there was any correlation between beak depth, seed availability and survival of the finches in these difficult conditions.

They found that, as the supply of seeds got less, the birds tended to specialise more and more in what they ate. Birds with big beaks, such as the large ground finch *G. magnirostris*, chose to eat the big seeds which other birds were not able to crack open. The medium ground finches, *G. fortis*, had more trouble. Some individual birds had particularly big beaks, and were able to cope with the big seeds, but others with smaller beaks could not. The Grants found that a difference of 0.5 mm in beak size could determine whether or not a *G. fortis* lived or died of starvation.

Through the drought of 1977, as the supply of seeds gradually went down, and the average size of the remaining seeds went up, hundreds of ground finches died. The numbers of *G. fortis* dropped from 1200 to 180, an 85% loss. Older birds survived better than younger ones, with no birds of less than one year old making it through the drought, and only one one-year-old bird surviving. Male birds survived better than female birds. Before the drought, the average beak depth of the birds in the *G. fortis* population had been 9.42 mm, but after the drought it was 9.96 mm. This was because many of the birds with beaks at the lower end of the size range had died. The bigger the beak, the more likely it was that the bird survived.

7.6 Beak depth – an example of natural selection
The details of the story which the Grants watched unfold between 1976 and 1978 can be summarised as a classic example of natural selection in action. Let us look at one species, the medium ground finch, *Geospiza fortis*, using some of the particular terminology used to describe the processes of natural selection.

In the population of *G. fortis* on Daphne Major, there was considerable **variation** in beak depth. When food supply was good, there was little stress on the finches, and finches with any beak size were equally likely to survive. But when food supply was short, it produced **competition** for food between the finches. Mortality rates increased, and finches with smaller beaks were more likely to die than finches with larger beaks. In other words, there was **differential survival**.

The food shortage acted as a **selection pressure** on the finch population, tending to select for survival those finches with beaks at the top end of the size range. Finches with big beaks had a **selective advantage** over those with small beaks.

7.7 The next generation

In 1978, it rained on Daphne Major. The plants seeded, and food supply was more abundant. And, of course, there were fewer finches around to eat it, so competition was much less. The finches responded by breeding.

Because of the differential mortality in the drought year between male and female finches, each female found herself with a choice of six possible males for a mate. The females chose the largest males with the largest beaks and the darkest plumage. The females themselves were the ones which had the largest beak sizes, because only they had survived the drought. As beak size has a strong genetic component, the offspring which were produced also tended to have large beaks. The average beak size of the new generation of *G. fortis* produced in 1978 was 4.5% greater than before the drought.

Evolution had happened. There had been a change, over time and from one generation to another, in the characteristics of the population of *G. fortis*. This evolution had occurred as a result of natural selection. As drought continued until 1982, beak size continued to increase.

7.8 Different selection pressures can act at different times

However, this proved not to be the end of the story. If it continued in this way, the average beak size of *G. fortis* would continue to get larger and larger. But this has not happened. There are two reasons why.

Firstly, even in drought years, it is not always an advantage to have a large beak. For *young* birds, a large beak is a positive *disadvantage*. They are not able to make use of their big beaks because their muscles have not yet developed enough to produce maximum force, and their beaks are not yet hard enough. But if they have big beaks they are likely to be big birds, and therefore need more food. So young birds with big beaks are actually more likely to die than young birds with small beaks when food is in short supply, because they starve to death more quickly.

Secondly, there is not always drought on Daphne Major. In 1982 it rained so much that there was flooding. It was so wet that many of the plants, especially cacti, which produced big seeds were killed. In the years following 1982, therefore, there were fewer big seeds on the island. Now there was no selective advantage for birds with big beaks. In fact they were at a disadvantage, because big birds need more food and so starve more easily.

So the average beak size of *G. fortis* on Daphne Major went down again after 1982. The selection pressures had changed, and swung the advantage back towards finches with small beaks.

These events on Daphne Major show clearly how advantageous it is to a species to have variation amongst its individual members. If all the *G. fortis* individuals had had the same size beaks, they might have all have died in the drought. If they had not died in the drought, they might all have died after the flood. By having variation, a species has more chance that at least some of its members will be able to survive under whatever pressures a changing environment produces.

7.9 Another example of natural selection – antibiotic resistance in bacteria

There are many other examples of natural selection, although few that have been measured so thoroughly or over such a long period of time as the studies on the ground finches in the Galapagos. One example which is of particular interest and importance to humans is the development of resistance to antibiotics in bacteria.

Many diseases are caused by bacteria. Before 1940, when penicillin was discovered, bacteria were a major cause of death. Wounds, for example, often became infected by bacteria which could spread into the blood system and cause death by blood poisoning. Penicillin is an **antibiotic**, a chemical which kills bacteria inside the body but does no harm to a person's own cells.

The use of antibiotics has introduced new selection pressures within bacterial populations. Like all organisms, bacteria vary from one another. Some individuals in a population, for example, may carry a gene which confers resistance to an antibiotic such as penicillin. (These resistance genes are often on plasmids (Section 5.12), rather than on the main DNA molecule in the cell.) If a person takes penicillin, then any such individual bacterium has a considerable selective advantage over the others. The non-resistant individuals will be killed, but the resistant bacterium will survive. It can then reproduce rapidly, producing a whole population of bacteria that also contain the gene which makes them resistant to penicillin.

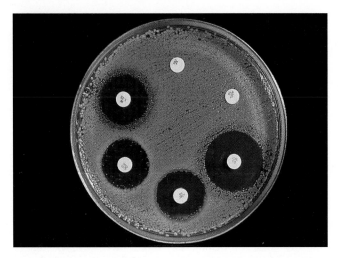

Fig. 7.9 Antibiotic resistance and sensitivity in *Escherichia coli*. A culture of these bacteria is growing on the agar. Filter paper discs containing six different antibiotics have been placed on the agar. The clear areas show where the antibiotic has stopped the bacteria growing. If the bacteria are resistant to the antibiotic, they can grow right up to the disc.

This has happened many times. Penicillin acts by inhibiting the synthesis of some parts of the bacterial cell wall. Some bacteria have genes which code for an enzyme called β lactamase which can break down penicillin and other antibiotics with a similar chemical structure. Other resistance genes may work by affecting the structure of proteins in the bacterium's membrane, stopping it from taking up the antibiotic at all, or by pumping it out after it has been taken up.

The pharmaceutical industry has a tremendous problem in trying to produce new antibiotics faster than bacteria evolve resistance to them. Most antibiotics have been developed from chemicals which are naturally synthesised by fungi which live in the soil; the fungi use them to prevent too many bacteria living and feeding close to them, as the bacteria might compete with the fungi for food. Now this source seems to have been almost exhausted and researchers are looking elsewhere. Frog skins might prove to be a fruitful hunting ground, as might microorganisms living in unusual environments. However, in the end bacteria are always likely to develop resistance to whatever antibiotics are used, and it will be a constant struggle to keep ahead of them.

7.10 Natural selection and allele frequency

Since Darwin first put forward his theory of evolution by natural selection, much evidence has accumulated to support it. Most of his ideas have turned out to be correct. However, we can now go a little further in explaining how natural selection happens, by considering not just how and why the *characteristics* of a population may change, but also the underlying causes of these characteristics – the *alleles of the genes* which are responsible for producing them.

Characteristics such as beak size in ground finches and antibiotic resistance in bacteria are caused by genes. We can think of selection pressures acting on the phenotypes produced by particular alleles, or combinations of alleles, of these genes. No-one knows exactly how many genes with how many alleles are responsible for determining beak size in ground finches, but it can be assumed that there are several genes, each with at least two alleles. In drought conditions, birds with alleles of these beak-size genes which code for large beaks are more likely to survive than birds with alleles which code for small beaks. These birds breed, and pass on the alleles for large beaks to their offspring. While drought continues, the frequency of the 'large beak' alleles in the population increases, and the frequency of the 'small beak' alleles decreases. The evolutionary change is a change in the allele frequency in the new generation.

In other instances where the effects of natural selection have been studied, we do know more about the alleles involved. One such example is the sickle cell allele in human populations.

The gene coding for the β polypeptide in haemoglobin has an allele which produces a 'wrong' form of the haemoglobin molecule, called sickle cell haemoglobin. (This allele and its effects are described in Section 5.7.) The allele is often given the symbol H^S, while the 'normal' allele is H^A. People who are homozygous for the sickle cell allele, $H^S H^S$, have sickle cell anaemia and are unlikely to live long or to reproduce successfully. Yet, in some parts of the world, this allele is quite common and many homozygous babies are born. Why, if natural selection really does work, does this happen? These people are at a great selective disadvantage, so it would be expected that natural selection would remove the sickle cell allele from the population.

Sickle cell anaemia is most common in parts of the world where malaria is found (Fig. 7.10). In some parts of Africa 1 in every 25 babies born has sickle cell anaemia. These babies each have two copies of the sickle cell allele. Many more are born who have one copy of the sickle cell allele and one copy of the normal allele. These heterozygous people, with the genotype $H^A H^S$, appear quite normal. Their red blood cells contain some normal

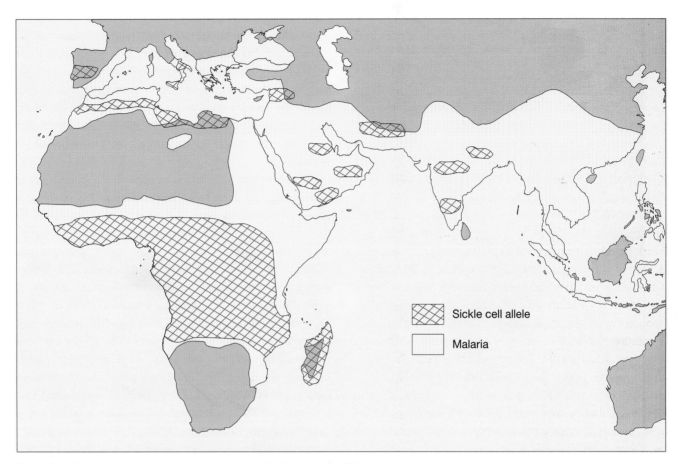

Fig. 7.10 Distribution of malaria and the sickle cell allele before 1930.

haemoglobin, and some sickle cell haemoglobin. They do not have sickle cell anaemia and will be quite unaware that they are heterozygous.

People who are heterozygous for the sickle cell allele have been found to be much less likely to suffer from malaria than people who are homozygous for the normal allele. Malaria is a disease caused by a protoctistan parasite called *Plasmodium* (Box 13.6), which is injected into a person's blood when an infected female mosquito bites. The parasites breed in red blood cells, causing fever and sometimes death. This happens most frequently in people with the genotype H^AH^A, as the parasites are able to breed most successfully in red cells in which all the haemoglobin is normal.

In people with the genotypes H^AH^S or H^SH^S, however, the malarial parasites do not do so well. This means that heterozygotes, with the genotype H^AH^S, have a great selective advantage over people with either of the other two genotypes in parts of the world where malaria is found. People with the genotype H^AH^A are more likely to die from malaria. People with the genotype H^SH^S are likely to die from sickle cell anaemia. But people with the genotype H^AH^S are unlikely to die from either of these two causes. They are the people who are most likely to live long lives and to reproduce.

Thus, the H^S allele is passed on, in each generation, to some of the children which are born. Some will be unlucky and get two copies of this allele, while others will get two copies of the normal allele. But some will get a copy of each allele, and be at an advantage in coping with the selection pressure exerted by the malarial parasite.

The co-existence of individuals in a population with different phenotypes caused by different genotypes, such as people who have or do not have sickle cell anaemia, is known as **polymorphism**.

7.11 Different types of selection

Natural selection is a process in which selection pressures act on a population so that individuals possessing a particular allele, or combination of alleles, are more likely to survive and pass on their alleles than other individuals. Natural selection may sometimes produce a *change*, or evolution, in a population, but this is by no means always the case.

Let us consider an imaginary population of leaf-eating insects, in which the major selection pressure is predation by a bird which hunts by sight. The insects are coloured yellow-green, to camouflage them against the yellow-green leaves on which they feed, and so avoid detection by birds. The colour of the insects is controlled by their genes. It is a polygenic characteristic, and there is a fairly wide range of colour variation (Fig. 7.11).

In a particular environment, the precise colour which best matches the leaves on which the insects live, and which therefore provides the best camouflage, lies near the middle of the range. Most insects will have this colour. Any insect with a colour either more green or more brown than this has a slightly greater chance of being eaten than an insect with the most common colour. Thus, in each generation, rather more of the insects with the combination of alleles giving the middle-range yellow-green survive than insects with other combinations of alleles. These middle-range insects are more likely to reproduce, and pass on their alleles to their offspring. In the next generation, the most common colour will again be the mid-range yellow-green, with relatively few individuals being born with dark green or brown colouration.

So, from generation to generation, natural selection will keep the range of colouration in the insect population about the same. Little, if any, change will occur. This is called **stabilising selection**. Stabilising selection does not lead to evolution. Probably, most populations most of the time are undergoing stabilising selection. If the population is already well adapted to its environment, then selection will maintain the favourable characteristics that enable it to be successful.

Now consider what might happen if there was a change in the environment. Imagine that some of the insects were transported to a new area, where the plants on which they chose to feed had leaves which were more brown. Now, the insects at the brown end of the colour range have the selective advantage. Greener and yellower insects are more likely to be eaten, and less likely to pass on their alleles to the next generation. Each generation, more brown insects than green and yellow-green insects are produced. The curve shifts to the right.

This type of selection is called **directional selection**. Directional selection produces a change, or evolution, in a population. Directional selection tends to occur when there is a change in the environment, or a change in an allele in a population – a mutation. Either of these changes may mean that the commonest form of an organism is no longer the one which is best adapted to the environment, and a different form is selected for. Over time, directional selection produces a change in the allele frequency of the population.

There is a third possibility. Imagine that a second type of bush, with very dark green leaves, also grows in the area where the brown-leaved bushes are found. Insects with dark green colouration will be well camouflaged against these dark green leaves, while those with brown colouration are well camouflaged against the brown leaves. Insects with yellow-green colouration stand out against both types of leaf, and are more likely to be eaten. So, each generation, few yellow-green insects will reproduce and pass on their alleles. The alleles for dark green and brown colouration are more likely to be passed on. Over time, the population may come to contain many dark green individuals, many brown individuals, but very few yellow-green individuals. This type of selection is called **disruptive selection**. Disruptive selection usually maintains polymorphism (Section 7.10) in a population.

Q1 The following are types of selection.

directional
stabilising
disruptive

Identify the type of selection that would best describe each of the examples below

(a) Early farmers selected cattle to produce some breeds that were horned and some that were hornless (1)

(b) There is a higher death rate among very light and very heavy human babies than among those of average mass at birth. (1)

AEB 1997 (specimen, modified)
(*Total 2 marks*)

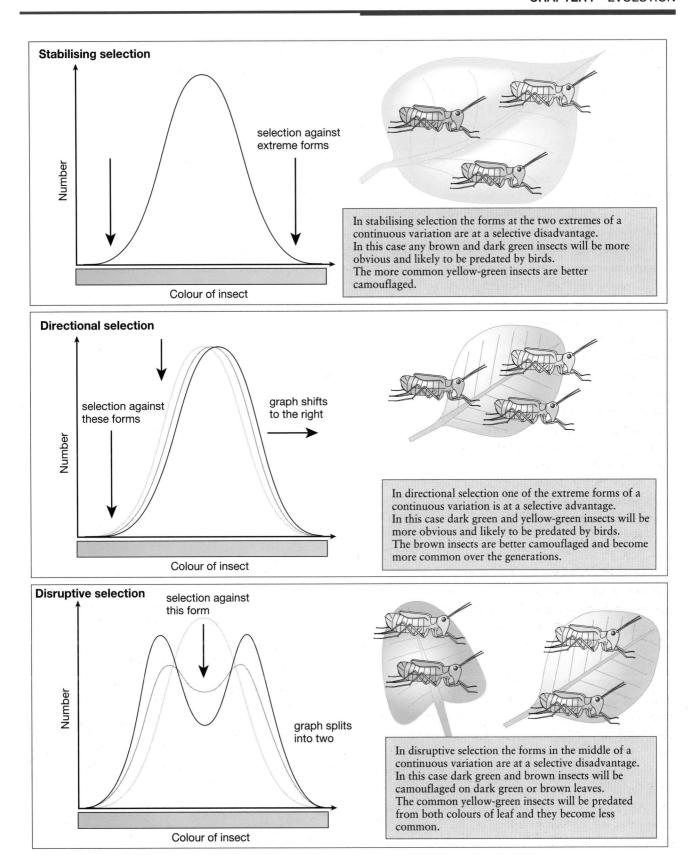

Stabilising selection

Number

selection against extreme forms

Colour of insect

In stabilising selection the forms at the two extremes of a continuous variation are at a selective disadvantage.
In this case any brown and dark green insects will be more obvious and likely to be predated by birds.
The more common yellow-green insects are better camouflaged.

Directional selection

Number

selection against these forms

graph shifts to the right

Colour of insect

In directional selection one of the extreme forms of a continuous variation is at a selective advantage.
In this case dark green and yellow-green insects will be more obvious and likely to be predated by birds.
The brown insects are better camouflaged and become more common over the generations.

Disruptive selection

selection against this form

Number

graph splits into two

Colour of insect

In disruptive selection the forms in the middle of a continuous variation are at a selective disadvantage.
In this case dark green and brown insects will be camouflaged on dark green or brown leaves.
The common yellow-green insects will be predated from both colours of leaf and they become less common.

Fig. 7.11 Types of selection within imaginary insect populations.

SELECTIVE BREEDING
7.12 Artificial selection

Long before anything was understood about genes, alleles, natural selection or evolution, humans began using a process very similar to natural selection to produce animals and plants which they could use for their own purposes. This process is **artificial selection**.

One of the earliest plants to be cultivated by humans was wheat. It was probably first used at least 10 000 years ago, in a very fertile region in what is now part of Iraq, Syria, Israel and Lebanon. Wild species of wheat were harvested and stored, to make flour and bread.

Wild wheat has grains that are firmly covered by a husk which protects the seeds. It also produces seed heads which shatter easily, to disperse the seeds as soon as they are ripe. Although both of these characteristics help the wheat to survive in the wild, they are both a nuisance to people who are trying to grow the wheat for food. These early farmers appear to have selected which grains they saved to sow for next season's crop. Rather than sowing just any grains, they chose those from plants which produced grain which was easy to separate from its husk, which did not shatter and drop the seed before harvest, and which produced good yields.

This selection of seeds continued for many generations. Over time, the characteristics of the wheat varieties changed, becoming more suitable for the purposes of the farmer, and less suitable for survival in the wild.

Selective breeding of wheat continues today. Desirable characteristics include high yield, short stem length (to reduce wastage, because straw produced from the stems has little value), resistance to pests such as fungi, and grain quality, especially the level of protein content.

Selective breeding of wheat is made easier because the plants naturally self pollinate, so that there is less likelihood of one plant fertilising another without the breeder deliberately causing this to happen. When a new variety of wheat is to be bred, the breeder usually begins by crossing two different varieties, which possess different alleles. He might, for example, choose one variety with a very high yield of high-protein grain, and another with excellent resistance to yellow rust disease. The crossing is done by removing the anthers from the flowers on one plant, and dusting pollen from another plant onto its stigmas (Fig. 7.13). The ears are then bagged, to stop any other pollen from getting onto the stigmas. The resulting seeds are collected, sown, and grown until the resulting plants have set seed themselves.

Fig. 7.12 The wild einkorn wheat, *Triticum monococcum*, was grown and harvested by early human populations in the Middle East.

Modern bread wheat, *Triticum aestivum*, has been bred to give much higher yields of grain than the wild varieties.

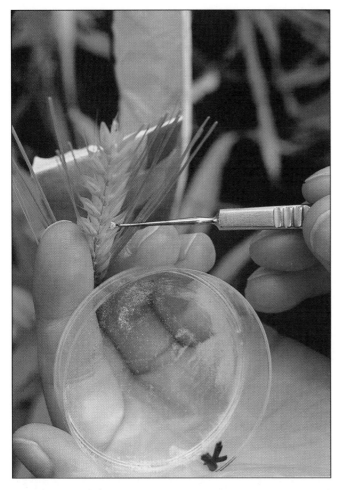

Fig. 7.13 The pollen in the petri dish has been collected from another plant. A metal seeker is being used to dust this pollen onto the stigma of the wheat flower. The flower's own anthers will have been removed long before their own pollen could be released, and the flowers will have been covered to ensure that no other pollen could get to them.

The breeders then select the individual plants from this first generation which most nearly have the characteristics they want – that is high yield, high protein content and high resistance to yellow rust. These plants are self-pollinated, and seed from them is saved, sown and grown to maturity. This process is continued for several generations, selecting the individuals for breeding each time. With each generation of self-pollination, variation becomes less and less, because some alleles are lost each time. Eventually, the individual plants become homozygous or true-breeding, producing offspring with alleles and therefore characteristics just like themselves. A new, marketable variety has been developed.

Similar techniques of artificial selection have been used to develop most of our farmed animals and crop plants, as well as animals used for other purposes, such as racehorses, dogs for hunting and companionship, and pigeons for racing. However, complete homozygosity has not developed in any of these animals.

In many ways, artificial selection is a very inexact art. This is because the characters we are looking for are often controlled by very many genes, and may also have a strong environmental component. Milk yield in cows, for example, appears to be influenced by a very large number of genes. It also has a strong environmental component, being affected by all sorts of factors such as food quality and quantity, and degree of stress. This has made selection for milk yield a very difficult process. It has been going on for several hundred years, and there is still no certainty that a cow bred from particular parents will inherit high milk yield.

7.13 Problems arising from inbreeding

Artificial selection often involves breeding closely related organisms together. This is called **inbreeding**. Inbreeding tends to reduce the variety of alleles in a population. In the breeding of wheat varieties, where self-pollination occurs, this is especially true, and any particular modern wheat variety is genetically entirely uniform – every individual has identical alleles.

This is, essentially, exactly what the breeder was aiming for. Each plant has identical characteristics. This makes it easier to harvest, because all the plants in a field grow to the same height (assuming they are growing in identical soil conditions), are ready to harvest at the same time, and produce grain of the same quality, making it easier to sell. The farmer can grow the same variety the next year, and know that he or she will – weather permitting – obtain a similar crop.

However, there are also major dangers associated with this genetic uniformity. The lack of genetic variability makes the wheat variety an evolutionary 'dead end'. If a breeder wishes to improve the plants' characteristics, he cannot, because there are no other alleles present which can produce anything different. Worse still, if a new disease arrives to which the plants have no natural resistance, then every plant may succumb. Because there is no genetic variability, not even a single plant will have resistance.

Plant breeders are therefore careful to maintain sources of genetic diversity in crop plants. While individual plant

Fig. 7.14 This seed bank contains many samples of seeds, which are kept in cold storage. Small samples of seeds are germinated and grown into adult plants at intervals, so that new, fresh seeds can be collected and stored.

Potatoes are propagated asexually, by tubers, and not usually by seeds. Potatoes originated in South America, and the International Potato Center in Peru has responsibility for maintaining the world's potato gene bank. They store tubers of many different potato varieties. Some of these may be used to produce new commercial varieties with different, useful characteristics such as resistance to disease.

varieties which are used commercially may be very inbred and genetically uniform, other varieties are kept which have different characteristics. These other varieties may have no commercial value in themselves, except as a source of new alleles for future breeding programmes. They may be wild forms, or they may be old varieties or ones grown in other countries. The form in which they are kept varies widely. Seeds from old or wild varieties of crop plants, such as wheat, cabbages, rice or carrots, are stored in seed banks. For species where seeds do not store well, such as rubber trees, individual plants can be grown and kept in a nursery, sometimes called a 'field gene bank'. Some of the many varieties of potato found in South America may be kept as tubers, some of which are grown each year to produce a continuous stock of fresh tubers.

Animal gene banks take different forms. Old varieties of farm animals, such as Tamworth pigs and Longhorn cattle, are kept as 'rare breeds'. Semen from male animals with different ancestries can be kept in a sperm bank, in which the semen is stored at very low temperatures. Embryos can be stored in a similar way.

7.14 Gene technology in plant and animal breeding

Artificial selection has been used for thousands of years, and it is still a very important technique in the production of new varieties of plants and animals for human use. However, in the last 30 years a new range of tools has developed, which have proved very helpful in enabling new varieties to be tailor-made.

The techniques of genetic engineering (Sections 5.10–5.13) enable a particular gene, or group of genes, to be transferred from one organism to another. So, for example, a gene for resistance to yellow rust could be taken from one plant – either of the same or a different species – and inserted into another. This technique can be used to produce crop varieties which are resistant to particular diseases.

However, the production of useful new varieties by genetic engineering is only possible where the desired characteristic is controlled by a single gene, or a group of genes on the same chromosome, which can be identified and manipulated. Many of the genes in wheat have now been mapped, and breeders are able to identify the positions of particular alleles. In other cases, however, such as milk yield in dairy cows, the genes involved have not been identified, and there is currently no alternative to the long-standing methods of artificial selection and selective breeding.

The identification of particular genes is not only useful in genetic engineering, but can also help to speed up selective breeding programmes. Individual wheat plants, for example, can be screened to see which ones contain genes for high protein content using DNA probes (Box 5.4). The breeder can then choose plants with these genes for breeding. This saves having to carry out time-consuming field tests.

SPECIATION

7.15 What is a species?

The term 'species' is one which is very widely used in biology, yet it is remarkably difficult to produce a definition of it which will satisfy every biologist.

We all have at least a vague idea of what we mean when we talk about a species. If two organisms belong to the same species, we would expect them to look fairly similar, to behave in fairly similar ways, and to have similar physiology (the way their bodies work). All these features would differ from organisms belonging to different species. But *how* similar do two organisms have to be to make them belong to the same species, and *how* different do they have to be to make them belong to a different one? Do plains zebras and Grevy's zebras (Fig. 7.15) belong to the same species, or to two different species, for example?

Most biologists define species according to their breeding behaviour. A good working definition of a species is *a group of organisms which, in natural conditions, breed successfully with each other, but not normally with members of other species*. According to this definition, the plains zebra and the Grevy's zebra are different species. They do not, in the wild, normally interbreed with each other.

Members of different species may, however, sometimes interbreed. This usually only happens under unusual conditions, such as in captivity. Lions and tigers, for example, have interbred in zoos. This does not make them the same species, because they do not *normally* interbreed, nor do they interbreed *in natural conditions*. Often, when individuals of different species do interbreed, the offspring are not fertile, so that the breeding is not *successful*.

7.16 Methods of reproductive isolation

By definition, species are **reproductively isolated** from each other. Members of one species do not normally breed with members of another species. What stops members of different species interbreeding successfully?

In most animals, sexual reproduction begins with courtship, and then moves on to mating and fertilisation. In plants, sexual reproduction involves pollination followed by fertilisation. Failure at any of these stages can produce reproductive isolation.

In animals, for example, differences in **appearance** or **behaviour** may prevent successful courtship. For example, many birds have complex and very precise courtship displays, to which only a bird of the same species will respond. This may include sounds, as well as visual displays. Insects such as moths also use scent; the scent produced by a female will only attract males of her own species. Individuals may also be prevented from getting anywhere near the mating stage because they are in the mood for reproduction at different **times** or in different **places**. An example of this is described in Section 7.18.

Mating and fertilisation in animals may be prevented by **physical** differences, for example if the male's genitalia do not fit the female's. Or the sperm of one species may not be able to survive in the genital tract of the female of another. Even if fertilisation is successful, the resulting zygote may not be able to live, because the **chromosomes** it has received from its two different parents do not give suitable instructions to produce a viable ('workable') organism. If it does survive, it may well be infertile, because the chromosomes from its two parents are not sufficiently alike to be able to pair and undergo meiosis.

Fig. 7.15 The plains or Burchell's zebra, *Equus burchelli*.

Grevy's zebra, *Equus grevyi*.

In plants, complex **pollination mechanisms** sometimes ensure that pollen from one flower is unlikely to be delivered to a flower of a different species. In many others, however, especially wind-pollinated flowers, there is nothing to stop this happening, except differences in **time** at which ripe pollen is produced. If the 'wrong' pollen does land on a stigma, successful reproduction is usually prevented because the pollen grain will not be stimulated to grow a tube (Box 18.1), so fertilisation does not occur. As in animals, even if fertilisation occurs it probably will not produce a viable or fertile offspring.

7.17 Problems in defining species

Although the definition of a species given in Section 7.15 may seem perfectly clear, it is extraordinarily difficult to apply in many circumstances.

For example, two similar organisms may live in very different parts of the world. They obviously do not interbreed, because they never come into contact with one another. But *would* they interbreed if they could?

Other organisms may never breed sexually at all, and so never interbreed even with members of their own species. Some plants, such as wild garlic, do this. How do you tell if two types of wild garlic belong to different species, or if they are just varieties of the same species? There are many plants which normally only reproduce asexually, and this makes it extraordinarily difficult to determine whether or not they belong to the same species. The classification of bacteria runs into similar problems. In these cases, decisions have to made solely on similarities in morphology and physiology, which – not surprisingly – leads to disagreement between different people!

How do new species arise? The appearance of a new species is called **speciation**. According to the definition given in Section 7.15, a species is a group of organisms which is reproductively isolated from other groups of organisms. For one species to produce a new species, a 'splinter group' of the old species must somehow become unable to interbreed with the rest. This process is very difficult to observe, and we have had to work out how it might happen by looking at the distribution and characteristics of species in the present time, and using what we see as clues to deduce what might have happened in the past.

7.18 Geographical isolation

One event which has undoubtedly been important in the production of many new species is **geographical isolation**. This process begins when a population becomes separated from the rest of its species by some form of geographical barrier. For example, a pair of lizards could drift over an ocean on a floating log, and be carried to a distant island where they could breed, separated by hundreds of miles of water from all the other lizards of that species. Or long-term changes in climate could cause most of the trees in a forest to die, leaving isolated pockets of trees in which marooned populations of spiders became isolated from all the other spiders of their species.

Two geographically separated populations will almost certainly be subjected to different selection pressures. This may produce directional selection (Section 7.11) in at least one of the populations. Over many generations, the frequency of particular alleles may become very different. Some alleles may be entirely lost from one population, while other new alleles may arise randomly by mutation. The characteristics of the two populations grow further and further apart. Eventually, they become so different that, even if the barrier between them breaks down, they will not or cannot interbreed successfully for any of the reasons described in Section 7.16. They have become different species.

There are many species in the world today which probably arose in this way. Darwin's finches, for example, appear to have evolved from a few birds belonging to a finch species, which arrived on the Galapagos islands from the mainland of South America between one and five million years ago. Separated from the rest of the species, and subjected to the different selection pressures on the islands, they evolved to produce different forms. There was little competition, because few other species were present, so all sorts of different sizes and forms of beaks proved to be successful. Thus many different species evolved from a single one, in a process called **adaptive radiation**.

Geographical isolation can even produce new species if the selection pressures on the two separated populations are very similar. If only two lizards (of different sexes) arrive on an island on a log, the number of different alleles they posses between them will be far fewer than the number possessed by the mainland population from which they have become isolated. When they reproduce, even some of this reduced number of alleles may be lost, just by chance, because only some will be passed on to their offspring, and only some of these offspring will survive. So the island population of lizards may come to be different from the mainland population largely due to chance. This process is called **genetic drift**, and it may have been a major factor in producing many island species.

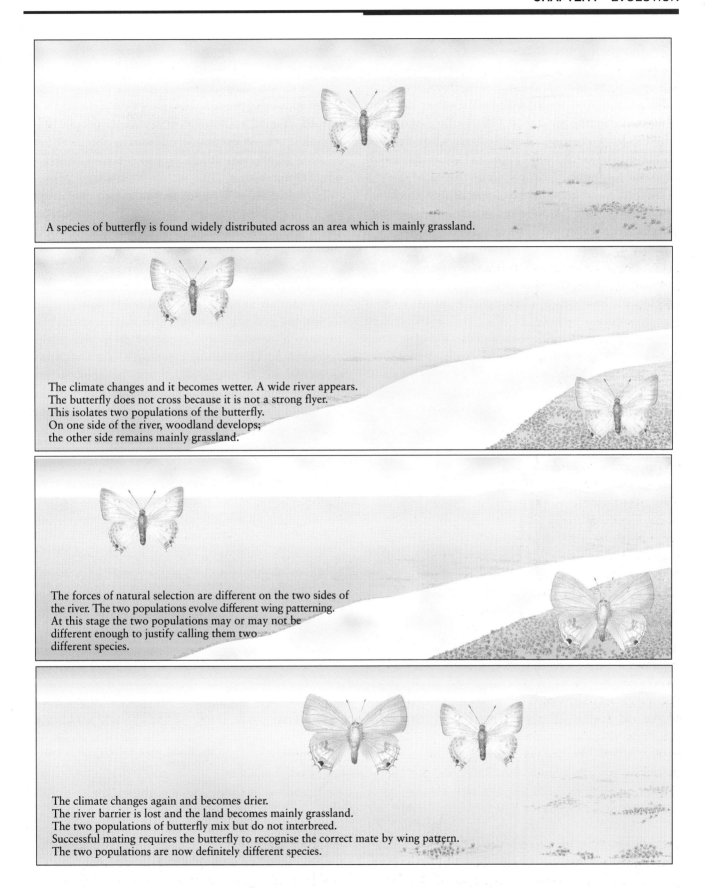

A species of butterfly is found widely distributed across an area which is mainly grassland.

The climate changes and it becomes wetter. A wide river appears.
The butterfly does not cross because it is not a strong flyer.
This isolates two populations of the butterfly.
On one side of the river, woodland develops;
the other side remains mainly grassland.

The forces of natural selection are different on the two sides of
the river. The two populations evolve different wing patterning.
At this stage the two populations may or may not be
different enough to justify calling them two
different species.

The climate changes again and becomes drier.
The river barrier is lost and the land becomes mainly grassland.
The two populations of butterfly mix but do not interbreed.
Successful mating requires the butterfly to recognise the correct mate by wing pattern.
The two populations are now definitely different species.

Fig. 7.16 Geographical isolation and how it may result in speciation.

7.19 Sympatric speciation – polyploidy

Geographical separation is not the only way in which a new species can arise. This can also happen when all the individuals involved are still living in the *same* place. This is called **sympatric speciation**. The kind of speciation resulting from geographical separation, where the two species evolve in *different* places, is sometimes called **allopatric speciation**.

The best understood method of sympatric speciation involves **polyploidy**. A polyploid organism is one which possesses more than two complete sets of chromosomes. If there are three sets of chromosomes, the organism is said to be triploid; if there are four, it is tetraploid and so on.

Polyploidy can create a new species in a single generation. Imagine, for example, a plant with 8 chromosomes in each of its cells. This is the diploid number of chromosomes, made up of two sets of 4. When the plant produces gametes, its cells divide by meiosis to produce haploid pollen and egg nuclei, each with a single set of 4 chromosomes. Two of these gametes fuse to form a zygote with the diploid number of 8 chromosomes.

However, sometimes, during early mitotic divisions of a newly fertilised egg, the chromosomes separate but the cell fails to divide. Instead of two cells each containing 8 chromatids being produced, one cell with 16 chromatids is formed. This cell has *four* sets of the 4 chromosomes. It is a tetraploid cell. As it repeatedly divides by mitosis to form an adult plant, every cell in the plant receives these four sets of chromosomes.

Tetraploid plants are often more vigorous than diploid ones, and the plant may grow strongly. Eventually, it may flower and produce gametes. During meiosis, each of the chromosomes will be able to find a homologous partner to pair with, because there is an even number of each kind of chromosome (Fig. 7.17). The gametes produced will each have two sets of chromosomes; they will be diploid.

Now imagine that a gamete from this tetraploid plant fertilises a normal haploid gamete from the original diploid plant. The resulting zygote will have *three* sets of chromosomes. It is triploid. It will be able to grow normally and to flower. However, it will run into difficulties when its cells attempt to divide by meiosis to

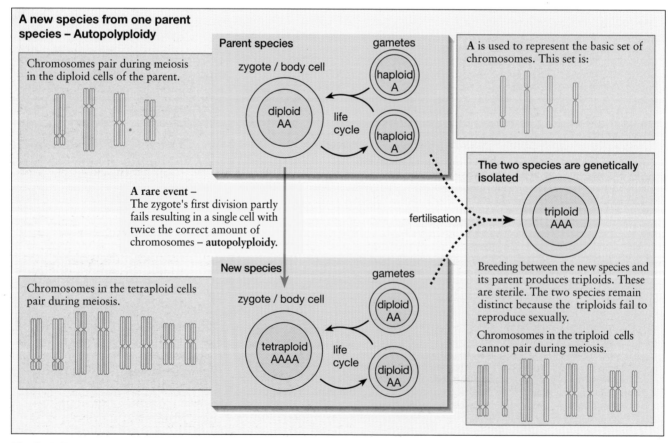

Fig. 7.17 Formation of new species by polyploidy.

produce gametes. There are three of each kind of chromosome, so they will not be able to pair up. Meiosis will be a disaster, and no functional gametes will be produced. The plant cannot reproduce sexually; it is sterile.

Thus, the original diploid plant and the tetraploid plant accidentally produced from it cannot successfully interbreed. They are different species. Natural selection had nothing to do with it; the whole process was just chance, and virtually instantaneous. However, natural selection will, of course, determine whether one or both of the two species survives or dies out, and will help to make 'fine adjustments' to their characteristics from generation to generation, making them better suited to their environment.

The kind of polyploidy described here involves a single original species of plant. It is known as **autopolyploidy** ('auto' means 'self'). Something similar can happen involving *two* different parent species. They may hybridise to produce a sterile, diploid hybrid (Fig. 7.17). If this can survive long enough (and, if it can reproduce asexually, it may well be able to do so) a time may come when it

accidentally produces a tetraploid offspring. This tetraploid is fertile, because it has two of each kind of chromosome, and so can undergo meiosis successfully. However, it cannot breed successfully with either of its original parents. The new, tetraploid plant is a new species. This kind of polyploidy is called **allopolyploidy**. An example of this actually happening is described in Box 7.1.

Polyploidy has been of great importance in the production of new plant species, and it is thought that it has been responsible for the origin of almost half of the known living species of flowering plants. It has also been important in plant breeding (Fig. 7.18). It seems, however, that polyploidy has not been so important in speciation in animals.

7.20 Other methods of sympatric speciation

Polyploidy may not be the only way in which sympatric speciation can occur. Speciation could theoretically happen if two populations of an organism become separated behaviourally, without any physical barrier coming between them.

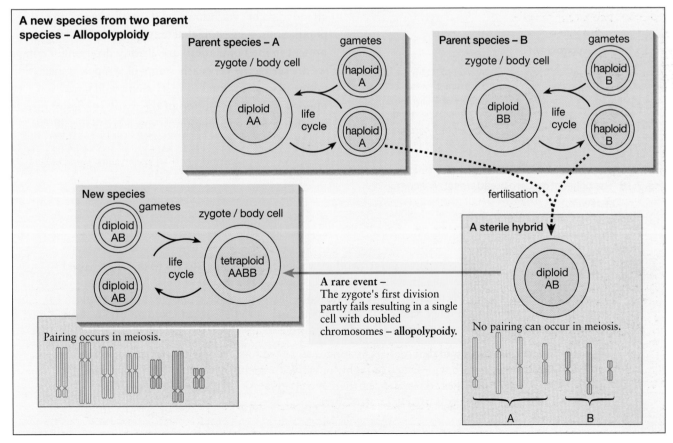

Fig. 7.17 *cont.*

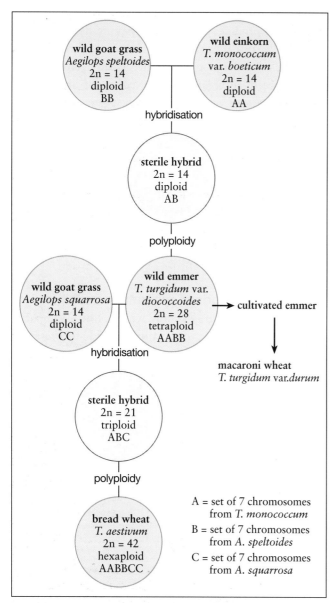

wild goat grass
Aegilops speltoides
2n = 14
diploid
BB

wild einkorn
T. monococcum
var. *boeticum*
2n = 14
diploid
AA

hybridisation

sterile hybrid
2n = 14
diploid
AB

polyploidy

wild goat grass
Aegilops squarrosa
2n = 14
diploid
CC

wild emmer
T. turgidum var.
diococcoides
2n = 28
tetraploid
AABB

→ cultivated emmer

macaroni wheat
T. turgidum var.*durum*

hybridisation

sterile hybrid
2n = 21
triploid
ABC

polyploidy

bread wheat
T. aestivum
2n = 42
hexaploid
AABBCC

A = set of 7 chromosomes from *T. monococcum*

B = set of 7 chromosomes from *A. speltoides*

C = set of 7 chromosomes from *A. squarrosa*

Fig. 7.18 The origin of modern bread wheat, *Triticum aestivum*.

In North America, there is a species of fruit fly, *Rhagoletis pomonella*, which lives on hawthorn trees. The larvae feed on the hawthorn fruits. The flies mate on the trees on which they feed.

In 1864, it was noticed that some *Rhagoletis* had begun to feed on apple trees in the Hudson River Valley. Soon, apple trees all over North America were being attacked by the flies. Other populations of the same species of fly began to infest cherry trees.

Because the flies only mate on the trees on which they feed, these three populations of *Rhagoletis pomonella* are reproductively isolated. A fly which was born in an apple will grow up to feed and mate on apple trees, which it can only do with other flies which were born on apple trees. It will not breed with a fly which was born on a hawthorn or cherry tree. The three fly populations are reproductively isolated not only in *space* (because they are on different kinds of trees), but also in *time* (because the three kinds of fruits mature at different times of year, so the flies breed at different times of year).

Some biologists think that these three populations of fruit flies may eventually become three separate species. Studies of 24 enzymes in the flies show that there are already slight variations in them between the three populations, suggesting that their gene pools (all the alleles present in the population) are already diverging. Perhaps we are seeing the very early stages of sympatric speciation taking place. This kind of speciation could have been very important in the evolution of the many species of insects which live only on a single host species of plant. ■

Q2 Until the early 1960s, plant breeders tried to produce varieties of wheat resistant to diseases caused by fungi by using a succession of simply inherited, major genes. The action of these genes was rapidly overcome by fungal pests. Fortunately, there are varieties of wheat which exhibit a more durable resistance, but this has a complex pattern of inheritance. Such varieties are attacked mildly by most of the major fungal diseases, but are not severely damaged and are unaffected by new fungal strains.

However, it has been suggested that there is no longer any need for breeders to spend time selecting for disease resistance, since a wide range of highly effective fungicides exists. Such a policy would be unfortunate. Apart from other consequences, there is a serious risk that fungal pests will develop strains tolerant of the chemicals used to control them.

Box 7.1 *Spartina anglica* – speciation by polyploidy

Spartina anglica is a grass which grows in salt marshes. It is a very vigorous, successful plant, which in many places is considered an invasive weed. Yet, until about 1830, this species did not even exist.

Until 1829, a native grass called *Spartina maritima* grew in salt marshes in southern England. This grass is at the northern limit of its natural distribution here, and does not spread vigorously. In 1829, a different species called *Spartina alterniflora* was accidentally introduced from America, perhaps in shipping ballast, in the area around Southampton. The two species hybridised, to produce a sterile, diploid hybrid called *Spartina × townsendii*. Despite being sterile, this species spread quite

widely, because these grasses naturally reproduce asexually by means of underground rhizomes (stems).

At some point in time, chromosome doubling occurred in *S. × townsendii*, to produce a tetraploid plant. This plant is an allopolyploid. It has two sets of chromosomes from *S. maritima*, and two sets from *S. alterniflora*. It is fertile, because each chromosome can find a partner during meiosis. It is suggested that this happened in 1892, because this is when the rapid spread of the hybrid was first noticed; presumably, this was when fertile seeds were first being produced.

Fig 7.19 The cord grass, *Spartina alterniflora*, growing in Cape Cod, from where it was accidentally introduced to Southampton Water, England.

The new, more vigorous species, *Spartina anglica*, is a tetraploid hybrid of *S. alterniflora* and the native English *S. maritima*, which it has largely replaced.

Q2 cont.

(a) (i) Explain the difference between *simply inherited major genes* and *complex pattern of inheritance*. (2)

    (ii) Predict the type of phenotypic variation produced by each of these two types of inheritance. (2)

(b) Suggest how the action of major resistance genes in wheat could be rapidly overcome by fungal pests. (3)

(c) Briefly explain how selective breeding can be used to produce disease-resistant plants. (4)

UCLES 1995   (*Total 11 marks*)

Q3 The beetles belonging to the genus *Colophon* are unable to fly and are found on hilltops in South Africa. The dotted lines on the map show the distribution of three species.

Suggest an evolutionary explanation for each of the following statements.

(a) All of these beetles are of very similar general appearance. *(1)*

(b) There are slight differences between the species of *Colophon* found in the three areas. *(2)*

(c) The fact that beetles of the genus *Colophon* are unable to fly has been important in the evolution of twelve different species of the genus in a small area of South Africa. *(2)*

AEB 1995 *(Total 5 marks)*

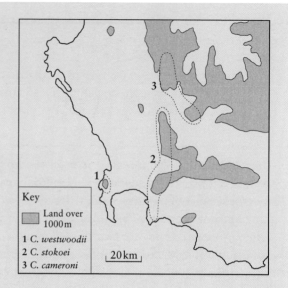

Key

Land over 1000m

1 C. *westwoodii*
2 C. *stokoei*
3 C. *cameroni*

20km

Q4 Rats and mice are common pests. Warfarin was developed as a poison to control rats and was very effective when first used in 1950.

Resistance to warfarin was first reported in British rats in 1958 and is now extremely common. Warfarin resistance in rats is determined by a single gene with two alleles W^S and W^R. Rats with the genotypes listed below have the characteristics shown.

$W^S W^S$ Normal rats susceptible to warfarin.

$W^S W^R$ Rats resistant to warfarin needing slightly more vitamin K than usual for full health.

$W^R W^R$ Rats resistant to warfarin but requiring very large amounts of vitamin K. They rarely survive.

(a) Explain why:

  (i) there was a very high frequency of W^S alleles in the British population of wild rats before 1950: *(1)*

  (ii) the frequency of W^R alleles in the wild rat population rose rapidly from 1958. *(2)*

(b) Explain what would be likely to happen to the frequency of W^R alleles if warfarin were no longer used. *(2)*

(c) Mice show continuous variation in their resistance to warfarin. What does this suggest about the genetic basis of warfarin resistance in mice? *(1)*

In humans, deaths from conditions where blood clots form inside blood vessels occur frequently in adults over the age of fifty. These conditions may be treated successfully with warfarin. However, some people possess a dominant allele which gives resistance to warfarin.

(d) Why would you not expect this allele to change in frequency? *(2)*

NEAB 1995 *(Total 8 marks)*

8 Photosynthesis and plant nutrition

All living organisms need energy to sustain life. This energy is obtained from organic molecules such as carbohydrates, fats and proteins. These molecules contain chemical energy. The initial formation of such molecules takes place in green plants which are able to transfer energy from sunlight into energy in carbohydrates. This process is called photosynthesis.

8.1 Energy and living organisms

Many processes which take place in living organisms require a supply of energy. These include:

- movement, for example locomotion of the whole organism using muscles or cilia (Section 3.13), circulation of fluids within animal bodies (Section 10.2) or movement of organelles within cells (Section 3.12),
- the synthesis of large molecules such as proteins from smaller molecules such as amino acids (Section 5.3),
- active transport of substances across cell surface membranes (Section 3.27),
- in mammals and birds, the production of heat for the maintenance of body temperature above that of the environment (Section 15.6).

For all of these processes except heat production, the immediate source of energy is almost always the chemical substance **adenosine triphosphate**, or **ATP**. The structure of ATP is shown in Fig. 1.23 on page 30. ATP molecules contain a relatively large amount of chemical energy in their molecular structure. This property is shared with many other molecules, but what makes ATP special is the ease with which living organisms can make use of some of this energy.

When one of the phosphate groups is removed from an ATP molecule, some energy is released.

$$ATP \longrightarrow ADP + P_i$$

released energy

The reaction is a hydrolysis reaction, and if it took place in a test tube the released energy would be dispersed, mostly as heat, to the environment. Living organisms, however, can use the energy that ATP releases in many different ways (Fig. 8.1).

You can think of ATP as the 'energy currency' of living organisms. Like money, it is constantly 'recycled'. ATP is the molecule from which energy can be quickly and easily used by a living cell. Other molecules, such as carbohydrates and fats, also contain a lot of energy, but the energy from these molecules cannot be accessed anywhere near as readily or directly as can the energy in ATP. Carbohydrates and fats act as energy *stores*, while ATP is energy *currency*.

Another advantage of ATP is that it provides energy in small 'packets'. The energy released from a single ATP molecule is often enough to supply the energy needs of a single chemical reaction.

As every cell needs a constant supply of energy, it must have a constant supply of ATP. Each cell has to make its own ATP. All living cells make ATP using energy from other molecules, especially glucose, in the process of **respiration**. Respiration is described in Chapter 9. In respiration, some of the chemical energy in the molecular structure of glucose is transferred to ATP. When ATP is used, this transferred energy is lost and so ATP has to be regenerated. The ATP is recycled.

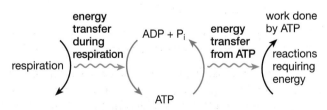

Energy from the breakdown of ATP

The coupling of ATP breakdown with another reaction

The breakdown of ATP releases energy.

By coupling the breakdown of ATP with a reaction that needs energy, energy can be transferred between the two reactions.

It is as if ATP breakdown 'drives' the energy-requiring reaction.

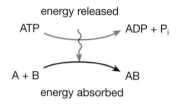

energy released

$$ATP \longrightarrow ADP + P_i$$

$$A + B \longrightarrow AB$$

energy absorbed

The coupling of the two reactions allows AB to be formed.

$$A + B \longrightarrow AB$$
an imaginary reaction that requires energy to occur

Movement of organelles along microtubules

ATP provides the energy to twist the heads of the kinesin molecules, causing the organelle's movement along the microtubule (Section 3.12).

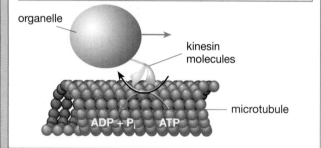

organelle

kinesin molecules

microtubule

ADP + P$_i$ ATP

Phosphorylation of glucose at the start of respiration

ATP activates glucose so that it is capable of being reorganised into fructose (Section 9.2).

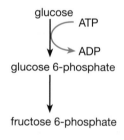

glucose

ATP

ADP

glucose 6-phosphate

fructose 6-phosphate

Active transport across the cell surface membrane

ATP provides the energy for the transport of a substance against the concentration gradient, which is opposite to the direction it would diffuse on its own accord.

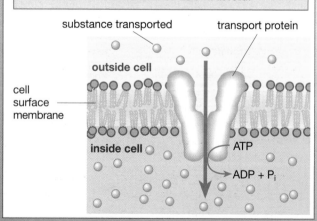

substance transported

transport protein

outside cell

cell surface membrane

inside cell

ATP

ADP + P$_i$

The activation of amino acids in protein synthesis

ATP provides the energy needed to join an amino acid to tRNA, which activates the amino acid so that it is capable of being linked to another in protein synthesis (Section 5.3).

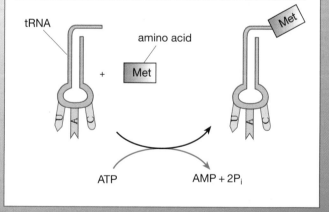

tRNA

amino acid

Met

+   Met

ATP

AMP + 2P$_i$

Fig. 8.1   The conversion of ATP to ADP or AMP supplies energy for many processes in living cells. A few examples are shown here.

PHOTOSYNTHESIS

8.2 Energy transfers in photosynthesis

In order to make large amounts of ATP, living cells need a supply of glucose or other organic molecules. Where do these glucose molecules come from? Where did the energy in the glucose molecules, which is transferred into the ATP molecules, originate?

Almost all the energy transferred to all the ATP molecules in living organisms originally came from energy in sunlight. (Read Box 8.1 if you would like to know why it is 'almost' all the energy, and not 'absolutely' all of it.) Green plants and some kinds of bacteria are able to transfer sunlight energy into energy trapped in the molecular structure of carbohydrates. This process is called **photosynthesis**.

In photosynthesis, green plants use the energy in sunlight to combine water and carbon dioxide to produce carbohydrates. The overall equation for this process is:

$$6CO_2 + 6H_2O \rightarrow C_6H_{12}O_6 + 6O_2$$
or
$$nCO_2 + nH_2O \rightarrow (CH_2O)_n + nO_2$$

Once carbohydrates such as glucose have been made, the plant can then convert some of them to other organic substances, such as oils, nucleic acids and proteins. Animals cannot make organic substances from inorganic ones, and rely entirely on plants for their supply of organic molecules. Without plants, animals would have no energy supply, nor a supply of carbon from which to build their bodies.

Photosynthesis happens inside chloroplasts, in the leaves of green plants. The structures of a leaf and a chloroplast are shown in Figs. 8.2 and 8.3.

8.3 A summary of photosynthesis

Photosynthesis uses two raw materials (**water and carbon dioxide**) and an energy source (**sunlight**). Some of the energy from sunlight is used to begin a chain of events in which hydrogen atoms from the water molecules are combined with carbon dioxide molecules to produce **sugars**. These sugars contain energy which was originally energy in the sunlight. The oxygen from the water molecules is given off as a waste product.

Box 8.1 Photoautotrophs and chemoautotrophs

An autotroph is an organism which can make all its own organic molecules from inorganic ones. It does not need to use organic molecules from somewhere else as an energy source; it gets its energy from a different source. Animals and fungi cannot do this and require organic food to supply them with energy. They are heterotrophs.

The autotrophs with which you will be most familiar are plants. Plants are photoautotrophs. Their energy source is sunlight, and they use this and two inorganic substances (water and carbon dioxide) to provide carbon, hydrogen and oxygen atoms to make carbohydrates. This process is photosynthesis. Many protoctists and some bacteria also photosynthesise.

There are other kinds of photoautotrophs which also use light as their energy source, but use different inorganic substances to provide the electrons and atoms they need to synthesise organic molecules. Some bacteria, for example, use carbon dioxide to provide carbon and oxygen and sunlight to provide energy (just as plants do), but use hydrogen sulphide, H_2S, instead of water to supply electrons. Just as oxygen is released as a waste product by green plants, so sulphur is a waste product of these bacteria.

Other autotrophs do not use light as an energy source, but use chemical energy sources. They are chemoautotrophs. There are many different chemicals which can be used. For example, nitrifying bacteria obtain energy by oxidising ammonia to nitrite, or by oxidising nitrite to nitrate. The nitrifying bacteria are a very important group of chemoautotrophs, and their central role in the nitrogen cycle is described in Section 19.7. They need no organic food materials, nor do they need light as an energy source. They do, however, require oxygen, because the reactions which provide their energy supply involve combining oxygen with nitrogen-containing ions.

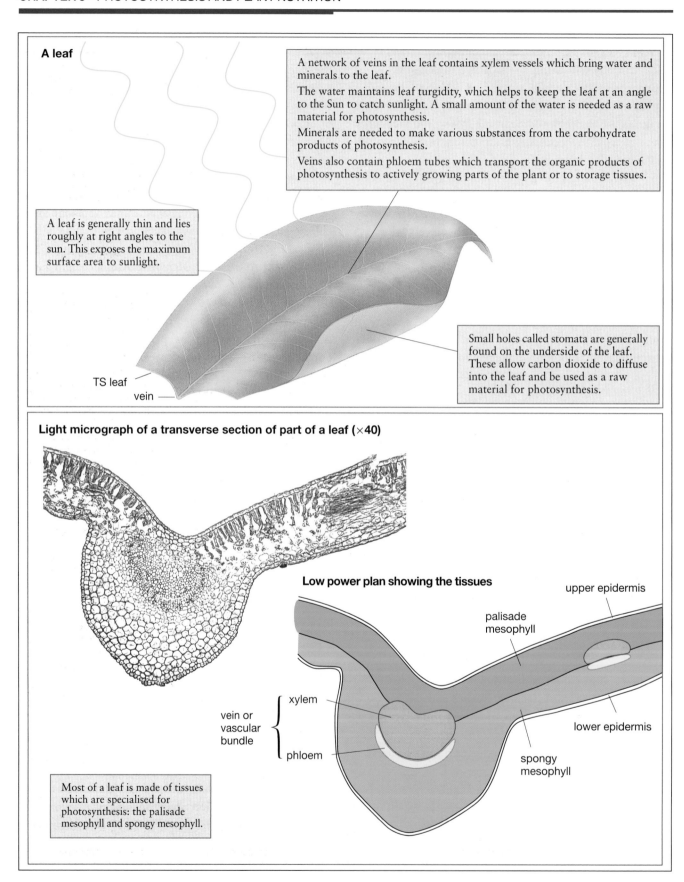

A leaf

A network of veins in the leaf contains xylem vessels which bring water and minerals to the leaf.

The water maintains leaf turgidity, which helps to keep the leaf at an angle to the Sun to catch sunlight. A small amount of the water is needed as a raw material for photosynthesis.

Minerals are needed to make various substances from the carbohydrate products of photosynthesis.

Veins also contain phloem tubes which transport the organic products of photosynthesis to actively growing parts of the plant or to storage tissues.

A leaf is generally thin and lies roughly at right angles to the sun. This exposes the maximum surface area to sunlight.

Small holes called stomata are generally found on the underside of the leaf. These allow carbon dioxide to diffuse into the leaf and be used as a raw material for photosynthesis.

TS leaf

vein

Light micrograph of a transverse section of part of a leaf (×40)

Low power plan showing the tissues

upper epidermis

palisade mesophyll

xylem

vein or vascular bundle

phloem

lower epidermis

spongy mesophyll

Most of a leaf is made of tissues which are specialised for photosynthesis: the palisade mesophyll and spongy mesophyll.

Fig. 8.2   The structure of a leaf.

High power detail of a transverse section of a leaf showing cells

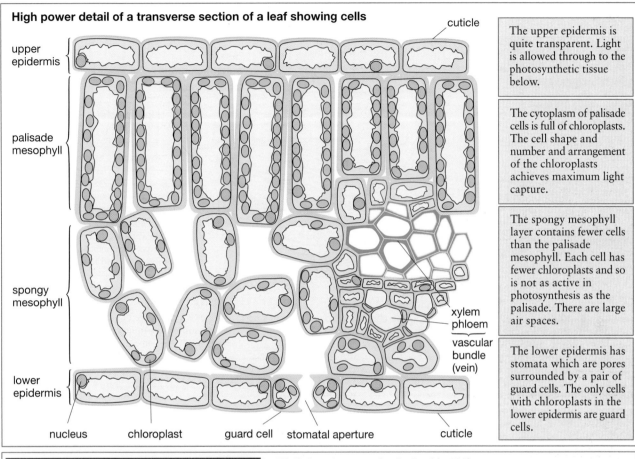

upper epidermis

palisade mesophyll

spongy mesophyll

lower epidermis

cuticle

xylem
phloem

vascular bundle (vein)

nucleus   chloroplast   guard cell   stomatal aperture   cuticle

The upper epidermis is quite transparent. Light is allowed through to the photosynthetic tissue below.

The cytoplasm of palisade cells is full of chloroplasts. The cell shape and number and arrangement of the chloroplasts achieves maximum light capture.

The spongy mesophyll layer contains fewer cells than the palisade mesophyll. Each cell has fewer chloroplasts and so is not as active in photosynthesis as the palisade. There are large air spaces.

The lower epidermis has stomata which are pores surrounded by a pair of guard cells. The only cells with chloroplasts in the lower epidermis are guard cells.

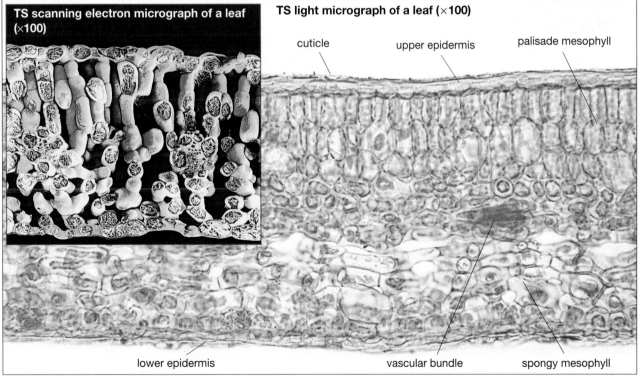

TS scanning electron micrograph of a leaf (×100)

TS light micrograph of a leaf (×100)

cuticle   upper epidermis   palisade mesophyll

lower epidermis   vascular bundle   spongy mesophyll

Fig. 8.2   cont.

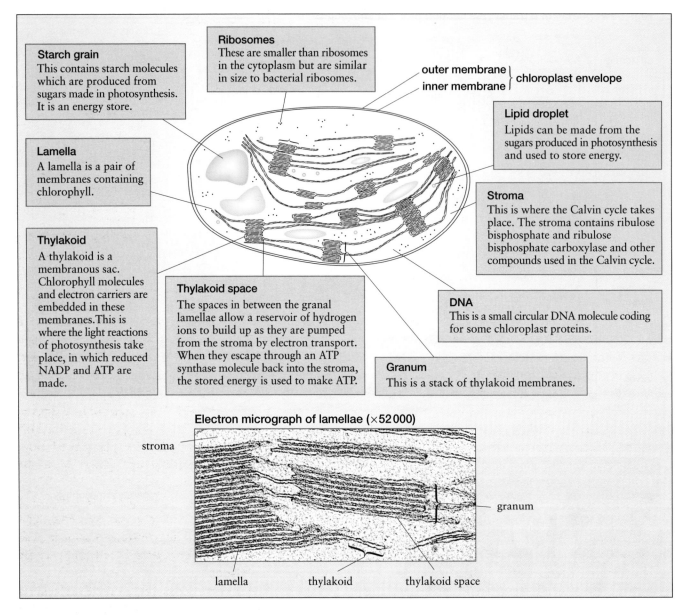

Starch grain
This contains starch molecules which are produced from sugars made in photosynthesis. It is an energy store.

Ribosomes
These are smaller than ribosomes in the cytoplasm but are similar in size to bacterial ribosomes.

outer membrane ⎫
inner membrane ⎭ chloroplast envelope

Lipid droplet
Lipids can be made from the sugars produced in photosynthesis and used to store energy.

Lamella
A lamella is a pair of membranes containing chlorophyll.

Stroma
This is where the Calvin cycle takes place. The stroma contains ribulose bisphosphate and ribulose bisphosphate carboxylase and other compounds used in the Calvin cycle.

Thylakoid
A thylakoid is a membranous sac. Chlorophyll molecules and electron carriers are embedded in these membranes. This is where the light reactions of photosynthesis take place, in which reduced NADP and ATP are made.

Thylakoid space
The spaces in between the granal lamellae allow a reservoir of hydrogen ions to build up as they are pumped from the stroma by electron transport. When they escape through an ATP synthase molecule back into the stroma, the stored energy is used to make ATP.

DNA
This is a small circular DNA molecule coding for some chloroplast proteins.

Granum
This is a stack of thylakoid membranes.

Electron micrograph of lamellae (×52 000)

stroma

granum

lamella   thylakoid   thylakoid space

Fig. 8.3   The structure of a chloroplast.

The conversion of water and carbon dioxide to sugars and oxygen takes place in several steps. These steps can be divided into two stages (Fig. 8.4).

● **The light reaction, or the light-dependent stage**
This is the first stage of photosynthesis. Its function is to make **reduced NADP** (NADPH) and to transfer light energy to **ATP**.

Energy from sunlight causes electrons to be emitted from **chlorophyll** molecules. Some of the energy from these electrons is used to make ATP molecules. Some is used to make reduced NADP. Water molecules are split to produce electrons, which replace the electrons that were ejected by light from the chlorophyll molecules, and hydrogen ions and electrons to help with the production of ATP. Oxygen is also produced and given off as a by-product.

● **The light-independent stage, or the Calvin cycle**
This stage incorporates the inorganic molecule carbon dioxide into a carbohydrate.

The reduced NADP and ATP which have been made in the light-dependent stage are used to convert carbon dioxide into sugars. No further input of light is needed for

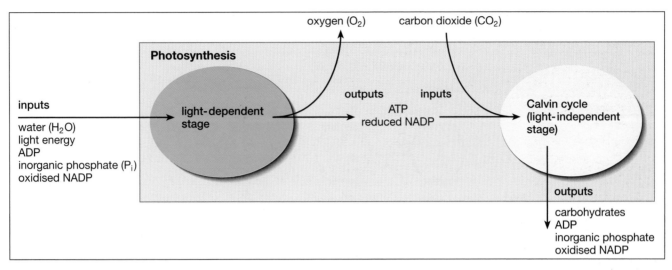

Fig. 8.4 Inputs and outputs in the stages of photosynthesis.

this stage, although, of course, it cannot take place unless the light-dependent stage is producing a good supply of reduced NADP and ATP.

In green plants these processes all occur inside **chloroplasts**, mostly in the leaves. The light-dependent stage takes place in the membranes inside the chloroplast, which form **thylakoids** that are stacked in layers called **grana**. The Calvin cycle takes place in the **stroma** of the chloroplast.

8.4 A more detailed look at the light-dependent reaction

White light, such as that which reaches the Earth from the Sun, is made up of light of many different wavelengths. We see different wavelengths of light as different colours. Light with short wavelengths, of around 450 to 500 nm, is seen as blue light, while longer wavelengths, of around 650 to 700 nm, appear as red light.

Green plants contain coloured substances, or **pigments**, which can absorb some wavelengths of light. The main pigment is **chlorophyll**, which looks green because it reflects green light. It can absorb most of the other wavelengths of light, especially red and blue light.

Chlorophyll molecules are found on the membranes inside chloroplasts. When light hits a chlorophyll molecule, some of the energy in the light is absorbed by the chlorophyll. This absorbed energy causes an electron to be emitted from the chlorophyll. The electron possesses some of the energy from the light. It is a high-energy electron (Fig. 8.5).

The electron is passed along a chain of **electron carriers**. These are molecules which can pick up the electron and

then pass it on to another molecule. When they pick up the electron they are **reduced**, and when they lose it again they are **oxidised**. In the chloroplast the electron carriers lie in the membrane of the thylakoid, so that the electron can easily be passed from one to the next.

As the electron is passed along, some of its energy is used to synthesise ATP. The making of ATP from ADP and inorganic phosphate (P_i) is called **phosphorylation**. As this is being done using energy from light, it is given the name **photophosphorylation**.

The electron is then passed on to a second, different chlorophyll molecule which has also been excited by light to emit an electron. Because the electron does not go back to where it came from, this process is called **non-cyclic photophosphorylation**.

The electron from the second chlorophyll molecule is not used to make ATP. Instead, two of these electrons (e^-) are taken up by a molecule of oxidised **NADP** (NADP$^+$), together with a hydrogen ion (H$^+$), to form **reduced NADP** (NADPH).

$$NADP^+ \qquad + H^+ + 2e^- \rightarrow \qquad NADPH$$
oxidised NADP $\qquad\qquad\qquad$ reduced NADP

The first chlorophyll molecule is still short of an electron. It gets one from a water molecule which is split to produce hydrogen ions, electrons and oxygen:

$$H_2O \rightarrow 2H^+ + 2e^- + \tfrac{1}{2}O_2$$

This water-splitting process is catalysed by an enzyme in the chloroplast. It only happens when light falls onto the chloroplast, and is called **photolysis** of water.

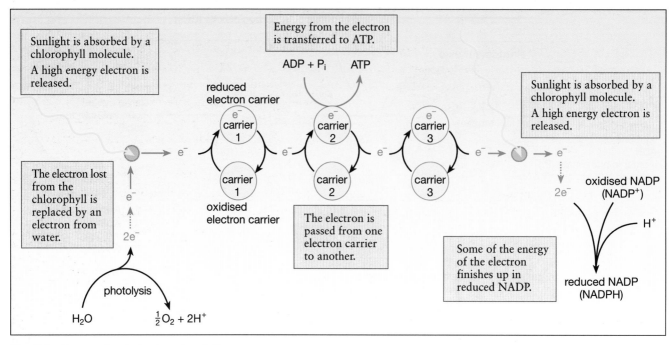

Fig. 8.5 Non-cyclic photophosphorylation.

Q1 The blue dye DCPIP can be converted to colourless reduced DCPIP by gaining electrons. This is summarised below.

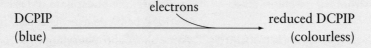

$$\underset{\text{(blue)}}{\text{DCPIP}} \xrightarrow{\text{electrons}} \underset{\text{(colourless)}}{\text{reduced DCPIP}}$$

A suspension of chloroplasts was made by grinding fresh leaves in buffer solution and centrifuging the mixture. Tubes were then prepared and treated in the following way.

Tube	Contents	Treatment	Colour at start	Colour after 20 minutes
A	1 cm³ chloroplast suspension 5 cm³ DCPIP	illuminated strongly	blue/green	green
B	1 cm³ buffer solution 5 cm³ DCPIP	illuminated strongly	blue	blue
C	1 cm³ chloroplast suspension 5 cm³ DCPIP	left in the dark	blue/green	blue/green

(a) (i) In tube **A**, from where do the electrons come that reduce the DCPIP? (1)

(ii) What normally happens to these electrons in a photosynthesising leaf? (1)

(b) The chloroplast suspension may be contaminated with mitochondria. Explain the evidence that the presence of mitochondria was not responsible for reduction of the DCPIP. (2)

AEB 1994 *(Total 4 marks)*

Box 8.2 Pigments, absorption spectra and action spectra

A pigment is a molecule which absorbs some wavelengths (colours) of light but not others. The wavelengths it does not absorb are either reflected, or transmitted through the substance. These unabsorbed wavelengths enter our eyes, so we see the pigment in these colours.

Chloroplasts contain several different pigments. The majority of the pigment molecules are **chlorophyll** *a* and **chlorophyll** *b* (Fig. 8.6). Both types of chlorophyll absorb similar wavelengths of light, but chlorophyll *a* absorbs slightly higher wavelengths than chlorophyll *b*. This is shown in Fig. 8.7; this kind of graph is called an **absorption spectrum**. You can see that neither of these chlorophylls absorb much light in the green region of the spectrum, which is why chlorophyll appears green.

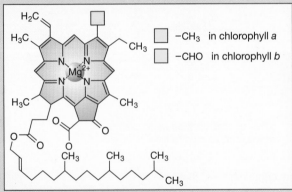

Fig. 8.6 Chlorophylls *a* and *b*.

Other pigments found in chloroplasts include **carotenoids**. These absorb a wide range of short-wavelength light, including more green light than is absorbed by the chlorophylls (Fig. 8.7). (What colour will carotenoids appear to be?) Carotenoids are **accessory pigments**. They help by absorbing wavelengths of light which otherwise could not be used by the plant, and passing on the energy from this light to chlorophyll (see Box 8.3). So, with both types of chlorophyll, and carotenoids, in a chloroplast, a wider range of wavelengths of light can be used in photosynthesis than with any one pigment alone.

If you supply a plant with light of a single wavelength and measure the rate of photosynthesis,

you find that the rate is greatest with wavelengths around 680 to 700 nm, with another, lower, peak at around 460 nm. A graph of rate of photosynthesis against wavelength is called an **action spectrum**, and is shown in Fig. 8.8. As you would expect, the shape of the action spectrum is very similar to the 'combined' shapes of the absorption spectra of the individual pigments shown in Fig. 8.7. This similarity can be taken as evidence that the light energy absorbed by the pigments is used in photosynthesis.

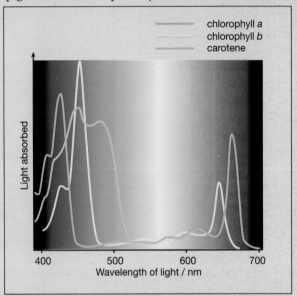

Fig. 8.7 Absorption spectra of chlorophylls *a* and *b* and carotene.

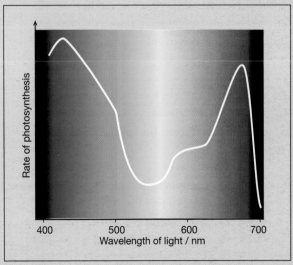

Fig. 8.8 Action spectrum for photosynthesis.

Box 8.3 Photosystems

Chlorophyll molecules do not act alone. In the thylakoid membranes, many chlorophyll and other molecules are grouped together to form a **photosystem**. When light falls onto a photosystem, the pigment molecules absorb energy and 'funnel' it to a pair of chlorophyll *a* molecules which emit electrons (Fig. 8.9).

photosystem I are combined with a hydrogen ion and picked up by NADP. Photosystem II is reoxidised by absorbing electrons from the photolysis of water.

Thus, electrons effectively flow from water, to photosystem II, along a chain of electron carriers

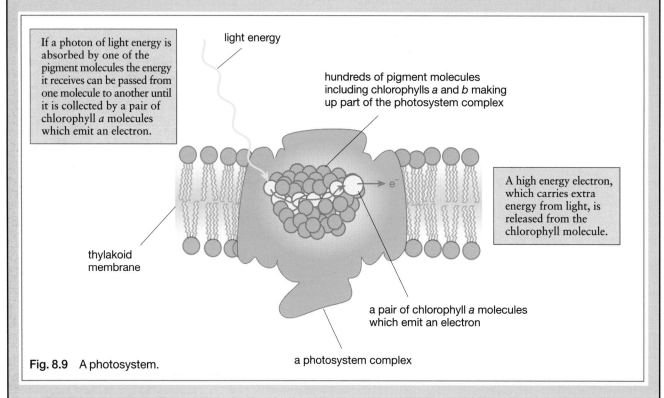

If a photon of light energy is absorbed by one of the pigment molecules the energy it receives can be passed from one molecule to another until it is collected by a pair of chlorophyll *a* molecules which emit an electron.

light energy

hundreds of pigment molecules including chlorophylls *a* and *b* making up part of the photosystem complex

A high energy electron, which carries extra energy from light, is released from the chlorophyll molecule.

e⁻

thylakoid membrane

a pair of chlorophyll *a* molecules which emit an electron

a photosystem complex

Fig. 8.9   A photosystem.

In the chloroplasts of green plants, there are two kinds of photosystems, containing slightly different collections of chlorophyll and other molecules arranged in different ways. **Photosystem I** absorbs light with wavelengths of 700 nm. **Photosystem II** absorbs light with wavelengths of 680 nm or less. Photosystem II also contains an enzyme which catalyses the splitting of water molecules.

In non-cyclic photophosphorylation, an electron emitted from photosystem II is passed along an electron transport chain and donated to photosystem I. Two of the electrons ejected from

(where some of their energy is used to make ATP), then to photosystem I and finally to NADP, forming reduced NADP. This pathway is shown in Fig. 8.10, which is often called the **Z scheme**. This diagram shows not only the pathway taken by an electron, but also its relative energy level. The energy level of the electron is raised twice: once when it is ejected from a chlorophyll molecule when photosystem II absorbs light energy, and again when it is ejected from a chlorophyll molecule when photosystem I absorbs light energy. It is these energy transfers which provide the energy to make ATP as the electrons pass along the chain of electron carriers, and also to make reduced NADP.

Box 8.3 Photosystems (cont.)

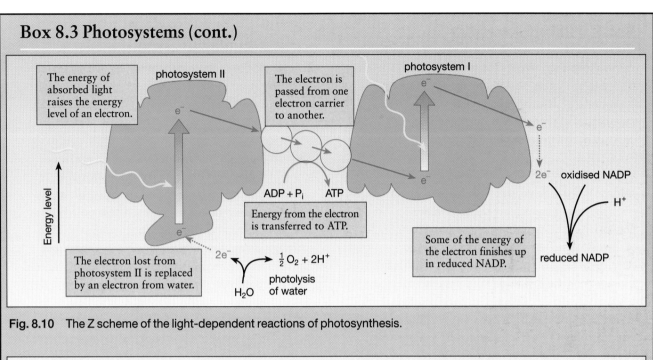

Fig. 8.10   The Z scheme of the light-dependent reactions of photosynthesis.

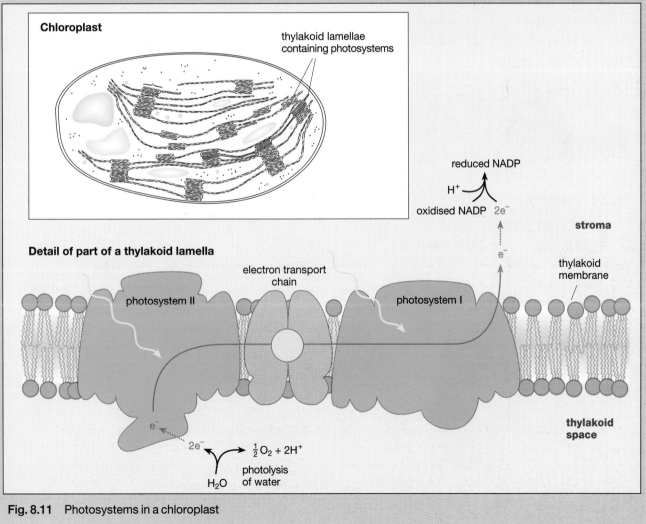

Fig. 8.11   Photosystems in a chloroplast

Box 8.4 Photophosphorylation

Photophosphorylation is the synthesis of ATP from ADP and inorganic phosphate, using the energy from sunlight. It happens on the thylakoid membranes of chloroplasts during the light-dependent reactions of photosynthesis.

When an electron has been emitted from a chlorophyll molecule, it is passed along a chain of electron carriers which are situated in the phospholipid bilayer that makes up the membrane of the thylakoid. As the carriers pick up the electrons, they also pick up hydrogen ions (protons) from *outside* the thylakoid, and pass them *into* the space inside the thylakoid. Thus, the passage of the electrons along the chain of carriers results in a build-up of hydrogen ions, which have a positive charge, inside the thylakoid space. In this way, a hydrogen ion and electrical potential gradient is set

up across the thylakoid membranes, with a high concentration in the thylakoid space and a lower concentration in the stroma of the chloroplast (Fig. 8.12).

Within the thylakoid membranes, there are large protein molecules called ATP synthase (or just ATPase). They are large enough to be visible as spheres in electron micrographs. These proteins span the membrane and allow hydrogen ions to pass through them, down their concentration gradient and electrical potential gradient, out of the thylakoid space and into the stroma. This movement provides enough energy for the ATP synthases to be able to add phosphate groups to ADP molecules to make ATP. The passage of approximately three hydrogen ions provides enough energy for the synthesis of one ATP molecule.

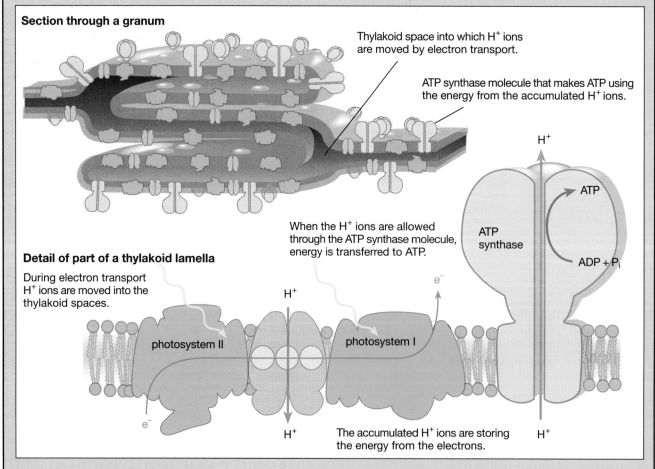

Section through a granum

Thylakoid space into which H$^+$ ions are moved by electron transport.

ATP synthase molecule that makes ATP using the energy from the accumulated H$^+$ ions.

When the H$^+$ ions are allowed through the ATP synthase molecule, energy is transferred to ATP.

Detail of part of a thylakoid lamella

During electron transport H$^+$ ions are moved into the thylakoid spaces.

H$^+$

ATP synthase

H$^+$

ATP

ADP + P$_i$

e$^-$

photosystem II

photosystem I

e$^-$

H$^+$

H$^+$

H$^+$

The accumulated H$^+$ ions are storing the energy from the electrons.

Fig. 8.12 Photophosphorylation.

Overall, the process can be summarised by the equation:

$$2NADP^+ + 2H_2O \rightarrow 2NADPH + O_2 + 2H^+$$

Some of the oxygen is used by the plant in respiration, but much of it is released to the environment as a gas.

So, at the end of the light-dependent reaction, two new substances have been made. Both of them – ATP and reduced NADP – contain energy which was derived from the sunlight which fell onto the chlorophyll molecules. These two substances will be used in the next stage – the light-independent reactions.

Q2 (a) Describe how ATP is produced as a result of light striking chlorophyll molecules. *(2)*

(b) ATP is made during photosynthesis, but plants also make ATP during respiration. Explain why this is necessary. *(2)*

AEB 1995 (modified)   *(Total 4 marks)*

8.5 A more detailed look at the light-independent reaction, or Calvin cycle

In the Calvin cycle, hydrogen is added to carbon dioxide to make carbohydrates. The hydrogen comes from reduced NADP, and the energy needed to drive the reactions comes from ATP and reduced NADP. The reduced NADP and ATP were made in the light-dependent reactions.

Fig. 8.13 shows the main stages in the Calvin cycle. Carbon dioxide from the air diffuses through the stomata into the leaf, into the air spaces in the mesophyll, into a palisade cell and into a chloroplast. Here, in the stroma, it meets an enzyme called **ribulose bisphosphate carboxylase**. This enzyme, otherwise known as **RuBP carboxylase**, or **Rubisco**, is thought to be the most abundant enzyme in the world. The stroma of every chloroplast in every green plant is full of this enzyme.

Rubisco catalyses the combination of carbon dioxide with a five-carbon sugar called **ribulose bisphosphate**, or **RuBP**.

At this point the carbon becomes part of a molecule made by the plant, and is said to be **fixed**. The addition of a carbon dioxide molecule to the ribulose bisphosphate briefly forms a six-carbon molecule, but this immediately splits to form two molecules which each contain three carbons. They are called **glycerate 3-phosphate**, or **GP** for short.

RuBP + carbon dioxide $\xrightarrow{\text{Rubisco}}$ 2 glycerate 3-phosphates
5 carbons   1 carbon   2 × 3 carbons

At this point, the products of the light-dependent reaction, reduced NADP and ATP, are needed. The reduced NADP and some of the ATP used supply energy and hydrogen atoms needed to reduce the GP to produce **triose phosphate**. Triose phosphate is a three-carbon phosphorylated sugar.

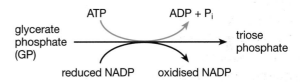

About one-sixth of the total amount of triose phosphate made is then used to make other carbohydrates (such as glucose, cellulose or starch), amino acids, fatty acids or glycerol. The remaining five-sixths is converted back to RuBP again. If this was not done, the plant would quickly run out of RuBP. The regeneration of RuBP uses up more of the ATP from the light reaction. It is this regeneration which makes this process a *cycle*.

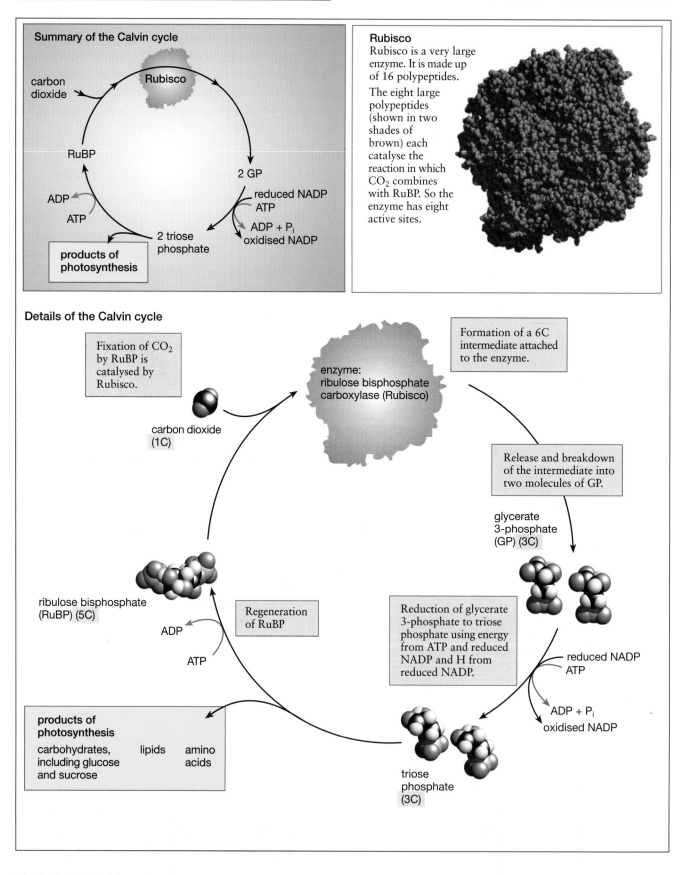

Fig. 8.13 The Calvin cycle.

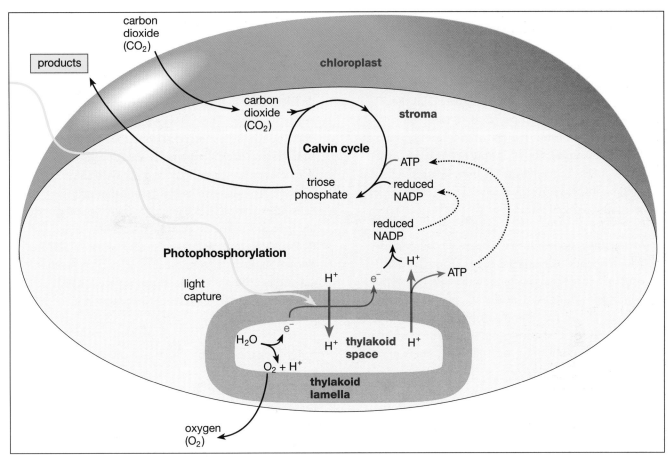

Fig. 8.14 Overview of the pathways of photosynthesis in a chloroplast.

Q3 The diagram shows the main stages of the light-independent reaction in photosynthesis.

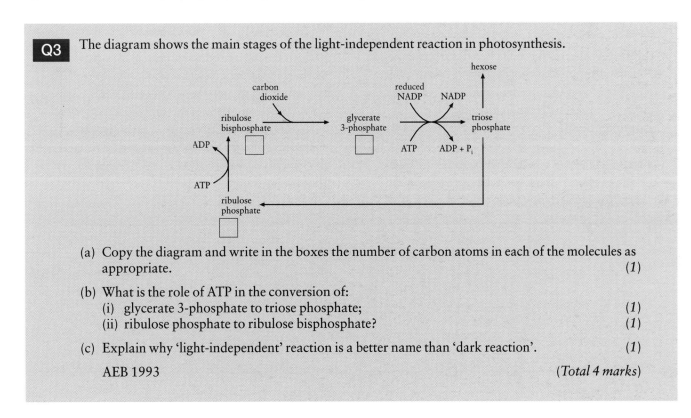

(a) Copy the diagram and write in the boxes the number of carbon atoms in each of the molecules as appropriate. *(1)*

(b) What is the role of ATP in the conversion of:
  (i) glycerate 3-phosphate to triose phosphate; *(1)*
  (ii) ribulose phosphate to ribulose bisphosphate? *(1)*

(c) Explain why 'light-independent' reaction is a better name than 'dark reaction'. *(1)*

AEB 1993 *(Total 4 marks)*

Box 8.5 C$_3$ and C$_4$ plants

To investigate the sequence of events in the Calvin cycle, a photosynthesising plant can be supplied with carbon dioxide in which the carbon is the heavy radioactive isotope ^{14}C. If you stop the process after various periods of time, and find out in which substances the ^{14}C is now present, you can work out the sequence in which these substances are made. This was how the events of the Calvin cycle were first worked out.

When this is done, the first detectable compound which is made using the labelled carbon dioxide is usually a three-carbon compound (GP). Plants in which this is the case are called C$_3$ plants. However, in some plants, for example tropical grasses and cereals, the first labelled compound to be made is a four-carbon compound, oxaloacetate. These plants are called C$_4$ plants.

Why should tropical grasses need to do something different?

The enzyme Rubisco is also able to catalyse the combination of *oxygen* with RuBP, rather than *carbon dioxide*. This results in the loss of RuBP which could be used for carbon dioxide fixation. The process also results in the loss of carbon dioxide from the plant. As this process has the overall effect of taking in oxygen and giving out carbon dioxide, and only happens in bright light, it is called **photorespiration**.

High light intensity and high temperatures increase the rate of photorespiration. Plants growing in the tropics live in just these conditions.

Tropical grasses manage to avoid photorespiration. They do this by keeping RuBP and Rubisco well away from high oxygen concentrations. The cells containing these two compounds are arranged around the vascular bundles and are called **bundle sheath cells** (Fig. 8.15). They have no direct contact with the air. Carbon dioxide is absorbed by another group of cells, the **mesophyll cells**, which *are* in contact with air spaces. These cells contain an enzyme called **PEP carboxylase**, which catalyses the combination of carbon dioxide from the air with a three-carbon substance called phosphoenolpyruvate, or **PEP**. The compound formed from this reaction is oxaloacetate.

Still inside the mesophyll cell, the oxaloacetate is converted to malate, and this malate is passed into the bundle sheath cells. Here, carbon dioxide is removed from the malate molecules and delivered to RuBP by Rubisco in the usual way. The Calvin cycle then proceeds as normal. Fig. 8.15 shows how the malate from the mesophyll cells is recycled to begin its carbon dioxide delivery round once again.

Some of the most productive crop plants in the world are C$_4$ plants. Sugarcane and maize are good examples. Sugarcane is especially efficient, converting around 8% of the sunlight energy which falls on a field of it into energy in carbohydrates. C$_3$ plants growing in a similar climate would be far less efficient, because of the wasteful process of photorespiration.

Box 8.5 C₃ and C₄ plants (cont.)

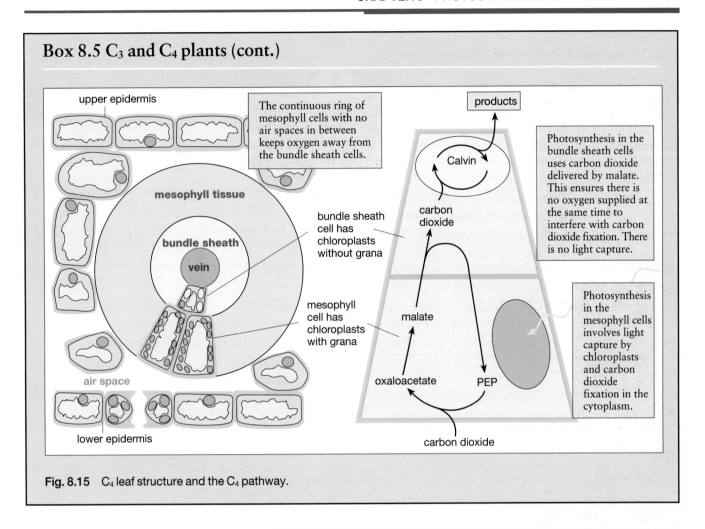

Fig. 8.15   C₄ leaf structure and the C₄ pathway.

Q4   The map below shows the distribution of grasses using the C₄ mechanism in different parts of North America. Each line shows the percentage of C₄ grasses compared with the total number of grasses in that region.

(a) Suggest a reason for the distribution of C₄ grasses in the figure. (2)

The graph below shows the distribution of C₃ and C₄ plants at different altitudes in Texas.

(b) (i) Examine the graph and find the approximate optimum altitude in metres for each type of plant. (2)

   (ii) Suggest reasons for the trends in distribution of each type of plant. (4)

UCLES 1992 (*Total 8 marks*)

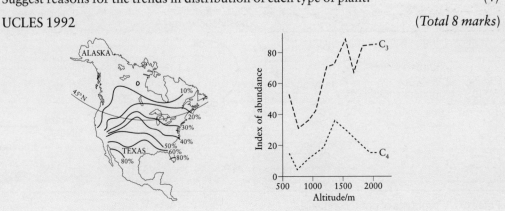

PLANT NUTRITION

8.6 Using triose phosphates to make other substances

The triose phosphate made in photosynthesis forms the basis of all the other carbon-containing substances in a green plant. These include other carbohydrates, lipids, proteins, nucleic acids and chlorophyll (Fig. 8.16).

● Carbohydrates

A large proportion of the triose phosphate is converted to hexose sugars, especially **glucose** and **fructose**. These may be used in respiration (Section 9.1) to provide ATP for the plant cell.

If carbohydrate is to be transported from the leaf cell where it was made to another part of the plant, then the disaccharide **sucrose** is made by linking together a glucose and a fructose molecule. The sucrose is then exported from the cell and loaded into the phloem sieve elements for translocation to other areas of the plant (Section 11.8).

For storage purposes, many glucose molecules are linked together to form **starch** molecules. These are stored as starch grains inside the chloroplast. Other storage tissues, such as potato tubers, store starch inside plastids called amyloplasts (Section 3.21).

If the plant is growing, then large amounts of **cellulose** are made, by linking together many glucose molecules, to form new cell walls.

● Lipids

Triose phosphates can be converted into **acetylcoenzyme A**, which is then converted into **fatty acids**. These are combined with glycerol from glycerol phosphate, formed from triose phosphate, to make **triglycerides** (mostly for storage) and **phospholipids** (for cell membranes).

● Proteins

To make amino acids (and hence proteins), plants need a nitrogen source. They are unable to use nitrogen from the air because it is much too unreactive. Most plants obtain their nitrogen as **nitrate ions**, NO_3^-, which they take up from the soil by active transport (Section 3.27). Inside the plant cells nitrate is reduced to **ammonium** ions, NH_4^+.

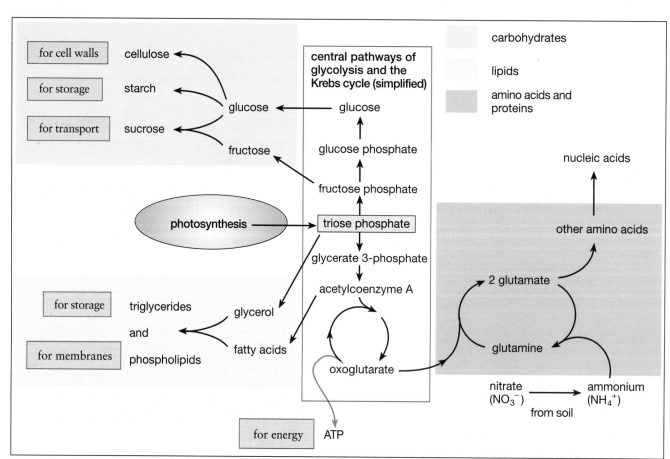

Fig. 8.16 Fates of the products of photosynthesis.

This may happen in the root, or the nitrate may first be transported to leaves, and ammonium made there.

The nitrogen from the ammonium ions is then transferred to a substance called oxoglutarate which is made from triose phosphate. (Oxoglutarate is formed in the Krebs cycle, so you can follow the pathway by which it is made from triose phosphate if you look at Fig. 9.3 - but you do not need to remember this!) This produces the amino acid **glutamine**. Other amino acids can then be made by transferring the amino group, NH_2, from one compound to another, in a process called **transamination**.

Once nitrogen has been incorporated into molecules in this way, the plant can use these molecules to make other nitrogen-containing compounds. These include **nucleotides** (e.g. in DNA and RNA) and also **chlorophyll**. Nucleotides also contain phosphate, while chlorophyll also contains magnesium. Both of these substances are obtained from the soil.

8.7 Factors affecting the rate of photosynthesis

The rate at which a plant converts carbon dioxide and water into sugars is affected by a number of factors. A limited supply of either of the two raw materials, **carbon dioxide** or **water**, or of the energy supply, **sunlight**, will

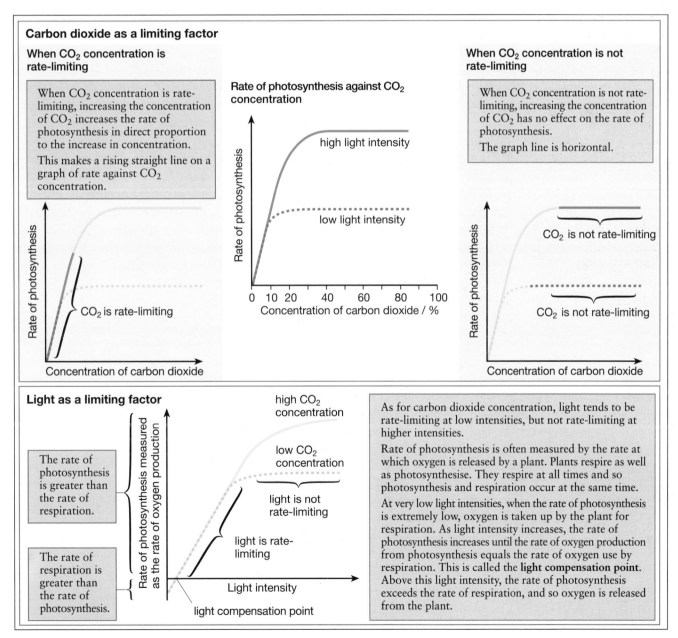

Fig. 8.17 Rate-limiting factors in photosynthesis.

put a limit on the maximum rate at which photosynthesis can proceed. **Temperature** may also affect the rate. The plant's own physiology and structure, for example the amount of chlorophyll in its leaves, can limit the rate of photosynthesis even when all these four factors are at ideal levels.

At any one time, the factor which is in the shortest supply is likely to be the one which is determining the rate at which photosynthesis can proceed, and this factor is said to be the **limiting factor**. For example, if a plant has plenty of light and water but only a very little carbon dioxide, then the rate of photosynthesis will be determined by the amount of carbon dioxide available. Carbon dioxide is the limiting factor. If the plant is provided with more carbon dioxide, it will photosynthesise faster (Fig. 8.17). However, if it is given more light, this will make no difference to the rate of photosynthesis, because it already has as much light as it can use at this concentration of carbon dioxide.

Over a warm 24-hour period in summer in a temperate country, when light intensity is high during daylight hours, the limiting factors for photosynthesis vary. At night, there is no photosynthesis as there is no light. As the sun rises and light levels gradually rise, photosynthesis begins, initially at a very low rate. The rate of photosynthesis increases as light increases, showing that at this time of day light is the limiting factor. By midday, with plenty of light available, carbon dioxide will probably become the limiting factor. The air normally contains only about 0.03% to 0.04% carbon dioxide, far less than a warm, well-watered plant with plenty of light could make use of. Growers of crops under glass often add extra carbon dioxide to the atmosphere in the glasshouses during the day, to increase photosynthetic rates and therefore crop yields.

If water is in short supply, then photosynthesis slows down. However, water has so many essential functions in a plant that this effect is not straightforward; long before the supply of water as a raw material for photosynthesis becomes a problem, the plant has probably already wilted (Section 16.2) and shut down some of its metabolic activities.

Temperature has little effect on the rate at which the light reaction of photosynthesis proceeds, because the energy driving these reactions is supplied by light, not heat. However, the Calvin cycle (light-independent reaction) is enzyme-controlled, and proceeds at a greater rate at higher temperatures, up to an optimum of about 25 °C or 30 °C; this varies in different species of plants. The situation is complicated because at high temperatures the enzyme Rubisco tends to catalyse a different reaction, as well as the fixation of carbon dioxide, resulting in the loss of carbon dioxide from the plant. This is called photorespiration, and is described in Box 8.5 together with a strategy which some plants have evolved to prevent it from happening. ■

Q5 In one approach to harnessing the Sun's energy, chemists mimic the photosynthetic process. A sensitiser (**S**) absorbs a photon of light and becomes excited. An electron passes from the excited sensitiser to an 'electron relay', methyl viologen (**MV**). This passes on an electron to a colloidal platinum catalyst (**P**). Here, water is split to produce hydrogen and hydroxyl ions.

$$\xrightarrow{\text{light}} S \xrightarrow{\text{electron}} MV \xrightarrow{\text{electron}} P \begin{cases} \longrightarrow H^+ \; OH^- \\ \longleftarrow H_2O \end{cases}$$

(a) State **three** ways in which this chemical system resembles photosynthesis. (3)

Methyl viologen (**MV**) is better known as the weedkiller, paraquat.

(b) Suggest how paraquat acts as a weedkiller. (2)

UCLES 1992 (modified) (*Total 5 marks*)

Q6 The graph below shows the effect of temperature on the rate of photosynthesis in two grasses, *Agropyron* and *Bouteloua*.

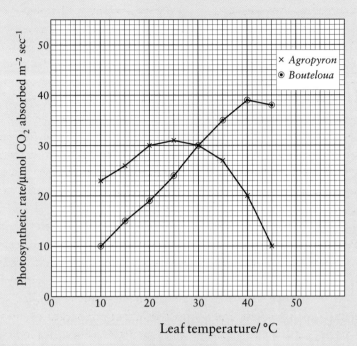

Leaf temperature/ °C

(a) From the graph, find the rate of photosynthesis at 22 °C for each of the grasses. (2)

(b) Suggest which of the two grasses is likely to grow faster in a tropical climate. Give a reason for your answer. (2)

(c) (i) Suggest why the rate of photosynthesis declines at high temperatures. (1)
   (ii) State **two** factors which can be limiting in photosynthesis. (2)

(d) Describe a simple method that you could use in the laboratory to investigate the effect of temperature on the rate of photosynthesis in an aquatic plant. (4)

London 1995 (*Total 11 marks*)

Q7 The diagram below shows the main steps in the light-independent stage of photosynthesis.

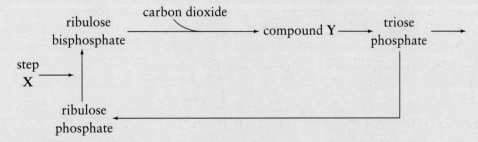

(a) For what is ATP used in step **X**? (1)

(b) Name compound **Y**. (1)

AEB 1995 (modified) (*Total 2 marks*)

Q8 The diagram below is a vertical section through the leaf of a plant.

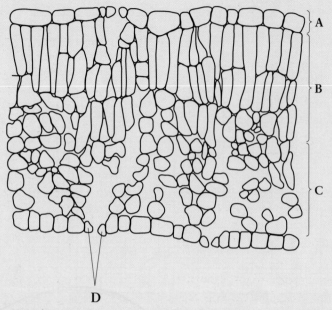

(a) (i) Name the tissues labelled **A** to **C** and state the main function of each. (6)

	Name	Main function
A		
B		
C		

(ii) Name **two** other tissues that are found in leaves. (2)

(b) (i) State the name of the cells labelled **D**. (1)

(ii) Describe briefly the function of these cells during the day and at night. (4)

UCLES 1994 *(Total 13 marks)*

9 Respiration

Respiration is a process which makes ATP using energy in organic molecules such as glucose. It has three main stages – glycolysis, the Krebs cycle and oxidative phosphorylation.

9.1 An outline of respiration

Glucose molecules contain energy. The energy in glucose originally came from sunlight which was captured by chlorophyll molecules and used to make glucose in photosynthesis (Chapter 8).

If glucose is placed in oxygen and set alight, it burns vigorously (Fig. 9.1). Large amounts of heat energy are released as the glucose molecules combine with oxygen to form carbon dioxide and water, and the energy from the glucose is rapidly transferred to heat energy. This is an oxidation reaction:

$$C_6H_{12}O_6 \ + \ 6O_2 \ \longrightarrow \ 6CO_2 \ + \ 6H_2O$$

In a living cell, a similar process takes place, but in a much more controlled way. The glucose molecule is dismantled steadily, in a series of reactions catalysed by enzymes. The energy in the glucose molecule is released in small stages, and some of this energy is used to make ATP. The whole dismantling sequence has about 25 individual steps. Such a sequence is called a **metabolic pathway**; you can think of it as being rather like a production line in a factory with each enzyme receiving its substrate, carrying out its own small part of the overall task by catalysing the conversion of the substrate to a product, and allowing the product to pass on to the next enzyme.

The metabolic pathway of respiration is divided into three main stages (Fig. 9.2).

- Firstly, in the cytoplasm of the cell, glucose is converted to pyruvate. This stage is called **glycolysis**.
- Next, inside mitochondria, pyruvate is fed into a cycle of reactions called the **Krebs cycle**.
- Finally, still inside mitochondria, electrons produced in the Krebs cycle are passed along an electron transport chain, producing ATP in a process called **oxidative phosphorylation**.

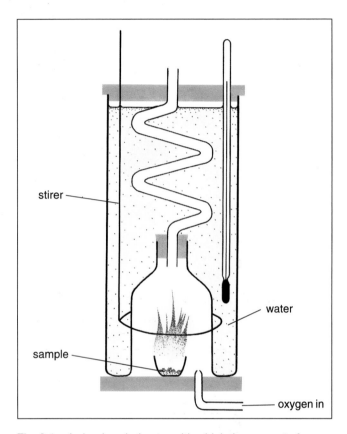

Fig. 9.1   A simple calorimeter with which the amount of energy released by the oxidation of glucose can be measured.

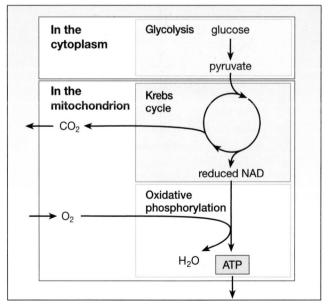

Fig. 9.2   The stages of respiration.

THE STAGES OF AEROBIC RESPIRATION
9.2 Glycolysis

Although they contain quite large amounts of energy, glucose molecules are relatively unreactive. They must be activated before glycolysis can proceed. This is done by the addition of a phosphate group to the glucose molecule, forming **glucose phosphate** (Fig. 9.3). The atoms in this molecule are then rearranged to form **fructose phosphate**, and another phosphate group added to form **fructose bisphosphate**.

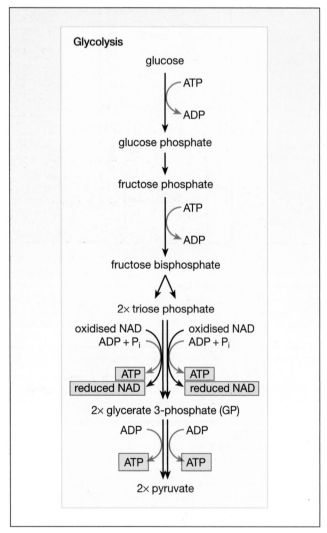

Fig. 9.3 Glycolysis.

Each of these additions of a phosphate group is done by transferring a phosphate group to the sugar from ATP. The ATP is converted into ADP in the process. So far then, far from *making* any ATP, glycolysis has actually used two ATP molecules! However, as you will see, more ATP molecules are made later, resulting in a net gain at the end.

Next, the six-carbon fructose bisphosphate molecule is split into two three-carbon molecules, **triose phosphate**. Each of these is then converted to **glycerate 3-phosphate (GP)** (Fig. 9.4) and then to **pyruvate** in a series of small steps. These steps release enough energy from the GP molecules to make some ATP.

Four molecules of ATP (two for each of the two triose phosphate molecules) are made directly, there and then in the cytoplasm, using energy released as the triose phosphate molecules are gradually changed to pyruvate. So, although two molecules of ATP were put into the process at the beginning, four have been made at the end.

However, this is not all the ATP which can be made in this process. The conversion of triose phosphate into GP also releases hydrogen ions (H$^+$) and electrons (e$^-$) which are transferred to the coenzyme **NAD** (nicotinamide adenine dinucleotide – you can see its structure in Fig. 1.24) to form reduced NAD. These hydrogen ions and high energy electrons are passed into a mitochondrion where they can be used to produce up to 5 ATP molecules in oxidative phosphorylation (described in Section 9.4). This, however, can only happen if oxygen is available.

The overall balance sheet for one molecule of glucose undergoing glycolysis is therefore:

ATP molecules produced	4
ATP molecules used	2
net gain of ATP molecules	2

In addition, the reduced NAD produced in glycolysis can yield up to 5 additional ATPs when oxygen is available.

9.3 The Krebs cycle

If oxygen is available, the pyruvate formed in glycolysis passes into a mitochondrion through the outer and inner mitochondrial membranes. Once in the matrix of the mitochondrion, pyruvate is converted to acetylcoenzyme A (Fig. 9.5). One hydrogen ion, two electrons and one carbon dioxide molecule are released during this process.

The acetyl group of acetylcoenzyme A, which contains two carbon atoms, then combines with a four-carbon compound called oxaloacetate. The resulting six-carbon

Box 9.1 Names for substances involved in glycolysis and the Calvin cycle

In recent years, there have been changes in the accepted names for two of the compounds which occur in both glycolysis and the Calvin cycle. The molecular structures of these two compounds, the names we have used in this book, and the other names which you may sometimes find used for them, are shown in Fig. 9.4.

You may like to look at the pathways of glycolysis and the Calvin cycle, and look for similarities and differences in them.

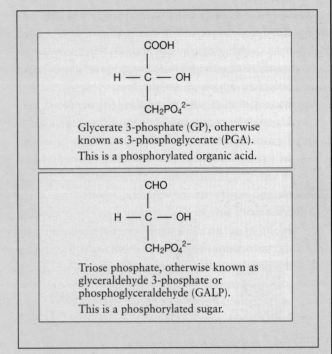

Glycerate 3-phosphate (GP), otherwise known as 3-phosphoglycerate (PGA). This is a phosphorylated organic acid.

Triose phosphate, otherwise known as glyceraldehyde 3-phosphate or phosphoglyceraldehyde (GALP). This is a phosphorylated sugar.

Fig. 9.4 The structures of glycerate 3-phosphate and triose phosphate.

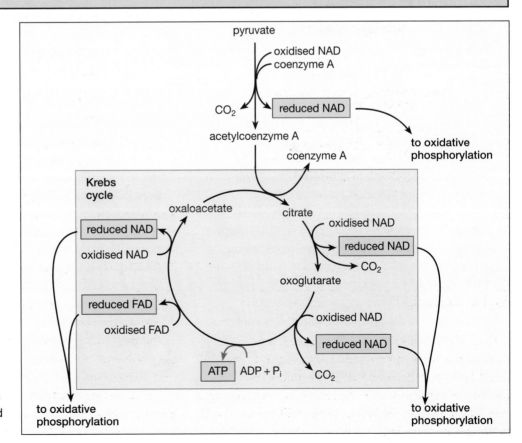

Fig. 9.5 The formation of acetylcoenzyme A from pyruvate, and the Krebs cycle.

compound, citrate (the same substance which forms the citric acid which give lemons their sharp flavour), is gradually re-converted to oxaloacetate. Many small steps are involved in this cyclic reaction. It is sometimes called the citric acid cycle (for obvious reasons), but sometimes the name Krebs cycle is used, after Hans Krebs who worked out the reactions in 1937.

At two stages in the Krebs cycle, carbon dioxide is removed from the compounds involved. This process is called **decarboxylation**. This carbon dioxide, plus that which was produced when pyruvate was converted to acetylcoenzyme A, diffuses out of the mitochondrion, out of the cell, and eventually out of the organism.

Other important products of the Krebs cycle are electrons and hydrogen ions which are both picked up by the oxidised form of the coenzyme NAD, and some by oxidised FAD (flavin adenine dinucleotide):

$$\underset{\text{oxidised NAD}}{NAD^+} + H^+ + 2e^- \longrightarrow \underset{\text{reduced NAD}}{NADH}$$

These coenzymes can hold electrons which will then be fed into the electron transport chain to make ATP, as described in Section 9.4.

When one glucose molecule is respired, two pyruvates are produced and they result in the production of six reduced NAD and two reduced FAD in the Krebs cycle. Two more reduced NAD molecules are produced in the conversion of pyruvate to acetylcoenzyme A.

In addition, one step in the Krebs cycle makes ATP directly. Two ATP molecules are produced in this way per original glucose molecule.

9.4   Oxidative phosphorylation

An important result of respiration is the formation of ATP. ATP is made by the addition of inorganic phosphate, P_i, to ADP, a **phosphorylation** reaction. In respiration, this process requires oxygen and so is known as **oxidative phosphorylation** (Fig. 9.6). (Compare this with the way in which ATP is made in the light-dependent stages of photosynthesis, where light is required for the process of *photo*phosphorylation.)

Box 9.2 Vitamins and respiration

Most vitamins are used to make substances which play essential roles in metabolism. Here, we will look at some which are involved in the reactions of glycolysis and the Krebs cycle.

Many vitamins are coenzymes, or are converted to coenzymes. These coenzymes are involved in reactions where an atom or group of atoms is transferred from one substance to another. The coenzyme holds the atom or group of atoms for a short time, helping with the transfer.

Riboflavin (vitamin B_2) is used to make FAD (flavin adenine dinucleotide). FAD is a coenzyme which acts as a hydrogen and electron acceptor in the Krebs cycle. It is a 'coenzyme' because the dehydrogenase enzyme catalysing the reaction which removes the hydrogens cannot do so unless FAD is available to accept them.

Niacin (nicotinic acid) is used to make NAD (nicotinamide adenine dinucleotide). This, like FAD, is a coenzyme acting as a hydrogen and

electron acceptor, which it does both in glycolysis and in the Krebs cycle. Both NAD and FAD act as coenzymes in other metabolic reactions besides those of respiration.

Pantothenic acid (vitamin B_3) is used to make one part of the large complex molecule coenzyme A. Coenzyme A transfers acyl groups, $R-C=O$, from one substance to another. When it is combined with the acetyl (ethanoate) group, $CH_3-C=O$, it is called **acetylcoenzyme A**. The pyruvate made in glycolysis provides an acetyl group, which combines with coenzyme A to produce acetylcoenzyme A. At the beginning of the Krebs cycle, acetylcoenzyme A transfers its acetyl group to oxaloacetate to produce citrate.

Thiamine (vitamin B_1) is converted in the body to thiamine pyrophosphate, **TPP**. This acts as a coenzyme in some reactions involving acyl group transfers, and is needed for the reaction in which pyruvate is converted to acetylcoenzyme A.

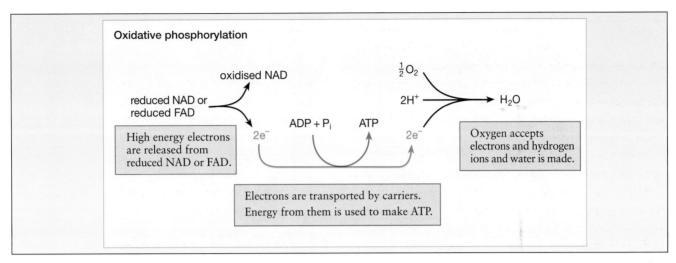

Fig. 9.6 Oxidative phosphorylation.

The Krebs cycle takes place in the matrix of a mitochondrion. The next stage, in which ATP is made, happens in the inner mitochondrial membrane. Within this membrane lie the components of the electron transport chain (Box 9.3).

Reduced NAD and FAD provide electrons for the synthesis of ATP. The electrons are used to provide energy for ATP synthesis as they are passed along the electron transport chain.

The electrons pass from the reduced NAD to the first member of this chain, and then from one carrier to the next. As the electrons are passed along, ATP is made (Box 9.3). It is not certain exactly how many ATP molecules are made using the energy of four electrons from every two

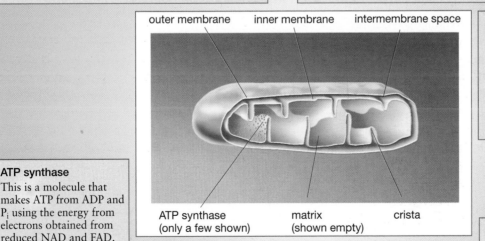

Outer mitochondrial membrane
The outer mitochondrial membrane is a barrier that stops large molecules from entering the mitochondrion and possibly interfering with the Krebs cycle and oxidative phosphorylation. However, it allows pyruvate needed for the Krebs cycle to cross freely into the matrix.

Inner mitochondrial membrane
This membrane has electron carriers and ATP synthase molecules embedded in it. The membrane is also a barrier which prevents many small molecules from the cytoplasm from entering the matrix and interfering with the Krebs cycle and oxidative phosphorylation. Pyruvate, however, is transported across it.

Intermembrane space
The activity of the electron carriers in the inner membrane causes a reservoir of H^+ ions to build up in the intermembrane space as a temporary energy store before the energy is used to make ATP.

ATP synthase
This is a molecule that makes ATP from ADP and P_i using the energy from electrons obtained from reduced NAD and FAD.

The molecule spans the inner membrane and has a channel in it which allows H^+ ions to pass through.

Matrix
The matrix is where the enzymes of the Krebs cycle are found. The Krebs cycle removes high energy electrons from the intermediates of the Krebs cycle and produces reduced NAD and FAD.

Crista
The inner mitochondrial membrane is highly folded. This creates a large surface area to hold electron carriers and ATP synthase molecules.

Fig. 9.7 Structure and function of a mitochondrion.

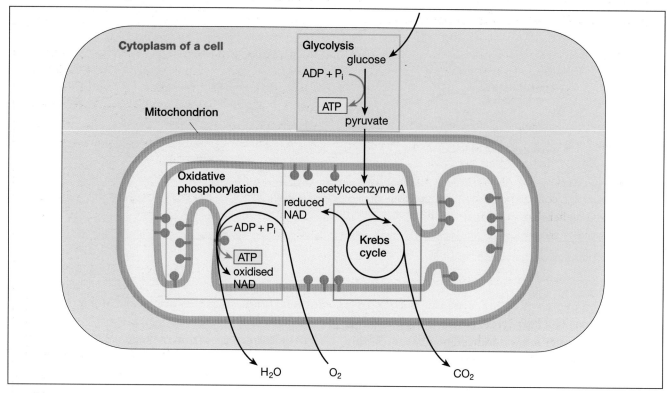

Fig. 9.8 Summary of respiration.

reduced NAD. It was originally thought to be six, but is now thought to be five or a little less.

You may have noticed that there has been no oxygen involved in any of these processes so far. It is only now, right at the end of the electron transport chain, that oxygen is needed. Its role is to combine with the electrons, as they come off the end of the chain, and with hydrogen ions to form water. If there is not enough oxygen available to do this, then the electron transport chain cannot work. This produces a complete traffic jam, stopping the Krebs cycle completely. Section 9.5 describes what happens in these circumstances.

Now that we have arrived at the end of all three stages of respiration, we can draw up a complete balance sheet to show how many ATP molecules are made from one glucose molecule when oxygen is available. This is shown in Table 9.1.

Process	ATP used	ATP produced
glycolysis	2	4
link reaction + Krebs cycle + oxidative phosphorylation (including reduced NAD from glycolysis)		29
total	2	33
maximum net ATP production		31

You may find some texts which give different numbers. This is because it is now known that fewer ATPs are produced during oxidative phosphorylation than was originally thought. There is still some uncertainty about the precise number, and it can vary between different tissues and different organisms.

Table 9.1 Balance sheet for ATP production, from one glucose molecule, when oxygen is available.

Box 9.3 Oxidative phosphorylation

Fig. 9.9 shows how the passing of electrons along the carriers in the inner mitochondrial membrane is used to produce ATP.

As the electrons are passed from one carrier to the next, some of their energy is used to move hydrogen ions (H^+, protons) from the matrix of the mitochondrion into the intermembrane space. This produces a high concentration of hydrogen ions here, much higher than in the matrix, and makes it more positively charged.

Within the inner membrane there are large protein molecules spanning the membrane from one side to the other. These are **ATP synthases**. They allow hydrogen ions to diffuse through them, down their electrical and concentration gradients, back into the matrix. This provides enough energy to make ATP from ADP and inorganic phosphate.

If you have already studied *photo*phosphorylation, you will notice how very similar these two processes are.

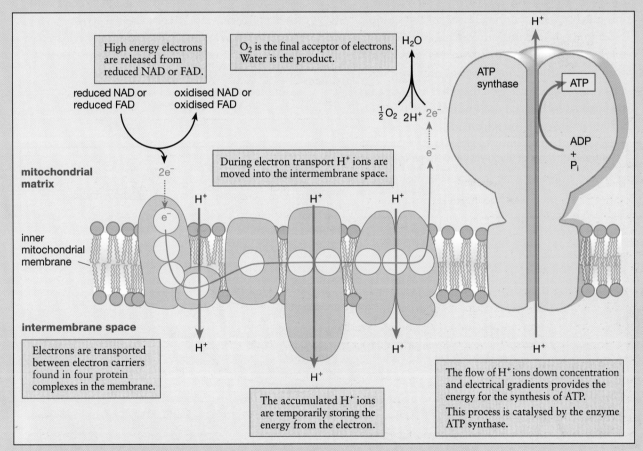

High energy electrons are released from reduced NAD or FAD.

O_2 is the final acceptor of electrons. Water is the product.

reduced NAD or reduced FAD → oxidised NAD or oxidised FAD

H_2O

$\frac{1}{2}O_2$ $2H^+$ $2e^-$

ATP synthase

ATP

ADP + P_i

mitochondrial matrix

$2e^-$

During electron transport H^+ ions are moved into the intermembrane space.

inner mitochondrial membrane

e^-

H^+ H^+ H^+

H^+

intermembrane space

Electrons are transported between electron carriers found in four protein complexes in the membrane.

H^+ H^+ H^+

H^+

The accumulated H^+ ions are temporarily storing the energy from the electron.

The flow of H^+ ions down concentration and electrical gradients provides the energy for the synthesis of ATP.

This process is catalysed by the enzyme ATP synthase.

Fig. 9.9   Detail of part of the inner mitochondrial membrane and oxidative phosphorylation.

Box 9.4 Respiratory substrates

In Sections 9.1 to 9.3, we have assumed that respiration always uses glucose as its starting point or substrate. This is not always so; different organisms, different tissues in the same organism, and even the same tissues at different times, use other molecules as their respiratory substrates. Fig. 9.10 shows at which points these compounds can enter the metabolic pathway of respiration.

In humans, for example, most tissues use glucose as their preferred respiratory substrate in the few hours after a meal, but may change over to fats once available carbohydrate runs low. Brain cells use only glucose, except during fasting or starvation. Red blood cells can only use glucose. (Red blood cells have no mitochondria. Look at Fig. 9.10 and work out why they cannot use any other respiratory substrate.) Muscle cells, on the other hand, readily use fatty acids. Heart muscle normally gets about 70% of its energy from fatty acids.

Another respiratory substrate is **ketone bodies**. Normally, the level of ketone bodies in the blood is low, but during fasting, starvation or in people with diabetes mellitus, concentrations can be relatively high. The reasons for this are as follows.

When blood glucose levels are low, the liver may make glucose from protein. At the same time fatty acids are broken down, producing acetylcoenzyme A. Acetylcoenzyme A would normally be fed into the Krebs cycle for ATP production. However, in the liver oxaloacetate is being used to make glucose and is therefore not plentiful enough to react with the acetylcoenzyme A. The excess acetylcoenzyme A is converted to ketone bodies which are released into the blood and can be used as a respiratory substrate by cells in some parts of the body, for example muscles and the brain.

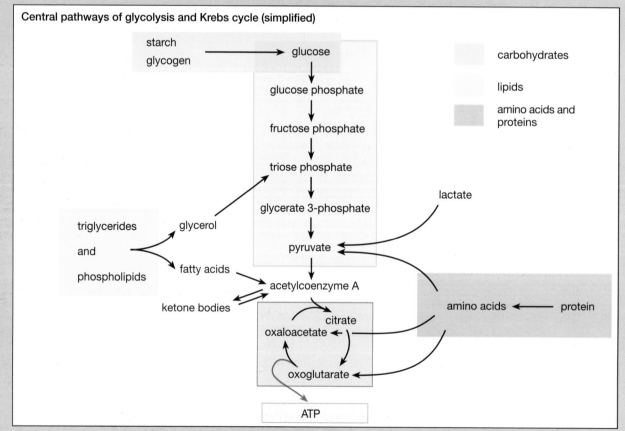

Fig. 9.10   The range of energy-containing substrates for respiration.

ANAEROBIC RESPIRATION

9.5 Respiration without oxygen

The sequence of reactions described in Sections 9.1 to 9.4 results in the complete oxidation of glucose. Oxygen is used as a final acceptor of electrons. As this oxygen comes from the air, the process is called **aerobic respiration**.

When oxygen is not available, however, oxidative phosphorylation and the Krebs cycle cannot take place. This is also true in organisms or cells which do not contain the machinery to carry these out; human red blood cells, for example, have no mitochondria, and so can only perform glycolysis. In these circumstances, respiration takes place without oxygen. It is **anaerobic**.

In anaerobic respiration, glycolysis takes place as usual, producing pyruvate and a small yield of ATP. If pyruvate were allowed to build up it would inhibit glycolysis, so it is converted to something else. More importantly, the reduced NAD which is produced in glycolysis must be oxidised back to NAD again or the cell would soon run out of it, bringing ATP production to a halt.

There are two different solutions to the problem, both of which get rid of the pyruvate, and regenerate NAD. These are **alcoholic fermentation**, which is used by fungi and plants, and **lactic fermentation**, which is used by animals.

● Alcoholic fermentation

Yeast converts pyruvate to **ethanol**. First, carbon dioxide is removed from pyruvate to produce ethanal (Fig. 9.11). Next, the enzyme alcohol dehydrogenase (working in the reverse direction to the one its name suggests) converts the ethanal to ethanol. This step requires hydrogen which is taken from reduced NAD.

This process has been used by humans for thousands of years. If yeast is provided with a supply of carbohydrate, it will carry out glycolysis and alcoholic fermentation. In bread making we provide it with starch in flour, and make use of the carbon dioxide it releases to make the bread rise. In the making of alcoholic drinks it is the ethanol which is required.

● Lactic fermentation

This process contributes to the discomfort you may experience in exhausted muscles. If muscle is exercising hard, it may run out of oxygen and have to respire anaerobically for a short period. The pyruvate produced by glycolysis is converted, in a single step, to **lactate**. The enzyme responsible for this conversion is lactate

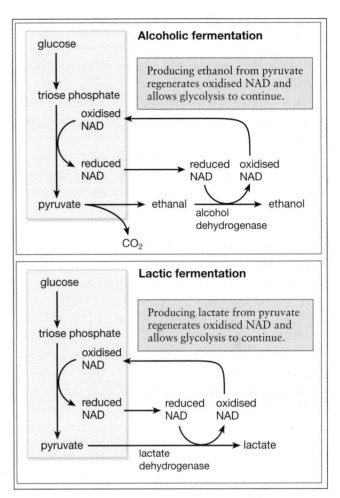

Fig. 9.11   What happens to pyruvate in anaerobic respiration.

dehydrogenase, and the process requires hydrogen from reduced NAD.

It is the build-up of lactate, which forms lactic acid, in muscles which causes the pain. The lactate must be broken down, and for this to take place it is transported in the blood to the liver. Here, some is converted back into glucose. This process requires oxygen, which is why you go on breathing deeply even when your strenuous exercise is over. You are supplying extra oxygen to the liver, to help it to deal with the lactate produced because of a *shortage* of oxygen earlier on. You are paying off an 'oxygen debt'.

Although lactic acid in muscles is unpleasant, we do enjoy lactic acid in other ways! Yoghurt, soured cream and cheese all contain lactic acid, which helps to give them their distinctive flavours. The lactic acid is produced during anaerobic respiration by bacteria such as *Lactobacillus bulgaricus*. The bacteria are added to milk where they use the sugar lactose as a respiratory substrate.

The lactic acid moves out of the bacteria into the surrounding milk. As well as providing flavour, the lactic acid lowers the pH of the milk, causing the proteins in it to coagulate.

Neither alcoholic fermentation nor lactic fermentation produce any additional ATP. So anaerobic respiration provides only two molecules of ATP for every glucose molecule. This is much less than the 31 molecules of ATP which can be produced if aerobic respiration, involving the Krebs cycle and oxidative phosphorylation, can be carried out (Table 9.1). ■

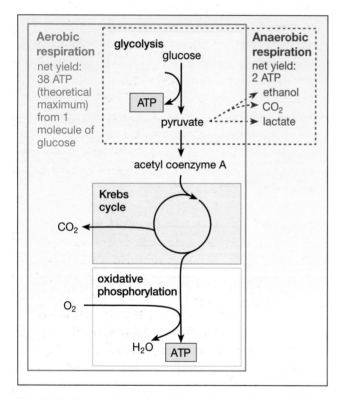

Fig. 9.12 Comparison of aerobic and anaerobic respiration.

Q1 The diagram below shows some of the stages of anaerobic respiration in a yeast cell.

```
                glucose
                   |
   stage 1         |------------> H
                   v
                pyruvate
                   |
   stage 2         |------------> compound X
                   v
                ethanal
              (acetaldehyde)
                   |
   stage 3         |
                   v
              compound Y
```

(a) (i) Identify compound **X**, produced at stage 2. *(1)*

 (ii) Identify compound **Y**, produced by stage 3. *(1)*

(b) State what happens to the hydrogen atoms produced by stage 1. *(2)*

(c) Name two products of anaerobic respiration in muscle. *(2)*

London 1995 *(Total 6 marks)*

Box 9.5 Respiratory quotients

When different respiratory substrates are used, the ratio of carbon dioxide given out to oxygen taken in may vary. This ratio is called the **respiratory quotient** or **RQ**.

RQ = volume of carbon dioxide given out
     volume of oxygen taken in

When glucose is the respiratory substrate, exactly the same number of molecules (and hence volume) of carbon dioxide and oxygen are produced and used respectively. This means that the RQ is exactly 1. However, if other substances are used as the main respiratory substrate, then the RQ is less than one. If fat is being respired, then on average only 70 carbon dioxide molecules are produced for every 100 oxygen molecules used. If protein is being used as the respiratory substrate, then 90 carbon dioxide molecules are produced for every 100 oxygen molecules used.

Respiratory substrate	RQ
carbohydrate, e.g. glucose	1.0
fat	0.7
protein	0.9

It is not difficult to measure the amount of oxygen which an organism uses and the amount of carbon dioxide which it gives out. Once you have done this, you can work out the RQ, which gives you a good clue about what the organism is using as its respiratory substrate. For example, in humans it is found that RQs just after a meal are usually very close to 1.0, indicating that carbohydrate is being

metabolised. If nothing is then eaten for around 7 to 10 hours, the RQ drops to about 0.7, indicating that fat is being metabolised. In people with severe diabetes mellitus (Section 15.5), where it is difficult for cells to absorb and use glucose, fat is the main respiratory substrate for most of the time, so the RQ is usually close to 0.7.

RQs can also show what respiratory substrates plants are using. Here, however, there is another possible range of values, because when plants respire anaerobically they release carbon dioxide. (If you look back at Section 9.5, you will see that this is not true for animals). If a plant respires anaerobically, it produces carbon dioxide but uses no oxygen, so its RQ is something divided by zero which is infinity. In practice, it will almost certainly be respiring at least partly *aerobically*, so at least some oxygen will be being used. This means that its RQ is high, but not actually infinity.

For example, pea seeds have a store of starch and protein, for use by the embryo plant in the early stages of germination (Section 18.10). At the start of germination, when the testa still covers the seed and it is difficult for oxygen to penetrate inside, respiration is partly anaerobic. At this stage the RQ is around 3 to 4. Later, the testa is shed and it becomes easier for oxygen to penetrate, so the RQ drops, eventually arriving at a value of around 1.0 as carbohydrate is respired aerobically. Seeds with large lipid stores, such as sunflower seeds, have RQs of around 0.7 or 0.8.

Q2 An experiment was carried out to measure the rate at which a sample of mitochondria used oxygen under different conditions. The mitochondria were placed in a well-oxygenated liquid with a water potential equal to the water potential of their contents.

At time **A**, an end-product of glycolysis was added to the liquid. At times **B**, **C** and **D**, ADP was added. The same amount of ADP was added each time.

The results of this experiment are shown in the graph.

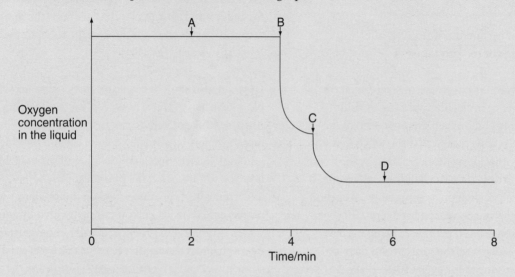

(a) Explain why the liquid used in the experiment should have the same water potential as the contents of the mitochondria. (3)

(b) (i) State the name of the end product of glycolysis which was added to the solution at **A**. (1)

(ii) Name the **two** stages of the respiratory process which take place inside the mitochondrion. (2)

(iii) State the role of oxygen in these respiratory processes. (1)

(c) Explain the result of adding ADP at the following points in the graph.
(i) **B** and **C**
(ii) **D** (4)

(d) Yeast cells can respire anaerobically using glucose as a substrate.
(i) State the end products formed from the glucose if oxygen is not available to the yeast cells. (2)
(ii) Explain why ADP is required in anaerobic respiration. (4)

AICE 1997   (*Total 17 marks*)

Q3 This question is about the metabolism of germinating seeds of a particular species.

(a) Make a **labelled** diagram of simple apparatus you could use to measure the rate of oxygen uptake of some germinating seeds. *(4)*

The endosperm of these seeds is a storage tissue containing lipids which are metabolised during germination. The main products, fatty acids, are broken down in a process which yields two-carbon fragments. These fragments may then enter one of two different biochemical pathways, the Krebs cycle or the glyoxylate cycle.

A typical equation for the metabolism of the fatty acid via the Krebs cycle is as follows:

$$C_{18}H_{34}O_3 + 25\,O_2 \rightarrow 18\,CO_2 + 17\,H_2O$$

A typical equation for the metabolism of the fatty acid via the glyoxylate cycle is as follows:

$$C_{18}H_{34}O_3 + 13\,O_2 \rightarrow C_{12}H_{22}O_{11} + 6\,CO_2 + 6\,H_2O$$

(b) Calculate the RQ (respiratory quotient) for the oxidation of the fatty acid via the
   (i) Krebs cycle;
   (ii) glyoxylate cycle. *(2)*

The figure below shows the RQs of the embryo and endosperm components of seeds germinating in the dark for the 12 days after sowing.

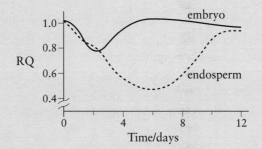

(c) Suggest an explanation in each case for the RQ values for the
   (i) embryo and endosperm from 0–2 days;
   (ii) endosperm from 2–12 days;
   (iii) embryo from 2–12 days. *(3)*

The table below gives results selected from analysis of germinating seedlings.

	Dry mass/mg per seedling		
	Lipid	Carbohydrate	Total
Day 4	250	51	390
Day 6	108	182	451

(d) (i) Explain what these changes in dry mass of lipids and carbohydrates suggest about the pathways of lipid metabolism in use at this time.
   (ii) The total dry mass is made up of components other than lipids and carbohydrates. Suggest what the other major component is likely to be and account for its presence in the germinating seed. *(3)*

JMB 1992 *(Total 12 marks)*

Q4 The diagram below shows apparatus that can be used to measure the rate of anaerobic respiration in yeast cells. The tube contains a yeast suspension in 1% glucose solution and a redox indicator. The pyrogallol solution absorbs oxygen.

(a) (i) Name one suitable redox indicator which could be used in this experiment. *(1)*

(ii) Give one change you would expect to observe during the experiment as the yeast respires and give a reason for your answer. *(2)*

(b) Describe how you could use the apparatus to investigate the effect of temperature on anaerobic respiration of glucose by yeast. *(3)*

London 1996   *(Total 6 marks)*

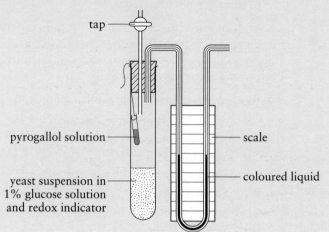

tap

pyrogallol solution

scale

yeast suspension in 1% glucose solution and redox indicator

coloured liquid

Q5 (a) Copy the table below.

Place a tick in the appropriate box in the table to show which of the statements (i) to (iii) applies to each of the three processes:

glycolysis (glucose ⟶ pyruvate);
the Krebs cycle;
oxidative phosphorylation.

If the statement does not apply, place a cross in the appropriate box. *(3)*

	Glycolysis	Krebs cycle	Oxidative phosphorylation
(i) Produces ATP			
(ii) Involves the production of carbon dioxide			
(iii) Occurs in a mitochondrion			

(b) The following are all types of enzyme:

A oxidoreductase
B transferase
C hydrolase

Using each letter once, more than once or not at all, identify the type of enzyme that would catalyse each of the reactions below.

(i) ATP + glucose ⟶ ADP + glucose 6-phosphate; *(1)*
(ii) glycogen + H_2O ⟶ glucose. *(1)*

AEB (specimen) 1997   *(Total 5 marks)*

10 Transport in mammals

All cells need a regular supply of water and nutrients (such as glucose), and most need oxygen. In a small organism, these substances can enter each cell fast enough by diffusion, directly from the environment. In a large organism, a transport system is needed to maintain an adequate supply to each cell. Mammals such as humans have a double circulatory system, in which blood is pumped by the heart through vessels, first to the lungs to collect oxygen, and then back to the heart to be pumped to all other parts of the body.

10.1 Size, surface area and the need for transport systems

Cells need regular, sometimes constant, deliveries of substances such as oxygen and nutrients. They also have waste products which must be taken away. These include carbon dioxide (produced in respiration) and, for animal cells, nitrogenous waste products such as urea (Section 15.11). For most cells, the substances which are most rapidly and most constantly taken in and out are oxygen, carbon dioxide and water.

In a single-celled organism, the substances the cell needs enter it directly from the external environment through the cell surface membrane. The waste substances leave the cell in the same way. This simple arrangement also works well for small organisms which have a relatively large proportion of their cells in direct contact with the outside environment, and not too many cells that are far away from the surface. Such organisms have a high **surface area to volume ratio**. In these organisms, oxygen just **diffuses** into the cells on the surface, and then to the cells deeper inside the body. If the organism is not very active (so does not use oxygen very rapidly in respiration) and not too 'thick', then diffusion can supply enough oxygen to the cells. Even large organisms can manage like this, so long as they have plenty of surface in contact with their environment. Plants, for example, have a branching shape and thin leaves, which means that no cell is very far from the air. As plants do not respire particularly quickly, diffusion can deliver oxygen to their cells as fast as is needed.

Most animals respire more rapidly than plants, and so need faster supplies of oxygen to their cells. In an animal,

enough oxygen can normally be supplied to cells by diffusion alone so long as the distance across which it has to diffuse is not greater than about 2 mm. Diffusion distances greater than this need some other arrangement. So large animals, and very active animals (even small ones), usually have a **transport system** to deliver oxygen as rapidly as possible to every individual cell. Rather than relying on the random movement of individual molecules of a substance (diffusion), the transport system delivers these substances in bulk, dissolved or suspended in a fluid which flows inside vessels. This is called **mass flow**.

The transport system also delivers the cells' other requirements, such as water, glucose and other nutrients, and removes waste products. Plants have transport systems too, which use mass flow like the animal systems. However, these do not deliver oxygen or carbon dioxide or take these gases away. They *do* deliver water, and nutrients such as sucrose and mineral ions.

As the needs of animals and plants are different, it is not surprising that they have evolved very different transport systems. Animals have **blood systems**, with a heart which keeps the fluid moving rapidly around the body. Plants have two separate systems – **xylem vessels** transport water and inorganic ions, mostly from roots to leaves, while **phloem tubes** transport sucrose and other organic substances, mostly from leaves to other parts of the plant. Neither of these two systems has an internal pump.

In this chapter we will look at the blood system of humans. Transport systems in plants are discussed in Chapter 11.

10.2 The double circulatory system

Fig. 10.1 shows a plan of the basic design of the human circulatory system. The diagram is drawn as though you were looking at a person who is facing you. This means that the person's left side is on the right-hand side of the diagram.

A pump, the **heart**, pushes a fluid, **blood**, along tubes called **vessels**. If you begin on the right side of the heart (the left side of the diagram), you can follow the pathway which blood would take as it flows first to the lungs, then back to the left side of the heart, then around the rest of the body and back to the right side of the heart again. As the blood passes twice through the heart on this single

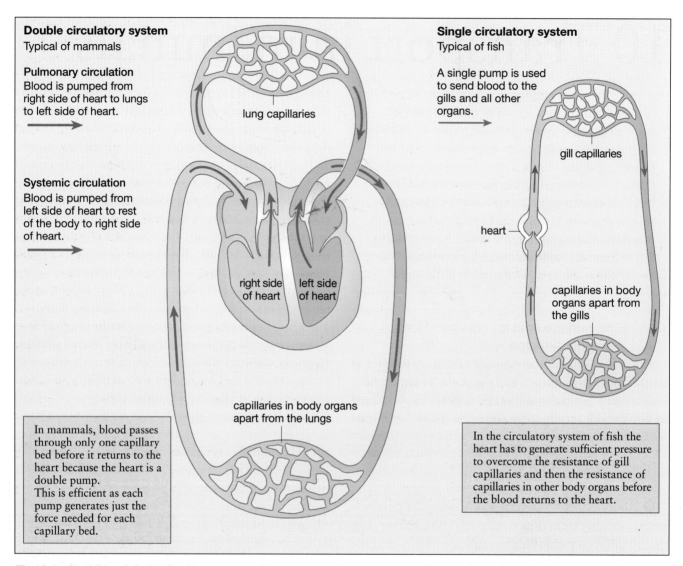

Double circulatory system
Typical of mammals

Pulmonary circulation
Blood is pumped from right side of heart to lungs to left side of heart.

⟶

Systemic circulation
Blood is pumped from left side of heart to rest of the body to right side of heart.

⟶

lung capillaries

right side of heart   left side of heart

capillaries in body organs apart from the lungs

In mammals, blood passes through only one capillary bed before it returns to the heart because the heart is a double pump.
This is efficient as each pump generates just the force needed for each capillary bed.

Single circulatory system
Typical of fish

A single pump is used to send blood to the gills and all other organs.

⟶

gill capillaries

heart

capillaries in body organs apart from the gills

In the circulatory system of fish the heart has to generate sufficient pressure to overcome the resistance of gill capillaries and then the resistance of capillaries in other body organs before the blood returns to the heart.

Fig 10.1   Double and single circulatory systems.

complete journey around the system, it is called a **double circulatory system**.

This arrangement ensures that every cell in the body gets as good a supply of oxygen as possible. The heart pushes blood out of its right side to the lungs. As the blood passes through the lungs, it absorbs oxygen from the air in alveoli (Section 12.5). The blood loses nearly all of its driving force (pressure) in lung vessels, but it flows back to the heart again (on the left side) to be pushed out once more, this time to the other parts of the body. Here it delivers oxygen to the cells which need it, before returning – at low pressure – to the heart to have its pressure boosted before starting around the circuit all over again. By passing through the heart again, after picking up oxygen

at the lungs, the blood is kept moving at high pressure, so that it moves fast towards the tissues which need its delivery of oxygen and arrives there with enough energy to pass through the tiny capillaries.

Fish have a simpler system. Blood leaves the heart and goes to the gills where it picks up oxygen. However, rather than going back to the heart at this stage, it continues directly onwards around the rest of the body, before returning to the heart to be pumped to the gills again. This arrangement does not supply oxygen as rapidly to the tissues. A double circulatory system provides oxygen to tissues more efficiently than does the fish's single circulatory system.

THE HEART
10.3 The structure of the human heart

Figs. 10.2 and 10.3 shows the structure of a human heart. An 'average' human heart weighs about 300 g. It is made almost entirely of muscle. The muscle is of a kind found nowhere else in the body, and is called **cardiac muscle**. You can find out something about the microscopic structure of this muscle, and how it works, in Chapter 16.

On the outside of the heart, various blood vessels are visible. These are called **coronary vessels**. The most obvious of these are usually the **coronary arteries**, which deliver oxygenated blood to the heart muscle.

Within the heart there are four chambers. The upper two receive incoming blood and are called **atria** (singular **atrium**). The lower two, which are much larger than the atria, pump blood out of the heart and are called **ventricles**. The left and right chambers are completely separated from each other by a **septum**, which prevents blood flowing from one side to the other.

The walls of these four chambers are made of cardiac muscle. The amount of muscle in the wall affects how forcefully a particular chamber can push blood out of itself as the muscle contracts. The two atria need only to provide a small amount of force, as they push blood into the ventricles just below them. They therefore have thin walls. The two ventricles, however, push blood to the lungs or to the rest of the body, which requires much more force, and so they have much thicker walls. Moreover, the left ventricle needs to produce much more force than the right one, because blood from the left ventricle travels all around the body, while blood from the right ventricle only goes to the lungs which are very close to the heart. So the wall of the left ventricle is much thicker than that of the right.

Between the atria and ventricles are **atrio-ventricular valves**. These are made of almost transparent, thin, but very tough, flaps of tissue. Strong **tendons** link the valves to little bumps of muscle protruding from the inner surface of the ventricles, called **papillae**. The valve on the left side of the heart has two flaps, and so is called the **bicuspid valve**; it also has the alternative name **mitral valve**. The one on the right side of the heart has three flaps and is called the **tricuspid valve**. Fig. 10.5 explains how these valves work.

A number of blood vessels enter and leave the heart. Two **pulmonary veins**, one from each lung, lead into the left atrium to deliver oxygenated blood. This blood flows

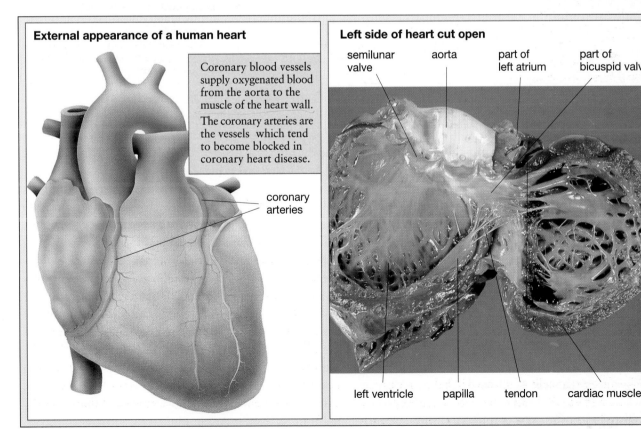

External appearance of a human heart

Coronary blood vessels supply oxygenated blood from the aorta to the muscle of the heart wall.

The coronary arteries are the vessels which tend to become blocked in coronary heart disease.

coronary arteries

Left side of heart cut open

semilunar valve   aorta   part of left atrium   part of bicuspid valve

left ventricle   papilla   tendon   cardiac muscle

Fig. 10.2 The structure of a human heart.

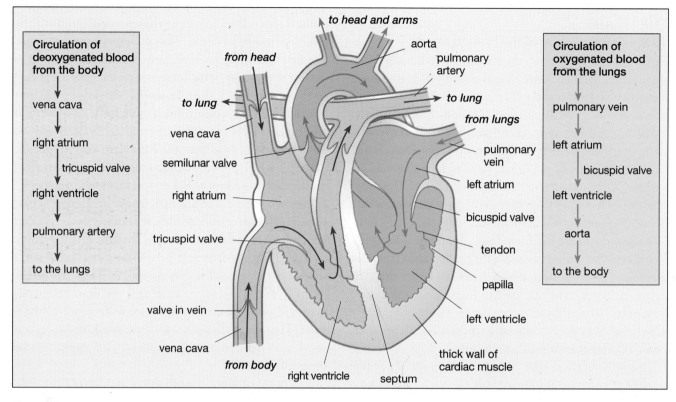

Fig. 10.3   Diagram of TS of a human heart.

through the left atrium and then into the left ventricle. From here, it is pumped out of the heart through the **aorta**, which is the first part of the route to all other parts of the body. The blood passes through body tissues and becomes deoxygenated, then returns from the body in one of the two **venae cavae** (singular vena cava), one from the head and one from the lower parts of the body, which lead into the right atrium. The blood flows from here into the right ventricle which pushes it out through the **pulmonary artery** to the lungs.

The aorta and pulmonary artery both contain valves. These valves are half-moon shaped and so are called **semilunar valves**.

10.4   The cardiac cycle

The heart pumps blood by rhythmic contraction of the cardiac muscle in its walls. At rest, a human heart contracts and relaxes about 70 times a minute. One complete sequence of contraction and relaxation is called a **cardiac cycle**.

Fig. 10.4 shows what happens during one cardiac cycle. Only one side of the heart is shown, to make it easier to follow. But you should realise that *both* sides of the heart are doing exactly the same thing at the same time.

The cycle can be divided into two stages – **systole** and

diastole. During systole the muscle contracts, and during diastole it relaxes. Fluids flow from a region of high pressure to a region of lower pressure. As the heart muscle contracts, it squeezes inwards on the blood in the chambers, decreasing the volume and increasing the pressure, which forces the blood out towards regions where the pressure is lower. The muscle then relaxes, allowing the volume of the chambers to increase again and the pressure to drop. Blood then flows in from regions where the pressure is higher.

The cycle begins as the atria contract. This stage is called **atrial systole**. The contraction of the atria pushes the blood inside the atria down into the ventricles, through the open atrio-ventricular valves.

Next, the ventricle muscles contract. This stage of the cardiac cycle is called **ventricular systole**. The ventricles contract much more forcefully than the muscles of the atria, producing a pressure of around 16 kPa in the left ventricle, and 4 kPa in the right ventricle. This is much greater than the pressure in the atria at this stage, which is around 1 kPa. This difference in blood pressure on the two sides of the atrio-ventricular valves pushes them upwards. They cannot flip right up like swing doors because the tendons hold them down (Fig. 10.5). So they slam shut, stopping the blood from passing back into the atria.

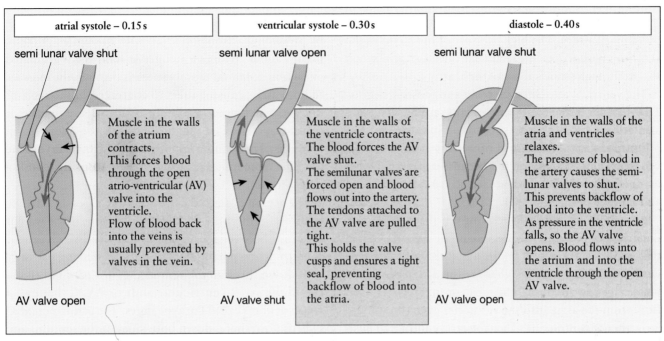

atrial systole – 0.15 s	ventricular systole – 0.30 s	diastole – 0.40 s

semi lunar valve shut

semi lunar valve open

semi lunar valve shut

Muscle in the walls of the atrium contracts.
This forces blood through the open atrio-ventricular (AV) valve into the ventricle.
Flow of blood back into the veins is usually prevented by valves in the vein.

Muscle in the walls of the ventricle contracts. The blood forces the AV valve shut.
The semilunar valves are forced open and blood flows out into the artery. The tendons attached to the AV valve are pulled tight.
This holds the valve cusps and ensures a tight seal, preventing backflow of blood into the atria.

Muscle in the walls of the atria and ventricles relaxes.
The pressure of blood in the artery causes the semi-lunar valves to shut.
This prevents backflow of blood into the ventricle. As pressure in the ventricle falls, so the AV valve opens. Blood flows into the atrium and into the ventricle through the open AV valve.

AV valve open

AV valve shut

AV valve open

Fig. 10.4   The cardiac cycle.

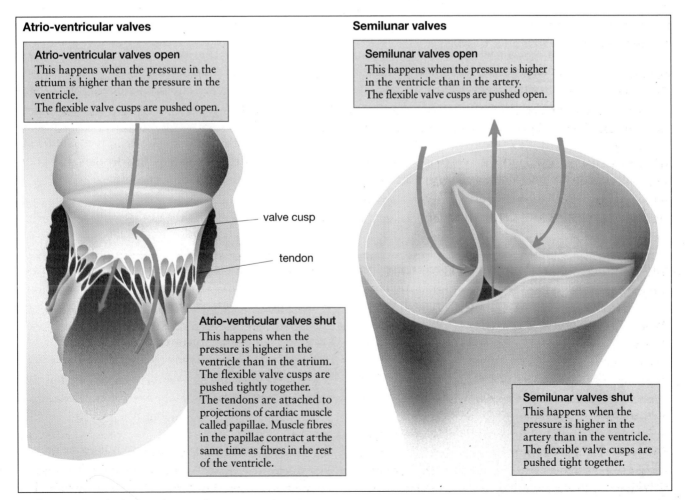

Atrio-ventricular valves

Atrio-ventricular valves open
This happens when the pressure in the atrium is higher than the pressure in the ventricle.
The flexible valve cusps are pushed open.

Semilunar valves

Semilunar valves open
This happens when the pressure is higher in the ventricle than in the artery.
The flexible valve cusps are pushed open.

valve cusp

tendon

Atrio-ventricular valves shut
This happens when the pressure is higher in the ventricle than in the atrium.
The flexible valve cusps are pushed tightly together.
The tendons are attached to projections of cardiac muscle called papillae. Muscle fibres in the papillae contract at the same time as fibres in the rest of the ventricle.

Semilunar valves shut
This happens when the pressure is higher in the artery than in the ventricle.
The flexible valve cusps are pushed tight together.

Fig. 10.5   How the heart valves work.

Instead, the blood flows up into the aorta and pulmonary artery. The high pressure of the blood in the ventricles pushes open the semilunar valves, and the blood shoots through them and out of the heart.

The ventricle muscles then relax and diastole begins. The pressure inside the ventricles falls rapidly. If it were allowed to, the high-pressure blood in the aorta and pulmonary arteries would now flow back into the ventricles, but it cannot do this because it gets trapped in the semilunar valves which are pushed shut by the blood and prevent any back-flow (Fig. 10.5).

As the pressure inside the relaxing ventricles gets lower, it quickly drops below the pressure inside the atria. When this happens, the blood on the atrial side of the atrio-ventricular valves has a higher pressure than the blood below them, so this pushes the valves open. Blood starts to flow from the atria into the ventricles even though the atria are not contracting. Then the atria contract to push the last bit of blood into the ventricles as the cycle begins all over again.

Fig. 10.6 shows the pressure changes in the left atrium, left ventricle and aorta during the cardiac cycle. It looks rather daunting at first but, if you take one line at a time, you should not find it too difficult to understand, though you do need to think carefully about it. Begin with the left ventricle and follow the pressure changes as it contracts (pressure up) and relaxes (pressure down). The little 'bump' in this curve just before the big rise is caused by the extra blood being forced into the ventricle as the atria contract. Then do the same for the atrium, which only has little pressure rises because it only has weak muscles. Finally, look at the pressure changes in the aorta.

10.5   Control of heart beat

It is very important that the sequence of events described in Section 10.4 takes place correctly, with the timing of contraction of atria and ventricles exactly right. If they all contracted at once, or in the wrong order, then blood flow through the heart would be very erratic, or might not even happen at all.

The muscles contract when a signal called an **action potential** arrives. (You can read about action potentials in Chapter 14.) The timing of arrival of the action potential at different parts of the heart determines the sequence in which these parts contract.

The signal begins in a small patch of muscle in the right atrium, called the **sino-atrial node**, or **SAN** (Fig. 10.7). Cardiac muscle has an in-built capacity to generate action potentials. The muscle in the SAN starts the cardiac cycle by producing action potentials with its own set rhythm, usually about 70 times a minute. As soon as it is generated an action potential rapidly spreads through the muscles of both atria, causing them to contract. Unlike skeletal muscle, which needs a stimulus from a nerve to make it contract, you can see that heart muscle provides its own stimulus. The stimulation for contraction is **myogenic** (coming from muscle) rather than **neurogenic** (coming from a nerve).

The action potential cannot spread directly into the ventricles as there is a band of fibrous tissue in the wall of the heart, between the atria and ventricles, which cannot conduct action potentials. The only conducting pathway runs down through the septum, from a patch of tissue called the **atrio-ventricular node** or **AVN**, through a group of fibres called **Purkyne fibres**. The action potential sweeps down here, down both sides of the septum, and then spreads upwards through the walls of the ventricles, causing the muscles to contract as it arrives.

This arrangement gives time for the atria to finish contracting, and to empty their contents into the ventricles, before the ventricles begin to contract. Conduction is slow through the AVN and this produces a delay. Ventricular contraction is stimulated from 0.12 to 0.20 seconds after the atria contract.

You can probably see why it is useful for the ventricles to contract from the bottom upwards. This squeezes the blood more efficiently up into the arteries than if all of the ventricle wall started to contract at once.

10.6   Cardiac output changes during exercise

The rate at which blood is pumped out of the heart depends not only on *how fast* the heart beats, but also on *how much blood* it pushes out with each beat. For example, if the heart beats at a rate of 72 beats per minute, and pumps out 80 cm^3 of blood with each beat, then it is moving $72 \times 80 = 5760$ cm^3 of blood per minute. This value is the **cardiac output**. Cardiac output can be increased either by increasing the rate at which the heart beats (**heart rate**), or the volume of blood pumped with each stroke (**stroke volume**).

cardiac output = heart rate $\times$ stroke volume

During exercise, the cardiac output must be greater than at rest. This is because exercising muscles need rapid supplies of oxygen for respiration to generate the ATP needed to fuel contraction. They also need their waste

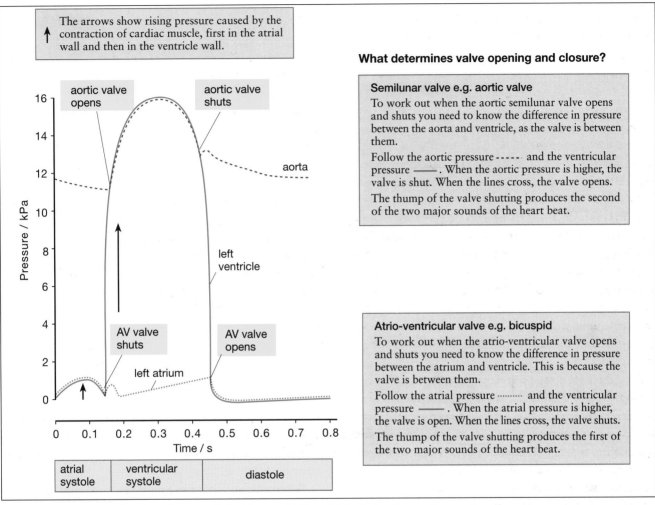

Fig. 10.6 Pressure changes in the aorta, left atrium and left ventricle during the cardiac cycle.

products, especially carbon dioxide, taken away more rapidly than usual.

Imagine a person has a normal, resting heart rate and stroke volume of 75 beats per minute and 75 cm³ respectively. If they undergo strenuous exercise, these can go up to 190 beats per minute and 110 cm³. This increases the cardiac output from 5625 cm³ of blood per minute at rest, to 20 900 cm³ of blood per minute during exercise.

If a person trains regularly, they increase the strength of their heart muscle and the volume of the heart chambers, so that their stroke volume becomes greater. (You can read more about the effects of training on this and other parts of the body in Box 16.3 on page 374). This means that their heart can pump the same volume of blood as in the 'untrained' person above at a lower heart rate. For example, a resting, fit marathon runner might have a heart rate of 50 beats per minute and a stroke volume of 105 cm³. This gives him a cardiac output of 5250 cm³ of blood per minute, very similar to that of the unfit person,

but with a much lower heart rate. During exercise, his stroke volume may go as high as 160 cm³, while his heart rate goes up to 180 beats per minute. That provides a cardiac output of 28 800 cm³ of blood per minute – significantly higher than that of the unfit person.

10.7 Regulation of cardiac output

What brings about the increase in cardiac output during exercise?

The heart is designed to pump out whatever flows into it, over quite a wide range of values. If an increased volume of blood returns to the heart in the veins, then the heart responds by pumping faster and harder to push it out. This happens because the incoming blood stretches the muscle in the heart wall, and the muscle responds by contracting harder than usual, increasing the stroke volume. At the same time, the stretching directly stimulates the SAN, which responds by firing action potentials slightly faster than usual, slightly increasing the heart rate.

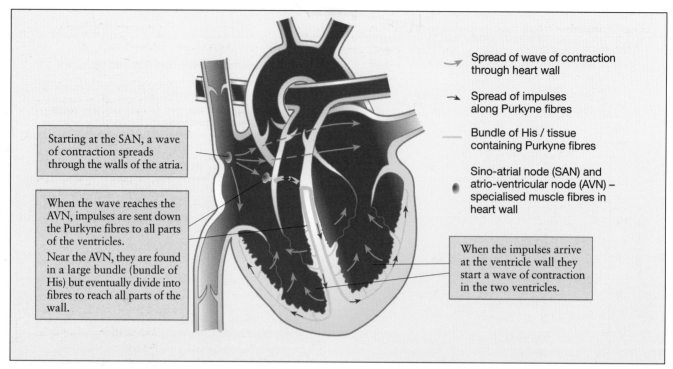

Starting at the SAN, a wave of contraction spreads through the walls of the atria.

When the wave reaches the AVN, impulses are sent down the Purkyne fibres to all parts of the ventricles.

Near the AVN, they are found in a large bundle (bundle of His) but eventually divide into fibres to reach all parts of the wall.

When the impulses arrive at the ventricle wall they start a wave of contraction in the two ventricles.

Spread of wave of contraction through heart wall

Spread of impulses along Purkyne fibres

Bundle of His / tissue containing Purkyne fibres

Sino-atrial node (SAN) and atrio-ventricular node (AVN) – specialised muscle fibres in heart wall

Fig. 10.7 The control of heart beat.

Therefore, anything which increases the rate at which blood returns to the heart will increase the cardiac output. This happens during exercise. An exercising muscle uses oxygen, and this reduces the oxygen concentration in the blood vessels in that muscle. This, together with the stress of extra blood flow on the cells lining the blood vessels, causes the release of nitric oxide. The nitric oxide causes the muscles in the blood vessel walls to relax which makes the vessels dilate (get wider). This increases the rate of flow of blood into the veins and thus into the heart, and so increases cardiac output. The extra demand for oxygen by working muscles therefore has the effect of increasing the rate at which blood is supplied to the muscle – a neat and very efficient arrangement.

This mechanism can only work up to a certain maximum cardiac output. However, nervous stimulation can alter the range over which the heart can cope with the blood returning to it. The heart has two types of nerves running to it, the **vagus** (a parasympathetic nerve) and **sympathetic nerves**. (You can read about the parasympathetic and sympathetic nervous systems in Chapter 14.) These nerves bring impulses from the cardiovascular centre in the medulla of the brain (Fig. 14.3). The vagus nerve brings impulses from the brain to the SAN and AVN, while the sympathetic nerves bring impulses to many areas of the muscle in the heart walls

(Fig. 10.8). If action potentials arrive along a sympathetic nerve, they speed up the heart rate and increase stroke volume. The parasympathetic nerve (vagus) has the opposite effect.

When you are about to begin exercise, your brain not only sends impulses to your muscles, but also along the sympathetic nerve to your heart, at the same time. This increases the rate of heart beat, even before the increased volume of blood returning to the heart does so, and prepares the heart to cope with the increased blood coming back to it during exercise. The hormone **adrenaline**, secreted from the adrenal glands in time of fear, stress or nervous anticipation, has similar effects to stimulation by the sympathetic nerves.

These nerves may also be affected by **blood pressure**. Inside the aorta, and also in the walls of the carotid arteries, are nerve endings which are sensitive to stretching. They are called **baroreceptors** or **stretch receptors**. If blood pressure rises, then this stretches the artery walls which stimulates these nerve endings. They fire off impulses to the brain, which then sends impulses down the vagus nerve to the heart. This slows the heart rate and stroke volume which can help to reduce the blood pressure. Low blood pressure has the opposite effect. In this case, the baroreceptors are not stretched and do not send impulses to the brain. The cardiovascular

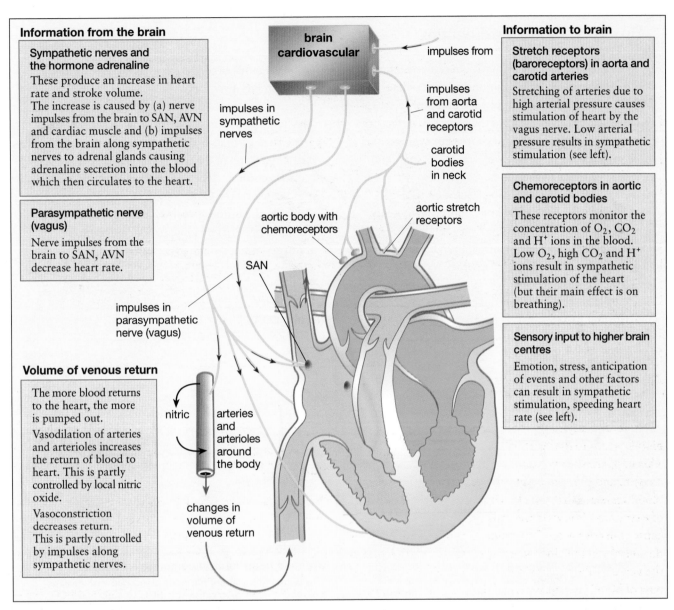

Information from the brain

Sympathetic nerves and the hormone adrenaline

These produce an increase in heart rate and stroke volume.
The increase is caused by (a) nerve impulses from the brain to SAN, AVN and cardiac muscle and (b) impulses from the brain along sympathetic nerves to adrenal glands causing adrenaline secretion into the blood which then circulates to the heart.

Parasympathetic nerve (vagus)

Nerve impulses from the brain to SAN, AVN decrease heart rate.

Volume of venous return

The more blood returns to the heart, the more is pumped out.
Vasodilation of arteries and arterioles increases the return of blood to heart. This is partly controlled by local nitric oxide.
Vasoconstriction decreases return. This is partly controlled by impulses along sympathetic nerves.

brain
cardiovascular

impulses from

impulses from aorta and carotid receptors

carotid bodies in neck

impulses in sympathetic nerves

aortic body with chemoreceptors

aortic stretch receptors

SAN

impulses in parasympathetic nerve (vagus)

nitric

arteries and arterioles around the body

changes in volume of venous return

Information to brain

Stretch receptors (baroreceptors) in aorta and carotid arteries

Stretching of arteries due to high arterial pressure causes stimulation of heart by the vagus nerve. Low arterial pressure results in sympathetic stimulation (see left).

Chemoreceptors in aortic and carotid bodies

These receptors monitor the concentration of O_2, CO_2 and H^+ ions in the blood. Low O_2, high CO_2 and H^+ ions result in sympathetic stimulation of the heart (but their main effect is on breathing).

Sensory input to higher brain centres

Emotion, stress, anticipation of events and other factors can result in sympathetic stimulation, speeding heart rate (see left).

Fig. 10.8 How cardiac output is regulated.

centre in the brain then sends messages along the sympathetic nerve, which increases cardiac output and thus blood pressure. Messages are also sent to muscles in the arteriole walls, which contract and narrow the arterioles (vasoconstriction), so increasing blood pressure.

Many factors affect blood pressure, both in the short term and long term. Your blood pressure briefly drops, for example, when you stand up after sitting down for a while. If you have been relaxing, your heart will be working at a fairly slow rate. When you stand up, blood pressure in the vessels in your head and upper body suddenly drops, which can sometimes make you feel faint. This is quickly remedied, as the baroreceptors

detect the drop in pressure and set off the processes which increase blood pressure, including an increase in cardiac output.

Yet another factor which can influence the rate of heart beat, through the action of nerves to the heart, is the concentration of carbon dioxide and oxygen in the blood. These are monitored by **chemoreceptors**, some of which are in the brain and others in the walls of the carotid arteries and aorta. High carbon dioxide concentrations or low oxygen concentrations can increase the rate of heart beat. However, this is usually of little importance compared with all the other factors controlling heart rate.

Box 10.1 Electrocardiograms

An electrocardiogram, or **ECG**, is a record of the voltage changes which occur during the cardiac cycle. Voltage changes occur as action potentials that spread from one part of the heart to another. Section 14.7 explains a little more about the reasons for such changes.

An ECG is made by attaching electrodes to the surface of a person's body and connecting these to an instrument which measures very small changes in voltage – the values are in millivolts. This in turn can be connected to a recorder which plots the voltage against time. An example of the result is shown in Fig. 10.9.

The first diagram in Fig. 10.9 shows a normal ECG. The letters P, Q, R, S and T are used to identify particular parts of the trace. The P wave occurs as the atria contract. The contraction of the ventricles is indicated by the Q, R, S section. The T wave occurs as the ventricles relax. An ECG which differs from this pattern can indicate that something abnormal is happening in the heart.

Normal ECG

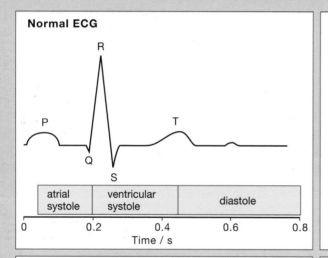

Normal ECG
recorded on a chart running at 25 mm s⁻¹

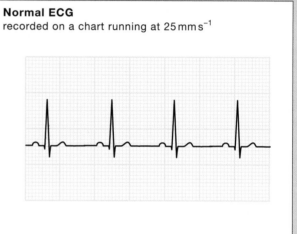

Ventricular fibrillation

This kind of chaotic electrical activity, showing no rhythm, can follow a serious heart attack and will be fatal without cardiopulmonary resuscitation because there is no cardiac output.

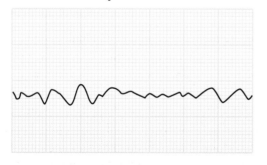

Dropped heart beat (incomplete AV block)

This is common and not normally associated with disease. Compare the PR interval in this ECG to a normal ECG. This is caused by a delay in conduction through the AVN.

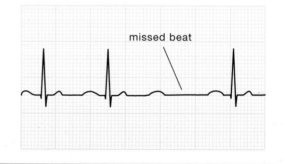

Fig. 10.9   ECG (electrocardiogram) records and the information that can be obtained from them.

Q1 The graph shows the pressure and volume changes that occur during the cardiac cycle.

(a) Make a copy of the graph and indicate on it the stages of the cardiac cycle.

(b) How does the graph of pressure in the atrium and ventricle explain the movement of blood into the ventricle at 0.13 s?

(c) What is causing the rapid rise in pressure at the start of the ventricular systole?

(d) During which stage of the cardiac cycle is the ventricle mostly filled?

(e) Why is the volume of the ventricle not changing at the start of ventricular systole, even though the pressure is rising rapidly inside the ventricle?

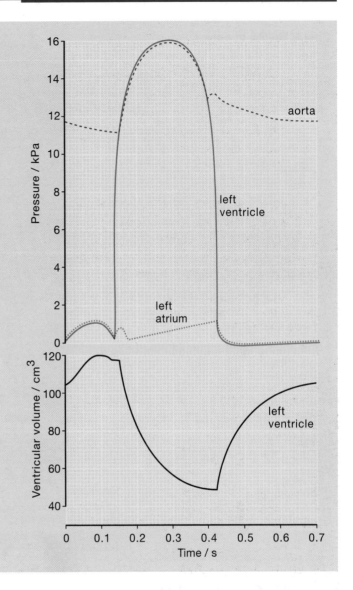

BLOOD VESSELS

10.8 The structure and functions of blood vessels

A blood vessel is a tube with a space in the centre, called the **lumen**, where the blood flows. Mammals have three types of blood vessels. **Arteries** carry blood away from the heart, and **veins** carry blood towards the heart. Linking the two, forming networks of tiny tubes in the tissues, are **capillaries**. Fig. 10.10 shows the structures of the walls of these three types of blood vessels.

Arteries carry blood which has recently been pumped out of the heart. The blood is at high pressure, travelling fast, and 'pulsing' – that is its pressure is fluctuating with the heart beat. You can feel this pulse if you rest your fingers on an artery in your neck or wrist. The walls of arteries are therefore *strong*, to withstand the high pressure of the blood inside them. They are also *elastic*, so that they can expand outwards to accommodate the increased flow of blood which accompanies each heart beat. As the elastic wall rebounds between each pulse of blood, it pushes inwards on the blood inside the vessel. This extra push, coming in between the surges of pressure from the heart, helps to smooth out the flow a little as the blood flows onwards through the arteries.

Arterioles are small arteries. As an artery gets closer to the tissue to which it is delivering blood it divides to form

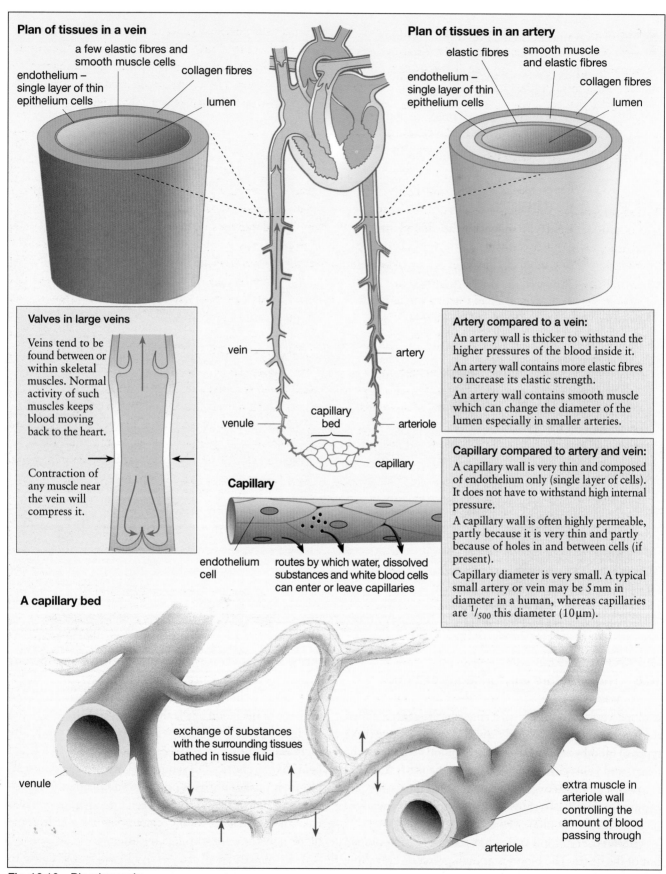

Plan of tissues in a vein

a few elastic fibres and smooth muscle cells

collagen fibres

endothelium – single layer of thin epithelium cells

lumen

Plan of tissues in an artery

elastic fibres

smooth muscle and elastic fibres

endothelium – single layer of thin epithelium cells

collagen fibres

lumen

Valves in large veins

Veins tend to be found between or within skeletal muscles. Normal activity of such muscles keeps blood moving back to the heart.

Contraction of any muscle near the vein will compress it.

vein

artery

venule

capillary bed

arteriole

capillary

Capillary

endothelium cell

routes by which water, dissolved substances and white blood cells can enter or leave capillaries

Artery compared to a vein:

An artery wall is thicker to withstand the higher pressures of the blood inside it.

An artery wall contains more elastic fibres to increase its elastic strength.

An artery wall contains smooth muscle which can change the diameter of the lumen especially in smaller arteries.

Capillary compared to artery and vein:

A capillary wall is very thin and composed of endothelium only (single layer of cells). It does not have to withstand high internal pressure.

A capillary wall is often highly permeable, partly because it is very thin and partly because of holes in and between cells (if present).

Capillary diameter is very small. A typical small artery or vein may be 5 mm in diameter in a human, whereas capillaries are $\frac{1}{500}$ this diameter (10 μm).

A capillary bed

venule

exchange of substances with the surrounding tissues bathed in tissue fluid

extra muscle in arteriole wall controlling the amount of blood passing through

arteriole

Fig. 10.10   Blood vessels.

many smaller vessels. These have a similar structure to large arteries but with less elastic tissue, as the blood flow has become smoother. They also have more smooth muscle. This muscle can widen (dilate) or narrow (constrict) the lumen of the arteriole. If the muscle contracts, the lumen gets narrower, so less blood can flow through that arteriole. If the muscle relaxes, then more blood can flow through. The body uses this mechanism to divert blood towards tissues which need it at a particular time, and away from tissues which have less urgent needs.

Box 10.2 Blood pressure

Blood pressure is the pressure which the blood exerts against the wall of the vessels through which it is flowing. Fig. 10.12 shows how the blood pressure gradually drops as the blood flows out of the heart and around the body. You can see how the pressure goes up and down in the arteries, but gradually smooths out as the blood gets further away from the heart. The blood pressure falls as the blood passes through the vessels because energy is used to overcome the friction of the blood against their walls. The biggest frictional resistance is in very small arterioles. The capillaries have an even smaller diameter, but there are so many of them that their total resistance to flow is much less than that of the arterioles, so the pressure drop within them is less than that in the arterioles.

You may have had your blood pressure measured with a **sphygmomanometer**. This measures the pressure in the brachial artery just above your elbow. A cuff is wrapped around the arm, and inflated with air so that it squeezes inwards tightly until it stops the blood flowing through the artery. The person taking the measurement places a stethoscope in the crook of the elbow to listen for the pulsing of the blood through the artery. The cuff is then slowly deflated. At first nothing can be heard, because no blood is flowing through. Then, as the pressure in the arm band continues to drop, the blood suddenly starts to get through and a sharp sound is heard. At this point, the pressure exerted by the cuff is the same as the maximum pressure in the artery. This value is the **systolic blood pressure**, the pressure produced during systole (contraction) of the heart. The blood is just managing to squirt through into the artery when it is at this maximum pressure.

The cuff is then gradually deflated even more, easing the pressure on the artery and letting blood through more and more easily. Eventually, the pressure on the cuff drops to a point at which the blood can get through even while it is at its minimum pressure. The sounds of the blood die away completely. This is the **diastolic pressure**, the pressure in the artery while the heart is relaxing.

Doctors measure blood pressure in units of millimetres of mercury, abbreviated to **mm Hg**. (1 mm Hg is equivalent to 0.13 kPa.) For a healthy person, the systolic blood pressure in the brachial artery while at rest is usually about 120 mm Hg, and the diastolic pressure about 80 mm Hg. This is written as 120/80. If your blood pressure at rest is much above this, you have high blood pressure.

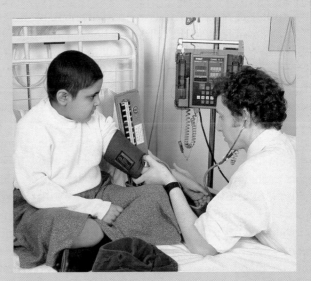

Fig. 10.11   Using a sphygmomanometer.

Box 10.2 Blood pressure (cont.)

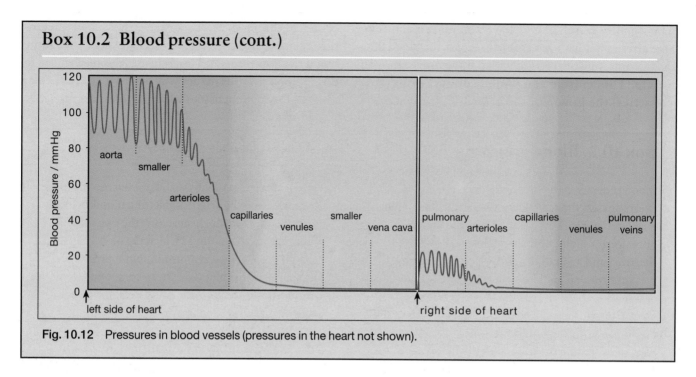

Fig. 10.12 Pressures in blood vessels (pressures in the heart not shown).

For example, during exercise, arterioles delivering blood to muscles dilate, while those delivering blood to the digestive system constrict.

Capillaries are very tiny, not visible to the naked eye. Many of them are only just wide enough for a red blood cell to squeeze through. An arteriole divides to form a spreading network of capillaries, called a **capillary bed** (Fig. 10.10). Almost every region of the body contains capillary beds.

Capillaries have the function of delivering blood as close as possible to all the cells in the body, a job which is obviously greatly helped by their small size. Most cells are no more than 1 mm away from a capillary. The tiny diameter of capillaries ensures that no part of their contents is far away from these cells. Their walls are very, very thin, with just a single layer of flattened cells separating them from the tissues in which they lie. Many of them have little gaps in their walls, which allow fluid from the blood to ooze out and fill the spaces between the cells. This allows exchange of materials by diffusion between the blood in the capillaries and the cells in the surrounding tissues. Water, nutrients such as glucose, and oxygen move into the tissues, while carbon dioxide moves into the blood. This exchange is described in more detail in Section 10.14.

Venules are small **veins** which collect blood after it has flowed through a capillary bed. The blood has now lost most of its pressure, so there is no need for venules, or the veins into which they deliver their blood, to have thick, elastic or muscular walls. Indeed, the pressure is now so low that the blood needs some extra help to make it flow back to the heart, especially if it is *below* the heart, for example in your feet. Many veins lie inside or between skeletal muscles, such as your leg muscles. When these muscles contract, they squeeze on the veins, pushing in on the blood and making it flow.

To ensure that the blood flows towards the heart in a vein, and not back to where it has just come from, many veins have **valves**. These are extensions of their inner wall, which have pockets that trap blood if it starts flowing backwards. The trapped blood pushes the valves shut, in a similar way to the semi-lunar valves illustrated in Fig. 10.4.

10.9 The human circulatory system

Fig. 10.13 shows the main arteries and veins in the human circulatory system. The ones going to and from the lungs make up the **pulmonary circulation**, and the ones going to and from the rest of the body form the **systemic circulation**.

In general, each organ is supplied with blood by an artery, and blood is taken away by a vein. These vessels are often named according to the organ they supply. For example the renal artery and vein supply the kidneys ('renal' means something to do with kidneys). Others have names of their own, such as the carotid artery and jugular vein.

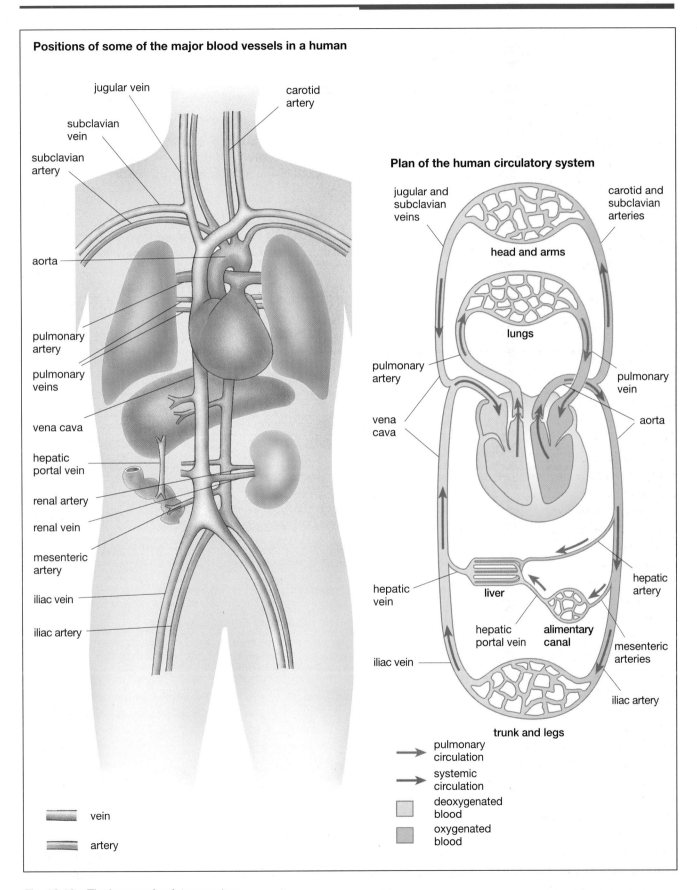

Positions of some of the major blood vessels in a human

- jugular vein
- carotid artery
- subclavian vein
- subclavian artery
- aorta
- pulmonary artery
- pulmonary veins
- vena cava
- hepatic portal vein
- renal artery
- renal vein
- mesenteric artery
- iliac vein
- iliac artery

vein

artery

Plan of the human circulatory system

- jugular and subclavian veins
- carotid and subclavian arteries
- head and arms
- lungs
- pulmonary artery
- pulmonary vein
- vena cava
- aorta
- liver
- hepatic artery
- hepatic vein
- hepatic portal vein
- alimentary canal
- mesenteric arteries
- iliac vein
- iliac artery

trunk and legs

→ pulmonary circulation
→ systemic circulation
☐ deoxygenated blood
☐ oxygenated blood

Fig. 10.13   The human circulatory system.

For most organs, the blood brought by the artery is oxygenated, and the blood taken away in the vein is deoxygenated. The only exception is the lungs, where the pulmonary artery brings deoxygenated blood and the pulmonary vein takes away oxygenated blood.

The liver is an exception to the basic design, because it has blood delivered in *two* vessels. One, as for all other organs except the lungs, branches off from the aorta and brings oxygenated blood. This is the hepatic artery. The other vessel brings blood which has first flowed along the mesenteric artery to the gut, where it travelled through a capillary bed and picked up soluble molecules resulting from the digestion of food. This blood then flows into the hepatic portal vein which carries it to the liver. In common with other organs, however, the liver has just one main vein taking blood away from it, called the hepatic vein.

Q2 The table below shows the diameter of the lumen and the rate of blood flow in a number of human blood vessels.

Vessel	Diameter of lumen	Rate of blood flow/ cm s^{-1}
Artery	0.4 cm	40–10
Arteriole	30.0 μm	10 –0.1
Capillary	8.0 μm	less than 0.1
Venule	20.0 μm	less than 0.3
Vein	0.5 cm	0.3 –5

(a) (i) Describe the general relation between the rate of blood flow and the diameter of the lumen of the blood vessel. *(1)*

    (ii) Explain how the diameter of a blood vessel affects the resistance to blood flowing through it. *(2)*

(b) (i) Which of the blood vessels mentioned has most elastic tissue in its walls? *(1)*

    (ii) How does the possession of elastic tissue affect flow through blood vessels? *(1)*

AEB 1994 *(Total 5 marks)*

Q3 A fish such as a trout has a single circulation while a mammal has a double circulation.

(a) Explain **one** advantage of a double circulation. *(2)*

(b) The table below shows how certain factors which affect the supply of oxygen to the tissues of a trout increase during maximum activity.

Factor	Number of times factor is increased from resting level
heart rate	1.36
heart stroke volume	2.24
oxygen released by haemoglobin	2.66

Suggest how the nervous system might produce the change in heart rate shown in the table.

(2)

AEB (part question) 1993 *(Total 4 marks)*

BLOOD
10.10   The composition of blood
Fig. 10.14 shows the different components of human blood. Just over half of its volume is a liquid called **plasma**. Plasma is mostly water which has a wide variety of substances dissolved in it. These include substances being transported from place to place, such as glucose, water and hormones, and also substances which remain in the blood for most of the time, especially **plasma proteins**. The most abundant plasma protein is **albumin** which has an important role in maintaining the solute potential of the blood, stopping too much water leaving it from the capillaries by osmosis (Section 3.26). Albumin and other proteins called **globulins** also help to transport substances such as iron and lipids in the plasma by combining with them. Some globulins, called **immunoglobulins**, help to fight against disease (Section 21.9). Other plasma proteins include **fibrinogen** and **prothrombin** which help in blood clotting (Section 21.6).

Suspended in the plasma are several different kinds of **cells**. The great majority of these are **red cells** which transport oxygen around the body. Some are **white cells** which function in protection of the body against disease. There are also small cell fragments surrounded by cell surface membranes. These are called **platelets** and they help in blood clotting and have various other roles.

In the next few sections we will look at the roles of blood plasma and red cells in transporting oxygen and carbon dioxide around the body. Some of the other substances transported in the blood are listed in Table 10.1. The roles of the white cells and platelets are described in Chapter 21.

10.11   The transport of oxygen
The blood transports oxygen from the lungs to the tissues where it is used in respiration. The way in which oxygen enters the blood is described in Section 12.5.

The great majority of oxygen is carried in combination with **haemoglobin** which is a reddish-purple pigment found inside red blood cells. Haemoglobin is a protein, each molecule of which is made up of four polypeptide chains (Fig. 10.15). These make up the globin part of the molecule. Each of these chains is associated with atoms that form a **haem** group with an iron(II) ion at its centre.

Substance	Where it enters the blood	Where it leaves the blood	Where you can read more about it
oxygen	alveoli of lungs	all respiring cells	pages 221 to 225
carbon dioxide	all respiring cells	alveoli of lungs	pages 228 to 230
dissolved nutrients, e.g. glucose, amino acids, inorganic ions	small intestine	the liver, and all other tissues	pages 282 to 283, and 327 to 328
water	colon	all tissues	page 284
urea	liver	kidneys	pages 337 to 338
plasma proteins	liver	most do not leave the blood	pages 482 to 483, 485, 487
hormones	endocrine glands	target organs	pages 323 to 330
antibodies	mostly from the lymph glands, via the lymphatic drainage	all tissues	page 487

Table 10.1   Some of the substances transported by human blood

Blood

Cells / cell fragments 45%

red cells

white cells
- monocytes
- lymphocytes
- granulocytes (neutrophils, eosinophils, basophils)

platelets

Plasma 55%

serum

fibrinogen

Scanning electron micrograph of red blood cells (×3500)

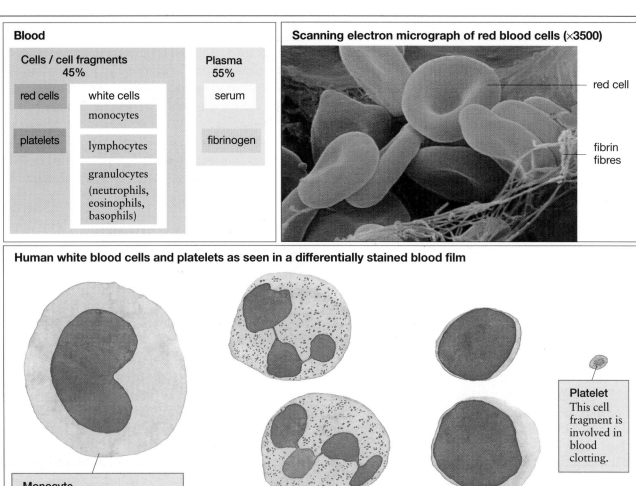

red cell

fibrin fibres

Human white blood cells and platelets as seen in a differentially stained blood film

Monocyte

This is a large cell with an indented nucleus.

The cell is phagocytic and ingests large cell fragments. It is also known as a macrophage.

Granulocyte

This cell has a lobed nucleus and granules in the cytoplasm. There can be 2–8 lobes.

The cell is phagocytic.

Lymphocyte

This cell has very little cytoplasm.

Lymphocytes are involved in defence against disease. Some of them secrete antibodies.

Platelet

This cell fragment is involved in blood clotting.

Differentially stained blood film (×570)

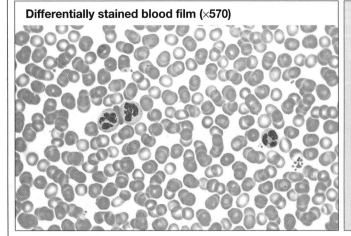

The blood film

A number of human diseases produce abnormal blood films and examination of stained films can help diagnosis. For example, a change from the normal proportions of different kinds of white cells can occur in disease. To provide this information a differential white cell count is needed.

You can perform a differential count by using a blood film stained with a special stain which differentiates between the white cells. The blood film is scanned systematically and the numbers of each type of white cell in a total of 200 white cells is noted.

Normal proportions are: granulocytes 40–75%, lymphocytes 20–45%, monocytes 2–10%.

This is a good example of the use which can be made of differential staining techniques.

Fig. 10.14 The structure and composition of blood.

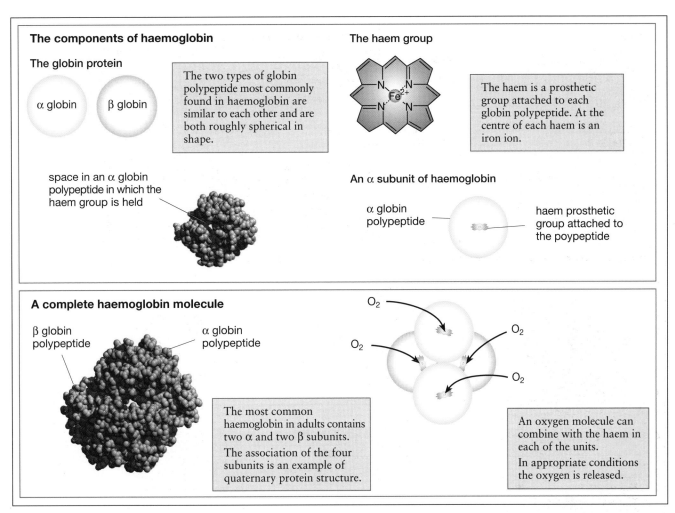

Fig. 10.15 The structure of haemoglobin.

It is these iron ions which bond with oxygen molecules. Each iron ion can bond with one oxygen molecule (which contains two oxygen atoms), so one haemoglobin molecule can bond with four oxygen molecules. When this happens, the haemoglobin molecule becomes **oxyhaemoglobin**. Oxyhaemoglobin is brighter red than haemoglobin.

Just as important as haemoglobin's ability to *bond* with oxygen is its ability to *drop* it again when it reaches a tissue that needs oxygen. Haemoglobin molecules bind rapidly with oxygen where the oxygen concentration is high, which in a human is in the lungs. They readily drop their oxygen where the oxygen concentration is low, for example in respiring tissues.

10.12 The haemoglobin dissociation curve

The graph in Fig. 10.16 is called a **haemoglobin dissociation curve**. The x axis shows the concentration of oxygen, measured as partial pressure in kilopascals.

('Partial pressure' is a measure of oxygen concentration.) The y axis shows the percentage saturation of the haemoglobin with oxygen. If all the haemoglobin molecules are combined with the maximum possible four molecules of oxygen each, then the haemoglobin is 100% saturated. If, on average, each haemoglobin molecule is combined with two molecules of oxygen, then the haemoglobin is 50% saturated, and so on.

The general trend of the curve is just as you would expect. The higher the concentration of oxygen, the greater the saturation of the haemoglobin molecules with oxygen. But what makes the curve S-shaped rather than a rising straight line, before levelling off? And is this of any significance?

A haemoglobin molecule is made up of four polypeptide chains, each with a haem group which is capable of combining with an oxygen molecule. When oxygen concentrations are very low, it is very unlikely that any of the four haem groups will do this. If the oxygen

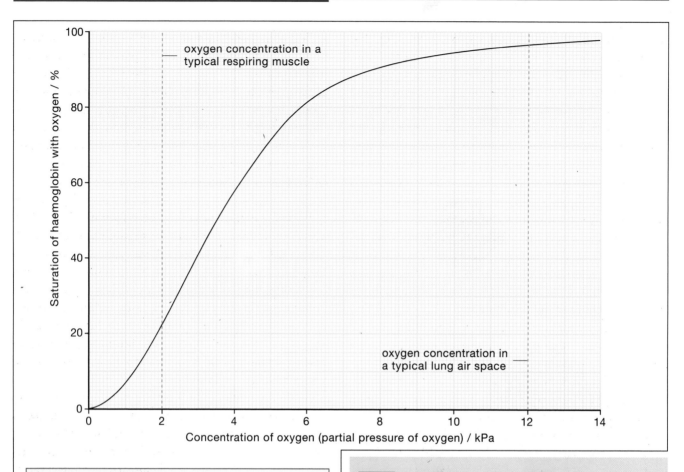

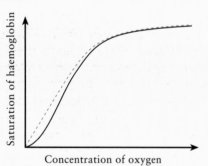

The S shape of the curve is unusual

The shape of the curve that you would expect of a molecule binding reaction would be like the red dashed line below:

The actual shape is shown in black and it shows that haemoglobin is less likely to bind oxygen at low oxygen concentrations than you would expect.

Fig. 10.16   The haemoglobin dissociation curve.

Q4

(a) What is meant by % saturation of haemoglobin with oxygen?

(b) Has haemoglobin at 30% saturation bound more oxygen than haemoglobin at 25% saturation?

(c) What is the saturation of haemoglobin in very active muscles where the oxygen concentration has fallen to 1 kPa?

(d) Make a copy of the graph shown above.

(e) On your graph draw a line to represent the 'expected' haemoglobin dissociation curve (not S-shaped).

(f) What would be the saturation of haemoglobin at an oxygen concentration of 1 kPa according to the curve drawn in (e)?

(g) Use the answers to (c) and (f) to explain the advantage of the S-shaped curve for haemoglobin dissociation.

(h) Explain why haemoglobin binds oxygen more readily once it has already bound some oxygen.

concentration is increased, then it becomes more likely that an oxygen molecule will combine with one haem group. When this happens the whole molecule slightly changes shape, making it much easier for another oxygen molecule to combine with one of the other haem groups in the molecule. This causes another shape change which makes it even easier for a third oxygen molecule to combine.

You can see the results of this property of haemoglobin if you look at the curve in Fig. 10.16. At the left-hand end of the x axis, where oxygen concentrations are very low, the percentage saturation of haemoglobin is also very low. However, if you move to the right, to a value of about 0.5 kPa partial pressure of oxygen, the curve starts to rise more rapidly. At about this point, quite a few of the haemoglobin molecules have picked up a molecule of oxygen. As they do so, they change their shape and become even more ready to combine with another oxygen molecule. So, if the partial pressure of oxygen rises only a little, the percentage saturation of haemoglobin rises a lot as each haemoglobin molecule readily and rapidly combines with two, three and eventually four oxygen molecules. Over this part of the curve, a small rise in partial pressure of oxygen causes a large rise in percentage saturation of haemoglobin. At partial pressures of 8 kPa and above, most haemoglobin molecules are fully combined with oxygen, so increasing the oxygen concentration above this does not have much effect and the curve stays relatively flat.

This also works in reverse, if you begin at the right-hand end of the curve (where oxygen concentrations are high) and work towards the left. At high oxygen concentrations most of the haemoglobin molecules are combined with four oxygen molecules. As oxygen concentration drops, one oxygen molecule may leave, which changes the shape of the oxyhaemoglobin and makes it easier for the next oxygen to leave, and so on.

How does this help with oxygen transport? In the lungs, oxygen concentrations are normally high. A typical partial pressure of oxygen is about 12 kPa. You can see from the curve that the haemoglobin in a red cell in a capillary in the lungs will be approximately 95% saturated with oxygen. The blood containing this oxyhaemoglobin will now flow along the pulmonary vein into the heart and out along the aorta. Along this route, the partial pressure of oxygen will not change much. In any case, the curve is very flat at high oxygen concentrations, so the % saturation of the haemoglobin will not change.

However, when the blood arrives at an exercising muscle, the partial pressure of oxygen will be much lower. A typical value might be 2 kPa. If you look at the curve, you will see that haemoglobin exposed to this concentration of oxygen is only just over 20% saturated. The haemoglobin molecules release much of their oxygen, releasing it into the blood plasma, from where it can diffuse to the muscle cells and be used in respiration.

Q5 Diagrams A, B and C below show three different types of white blood cell.

Copy the table below and complete it by identifying cells **A**, **B** and **C** and giving *one* function of each.

	Type of cell	Function of cell
A		
B		
C		

London 1995   (*Total 6 marks*)

Q6 Copy the table below which refers to three components of human blood. If the statement is correct for the component, place a tick (✓) in the appropriate box and if the statement is incorrect, place a cross (✗) in the appropriate box.

Function	Red blood cell	Platelet	Plasma
Transports carbon dioxide			
Contains enzymes involved in clotting			
Forms antibodies			
Transports hormones			
Carries out phagocytosis			

London 1994   (*Total 5 marks*)

Box 10.3 Other respiratory pigments

Fetal haemoglobin

In a human fetus, the globin in the haemoglobin molecules is slightly different from that in adult haemoglobin. This has the effect of making fetal haemoglobin more likely to combine with oxygen. We say that it has a **higher affinity** for oxygen than does adult haemoglobin. The left-hand diagram in Fig. 10.17 shows the two dissociation curves. You can see that, at any oxygen concentration, the fetal haemoglobin is more saturated with oxygen than the adult haemoglobin. This helps the fetus to obtain oxygen. A fetus obtains all its oxygen through the placenta, from its mother's blood, where it is being carried as oxyhaemoglobin. The difference in affinity means that enough oxygen will leave the mother's haemoglobin, and combine with the fetus's, to supply the fetus with all its oxygen requirements.

Myoglobin

Myoglobin is a dark red pigment found in muscle cells. It is not found in the blood, and has no role in oxygen transport. It is an oxygen store. Fig. 10.17 also shows the dissociation curve for myoglobin, with the haemoglobin dissociation curve for comparison. Myoglobin has a very high affinity for oxygen, so the curve is to the left of that for haemoglobin. You can see that, even at very low oxygen concentrations, myoglobin is highly saturated with oxygen. Myoglobin picks up oxygen very readily, but will only give up its oxygen when oxygen concentrations drop to very low levels. In a very active muscle, the oxygen delivered by the blood may not be enough to keep up with its demands, and the oxygen concentrations in the muscle can easily drop to below 0.5 kPa. The myoglobin will then release its oxygen, providing a reserve supply to keep the muscle going for a bit longer. Eventually, of course, the myoglobin has no more oxygen to give up, and the muscle will have to respire anaerobically.

The shape of myoglobin's dissociation curve is due to its molecular structure. A myoglobin molecule contains only one polypeptide chain (which is very similar to the polypeptide chains in haemoglobin) and one haem group. At oxygen tensions above about 1 kPa, the iron ion in this haem group combines with oxygen. At oxygen tensions much below this, it does not combine. There is no gradual combination with more and more oxygen molecules as there is in haemoglobin. Thus, the curve for myoglobin just goes almost straight up over a narrow range of oxygen concentration.

Fetal haemoglobin

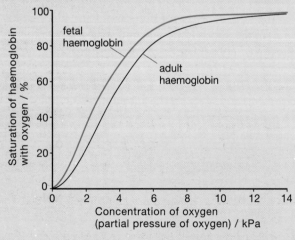

Myoglobin

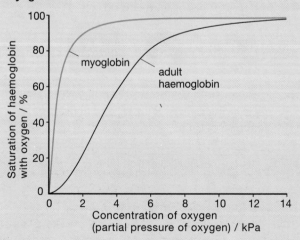

Fig. 10.17 Dissociation curves for fetal haemoglobin and myoglobin.

Box 10.3 Other respiratory pigments (cont.)

Respiratory pigments in other animals

All vertebrates (except for a few species of fish which have no respiratory pigment at all) have **haemoglobin** in their blood. Haemoglobin is also found in some non-vertebrates, including many species of annelid worms, such as the common earthworm *Lumbricus*, and in some insects. There are many different types of haemoglobin, varying from one another in the structure of their polypeptide chains and in their properties. For example, in the mud-dwelling lugworm, *Arenicola*, which spends much of its time in a burrow where oxygen concentrations drop very low between tides, the dissociation curve for its haemoglobin looks very like that for human myoglobin. This ensures that the haemoglobin can pick up oxygen even at relatively low concentrations, and this outweighs the disadvantage that it will not give it very readily to the worm's tissues.

Some marine annelids have a green respiratory pigment called **chlorocruorin**. The molecular structure of this pigment is quite similar to haemoglobin and also contains iron. Despite its name, however, the pigment **haemocyanin** is much less like haemoglobin. Haemocyanin contains copper, not iron, and the copper is bound to the protein, not to a prosthetic group. Haemocyanin is blue when oxygenated. It is found in many molluscs, including the common garden snail, and also in arthropods, especially crustaceans such as crabs and lobsters.

Q7 The graph below shows an oxygen dissociation curve for human haemoglobin.

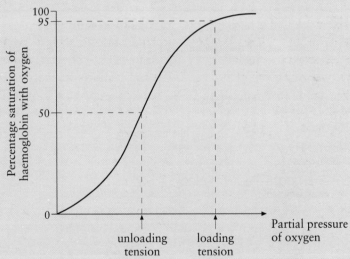

The loading tension is the partial pressure at which the haemoglobin is 95% saturated with oxygen. The unloading tension is the partial pressure at which the haemoglobin is 50% saturated.

(a) (i) What would be the effect on the unloading tension of an increase in the partial pressure of carbon dioxide? *(1)*

    (ii) Explain how this may be of value in supplying tissues with oxygen. *(2)*

(b) The prairie dog is a small mammal that spends much of its life in an extensive system of burrows where the air may have a low partial pressure of oxygen.

    (i) Copy the graph above and sketch on another curve which would represent an oxygen dissociation curve for prairie dog haemoglobin. *(1)*

    (ii) Explain why you have drawn the curve in this position. *(2)*

AEB 1993 *(Total 6 marks)*

10.13 Carbon dioxide transport and the Bohr effect

As well as transporting oxygen from the lungs to the tissues, the blood also transports carbon dioxide from tissues to the lungs. There are three ways in which the carbon dioxide is carried (Fig. 10.18), one of which helps considerably in the release of *oxygen* from haemoglobin to the tissues.

● As hydrogencarbonate ions

This is the most important method of carbon dioxide transport. About 85% of it is carried in this way.

Carbon dioxide produced by a respiring cell diffuses into the plasma in a blood capillary. Some then diffuses into red blood cells. Inside these cells there is an enzyme called **carbonic anhydrase**, which catalyses the reaction:

$$CO_2 + H_2O \xrightleftharpoons{\text{carbonic anyhdrase}} H_2CO_3$$

carbon dioxide + water ⇌ carbonic acid

Carbonic acid is a weak acid. It dissociates to produce hydrogen ions:

$$H_2CO_3 \rightleftharpoons H^+ + HCO_3^-$$

carbonic acid → hydrogen ions + hydrogencarbonate ions

Haemoglobin very readily combines with the hydrogen ions. It forms **haemoglobinic acid**. This has two useful effects. Firstly, it removes the hydrogen ions from solution, so preventing an increase in acidity (drop in pH). The haemoglobin is acting as a **buffer**, helping to keep a constant pH in the blood. Secondly, as the haemoglobin combines with the hydrogen ions, it releases some of the oxygen which it is carrying. This is just what is required because, if carbon dioxide is around in any quantity, this must mean that cells are respiring and in need of oxygen.

You can see the effect of high carbon concentrations on the haemoglobin dissociation curve in Fig. 10.19. With carbon dioxide present, the haemoglobin is *less* saturated

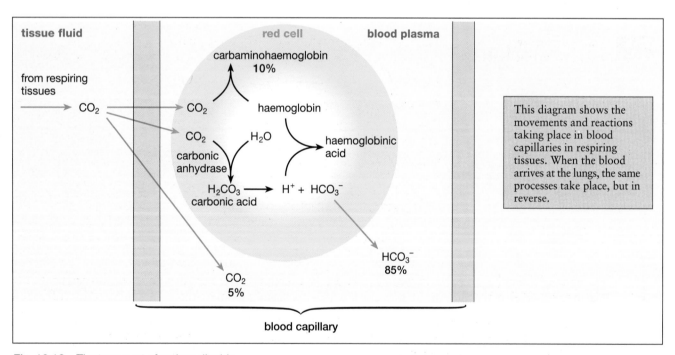

Fig. 10.18   The transport of carbon dioxide.

> **Q8** (a) Using Fig. 10.18 as a guide, make a similar diagram to show how carbon dioxide is released from the blood in lung capillaries
>
> (b) Explain how the behaviour of haemoglobin as a buffer helps in carbon dioxide transport.
>
> (c) What is the role of carbonic anhydrase in carbon dioxide transport?

The effect of changes in carbon dioxide concentration on haemoglobin saturation

How changes in carbon dioxide concentration affect oxygen transport

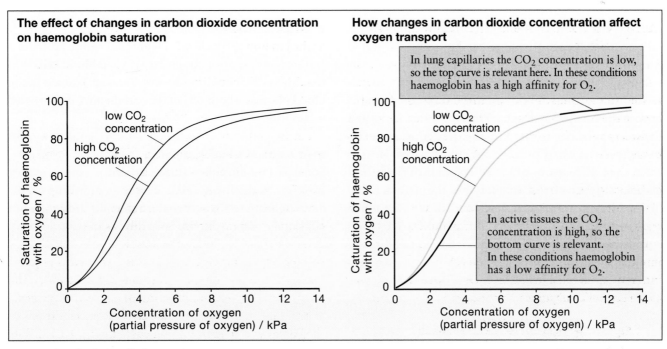

Fig. 10.19   The Bohr effect.

Q9   The figure below shows the oxygen dissociation curve of human haemoglobin. The curve is labelled **A**.

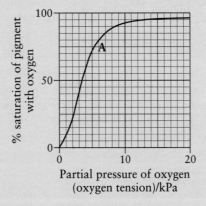

(a)   Over what range of partial pressures of oxygen does the greatest change in percentage saturation of haemoglobin occur?   (2)

(b)   Copy the figure and draw a dissociation curve to indicate
   (i)   the effect of higher partial pressure of carbon dioxide on the dissociation of human haemoglobin. Label this curve **B**.
   (ii)   the dissociation curve for myoglobin. Label this curve **C**.   (2)

(c)   Explain the significance of the differences between curves **A** and **B**.   (4)

(d)   Explain the significance of the shape of curve **C** in terms of oxygen tension and muscle activity in the body.   (3)

UCLES 1994   *(Total 11 marks)*

with oxygen at any given oxygen concentration. This is called the **Bohr effect**, after Christian Bohr who discovered it in 1904.

If you look back at the two equations above, you will see that the carbon dioxide which entered the blood is now in the form of hydrogencarbonate ions. Although these are initially formed inside the red blood cells (because that is where the carbonic anhydrase is), most of them then diffuse out of the cells and into the blood plasma. They are carried, in solution in the plasma, to the lungs. Here the reactions described above all go into reverse, and carbon dioxide gas diffuses out of the blood and into the alveoli, ready to be expired.

● As carbon dioxide molecules

Some carbon dioxide which enters the blood from a respiring tissue does not go into the red blood cells, but remains as carbon dioxide molecules, dissolved in the blood plasma. About 5% of the carbon dioxide is carried in this way.

● As carbaminohaemoglobin

Some carbon dioxide diffuses into the plasma and then into the red blood cells, where it combines with haemoglobin to form **carbaminohaemoglobin**. About 10% of the carbon dioxide is carried in this way.

Q10 Read the passage.

Substitute for blood to be tested

Trials are about to begin in England of a blood substitute that might replace 10 to 20% of transfusions, while making use of blood donations that have passed their 'use-by' date.

The artificial blood is a haemoglobin solution made from the oxygen carrying part of the red cells in human blood and is being tested in trauma cases. Because the red cell surfaces are missing, patients do not have to be typed and the blood cross-matched before transfusion.

The product has been developed by the US-based Baxter Healthcare which has overcome the problem that pure haemoglobin naturally tends to break into two molecules and be rapidly lost from the body. Baxter has found a way of locking the two sub-units together that makes the haemoglobin an efficient oxygen deliverer and allows it to be heat treated to destroy viruses. The company is taking the haemoglobin from blood donations that have passed their 35-day shelf life – a fate that on average happens to about 5% of donations in England.

Apart from being used in accident, injury and shock cases where oxygen delivery and fluid bulk is needed, one of the artificial blood's most exciting possibilities is that it may offer treatment for strokes. In animal studies, the haemoglobin solution has been able to go round blood clots and reach the parts of the brain being oxygen-starved by the clot. Infusion of the solution soon after a stroke appears to reduce the damage done to brain tissue and thus the effects of the stroke, which in humans can leave the victim paralysed, or their speech affected.

The blood substitute will not reduce the need for donors because it is derived from human haemoglobin. But it will cut out the waste of out-dated blood, allow blood to be used more flexibly and the resulting artificial blood to be stored for long periods.

adapted from an article in the Independent (7/5/94)

(a) The reason blood has a 'use-by' date is that red blood cells have a much shorter life span than the other cells in the body. Suggest **one** reason, connected with their structure, why red blood cells have a short life span. *(1)*

(b) Explain why artificial blood 'can reach the parts of the brain being oxygen-starved by the clot'. *(2)*

(c) Apart from its use in stroke victims, give **two** other advantages of using artificial blood rather than natural whole blood. *(2)*

(d) Explain the role of haemoglobin in the loading, transport and unloading of oxygen. *(7)*

NEAB 1995 *(Total 12 marks)*

TISSUE FLUID AND LYMPH

10.14 The formation of tissue fluid

Capillaries take blood into every tissue of the body. Here, fluid escapes from the capillaries and fills the spaces between the cells. This fluid is called **tissue fluid**.

Fluid can get out of capillaries because they have tiny gaps in their walls. The number of these gaps varies a great deal between capillaries in different parts of the body. In many capillaries there are gaps where two of the cells making up the capillary wall meet. These gaps are easily big enough to let quite large molecules through, but too small for red blood cells to pass through. Some capillaries, such as those in the wall of the small intestine and in the glomeruli of renal capsules in the kidneys, also have holes actually running through the cells in their walls. This makes them even more permeable. In contrast, capillaries in the brain are very tightly sealed, allowing very little to pass through except essentials such as water, oxygen and glucose. (This arrangement is called the 'blood–brain barrier', and helps to stop potentially harmful substances, including viruses, from entering the brain.) Fluid tends to leave capillaries at the end of a capillary bed nearest to an arteriole, and to re-enter them at the end nearest to a venule. (Box 10.4 explains why this happens.)

Tissue fluid is the medium through which substances are exchanged between blood and cells. Most of this exchange is through **diffusion**. As capillaries are so tiny, with very thin walls, and as they come so close to almost every cell, the distances involved are very small. In the heart muscle, for example, an oxygen molecule only has to diffuse a distance of about 13 μm to get from a capillary to the most distant mitochondrion.

Another important function of tissue fluid is that it maintains a relatively constant environment around the body cells. Many processes help to keep the concentrations of important substances, such as glucose, water and hydrogen ions, constant in the blood plasma, and therefore in the tissue fluid which is formed directly from it. Temperature is also closely regulated. Keeping such conditions nearly constant is called homeostasis, and is described in Chapter 15. By regulating the composition and temperature of tissue fluid, the immediate environment of body cells is kept constant, enabling the cells to function much more efficiently than if their surroundings were liable to sudden change.

10.15 Lymph

You have seen that much of the fluid which leaks from capillaries at one end of a capillary bed returns to them at the other end. However, in most capillary beds less fluid returns than is lost, and in some only a very little returns. If nothing was done about this, then the blood would lose fluid, and the build-up of fluid in the tissues would cause swelling, which is known as oedema.

This excess tissue fluid is returned to the blood via the **lymphatic system**. This is a network of vessels called **lymphatics** (Fig. 10.20) which spread all over the body. However, unlike the vessels of the blood system, they do not form a continuous circulatory system. The lymphatic

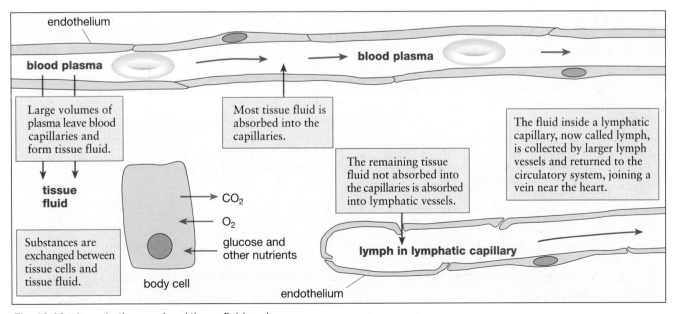

Fig. 10.20 Lymphatic vessel and tissue fluid exchange.

capillaries begin in the tissues as tiny blind-ending tubes, with valves in their walls which allow tissue fluid to flow in, but not to escape. Once inside the vessel, the fluid is called **lymph**. These lymphatic capillaries lead into larger vessels which eventually join with the subclavian veins. The lymph is therefore returned to the blood system.

There is no pump in the lymphatic system. Rather like veins, lymphatic vessels often lie within and between muscles whose contractions squeeze inwards on the lymph. Also like veins, they have valves in them to prevent backflow of lymph. Fluid movement within them is very slow but, nevertheless, in one day the lymphatic system transfers a volume of fluid equivalent to the total volume of plasma in the blood system. ■

Q11 (a) What is the role of blood capillaries in the transport system of a mammal? (2)

(b) Distinguish between the following pairs of terms.
   (i) *blood* and *lymph* (2)
   (ii) *plasma* and *tissue fluid* (2)

(c) Mammalian fetal haemoglobin has a dissociation curve which lies above and to the left of that of adult haemoglobin. Explain the significance of this. (4)

UCLES 1994 (*Total 10 marks*)

Q12 A student cycled strenuously on an exercise bicycle for 10 minutes. During this time blood pressure measurements were taken. These measurements continued for a further 5 minutes after the exercise had finished. After the 10 minutes cycling, the student was near exhaustion and felt very faint. The changes in the student's blood pressure are shown in the figure below.

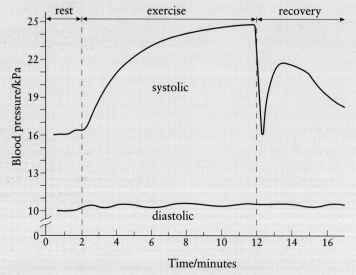

(a) Distinguish between *systolic* and *diastolic* blood pressure. (2)

(b) With reference to the figure, describe the changes in systolic blood pressure between
   (i) 2 and 12 minutes;
   (ii) 12 and 14 minutes. (3)

(c) Explain the change in systolic blood pressure during exercise. (3)

(d) (i) With reference to blood pressure, suggest why the student felt faint immediately after exercise. (2)
   (ii) Suggest how the student might avoid feeling faint at the end of strenuous cycling. (1)

UCLES 1995 (*Total 11 marks*)

Box 10.4 Movement of fluids into and out of capillaries

Fluid tends to leave a capillary as the blood enters it from an arteriole, and to enter it at the other end of the capillary bed, before the blood enters a venule (Fig. 10.21). The direction of movement of the fluid is determined by the balance between **hydrostatic pressure** (pressure of a liquid) and the **solute potential** inside and outside the capillary, which between them determine the water potential of the fluids (Section 3.26).

water potential = solute potential + hydrostatic pressure

As the blood enters a capillary bed from an arteriole, it is at a relatively high hydrostatic pressure. The hydrostatic pressure raises its water potential above that of the fluids outside the

capillary so that fluid moves out, contributing to the tissue fluid. Many of the contents of the blood plasma pass out in this way, but most of the larger molecules, especially albumin, cannot. Most of the albumin remains dissolved in the plasma inside the capillary.

So, as the blood flows along the capillary, it loses water but not albumin. Its solute potential becomes more negative, decreasing its water potential. At the same time, because it has lost fluid earlier in the capillary, its hydrostatic pressure drops, which also decreases its water potential. By the time it reaches the venous end of the capillary bed, the water potential inside the capillary is lower than that outside, so fluid moves into the capillary from the tissue fluid.

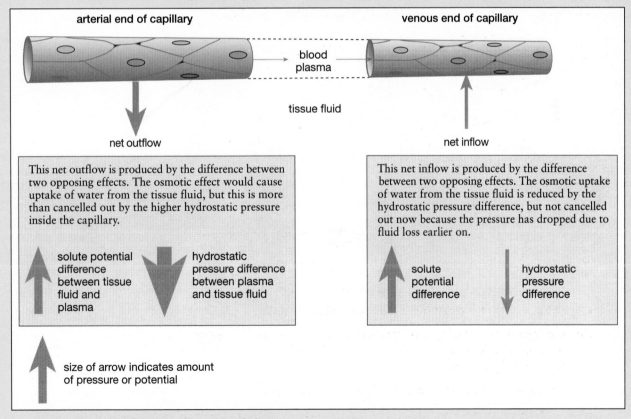

Fig. 10.21   How tissue fluid forms from blood plasma.

Q13 The cardiac output is the volume of blood pumped by each ventricle per minute. The cardiac output depends on the volume of blood pumped by each contraction of a ventricle, the stroke volume.

The figure below shows the events of the heartbeat of a mammal over time.

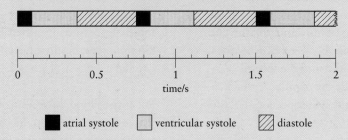

(a) Assuming 70 cm³ of blood is ejected from the heart with each beat, use the figure to calculate the cardiac output. Show your working. (2)

As blood flows into the ventricles of the heart during diastole it causes their walls to stretch. The amount of stretching depends on the volume of blood in the ventricle just before systole, which is called the ventricular end-diastolic volume.

The figure below shows the relationship between ventricular end-diastolic volume and stroke volume.

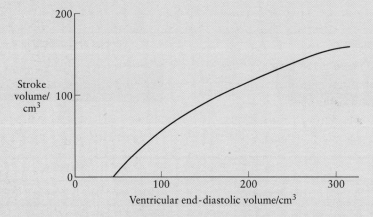

(b) (i) With reference to the figure **explain** the effect of increasing ventricular end-diastolic volume on stroke volume. (2)

(ii) Outline the significance of this effect on the body. (2)

UCLES 1995 (*Total 6 marks*)

11 Transport in plants

There are many similarities between the ways in which substances are transported in plants and in mammals. In both kinds of organism, fluids carry substances in solution from one part to another, moving by mass flow inside vessels. In plants, however, there is no pump. Another difference is that plants have two different transport systems – xylem and phloem.

11.1 Vascular tissues in plants

Plants have two quite separate **vascular tissues** which transport substances from one part to another. **Xylem tissue** transports water, inorganic ions (minerals) and a few small organic molecules from the roots upwards. **Phloem tissue** transports organic substances which have been made by the plant, such as sucrose, mostly from leaves to storage organs or places where these substances are being used in metabolic reactions.

Figs. 11.1 and 11.2 show the positions of these vascular tissues in the roots and stems of a young herbaceous (non-woody) plant. Xylem and phloem tissue usually run quite close to each other, forming a group of cells called a **vascular bundle** in leaves and stems and a **stele** in roots.

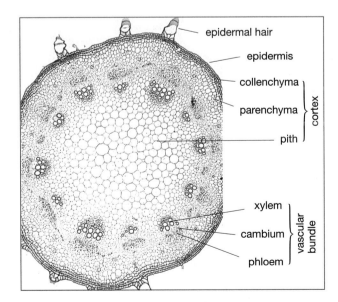

Fig. 11.1 Light micrograph of TS of a stem of *Helianthus* (sunflower) (×50).

THE TRANSPORT OF WATER AND MINERAL IONS

11.2 The structure of xylem tissue

Fig. 11.3 shows the structure of xylem tissue. This tissue contains several kinds of cells, including **fibres**, **parenchyma cells** and **xylem vessel elements**. Fibres are long cells with thickened walls which help to provide structural support for the plant. Parenchyma cells are 'general-purpose' cells which can be used for storing substances such as starch. The cells which are involved in transport of water are the xylem vessel elements.

A vessel element is a long cell with absolutely no cell contents. It is dead. Vessel elements begin as normal living cells with cellulose cell walls, which then elongate. Their cytoplasm gradually breaks down, and their walls become thickened with a substance called **lignin**. Lignin is a very strong substance which is impermeable to water. The end walls of the elements break down, providing an uninterrupted pathway between one element and the next. These continuous tubes run all the way from the roots to the very top of the plant. They are called **xylem vessels**.

The diameter of a typical xylem vessel is about 100 μm, although they can be much smaller or larger than this. An oak tree, for example, may contain xylem vessels as wide as 500 μm, which you can easily see with the naked eye. Variation in the size of vessels produced at different times of year gives rise to the growth rings visible in a section of a tree trunk.

Although water cannot leak out of a xylem vessel through its lignified walls, there are gaps in these walls, called **pits**, which allow sideways movement of water. These are important in allowing water to move from one xylem vessel to another, and also from xylem vessels to living tissues nearby.

Q1	How do the structures of xylem vessels, fibres and xylem parenchyma cells relate to their functions?

11.3 Transpiration

The xylem vessels of a large tree may carry around 250 dm^3 of water from the roots to the leaves every hour, over a distance of perhaps 15 metres. What is the force which causes this movement?

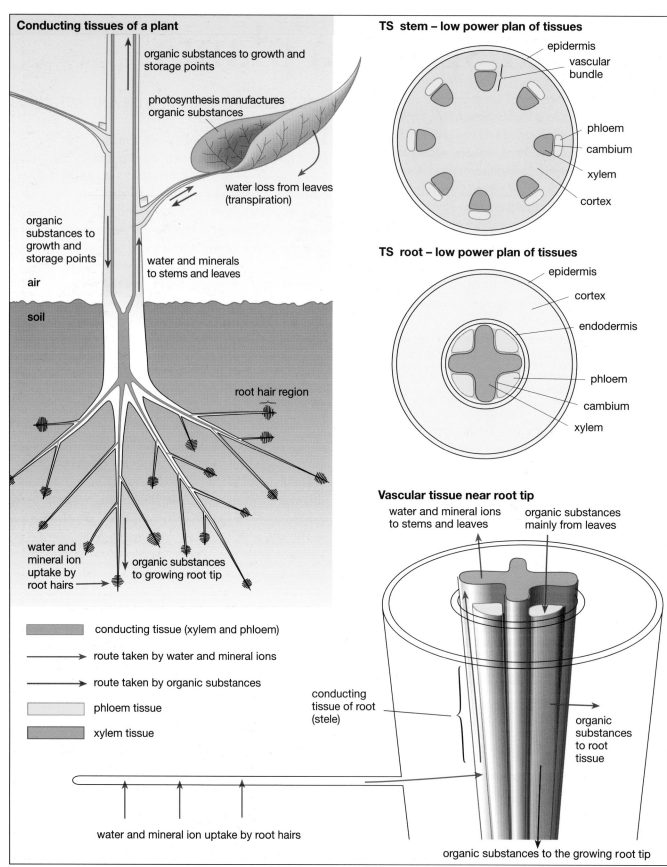

Conducting tissues of a plant

organic substances to growth and storage points

photosynthesis manufactures organic substances

water loss from leaves (transpiration)

organic substances to growth and storage points

air

soil

water and minerals to stems and leaves

root hair region

water and mineral ion uptake by root hairs

organic substances to growing root tip

conducting tissue (xylem and phloem)

route taken by water and mineral ions

route taken by organic substances

phloem tissue

xylem tissue

TS stem – low power plan of tissues

epidermis

vascular bundle

phloem

cambium

xylem

cortex

TS root – low power plan of tissues

epidermis

cortex

endodermis

phloem

cambium

xylem

Vascular tissue near root tip

water and mineral ions to stems and leaves

organic substances mainly from leaves

conducting tissue of root (stele)

organic substances to root tissue

water and mineral ion uptake by root hairs

organic substances to the growing root tip

Fig. 11.2   Conducting tissues in a plant.

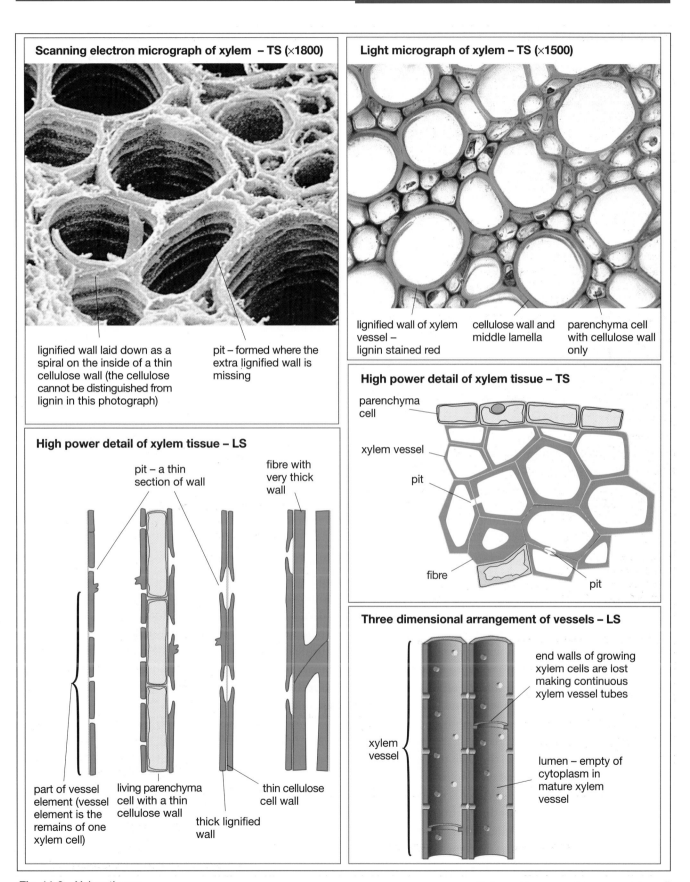

Scanning electron micrograph of xylem – TS (×1800)

lignified wall laid down as a spiral on the inside of a thin cellulose wall (the cellulose cannot be distinguished from lignin in this photograph)

pit – formed where the extra lignified wall is missing

Light micrograph of xylem – TS (×1500)

lignified wall of xylem vessel – lignin stained red

cellulose wall and middle lamella

parenchyma cell with cellulose wall only

High power detail of xylem tissue – TS

parenchyma cell

xylem vessel

pit

fibre

pit

High power detail of xylem tissue – LS

pit – a thin section of wall

fibre with very thick wall

part of vessel element (vessel element is the remains of one xylem cell)

living parenchyma cell with a thin cellulose wall

thick lignified wall

thin cellulose cell wall

Three dimensional arrangement of vessels – LS

end walls of growing xylem cells are lost making continuous xylem vessel tubes

xylem vessel

lumen – empty of cytoplasm in mature xylem vessel

Fig. 11.3 Xylem tissue.

Water enters the xylem vessels in the roots of the plant. (Section 11.5 explains how this happens.) Most of this water leaves the xylem vessels in the leaves, from where it evaporates and diffuses as water vapour into the atmosphere. This process is called **transpiration**. The removal of water from the top of the xylem vessels in this way reduces the hydrostatic pressure in the vessels. This causes a difference in pressure between the top and base of the xylem vessels. Water therefore moves up the xylem vessels by mass flow, from the region of relatively high hydrostatic pressure at the base to the region of relatively low hydrostatic pressure at the top.

Fig. 11.4 shows how transpiration happens. The mesophyll cells in a leaf have moist cell walls because cellulose is freely permeable to water. Most of these cells are in contact with the air spaces in a leaf, and some of the liquid water in their cell walls evaporates, producing a high concentration of water vapour in these air spaces. If the stomata (Box 12.3) are open, and if the concentration of water vapour in the air outside the leaf is less than that inside, then water vapour will diffuse out through the stomata into the air.

The rate of transpiration depends to a large extent on the environmental conditions around the plant. Very dry air – that is, low humidity – will increase the concentration gradient for water vapour between the inside of the leaf and the air, and so will increase the rate of transpiration. High temperatures tend to increase the rate of transpiration, partly because molecules move more rapidly at higher temperatures, and partly because warm air can hold more water vapour than cold air. Windy conditions increase transpiration rates (Box 11.1).

Transpiration is an important process to plants, because it provides the force to pull water and mineral ions up the xylem vessels. However, if water is in short supply, transpiration may allow more water to be lost from the plant than can be replaced by absorbing water from the soil. If this happens, cells lose water and become flaccid (Section 16.2). Over very short periods of time, this is unlikely to do much harm to most plants, but if it continues for long periods then the plant may die.

Most plants are therefore adapted to be able to reduce the rate of transpiration when water is in short supply. The most obvious method of doing this is to close the stomata. This is done by the guard cells. When the guard cells are turgid, they curve apart from each other, opening the stoma between them. When they are flaccid, their curvature decreases, and their inner edges lie close

together which closes the stoma. (This is described in more detail in Box 12.3.) With the stomata closed, transpiration is virtually stopped, as only a tiny amount of water vapour escapes through the rest of the leaf surface. However, closed stomata also means no carbon dioxide can enter for photosynthesis, so plants have to strike a balance between preventing water loss and allowing photosynthesis to take place.

Plants which live in environments where water is regularly in short supply usually have permanent structural and physiological features which reduce the rate of water loss from leaves. These plants are called **xerophytes**. Fig. 11.5 shows some xerophytic adaptations.

11.4   The cohesion–tension theory of water movement

The mechanism for water movement in xylem vessels outlined in Section 11.3 is known as the **cohesion–tension theory**. It was first suggested in 1914, and since then so much evidence has accumulated to support it that many biologists would now consider that it is no longer a 'theory', but fact.

The 'tension' part of the name refers to the fact that the water in the xylem vessels is being *pulled* – that is it is under tension. As you have seen, the pull is provided by transpiration in the leaves, and it is often known as **transpiration pull**.

The 'cohesion' part of the name refers to the cohesion, or 'stickiness' of the water molecules. For the process to work, the xylem vessels must contain an unbroken column of water so that, when the top of the column is pulled, the pull is transmitted all the way down to the bottom of the column and moves the water up as an unbroken stream. Water molecules have dipoles which provide a force of attraction between them (Section 1.1). This helps water molecules to stick together, making it relatively difficult to break the water column.

Air bubbles do sometimes develop inside a column of water in a xylem vessel, forming an air lock. Unlike liquid water, air will 'stretch' when tension is applied to it, so the force produced by the loss of water from the top of the vessel is not transmitted to the water column below the bubble. This stops water movement *up* that vessel. However, water below the air bubble can still move *sideways*, through a pit and into a xylem vessel running alongside. The air bubble can thus be bypassed.

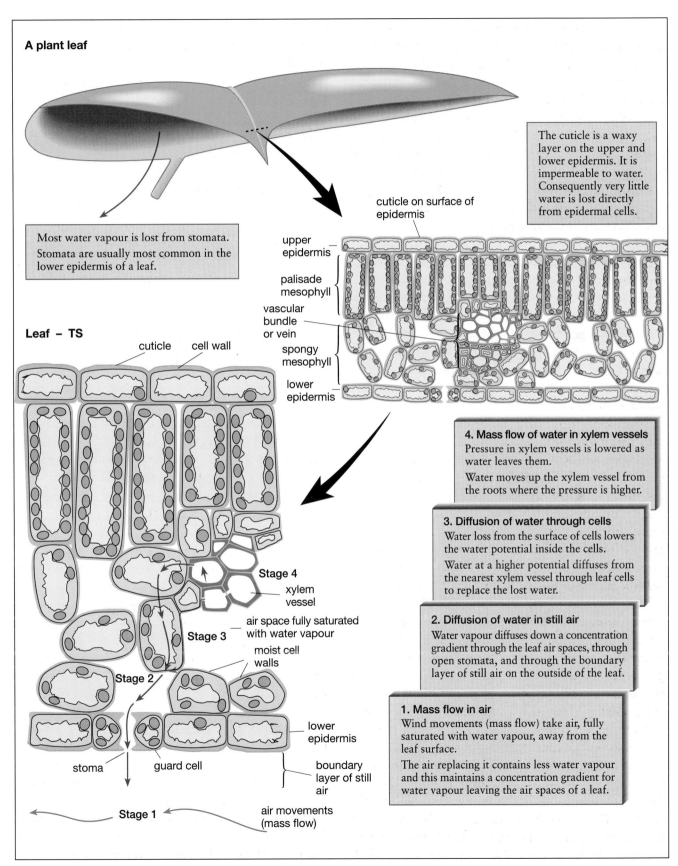

A plant leaf

Most water vapour is lost from stomata. Stomata are usually most common in the lower epidermis of a leaf.

The cuticle is a waxy layer on the upper and lower epidermis. It is impermeable to water. Consequently very little water is lost directly from epidermal cells.

cuticle on surface of epidermis

upper epidermis

palisade mesophyll

vascular bundle or vein

spongy mesophyll

lower epidermis

Leaf – TS

cuticle   cell wall

Stage 4

xylem vessel

air space fully saturated with water vapour

Stage 3

moist cell walls

Stage 2

lower epidermis

stoma   guard cell

boundary layer of still air

Stage 1   air movements (mass flow)

4. Mass flow of water in xylem vessels
Pressure in xylem vessels is lowered as water leaves them.

Water moves up the xylem vessel from the roots where the pressure is higher.

3. Diffusion of water through cells
Water loss from the surface of cells lowers the water potential inside the cells.

Water at a higher potential diffuses from the nearest xylem vessel through leaf cells to replace the lost water.

2. Diffusion of water in still air
Water vapour diffuses down a concentration gradient through the leaf air spaces, through open stomata, and through the boundary layer of still air on the outside of the leaf.

1. Mass flow in air
Wind movements (mass flow) take air, fully saturated with water vapour, away from the leaf surface.

The air replacing it contains less water vapour and this maintains a concentration gradient for water vapour leaving the air spaces of a leaf.

Fig. 11.4   Transpiration (water loss from leaves) and its consequences.

Mesembryanthemum grows in dry areas in southern Africa. It is a succulent, which means that it has fleshy leaves which store water. These thick leaves have a relatively low surface area to volume ratio, reducing loss of water by transpiration.

Euphorbia obesa is a South African succulent. The fat, rounded stem growing close to the ground reduces surface area. The stem is the main photosynthetic organ, and the leaves very tiny – they are arranged in rows down the stem.

Azorella is a cushion plant which grows at heights well over 4000 m in Peru. It survives exposure to cold, drying winds by growing close to the ground; this growth form reduces its surface area.

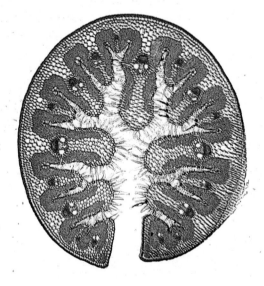

A section through a rolled leaf of marram grass, *Ammophila*. Marram grass grows on sand dunes. In dry conditions, the leaves roll with the lower surface inside, so that the stomata open into an enclosed space. Water vapour can accumulate here and reduce the diffusion gradient. The spines increase the width of the boundary layer.

Opuntia bigelovii, or teddy bear cholla, grows in dry areas in California. The swollen stems store water, and are the main photosynthetic organs. The leaves are just spines, which protect the plant from grazing animals.

Fig. 11.5 Xerophytic adaptations.

Box 11.1 Fick's Law and rates of diffusion

Diffusion is the net movement of molecules from a region of high concentration to a region of low concentration, caused by the random movement of individual molecules.

The rate of this net movement depends on many factors, one of the most important of which is temperature. High temperatures increase diffusion rates, because they increase the speed of movement of individual molecules.

If temperature remains constant, however, the rate of diffusion is determined by three factors. These are:

• *the surface area* across which diffusion is able to take place – the greater the surface area, the greater the rate of diffusion.

• *the difference in concentration* – the greater the concentration gradient, the greater the rate of diffusion.

• *the length of the diffusion path* – the greater the distance the substance has to diffuse, the lower the rate of diffusion.

The effect of these three factors can be summarised in **Fick's law**, which states that the rate of diffusion is proportional to

$$\frac{\text{surface area} \times \text{difference in concentration}}{\text{length of diffusion path}}$$

Fick's law can help to explain how humidity, wind speed and leaf shape affect the rate of transpiration from a plant.

The humidity of the air inside a leaf is usually close to 100%, while the humidity of the air outside may be considerably lower than this. High humidities in the air outside the leaf reduce the concentration gradient, so decreasing the rate of diffusion.

The length of the diffusion path from the inside of a leaf to the air outside depends partly on the thickness of the leaf. Thin leaves obviously have smaller diffusion distances, and so tend to lose water vapour more quickly than thick leaves (other factors being equal). Xerophytic plants often have thick leaves to reduce the rate of diffusion. However, the total diffusion distance also includes a layer of undisturbed air on the outside of the leaf, called the **boundary layer**, through which water vapour has to diffuse to reach the wide open spaces outside. The thickness of this boundary layer can be increased, for example, by hairs on the surface of the leaf which trap air and so increase the diffusion distance. Many xerophytic plants use this method of reducing the rate of transpiration.

The thickness of the boundary layer is also affected by wind speed. Increasing wind speed decreases the thickness of the boundary layer and so speeds up diffusion.

Q2 Explain how the boundary layer and mass flow of air are relevant to the uptake of carbon dioxide in a photosynthesising leaf.

Box 11.2 Other theories for movement of water in xylem – root pressure and capillarity

The cohesion–tension theory for water movement up xylem vessels has a considerable amount of evidence to support it, and most biologists would consider that it is by far the most important mechanism. In particular, it is found that the rate of water movement up xylem vessels is usually very closely correlated with the rate of transpiration from leaves. Another piece of supporting evidence is that the water in xylem vessels is usually found to be under tension. For example, if you hold an intact stem in a container of coloured liquid and cut it, the coloured liquid is instantly pulled into the ends of the cut xylem vessels. Yet another – rather surprising – piece of evidence is that the diameters of stems decrease quite significantly when the leaves are transpiring rapidly, indicating that the tension in the water columns in the xylem vessels is pulling their walls inwards. Although each individual xylem vessel is only pulled inwards by a very small amount, the added effect of all of them makes a measurable difference to the diameter of the stem.

However, this evidence does not necessarily mean that transpiration pull is the *only* way in which water is moved up xylem vessels, nor that it is *always* the way in which this is achieved.

Root pressure is undoubtedly a significant force in herbaceous plants in some circumstances. In the roots, a ring of cells called the **endodermis** surrounds the xylem vessels in the middle of the root (Fig. 11.6). These cells actively transport mineral ions into the xylem, which has the effect of reducing the water potential in the xylem. This draws water into the xylem, so increasing its hydrostatic pressure. By raising the hydrostatic pressure at the base of the xylem in this way, a pressure difference can be created between the base and the top of the water column, pushing the water upwards.

You can show that root pressure does exist by cutting the stem of a well-watered herbaceous plant. Water will ooze out of the top of the cut xylem vessels, indicating that it is being pushed upwards from below. However, the magnitude of the pressure is usually very low, and would be nowhere near enough to push water all the way to the top of a tree. Root pressure is probably only significant in small, herbaceous plants in conditions where rates of transpiration are low.

Capillarity has also been put forward as a mechanism causing the rise of water in xylem vessels. You have probably seen how water will 'climb' up inside a narrow glass tube. This happens because the water molecules are attracted to polar molecules in the wall of the tube, an attraction called **adhesion**. As the water molecules flow upwards along the wall, the strong cohesive forces between them pull up an entire column of water.

The height to which the water column can climb is inversely proportional to the radius of the tube. In a small xylem vessel with a diameter of 50 μm, capillarity could cause water to rise to a height of about 60 cm. This could be useful in a small plant, but is obviously of little help to a tree 100 m high!

11.5 The movement of water into and across the root

Water enters a plant through its roots. The roots of a plant often make up a very large proportion of its total body mass, frequently more than half of it. They branch and spread through the soil, providing a very large surface area for the absorption of water. One rye plant, growing in a container measuring $30 \times 30 \times 56$ cm, was found to have roots with a total length of 623 km and a surface area of 639 m².

However, not all of the root surface is important in absorbing water. Most water is absorbed in a region between about 0.5 cm and 10 cm from the tip of the root. Nearer the tip than this is the **root cap**, which is a strong protective layer designed to withstand the forces generated as the root grows through the soil. Further away from the tip, the outer layers of the root become full of two impermeable substances, **lignin** and **suberin**.

In the absorbing region of the root, most plants have

root hairs. These are extensions of the cells which make up the outer layer, or **epidermis**, of the root. Root hairs are very thin, with diameters around 10 µm, but they may be up to 1 cm long. They greatly increase the surface area of the root.

Water enters the root by osmosis, moving down a water potential gradient (Section 3.26) from the soil into the root hairs. From here, it crosses the root, moving down a water potential gradient towards the xylem vessels in the centre. Some water travels along the cell walls and through the spaces between the cells, a route known as the **apoplast** pathway. Some travels into and through the cells themselves, moving from one cell to another through their cell surface membranes and cell walls, or through plasmodesmata. This route is known as the **symplast** pathway.

As the water nears the xylem, the apoplast pathway is blocked by a layer of cells, called the **endodermis**, whose walls are thickened with suberin. Suberin is impermeable to water, and it forms a band all around the cells called a **Casparian strip** (Fig. 11.6). The cells are tightly packed together so that there is no pathway between them through which water can pass. At this point in its journey, therefore, the water must enter the cells and pass through them to get to the other side. The function of this arrangement may be to allow the plant some control over the mineral ions which enter the xylem. Active transport of these ions out of the endodermal cells may help to provide root pressure (Box 11.2).

Finally, the water enters the xylem vessels through pits in their walls, before beginning its journey up the xylem and into the leaves.

11.6 The uptake of mineral ions into the roots

Most plants obtain most of their mineral ions from the soil. There are exceptions, however. Carnivorous plants, for example, absorb various substances from trapped insects in their leaves. And several species of plants, especially legumes (peas and beans) have symbiotic bacteria in their roots which provide them with fixed nitrogen (Box 13.5).

Roots are highly selective about which ions they take up in any quantity from the soil. Most ions enter root hair cells through **transporter proteins** in the cell surface membrane (Figs. 3.28 and 3.32). They may move into the root down their concentration gradient, by facilitated diffusion, or against their concentration gradient, by active transport. Roots also use active transport to pump ions such as sodium *out* of the root. As sodium ions have a positive charge, this can create an electrical gradient which can help the uptake of other positively charged ions.

In addition to root hairs, many plants have a symbiotic relationship with fungi. These grow in close association with the roots to form **mycorrhizae**. The mycorrhizae appear to help the plant to take up mineral ions from the soil.

Once in the root, the mineral ions move across the root by the same pathways as water, in solution in the water. They pass through the endodermal cells, and are probably actively transported out of these cells and into the xylem. They are then carried, in solution, in the xylem to all parts of the plant.

Q3 (a) Explain why a water column in the xylem of a transpiring shoot is under tension. (2)

The diagram on the right shows how the middle of a transpiring shoot was pushed below the surface of a dye solution in a beaker and cut with a pair of scissors. The two ends of the shoot on either side of the cut were left below the surface for 10 minutes and then examined. It was found that the dye had moved away from the two cut surfaces in the directions indicated by the arrows.

(b) How does the movement of the dye in the lower part of the shoot after it has been cut provide support for the cohesion–tension theory? (3)

AEB 1994 (*Total 5 marks*)

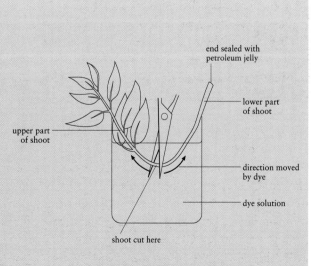

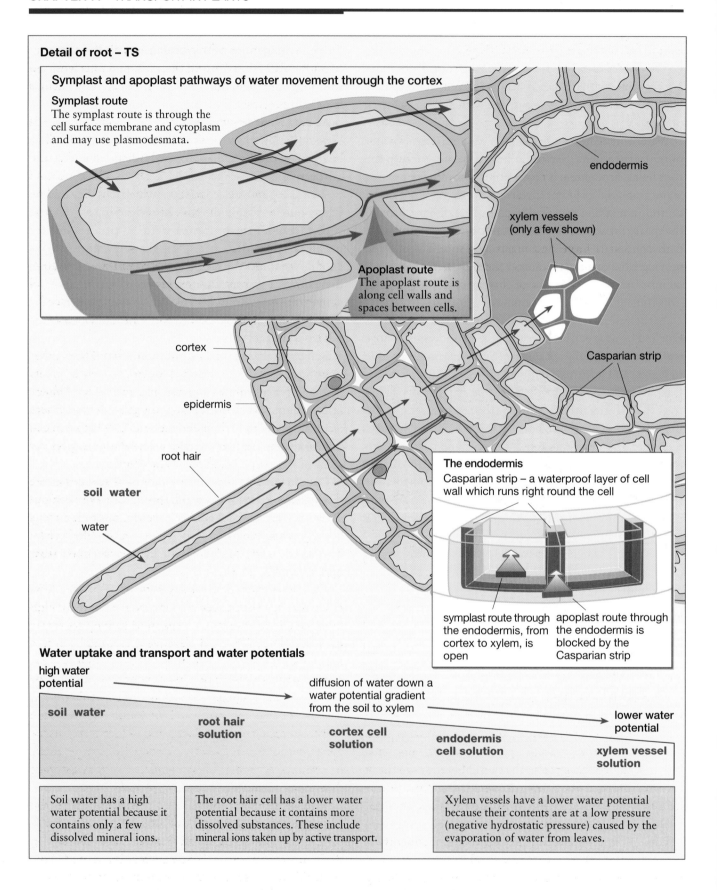

Detail of root – TS

Symplast and apoplast pathways of water movement through the cortex

Symplast route
The symplast route is through the cell surface membrane and cytoplasm and may use plasmodesmata.

Apoplast route
The apoplast route is along cell walls and spaces between cells.

endodermis

xylem vessels (only a few shown)

Casparian strip

cortex

epidermis

root hair

soil water

water

The endodermis
Casparian strip – a waterproof layer of cell wall which runs right round the cell

symplast route through the endodermis, from cortex to xylem, is open

apoplast route through the endodermis is blocked by the Casparian strip

Water uptake and transport and water potentials

high water potential

diffusion of water down a water potential gradient from the soil to xylem

lower water potential

soil water

root hair solution

cortex cell solution

endodermis cell solution

xylem vessel solution

Soil water has a high water potential because it contains only a few dissolved mineral ions.

The root hair cell has a lower water potential because it contains more dissolved substances. These include mineral ions taken up by active transport.

Xylem vessels have a lower water potential because their contents are at a low pressure (negative hydrostatic pressure) caused by the evaporation of water from leaves.

Fig. 11.6 Mechanism and pathway of water uptake by roots.

THE TRANSPORT OF ORGANIC SUBSTANCES

11.7 The structure of phloem tissue

Fig. 11.7 shows the structure of phloem tissue. The cells through which substances are transported are called **sieve elements**. As in xylem vessels, these cells lie end to end forming a continuous vessel called a **sieve tube**. However, the sieve elements differ greatly from xylem elements. Sieve elements are living cells with active cytoplasm, although in a mature sieve element there is no nucleus, Golgi or ribosomes. Their walls do not contain lignin. And they still have end walls, although these are perforated with numerous pores, forming **sieve plates**.

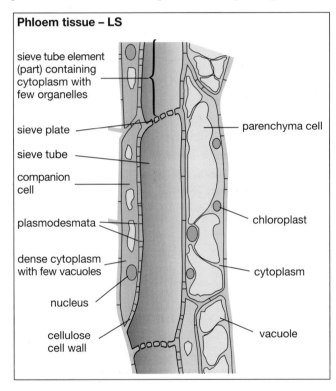

Phloem tissue – LS

sieve tube element (part) containing cytoplasm with few organelles

sieve plate

sieve tube

companion cell

plasmodesmata

dense cytoplasm with few vacuoles

nucleus

cellulose cell wall

parenchyma cell

chloroplast

cytoplasm

vacuole

Fig. 11.7 Structure of phloem tissue.

Sieve elements contain quite large amounts of a protein known as **phloem protein**, or **P-protein**. In phloem tissue which has been prepared for examination with a microscope, this protein may appear as long strands in the cell, or even blocking the sieve pores. However, it is now known that, in living sieve elements, the P-protein is mostly found near the side walls and certainly does not block the pores in the sieve plate.

Each sieve element lies in close association with a **companion cell**. The sieve element and its companion cell were formed by division of the same parent cell. Many plasmodesmata (Section 3.19) connect the cytoplasm of the sieve element and the companion cell. Companion cells have all the usual organelles, including a nucleus, and are thought to 'help out' the sieve tube cell with various metabolic processes.

At the tips of the veins in leaves, the companion cells look rather different from elsewhere in the plant. They have very folded cell walls and cell surface membranes, giving them a large surface area. These cells are called **transfer cells**, and are thought to be involved with loading sucrose by active transport into the phloem vessels (Section 11.8).

11.8 How substances are transported in phloem

Phloem tissue transports substances made in leaves to all other parts of the plant. Box 11.3 outlines the evidence for this. The transport of these substances is known as **translocation**.

By far the most abundant substance in phloem (other than water) is **sucrose**, which is the form in which plants transport carbohydrate from one place to another. Phloem also transports **amino acids**, **plant growth substances** (such as auxin, cytokinin and gibberellin which you can read about in Chapter 15) and **mineral ions**, especially potassium, phosphate, sulphate and chloride.

It is still not clear just how these substances move through sieve tubes. Several hypotheses have been put forward over the last 60 or 70 years, but evidence is building that one of these theories is more likely to be correct than any of the others. This is the **mass flow hypothesis** (Fig. 11.8).

The mass flow hypothesis suggests that fluids can flow freely through sieve tubes, moving from a region of high hydrostatic pressure to a region of low hydrostatic pressure. The pressure difference is created by active loading of sucrose into the sieve tube at a **source**. This source will usually be in a photosynthesising leaf, or perhaps in a storage organ such as a potato tuber when the stores are being mobilised for use elsewhere in the plant. Sucrose is unloaded at a **sink**, which is any tissue where sucrose is being used as an energy source, or where it is being converted into something else, such as a storage substance.

Where sucrose is loaded into the sieve tube at the source, it lowers the water potential of the sieve tube's contents. Water therefore flows into the sieve tube, raising the hydrostatic pressure. Where sucrose is removed at the sink, this increases the water potential, so that water moves out of the sieve tube into the surrounding tissues.

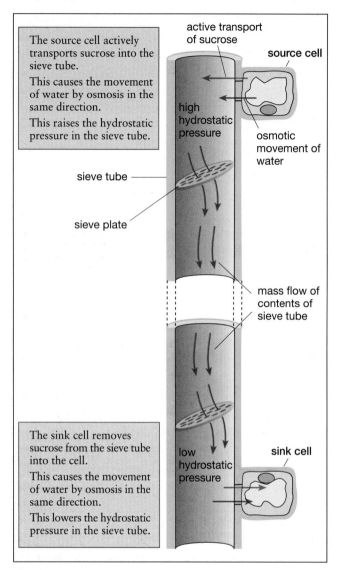

The source cell actively transports sucrose into the sieve tube.

This causes the movement of water by osmosis in the same direction.

This raises the hydrostatic pressure in the sieve tube.

active transport of sucrose

source cell

high hydrostatic pressure

osmotic movement of water

sieve tube

sieve plate

mass flow of contents of sieve tube

The sink cell removes sucrose from the sieve tube into the cell.

This causes the movement of water by osmosis in the same direction.

This lowers the hydrostatic pressure in the sieve tube.

low hydrostatic pressure

sink cell

Fig. 11.8 Mass flow in phloem.

This reduces the hydrostatic pressure in the sieve tube. This difference in pressure causes the fluid inside the sieve tube to flow from the source to the sink.

There is considerable circumstantial evidence that this *is* the mechanism causing movement of fluids in phloem. For example, it is found that concentrations of sucrose in the sieve tubes are greater near to a source than to a sink. The pressure differences which are created by these concentration differences are more than enough to explain the measured rates of flow in the phloem, even taking into consideration the resistance which would be provided by the sieve plates. And the structure and physiology of transfer cells (Section 11.7) suggests that they do actively load sucrose into sieve tubes.

However, there are still a few problems to be solved. Why, for example, if fluids travel by mass flow in sieve tubes, do the cells making up these tubes need cytoplasm? Why are they not completely empty, like xylem vessels? And why do they have sieve plates between them, rather than open ends like xylem elements?

One suggestion is that these features help to stop too much loss of valuable sucrose, and other substances being carried in the phloem, if the sieve tube is damaged. Moreover, a leaking phloem sieve tube would provide an excellent feeding and growing site for microorganisms which could be pathogenic and infect the plant. To prevent this, if phloem tissue is cut into, P-protein and a carbohydrate called **callose** rapidly plug the pores in the sieve plates. This seals off the sieve tube, stopping its contents flowing out. The mobilisation of P-protein and the formation of callose plugs could only be done in a living cell, which may be why sieve elements contain cytoplasm.

Another feature of phloem transport which has been considered to be evidence *against* the mass flow hypothesis is that phloem tissue frequently transports substances in opposite directions at the same time. This is clearly impossible, if you try to imagine fluids flowing in two directions in the same sieve tube! However, it is easy to explain if you consider that phloem tissue contains many sieve tubes, and it is obviously possible for fluids to be travelling in opposite directions in two different, but nearby, sieve tubes. They would need to be 'plugged in' to different sources and sinks, because the different direction of flow would be caused by opposite pressure gradients in the two sieve tubes. ■

Box 11.3 Evidence that phloem transports organic substances

There are three lines of evidence which indicate that phloem tissue transports substances made in leaves by photosynthesis.

Ringing experiments

Phloem tissue is situated quite near to the outside of a young woody stem, just beneath the bark. If a ring of bark is removed, the phloem comes away with it. This is called ringing. A similar result is obtained if steam is applied around the stem, as the high temperature kills the phloem cells.

In either case, the young plant continues to grow, and there is clearly no interruption to the flow of water from the roots to the leaves. This is what would be expected, because xylem vessels lie deeper in the stem and also they are dead cells which cannot be damaged by steam. However, analysis of the tissues just above the ring where the phloem was damaged shows that sucrose and other organic substances accumulate there, their pathway blocked by the missing or dead phloem. The stem often swells noticeably in this region (Fig. 11.9). Over a long period of time, the plant will die, as the roots are starved of nutrients from the leaves.

Using sap-sucking insects

Several kinds of insects, such as aphids (greenfly), feed by inserting tubular mouthparts, called **stylets**, into sieve tubes. The pressure in the sieve tube pushes its contents out through the stylets and into the insect. All the insect has to do is to sit still, plugged into a self-replenishing supply of sugar and amino acid solution which pours into its body with no effort from itself.

An insect with its stylets inserted into a sieve tube can be anaesthetised (usually with carbon dioxide) and its stylets cut off. Fluid continues to flow through the stylets, and can be collected and analysed. A typical analysis shows the solutes in the

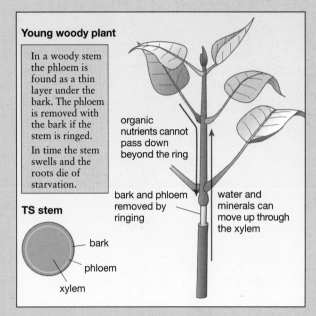

Young woody plant

In a woody stem the phloem is found as a thin layer under the bark. The phloem is removed with the bark if the stem is ringed.

In time the stem swells and the roots die of starvation.

organic nutrients cannot pass down beyond the ring

bark and phloem removed by ringing

water and minerals can move up through the xylem

TS stem

bark
phloem
xylem

Fig. 11.9   The effects of ringing a plant.

fluid to be mostly sucrose, with some protein and amino acids (mostly glutamic acid and aspartic acid), a small amount of plant growth substances and some mineral ions.

Using radioactive tracers

The heavy isotope of carbon, ^{14}C, is radioactive. Plants can be exposed to an atmosphere in which the carbon dioxide contains this isotope. The plants use the $^{14}CO_2$ to make carbohydrates in photosynthesis.

The contents of the phloem can then be investigated to see if the ^{14}C is being transported in them. For example, a cross-section of a stem can be cut and placed on an X-ray film. The film blackens where radioactivity strikes it. It is found that the blackened areas correspond exactly to the position of the phloem in the stem, indicating that the substances made by photosynthesis in the leaf are being transported exclusively in the phloem.

Q4 A cotton plant was treated by removing a ring of phloem from the stem as shown in the diagram below.

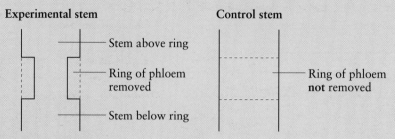

Experimental stem — Stem above ring / Ring of phloem removed / Stem below ring

Control stem — Ring of phloem **not** removed

A control plant was left untreated.

The graphs show changes in the total sugar content of the phloem and of the xylem over a period of 18 hours.

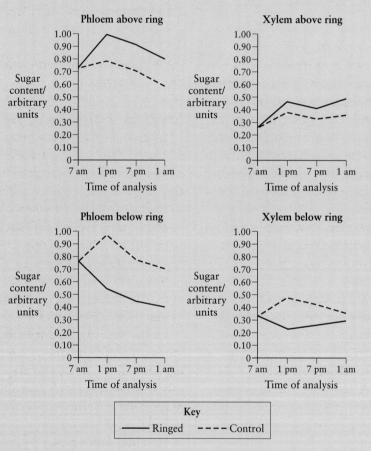

(a) Explain why you would expect there to be a variation in the sugar content in the phloem of a plant over the period shown. (2)

(b) Suggest an explanation for the difference in the sugar content of the ringed and control stems:
  (i) in the phloem above the ring; (1)
  (ii) in the phloem below the ring. (1)

(c) Explain the evidence from the graphs to support the hypothesis that although sugars can move laterally in xylem, they do not move downwards in it. (2)

AEB 1995 *(Total 6 marks)*

12 Gas exchange

All living organisms take in gases from their environment and return gases to it. Organisms which respire aerobically take in oxygen and give out carbon dioxide. Photosynthesising plants take in carbon dioxide and give out oxygen. Many organisms have specialised surfaces through which this gas exchange occurs.

12.1 Size, surface area and gas exchange

All living organisms that respire aerobically require supplies of oxygen which they obtain from their environment. They produce carbon dioxide as a waste product which leaves their bodies. In daylight, plants usually exchange gases in the opposite direction, as carbon dioxide is required for photosynthesis and oxygen is produced as a by-product. In most of this chapter, we will be considering the intake of oxygen and loss of carbon dioxide for respiration.

This exchange of gases between an organism and its environment takes place by diffusion. The part of the organism across which the exchange takes place is called a **gas exchange surface**.

The amount of oxygen which an organism needs is determined by the amount of living cells in its body, and the rate at which they are respiring. The rate at which oxygen can enter the body is determined by the surface area and thickness of the gas exchange surface. (Box 11.1 describes this in terms of Fick's law.) So, the requirement for oxygen is partly related to the **volume** of the organism, while the rate at which it can be supplied depends on its **surface area**.

In a small organism, such as *Amoeba* or a sea anemone, the ratio of surface area to volume is high. Small organisms can obtain all the oxygen they need by diffusion through their body surface. In large organisms, however, such as humans, the ratio of surface area to volume is much smaller (Fig. 12.1). The external surface area of the body is not large enough for diffusion of oxygen through it to take place rapidly enough to supply the cells with the oxygen they need.

Large organisms, therefore, usually have special, 'extra', surfaces designed just for gas exchange. These surfaces have large areas, and are as thin as possible, to allow rapid diffusion of gases across them. These organisms often also have a transport system (Section 10.1) to take gases to and from the gas exchange surface. This not only ensures that the gases are moved rapidly between the body cells and the gas exchange surface, but also maintains a concentration gradient for the gases across the exchange surface. The greater the concentration gradient, the more rapidly diffusion occurs.

12.2 Gas exchange problems for land organisms

Terrestrial (land-living) organisms obtain their oxygen from the air. Atmospheric air contains about 20% oxygen.

A high percentage of any organism's body is made up of water. When living cells are exposed to air, water molecules evaporate from the cells and diffuse into the air. Unprotected cells rapidly dehydrate. Some terrestrial animals, such as earthworms, avoid this problem by restricting their habitats to places where the air is always very moist, such as in damp soil. Most, however, have evolved waterproof coverings which cut down the amount of water loss. Humans, for example, have a waterproof layer of keratin covering their skin. Insects have a covering of chitin with a waxy, waterproof layer on the surface.

If a surface has a waterproof covering, this virtually stops the diffusion of oxygen through it. Terrestrial organisms therefore have to keep some parts of their body surface non-waterproofed, to allow gas exchange to take place. Different groups of organisms achieve this in different ways.

Humans, like all mammals, have **lungs**, in which the gas exchange surface is tucked away deep inside their bodies, thus greatly reducing the amount of water loss from it. This means that they have to make **breathing movements** to bring fresh supplies of air into contact with this surface.

Insects have a completely different system, in which tubes called **tracheae** penetrate deep into their bodies, carrying air close to every tissue. Gas exchange takes place at the ends of each of the smallest branches of these tubes. Many insects, like mammals, make breathing movements to move air in and out of these tubes.

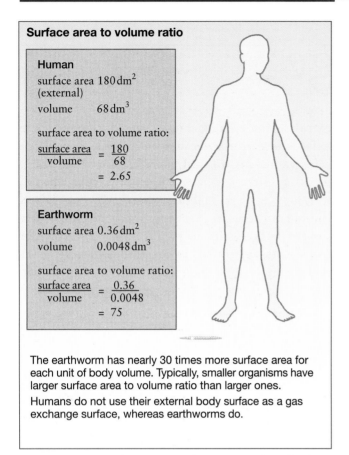

Surface area to volume ratio

Human
surface area 180 dm^2
(external)
volume   68 dm^3

surface area to volume ratio:
$$\frac{\text{surface area}}{\text{volume}} = \frac{180}{68}$$
$$= 2.65$$

Earthworm
surface area 0.36 dm^2
volume   0.0048 dm^3

surface area to volume ratio:
$$\frac{\text{surface area}}{\text{volume}} = \frac{0.36}{0.0048}$$
$$= 75$$

The earthworm has nearly 30 times more surface area for each unit of body volume. Typically, smaller organisms have larger surface area to volume ratio than larger ones.

Humans do not use their external body surface as a gas exchange surface, whereas earthworms do.

Fig. 12.1   How surface area to volume ratio varies with size.

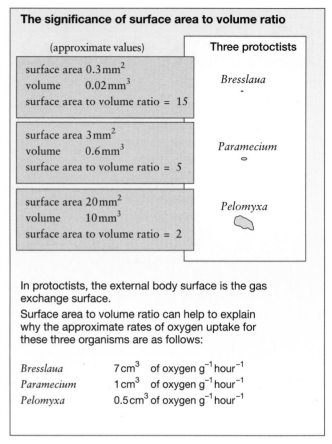

The significance of surface area to volume ratio

(approximate values)   **Three protoctists**

surface area 0.3 mm^2
volume   0.02 mm^3 *Bresslaua*
surface area to volume ratio = 15

surface area 3 mm^2
volume   0.6 mm^3 *Paramecium*
surface area to volume ratio = 5

surface area 20 mm^2
volume   10 mm^3 *Pelomyxa*
surface area to volume ratio = 2

In protoctists, the external body surface is the gas exchange surface.

Surface area to volume ratio can help to explain why the approximate rates of oxygen uptake for these three organisms are as follows:

Bresslaua   7 cm^3 of oxygen g^{-1} hour^{-1}
Paramecium   1 cm^3 of oxygen g^{-1} hour^{-1}
Pelomyxa   0.5 cm^3 of oxygen g^{-1} hour^{-1}

Q1   Suggest two reasons why humans do not use their external body surfaces for gas exchange.

Q2   (a) Explain how the surface area to volume ratio of *Bresslaua*, *Paramecium* and *Pelomyxa* could explain the rate of oxygen uptake in these organisms.

(b) Give another possible reason for the differences in the rates of oxygen uptake other than surface area to volume ratio.

Plants have highly branched shapes, with leaves which are designed to maximise gas exchange both for photosynthesis and respiration. The leaves have large surface areas inside them in contact with air spaces which connect to the external atmosphere via stomata. Large amounts of water vapour are lost from leaves by transpiration (Section 11.3), but this is kept under control both by waterproofing of most of the leaf surface with a layer of wax, and also by closing stomata when water loss is reaching levels which are dangerous to the plant.

12.3 Gas exchange problems for aquatic organisms

Aquatic (water-living) organisms obtain their oxygen from that which is dissolved in water. (They do *not* take oxygen from water molecules.)

There is much less oxygen available in water than in air. Oxygen is not very soluble in water, and a given volume of water can only contain about one-thirtieth the amount of oxygen as the same volume of air. Some of the dissolved oxygen in water comes from the air; oxygen molecules diffuse into water from the air at the water surface. If this surface is very still, then oxygen diffuses in only slowly. A moving water surface speeds up the rate of diffusion of oxygen from air into the water in two ways. Firstly, it exposes more surface area to the air. Secondly, moving water constantly takes away dissolved oxygen by mass flow, so helping to maintain a concentration gradient. Moving water is therefore often better oxygenated than still water.

Some of the dissolved oxygen in water comes from photosynthesising aquatic plants. This is often the major source of oxygen in still water during the day and without it aerobically respiring aquatic animals would be unable to survive. However, at night respiration by the same plants can cause the dissolved oxygen levels to fall substantially.

Temperature greatly affects the amount of oxygen which can dissolve in water. At higher temperatures, oxygen becomes *less* soluble in water. This means that, on a hot day, a pond containing large numbers of respiring animals can become very short of dissolved oxygen.

Oxygen diffuses about 1000 times more slowly in water than it does in air. Deep lakes, and also the deeper regions of the sea, have very low levels of dissolved oxygen, because these areas are a long way from the surface at which oxygen enters the water. Moreover, there are no plants to produce oxygen in these regions because light cannot penetrate to any great depth in water.

Terrestrial organisms have to balance their needs for rapid gas exchange with the prevention of too much water loss, whereas this is not a problem at all for aquatic organisms. However, aquatic organisms have different problems because oxygen may be in much shorter supply than it is on land.

Thus, aquatic organisms have just as great a need – if not more so – as terrestrial organisms for large surfaces for gas exchange. Even small aquatic organisms often have specialised gas exchange surfaces, with large surface areas. As there is no problem with water loss, these surfaces can be on the outside of the body, for example the external gills of young frog tadpoles. However, such thin, delicate surfaces hanging out from the body are in danger of mechanical damage, and so many aquatic organisms have evolved gas exchange surfaces which are inside the body. The gills of fish are an example of this strategy.

In this chapter, we will look in detail at how four different kinds of organisms – humans, fish, insects and terrestrial plants – have solved the problems of gas exchange in four very different ways.

Q3 *Arenicola* is a worm that lives in a burrow in the sand on the sea shore as shown below. It uses gills to obtain oxygen from sea water that it pumps through its burrow.

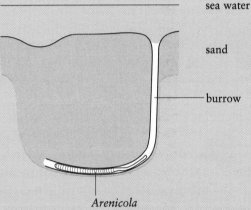

(a) The figure below shows a cross section through the body and gills of the worm.

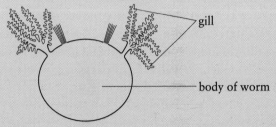

Using information from the second figure explain how the shape of the gill makes it an efficient structure for absorbing oxygen. (2)

(b) Explain in terms of gas exchange the advantage to the animal of pumping sea water through its burrow. (2)

NEAB (part question) 1995 *(Total 4 marks)*

GAS EXCHANGE IN HUMANS

12.4 The gross structure of the human gas exchange system

Fig. 12.2 shows the structure of the lungs and associated organs in a human. Most of the gas exchange system lies inside the thorax, protected by the ribs, sternum and vertebral column.

Air can enter this system through either the mouth or nose, from where it passes through the **larynx** and into the **trachea**. The wall of the trachea contains C-shaped rings of cartilage, which give it support and prevent it collapsing if air pressure inside it is low.

The trachea branches into two **bronchi**, which in turn branch into smaller tubes called **bronchioles**. The bronchioles end in millions of tiny interconnected cavities called **alveoli**. These form the gas exchange surface.

The lungs are surrounded by two thin, slippery **pleural membranes** which form an airtight barrier around them. The membranes secrete small amounts of a slimy liquid called **pleural fluid**, which fills the space between them and allows them to slip over each other as the lungs expand and deflate during breathing.

Just below the lungs, dividing the thorax from the abdomen, lies a sheet of muscle and fibrous tissue called the **diaphragm**. This helps to produce breathing movements. The other muscles involved in breathing are the **intercostal muscles**, which stretch between the ribs.

12.5 Gas exchange between alveolar air and blood

Gas exchange takes place by diffusion. Carbon dioxide diffuses from the blood inside the capillaries in the lungs, into the air inside the alveoli. Oxygen diffuses in the opposite direction, into the red blood cells, where it combines with haemoglobin (Section 10.11).

Fig. 12.3 shows the structure of the alveoli. Each alveolus is about 100 μm in diameter, with a wall approximately 0.1 μm to 0.5 μm thick. Blood capillaries are very closely associated with the alveoli; their walls are also very thin, so that the distance separating an oxygen molecule in an alveolus from a haemoglobin molecule in a red blood cell inside a capillary is only about 1.5 μm.

The total surface area of the alveoli in your lungs is approximately 70 m². (Compare this with the total surface area of your skin, which is approximately 1.8 m².) Approximately 80% of the alveolar walls is covered with blood capillaries. Because the diffusion distance is so small, and because the surface area of contact is so great,

equilibrium is very quickly reached between the concentrations of gases in the alveoli and their concentrations in the blood. Even though it takes only about one second or less for blood to pass through the capillaries in the lungs, this is more than enough time for the concentrations of gases in the alveoli and the capillaries to become equal.

The walls of the alveoli are covered with a thin layer of liquid. If this was water, or even tissue fluid, it would cause great problems because of its surface tension. Alveoli have concave inner surfaces, and the surface tension in the film of liquid would tend to pull the walls together so that the alveoli would collapse. To prevent this, the liquid contains a detergent-like substance, or **surfactant**. The surfactant is a phospholipid, which is secreted by cells in the wall of the alveolus. These cells do not begin to function in a developing fetus until it is 20 weeks old, and are not fully working until it is 30 weeks old. Premature babies, therefore, often do not have enough surfactant and may have collapsed alveoli. They suffer from respiratory distress syndrome, in which each breath takes an enormous effort in order to inflate the lungs.

12.6 Breathing movements

Fresh air is supplied to the alveoli by rhythmical changes in the volume of the thorax (Fig. 12.4). This is done by the muscles in the diaphragm and the intercostal muscles. (The lungs themselves have no muscles at all.)

To inspire, the two sets of muscles act to increase the volume inside the thorax. The diaphragm muscles contract, flattening the dome. In relaxed breathing, the centre of the diaphragm moves down by about 1 to 2 cm, but this can be as much as 10 cm in heavy breathing. At the same time, the external intercostal muscles also contract. They swing the ribcage upwards and outwards.

These movements of the diaphragm and ribcage result in an increase in volume of the thorax. This causes the pressure inside the thorax to decrease to below the pressure of the air outside the body. Air therefore flows into the thorax by mass flow, from the area of high pressure to the area of lower pressure, along the only route open to it – through the mouth or nose, down the trachea and into the air spaces in the lungs.

To expire, both the diaphragm and external intercostal muscles relax. The lungs contain elastic fibres, which were stretched as they were inflated during inspiration. Now these fibres recoil to their relaxed length, causing the lungs

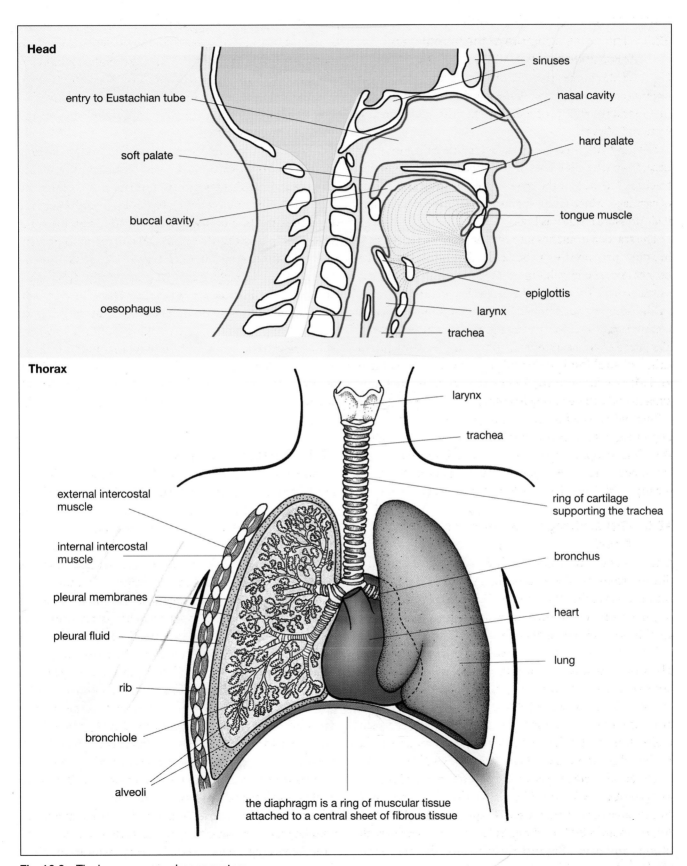

Fig. 12.2 The human gas exchange system.

Alveoli in TS and 3D

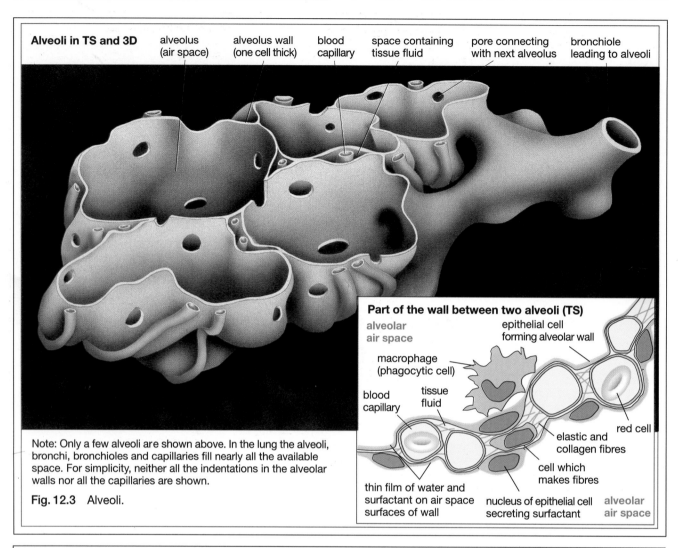

alveolus (air space) · alveolus wall (one cell thick) · blood capillary · space containing tissue fluid · pore connecting with next alveolus · bronchiole leading to alveoli

Note: Only a few alveoli are shown above. In the lung the alveoli, bronchi, bronchioles and capillaries fill nearly all the available space. For simplicity, neither all the indentations in the alveolar walls nor all the capillaries are shown.

Fig. 12.3 Alveoli.

Part of the wall between two alveoli (TS)

alveolar air space · epithelial cell forming alveolar wall · macrophage (phagocytic cell) · blood capillary · tissue fluid · red cell · elastic and collagen fibres · cell which makes fibres · thin film of water and surfactant on air space surfaces of wall · nucleus of epithelial cell secreting surfactant · alveolar air space

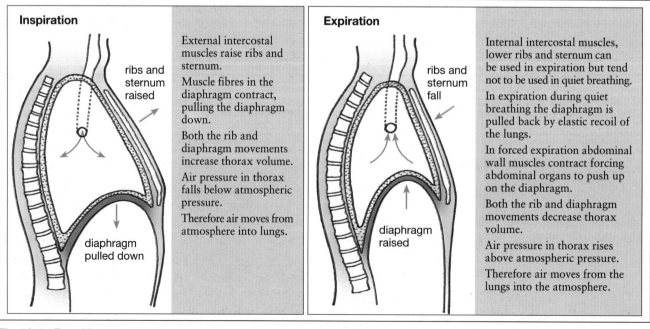

Inspiration

ribs and sternum raised

diaphragm pulled down

External intercostal muscles raise ribs and sternum.

Muscle fibres in the diaphragm contract, pulling the diaphragm down.

Both the rib and diaphragm movements increase thorax volume.

Air pressure in thorax falls below atmospheric pressure.

Therefore air moves from atmosphere into lungs.

Expiration

ribs and sternum fall

diaphragm raised

Internal intercostal muscles, lower ribs and sternum can be used in expiration but tend not to be used in quiet breathing.

In expiration during quiet breathing the diaphragm is pulled back by elastic recoil of the lungs.

In forced expiration abdominal wall muscles contract forcing abdominal organs to push up on the diaphragm.

Both the rib and diaphragm movements decrease thorax volume.

Air pressure in thorax rises above atmospheric pressure.

Therefore air moves from the lungs into the atmosphere.

Fig. 12.4 Breathing movements.

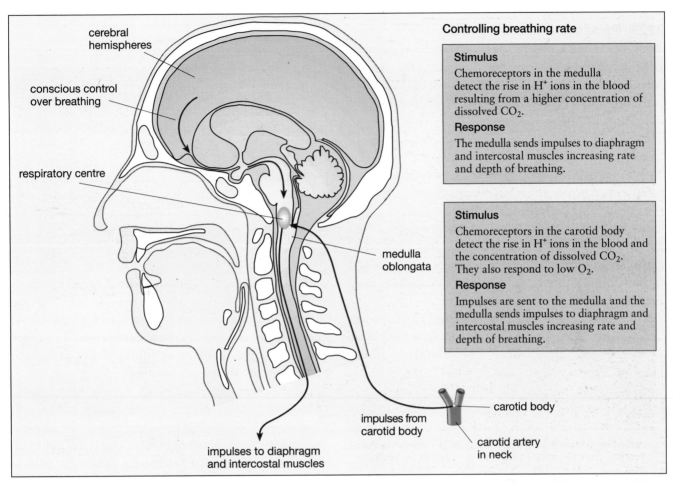

Controlling breathing rate

Stimulus

Chemoreceptors in the medulla detect the rise in H^+ ions in the blood resulting from a higher concentration of dissolved CO_2.

Response

The medulla sends impulses to diaphragm and intercostal muscles increasing rate and depth of breathing.

Stimulus

Chemoreceptors in the carotid body detect the rise in H^+ ions in the blood and the concentration of dissolved CO_2. They also respond to low O_2.

Response

Impulses are sent to the medulla and the medulla sends impulses to diaphragm and intercostal muscles increasing rate and depth of breathing.

cerebral hemispheres

conscious control over breathing

respiratory centre

medulla oblongata

carotid body

impulses from carotid body

carotid artery in neck

impulses to diaphragm and intercostal muscles

Fig. 12.5   The control of breathing in humans.

to deflate. Expiration is therefore often a passive process, relying on the elasticity of the lungs.

Sometimes, however, a more active expiration is needed, for example when coughing, sneezing or blowing. The most important muscles involved here are the muscles of the abdomen. They contract, squeezing the contents of the abdomen up against the diaphragm, which pushes it upwards. This reduces the volume in the thorax, and forces air out of the lungs. You can feel this happening when you cough. The internal intercostal muscles can also help by contracting, pulling the ribcage downwards and inwards.

12.7   Control of breathing

At rest, you probably take about 12 breaths per minute, each one moving about 0.5 dm^3 of air into and out of your lungs. Thus, you move 6 dm^3 of air into and out of your lungs each minute; this is your **ventilation rate**.

The part of the brain which controls breathing is in the medulla (Fig. 12.5). Rhythmic breathing is produced by a

steady pattern of impulses along nerves from the medulla to the diaphragm and intercostal muscles, causing them to contract and relax.

In most mammals, as the lungs inflate during inspiration, stretch receptors in the walls of the airways are stimulated, and they send messages up to the medulla. This briefly cuts off the 'inspiration' signals from the medulla, and so helps to set the timing and rhythm of the pattern of impulses. However, in humans these stretch receptors are not important in quiet breathing, only coming into play when breathing is heavier such as during exercise. At rest, the rhythm of breathing is switched on and off in the brain.

We also have conscious control over breathing, and can make ourselves breathe faster or slower if we wish. However, if the body gets really short of oxygen, then automatic control systems override any attempts at voluntary control.

12.8 Regulation of breathing rate

Both the rate and the depth of breathing are affected by the concentrations of carbon dioxide in the air you breathe, and also by the concentration of oxygen. High concentrations of carbon dioxide, or low concentrations of oxygen, increase breathing rate.

Chemoreceptors in the medulla detect any rise in carbon dioxide concentration in the blood. They do this by being sensitive to the concentration of hydrogen ions, which rises when more carbon dioxide dissolves in water (Section 10.13). There are other carbon dioxide-sensitive chemoreceptors in the walls of the carotid arteries. When they are stimulated, they cause an increase in the rate of signals from the medulla to the intercostal muscles and diaphragm. This increases both the rate and depth of breathing.

Chemoreceptors in the carotid arteries and the aorta are also sensitive to oxygen concentration in the blood. Low oxygen concentrations stimulate these chemoreceptors, which send impulses to the medulla, causing an increase in rate and depth of breathing.

Ventilation rate needs to change with the needs of your tissues. For example, during exercise, much more oxygen is needed to supply hard-working muscles, so ventilation rate must rise (Fig. 12.6). In really strenuous exercise, ventilation rate can be as high as $120 \, dm^3$ per minute – 20 times greater than at rest.

When you exercise, your muscles respire more rapidly than usual, using up more oxygen and producing more carbon dioxide. This affects the oxygen and carbon

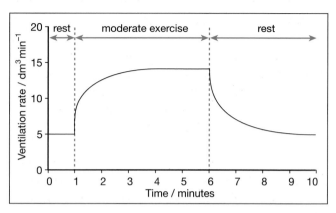

Fig. 12.6 Change in ventilation rate with exercise.

dioxide concentrations in the blood in the veins which are transporting blood *away* from the muscles, but it does *not* affect their concentrations in arteries which have not yet reached them. The carbon dioxide and oxygen concentration in arterial blood depends on the concentrations of these gases in the lungs.

But the chemoreceptors which respond to changes in blood oxygen concentration and blood carbon dioxide concentration sense these concentrations in the blood in the *arteries*, and these concentrations hardly change, even during vigorous exercise. So far, similar receptors in the veins have not been found. The precise mechanism by which ventilation rate increases during exercise remains a mystery. It may involve a direct signal to the medulla from the cerebrum at the same time that the cerebrum sends signals to the skeletal muscles to carry out the exercise.

Q4 (a) Give the letter of the factor from the following list whose value should be as low as possible in an efficient gas exchange system.

    A   surface area

    B   thickness of membrane

    C   temperature

    D   difference in concentration   *(1)*

(b) Explain why, in terrestrial organisms, water is always lost from the gas exchange surface.   (2)

(c) In a mammal, describe one way in which:
    (i) a large surface area for gas exchange is achieved;   *(1)*
    (ii) water loss is minimised from the gas exchange system.   *(1)*

AEB 1995   *(Total 5 marks)*

Box 12.1 Lung volumes

You may be able to make some measurements on the volumes of air moved in and out of your lungs during different kinds of breathing. Here, we will describe how these measurements can be made using a **spirometer** (Fig. 12.7).

Several dm³ of air are trapped over water in a hinged chamber. A flexible tube runs from the chamber to a mouthpiece, through which you can breathe this air. A second tube runs back from the mouthpiece, through a carbon dioxide-absorbing substance (such as soda lime) and back into the chamber. A valve in the mouthpiece ensures that the air you breathe in, and the air you breathe out, move in the correct tubes.

As you breathe in, you reduce the volume of air in the chamber and it drops. The movement of the chamber is recorded in some way, often on a revolving drum. In this example, a downward movement of the chamber produces a downward movement of the pen on the chart. (Other recording methods may produce lines going in the opposite direction.)

The distance the pen moves vertically is proportional to the vertical movement of the lid of the hinged chamber, which in turn is proportional to the volume of the air you breathe out of it, or into it. This needs to be calibrated, by introducing a known volume of air into the chamber and measuring the resulting movement of the pen.

Fig. 12.7 shows the kind of results you might obtain. The first few traces on the chart show the volumes of air moved in and out of the lungs during normal, relaxed breathing. This is called the **tidal volume,** and is usually approximately 0.5 dm³. The subject then breathed out as much air as possible from their lungs. The extra air breathed out, beyond the normal amount breathed out, is called the **expiratory reserve volume.** They then took a very deep breath in. The extra air taken in is called the **inspiratory reserve volume.** The total amount of air moved in and out during these very large in-and-out breaths is called the **vital capacity.** Your vital

capacity is the maximum amount of air you can move in and out of your lungs.

Even when you have pushed as much air as possible out of your lungs, quite a lot of air still remains, because your lungs never do collapse completely. This remaining air is called the **residual volume.** It is not possible to measure your residual volume.

When the subject breathes normally, the trace does not remain level, but slowly drops. This is because all the carbon dioxide in the air being breathed back into the chamber is being removed. Each time the subject breathes in, they use some of the oxygen in the air. The drop in volume represents the volume of oxygen being used.

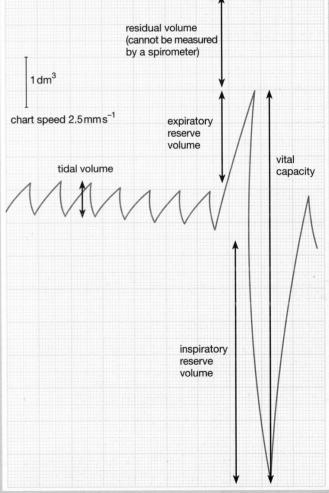

Fig. 12.7 Spirometer trace.

12.9   Keeping foreign materials out of the lungs

The surfaces of the alveoli are very vulnerable to infection or damage from substances in the air. Unlike almost all the other surfaces of the body which are in direct contact with air, they have no protective layers over them. The airways leading to them are therefore designed to remove as many of the potentially dangerous substances in the air as possible, before these substances reach the lungs.

Fig. 12.8 shows the structure of the wall of a bronchus. The inner layer of the wall (nearest to the lumen) is the **epithelium**, and the layer beneath this is called the **lamina propria.**

The epithelium of both the bronchus and the bronchiole contains **goblet cells** which secrete **mucus**. Mucus is a glycoprotein, with molecules made up of long polypeptide chains with sugars attached to them. The glycoprotein molecules interact with each other to form intertwined networks in solution, which makes the solution very viscous. The wall of the bronchus also contains mucus-secreting glands in the lamina propria. Mucus is continuously secreted onto the surface of the epithelium where it forms a sticky, protective coating over the cells. Much of the dust and microorganisms in the air which is breathed in is trapped in this mucus. Antibodies (Section 21.9) are secreted into the mucus to help to kill microorganisms.

The most numerous cells in the epithelium of the bronchus and bronchioles are **ciliated cells**. The cilia (Section 3.13) beat rhythmically, gradually sweeping the mucus up towards the back of the throat, where it is swallowed.

In the lamina propria of both the bronchus and the bronchiole there is **smooth muscle**. This type of muscle is involuntary; you have no control over its contraction. When these muscles contract, they narrow the airways. No-one is really certain what the normal function of these muscles is. In people who suffer from asthma, their contraction causes considerable problems with breathing (Box 12.2).

Despite the action of goblet cells and cilia, foreign particles and microorganisms do still reach the lungs. The surfaces of the alveoli are constantly patrolled by phagocytic white cells which engulf and destroy these invaders.

Smoking causes considerable damage to the surfaces of the airways, increasing mucus production, decreasing the efficiency of cilia, and increasing the chances of infections and cancerous growths.

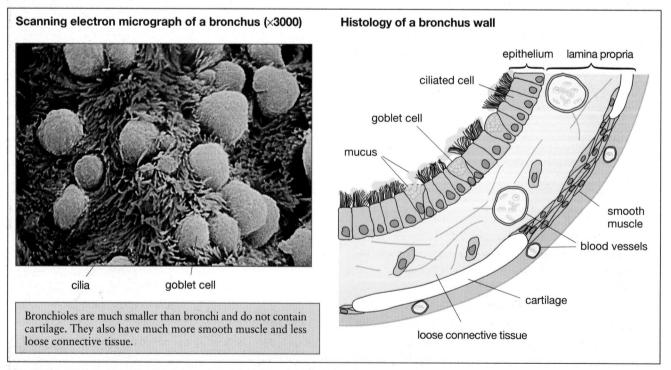

Scanning electron micrograph of a bronchus (×3000)

cilia   goblet cell

Bronchioles are much smaller than bronchi and do not contain cartilage. They also have much more smooth muscle and less loose connective tissue.

Histology of a bronchus wall

epithelium   lamina propria

ciliated cell

goblet cell

mucus

smooth muscle

blood vessels

cartilage

loose connective tissue

Fig. 12.8   The structure of bronchi and bronchioles.

Box 12.2 Asthma

Asthma is one of the few diseases which is becoming increasingly common. In the United Kingdom, almost 1 in 10 people suffer from asthma at some time in their lives. The reasons for this increase are not clear. One possible theory is that young children are now exposed to fewer sources of infection. Asthma is a disease involving the body's defence (immune) system, as are eczema and hay fever. All of these three diseases are increasing, and it may be that this is because the immune system develops differently if it does not have many infections to deal with when a child is small. Evidence for this includes the observation that asthma is increasing all over the world in areas whenever living standards improve; that it is more common in affluent households than in poor ones, and in small families than in large ones; and that it seems to be more common in isolated rural communities than in dense urban populations.

An attack of asthma may be triggered by a particular stimulus, such as exposure to faeces of the house dust mite, an allergen such as pollen or dog hair, a viral infection, or exposure to nitrogen oxides and other gases in vehicle exhaust fumes. However, it is probable that none of these triggers actually *causes* asthma, but only sets off the symptoms of an attack in someone who suffers from the disease. Adults may have chronic asthma, where the symptoms are always with them even if there has been no immediate stimulus.

During an asthma attack the smooth muscle in the airways contracts, narrowing the pathway along which air can move and making breathing very difficult. Extra mucus is produced, which also contributes to the blocking of the airways. Blood vessels in the walls of the airways dilate (vasodilation). This all happens within minutes of exposure to the stimulus.

Later, large numbers of white cells from the immune system (Section 21.7) accumulate. They behave as though there has been a massive invasion of pathogenic (disease-causing) microorganisms,

and they secrete a variety of substances. Some of these stimulate other white cells, while others damage the epithelial cells lining the airways. Over time, the epithelium may become very badly damaged and detach from the wall, further blocking the airways.

Most people who are susceptible to asthma attacks carry an inhaler. This contains one or more drugs which cause the smooth muscles in the bronchi and bronchioles to relax so that the airways dilate. Inhalers usually work very quickly, easing breathing within two minutes or so.

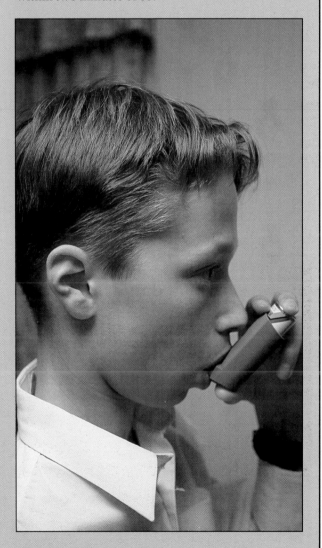

Fig. 12.9 Using an inhaler quickly relieves the symptoms of asthma.

Q5 A spirometer is used to measure the volumes of gas breathed in and out of the lungs. A person breathes through a length of tubing connected to an oxygen chamber and soda lime is used to absorb all the carbon dioxide in the expired air. As a person breathes in and out, the oxygen chamber goes down and up respectively. These movements are recorded on a revolving drum. The figure below shows the spirometer trace of a person who breathed normally at rest and then took a deep breath.

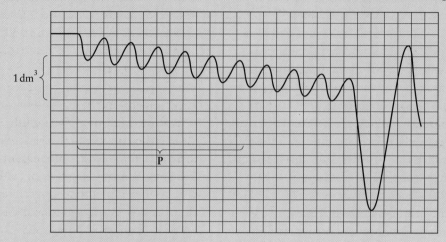

(a) Using the spirometer trace in the figure, determine the person's
 (i) tidal volume;
 (ii) vital capacity;
 (iii) expiratory reserve volume;
 (iv) inspiratory reserve volume. (4)

(b) Calculate the total volume of gas that the person breathed in during the period indicated by **P**. Show your working. (2)

(c) Explain why only some of the gas taken in with each breath reaches the gaseous exchange surface. (2)

(d) Explain why the spirometer cannot be used to measure the **total** volume of the lungs. (2)

The muscles used in breathing movements are controlled by motor nerves which originate in the spinal cord. During normal breathing at rest, nerve impulses pass to the diaphragm and intercostal muscles. The activity of these nerves can be monitored.

(e) (i) State the pattern of activity which you would expect in the nerves leading to the diaphragm muscles. (1)
 (ii) Explain why the nerves to the internal intercostal muscles show no activity during normal breathing at rest. (3)

UCLES 1995 *(Total 14 marks)*

GAS EXCHANGE IN FISH

12.10 The structure of gills

Fish, like mammals, have a gas exchange surface at which blood is brought very close to the external environment so that oxygen can diffuse in and carbon dioxide diffuse out. In fish, this gas exchange surface is the **lamellae** of the **gills** (Fig. 12.10).

In teleost (bony) fish, the gills are covered by a bony flap called an **operculum**. In cartilaginous fish, such as sharks, there is no operculum. The gills are supported by a **gill bar**, containing either bone or cartilage. The spaces between the gill bars, through which water flows, are called **gill slits**. Most fish have five gill slits.

Each gill has two rows of thin, flat, dark red **gill filaments**, projecting into the slits. The upper and lower surface of the filaments are covered with folds called **gill lamellae**. Each lamella is about 0.5 mm high and has an excellent blood supply. The lamellae are covered with a thin sheet of epithelial cells. They have a very large surface area.

12.11 Gas exchange

As water passes through the gills, it flows between the gill lamellae where gas exchange occurs. The diffusion distance between the surface of the lamella and a red blood cell inside a gill lamella is only about 5 μm.

The tiny lamellae lie very close together, with only narrow spaces between them through which the water can flow. These channels are often around 0.05 mm wide, so the maximum distance of a dissolved oxygen molecule from the surface of the lamella is only 0.025 mm.

The blood flows through the gill lamellae in the opposite direction to that in which water flows over them. This is called a **countercurrent** arrangement. Fig. 12.11 shows how this helps to maximise the amount of oxygen which is extracted from the water.

12.12 Ventilation

Water flows in through the mouth of a fish, through its gills and then out through the openings of the gill slits. Many fish achieve this movement just by swimming forwards with their mouth open. Others, such as trout, lie with their heads pointing upstream in flowing water. But fish which live in still water, and are not fast swimmers, have to make breathing movements.

To take water into the mouth, the floor of the mouth cavity is lowered, which increases its volume and reduces pressure. Water therefore moves into the mouth as it moves from an area of relatively high pressure outside. During this stage, the operculum is kept closed.

The mouth then closes and the floor is raised, decreasing the volume and increasing the pressure. At the same time the operculum is opened. Water is therefore pushed out, over the gills and out through the operculum.

Q6 The table below shows some features of gills in several species of fish.

Species	Thickness of lamellae/ μm	Number of lamellae per mm	Distance between lamellae/μm	Distance between blood and water/μm	Activity
icefish	35	8	75	6	slow-moving
bullhead	25	14	45	10	slow-moving
sea scorpion	15	14	55	3	active
trout	15	20	40	3	active
roach	12	27	25	2	active
coalfish	7	21	40	<1	active
herring	7	32	20	<1	very active
mackerel	5	32	20	<1	very active

(a) Use information from the table to describe **two** ways in which the structure of the gills is related to the activity of the fish. (2)

(b) Explain how the structure of the gills in the mackerel enables it to be far more active than the bullhead. (3)

NEAB (part question) 1995 *(Total 5 marks)*

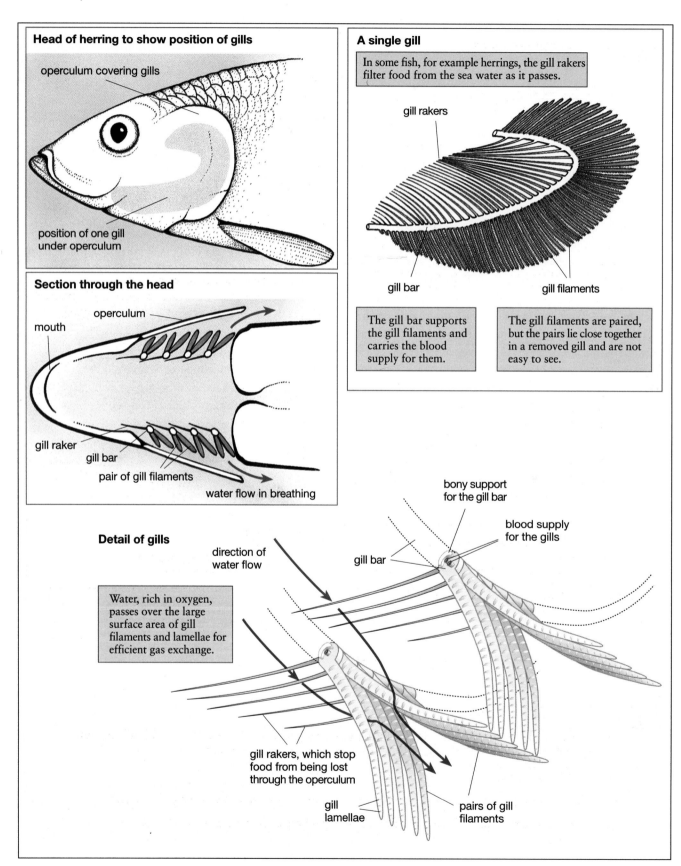

Head of herring to show position of gills

operculum covering gills

position of one gill under operculum

Section through the head

mouth

operculum

gill raker

gill bar

pair of gill filaments

water flow in breathing

A single gill

In some fish, for example herrings, the gill rakers filter food from the sea water as it passes.

gill rakers

gill bar

gill filaments

The gill bar supports the gill filaments and carries the blood supply for them.

The gill filaments are paired, but the pairs lie close together in a removed gill and are not easy to see.

Detail of gills

direction of water flow

Water, rich in oxygen, passes over the large surface area of gill filaments and lamellae for efficient gas exchange.

bony support for the gill bar

blood supply for the gills

gill bar

gill rakers, which stop food from being lost through the operculum

gill lamellae

pairs of gill filaments

Fig. 12.10   The structure of gills in a bony fish.

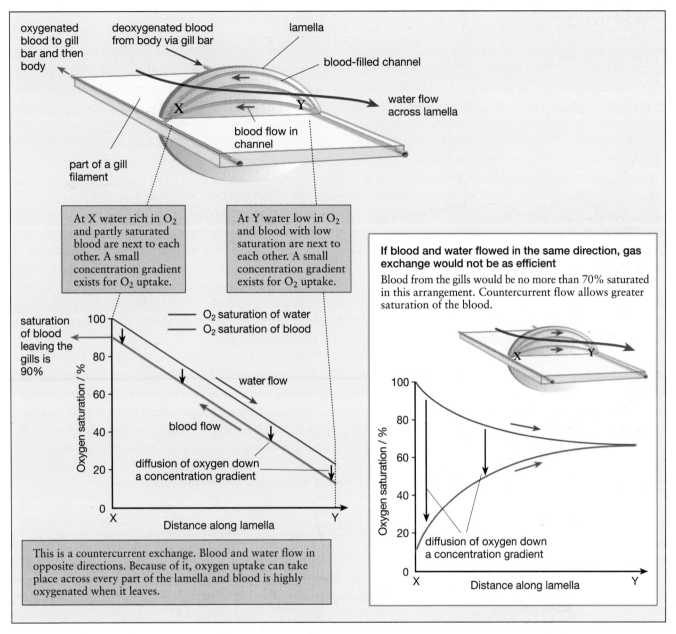

Fig. 12.11 Countercurrent mechanism of gas exchange in gills.

Q7 (a) Why do fish need gills?

(b) In the graphs in Fig. 12.11, what is the degree of oxygenation of blood leaving the gills in reality, and what would it be if blood and water flowed in the same direction?

(c) Explain the term **countercurrent exchange**.

(d) What is the advantage of countercurrent exchange of oxygen and carbon dioxide in fish?

(e) Why is it not possible to have a countercurrent mechanism in human gas exchange?

GAS EXCHANGE IN INSECTS

12.13 Structure of the tracheal system

Insects have a very different method of gas exchange, compared with fish and mammals. Insects do not use blood to transport their respiratory gases from a single gas exchange surface. They have many small gas exchange surfaces all over the body, close to every tissue which actively respires. Air is moved to and from these gas exchange surfaces through the **tracheal system**.

Fig. 12.12 shows the structure of an insect's tracheal system. Along the side of the insect's body are a number of openings called **spiracles**, which are the entrances to tubes called **tracheae**. The spiracles often have valves which can open and close them; closing the spiracles can help to stop water loss if the air is dry. Many species of insects have hairs or spines in the opening of the trachea just inside the spiracle, to trap dust.

An insect's body is covered with an exoskeleton or **cuticle** made of a nitrogen-containing substance called **chitin**. The tracheae develop as ingrowths of the surface of the insect's body, and so they too are lined with cuticle. This is often spirally thickened, which helps to support the trachea if the air pressure inside is reduced.

In most species of insect, the tracheae from each spiracle join on to a large longitudinal trachea. From here, tracheae spread to every tissue.

As they near their destination, the tracheae divide to form smaller, blind-ending tubes called **tracheoles**. These are very small, usually only about 0.1 μm to 1 μm in diameter. Tracheoles penetrate into every tissue and often make indentations in cell surfaces, especially in muscle cells. They do not, however, penetrate cell surface membranes. The endings of tracheoles may contain either air or fluid.

12.14 Gas exchange

Gas exchange takes place by diffusion, between the air in the tracheoles and the tissues which they penetrate.

As the tracheoles are so small, and there are so many of them, their total surface area is very large. It is uncommon for any cell to be more than three cells away from a tracheole. The walls of the tracheoles are only about 50 nm thick, so diffusion across them can take place very rapidly.

The tips of many tracheoles are filled with fluid. Oxygen diffuses much more slowly through fluid than through air, so this greatly reduces the rate at which gas exchange can take place. If the tracheole is supplying a muscle, this fluid may be withdrawn into the surrounding tissues when the muscle is active. This happens because the activity of the

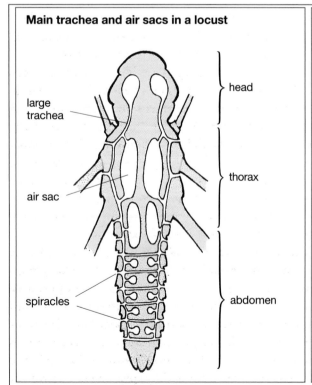

Main trachea and air sacs in a locust

- head
- large trachea
- air sac
- spiracles
- thorax
- abdomen

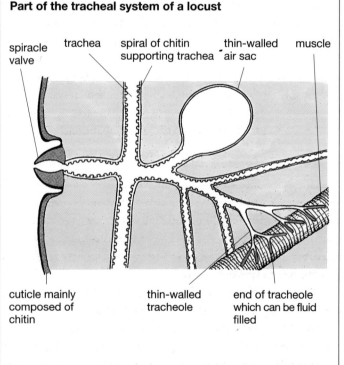

Part of the tracheal system of a locust

- spiracle valve
- trachea
- spiral of chitin supporting trachea
- thin-walled air sac
- muscle
- cuticle mainly composed of chitin
- thin-walled tracheole
- end of tracheole which can be fluid filled

Fig. 12.12 The tracheal system of a locust.

Spiracle opening and closure

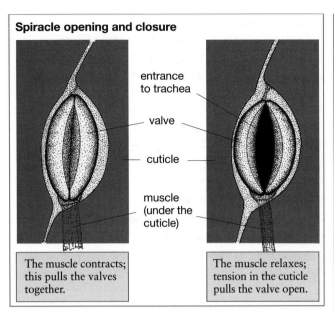

entrance
to trachea

valve

cuticle

muscle
(under the
cuticle)

The muscle contracts;
this pulls the valves
together.

The muscle relaxes;
tension in the cuticle
pulls the valve open.

Fig. 12.13 Ventilation in a locust.

Breathing movements in a resting locust
Inspiration

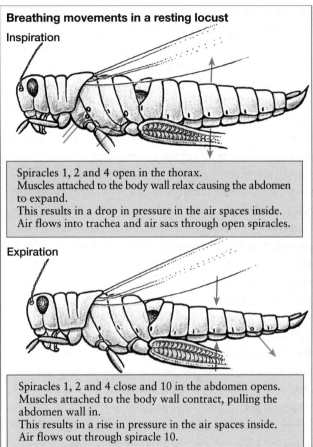

Spiracles 1, 2 and 4 open in the thorax.
Muscles attached to the body wall relax causing the abdomen
to expand.
This results in a drop in pressure in the air spaces inside.
Air flows into trachea and air sacs through open spiracles.

Expiration

Spiracles 1, 2 and 4 close and 10 in the abdomen opens.
Muscles attached to the body wall contract, pulling the
abdomen wall in.
This results in a rise in pressure in the air spaces inside.
Air flows out through spiracle 10.

muscle produces lactic acid which decreases the water potential of the tissue fluid in the muscle as it dissolves in it. This creates a water potential gradient between the fluid in the tracheole and the tissue fluid, so water moves out of the tracheole down this gradient. The removal of the fluid from the end of the tracheole speeds up the rate at which oxygen can diffuse along it, and so increases the rate at which oxygen can be supplied to the respiring muscle.

12.15 Ventilation

In small insects, diffusion along the trachea and tracheoles is enough to supply all the tissues with their oxygen requirements. Large insects, especially active ones which fly, require very large amounts of energy and hence large amounts of oxygen. In these insects, air must be moved along the trachea by mass flow.

You may be able to watch breathing movements in a locust. At rest, air flows in through spiracles 1, 2 and 4 (near the front) and out through spiracle 10 (Fig. 12.13).

Firstly, spiracles 1, 2 and 4 open, as the muscles in the abdomen relax. After a second or so these spiracles close, and the abdominal muscles begin to contract. This

increases the pressure of the air inside the tracheae. Next, spiracle 10 opens, while the abdominal muscles are still contracting, so the air in the tracheae is forced out.

When a locust is flying, it needs almost 400 times as much oxygen per minute as it does at rest. To help to supply this, it opens more of its spiracles to allow air in and out, and increases the speed and size of the contractions of its abdominal muscles. But the most important mechanism of supplying extra oxygen to the flight muscles uses the effects of these muscles themselves. As they contract and relax to pull the wings up and down, they cause pumping movements of the thorax, which bring large volumes of air into the tracheae.

The rate at which breathing movements takes place is controlled by the central nervous system. Ganglia (groups of nerve cells) in each segment of the insect's body produce rhythmical impulses which travel to the muscles and spiracles, causing their repeating and coordinated patterns of movement. The ganglia are sensitive to concentrations of carbon dioxide. If carbon dioxide builds up in the insect's body, they respond by speeding up the rate at which they send impulses, so ventilation rate increases.

GAS EXCHANGE IN PLANTS

12.16 Gas exchange in leaves

Plants, like animals, respire aerobically. They therefore require oxygen, and produce carbon dioxide. However, in daylight they also photosynthesise, and they do this at a faster rate than they respire. The oxygen produced in photosynthesis is more than enough to supply the requirements of leaf cells for respiration. The carbon dioxide produced in respiration, however, is not enough to supply their requirements for photosynthesis. So, in daylight, leaves take in carbon dioxide and give out oxygen.

In darkness there is no photosynthesis, but cells continue to respire. So, at night, leaf cells take in oxygen and give out carbon dioxide, just as animals do.

Plants do not use their transport systems to carry oxygen or carbon dioxide to the cells which require it. Each cell obtains the gases it needs by diffusion, usually directly from the external environment.

Fig. 8.2 shows the structure of a leaf. The gas exchange surface is the surfaces of the mesophyll cells in contact with the air spaces in the leaf. The surface area is large and diffusion distances are small; carbon dioxide or oxygen molecules only have to travel from an air space across a single cell wall to get into the cytoplasm of a cell.

Like all terrestrial organisms, plants have the problem of losing water by evaporation from the gas exchange surface. Water evaporates from the wet cell walls in contact with the air spaces in the leaf and is lost by transpiration. Section 11.3 and Fig. 11.4 describe some of the mechanisms used by plants to keep this loss within reasonable limits.

12.17 How stomata open and close

Carbon dioxide and oxygen diffuse in and out of leaves through small openings called **stomata**. Most stomata are on the underside of the leaf. A stoma is surrounded by two **guard cells**, which control the opening and closure of the hole between them. By opening and closing its stomata, a leaf controls the diffusion of carbon dioxide into the leaf and of water vapour out of it.

Fig. 12.14 shows the structure of a stoma and its bean-shaped guard cells. Most guard cells, unlike other cells in the leaf epidermis, have chloroplasts. Their cell walls are especially rigid on the inner surface (the surface nearest the stoma).

When a cell absorbs water, it expands and becomes turgid (Fig. 3.31). When guard cells do this, their rigid inner wall resists expansion and they become more curved. (Try sticking a piece of elastoplast on one side of a long balloon and then blowing it up – you will get a similar effect.) So, when guard cells are turgid, they are curved away from each other and the stoma between them is open. When they lose water and become flaccid, they collapse together and the stoma between them is closed.

Guard cells become turgid by actively transporting potassium ions, K^+, from outside the cell into the cytoplasm. This decreases the water potential in the cell, so water is drawn in by osmosis.

12.18 Control of stomatal movements

The main role of stomata is to allow carbon dioxide into a leaf when it is photosynthesising, but not to let too much water vapour out. This can be quite a difficult balancing act.

In general, stomata tend to open in the light, to allow carbon dioxide into the leaf for photosynthesis. If carbon dioxide levels are especially high, then the stomata may partially close. This still allows plenty of carbon dioxide in, yet conserves water. If water is in very short supply, then the need to conserve water overrides everything else and the stomata will close, even if this means shutting down photosynthesis.

What makes stomata open and close at particular times? In some plants, there seems to be an inbuilt **circadian rhythm** of stomatal opening and closure. 'Circadian' means 'about a day', and circadian rhythms are repeating, daily patterns which appear to run by a kind of internal clock. *Tradescantia* plants, for example, open and close their stomata in a regular pattern over a 24-hour period, even when they are kept in absolutely constant conditions of light and carbon dioxide concentration.

However, in many plants the opening and closure of stomata is controlled by changes in the external environment (the air outside the leaf) and the internal environment (the air in the air spaces inside the leaf). Carbon dioxide and water availability are the most important factors. Light also plays a part, although this is probably indirectly, as light increases the rate of photosynthesis and therefore affects carbon dioxide concentrations inside the leaf.

● **Carbon dioxide and light**

Guard cells are sensitive to the concentration of carbon dioxide in the air spaces in the leaf. When this is low they

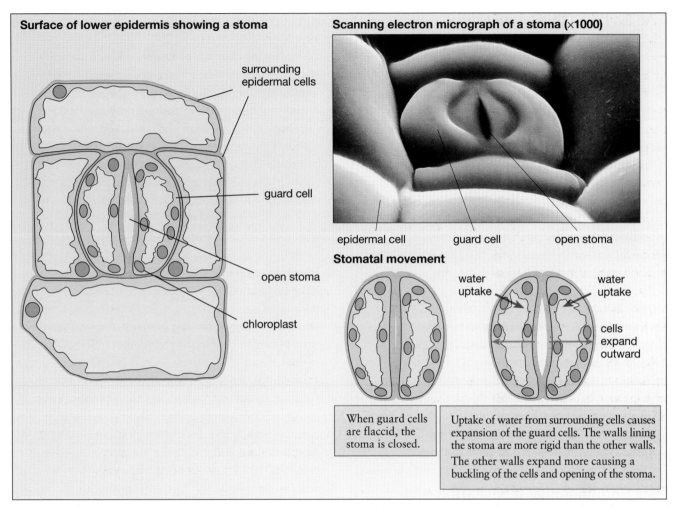

Fig. 12.14 Stomatal structure and movements.

open, and when it is high they close. Stomata therefore tend to open at dawn, when photosynthesis lowers carbon dioxide concentrations in the leaf's air spaces, and close at dusk when photosynthesis stops and carbon dioxide produced in respiration begins to build up. The carbon dioxide concentration presumably switches the potassium pumps in the guard cell membranes (Box 12.3) on and off, but nothing is yet known about how this is done.

● **Water availability**

If a plant becomes very short of water, then the guard cells may lose water by evaporation to the surrounding air faster than this water can be replaced. The guard cells therefore become flaccid and the stomata close, even if the sun is shining and carbon dioxide concentrations in the leaf are low. The harm which would be done by loss of too much water is far greater than that caused by shutting down photosynthesis for a while.

Another way of closing the stomata when water is in short supply is by means of the hormone **abscisic acid, ABA**. ABA is made in leaf mesophyll cells, and stored in the chloroplasts. When leaf cells become short of water, ABA is released and passes to the guard cells where it causes them to become flaccid and close the stomata.

12.19 Gas exchange in other parts of plants

It is not only leaf cells which need to exchange gases with their environment. Cells in stems and roots are constantly respiring, and they need to take in oxygen and get rid of carbon dioxide.

Rates of respiration in cells in plant stems are usually quite low. In herbaceous (non-woody) plants the stems are not very wide, and diffusion is adequate to supply oxygen from the air outside the stem to all the cells within it. Woody plants may have much wider stems. Also, these are covered with a layer of **cork**, which is made of dead

Box 12.3 Theories of the mechanism of stomatal movement

Stomata are opened and closed by changes in the shape of the guard cells. These shape changes are produced by turgor changes; turgid guard cells open the stoma between them, while flaccid ones close it.

However, the exact mechanism which produces these turgor changes is still not understood. For many years it was suggested that when the chloroplasts in guard cells photosynthesised they produced sugars. The sugars would dissolve in the cell contents, reducing the water potential and causing water to be drawn in by osmosis. This could explain how stomata opened in the light.

This theory no longer has any real support. One difficulty with it is that many plants, such as variegated *Pelargonium*s, have no chloroplasts in their guard cells, yet their stomata work perfectly. Other investigations suggest that the chloroplasts in the guard cells of many species do not contain Rubisco (Section 8.5) and so do not fix carbon at all. Moreover, it does not explain other observed differences between turgid and flaccid guard cells, such as their higher concentrations of potassium ions, K^+, and malate.

In the 1940s and 1950s, Japanese scientists discovered that potassium ions accumulated in the guard cells of open stomata. European and American researchers were not aware of the Japanese work until the late 1960s, and since then a considerable amount of evidence has been found that the uptake of potassium ions does lead to the increase in guard cell turgidity which opens stomata. Concentrations of potassium ions are often around five times greater in 'open' guard cells than in 'closed' ones.

The uptake of potassium ions is thought to be driven by an ATP-powered pump, which actively removes hydrogen ions from the cell to the outside (Fig. 12.15). This lowers the electrical potential of the cell inside compared to outside, which causes potassium ion channels in the cell surface membrane to open. (You can read about similar effects in the generation of action potentials in neurones in Section 14.7.) Potassium ions then enter passively, drawn in to the cell because they are positively charged and the inside of the cell has a relative negative potential. Evidence for this mechanism includes the fact that chemicals known to stimulate or inhibit hydrogen ion pumps also stimulate or inhibit stomatal opening.

In order to make sure that the inside of the cell does not gain too much positive charge as a result of the potassium ions entering it, some negative ions must be produced inside the cell. In many plant species, this appears to be done by changing starch into **malate**, which is an anion. There is considerable evidence for this. For example, guard cells of open stomata may contain six times as much malate as guard cells of closed stomata, whereas their starch content is much less. Moreover, guard cells contain large amounts of **PEP carboxylase** (Box 8.5) which catalyses the conversion of starch to malate.

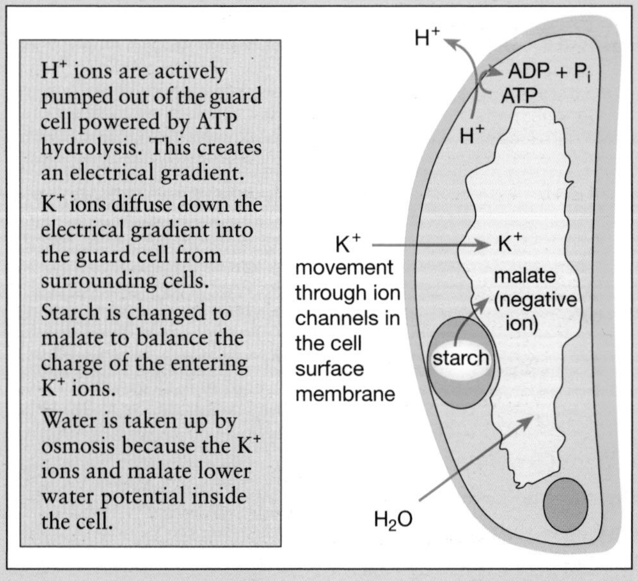

H^+ ions are actively pumped out of the guard cell powered by ATP hydrolysis. This creates an electrical gradient.

K^+ ions diffuse down the electrical gradient into the guard cell from surrounding cells.

Starch is changed to malate to balance the charge of the entering K^+ ions.

Water is taken up by osmosis because the K^+ ions and malate lower water potential inside the cell.

Fig. 12.15 Mechanisms of stomatal movement.

hollow cells with walls containing **suberin** (Section 11.5). The cork layer is impermeable to air. To allow oxygen in to the living cells beneath, gaps known as **lenticels** are present (Fig. 12.16).

In a large tree with a thick trunk, diffusion could never supply oxygen fast enough to the centre of the trunk. However, this is not necessary because the centre contains only dead cells (mostly xylem and fibres) which do not need oxygen. The living cells are all quite near to the surface of the trunk.

Cells in roots obtain their oxygen by diffusion from air spaces in the soil. Root cells may have quite high demands for oxygen, because they use respiration to supply the ATP they need for the active uptake of mineral ions. Roots have a very large surface area to volume ratio, and so gas exchange can occur rapidly across their surfaces. Most roots have air spaces inside them through which oxygen can diffuse fast enough to reach all cells. However, problems can occur if the soil becomes even partially flooded, which greatly reduces oxygen availability. ■

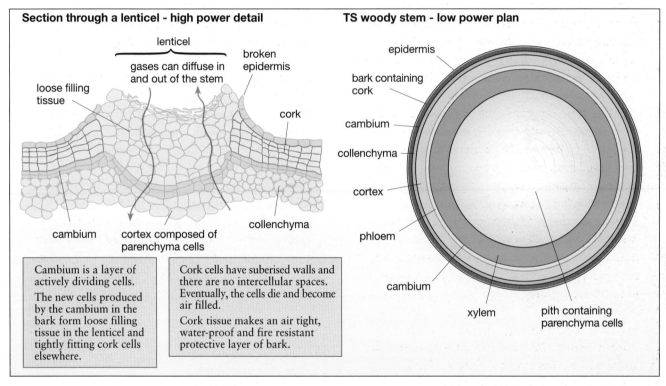

Fig. 12.16   Lenticel and stem histology of a young woody stem of *Sambucus* (elder).

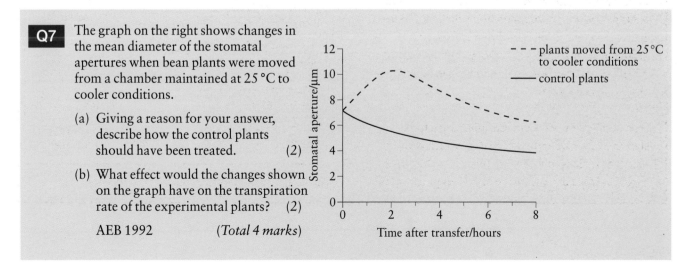

Q7   The graph on the right shows changes in the mean diameter of the stomatal apertures when bean plants were moved from a chamber maintained at 25 °C to cooler conditions.

(a) Giving a reason for your answer, describe how the control plants should have been treated.   (2)

(b) What effect would the changes shown on the graph have on the transpiration rate of the experimental plants?   (2)

AEB 1992   (*Total 4 marks*)

Q8 The diagram shows the stomatal aperture changes in two plants, **A** and **B**, in different conditions.

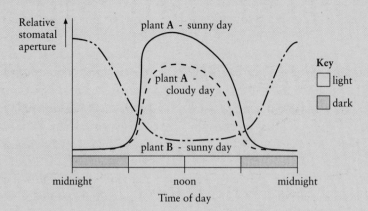

(a) Stomata open when guard cells absorb water because of a change in the water potential of their cell contents.

Give **one** explanation for the mechanism that results in
(i) a change in water potential of the guard cells in plant **A** between 06.00 and noon. (3)
(ii) the stomata of plant **A** not opening as widely on the cloudy day as on the sunny day. (2)

(b) Plant **B** is a succulent plant that lives in dry conditions.
(i) Give **one** advantage to plant **B** of the different behaviour of its stomata. (1)
(ii) Give one disadvantage to plant **B** of the different behaviour of its stomata. (1)

NEAB 1995 (*Total 7 marks*)

Q9 The drawing shows a section through the leaf of *Nerium*, an evergreen shrub which lives in dry conditions.

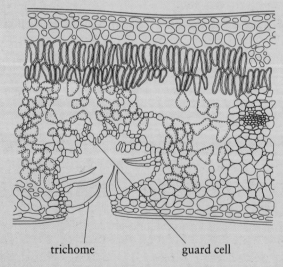

trichome   guard cell

Describe **three** features of a *Nerium* leaf and explain how each feature helps to reduce the rate of transpiration.

NEAB 1995 (*Total 6 marks*)

13 Heterotrophic nutrition

Heterotrophic organisms need to take in organic nutrients which have originally been produced by plants. Humans and all other animals are heterotrophs, and so are fungi. Heterotrophs first digest and then absorb food. The digestive enzymes produced by all kinds of heterotrophs work in very similar ways, but the precise way in which feeding and digestion takes place varies greatly between different kinds of heterotrophic organisms.

13.1 Autotrophic and heterotrophic nutrition

Humans, like all animals, eat food which has been made by other organisms. The food we eat contains **organic** substances, especially carbohydrates, fats and proteins, which have been made by plants. Plants are able to make these organic substances from **inorganic** ones; they use carbon dioxide and water to make carbohydrates by photosynthesis (Chapter 8). The addition of a few inorganic mineral ions, such as nitrates and phosphates, enables them to synthesise all the other substances which they require, such as proteins and nucleic acids.

All animals depend on organic substances which have originally been made by plants, both for their source of energy and for materials from which to build their bodies. Animals are therefore said to be **heterotrophic**, while plants are **autotrophic**. ('Hetero' means 'different' or 'other', whereas 'auto' means 'self.) Animals are dependent on food produced by *other* organisms, but plants (apart from a few parasitic ones) can make their own food.

Animals are not the only group of organisms which feed heterotrophically. Fungi are also heterotrophs, as are many protoctists and prokaryotes. All of them are dependent on food made by autotrophs.

13.2 Types of heterotrophic nutrition

Heterotrophic organisms have evolved many different ways of obtaining the organic nutrients they need. In this chapter, we will look at three of these methods. These are:
- **holozoic nutrition**, which is the method by which humans and other mammals feed, as well as many other animals such as insects. Food, in solid or liquid form or both, is taken into a tube called the **alimentary canal** where it is digested (Section 13.3) and absorbed into the body.
- **saprotrophic nutrition**, which is the method by which fungi and many prokaryotes feed. They live and grow on or in their food substance, which can be anything organic, such as milk, bread or a dead body. They secrete enzymes from their bodies, and digest the food material around them before absorbing it.
- **parasitic nutrition**, which is a method of feeding which has evolved in many different groups of organisms, including various kinds of worms and fungi and a few plants. Parasites feed on, and live in close association with, a living organism of a different species, called their host. They can feed either holozoically, biting their host or sucking fluids from it (for example fleas on a cat or greenfly on a rose plant); or they can feed saprotrophically, absorbing soluble food into their bodies (for example a tapeworm inside a dog's digestive system).

13.3 Digestion and absorption

Nutrients must enter cells before they can be of any use to an organism. The entry of nutrients into an organism's cells, or into its transport system, is called **absorption**.

To be absorbed, nutrients must at some stage cross a cell surface membrane, by one of the methods described in Sections 3.24 to 3.28. Clearly, large lumps of food cannot do this! Nor, in most cases, can large *molecules* do this. With few exceptions (some of which are described in Section 13.10) only relatively small molecules are able to move into living cells.

All heterotrophic organisms therefore need to **digest** food. Digestion involves the breaking down of food into molecules which are small enough to be absorbed into an organism's cells or transport system.

Organisms which feed on solid food may use some form of **mechanical breakdown** as a first method of attack on their food. This involves physically breaking down large pieces of food into smaller ones. Humans, for example, use teeth to do this, and also muscles in the wall of the alimentary canal.

All heterotrophs use **chemical digestion**, which breaks down large food molecules into smaller ones. The reactions involved are **hydrolysis** reactions (Section 1.8), in which water molecules are added when the bonds between different parts of the molecule are broken. These reactions are catalysed by enzymes. **Carbohydrases** catalyse the hydrolysis of polysaccharides (such as starch) and disaccharides (such as maltose). **Proteases** catalyse the hydrolysis of proteins, and **lipases** catalyse the hydrolysis of lipids. Fig. 13.1 illustrates the sequences in which these three groups of molecules are digested to smaller molecules. Vitamins, minerals and water need no digestion.

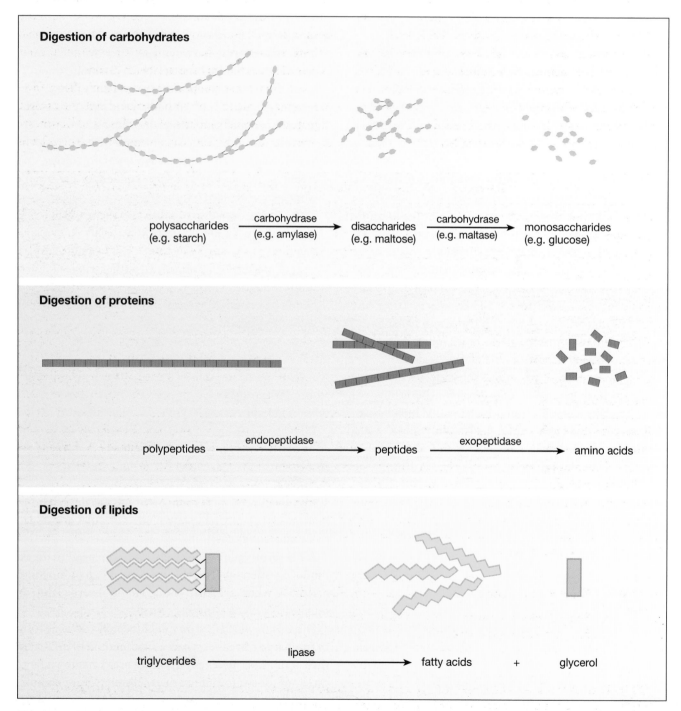

Digestion of carbohydrates

polysaccharides → carbohydrase → disaccharides → carbohydrase → monosaccharides
(e.g. starch)   (e.g. amylase)   (e.g. maltose)   (e.g. maltase)   (e.g. glucose)

Digestion of proteins

polypeptides → endopeptidase → peptides → exopeptidase → amino acids

Digestion of lipids

triglycerides → lipase → fatty acids + glycerol

Fig. 13.1 Summary of chemical digestion.

HOLOZOIC NUTRITION – FEEDING IN HUMANS

13.4 The human diet

Humans, like all animals, require many different organic nutrients in their diet. **Carbohydrates**, **fats** and **proteins** are all required in relatively large amounts. Vitamins are required in much smaller quantities (Table 13.1). You can read about the functions of carbohydrates, fats and proteins in the body in Chapter 1. The functions of some of the major vitamins are summarised in Table 13.2.

We also require some inorganic nutrients. These include **inorganic ions**, sometimes called **minerals**. Some of these, such as sodium, potassium, iron, calcium and iodine, are needed in relatively large amounts while others, such as molybenum and selenium, are needed in such tiny quantities that they are sometimes called **trace elements**.

The functions of some of the most important inorganic ions are summarised in Table 13.3.

Water is also an essential component of every diet. The functions of water in living organisms are described in Sections 1.2 to 1.6.

As well as these essential types of food substances, we can also make use of others. **Ethanol** (alcohol), for example, can be used as an energy source. **Nucleic acids** can also be digested and absorbed. We do not actually need either of these substances, however. Most foods can be used as an energy source, and we are able to make our own nucleic acids from other nutrients in food.

A very important component of a person's diet is **fibre** or roughage. Fibre is plant material which we cannot digest, and consists mostly of cellulose and lignin. Its presence in the alimentary canal stimulates the muscles in

	Energy/kJ	Protein/g	Calcium/mg	Iron/mg	Vitamin A/µg	Vitamin C/mg
girl aged 1 year	4000	14.5	350	8.0	350	25
boy aged 1 year	5150	14.5	350	7.0	400	30
girl aged 10 years	7280	28.3	550	8.7	500	30
boy aged 10 years	8240	28.3	550	8.7	500	30
woman aged 19 years	8100	45.0	700	15.0	600	40
man aged 19 years	10 600	55.5	700	8.7	700	40
pregnant woman	8900	51.0	700	14.8	700	50
breast-feeding woman	10 050	53.0	1250	14.8	950	70
woman aged 75 years	7610	46.5	700	8.7	600	40
man aged 75 years	8770	53.3	700	8.7	700	40

Research into people's dietary requirements has resulted in recommendations for the amounts of each type of nutrient which should be included in each day's food intake. The recommendations for energy intake are **average** values. The values given in this table for the five nutrients are **Reference Nutrient Intakes** (**RNIs**). This is the level of intake which should supply almost everyone with their needs. There will be a few (approximately 2.5%) of the population who need more than this, but most people will need less, and some will need substantially less. RNIs are not given for fat and carbohydrate; these are rarely too low in a diet.

Table 13.1 Dietary requirements

(a) What kind of people or organisations are likely to be interested in RNIs?

(b) Suggest why it is most useful for RNIs to be calculated as described above, and not as *average* requirement of the population.

Q2 Discuss the figures in Table 13.1, pointing out similarities and differences in requirements at different ages and for different sexes, and suggesting reasons for them.

Vitamin	Chemical name	Types of food which contain it	Functions in the body	Where you can find more about it
A	retinol	most meat products e.g. liver, milk, egg yolk; the orange pigment carotene, in carrots, can be converted to retinol	formation of rhodopsin, the light-sensitive pigment in rod cells	Section 14.12 and Box 14.5
B_1	thiamine	outer layers of cereal grains, e.g. in brown rice; beans, nuts, bread, breakfast cereals	formation of TPP, which is a coenzyme in many reactions	Box 9.2
B_2	riboflavin	milk, eggs, yeast products, outer layers of cereal grains, bread, breakfast cereals, liver	formation of FAD, a coenzyme required in respiration	Box 9.2
B_3	pantothenic acid	found in a wide variety of food	formation of coenzyme A	Box 9.2
B_{12}	cobalamin	meat, especially liver; also synthesised in the gut by mutualistic bacteria	needed for thymine formation, and therefore for DNA; especially important in blood cell formation	Box 21.4
C	ascorbic acid	most fresh fruits and vegetables, especially citrus fruit	many different roles in metabolism, where it functions as an electron carrier; helps, for example, in the formation of collagen, in the use of iron (so preventing anaemia) and in stimulating the immune system	
D	cholecalciferol	made in the human skin by the action of sunlight; eaten in dairy products, oily fish and egg yolk	formation of a hormone which controls the uptake of calcium by cells	
	nicotinic acid/ niacin	liver, yeast products, oily fish, breakfast cereals, peanuts	formation of the coenzyme NAD	Box 9.2

Shaded rows are fat-soluble vitamins; unshaded rows are water-soluble vitamins.

Table 13.2 Some vitamins required in the human diet

Inorganic ion	Foods which contain it	Function in the body	Where you can find more about it
calcium, Ca^{2+}	milk products, shellfish, fish bones (e.g. in sardines), treacle, flour, eggs	formation of bones, blood clotting, muscle contraction, transmission of signals across synapses	Sections 14.10, 16.7, Box 16.2, Fig. 21.5
iron, Fe^{3+}	red meat, beans, chocolate and cocoa, shellfish, breakfast cereals, eggs	formation of haemoglobin and myoglobin, and of cytochrome oxidase (an enzyme in the electron transport chain)	Section 10.11, Box 9.3
iodine, I^-	sea food, iodised salt, drinking water	formation of thyroxine	Section 15.2
phosphate, PO_4^{3-}	milk products, fish bones (e.g. sardines)	bone formation	Section 16.7

Table 13.3 Some inorganic ions (minerals) important in the human diet

the walls, speeding up the rate at which they push food through. This not only has the obvious effect of preventing constipation, but also appears to lower the risk of suffering from many diseases of the digestive system, including bowel cancer. This may be because the bulky fibre absorbs potentially harmful chemicals in the food, keeping it away from living cells. Fibre is not, of course, a *nutrient*, because it is not absorbed into the body; it just goes in at one end and out of the other.

13.5 The structure of the human alimentary canal

The **alimentary canal** is a long hollow tube which runs from the mouth to the anus. Together with several other organs, including the **liver** and the **pancreas**, it makes up the **digestive system** (Fig. 13.2).

The lumen (Fig. 13.3) of your alimentary canal is, strictly speaking, part of the outside world and not part of you at all. An object can enter your mouth, pass through the whole length of the alimentary canal and out of the anus without ever crossing any physical barrier. (This fact is frequently illustrated by young children who swallow small items such as toys.) It is not until food has passed into the cells which make up the wall of the alimentary canal that it can be said to be truly *inside* the body.

The total length of the human alimentary canal is between 5 and 6 m, from mouth to anus. To fit this considerable length into the body, parts of the canal are folded and coiled inside the abdomen.

If you could travel through the alimentary canal, you would find yourself inside a dark slippery tube. The slipperiness is caused by **mucus**, a substance secreted along the whole length of the tube by cells lining its walls. Mucus helps food to slide through the canal without doing too much damage to the lining. It also forms a protective covering which keeps the digestive juices, which are inside the lumen of the canal, from coming into contact with the living cells of the walls. Nevertheless, the cells lining the alimentary canal do get damaged and have a very short life span.

Along the whole length of the alimentary canal there are **muscles** in the walls. These produce waves of contraction and relaxation called **peristaltic waves**, which move food along the alimentary canal and help to mix the contents.

Each region of the alimentary canal is adapted to carry out a particular function and, as you will see, the different regions have different structures. However, these differences are all just variations on a common theme; the structure of the whole of the alimentary canal, except the mouth, has the same basic design. This is shown in Fig. 13.3. (The names of the different layers are derived from Latin, which can make them seem rather strange.)

There are four basic layers in the wall of the alimentary canal. Working from the inside (nearest to the lumen) outwards, these are:

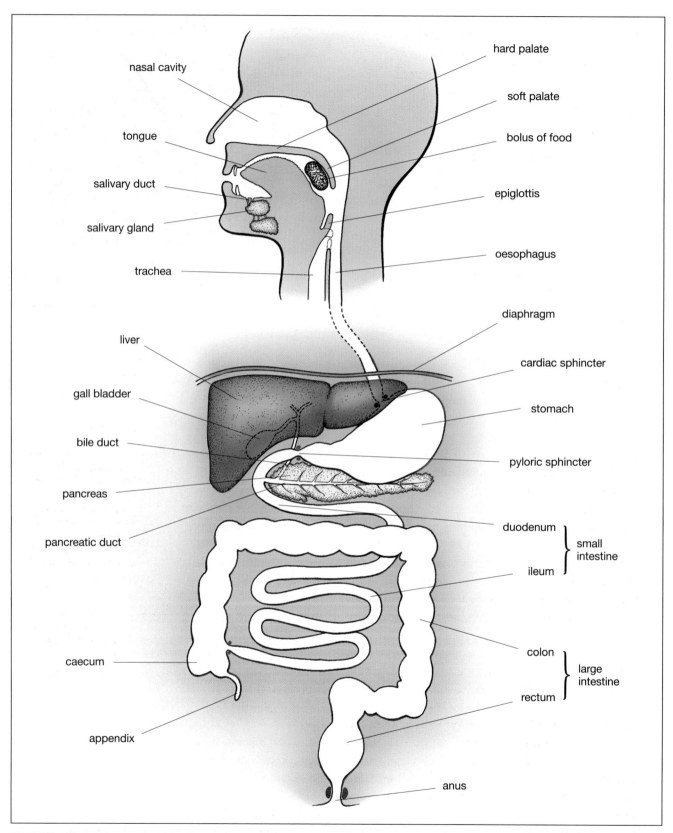

Fig. 13.2 The structure of the human digestive system.

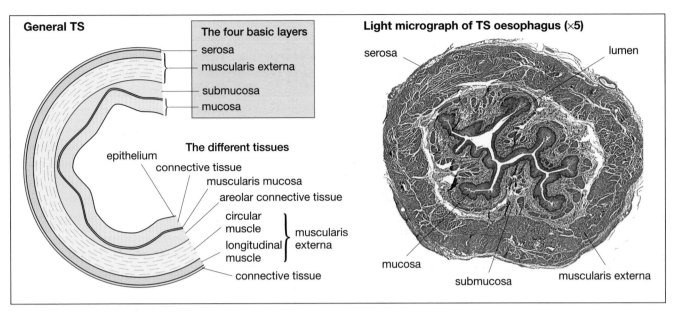

Fig. 13.3 The structure of the alimentary canal wall.

- the mucosa,
- the submucosa,
- the muscularis externa,
- the serosa.

The **mucosa** is made up of three layers. The innermost layer is the **epithelium**. The structure of the epithelium varies considerably in different parts of the alimentary canal, but it always contains cells which secrete mucus. Beneath it is a layer of **connective tissue** (sometimes called the lamina propria, which means 'closest layer'), and beneath that is a layer of smooth muscle (Box 16.1) called the **muscularis mucosa** ('muscle in the mucosa layer').

The **submucosa** is made up of **areolar connective tissue**. This is an open-textured stretchy tissue, containing many elastic fibres and collagen fibres. Running through it are numerous blood vessels and nerves.

The **muscularis externa** ('muscle in the outside layer') is made of two layers of muscle. The innermost layer has fibres running *around* the tube, and is called **circular muscle**. The outermost layer has fibres running *along* the tube, and is called **longitudinal muscle**. It is these muscles which produce peristaltic waves (Fig. 13.4).

The **serosa** is a very thin layer, made up of connective tissue covered with a single layer of thin, smooth closely-fitting cells.

We will look at each part of the human alimentary canal in detail, following the sequence which food would follow as it passes through.

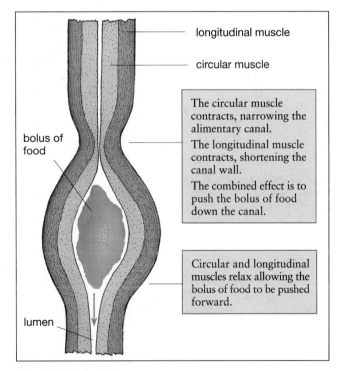

Fig. 13.4 Peristalsis.

The circular muscle contracts, narrowing the alimentary canal.

The longitudinal muscle contracts, shortening the canal wall.

The combined effect is to push the bolus of food down the canal.

Circular and longitudinal muscles relax allowing the bolus of food to be pushed forward.

13.6 The mouth

Taking food into the mouth is called **ingestion** (not to be confused with indigestion!). We use lips, tongue and teeth – especially incisors and canines – for this purpose. The tongue is also important in tasting food, to tell you whether it is good to eat; if not, it will be ejected from the mouth rather than swallowed.

The main purpose of human teeth is to break up large pieces of food, thus beginning the process of mechanical digestion. This is done by chewing, or **mastication**. Strong muscles in the jaws move the lower jaw up and down and from side to side, grinding the teeth in the lower jaw against those in the upper jaw. The premolar and molar teeth have ridges and grooves, which trap food between them and crush it as you chew. Mastication greatly increases the surface area of the food, bringing more of it into direct contact with enzymes in the digestive juices and so speeding up chemical digestion.

Three pairs of **salivary glands** secrete the watery liquid **saliva**, which pours along ducts into the mouth. Approximately 1 dm³ of saliva is secreted each day. Like

all secretions along the alimentary canal, saliva is mostly water. It contains **mucus**, which mixes with the food as it is chewed, helping to glue it loosely together into a ball called a **bolus**. The mucus also makes the bolus slippery, so that it is easier to swallow.

Saliva contains the enzyme **amylase,** which catalyses the hydrolysis of starch. It breaks the α1-4 links (Fig. 1.6) between glucose molecules within starch molecules, but is not able to break the links of the glucose molecules on the end of a chain. Thus, digestion by amylase produces maltose (a disaccharide) and small chains made up of three, four or more glucose molecules linked together, but it does not produce individual glucose molecules.

Saliva also contains an enzyme called **lysozyme**. This enzyme, which is also found in tears, can destroy several types of bacteria which can cause infections in the mouth and throat, including *Staphylococcus* and *Streptococcus*.

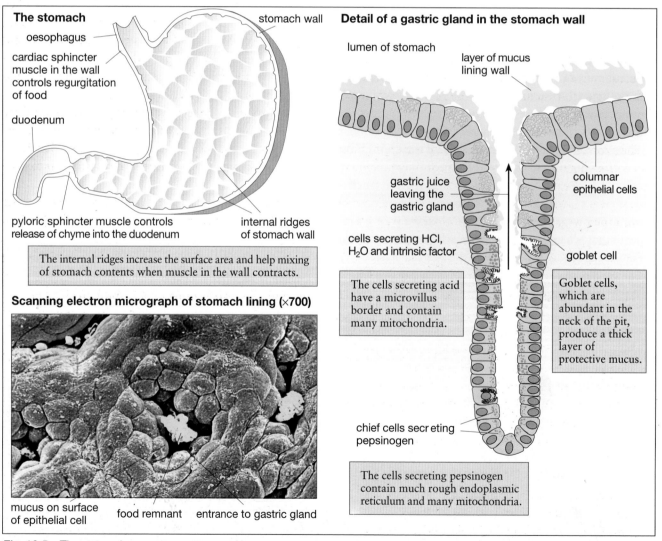

Fig. 13.5 The stomach.

The lysozyme, together with a general 'washing' action of saliva, and a small amount of hydrogencarbonate ions in it (which partly neutralises acids on teeth) appear to help reduce the incidence of tooth decay.

13.7 The stomach

When a bolus of food is swallowed, it is moved swiftly down the oesophagus by peristalsis and into the stomach.

The stomach (Fig. 13.5) is a muscular sac, with a capacity of up to 5 dm³. In some parts of the stomach the muscle layers of the muscularis externa are thicker than in most other parts of the alimentary canal. They produce strong, rhythmic, churning movements when there is food in the stomach (and sometimes when there isn't and you are feeling hungry!). This not only mixes the food with the juices secreted in the stomach, but also helps to continue the process of mechanical breakdown begun by chewing in the mouth.

The inner layer of the stomach wall, the mucosa, is specialised to produce large quantities of **gastric juice**, up to 2 dm³ each day. Gastric juice contains **protease** and **lipase**, as well as **hydrochloric acid (HCl)**. To protect the cells in the wall from damage by the acid and proteases, they are covered with a slimy coat of mucus containing hydrogencarbonate ions which neutralise the acid.

The protease secreted in gastric juice is **pepsin**. (The way in which pepsin hydrolyses proteins is described in Section 2.1.) Pepsin is secreted from large cells in the gastric glands called **chief cells**. It is secreted in an inactive form, as **pepsinogen**, to prevent it from digesting proteins in the cells which produce it. Pepsinogen is a larger molecule than pepsin, and it is activated by removing a strip of several amino acids from it. This happens automatically when it is exposed to the acidic conditions inside the stomach. It is also achieved by pepsin molecules which have already been activated; they 'digest' pepsinogen molecules to convert them into more pepsin.

Pepsin catalyses the hydrolysis of peptide bonds within protein molecules; it does not break the bonds holding the 'end' amino acids of the polypeptide chains. Proteases which do this are called **endopeptidases** ('endo' means 'within'). Pepsin therefore breaks protein molecules into short chains of amino acids (called peptides), but produces almost no individual amino acid molecules.

Pepsin molecules are unusual proteins in that they are only stable in acidic conditions. The optimum pH for the pepsins found in the human stomach is about 2 or 3. This is, of course, the pH which is found in the stomach when gastric juice has been secreted because this juice contains large amounts of hydrochloric acid. Hydrochloric acid helps to destroy many potentially harmful micro-organisms which might be present in food. It is secreted from **parietal cells** in the gastric glands.

The lipase in gastric juice begins to hydrolyse triglycerides into fatty acids and glycerol. However, the majority of the digestion of triglycerides (Section 1.18) and other lipids happens later, in the small intestine (Section 13.9).

Gastric juice also contains a substance called **intrinsic factor**. This is a glycoprotein (Section 3.6) which binds to

---

Box 13.1 Absorption in the stomach

The wall of the stomach is not designed to allow absorption to occur, but there are a few substances which do enter the blood vessels in the stomach wall from the lumen. These include **alcohol** and **aspirin**. Alcohol is a small molecule, which is soluble in lipids and therefore can easily move through cell surface membranes. Aspirin will dissolve in lipid when it is in acidic conditions, but not when it is in neutral conditions. So, in the acidic conditions in the stomach, aspirin can easily move across the cell surface membranes of the cells lining the walls. Once it has crossed these membranes it is in neutral conditions and becomes lipid-insoluble, so it cannot diffuse back again. You might like to think of this next time you are waiting for an aspirin to take effect. If it could not be absorbed in the stomach, you would have to wait much longer until it made its way into the small intestine.

Unfortunately, aspirin has a potentially dangerous side-effect on the stomach lining. It inhibits the secretion of mucus and hydrogencarbonate ions, which increases the likelihood that the stomach wall will be damaged by hydrochloric acid and pepsin. This can result in ulcers. Anyone with an ulcer should avoid aspirin and choose a different type of painkiller.

vitamin B_{12} and protects it from being digested. Later, in the ileum, the intrinsic factor–vitamin B_{12} complex sticks to the surfaces of the cells of the ileum wall, which absorb it. People who do not secrete intrinsic factor cannot absorb vitamin B_{12}, however much they eat in their diet. They suffer from **pernicious anaemia**, an illness in which not enough red blood cells are formed.

Food may be kept in the stomach for several hours. The acidic mixture of partly digested food and water, called **chyme**, cannot pass on to the next part of the alimentary canal, the duodenum, until a band of muscle called the **pyloric sphincter** relaxes. When this happens depends on many factors which seem to relate to how quickly the duodenum will be able to deal with what is being sent into it. For example, if there is a lot of fat in the chyme, it will be allowed into the duodenum only in small amounts at a time, to give the duodenum (Section 13.8) a chance to deal with it.

13.8 The small intestine

The duodenum and the ileum together make up the **small intestine**. (The first part of the ileum is sometimes known as the jejunum.) The overall length of the small intestine is about 5 m, of which the duodenum makes up the first 25 cm. It is within the duodenum and the ileum that most digestion and absorption occurs.

The mucosa of the whole of the small intestine is greatly folded, forming tiny projections called **villi** (Fig. 13.6). In the duodenum, these are flattened with a rather leaf-like shape, while in the ileum they are more finger-like. A villus is about 0.5 mm to 1.0 mm long; villi are very thin and make the inner surface of the small intestine look rather like velvet. As in the mucosa layer of all parts of the alimentary canal, this mucosa is made up of three layers – an epithelium, a layer of connective tissue and the muscularis mucosa. The muscles of the muscularis mucosa contract and relax, so that the villi sway about. This helps to bring their surfaces into contact with more of the contents of the small intestine than if they remained still.

The cells which make up the epithelium of the villi have a very folded cell surface membrane on the side nearest to the lumen of the small intestine; these little folds are called **microvilli** (Fig. 13.6). Seen under the microscope, the

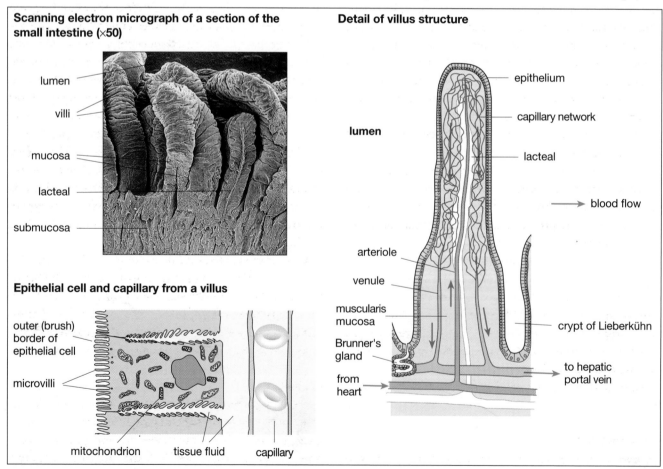

Scanning electron micrograph of a section of the small intestine (×50)

lumen
villi
mucosa
lacteal
submucosa

Epithelial cell and capillary from a villus

outer (brush) border of epithelial cell
microvilli
mitochondrion   tissue fluid   capillary

Detail of villus structure

epithelium
capillary network
lacteal
lumen
blood flow
arteriole
venule
muscularis mucosa
Brunner's gland
from heart
crypt of Lieberkühn
to hepatic portal vein

Fig. 13.6   The small intestine.

surface of the cell looks like the bristles of a brush and is often called a **brush border**. The villi and their microvilli produce an enormous surface area within the small intestine, which greatly increases the rate at which absorption can take place.

In the 'troughs' between the villi in the duodenum are glands, known as **crypts of Lieberkühn,** which secrete mucus. The crypts also constantly produce new cells, which move up the villi until they 'fall off' at the top. This constant replacement of the surface cells is essential, as individual cells do not last long. Deeper in the walls of the duodenum, in the submucosa, **Brunner's glands** are found. These glands secrete a watery mucus that contains hydrogencarbonate ions to help neutralise the acidic chyme flowing into the duodenum from the stomach.

13.9   Digestion in the small intestine

Digestion in the small intestine is brought about by enzymes from two sources. One of these is the cells which cover the surface of the villi, and the other is the **pancreas**.

The pancreas secretes **pancreatic juice**. This flows into the duodenum along the pancreatic duct (Fig. 13.2). (The pancreas also has another, quite different, role as part of the endocrine system, where it helps in the regulation of blood glucose levels. You can find information about its structure in Fig. 15.5.) Pancreatic juice contains hydrogencarbonate ions (to neutralise the acidic chyme from the stomach) and a number of enzymes, especially **amylase**, the three proteases **trypsin, chymotrypsin** and **carboxypeptidase,** and **lipase.**

The enzymes in pancreatic juice continue to digest the partly digested substances which flow into the small intestine from the stomach. Digestion is completed by enzymes which are produced by the cells on the surface of the villi and remain on their surfaces. Indeed, some of the pancreatic enzymes become adsorbed onto (attached to) these surfaces, so that much of the digestion in the small intestine takes place on the brush border of the villi. This is useful because it means that the products of digestion are right next to the surface across which they can be absorbed, which probably increases the speed at which they are taken up into the cells.

We will look at the digestion of each kind of food in turn.

● Carbohydrates

Amylase from the pancreas acts in a very similar way to the amylase in saliva, catalysing the hydrolysis of **starch** to maltose. This happens partly in the lumen of the small intestine, but also on the brush border of the villi because quite a lot of the pancreatic amylase becomes adsorbed onto these surfaces.

The cells on the villi also produce several carbohydrase enzymes of their own, which also do their work within the brush border. They include **maltase**, which catalyses the hydrolysis of maltose to glucose; **sucrase**, which hydrolyses sucrose to glucose and fructose; and **lactase,** which hydrolyses lactose (a disaccharide found in milk) to glucose and galactose. Although all young children have lactase, in most people the levels of this enzyme drop as they get older. However, in some North European and African populations, lactase remains active throughout adult life.

● Proteins

Trypsin and chymotrypsin, like pepsin in the stomach, are secreted by the pancreas in inactive forms, as trypsinogen and chymotrypsinogen. Like pepsinogen, these inactive forms are larger molecules than the active enzymes and need to have a piece removed before they can begin to digest proteins. A substance called **enterokinase**, which is secreted by the walls of the duodenum, performs this role. Once some trypsin and chymotrypsin have been produced, they can act on their inactive forms and convert them into active ones. Both of these proteases are endopeptidases (Section 13.7), producing peptides from protein molecules.

Carboxypeptidase, however, is an **exopeptidase**. It catalyses the removal of single amino acids, one at a time, from the end of a peptide chain with a free carboxyl group. (Like all the other proteases, carboxypeptidase is released in an inactive form. It is activated by trypsin removing part of its molecule.) So, carboxypeptidase produces free amino acids.

Most of the peptides produced by the action of pepsin, trypsin and chymotrypsin are adsorbed onto the brush border of the cells on the villi. Here **peptidases** secreted by these cells break the peptides down to individual amino acids. Some peptides are taken into the cells intact, and their digestion is completed by peptidases *inside* the cytoplasm.

● Lipids

The enzyme **lipase,** which is present in pancreatic juice, catalyses the hydrolysis of some triglycerides to fatty acids and glycerol. Other triglycerides are only partly broken down, leaving one fatty acid still attached to glycerol; this kind of molecule is called a **monoglyceride.**

Lipids are, in some ways, the most difficult type of nutrient to digest because they are not water soluble. They tend to separate out in water to form big droplets, or even a layer of lipid lying on top of the watery contents of the alimentary canal. Lipase is water soluble, so it would be very difficult for it to carry out its function if the lipids were present in a separate layer or in big droplets, because there would be very little surface at which the lipase could make contact with the lipid molecules.

Mechanical mixing in the stomach breaks large drops of lipid into tiny droplets that are no more than 1 μm in diameter, which become suspended in the watery chyme. This sort of mixture, made up of tiny droplets of one insoluble liquid suspended in another liquid, is called an **emulsion**. Lipase can readily act on lipids in a lipid–water emulsion, because a large surface area of lipid droplets is in contact with the watery part of the liquid in which the lipase molecules are found.

Once the chyme leaves the stomach, the tiny droplets would rapidly coalesce back into big droplets again if it were not for the presence of several **emulsifying agents**. These are present in **bile**, a greenish liquid produced by the liver, which flows into the duodenum from the gall bladder. The most important ones are **bile acids**, **lecithin** (this is a phospholipid which you may have noticed on food labels as it is often used as an emulsifying agent) and **cholesterol**.

Once lipase has hydrolysed the triglycerides to monoglycerides, fatty acids and glycerol, the bile acids continue to help out with the next stage of digestion. Fatty acids and monoglycerides are not very soluble in water, so it would be difficult for them to be carried to the surface of the villi and be absorbed. Molecules of bile acids, however, associate with monoglycerides and cholesterol to form into groups called **micelles** (Fig. 13.7), with hydrophobic areas pointing inwards and hydrophilic areas pointing outwards into the watery contents of the alimentary canal. Each micelle is very tiny, only about 5 nm in diameter. Inside the micelles, fat-soluble substances such as fatty acids and the fat-soluble vitamins A and D are carried to the surface of the villi. Here, the contents of the micelle are released and can be absorbed into the cells. The bile acids are also absorbed, ready to be taken back to the liver, recycled and used to help with digestion again.

13.10 Absorption in the small intestine

The small intestine is the area of the alimentary canal in which almost all absorption of nutrients occurs. (Some absorption also occurs in the colon, which is described in

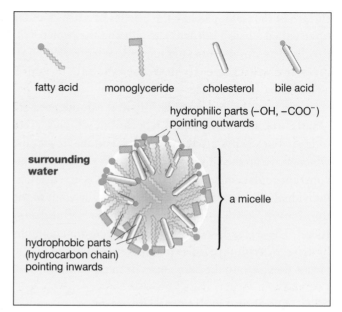

fatty acid   monoglyceride   cholesterol   bile acid

hydrophilic parts (–OH, –COO⁻) pointing outwards

surrounding water

a micelle

hydrophobic parts (hydrocarbon chain) pointing inwards

Fig. 13.7   A micelle.

Section 13.11.) The very large surface area provided by the villi, and the microvilli on the surfaces of the cells which cover them, greatly speeds up absorption. Inside each villus is a blood capillary, which can transfer absorbed nutrients to a branch of the hepatic portal vein. There is also a lymph vessel, called a **lacteal**, which you will see is important in the absorption of lipids.

To get into either the blood capillary or the lacteal, nutrient molecules must first cross the cell surface membrane on the 'outer' (brush border) surface of one of the cells on the surface of a villus. Then they must cross the cell and leave it across the cell surface membrane on the side furthest away from the lumen (Fig. 13.8). They then have to cross either the wall of the blood capillary or the wall of the lacteal. This last part of the journey does not cause too many difficulties, as these walls are adapted to allow various substances to pass in and out. (You can read more about this in Section 10.14.)

Molecules cross the cell surface membranes of the villus cells by diffusion, facilitated diffusion, active transport (both direct and indirect) and endocytosis (Sections 3.24 to 3.28).

Glucose is absorbed into the cells by indirect active transport, involving the co-transport of sodium ions. This process is shown in Fig. 3.32. The glucose then moves out of the opposite side of the cell by facilitated diffusion and simple diffusion, into the tissue fluid inside the villus and then into the blood capillary.

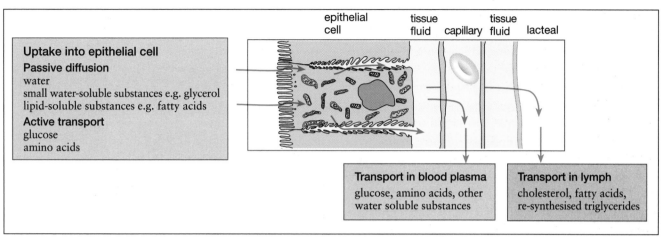

Fig. 13.8 Absorption across the villus epithelium.

Amino acids are absorbed into the villus cells by active transport, and pass out of the opposite side by diffusion. In a fetus and newly born baby, some entire undigested proteins can be absorbed by pinocytosis. This is how babies are able to absorb some of their mother's antibodies from breast milk. (Antibodies are proteins.) This can also happen to a small extent in adults.

Fatty acids and **glycerol** are easily absorbed across the cell surface membranes of the villus cells because they are lipid-soluble; they move across by simple diffusion. Once inside the cell, they are taken to the smooth endoplasmic reticulum where some are reconverted to triglycerides. They are moved to the Golgi apparatus, where they are surrounded in a coat of protein, phospholipid and cholesterol to form **chylomicrons** (Fig. 13.9). These tiny structures, ranging from 100 to 600 nm in diameter, are moved out of the far side of the cell into the tissue fluid in the villus by exocytosis. Although they are very small, they are too big to get through the even smaller holes in the walls of the blood capillaries, and so they do not enter the blood. They can, however, readily enter the lacteals. The chylomicrons suspended in the lymph inside the lacteals form a milky emulsion, which is what gives these structures their name. ('Lact' means 'to do with milk'.)

Considerable amounts of **water** and **inorganic ions**, such as **sodium, chloride, calcium** and **iron**, are also absorbed in the small intestine. The absorption of calcium is helped by the presence of vitamin D. The absorption of iron is helped by citrate ions and ascorbic acid, both of which are found in citrus fruits. This is probably why fresh fruits and vegetables in the diet can help to prevent anaemia. On the other hand, drinking too much tea can hinder iron absorption, because tannins in the tea react

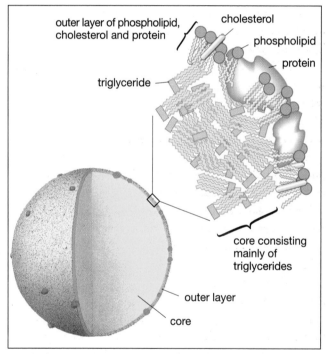

Fig. 13.9 A chylomicron.

with iron to produce compounds which cannot be absorbed.

Vitamins are also absorbed in the small intestine. The fat-soluble vitamins **A**, **D** and **E** can simply cross the cell surface membranes by diffusion; you have seen how bile salts help to bring them to the surfaces of the villi along with fatty acids. The water-soluble vitamins, such as vitamin **C** and the many types of **B** vitamins are moved across the cell surface membranes by specific transporters, often by active transport. Vitamin B_{12} can only be absorbed in combination with intrinsic factor (Section 13.7).

13.11 The colon and rectum

By the time the food has reached the end of the small intestine, virtually everything which could be absorbed has entered the villi. What is left? The undigested, unabsorbed remains are mostly fibre; humans cannot digest cellulose or lignin. There is also quite a lot of water (some of it recently drunk, but much of it from the secretions such as saliva and gastric juice from earlier parts of the alimentary canal), some remains of old cells sloughed off from the inner surface of the alimentary canal and many bacteria.

At the entrance to the **colon** from the small intestine, there is a blind-ending side branch – the **caecum** and **appendix**. The appendix has no function in humans. The colon, however, is very important indeed as it is here that much of the remaining water is absorbed into the blood, together with sodium and chloride ions. These processes also occur in the caecum. The colon has no villi, but it does have a large surface area produced by many folds in its wall, to increase the efficiency of absorption.

The **rectum** is a short straight section of the alimentary canal, which leads from the colon to the anus and thus to the outside world. It is usually empty, only receiving the contents of the colon – now called **faeces** – when they are ready to be passed out of the anus.

13.12 The control of secretions in the alimentary canal

As food passes along the alimentary canal, numerous secretions are produced to help to digest it. It is important that these secretions are only produced when needed, that when they *are* needed they are ready and waiting for the food when it arrives, and that they contain suitable amounts of whatever enzymes are needed. Various mechanisms are used to ensure that this happens.

Saliva is produced by a reflex action (Section 14.15) resulting from a stimulus of the thought, sight, smell or taste of food.

Gastric juice, like saliva, begins to be secreted even before anything has been eaten, just at the thought or smell of food. This is brought about by impulses carried from the brain and along a branch of the **vagus nerve** (Section 14.3) to the gastric glands. In animals such as dogs, these impulses also cause the release of a hormone (Section 15.2) called **gastrin**, which is produced by cells in the mucosa of the stomach, but this is less important in humans. Like all hormones, gastrin is secreted into the blood, and it is carried in the blood to the gastric glands.

The arrival of gastrin causes these glands to increase their secretion of hydrochloric acid and pepsinogen. When the anticipated food actually reaches the stomach, its arrival stimulates the secretion of even larger amounts of gastrin, thus increasing the secretion of gastric juice.

The secretion of **pancreatic juice** into the duodenum is controlled in a similar way. Once again, the very thought of food can cause this to begin, in a similar way to that described above. However, most secretion only happens when chyme from the stomach enters the duodenum. Acid entering the duodenum causes cells in its walls to secrete a hormone called **secretin**, which is carried in the blood to the pancreas and increases the production and release of pancreatic juice especially rich in hydrogencarbonate ions. (Secretin was the first hormone ever to be discovered, in 1902, well before any of the more well-known ones such as insulin or oestrogen.)

Another hormone with a similar effect to secretin is called **cholecystokinin**, or **CCK**. (You may also come across it under its old name, **pancreozymin**. You may also meet CCK in other contexts; it is, for example, found in the brain, and may be involved in controlling the sleeping–waking cycle.) Like secretin, CCK is secreted by the walls of the duodenum when chyme enters from the stomach. However, in this case it appears to be the presence of products of fat and protein digestion which triggers its release, rather than acidity. CCK stimulates the secretion of bile, which it does by causing contraction of the walls of the gall bladder. It also stimulates the production of pancreatic juice especially rich in enzymes.

Q3 Read through the following account of carbohydrate digestion then copy it, filling in the most appropriate word or words to complete the account.

Digestion of starch starts in the .... where it is hydrolysed to .... by the enzyme .... This process is halted in the stomach but continues in the duodenum, catalysed by an enzyme secreted by the .... Also in the duodenum, sucrose is hydrolysed to .... and .... by enzymes produced by secretory cells in the duodenum wall.

London 1996   (*Total 6 marks*)

Q4 One kind of 'heartburn' is caused when the acid contents of the stomach pass up into the oesophagus, a condition called acid-reflux. To find out if acid-reflux was the cause of a patient's 'heartburn', a pH probe was inserted into the oesophagus and pH levels in the oesophagus were recorded over a period of 24 hours. The patient was asked to record the times at which drinks were taken during the 24-hour period. The graph shows the results of this investigation.

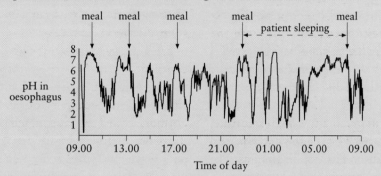

(a) Suggest how the stomach contents are normally prevented from passing into the oesophagus. (2)

(b) (i) Describe the relationship between taking a meal and the pH in the oesophagus. (1)
    (ii) Suggest why the pH in the oesophagus was very low between 02.00 and 04.00, but high between 05.00 and 07.00. (2)

(c) The secretion of acid by the stomach is partly controlled by the hormone gastrin.
    (i) Describe the general characteristics of hormones. (3)
    (ii) Describe the role of gastrin in the control of gastric secretions. (4)

NEAB 1995   (*Total 12 marks*)

Q5 The diagram below shows the structure of a villus as seen in longitudinal section.

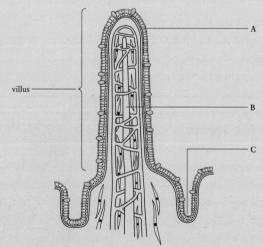

(a) Name the parts labelled **A**, **B** and **C**. (3)

(b) The magnification of this diagram is x 90. Calculate the actual height of this villus. Show your working. (2)

(c) Describe **one** way in which the structure of the villus is adapted for the functions it performs. (2)

London 1995   (*Total 7 marks*)

Box 13.2 Filter feeding

Many organisms which live in the sea or in fresh water feed on the tiny organisms and debris which float in the water. In some areas, such as the upper layers of the sea, this food source can be present in large enough quantities to form the entire diet of many species, including whales. The whale simply swims through the water with its mouth open; the water is allowed to flow out, while the tiny organisms within it are filtered out and swallowed.

Fig. 13.10 shows how a much smaller organism, the mussel *Mytilus edulis*, filter feeds. Mussels are **sedentary** organisms, which means that they remain in one place. They wait for food to come to them, carried on water currents and tides. *Mytilus* lives in shallow water, attached firmly to rocks, often in large colonies.

Mytilus makes use of the natural movement of the water in which it lives, but it also uses cilia to move a steady current of water through its filter system. This system is formed from its gills. The gills thus carry out two functions – gas exchange and also the extraction of food particles from the water.

The gills are made up of many fine **filaments** which provide a large surface area. Cilia on the surfaces of the filaments draw water through between them. Food particles are trapped in mucus on the gill surfaces, and swept by the cilia towards a 'food groove'. This leads to the mouth and the rest of the alimentary canal.

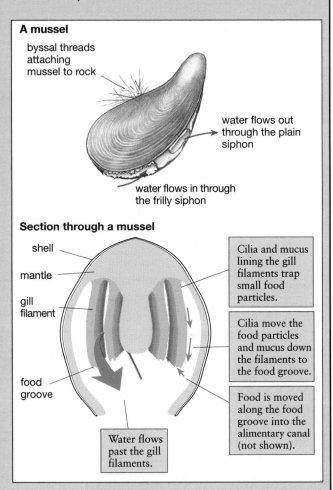

A mussel

byssal threads attaching mussel to rock

water flows out through the plain siphon

water flows in through the frilly siphon

Section through a mussel

shell

mantle

gill filament

food groove

Cilia and mucus lining the gill filaments trap small food particles.

Cilia move the food particles and mucus down the filaments to the food groove.

Food is moved along the food groove into the alimentary canal (not shown).

Water flows past the gill filaments.

Fig. 13.10 Filter feeding in a mollusc.

Box 13.3 Digestion in ruminants

Humans, like most animals, do not produce the enzyme cellulase which catalyses the hydrolysis of cellulose. Cellulose molecules are made up of long chains of β glucose molecules, and the glycosidic bonds between them are difficult to break. This means that we cannot digest and make use of the cellulose which we eat.

Most herbivorous animals, however, have evolved ways of making use of cellulose in their diet. In cattle, for example, a very high proportion of the food they eat is made up plant cell walls which contain large amounts of cellulose. Although cattle cannot make cellulase, an arrangement has evolved in which microorganisms (mostly bacteria) which *do* make this enzyme live in the stomach. Both the cattle and the bacteria benefit from this arrangement (although, as you will see, many individual bacteria are sacrificed in the cause). This kind of mutually beneficial association between organisms of different species is called **mutualism**.

Box 13.3 Digestion in ruminants (cont.)

Fig. 13.11 shows the structure of the stomach of a cow. It has four chambers. The **reticulum** has honeycomb-like walls (you may have seen these in butcher's shops as 'honeycomb tripe'). When food is first swallowed, it passes into the reticulum and a large chamber called the **rumen**.

Inside the rumen and reticulum, a large community of microorganisms lives and feeds on the cellulose which the cow eats. Cattle, like all mammals, are homeothermic (Section 15.6) and the contents of the rumen and reticulum remain at a relatively constant temperature of 39 °C, and pH of 6 to 7. There is no oxygen present, so all the activities of the microorganisms are anaerobic. They first break down cellulose to cellobiose (a two-unit sugar made up of two glucose molecules linked by a β 1-4 glycosidic bond) and glucose. The microorganisms then convert these sugars to fatty acids, producing large amounts of carbon dioxide and methane as by-products. These gases pass up the cow's oesophagus and into the outside world; the total carbon dioxide and methane production of all the world's cattle makes a significant contribution to the greenhouse effect (Section 20.2).

The fatty acids which are produced in the rumen can be absorbed directly through its walls. Ruminants (animals with a rumen) such as cattle often rely on fatty acids as their main respiratory substrate.

At intervals, some of the food in the rumen and reticulum is passed back up the oesophagus into the cow's mouth, where it is rechewed. Cattle spend many quiet hours 'chewing the cud' in this way. The rechewed food is swallowed again, to continue digestion in the rumen and reticulum. There is a constant trickle of partly digested food into the third and then the fourth chambers, the **omasum** and **abomasum**. The abomasum is the equivalent of the stomach in a human and has a very similar structure. The food which enters it contains large

numbers of microorganisms that are mixed up with the regurgitated and reswallowed food; the cow digests these, and obtains most of its amino acids by digesting the proteins in them. Many of the microorganisms in the rumen are able to synthesise their own amino acids using substances such as urea as a nitrogen source, and urea is often added to cattle feeds to allow them to do this. There are also, of course, proteins in the plant food which the cow eats.

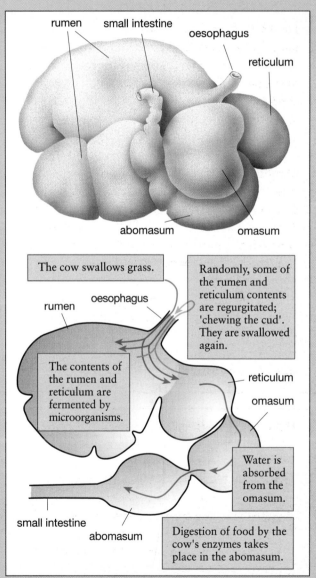

Fig. 13.11 The stomach of a cow.

Box 13.4 *Rhizobium* – an example of mutualism

Plants need supplies of nitrogen, in order to make amino acids and proteins (Section 8.6). Nitrogen gas, N_2, is useless to them, because the two atoms in the molecule are held by a triple bond, making it very stable. Most plants absorb nitrogen in the form of nitrate or ammonium ions from the soil.

However, many species of plants in the family Leguminosae (which includes the Papilionoideae) have evolved very close relationships with bacteria which are able to break the bonds between the atoms in nitrogen molecules and produce ammonium ions. This process is called **nitrogen fixation**, and the bacteria which do it are **nitrogen-fixing bacteria**. There are many different species of nitrogen-fixing bacteria, but we will concentrate on one which has especial economic importance.

Rhizobium is a genus (Section 22.1) of bacteria that contains many different species. They live freely in the soil where they feed saprotrophically. However, if roots of a suitable plant are present in the soil, the bacteria are attracted towards them by chemicals given out by the plant. Particular species of *Rhizobium* become associated with particular plants. For example, *R. leguminosarum* is attracted to roots of the garden pea, *Pisum sativum*.

The presence of the bacteria around the roots of the pea plant stimulates it to grow extra root hairs which branch and curl. The bacteria attach to the surface of the root hairs. Chemical linkages form between proteins called **lectins** that are produced by the pea plant and complex **polysaccharides** on the surface of the bacteria. The linkages will only form between a particular lectin and a particular polysaccharide, so only a particular kind of bacterium will attach to a particular species of plant.

The bacteria penetrate the cell walls of the pea plant's root hairs, probably by secreting enzymes such as cellulase. The cell surface membrane of the pea cell becomes deeply infolded, carrying bacteria deeply into the cell. The membrane buds off to form many small vesicles, each containing bacteria (Fig. 13.12).

The presence of the bacteria stimulates the pea's root cells to divide to form swellings or **nodules**. The bacteria inside the cells of the nodules synthesise the enzyme **nitrogenase**, which catalyses the conversion of nitrogen gas (obtained by diffusion from air spaces in the soil) to ammonia:

$$8H^+ + 8e^- + N_2 + 16ATP \rightarrow 2NH_3 + H_2 + 16ADP + 16\,P_i$$

You can see that this reaction requires very large amounts of energy, hydrogen ions and electrons. These are all supplied by respiration in the bacterial cells, using carbon compounds produced by the pea plant's photosynthesis as respiratory substrates. *Rhizobium* would find it very difficult to supply all this energy itself, which is why it does not fix nitrogen when it is living freely in the soil.

The ammonia produced is converted to amino acids (Section 8.6), and transported to other parts of the plant in the xylem vessels. Thus, for a rather large energy investment, the pea plant gains a good supply of amino acids. This means that the plants grow well on soils where nitrate or ammonium ions are in short supply.

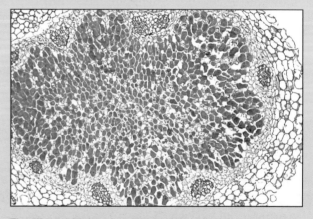

Fig. 13.12   Light micrograph of a section through a root nodule ($\times 90$). The red colour is caused by leghaemoglobin in the cytoplasm of cells containing *Rhizobium*.

As well as providing a place to live for the *Rhizobium*, and a supply of energy to fuel the nitrogen-fixing reaction, the pea plant has one other major investment to make in the partnership. The nitrogenase enzyme can only function in an environment where oxygen concentrations are very low. The cells in the pea's root nodules synthesise large amounts of a pink pigment called **leghaemoglobin**, which is very similar to haemoglobin (Section 10.11) and has a similar function – it absorbs oxygen. Leghaemoglobin releases oxygen only at relatively low oxygen concentrations, providing the bacteria with just enough oxygen to allow them to respire aerobically (which they must do to provide all the ATP, hydrogen ions and electrons needed to fix nitrogen), but not enough to stop nitrogenase from working.

SAPROTROPHIC NUTRITION

13.13 Feeding in *Rhizopus*

Fig. 13.13 shows the structure of the fungus *Rhizopus*. Like all fungi, this organism feeds by secreting enzymes which digest the material on which it lives. The digested nutrients are then absorbed into its body. This method of feeding is called **saprotrophic** feeding. Organisms which feed in this way are called **saprotrophs**, **saprobionts** or **saprophytes;** these words are all used interchangeably.

Rhizopus lives and feeds on living green plants, for example on the leaves and ears (seed heads) of grasses and cultivated grains. It also grows very well in a laboratory on agar jelly containing suitable nutrients. Several different species of *Rhizopus* are used in Indonesia to make the fermented food products called tempe, by allowing the fungus to feed on various foods such as soya beans.

Like all fungi, *Rhizopus* requires organic carbon compounds; it is not able to make these for itself. *Rhizopus* grows well on agar containing material extracted from potato tubers (containing starch and some protein) plus glucose. It also needs various inorganic mineral ions, such as zinc, and a number of vitamins.

Rhizopus secretes enzymes, including carbohydrases and proteases, from its hyphae which catalyse the hydrolysis of proteins, carbohydrates and lipids in a similar way to human enzymes. This produces smaller molecules such as amino acids and glucose, which are absorbed into the hyphae.

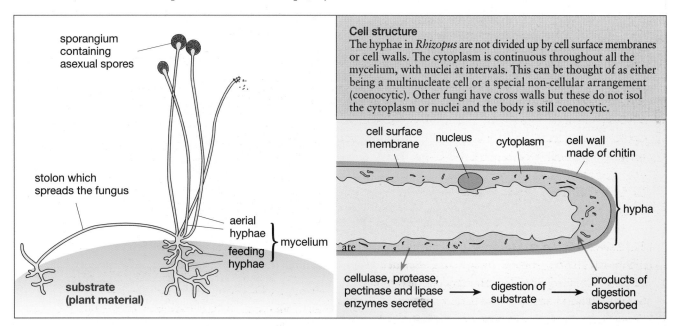

Cell structure

The hyphae in *Rhizopus* are not divided up by cell surface membranes or cell walls. The cytoplasm is continuous throughout all the mycelium, with nuclei at intervals. This can be thought of as either being a multinucleate cell or a special non-cellular arrangement (coenocytic). Other fungi have cross walls but these do not isol the cytoplasm or nuclei and the body is still coenocytic.

Fig. 13.13 Structure and feeding in *Rhizopus*.

Box 13.5 Feeding in other fungi

Many fungi feed on dead plant and animal material, such as dead trees or animal dung. The digestion of this material by saprotrophic fungi is an extremely important process. If it did not happen, the material would simply lie unused and collect in large quantities, with nutrients trapped within it which could otherwise be used by other organisms. Fungi are therefore vital components of food chains and nutrient cycles, such as the carbon and nitrogen cycles (Sections 19.6 and 19.7).

Several types of fungi specialise in feeding on dead wood. Wood is not easy to digest, because it is made up mostly of cellulose and lignin. Cellulose is a polymer of β1-4 glucose; each glucose unit is the same and is joined to the next in just the same way, so it is possible for one type of enzyme – cellulase – to catalyse the hydrolysis of all of the glycosidic bonds within it. Lignin is a different problem altogether because it is a very complex substance, containing three different monomers and at least three different linkages between these monomers.

In addition, these bonds cannot easily be broken by hydrolysis, unlike in polysaccharides for example. There is no 'lignase' enzyme which can digest lignin. Many different enzymes are involved, and the way in which they catalyse the breakdown of lignin is not yet understood. However it is done, it is a slow process and, even in warm humid climates where fungal activity is at its maximum, wood rots only relatively slowly compared with other dead plant material. Despite this, wood-digesting fungi such as **dry rot** cause considerable damage to structural timbers in houses.

Yeast is a fungus which feeds on sugars that are often produced by fruits. Yeast has been used for thousands of years by humans for making bread and alcohol. In bread-making it feeds on sugars produced by the digestion of starch in flour. In making alcoholic drinks, yeast is provided with fruits, such as grapes, which contain sugars; or with partly germinated grains, such as barley, which contain maltose.

Fig. 13.14 Dry rot, *Serpula lacrymans*, is a fungus which can do tremendous damage to timberwork in houses. It is able to grow in, and feed on, timber with a very low moisture content. It sends out hyphae which are able to penetrate not only wood but also masonry. In very damp conditions, it forms cotton-wool like mycelia. Attack by dry rot causes timber to become brittle and break up. Here the fungus has produced wrinkled 'fruiting bodies' (the equivalent of 'toadstools') which release hundreds of thousands of rust-coloured spores.

PARASITIC NUTRITION

13.14   The parasitic lifestyle

Many species of living organisms have evolved lifestyles where they live in close association with another organism of a different species. This type of association is known as **symbiosis**, which simply means 'living together'.

Frequently, both partners in the arrangement gain some benefit from it. If this is the case, then the relationship is known as **mutualism**. The association between the bacterium *Rhizobium* and the plant in whose roots it lives, which is described in Box 13.4, is an example of mutualism. Some hermit crabs carefully place sea anemones on their shells; this too is a mutualistic relationship, as the crab gains protection because of the anemone's stinging tentacles while the anemone picks up remnants of food from the crab's meals.

In other cases, only one of the two species in the symbiotic relationship gains any benefit, while the other is harmed. Such a relationship is known as **parasitism**. A **parasite** is an organism which lives and feeds on another living organism, the **host**. The parasite gains from this relationship, while the host is harmed.

How does a parasite differ from a predator? It is not always easy to draw a clear dividing line, but in general a parasite has a close and relatively long-term relationship with its host, while a predator meets its prey only briefly. Parasites do not normally kill their hosts outright, as it is in their best interests to keep them alive, to provide a steady food supply. Predators kill their prey and eat it. Their next meal will come from elsewhere.

Parasites which live on the surface of their host are called **ectoparasites**. Fleas, ticks and lice are all ectoparasites. **Endoparasites** live inside the host's body. Tapeworms (Section 13.15) and the malarial parasite *Plasmodium* (Box 13.6) are endoparasites.

In some ways, you could consider that a parasite has an easy life, because it has a supply of food on its doorstep. Endoparasites such as tapeworms do not even need to digest their food, as they are surrounded by digested food in the host's alimentary canal, and only have to absorb it. Nor, once in position, do most endoparasites need to move very much. They often, therefore, have greatly reduced digestive or locomotory systems. This is not usually the case with ectoparasites, and the jumping powers of fleas are legendary.

However, life is not really all that easy for most parasites. Their host will do its best to get rid of them, so parasites must have adaptations for gripping firmly in position, and for fending off attempts by the host's immune system to destroy them. These adaptations are generally finely tuned to cope with conditions on a particular species of host, and so most parasites can only survive on one or two different host species.

Another problem for a parasite is to ensure that at least some of its offspring can find their way to a new host. Complex life cycles have evolved in many cases, to increase the chances that this will happen. These cycles often involve a second host, of a completely different species, and some have many different hosts.

13.15   The human tapeworm, *Taenia solium*

Tapeworms belong to the phylum Platyhelminthes, or flatworms (Section 22.14). The human tapeworm is now very rare in most parts of the world (a fact for which you will be grateful when you have read about it), but it provides an excellent example of the problems faced by an endoparasite and how they can be solved.

An adult *T. solium* can be up to 3 m long. It lives in the small intestine of humans.

At the anterior part of the tapeworm is the **scolex** (Fig. 13.15), which is adapted for clinging firmly to the intestine wall. An array of hooks and suckers helps to hold it in position, despite the peristaltic movements which would otherwise move it out of the alimentary canal. Behind the scolex is a long chain of flattened segments called **proglottids**. New proglottids are produced just behind the scolex, and added to the chain as the tapeworm grows.

The proglottids contain nerves and excretory organs, but there is no digestive system and only very weak muscles. Neither digestion nor much movement are necessary. Nutrients are absorbed from the contents of the host's alimentary canal directly through the body wall.

The body wall is covered with a non-living **cuticle**, which protects the living cells beneath from the host's enzymes. Gas exchange takes place through the cuticle, but there is almost no oxygen in the lumen of the small intestine so the tapeworm respires anaerobically.

Tapeworms reproduce sexually. Each proglottid contains reproductive organs. *T. solium* is hermaphrodite, which means that it has both egg-producing and sperm-producing organs in the same individual. However, normally self-fertilisation does not take place. Two different worms mate, exchanging sperm and fertilising each other's eggs. The fertilised eggs are contained within the proglottids.

The oldest proglottids, which are the ones furthest from the scolex, break away from the rest of the worm and are carried out of the host's body with the faeces. If they are to develop any further they must be eaten by a pig, in which they hatch and develop inside the pig's muscle as a **cysticercus** (Fig. 13.15). If undercooked pork infected with tapeworms is eaten by a person, the cysticercus hatches inside the alimentary canal, attaches itself to the wall of the intestine, and grows into an adult tapeworm.

Pork is inspected for any signs of tapeworm infection, which is one of the reasons why *T. solium* has become very rare. Cooking pork thoroughly also helps to prevent infection. However, good sewage treatment systems, which ensure that human faeces cannot come into contact with pig food, are probably the best method of breaking the life cycle of this parasite. ∎

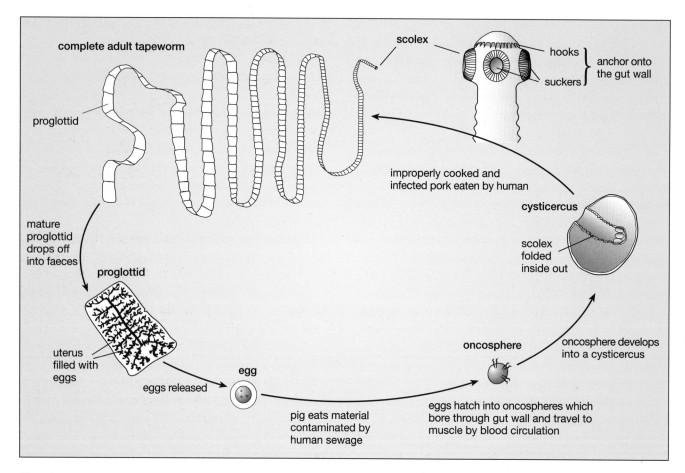

Fig. 13.15 Life cycle of *Taenia solium*, an endoparasite in the human gut.

Q6 The drawings below show three parasitic worms that may be found in the alimentary canal of a frog.

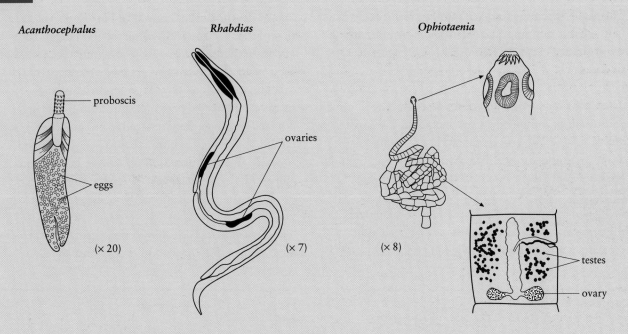

Acanthocephalus   *Rhabdias*   *Ophiotaenia*

proboscis

eggs

(× 20)

ovaries

(× 7)

(× 8)

testes

ovary

(a) (i) What are the main problems that a parasite must overcome in order to live in the gut of a frog?   (3)

   (ii) Briefly describe how **three** features shown in the drawings enable the parasites to overcome these problems.   (3)

(b) (i) What is the main difference in the way in which *Rhabdias* and *Ophiotaenia* obtain their food? Give the evidence from the drawings that supports your answer.   (2)

   (ii) Suggest an explanation for the fact that *Ophiotaenia* is confined to the intestinal region of the host's gut, while *Rhabdias* may be found throughout its length.   (3)

A particular species of parasite may be found in the lens of its fish host. The table shows the percentage of parasites in various parts of the fish's body at different times after infection.

Time after infection	Percentage of parasites in			
	epithelium of pharynx	connective tissue and muscle	blood	lens
15 minutes	84.2	0	0	0
1 hour	19.5	59.0	3.1	0
5 hours	12.8	20.7	2.8	5.1
19 hours	3.4	3.4	3.4	72.6
139 hours	0	0	0	92.7

(c) Giving evidence for your answer, describe the route taken by most of the parasites once they have penetrated the body.   (3)

AEB 1997 (specimen)   (*Total 14 marks*)

Box 13.6 *Plasmodium* – a parasitic protoctist

Plasmodium is a single-celled organism which causes great suffering, and often death, in millions of people each year. It is the organism which causes **malaria**.

There are four species of *Plasmodium* which can cause malaria, although only two of these, *P. vivax* and *P. falciparum*, are common. They cause illness as they reproduce inside red blood cells, eventually bursting out of them and releasing chemicals which cause fever. They then reinfect more red blood cells, breed and burst out again. The symptoms of malaria therefore include repeated bouts of fever, each time the parasites burst from the red blood cells.

Fig. 13.16 shows the life cycle of *Plasmodium*. Like that of the tapeworm *Taenia*, it involves two hosts and several different stages. The second host is a female mosquito of the genus *Anopheles* which takes up gametocytes of *Plasmodium* when she feeds on an infected person. (Male mosquitoes do not feed on blood; females need to because they require the protein in blood to make eggs.) Many stages of reproduction of *Plasmodium*, both sexual and asexual, take place inside the mosquito, producing millions of sporozoites. These may be injected into a person when the mosquito feeds, as her saliva contains an anti-clotting agent, and she injects saliva into the wound to allow her to feed more easily.

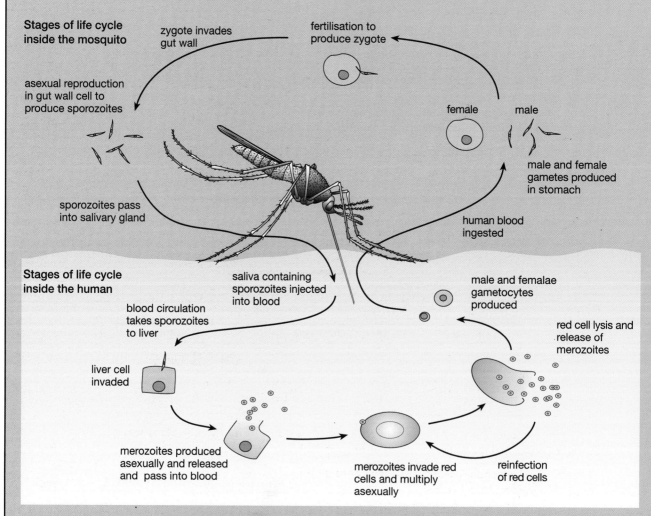

Stages of life cycle inside the mosquito

zygote invades gut wall

fertilisation to produce zygote

asexual reproduction in gut wall cell to produce sporozoites

female   male

male and female gametes produced in stomach

sporozoites pass into salivary gland

human blood ingested

Stages of life cycle inside the human

saliva containing sporozoites injected into blood

male and femalae gametocytes produced

blood circulation takes sporozoites to liver

red cell lysis and release of merozoites

liver cell invaded

merozoites produced asexually and released and pass into blood

merozoites invade red cells and multiply asexually

reinfection of red cells

Fig. 13.16 Life cycle of the malarial parasite, *Plasmodium*.

Box 13.6 *Plasmodium* – a parasitic protoctist (cont.)

Inside the human, the sporozoites travel in the blood to the liver, where they invade liver cells and multiply yet again. Millions of merozoites are released from the liver cells into the blood about eight days after infection, where they invade red cells.

This complex life cycle, involving many different stages adapted for different things (living in liver cells, living in red blood cells, living in mosquitoes, reproducing sexually, and reproducing asexually) is typical of many parasites. The complexity of the cycle has evolved to increase the chance that the offspring of a *Plasmodium* have a good chance of arriving in another host. It would not be easy,

without some intermediary such as a mosquito, to get from a blood cell in one human to a blood cell in another. (However, this is obviously not impossible; you have only to think of HIV.) The many reproductive stages produce very large numbers of offspring, making it more likely that at least some of them will end up in a suitable host. The many different forms which occur in the life cycle are each adapted to living in a particular host cell; they need to be well adapted, to be able to combat whatever mechanisms the host has of dealing with invaders.

The relationship between the global distribution of malaria and the inherited disease sickle cell anaemia is described in Section 7.10.

Q7 (a) Copy the table and complete it to show **two** general differences between parasites and predators. (2)

Parasite	Predator

The diagram shows the life cycle of *Schistosoma mansoni*, an important platyhelminth parasite which has two larval stages, miracidia and cercariae.

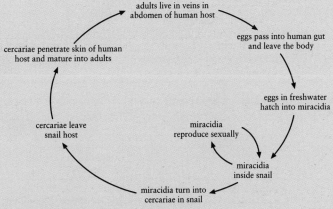

(a) Explain the possible advantage to the parasite of:
   (i) having two larval stages (2)
   (ii) the miracidia reproducing asexually. (2)

   AEB 1995 (modified) (*Total 6 marks*)

Q8 Curve **A** on the graph below represents the change in pH which occurred when a mixture of olive oil and water was incubated with the enzyme lipase. Curve **B** shows the results obtained when the experiment was repeated with the addition of bile salts, an emulsifying agent.

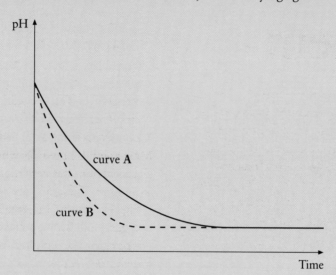

(a) Explain the change in pH shown by curve **A**. (2)

(b) Explain why the addition of bile salts:
(i) produces a faster fall in curve **B** over the first part of the experiment; (2)
(ii) does not alter the final pH. (1)

AEB 1994 (*Total 5 marks*)

Q9 (a) Outline the roles in the body of
(i) vitamin A; (2)
(ii) vitamin D. (2)

(b) Copy and complete the table below by naming a deficiency disease associated with vitamins A and D, and stating **one** symptom of each disease. (4)

Vitamin	Deficiency disease	Symptom
A		
D		

During pregnancy, women are advised to increase their dietary intake of calcium and iron.

(c) Explain why it is important to increase the dietary intake of calcium and iron during pregnancy. (2)

UCLES 1995 (*Total 10 marks*)

14 The mammalian nervous system

Information can be transferred from one part of a mammal to another as signals along neurones. This information travels along a neurone as an electrical signal known as an action potential, and passes between neurones as a chemical signal. Signals may originate at receptors, which are cells specialised to respond to changes in their environment by generating action potentials in sensory neurones.

14.1 Information transfer in living organisms

All living organisms must be able to respond to their environment. *Amoeba* finds food by sensing chemical gradients in the water, and moving towards the source of the chemical. You avoid harm to your eye by blinking or moving your head away if you see an object flying towards you. The shoot of a plant grows towards the direction from which most light comes, enabling it to make use of this light in photosynthesis.

Each of these responses involves three stages. Firstly, the information about the environment is **sensed** and converted into a form which the body can use. Secondly, the information is **transmitted** from the part of the organism which sensed it to the part which will respond to it. Lastly, a **response** is carried out or effected.

In multicellular organisms, specialised cells and organs are usually involved in these stages. An object flying towards your eye is sensed by light-sensitive cells in the retina of your eye. These are called **receptors**. The information is transmitted from these cells as electrical impulses along **neurones** (nerve cells) to the brain, and then to muscle cells in your eyelid which contract and close your eye. These muscle cells are **effectors**.

In this chapter, we will concentrate on how information is received and transmitted by the nervous system in mammals. Another method of transmitting information within an organism's body, using chemicals rather than electrical impulses, is described in Chapter 15, which also looks at a few responses in plants. The mechanism by which muscle cells contract is described in Chapter 16.

THE STRUCTURE OF THE MAMMALIAN NERVOUS SYSTEM

14.2 Neurones and nerves

Most animals have cells which are specialised to transmit electrical impulses very rapidly from one part of the body to another. These cells are called **nerve cells** or **neurones**.

Fig. 14.1 shows the structure of three types of neurone in a mammal. The top illustration is of a **motor neurone**, which transmits impulses from the brain or spinal cord to an effector such as muscle. It has a very long **axon** which carries impulses away from the neurone's **cell body**, and many short **dendrites** which carry impulses towards the cell body. **Sensory neurones** and **interneurones** (sometimes called intermediate neurones or relay neurones) have the same basic structure as a motor neurone, but a sensory neurone has a long axon on each side of the cell body and an interneurone may have many short axons. Axons are always very thin, but may be more than 1 m long in some parts of the body.

The axon of the motor neurone in Fig. 14.1 has a **myelin sheath**, which is formed from many layers of membrane produced as a **Schwann cell** wrapped itself round and round the axon. In humans many, but not all, neurones are myelinated. Myelin helps to increase the rate at which an electrical impulse is transmitted along an axon, and this is described in Section 14.9.

The axons of sensory and motor neurones run through the body in bundles, forming **nerves**. A nerve may contain several hundred axons, from both sensory and motor neurones. These are arranged in bundles surrounded by a **perineurium**. Blood vessels lie between and within the bundles (Fig. 14.2), and the whole structure is surrounded by a tough outer covering called the **epineurium**.

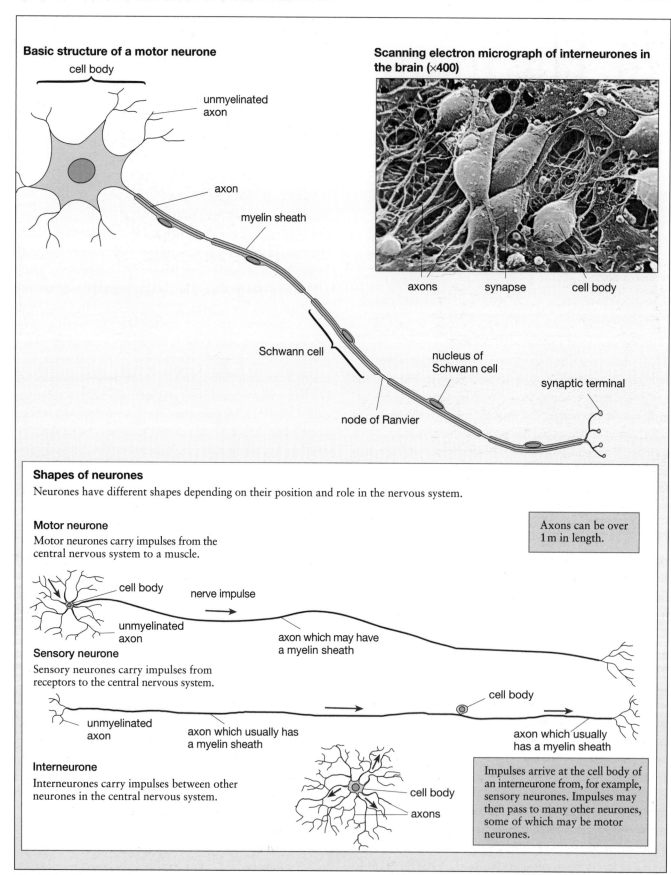

Basic structure of a motor neurone

cell body

unmyelinated axon

axon

myelin sheath

Schwann cell

node of Ranvier

nucleus of Schwann cell

synaptic terminal

Scanning electron micrograph of interneurones in the brain (×400)

axons   synapse   cell body

Shapes of neurones

Neurones have different shapes depending on their position and role in the nervous system.

Motor neurone

Motor neurones carry impulses from the central nervous system to a muscle.

cell body

nerve impulse

unmyelinated axon

axon which may have a myelin sheath

| Axons can be over 1 m in length. |

Sensory neurone

Sensory neurones carry impulses from receptors to the central nervous system.

unmyelinated axon

axon which usually has a myelin sheath

cell body

axon which usually has a myelin sheath

Interneurone

Interneurones carry impulses between other neurones in the central nervous system.

cell body

axons

Impulses arrive at the cell body of an interneurone from, for example, sensory neurones. Impulses may then pass to many other neurones, some of which may be motor neurones.

Fig. 14.1   Structure of neurones.

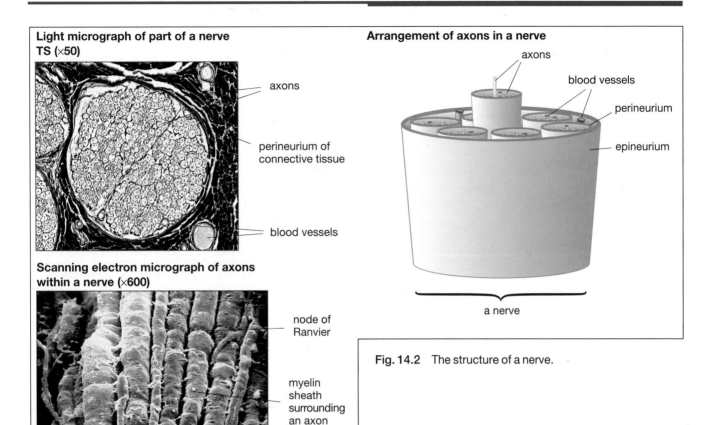

Light micrograph of part of a nerve TS (×50)

— axons

— perineurium of connective tissue

— blood vessels

Scanning electron micrograph of axons within a nerve (×600)

— node of Ranvier

— myelin sheath surrounding an axon

— blood capillary

Arrangement of axons in a nerve

axons

blood vessels

perineurium

epineurium

a nerve

Fig. 14.2 The structure of a nerve.

14.3 The central and peripheral nervous systems

The **central nervous system** or **CNS** is made up of the **brain** and the **spinal cord**. Nerves run between the CNS and the rest of the body, and these make up the **peripheral nervous system**.

Fig. 14.3 shows the structure of the brain and the spinal cord. Both are protected by bone, and by three membranes called **meninges** (Box 14.1). These membranes help to secrete **cerebrospinal fluid**, which fills the spaces between the brain and spinal cord and the bone which surrounds them, and also spaces inside them. The blood capillaries supplying the brain lie in the meninges and do not penetrate the brain tissue itself. The walls of these capillaries have no gaps in them and so are much less permeable than those of other capillaries, forming a **blood–brain barrier**. This prevents pathogens and most large molecules from entering the brain from the blood. Only glucose, respiratory gases and a few other essential substances can pass through. The blood–brain barrier protects the brain from harmful pathogens and chemicals which may be present in other parts of the body.

Sections through the brain or the spinal cord show differences in colour in their outer and inner regions. In the brain, the outer layers are grey, while the inner layers are white; this pattern is reversed in the spinal cord. The white areas are produced by myelin around axons, while the grey areas indicate the presence of non-myelinated nerve cell bodies and interneurones.

Nerves from the brain are called **cranial nerves**; nerves from the spinal cord are **spinal nerves**. In humans, there are twelve pairs of cranial nerves. Some of these are very short, for example the optic nerves which carry impulses to and from the eyes. Others are much longer, for example the vagus ('wandering') nerve which carries impulses to and from many parts of the body, including the heart, lungs and organs in the abdomen.

A pair of spinal nerves leaves the spinal cord between each pair of vertebrae. Each spinal nerve is attached to the spinal cord by two 'roots'. The upper or **dorsal** root carries axons and cell bodies of sensory neurones, while the lower or **ventral** root carries axons of motor neurones.

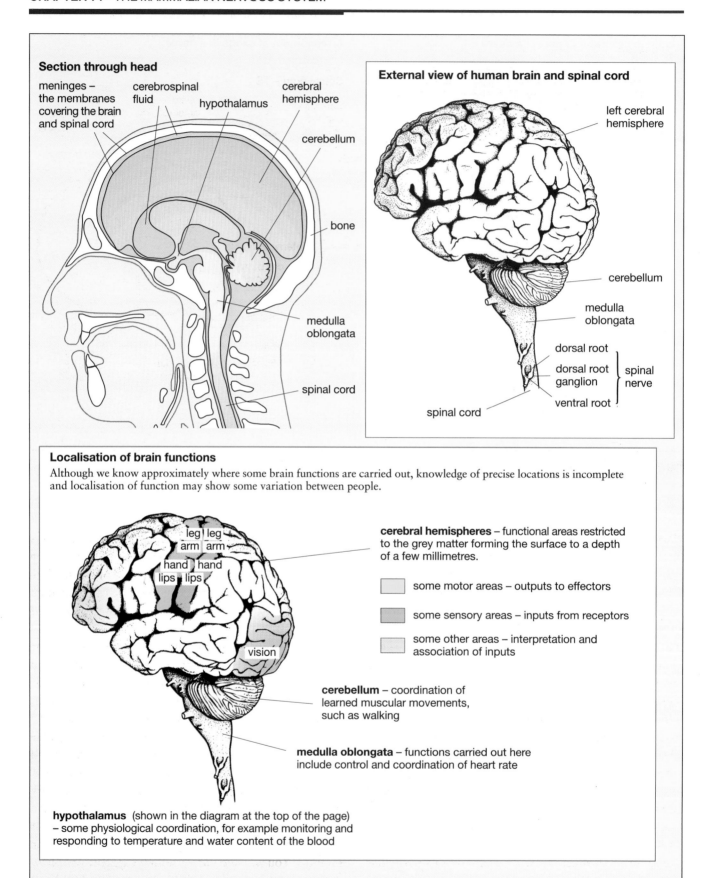

Section through head

meninges – the membranes covering the brain and spinal cord

cerebrospinal fluid

hypothalamus

cerebral hemisphere

cerebellum

bone

medulla oblongata

spinal cord

External view of human brain and spinal cord

left cerebral hemisphere

cerebellum

medulla oblongata

dorsal root

dorsal root ganglion

ventral root

} spinal nerve

spinal cord

Localisation of brain functions

Although we know approximately where some brain functions are carried out, knowledge of precise locations is incomplete and localisation of function may show some variation between people.

leg leg
arm arm
hand hand
lips lips

vision

cerebral hemispheres – functional areas restricted to the grey matter forming the surface to a depth of a few millimetres.

some motor areas – outputs to effectors

some sensory areas – inputs from receptors

some other areas – interpretation and association of inputs

cerebellum – coordination of learned muscular movements, such as walking

medulla oblongata – functions carried out here include control and coordination of heart rate

hypothalamus (shown in the diagram at the top of the page) – some physiological coordination, for example monitoring and responding to temperature and water content of the blood

Fig. 14.3   Structure of the central nervous system.

Reflex arc

If the hand touches a hot object, pain receptors in the skin are stimulated. Impulses pass down sensory neurones to the nearest part of the spinal cord. Impulses are sent to the biceps muscle along motor neurones and the muscle contracts, pulling the hand away from the hot object.

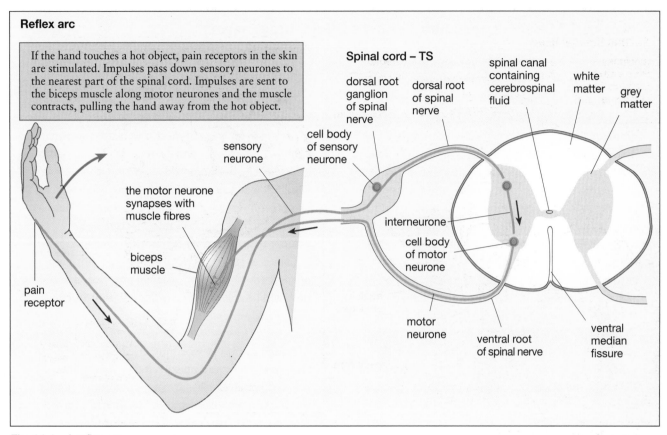

Fig. 14.4   A reflex arc.

14.4   The reflex arc

Fig. 14.4 shows a simple pathway along which information is transferred from a receptor to an effector. This pathway is called a **reflex arc**. The information is picked up by a receptor, and carried along a sensory neurone as an electrical impulse to the spinal cord. Here, it may be passed to an interneurone and then to a motor neurone. In some reflex arcs there is no interneurone involved, and the impulse passes directly from sensory to motor neurone.

The cell body of a sensory neurone is always in a swelling, or **ganglion**, in the dorsal root of a spinal nerve. The interneurone lies entirely within the spinal cord. The motor neurone's cell body is in the spinal cord, and its long axon passes out through the ventral root of a spinal nerve.

A reflex arc is a very simple pathway that transmits information in a very straightforward and rapid way from a receptor to an effector. This is useful when a particular stimulus always needs a particular response which should happen as quickly as possible. A good example is the sight of an object flying rapidly towards your eye, when it is obviously a great advantage if your eye closes as quickly as possible without you having to think about it. This kind of action is called a **reflex action**. You can read more about reflex actions and other more complex types of behaviour in Section 14.15.

There is no direct contact between the different neurones in a reflex arc. Each neurone is separated from the next by a tiny gap called a **synaptic cleft**. This cleft, and the regions of the two neurones on either side of it, make up a structure called a **synapse**. Interneurones have many synapses with other neurones, so an impulse arriving along a sensory neurone and then passing to an interneurone can proceed along many different pathways. Impulses will be passed up to the brain, as well as along the motor neurone to an effector. Moreover, impulses can be passed down *from* the brain to the interneurone, to modify the response which the effector makes to the stimulus. You will find out more about synapses and how they can modify actions in this way in Section 14.10 and Box 14.3.

Box 14.1 Meninges, meningitis and the blood–brain barrier

The brain and spinal cord are surrounded by three membranes called **meninges**. The outermost of these membranes, the **dura mater**, lies closely against the skull or the vertebrae which protect the brain and spinal cord from mechanical damage. The inner membrane, the **pia mater**, follows the folded surface of the brain very closely, dipping deeply into it in places. In between these two is the **arachnoid** ('spidery') **layer**, so called because it contains spidery webs of connective tissue. Both the pia mater and the arachnoid layer contain many small blood vessels which supply the brain and spinal cord with oxygen and nutrients. A fluid, called **cerebrospinal fluid,** is secreted by the pia mater and arachnoid layer and fills the space between them. Cerebrospinal fluid also fills large spaces in the brain, called **ventricles**, and a central canal in the spinal cord. The cerebrospinal fluid helps to cushion the brain and spinal cord, helping to support them and buffering them from knocks and blows.

Meningitis is an illness in which the meninges of the brain become infected and inflamed. Meningitis can be caused either by bacteria or viruses. The type of meningitis caused by bacteria is the most dangerous, and can kill within a day of the first symptoms being noticed.

In bacterial meningitis, bacteria somehow cross the normally impermeable blood–brain barrier, enter the cerebrospinal fluid and breed rapidly. The meninges become inflamed, and the sufferer experiences fever, a stiff neck and headache, often culminating in coma and death as the brain itself is affected. The bacteria produce toxins which make capillary walls more permeable than usual, which can cause a serious loss of blood pressure as fluid leaks from the capillaries into the tissues. Very prompt treatment with antibiotics is essential if the patient is to survive. Very large doses of antibiotics are needed, because only a small proportion of the dose will be able to cross the blood–brain barrier and reach the bacteria.

Meningitis is a very worrying disease because it can strike so rapidly and unexpectedly. Some of the bacteria which cause it are very common, but only rarely cause any problems. In Britain it is a rare disease, but small groups of two or three cases sometimes occur in a school or town. In developing countries, meningitis epidemics may flare up, where thousands of people suffer from the disease within a few weeks. No-one yet knows exactly why a bacterium which is always present in a population can suddenly cause fatal outbreaks of disease.

14.5 The autonomic nervous system

Motor neurones which carry impulses from the brain or spinal cord to skeletal muscles (muscles attached to your bones) are sometimes known as **somatic motor neurones**. Motor neurones which supply other parts of the body, such as the heart, glands and the wall of the alimentary canal are called **autonomic motor neurones**, and they make up the **autonomic nervous system.**

The autonomic nervous system can be divided into two sets of motor neurones which work in a different way from each other and have different effects on the organs they supply. These are the **sympathetic** nervous system and the **parasympathetic** nervous system. (They have different effects because they use different neurotransmitters, which are described in Box 14.4.) All the sympathetic neurones originate in the spinal cord, while many parasympathetic neurones originate in the brain. The vagus nerve, for example, contains parasympathetic neurones, as well as sensory neurones taking impulses back from the body organ to the brain. Table 14.1 lists some of the effects of impulses from the two divisions of the autonomic nervous system.

Organ	Effect of stimulation by sympathetic neurone	Effect of stimulation by parasympathetic neurone
heart muscle	increases heart rate and force of contraction	decreases heart rate
muscles in bronchioles	relax	contract
smooth muscle in walls of blood vessels	most contract (to constrict blood vessels)	most relax (to dilate blood vessels)
erector muscles (for hairs) in skin	contract (to raise hairs)	no effect
ciliary muscle in eye	relax (for distant vision)	contract (for near vision)
salivary glands	secrete amylase	no effect
tear glands	no effect	secrete tears

Table 14.1 Examples of the effects of the autonomic nervous system

HOW INFORMATION IS TRANSMITTED ALONG NEURONES

14.6 Resting potentials and depolarisation

Information is carried along a neurone as an electrical impulse. It is not, however, an electric current – that is, a flow of electrons along the neurone. The signal is a fleeting change in the electric potential difference across the cell surface membrane of the neurone which sweeps along the neurone from one end to the other.

When a neurone is not transmitting a signal it is said to be **resting**. However, a 'resting' neurone is really very active. As in all body cells, the cell surface membranes of axons contain a **sodium–potassium pump** (Fig. 3.32), which uses energy from ATP to move sodium ions (Na^+) out of the cell and potassium ions (K^+) in. Three sodium ions are pumped out for every two potassium ions pumped in, resulting in a slightly higher positive charge outside than inside.

Potassium ions are able to diffuse freely back out of the cell, down their concentration gradient. But the permeability of the cell surface membrane to sodium ions is much less, so they can diffuse back in only very slowly. This results in the tissue fluid outside the cell containing more positive ions than the cytoplasm inside it. There is

therefore a negative electrical charge inside compared with outside. In a resting neurone, this difference in charge, or **potential difference**, is about –70 mV (millivolts) inside compared with outside. This is the neurone's **resting potential** (Fig. 14.5).

If something happens to reduce this difference in charge across the membrane, then the neurone is said to be **depolarised**. Depolarisation can be caused by a stimulus from the environment, which is received by a receptor. Receptor cells are able to use the energy from a stimulus, such as sound, to depolarise a sensory neurone. Section 14.11 explains how the stimulus of pressure can do this. If the depolarisation is quite large, say to –40 mV or more, then an **action potential** is created.

14.7 Action potentials

The cell surface membrane of a neurone contains proteins which act as specific channels for sodium and potassium ions. These channels are sensitive to potential difference, or voltage, and so they are known as **voltage-gated channels**. When the neurone is resting, with a potential difference of –70 mV inside, these channels are closed. However, when the membrane is depolarised and the charge difference between the inside and outside becomes

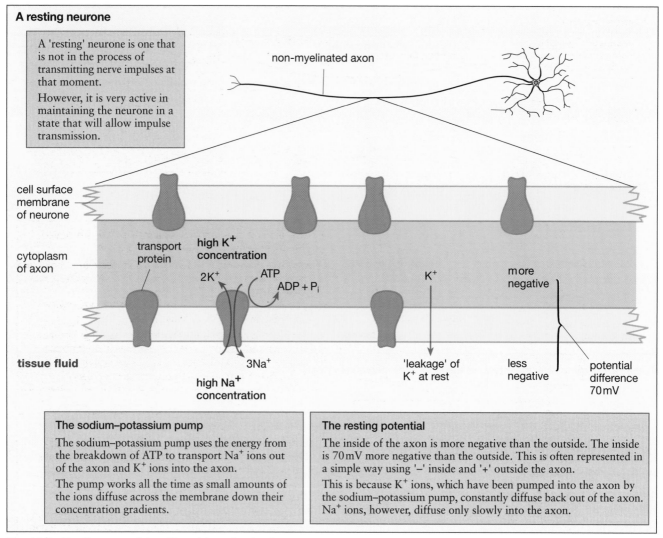

A resting neurone

A 'resting' neurone is one that is not in the process of transmitting nerve impulses at that moment.

However, it is very active in maintaining the neurone in a state that will allow impulse transmission.

non-myelinated axon

cell surface membrane of neurone

cytoplasm of axon

transport protein

high K⁺ concentration

2K⁺

ATP

ADP + Pᵢ

3Na⁺

high Na⁺ concentration

tissue fluid

K⁺

'leakage' of K⁺ at rest

more negative

less negative

potential difference 70 mV

The sodium–potassium pump

The sodium–potassium pump uses the energy from the breakdown of ATP to transport Na⁺ ions out of the axon and K⁺ ions into the axon.

The pump works all the time as small amounts of the ions diffuse across the membrane down their concentration gradients.

The resting potential

The inside of the axon is more negative than the outside. The inside is 70 mV more negative than the outside. This is often represented in a simple way using '–' inside and '+' outside the axon.

This is because K⁺ ions, which have been pumped into the axon by the sodium–potassium pump, constantly diffuse back out of the axon. Na⁺ ions, however, diffuse only slowly into the axon.

Fig. 14.5 Resting potential and how it is maintained.

less than −40 mV, the sodium ion channels suddenly open.

The activities of the sodium–potassium pump in the resting neurone have built up a concentration gradient for sodium ions, with a higher concentration outside the cell surface membrane than inside. In addition, the relative permeability of the cell surface membrane to sodium and potassium ions produces a negative charge inside compared with outside. This creates both a concentration gradient and an electrical gradient for the sodium ions, from the outside to the inside of the membrane. When the membrane is depolarised, the sodium ions can get through their open channels, down this **electrochemical gradient**, and into the cytoplasm of the neurone. Their positive charge depolarises the membrane even more, so that even more sodium ion channels open. So many sodium ions move in so quickly that, within less than a millisecond, the

potential difference across the membrane changes from −40 mV inside to +40 mV.

At this point the sodium ion channels begin to close. The combination of fewer open channels, and the smaller electrochemical gradient for sodium ions, means that sodium ions stop moving in. Now the voltage-gated potassium ion channels open, and potassium ions flow rapidly *out*, down their electrochemical gradient. As the potassium ions take positive charge out of the neurone, the potential difference across the membrane swings back again to a value of about −75 mV inside – slightly overshooting the resting value. The voltage-gated potassium ion channels now close and the resting potential is restored once more.

This whole process lasts about 4 ms. It is called an **action potential**. Fig. 14.6 shows the changes in the

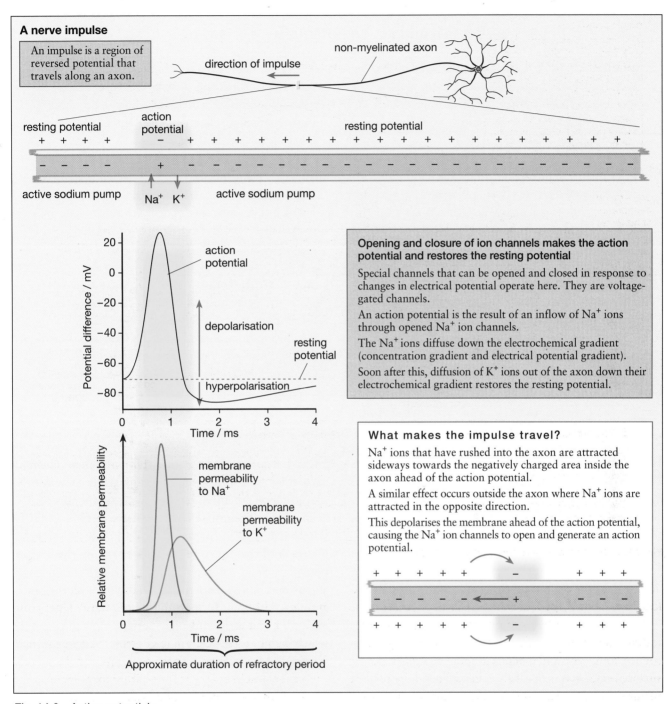

A nerve impulse

An impulse is a region of reversed potential that travels along an axon.

non-myelinated axon

direction of impulse

resting potential

action potential

resting potential

active sodium pump

Na⁺ K⁺

active sodium pump

Opening and closure of ion channels makes the action potential and restores the resting potential

Special channels that can be opened and closed in response to changes in electrical potential operate here. They are voltage-gated channels.

An action potential is the result of an inflow of Na^+ ions through opened Na^+ ion channels.

The Na^+ ions diffuse down the electrochemical gradient (concentration gradient and electrical potential gradient).

Soon after this, diffusion of K^+ ions out of the axon down their electrochemical gradient restores the resting potential.

What makes the impulse travel?

Na^+ ions that have rushed into the axon are attracted sideways towards the negatively charged area inside the axon ahead of the action potential.

A similar effect occurs outside the axon where Na^+ ions are attracted in the opposite direction.

This depolarises the membrane ahead of the action potential, causing the Na^+ ion channels to open and generate an action potential.

Approximate duration of refractory period

Fig. 14.6 Action potentials.

potential difference across the membrane, and also the changes in the membrane's permeability to sodium and potassium ions during an action potential.

When an action potential has just taken place at a particular point in a neurone, that point is unable to fire a second action potential. This is because its sodium ion channels are closed and cannot immediately reopen. The membrane must wait until at least a good proportion of these channels are capable of reopening, before it can respond to another depolarisation by producing an action potential. The time while the membrane is unable to fire another action potential is called the **refractory period**.

Box 14.2 Snakes, puffer fish and action potentials

Some of the most deadly venoms produced by animals are nerve poisons. Some of these work by blocking the sodium or potassium channels in cell surface membranes, thus preventing action potentials being produced.

Puffer fish belonging to the family Tetraodontidae are considered a great delicacy in Japan. However, their skin and several organs contain a toxin (poison) called **tetrodotoxin**, which blocks sodium channels and prevents them from opening. If a person swallows this toxin, their neurones become unable to transmit action potentials, and they die. Chefs who prepare puffer fish for the dish called *fugu* are highly trained to ensure that they remove every trace of the organs containing the toxin and do not serve their customers a lethal meal.

The black mamba snake, which lives in Africa, has one of the most deadly venoms of any snake. The venom contains a toxin called **dendrotoxin** which blocks potassium channels. Once again, this stops the transmission of nerve impulses.

There are many other organisms which have evolved venoms which block sodium or potassium channels. For example, some species of South American frogs secrete such venoms from their skin, and humans have long used these as arrow poisons. Scorpion venom contains potassium-channel blockers, amongst several other toxins. And some kinds of plankton secrete sodium-channel blocking toxins into the water which may be concentrated by filter-feeding molluscs (Box 13.3) such as mussels. When population explosions of these plankton occur, eating mussels which have fed on them can be fatal.

14.8 How action potentials transfer information

The action potential described in Section 14.7 was happening at one point in the cell surface membrane of a neurone. Once an action potential is generated, it sweeps along the cell surface membrane. Fig. 14.6 shows how this happens. When sodium ions have rushed in to a depolarised region of the neurone they are attracted sideways, as the regions on either side of the depolarised area have a more negative charge. This depolarises these regions, and so the action potential travels along the neurone.

The action potential remains exactly the same size as it travels along the neurone. Moreover, all action potentials in a particular neurone are always the same size. When a resting neurone is depolarised, the depolarisation is either enough to produce a full-sized action potential or not big enough to produce any action potential at all. You cannot have big or small action potentials – you either have a 'standard' one, or none at all.

So, if all action potentials are the same size, how do they transfer different kinds of information?

Information about the *strength* of the stimulus which started off the action potentials is contained in the *frequency* of the action potentials in the neurone (Fig. 14.7). Lots of action potentials following closely behind each other indicate a strong stimulus, while a few widely spaced action potentials represent a weak stimulus.

The brain recognises the *type* of stimulus – that is whether it is light, pressure, sound or so on – by the *position* of the neurone which is carrying the action potentials. So, if action potentials arrive in the brain along a neurone coming from the retina of your eye, the brain assumes that the information is about light. This is not always so, of course; you might suffer a blow to your eye, which stimulates the cells in your retina. You might then see stars, even though there are no stars to see!

14.9 Speed of conduction

The speed at which the axon of a neurone can transmit action potentials depends on a number of factors. The most important of these are the diameter of the axon and whether or not it has a myelin sheath around it.

Fig. 14.8 shows how these two factors affect conduction velocity. You can see that large diameter axons transmit action potentials faster than small diameter ones, and that myelinated axons transmit action potentials faster than non-myelinated ones. Non-vertebrate animals, such as squid, do not have myelin. Instead, they have evolved very

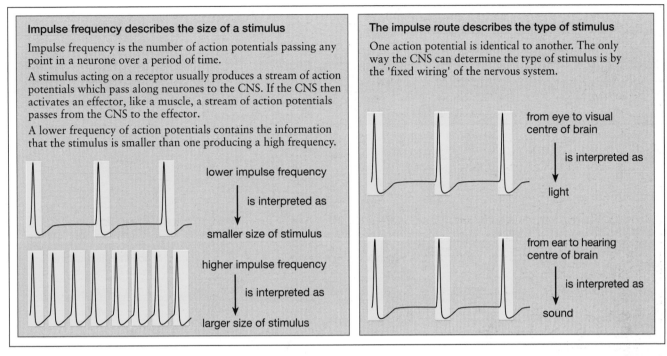

Impulse frequency describes the size of a stimulus

Impulse frequency is the number of action potentials passing any point in a neurone over a period of time.

A stimulus acting on a receptor usually produces a stream of action potentials which pass along neurones to the CNS. If the CNS then activates an effector, like a muscle, a stream of action potentials passes from the CNS to the effector.

A lower frequency of action potentials contains the information that the stimulus is smaller than one producing a high frequency.

lower impulse frequency

↓

is interpreted as

smaller size of stimulus

higher impulse frequency

↓

is interpreted as

larger size of stimulus

The impulse route describes the type of stimulus

One action potential is identical to another. The only way the CNS can determine the type of stimulus is by the 'fixed wiring' of the nervous system.

from eye to visual centre of brain

↓

is interpreted as

light

from ear to hearing centre of brain

↓

is interpreted as

sound

Fig. 14.7 How action potentials transfer information.

large axons to enable rapid transfer of action potentials from one part of their body to another. But they still do not achieve the very fast speeds, up to 100 m s⁻¹, that can be achieved in a myelinated axon. The maximum conduction velocity in a squid giant axon, with a diameter of 500 μm, is only about 20 m s⁻¹.

Myelin has this effect because it effectively insulates the axon, preventing changes in potential difference across the axon's cell surface membrane. Moreover, there are usually very few sodium channels in the myelinated parts of the axon. In a myelinated axon, unmyelinated gaps called **nodes of Ranvier** occur roughly every 1 to 2 mm, and it is only here that there are significant numbers of sodium channels. The changes in potential difference which produce action potentials can therefore take place only at these nodes. An action potential occurring at one node of Ranvier sets up a local circuit which depolarises the membrane at the next node of Ranvier, but has no effect on the membrane in between. The action potential therefore effectively 'jumps' from one node to the next. This is sometimes known as **saltatory** or 'jumping' conduction (Fig. 14.9).

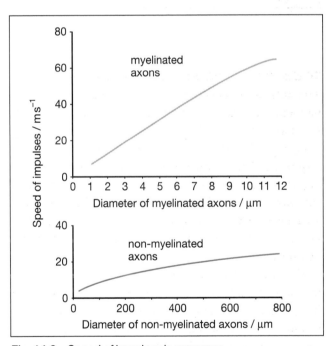

Fig. 14.8 Speed of impulses in neurones.

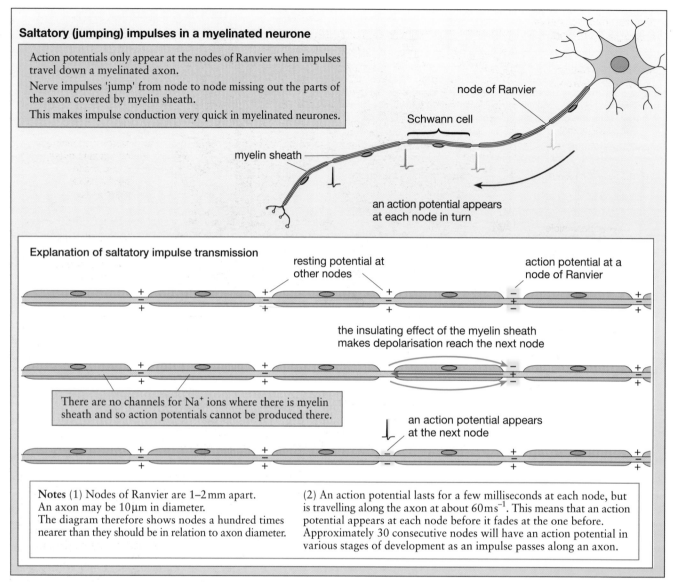

Saltatory (jumping) impulses in a myelinated neurone

Action potentials only appear at the nodes of Ranvier when impulses travel down a myelinated axon.

Nerve impulses 'jump' from node to node missing out the parts of the axon covered by myelin sheath.

This makes impulse conduction very quick in myelinated neurones.

node of Ranvier

Schwann cell

myelin sheath

an action potential appears at each node in turn

Explanation of saltatory impulse transmission

resting potential at other nodes

action potential at a node of Ranvier

the insulating effect of the myelin sheath makes depolarisation reach the next node

There are no channels for Na⁺ ions where there is myelin sheath and so action potentials cannot be produced there.

an action potential appears at the next node

Notes (1) Nodes of Ranvier are 1–2 mm apart. An axon may be 10 μm in diameter. The diagram therefore shows nodes a hundred times nearer than they should be in relation to axon diameter.

(2) An action potential lasts for a few milliseconds at each node, but is travelling along the axon at about $60\,\text{ms}^{-1}$. This means that an action potential appears at each node before it fades at the one before. Approximately 30 consecutive nodes will have an action potential in various stages of development as an impulse passes along an axon.

Fig. 14.9 Saltatory conduction in a myelinated neurone.

14.10 Transmission of information across a synapse

A tiny gap, called a **synaptic cleft**, separates one neurone from the next. Action potentials are not able to cross this gap. The information crosses as a chemical signal.

Fig. 14.10 shows the structure of a **synapse**, a meeting point between two neurones. The first, or **presynaptic**, neurone contains many tiny vesicles full of a chemical known as a **neurotransmitter**. In this example, the chemical is **acetylcholine**.

When an action potential sweeps down the cell surface membrane of the presynaptic neurone, the change in potential difference opens **calcium ion channels** in the membrane. Calcium ions rush in to the neurone through

these channels, and this causes some of the vesicles of acetylcholine to fuse with the presynaptic membrane. Each time a vesicle does this, a very small amount of acetylcholine is released into the synaptic cleft.

The acetylcholine molecules diffuse across the cleft and lock into **acetylcholine receptors** in the postsynaptic membrane. These receptors are proteins which also act as sodium channels, and the arrival of acetycholine causes them to open. As the postsynaptic neurone had been maintaining a resting potential, there was an electrochemical gradient for sodium ions. They now rush into the postsynaptic neurone. This depolarises the neurone and sets off an action potential in that neurone.

The acetylcholine molecules in the cleft are rapidly

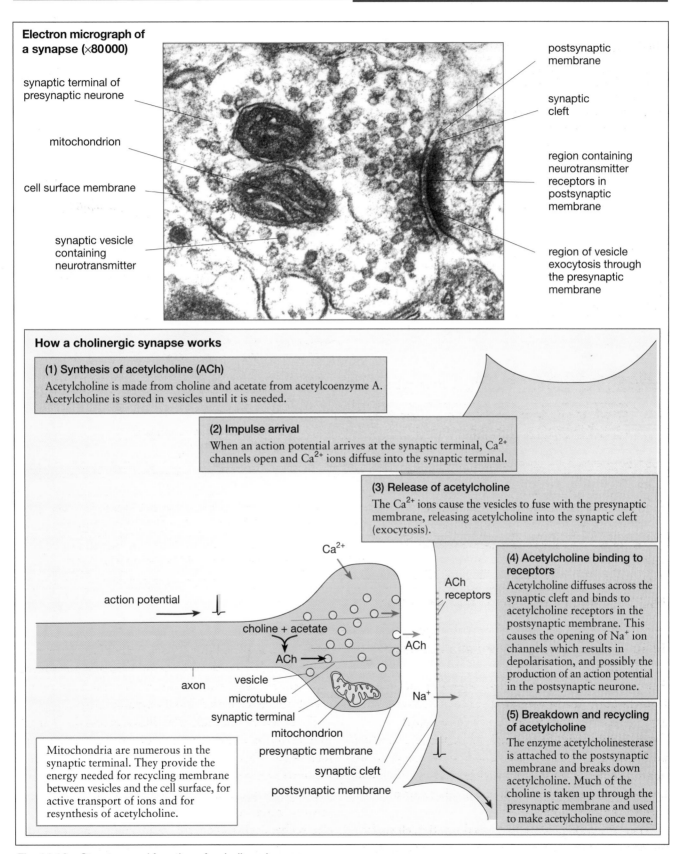

Electron micrograph of a synapse (×80 000)

synaptic terminal of presynaptic neurone

mitochondrion

cell surface membrane

synaptic vesicle containing neurotransmitter

postsynaptic membrane

synaptic cleft

region containing neurotransmitter receptors in postsynaptic membrane

region of vesicle exocytosis through the presynaptic membrane

How a cholinergic synapse works

(1) Synthesis of acetylcholine (ACh)

Acetylcholine is made from choline and acetate from acetylcoenzyme A. Acetylcholine is stored in vesicles until it is needed.

(2) Impulse arrival

When an action potential arrives at the synaptic terminal, Ca^{2+} channels open and Ca^{2+} ions diffuse into the synaptic terminal.

(3) Release of acetylcholine

The Ca^{2+} ions cause the vesicles to fuse with the presynaptic membrane, releasing acetylcholine into the synaptic cleft (exocytosis).

(4) Acetylcholine binding to receptors

Acetylcholine diffuses across the synaptic cleft and binds to acetylcholine receptors in the postsynaptic membrane. This causes the opening of Na^+ ion channels which results in depolarisation, and possibly the production of an action potential in the postsynaptic neurone.

(5) Breakdown and recycling of acetylcholine

The enzyme acetylcholinesterase is attached to the postsynaptic membrane and breaks down acetylcholine. Much of the choline is taken up through the presynaptic membrane and used to make acetylcholine once more.

Ca^{2+}

ACh receptors

action potential

choline + acetate

ACh

ACh

axon

vesicle

microtubule

synaptic terminal

mitochondrion

presynaptic membrane

synaptic cleft

postsynaptic membrane

Na^+

Mitochondria are numerous in the synaptic terminal. They provide the energy needed for recycling membrane between vesicles and the cell surface, for active transport of ions and for resynthesis of acetylcholine.

Fig. 14.10   Structure and function of a cholinergic synapse.

broken down by an enzyme called **acetylcholinesterase**. This prevents the acetylcholine from continuing to bind with the receptors, so the sodium channels remain open only very briefly. If this did not happen, then the acetylcholine molecules would keep binding with the receptors and action potentials would continuously be produced in the postsynaptic neurone. Many organophosphorous compounds produce this effect, by inhibiting acetylcholinesterase. They are used as insecticides (for example malathion) and nerve gases (such as sarin).

The events described above also take place when a nerve impulse is passed from a motor neurone to a muscle. The synapse between the motor neurone and the muscle is known as a **motor end plate**, and the postsynaptic membrane is the cell surface membrane of the muscle cell. You can read about what happens when acetylcholine arrives at this membrane in Section 16.12.

Acetylcholine is only one of many neurotransmitters used in the human body. Box 14.4 describes some more of these, and also outlines some of the problems which can occur if too much or too little of them are synthesised, or if other substances interfere with their normal effects.

Q1 The figure below shows part of a sensory neurone and a motor neurone in a simple reflex arc. The potential differences across the axon membranes at the nodes of Ranvier are shown.

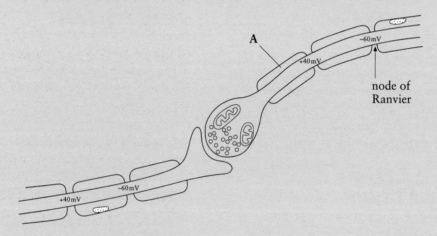

(a) Copy the diagram and label each of the following. In each case, explain how you made your decision.
  (i) Where you would find receptors for a transmitter substance (2)
  (ii) The axon of the motor neurone (2)
  (iii) Where an action potential is occurring (2)

(b) State the name of, or write the chemical symbol for, an ion which
  (i) diffuses into the presynaptic neurone when an action potential arrives, and causes the vesicles to fuse with the presynaptic membrane; (1)
  (ii) is in a higher concentration outside a resting neurone than inside it, and floods into the neurone when an action potential is generated. (1)

(c) (i) Name part **A**. (1)
  (ii) What is part **A** made of? (2)
  (iii) What effects does part **A** have on the transmission of action potentials along the neurone? (2)

(d) In certain diseases, the motor neurones are progressively damaged.

  Suggest **two** ways in which a person with such a disease may be affected. (2)

UCLES 1996   (*Total 15 marks*)

Box 14.3 Integration at synapses

Section 14.10 describes a straightforward transmission of an impulse across a synapse. A single action potential arriving along the presynaptic neurone produces a single action potential in a postsynaptic neurone. If this was all that synapses could do, there would be little advantage in having them. The impulse could be transmitted much more quickly from one neurone to the next if the two neurones were directly joined.

In fact, synapses provide a capability for complex behaviour and responses to stimuli which would not be possible without them. A particular *input* to a synapse (in the form of action potentials in a presynaptic neurone) can have many different *outputs* (in the form of action potentials in a postsynaptic neurone or muscle cell), depending on the type of synapse involved and what other inputs are arriving at the same time. Synapses are rather like components in an electronic circuit, integrating different inputs to provide the required output.

The transmission of an impulse across a synapse described in Section 14.10 is the simplest situation, and is known as a **one-to-one synapse**. But most neurones have many synapses with others; neurones in the brain, for example, may have thousands of synapses with other neurones. What happens at one of these synapses is affected by what is happening at all the others as well.

Consider a motor neurone in the spinal cord, which will probably have over 100 synapses with axons from other neurones. At some of these synapses, the neurotransmitter will act as previously described, causing depolarisation of the motor neurone's membrane. These are **excitatory** synapses. At other synapses, the neurotransmitter released from the presynaptic neurone does not cause depolarisation of the postsynaptic membrane of the motor neurone but does exactly the opposite – it makes it more negative inside, or **hyperpolarises** it. These are called **inhibitory** synapses. When action potentials are arriving at many of these synapses, the balance between the activity of the excitatory and inhibitory synapses will determine whether or not the motor neurone's membrane is depolarised enough to set off an action potential. In effect, the motor neurone's membrane is **integrating** all of the different inputs.

This integration of inputs can happen in either space or time. For example, if two separate action potentials arrive at two excitatory synapses on the same neurone at the same time, two lots of neurotransmitter will be released, which will cause twice as much depolarisation as if only one action potential had arrived. If one action potential arrives at an excitatory synapse at the same time as another arrives at an inhibitory synapse on the same neurone, the two will cancel each other out. This is **spatial summation**.

If two action potentials arrive at an excitatory synapse in very rapid succession, then the depolarisation caused by the second one may overlap the first one in time. This will make the depolarisation greater than if only one had arrived. This is **temporal summation**.

You can imagine, for example, a motor neurone with an axon running to a muscle in your hand, with many synapses at its cell body in the spinal cord. Impulses are originating in a sensory cell in a finger, stimulated by contact with a very hot plate. These would arrive at the motor neurone via excitatory synapses. At the same time, signals which originated in your eyes which have been processed by your brain and recognised as 'my favourite meal', plus other signals originating in your brain meaning 'I am very hungry' might be arriving via inhibitory synapses. Whether or not an action potential will be set up in the motor neurone, causing the muscle to contract and the plate to be dropped, will depend on the balance between these excitatory and inhibitory signals.

Box 14.4 Neurotransmitters, toxins and disease

Synapses using acetylcholine are known as **cholinergic synapses**. They occur in many parts of the nervous system, including the brain. In some people, a group of cells in the brain which normally produce acetylcholine degenerate as they get older, resulting in a shortage of acetylcholine in these brain cells. This produces the symptoms of Alzheimer's disease, which include the progressive deterioration of memory. No-one yet knows just why these cells degenerate in some people and not others, and at different ages. Current treatments for Alzheimer's disease focus on inhibiting acetylcholinesterase, to try to maintain levels of acetylcholine as high as possible for as long as possible.

Several toxins act by affecting events at cholinergic synapses. The drug nicotine is one of these. Nicotine binds with the receptors on the postsynaptic membrane at one type of cholinergic synapse, fixing the sodium channels in the open position. While small doses of nicotine act as a stimulant, in large doses it is a lethal poison, and has long been used as an insecticide. The fly agaric toadstool, *Amanita muscaria*, contains a substance called muscarine, which has a similar effect at other cholinergic synapses; its effects are extremely unpleasant and can be fatal. Curare (a South American arrow poison) and atropine (from deadly nightshade) have the opposite effect at synapses, binding to the receptors and keeping the sodium channels closed.

The black widow spider produces a venom containing a substance which causes a burst of acetylcholine to be released at synapses, and prevents the vesicles in the presynaptic neurone being refilled. A victim therefore first suffers muscular spasms, followed by paralysis. However, despite the bad reputation of these spiders, a bite rarely causes death. The bacterium *Clostridium botulinum*, which sometimes breeds in anaerobic conditions in food, produces a toxin called botulin. This is the most lethal natural toxin known, and it acts by inhibiting acetylcholine release.

Noradrenaline, **adrenaline** and **dopamine** belong to a group of neurotransmitters called **catecholamines**. Noradrenaline is the transmitter used at the junctions between sympathetic neurones and smooth muscle. Dopamine is mostly used in the brain, and there is a great deal of interest in it because it appears to be implicated in several diseases, including schizophrenia and Parkinson's disease. In schizophrenia, it is thought that receptors in the brain may become over-sensitive to dopamine, or too much dopamine may be produced; no-one is yet sure how or why this might happen. Drugs used to treat schizophrenia work by blocking dopamine receptors. In Parkinson's disease, however, neurones which should produce dopamine are lost, so not enough dopamine is made. The symptoms of the disease are muscular rigidity and weakness, and these can be relieved by giving the patient drugs which mimic the action of dopamine.

The amino acid **glutamate** also acts as a neurotransmitter, and is probably the most widely used excitatory transmitter within the brain. Gamma aminobutyric acid, or **GABA**, is an inhibitory transmitter, and is the most common transmitter in the brain. GABA is important in the regulation of many behavioural control pathways in the brain. In the hereditary disease Huntington's chorea there is not enough GABA in some parts of the brain, and this results in uncontrolled movements. GABA works by opening chloride channels in the postsynaptic membrane, allowing chloride ions to flood in and hyperpolarising the postsynaptic neurone. The effects of ethanol (alcohol) on the brain may be partly due to the fact that ethanol appears to open the GABA receptor chloride channels. Barbiturates also act on GABA receptors, and this may be one reason why alcohol and sleeping pills taken together can have very serious effects on the brain and may kill. However, we still have much to learn about exactly how these and other drugs affect the brain.

Q2 Reflexes are found in all animals that have a nervous system.

(a) What is a reflex? *(1)*

(b) Copy and complete the diagram below by adding and labelling the structures and pathway involved in a spinal reflex. *(4)*

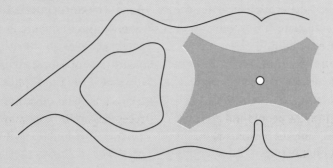

(c) Suggest why you may feel pain when you touch a hot object even if you move your hand away quickly. *(1)*

AEB 1993 *(Total 6 marks)*

Q3 Read through the following passage about the mammalian nervous system, then copy it, filling in the dotted lines with the most appropriate word or words to complete the account.

The nervous system contains several types of neurones. Of these,

.... neurones carry impulses to muscles and glands while

.... neurones carry impulses from receptor cells to the central

nervous system. The interior of a nerve fibre has a lower concentration of

.... ions than its surroundings, as a result of the action of a

.... in its membrane. This imbalance of ions creates a

.... potential in the fibre, which is reversed during the passage of

an impulse. When this happens, ... ions flood into the fibre, after

which there is a compensating outward movement of .... ions.

London 1996 *(Total 7 marks)*

Q4 (a) Describe the structure of a motor neurone. *(10)*

(b) Explain how a nerve impulse is generated in and transmitted along the axon of a neurone. *(13)*

UCLES 1995 *(Total 23 marks)*

RECEPTORS

14.11 How receptors produce action potentials

A receptor is an organ which is able to respond to its environment by generating action potentials if the environment changes. Receptors cells in humans are specialised to respond to many different aspects of the environment, such as light, sound, temperature, chemicals (in taste and smell) and pressure.

Fig. 14.11 shows the structure of a pressure or vibration receptor in human skin, called a Pacinian corpuscle. It contains a nerve ending of a sensory neurone. The cell body of this neurone is a long way from the receptor, inside a ganglion of the dorsal root of a spinal nerve. The neurone has a long axon running between the cell body and the nerve ending in the Pacinian corpuscle.

The end of the neurone maintains a normal resting potential of about –70 mV inside. When pressure is applied to the Pacinian corpuscle, sodium ion channels are opened in the cell surface membrane near the end of the neurone. Sodium ions flood into the neurone and the cell membrane is depolarised. The change in potential difference across the membrane is called the **receptor potential**. If the depolarisation is not very great, then nothing else happens. However, if it reaches a **threshold value** then an action potential is triggered and sweeps along the axon and into the spinal cord.

The size of the receptor potential depends on the strength of the stimulus. A gentle touch might not produce a high enough receptor potential to trigger an action potential. A very strong pressure would produce a much higher receptor potential, which would trigger many action potentials following each other in rapid succession.

14.12 How rod cells produce action potentials

A Pacinian corpuscle is a very simple receptor. The vertebrate eye, on the other hand, is a highly complex structure containing many receptor cells. The receptor cells, called **rods** and **cones**, are situated in the **retina**. The rest of the eye is concerned with bringing light to a focus on these cells, or with protection. Fig. 14.12 shows the structures and functions of these parts of the eye.

Fig. 14.13 shows the structure of a rod cell and its position in relation to other cells in the retina. A rod cell is about 40 µm long and about 1 µm in diameter. In the **outer segment**, there is a stack of flattened vesicles. These membranes are packed with molecules of **rhodopsin**. A single rod cell probably contains about 30 million molecules of rhodopsin. Rhodopsin is a pigment that appears pinkish-purple when white light is shone on to it. It is sometimes called 'visual purple'.

When light falls on a rhodopsin molecule, it causes it to change shape. This affects the permeability of the cell surface membrane of the rod cell, which in turn affects the secretion of a transmitter substance from the rod cell. These changes produce an action potential in a **ganglion cell** (Fig. 14.13) which is transmitted along the ganglion cell's axon in the optic nerve to the brain. (This process is described more fully in Box 14.5.)

Rod cells are extremely sensitive. Even a single photon of light can cause enough hyperpolarisation to produce an action potential in a ganglion cell. We rely on rod cells to see in dim light. The old saying that eating plenty of carrots will help you to see in the dark is based on the fact that the orange pigment carotene is converted in the body to retinene (vitamin A) which is used in the body to make rhodopsin. People who are short of vitamin A in their diet may suffer from night blindness. This is no longer a problem in Britain, but does occur still in some developing countries.

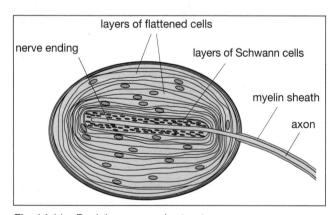

Fig. 14.11 Pacinian corpuscle structure.

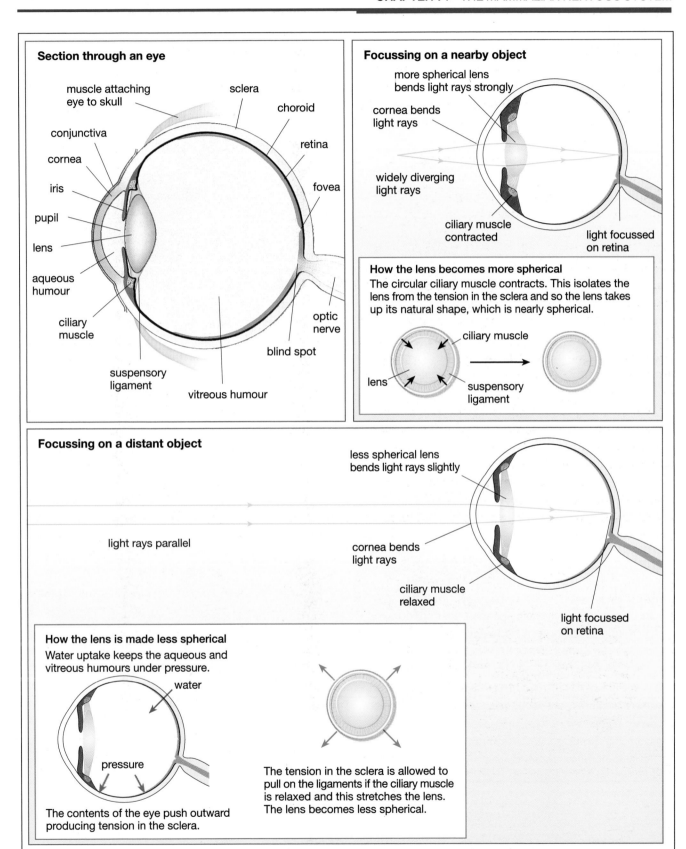

Section through an eye

muscle attaching eye to skull

sclera

choroid

conjunctiva

retina

cornea

iris

fovea

pupil

lens

aqueous humour

optic nerve

blind spot

ciliary muscle

suspensory ligament

vitreous humour

Focussing on a nearby object

more spherical lens bends light rays strongly

cornea bends light rays

widely diverging light rays

ciliary muscle contracted

light focussed on retina

How the lens becomes more spherical

The circular ciliary muscle contracts. This isolates the lens from the tension in the sclera and so the lens takes up its natural shape, which is nearly spherical.

ciliary muscle

lens

suspensory ligament

Focussing on a distant object

less spherical lens bends light rays slightly

light rays parallel

cornea bends light rays

ciliary muscle relaxed

light focussed on retina

How the lens is made less spherical

Water uptake keeps the aqueous and vitreous humours under pressure.

water

pressure

The contents of the eye push outward producing tension in the sclera.

The tension in the sclera is allowed to pull on the ligaments if the ciliary muscle is relaxed and this stretches the lens. The lens becomes less spherical.

Fig. 14.12 The eye.

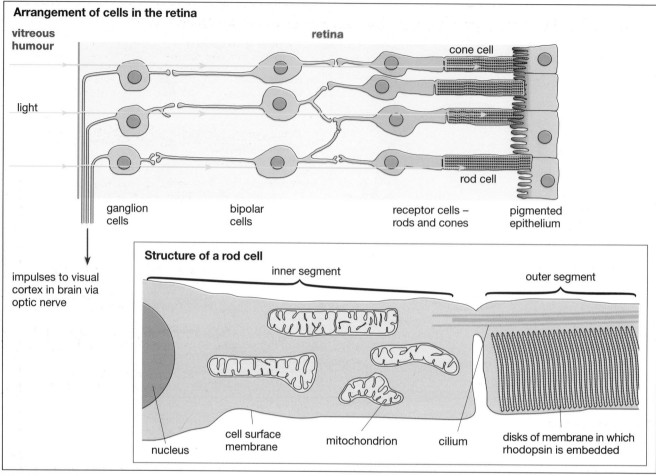

Arrangement of cells in the retina

vitreous humour

retina

cone cell

light

rod cell

impulses to visual cortex in brain via optic nerve

ganglion cells

bipolar cells

receptor cells – rods and cones

pigmented epithelium

Structure of a rod cell

inner segment

outer segment

nucleus

cell surface membrane

mitochondrion

cilium

disks of membrane in which rhodopsin is embedded

Fig. 14.13   The structure of the retina.

Box 14.5 How light produces action potentials in ganglion cells

Rod cells contain a visual pigment called rhodopsin. A rhodopsin molecule is formed from a molecule of the protein **opsin** and a molecule of **11-*cis*-retinal**.

Rod cells, like neurones, maintain a resting potential across their cell surface membranes. In the inner segment (Fig. 14.13), just as in a resting neurone, the cell surface membrane is permeable to potassium ions and they constantly flow out of the cell down their electrochemical gradient. However, the rod cell's membrane in the outer segment is highly permeable to sodium ions. Sodium ions therefore constantly flow into the cell in this region. This constant flow of charge into and out of the cell in different regions generates a circulating electric current (Fig. 14.14). 'Resting' rod cells are really extremely active!

Box 14.5 How light produces action potentials in ganglion cells (cont.)

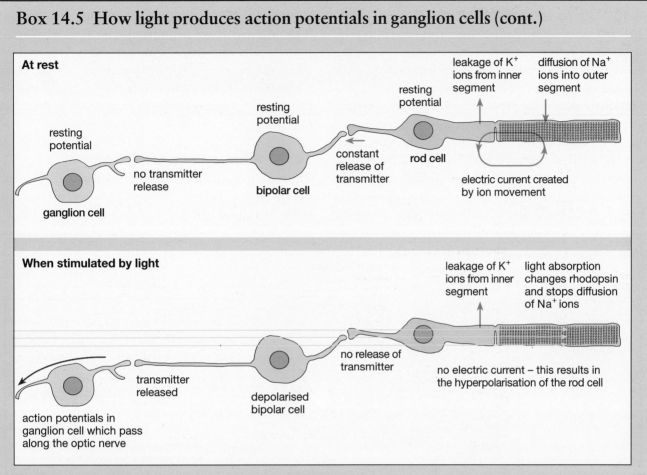

Fig. 14.14   How light generates an action potential in a ganglion cell.

Another feature of rod cells makes them very different from neurones. When 'resting', they secrete a steady stream of the neurotransmitter **glutamate**. This diffuses across the synaptic cleft between the rod cell and a **bipolar cell**. This transmitter has exactly the opposite effect to acetylcholine – it *prevents* the bipolar cell from becoming depolarised.

When light falls onto a rod cell, the rhodopsin absorbs light and changes shape; the 11-*cis*-retinal changes to all-*trans*-retinal. This interacts with other proteins in the rod cell's membrane, which causes the sodium channels to close suddenly. The circulating current therefore stops, and the cell becomes even more negative inside than usual. It is **hyperpolarised**.

The hyperpolarisation of the rod cell membrane causes it to stop releasing the neurotransmitter. The bipolar neurone now becomes depolarised, and this causes the generation of an action potential in a **ganglion cell** (Fig. 14.13). The ganglion cell has an axon running right along the **optic nerve** and into the brain.

Once a rhodopsin molecule has absorbed a photon of light and changed shape, it can no longer absorb light. In bright light, most of your rhodopsin molecules will undergo this shape change within seconds. After some minutes, they will break down into opsin and retinal. If you walk from a well-lit street into a dark cinema, it usually takes several minutes before you can see at all clearly. During this time, the opsin and retinal molecules in your rod cells are recombining to form rhodopsin. The process is called **dark adaptation**.

14.13 Cones and colour vision

Cone cells have a very similar structure to rod cells (Fig. 14.15). Cone cells are most densely packed in a part of the retina called the **fovea**. This is where light rays are focussed when you are looking directly at an object.

Humans have three types of cone cells, each with a different kind of opsin in their pigments. These opsins absorb different wavelengths of light, in the blue, green and red areas of the spectrum. No-one is quite sure exactly how colour vision works, but certainly the relative degree of stimulation of the three types of cones is important. If, for example, only your 'blue' cones are

stimulated, then you see the colour blue, while if both 'blue' and 'red' cones are stimulated then you see purple.

Cone cells need more light than rod cells in order to generate action potentials in the axons in the optic nerve. Cones therefore work only in bright light. This is why you cannot see colours in dim light, when only rod cells can function.

14.14 Rods, cones and resolution

The resolution of an image is the degree of detail which can be seen in it (Fig. 3.5). If you think of an image as being made up of lots of tiny dots, the degree of detail will

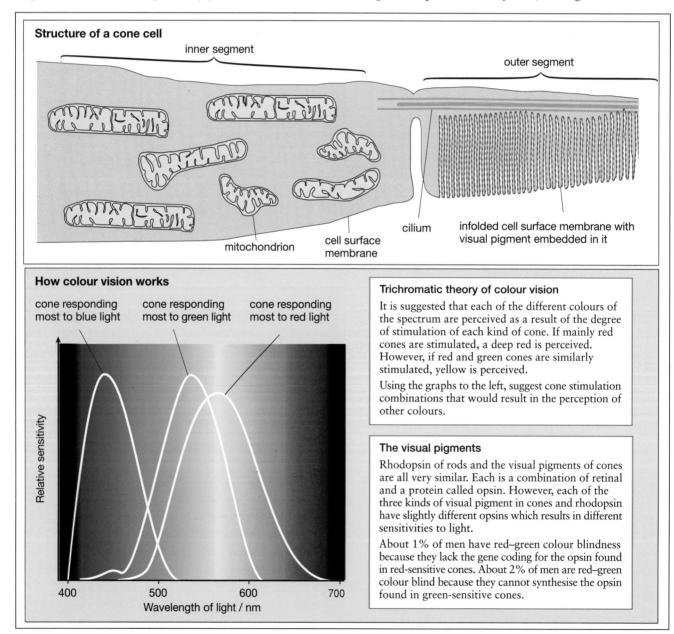

Fig. 14.15 Cone cells and colour vision.

depend on the size of the dots and how closely packed they are. The smaller the dots, and the closer they are packed, the better the resolution.

Cone cells are designed to provide the brain with enough information to visualise a very high resolution image. Cone cells are very small and are densely packed in the fovea, so light coming from parts of an object which are very close together will be picked up by different cone cells. Each cone cell in the fovea synapses with just one bipolar cell (Fig. 14.13), so the information from each individual cone cell is kept separate as it travels to the brain.

Rod cells do not provide such high resolution; you have probably noticed that you cannot see such good detail in dim light as in bright light. Although rod cells, like cone cells, are small and tightly packed, many of them converge on one bipolar cell (Fig. 14.13). The information from several rod cells is therefore pooled and the brain only knows that light fell in a general area of the retina, not that it fell on a particular rod cell. The image which can be built up in the brain is therefore less sharp than that which can be formed when cones are being stimulated.

Q5 The diagram below shows a rod cell from the retina of a mammal.

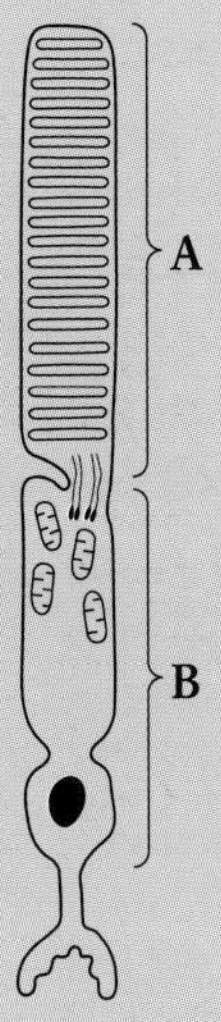

(a) Name the regions labelled **A** and **B**. (2)

(b) State the location of most of the rod cells in the human retina. (1)

(c) (i) Give the name of the light-sensitive pigment contained in the rod cells. (1)
   (ii) Copy the diagram and add the label **P** to show the region of the rod cell in which this pigment is located. (1)

London 1996 *(Total 5 marks)*

HOW ANIMALS RESPOND TO STIMULI

Humans have extremely complex behaviour. We can respond to the same stimulus in many different ways, and this is also true of many other animals. But in this section we will concentrate on some very simple examples of behaviour in humans and in some non-vertebrate animals.

14.15 Reflex actions

A reflex action is a fast automatic response to a stimulus. No conscious thought is required to bring about the response, and the same stimulus always produces the same response. For example, the presence of food in your mouth always produces a response by your salivary glands and gastric glands (Section 13.12), both of which secrete juices which will help to digest the food.

You may have had your **knee-jerk** reflex tested. If you sit with one leg crossed over the other and someone gives you a sharp tap on your knee, muscles contract and lift your lower leg upwards. The tap stimulates **stretch receptors**, each of which sends an action potential along a sensory neurone to your spinal cord and then to a motor neurone which carries an action potential to the muscles. This pathway is a **reflex arc** (Fig. 14.4).

The knee-jerk reflex is one of several innate reflexes which humans have. An **innate** reflex is one which you are born with. The 'wiring' for the reflex is already in position and you do not have to learn how to respond to the stimulus. Babies have several innate reflexes, such as turning the head towards a gentle touch on the side of the cheek, or curling the fingers when the palm of the hand is stimulated.

Other reflexes are learned as we experience new situations. They are **learned** or **conditioned** reflexes. For example, when walking, your muscles automatically respond to signals coming in from your eyes, touch receptors in your feet and stretch receptors in your leg muscles, to keep your legs moving forward one at a time and to stop you from falling over. You do not (usually!) have to think about these responses, which happen quickly and automatically. But you did have to learn them, just as you have to learn the reflexes required to ride a bicycle or to play a musical instrument.

There is probably no clear dividing line between innate and conditioned reflexes. While some reflexes are obviously learned, it is less certain whether reflexes which seem to be innate really are always pre-programmed into the brain, requiring no learning experiences. For example, a newborn baby withdraws its legs if it is given a small pin-prick on the sole of the foot and this is classed as an innate reflex. But the response to this stimulus is affected by the position of the baby's legs during the later stages of pregnancy and during birth. It seems that some apparently innate reflexes may be at least partly learned during the baby's time in the uterus.

We know only very little about what takes place in the nervous system as something new is learned. One thing which is certain is that synapses are involved. During learning, changes take place in the activities, and even the structure, of synapses between one neurone and another.

Reflex actions are extremely valuable to animals. As the conscious, decision-making parts of the brain are not involved, the pathways along which the action potentials travel are as short as possible, so that the response happens very quickly. In situations where the most useful response to a stimulus is always the same, a reflex action is ideal.

14.16 Kineses and taxes

Kineses and taxes (singular kinesis and taxis) are two simple behavioural patterns in which an organism's direction or rate of movement is affected by a stimulus. In a **kinesis**, the stimulus produces a change in either the rate of movement or the rate of turning. In a **taxis**, the organism senses the direction from which the stimulus is coming and moves either towards or away from it (Fig. 14.16).

Woodlice, for example, tend to move more slowly in a damp environment than in a dry one. If you put a woodlouse into a chamber in which one half has a damp atmosphere and the other half a dry atmosphere, it will probably eventually come to rest in the damp half. This is not because it moved purposefully towards this area; it simply moved more when it was in the dry part and less in the wet part. This is an example of a **kinesis**. In this case, it has the effect of ensuring that the woodlouse rests in areas in which it is least likely to dry out.

A **taxis** achieves a similar effect in a more direct way. Maggots (fly larvae) have light-sensitive receptors on each side of their head. When a maggot moves forward, it turns its head from side to side and positions its body until the light shining on each receptor is equal and as little as possible. This means that it is facing and moving directly away from the light.

Many non-vertebrate animals have very simple patterns of behaviour like those described here. Their actions are largely determined by reflexes; you can be fairly sure that

Kinesis – a response involving changed level of activity

Woodlice tend to spend more time in humid areas, if they have previously been in an area that is too dry.

The woodlouse moves more slowly in more humid conditions and randomly turns more frequently in more humid conditions. The combined effects of this mean the woodlouse will spend most time in the humid area. This response is a hygrokinesis.

Taxis – a directional locomotory response

Fly maggots move directly away from a light source. This response is a phototaxis. As it is away from the light, it is a negative phototaxis.

Maggots have two light receptors at the anterior end. As the maggots move they wave their heads from side to side. If the light reaching the two receptors is not equal in strength, the maggot turns. If the light is equal in strength at the two receptors, the maggot keeps moving straight on.

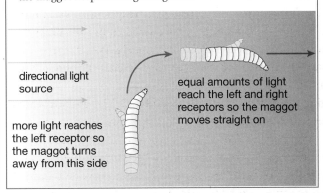

moves quickly turns less

dry area

humid area

moves slowly turns more

directional light source

more light reaches the left receptor so the maggot turns away from this side

equal amounts of light reach the left and right receptors so the maggot moves straight on

Fig. 14.16   Kinesis and taxis.

they will always respond in a particular way to a particular stimulus. However, these two examples describe what happens in very simple laboratory situations. In its natural environment, an organism will have many stimuli reaching it at once, and its behaviour will be more complex. ■

Q6   The earthworm, *Lumbricus terrestris* is a nocturnal annelid. It feeds at night on dead leaves on the soil surface and spends the day underground in a burrow.

(a) In the laboratory, *L. terrestris* can be shown to move directly from the dark towards light of low intensity.
   (i) What sort of behavioural response is being shown in this case? (1)
   (ii) Explain the importance of this response in the life of *L. terrestris*. (1)

(b) In very dry conditions, *L. terrestris* burrows deeper into the soil and curls into a ball. How does this curling into a ball increase the animal's chance of survival? (2)

(c) If the worm is touched, it responds by contracting all its segments rapidly. How can this movement be related to the fact that the nerve cord of the worm contains a number of axons which have a very large diameter? (1)

AEB 1995   (*Total 5 marks*)

Q7 The diagram below represents an enlarged section of part of the retina of a human eye.

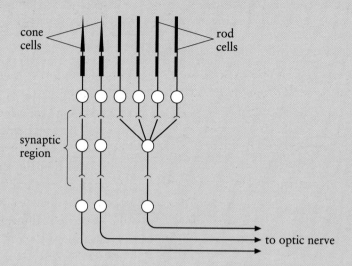

(a) Draw an arrow on the diagram to represent the direction of incoming light. (1)

(b) Explain how, in the synaptic region:
   (i) the connections of the rod cells enable us to see in conditions of low light intensity. (2)
   (ii) the connections of the cone cells enable us to distinguish between objects close together. (2)

NEAB 1995 *(Total 5 marks)*

Q8 A petri dish was divided in two. Half was illuminated and the other half kept in the dark. The drawing shows the path of a free-living aquatic flatworm plotted for five minutes in each condition.

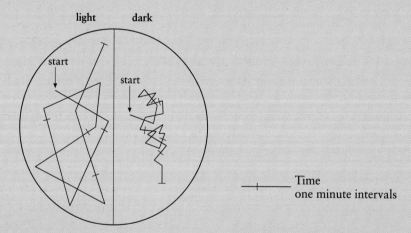

(a) Describe **two** differences between the movement of the flatworm in the light and in the dark. (2)

(b) (i) What type of response is shown by the flatworm in this investigation? (1)
   (ii) Explain the importance of this response in the life of the flatworm. (2)

AEB 1997 (specimen) *(Total 5 marks)*

15 Regulation and control

Many animals at least partially control the content of the fluids which surround the cells within their bodies – their internal environment. Mammals do this especially well, controlling not only the concentrations of many substances within their body fluids, but also body temperature. Endocrine glands, which secrete hormones, and the kidneys have particularly important roles in this control, which is called homeostasis. Plants exert less control over their internal environment, but they do use hormone-like substances to control a wide variety of physiological processes.

REGULATORY MECHANISMS IN ANIMALS

15.1 The role of negative feedback in homeostasis

Humans, like all mammals, maintain many features of their internal environment at almost constant levels. For example, we regulate our internal temperature, the concentration of glucose in blood and tissue fluid, and the amount of water in the blood. This regulation is called **homeostasis**. Homeostasis means 'staying the same'.

Homeostasis provides cells within the body with a relatively constant environment, and this helps them to work efficiently, no matter what is going on outside the body. Whatever the air temperature around you, the temperature around a cell in your liver is always just below 38 °C. However much or little carbohydrate you have eaten, the concentration of glucose in your body fluids does not normally fluctuate very far from 800 mg per dm^3. In this chapter you will see how these and other features of body fluids are kept within narrow limits. If these controls did not take place, many functions of cells, especially those involving membrane transporters and enzymes, would not be able to take place effectively.

Processes which aim to keep a potentially fluctuating feature within narrow limits use **negative feedback mechanisms**. This is true not only of living organisms but also of many technical devices, such as a central heating system, or the machinery which rolls out sheets of metal to a particular thickness.

In a negative feedback system (Fig. 15.1), there needs to be a **detector**, which measures the value of the feature to be controlled – for example the thickness of the metal, or the temperature of your blood. If the detector finds that the value is higher than it should be, it sends this information to an **effector**, which does something to lower the value back towards the correct level. It keeps on doing this until the detector, which is still measuring the value, finds that the value is now *too* low, and sends information to the effector telling it to stop doing whatever it is doing and start doing something to *raise* the value once more. Information is therefore fed back to the detector from the effector. The feedback is called 'negative' because it stops the effector doing one thing and stimulates it to do the opposite.

Negative feedback mechanisms in living organisms do not usually succeed in keeping a particular feature absolutely constant. There is usually some fluctuation or oscillation about an 'ideal' level or 'set point'. This happens because it takes time for information to be passed from the detector to the effector, and for the actions of the effector to have their effect. The longer this time delay, the greater the fluctuations will be.

In humans, the detectors are specialised cells. Some of these cells are in the brain, but cells in other organs, such as the pancreas, also act as detectors for particular substances. Many different organs act as effectors. For example, the skin is an effector in temperature regulation, while the kidneys are effectors in the regulation of water content. Information passes from detectors to effectors either along nerves (as in temperature regulation for example) or via the blood as chemicals called **hormones** (as in the regulation of water content for example).

15.2 Hormones in animals

A hormone is a chemical substance which is used to carry information from one part of the body to another. Hormones are secreted by **endocrine glands**; Fig. 15.2 shows the position of the most important of these glands in the body. An endocrine gland differs from other types of glands because it does not have a duct carrying its secretions to a particular point (as, for example, the salivary glands do). For this reason, endocrine glands are sometimes called **ductless glands**. The hormones which they secrete pass directly into the blood which flows through the many capillaries in the gland.

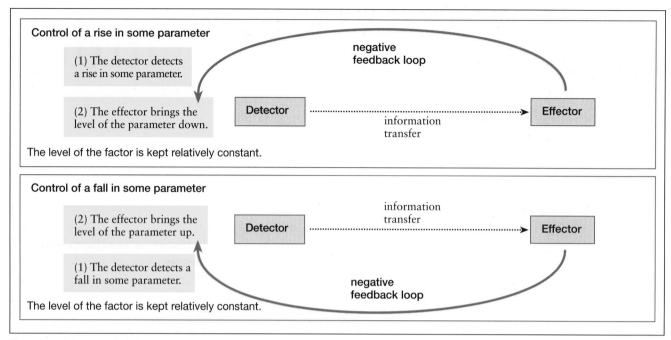

Fig. 15.1 Negative feedback.

Animal hormones fall into three main groups:

- **amino acids** and the closely related substances **catecholamines**. These are all water-soluble molecules. Examples of this type of hormone include **thyroxine** (Fig. 1.10) which is an amino acid and **adrenaline** which is a catecholamine.
- **proteins**. These are water soluble and include the hormones **insulin** (Fig. 1.12) and **glucagon**.
- **steroids**. These are lipids. They are fat-soluble molecules, often made from cholesterol. Examples of steroid hormones include **oestrogen** and **testosterone** (Fig. 15.3).

Hormones are transported in the blood from the endocrine gland where they are made to all parts of the body. They affect particular cells called **target cells**. These cells have receptors to which the hormone can bind; cells without the receptor for a particular hormone are unaffected by it.

Protein and catecholamine hormones, such as insulin and adrenaline, do not enter their target cells. They bind with receptors on the cell surface membrane, and this sets off a series of events inside the cell (Box 15.1). These events can happen very quickly, often within minutes. Thyroxine and the steroid hormones, on the other hand, pass through the cell surface membrane and into the cell where they bind with receptors in the nucleus. The hormone–receptor complex can bind with DNA, regulating transcription (Section 5.3). So these hormones affect the kinds of proteins being produced in a cell. This takes time, usually several hours or even longer. However, recent evidence suggests that at least some steroid hormones do also act at cell surface membranes where they may affect ion channels, and these effects occur very rapidly.

Hormones are often effective in extremely small amounts. For example, the average concentration of insulin in the blood of a healthy person is about 10^{-5} g per cm^3. Most hormones are rapidly removed from the blood, partly by means of excretion in urine and partly as they are broken down by enzymes. Insulin, for example, has a 'half-life' of just under 9 minutes; that is, if 1 µg of insulin is secreted into the blood, there will only be 0.5 µg present after 9 minutes. If a hormone is required to act for a long time, then it is continually secreted by the endocrine gland.

Some hormones are identical, or almost identical, with some neurotransmitter substances (Section 14.10). For example, the hormone **adrenaline** is extremely similar to the neurotransmitter **noradrenaline**. Not surprisingly, these two chemicals have very similar effects on the body, such as increasing the rate of heart beat.

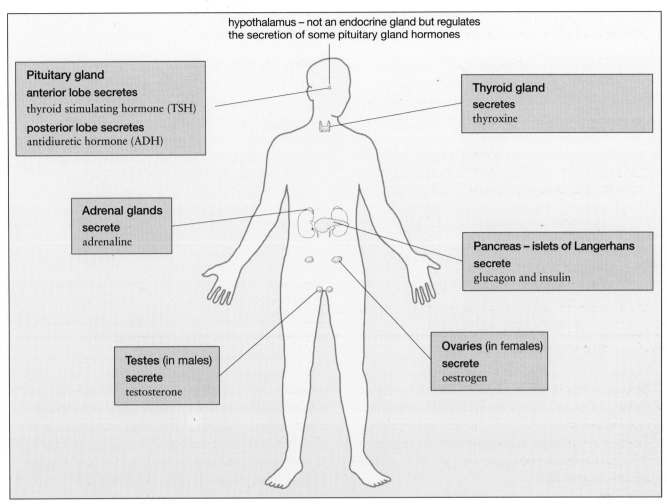

Fig. 15.2   The major endocrine glands and some of their secretions.

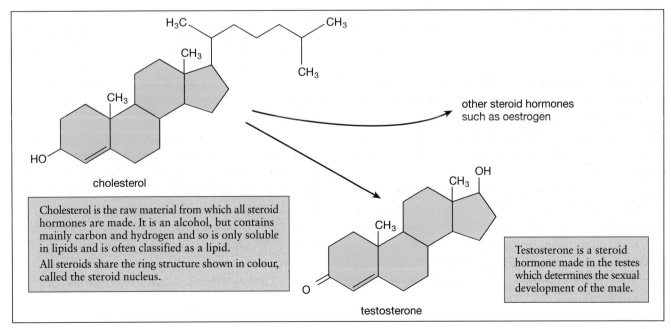

Fig. 15.3   Molecular structure of steroid hormones.

Box 15.1 How adrenaline affects its target cells

Adrenaline is a catecholamine hormone which is secreted by the adrenal glands in times of stress. Many different types of cells, for example smooth muscle cells and liver cells, have glycoprotein receptors for adrenaline in their cell surface membranes. Adrenaline has many different effects on these cells. For example, liver cells are stimulated to break down glycogen to glucose and release it into the blood, while smooth muscle cells that are responsible for peristalsis in the alimentary canal are inhibited from contracting. Adrenaline also increases heart rate (Section 10.7). We will look at the way in which adrenaline causes muscle cells to convert glycogen to glucose.

When adrenaline binds to its receptor, it causes a shape change which affects a protein on the inner surface of the membrane called a **G protein**. The G protein activates an enzyme called **adenylyl cyclase** which catalyses the production of **cyclic AMP** from ATP. (AMP stands for adenosine monophosphate; it is called 'cyclic' because the phosphate group is bonded to two different parts of the adenosine molecule.)

If the adrenaline is the 'first messenger' bringing information to the surface of the liver cell, then cyclic AMP can be thought of as the 'second messenger', which hands on the information to molecules inside the cell. Cyclic AMP activates an enzyme in the cytoplasm that catalyses a reaction which activates another enzyme, and so on in a 'chain' of enzymes (Fig. 15.4) culminating in the activation of **glycogen phosphorylase**. This enzyme catalyses the conversion of glycogen to glucose phosphate.

For every molecule of the first enzyme activated by cyclic AMP, many molecules of phosphorylase will eventually be activated. This happens because each enzyme in the chain can catalyse many reactions; thus one molecule of the first enzyme can catalyse the activation of many molecules of the second enzyme, and so on down the chain. This is called a **cascade** effect. It means that just a few molecules of adrenaline arriving at a cell surface membrane can result in the production of a very large number of glucose phosphate molecules in the cell. The cascade effect **amplifies** the signal arriving at the cell.

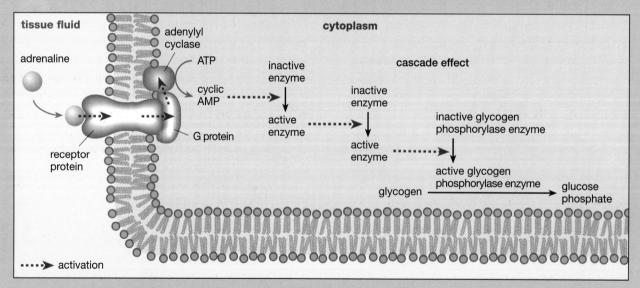

Fig. 15.4   How adrenaline affects glucose production in a cell.

THE CONTROL OF BLOOD GLUCOSE CONCENTRATION

15.3 The importance of blood glucose concentration

Glucose is the form in which carbohydrates are transported in an animal's body. It is carried in solution in the blood plasma. It is a small molecule, and easily moves out of blood capillaries into tissue fluid (Section 10.14). In a healthy person, the concentration of glucose in the blood is maintained at around 800 mg per dm³.

Many cells need a constant supply of glucose as a respiratory substance. Without it, they cannot produce ATP. Brain cells are especially sensitive to any drop in the amount of glucose in the blood. If blood glucose concentration drops below about 600 mg per dm³, a person suffers from **hypoglycaemia** which can rapidly cause loss of consciousness.

On the other hand, very high concentrations of glucose, a condition known as **hyperglycaemia**, cause problems as well. A high concentration of any solute lowers water potential (Section 3.26) and tends to draw water out of cells. Glucose is also lost in urine which should not normally happen (Section 15.14). This causes excessive water loss in urine that can result in a 'circulatory shock' in which not enough blood returns to the heart for adequate blood circulation.

Glucose can be added to the blood in several ways.

- When carbohydrate-rich foods are eaten, these are digested to monosaccharides in the alimentary canal. The monosaccharides, most of which are glucose, are absorbed into the blood in the capillaries in the villi.
- Liver cells contain stores of the polysaccharide **glycogen**. This can be hydrolysed to glucose, which can then leave the cells and enter the blood.
- Amino acids, and glycerol from triglyceride lipids, can be converted to glucose. This usually happens in the liver.

Glucose can also be removed from the blood in several ways.

- Many cells use glucose as their main respiratory substrate, breaking it down to carbon dioxide and water.
- Liver and muscle cells convert glucose to glycogen, for storage.
- Glucose can be converted to fat, for storage.

The regulation of the glucose content of the blood is done by speeding up or slowing down these processes, so that a balance is achieved between the addition and removal of glucose from the blood.

15.4 Insulin and glucagon

The two major hormones involved in the control of blood glucose concentration are **insulin** and **glucagon**. (Take care not to confuse *glucagon*, which is a protein hormone, with *glycogen*, which is a storage polysaccharide.) Both of these hormones are proteins. They are both secreted by cells in the **pancreas**.

The pancreas has two very different functions. One function is the secretion of pancreatic juice, containing enzymes and sodium hydrogencarbonate, into the duodenum (Section 13.9). The second function is the detection of blood glucose concentration, and the secretion of the two hormones which control this concentration.

Fig. 15.5 shows the microscopic structure of the pancreas. The cells which secrete insulin and glucagon are arranged in patches called **islets of Langerhans**. Within the islets, there are different types of cells. Insulin is secreted by β **cells**, and glucagon by α **cells**.

The islets in the pancreas have an excellent blood supply; although they make up only 1% of the tissue in the pancreas, they receive 10% of the blood supply. The α and β cells are able to sense the concentration of glucose in the tissue fluid around them, which is formed from the blood. They respond to changes in blood glucose concentration by switching on or switching off the secretion of glucagon or insulin respectively.

Let us consider what happens if a person eats a meal containing a lot of carbohydrate. This is digested and large amounts of glucose enter the blood capillaries in the villi. The α and β cells in the pancreas sense the raised glucose concentration in the blood which flows past them. The α cells respond by *not* secreting glucagon, while the β cells respond by secreting insulin.

The insulin is secreted into the tissue fluid and passes directly into the capillaries in the islets. The insulin is carried in the blood plasma to all parts of the body, where it binds to glycoprotein receptors in the cell surface membranes of its target cells. This causes changes in the cells which have several effects, including:

- an increased rate of uptake of glucose by muscle and fat cells, achieved by increasing the number of glucose channels in the cell surface membranes.
- an increased rate of use of glucose by the cells. This is

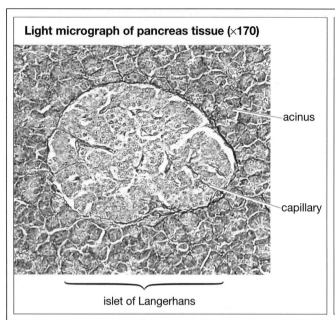

Light micrograph of pancreas tissue (×170)

acinus

capillary

islet of Langerhans

Diagram of pancreas structure

acinus – a group of cuboid secretory cells around the end of a branch of the pancreatic duct. The cells secrete pancreatic juice.

islet of Langerhans containing α and β cells

capillary

glucagon and insulin secreted into blood capillaries and then into general circulation

pancreatic duct

pancreatic juice to the alimentary canal

Fig. 15.5   Structure of the pancreas.

done by increasing the rate at which glucose is used in respiration, especially in muscle cells, and increasing the rate at which glucose is converted to glycogen in liver and muscle cells.

These responses by the cells take glucose out of the blood. If no more food is eaten then, as the blood continues to flow around the body, eventually the level will drop below its 'normal' level of 800 mg per dm³. When this is sensed by the β cells, they stop secreting insulin. However, the α cells respond to this low blood glucose concentration by secreting glucagon.

When glucagon arrives at the liver cells, it binds with its glycoprotein receptor on their cell surface membranes and sets off a chain of events which are almost the opposite to those stimulated by insulin. The effects include:

- activating the enzyme which breaks down glycogen to glucose.
- speeding up the rate at which amino acids and other substances are converted to glucose.
- reducing the rate of respiration.

The way in which these effects are brought about is very similar to that for adrenaline, which is shown in Fig. 15.4.

All of these effects prevent the blood glucose levels from falling any further. When food is next eaten, blood glucose concentrations rise, and this is detected by the α and β cells. The β cells respond by secreting insulin, and so on.

You can see that we have gone back to where we began. This is a typical negative feedback control mechanism. It is a little more sophisticated than some because there are two different hormones involved. One (insulin) brings about positive actions to bring down blood glucose levels, and one (glucagon) brings about positive actions to stop them falling too low. If you imagine having only *one* of these hormones – insulin, say – then you would still get a rapid response bringing blood glucose concentration down whenever it went too high. But if it went too low, all that would happen would be that insulin secretion would be switched off. Nothing positive would happen to allow blood glucose concentration to rise again, so it would just stay low, until you ate a carbohydrate-rich meal again. Having the two hormones acting in opposite ways speeds up the response to changes in blood glucose concentration, and so reduces the magnitude of these changes.

15.5   Diabetes mellitus

Diabetes mellitus, often known simply as diabetes, is a disease in which the body can no longer control blood glucose concentration so that it remains within safe levels. There are two different forms of diabetes, with similar symptoms but different causes and different methods of treatment.

Type 1 diabetes, also known as insulin-dependent or juvenile-onset diabetes, is caused by the inability of the β cells to secrete sufficient insulin. The exact reason for this

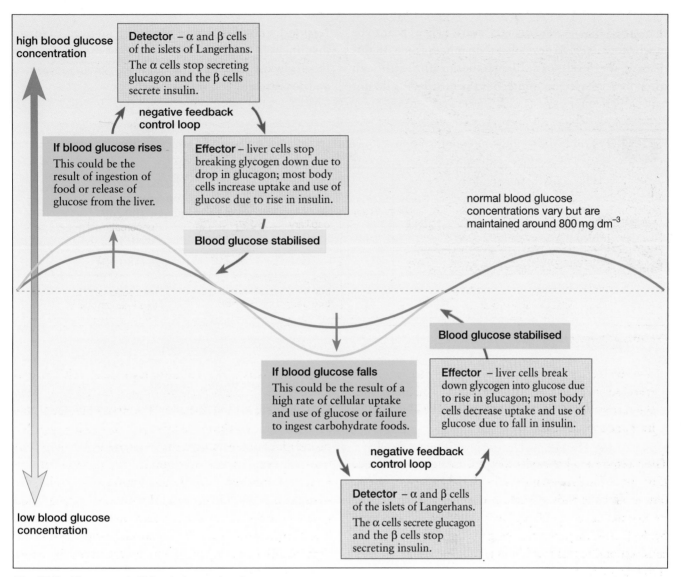

Fig. 15.6 The control of blood glucose level.

is not understood, but it seems that the body's own immune system attacks and destroys the β cells. As with many diseases, there appears to be a genetic component to the illness; some people inherit genes which make them more prone to develop it than others, but even with these genes they will not definitely develop diabetes. This type of diabetes usually develops very early in a person's life.

With no, or very little, insulin being secreted, a glucose-rich meal sends blood glucose concentration soaring far above the norm of 800 mg per dm^3. The kidneys are unable to remove all of this glucose from the urine, and glucose in the urine is an early sign of diabetes. Glucose cannot be stored as glycogen as there is no insulin to stimulate this, so any extra glucose eaten just makes the problem worse. Fats are metabolised more rapidly than

usual, resulting in the production of substances called ketoacids. These accumulate in the blood, lowering its pH. This is very dangerous, as a person can die from acidosis if the pH of the blood drops below about 7.0.

A person with type 1 diabetes regularly measures their blood glucose concentration; small and easy-to-use biosensors or dipsticks (Box 2.2) can be used for this. Such a person must watch their diet very carefully, never eating large amounts of carbohydrate, but always having a supply of sugary food to hand in case blood glucose concentration should drop too low. They inject insulin into their bloodstream each day.

Type 2 diabetes, also known as non-insulin dependent or late-onset diabetes, usually develops much later in life than type 1. People who are very overweight appear to be much more likely to develop it than other people. In this disease, the β cells can still produce insulin, although often in decreased amounts, but the target cells do not respond well to it. There is usually no need to inject insulin, at least in the earlier stages of the disease, but blood glucose concentrations must be regularly measured and diet carefully controlled.

Q1 The table shows how the concentrations of insulin and glucose in the plasma vary at different times.

When measurement taken	Plasma insulin concentration/ units per cm³	Plasma glucose concentration/ mg per 100 cm³
during overnight fast	10	60–100
during a meal	70	110–180
after a meal	10	60–100
during prolonged fasting	5	50–70

(a) Describe the relationship between glucose concentration and insulin concentration in the plasma. *(1)*

(b) Explain the rise in plasma glucose and insulin levels that occurs during the meal. *(3)*

(c) Use information from the table to explain how the control of insulin production is an example of negative feedback. *(2)*

(d) The plasma glucose level is maintained at a minimum of 50 mg per 100 cm³ during prolonged fasting. Suggest how this might be achieved. *(2)*

NEAB 1995 *(Total 8 marks)*

Q2 Suggest explanations for the following aspects of diabetes mellitus and its treatment.

(a) Glucose may be present in the urine of a diabetic. *(2)*

(b) A diabetic cannot take insulin orally in tablet form, it must be injected. *(2)*

(c) A person whose diabetes is treated by diet and not by insulin injection must not eat pure sugars but should obtain carbohydrate from bread, potatoes etc. *(2)*

AEB 1993 *(Total 6 marks)*

TEMPERATURE REGULATION
15.6 Endotherms and ectotherms

Most animals are not able to regulate their body temperatures precisely. Non-vertebrates, and also fish, amphibians and reptiles, are usually the same temperature as their environment. Most of the heat which warms the bodies of these animals comes from *outside* the body, and so they are known as **ectotherms** ('outside heat'). Another term used to describe them is **poikilotherms**, which means 'variable temperature'. Their body temperature goes up and down as the temperature of their environment goes up and down.

Mammals and birds differ from all other animals in being able to produce enough heat inside their bodies to maintain a constant body temperature, above that of their surroundings. They are known as **endotherms** ('inside heat'). They regulate their body temperature, keeping it close to a particular value, which varies slightly between different species. Humans, for example, maintain an internal body temperature (core temperature) of about 37 °C, while many birds keep their temperature around 40 °C. Mammals and birds can also be described as **homeotherms**, which means 'same temperature'. Their temperature remains almost constant, despite changes in the temperature of their environment (Fig. 15.7).

You have probably heard the words 'cold-blooded' and 'warm-blooded' used to describe these animals, but these are not scientific terms and you should avoid them. It is true that in a cool climate ectothermic animals do feel cool to touch, but a fish living in warm tropical water feels warm to touch! An ectothermic animal can have blood as warm as that of an endothermic animal if its environment is warm.

Endothermic animals have considerable advantages over ectothermic animals. Temperature affects the rate of chemical reactions, including metabolic reactions. Low temperatures slow down reactions, while high temperatures speed them up; very high temperatures denature enzymes, and therefore stop metabolic reactions from taking place. The activity of an animal is affected by the rate of its metabolic reactions. An animal with a very low internal body temperature has a very low rate of metabolism and will be unable to move around quickly.

Endothermic animals are able to maintain their body temperature at a value close to the optimum for their enzymes. These animals can therefore remain active in both day and night, summer and winter, in very warm climates and in very cold ones. Ectothermic animals have

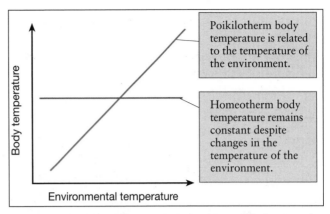

Fig. 15.7 Body temperature variation in a poikilotherm and a homeotherm.

Poikilotherm body temperature is related to the temperature of the environment.

Homeotherm body temperature remains constant despite changes in the temperature of the environment.

much less control over their body temperature. In a temperate climate, many insects, for example, are only active during summer days, becoming slow-moving as temperatures drop at night and during the winter.

There is, however, also one major *dis*advantage in being an endotherm. Large amounts of food must be eaten to provide fuel for the generation of heat within the body. An endothermic animal has to eat a far greater amount of food each day than does an ectothermic animal of the same body weight.

This is especially significant for small animals living in cold climates. Heat is generated within the body, but is lost through the surface. Very small animals have a high surface area to volume ratio, and therefore their bodies have to work extremely hard to generate enough heat to replace that which is lost through the surface. Tiny birds and mammals, such as hummingbirds and shrews, are unable to live in very cold climates, as they simply cannot eat enough to provide the fuel to produce enough heat within their bodies. In Britain, small mammals may hibernate if they are not able to find enough food to maintain their body temperature in very cold weather. In extremely cold climates, even large animals such as bears hibernate.

15.7 Temperature control by ectotherms

Although ectotherms, by definition, are not able to generate enough heat within their bodies to keep their temperature constant, they can use behavioural means to adjust their temperatures. For example, a lizard living in a desert may bask in the sun on a warm rock first thing in the morning, to help to raise its body temperature high enough to enable it to become active. In the middle of the day, it may move into the shade or a deep burrow where the temperature is lower. Honeybees cluster in a ball in their hive during winter, so that heat lost from the 'inside' bees helps to keep the surrounding bees warm. Those on the outside lose heat to the environment, but they slowly crawl back into the cluster, exchanging places with the bees nearer the centre.

15.8 Temperature regulation in humans

Humans, like all mammals, are endotherms and can keep their internal body temperature almost constant. This is done by maintaining a balance between heat gain and heat loss.

Heat is gained by:
- heat generated from metabolic reactions in cells.
- heat gained from the environment through radiation (for example infrared radiation from the Sun) or conduction (for example sitting on a hot radiator).

Heat is lost by:
- infrared radiation from the skin.
- evaporation of water from the skin.
- conduction to air or solid objects next to the skin.
- warm substances leaving the body, such as air being breathed out and the loss of urine.

In mammals, the negative feedback loop which controls body temperature (Fig. 15.8) centres on the **hypothalamus**, which is a small area at the base of the brain just above the pituitary gland (Fig. 14.3). The hypothalamus constantly monitors the temperature of the blood which flows through it, and so has a steady supply of information about the *internal* body temperature. It also receives information from temperature receptors in the skin which give information about the *external* temperature. The hypothalamus responds to this information by sending impulses along nerves to various parts of the body, causing a decrease or increase in heat-producing or heat-losing activities. Because it receives information about external temperature as well as internal temperature, the hypothalamus is usually able to make these adjustments well before the internal temperature changes significantly. For example, if sensors in the skin report that the air temperature is very cold, then the hypothalamus will turn up heat production in the body, and slow down heat loss, before the internal temperature has had time to drop.

15.9 Responses to prevent lowering of body temperature

In an environment with a temperature lower than 37 °C, heat will be lost from the body to the environment. A constant generation of heat within the body is needed, in order to maintain a steady internal temperature.

If the internal temperature is in danger of dropping, then several mechanisms come into play to increase heat gain and decrease heat loss.

● Decreasing heat loss

A considerable amount of heat is lost by radiation from the warm blood in capillaries just below the skin surface, to the surrounding air (Fig. 15.9). This heat loss can be greatly reduced by restricting the amount of blood that flows through these surface capillaries. This is done by closing off the arterioles which carry blood to the capillaries. This is called **vasoconstriction**. The blood then flows through capillaries much deeper in the skin, often beneath a layer of fat or **adipose tissue** which is an excellent insulator. Vasoconstriction is brought about by impulses arriving along sympathetic nerves from the hypothalamus.

In most mammals, loss of heat by radiation can be reduced by raising hairs on end; this traps a layer of air (which is a poor conductor of heat) next to the body. Humans have so little hair that, although the hairs do stand on end when we are cold, this has virtually no effect on the rate of heat loss. Instead, we rely on clothes to provide this effect. Behavioural mechanisms, such as putting on more warm clothes, moving to a warmer place or huddling next to others, are very important in reducing heat loss in humans.

● Increasing heat gain

Shivering can generate significant amounts of heat; during shivering, body heat production can be five times as great as normal. Shivering is the non-coordinated contraction and relaxation of skeletal muscles (muscles attached to bones). The energy transfers taking place in the muscles (chemical energy in glucose to ATP; chemical energy in ATP to movement energy in the muscle fibres) produce heat which warms the blood as it passes through the muscles. The blood then transfers the heat around the body. Shivering is stimulated by the hypothalamus, which sends impulses along motor neurones, via the spinal cord, to the muscles. The hypothalamus sends these impulses when it receives 'cold' signals from temperature receptors in the skin.

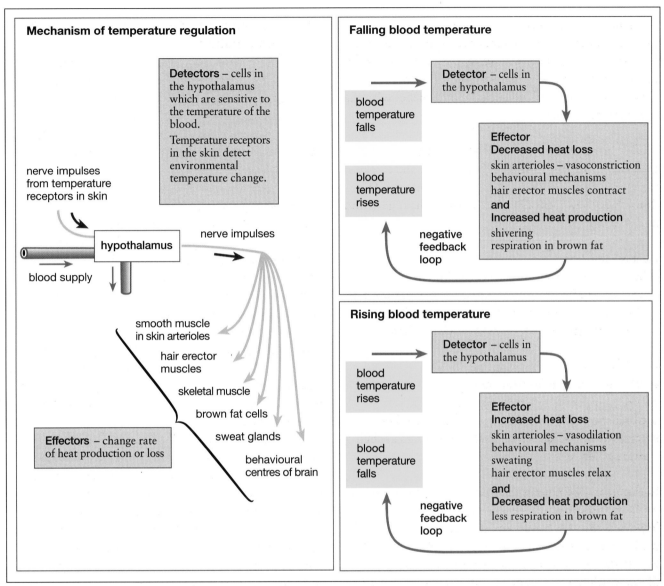

Mechanism of temperature regulation

Detectors – cells in the hypothalamus which are sensitive to the temperature of the blood.

Temperature receptors in the skin detect environmental temperature change.

nerve impulses from temperature receptors in skin

hypothalamus

blood supply

nerve impulses

smooth muscle in skin arterioles

hair erector muscles

skeletal muscle

brown fat cells

sweat glands

behavioural centres of brain

Effectors – change rate of heat production or loss

Falling blood temperature

Detector – cells in the hypothalamus

blood temperature falls

blood temperature rises

Effector
Decreased heat loss
skin arterioles – vasoconstriction
behavioural mechanisms
hair erector muscles contract
and
Increased heat production
shivering
respiration in brown fat

negative feedback loop

Rising blood temperature

Detector – cells in the hypothalamus

blood temperature rises

blood temperature falls

Effector
Increased heat loss
skin arterioles – vasodilation
behavioural mechanisms
sweating
hair erector muscles relax
and
Decreased heat production
less respiration in brown fat

negative feedback loop

Fig. 15.8 Negative feedback loop for the regulation of temperature.

Heat is also generated by the reactions of **respiration** within cells. This happens especially in cells in **brown fat**, which have special mitochondria. Instead of using energy released in oxidative phosphorylation (Section 9.4) to make ATP, these mitochondria release the energy as heat. The brown fat cells are stimulated to respire faster, generating extra heat, by impulses arriving along sympathetic nerves from the hypothalamus. Brown fat is especially important in very young children, but adults have almost no brown fat.

As well as these rapid, short-term responses to a threatened drop in internal body temperature, there is also a long-term response. If a mammal is exposed to cold for several weeks, then the hypothalamus increases its output of a hormone called **thyrotropin releasing hormone**. This causes the **thyroid gland** to enlarge and secrete more **thyroxine**. Thyroxine increases the metabolic rate, so this response results in an increase in the amount of heat produced inside the body. (Box 15.2 explains more about the secretion and effects of thyroxine.)

15.10 Responses to prevent raising of body temperature

Body temperature tends to rise if external temperatures are above 37 °C, or during exercise when heat is generated within muscles. Heat loss needs to be increased in order to stop the internal body temperature rising.

The arterioles supplying the surface capillaries widen, a

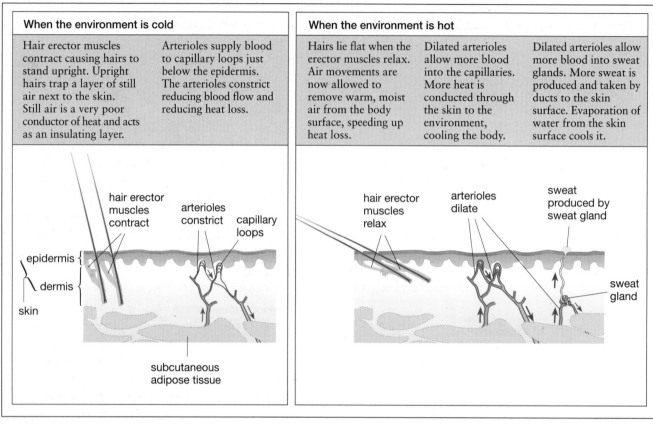

When the environment is cold		When the environment is hot		
Hair erector muscles contract causing hairs to stand upright. Upright hairs trap a layer of still air next to the skin. Still air is a very poor conductor of heat and acts as an insulating layer.	Arterioles supply blood to capillary loops just below the epidermis. The arterioles constrict reducing blood flow and reducing heat loss.	Hairs lie flat when the erector muscles relax. Air movements are now allowed to remove warm, moist air from the body surface, speeding up heat loss.	Dilated arterioles allow more blood into the capillaries. More heat is conducted through the skin to the environment, cooling the body.	Dilated arterioles allow more blood into sweat glands. More sweat is produced and taken by ducts to the skin surface. Evaporation of water from the skin surface cools it.

Fig. 15.9   How the skin helps to regulate body temperature.

process called **vasodilation**. Blood now flows freely through these capillaries, and heat is lost from it to the air, by radiation (Fig. 15.9). The amount of heat loss by radiation can also be increased by behavioural means, such as removing clothing.

The skin in most parts of the body contains **sweat glands**. These are stimulated by sympathetic nerves from the hypothalamus, which cause them to secrete a liquid containing water with urea, lactic acid and sodium, potassium and chloride ions dissolved in it. This liquid passes up the duct of each gland and onto the surface of the skin through a pore. As the water evaporates from the skin surface, heat is lost from the skin. Sweating is the only way in which a person can lose heat from their body when the environmental temperature is greater than their skin temperature. When the air is very humid, water evaporates only very slowly or not at all and the cooling effect is lost; the sweat just lies on your skin. You tend to feel much more uncomfortable in hot, humid air than in equally hot, dry air.

Many mammals increase heat loss by evaporation by **panting**. Dogs, for example, draw air in through the nose and into the mouth, where it comes into contact with the wet surface of the mouth and tongue. Moisture from these surfaces evaporates into the air; the 'wet' air is moved out of the mouth and dryer air brought in, so that water will continue to evaporate.

Humans have many behavioural means of keeping cool, as well as the removal of clothes mentioned above. If water is available, it can be splashed onto the skin and left to evaporate; this has the same effect as sweating. Moreover, a body of water, such as a river or the sea, is almost always cooler than the air, so swimming can reduce your body temperature to a more comfortable level. Cold drinks do not, though, have much effect on your body temperature, although they may be very necessary to replace the water you lose by sweating.

Box 15.2 Thyroid hormones and the control of metabolic rate

The thyroid gland lies on either side of the trachea in the neck. It secretes three hormones, all of which are secreted together and have similar effects. The most abundant of these is **thyroxine**, otherwise known as **tetraiodothyronine** or **T₄.**

Fig. 15.10 shows the structure of the thyroid gland. It contains many blood capillaries running between spherical **follicles**, each of which consists of a single layer of cells. These cells secrete a polypeptide called **thyroglobulin** into the lumen of the follicle. Thyroglobulin contains iodine.

When thyroxine is to be secreted into the blood, the cells take up droplets of thyroglobulin by phagocytosis. Lysosomes fuse with the vesicles containing thyroglobulin, and proteases then hydrolyse it to produce thyroxine. The thyroxine then leaves the cell and passes into a blood capillary.

Thyroxine passes through the cell surface membranes of its target cells, and then binds with a receptor molecule in the nucleus. The thyroxine–receptor complexes stimulate the transcription of many different genes, including those which code for the production of growth hormone and myosin (one of the proteins in muscle). Thyroxine causes an increased production of mitochondria in the cell, and an increased production of many of the enzymes involved in respiration. A major effect of thyroxine on a cell is therefore to increase the rate of respiration within it. These effects are not immediate because it takes time for a gene to be transcribed to produce mRNA, for the mRNA to be translated in protein synthesis, and for the newly made protein to begin to carry out its function in the cell.

Apart from its effect on the rate of respiration in cells, thyroxine has a wide range of other effects on the body, many of which are not yet understood. For example, it stimulates tooth development and bone growth in children, and the normal cycle of skin replacement and hair growth in both children and adults. It increases the activity of the muscles in the wall of the alimentary canal, increases the speed of reflex actions and affects many brain functions, such as wakefulness, memory and learning capacity.

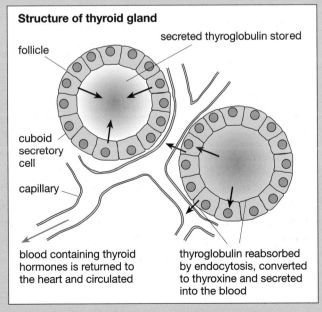

Structure of thyroid gland

follicle

secreted thyroglobulin stored

cuboid secretory cell

capillary

blood containing thyroid hormones is returned to the heart and circulated

thyroglobulin reabsorbed by endocytosis, converted to thyroxine and secreted into the blood

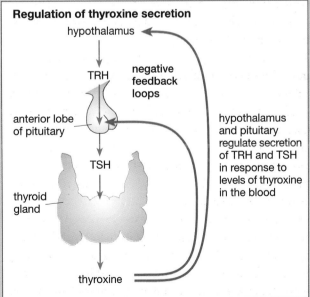

Regulation of thyroxine secretion

hypothalamus

TRH

negative feedback loops

anterior lobe of pituitary

TSH

thyroid gland

thyroxine

hypothalamus and pituitary regulate secretion of TRH and TSH in response to levels of thyroxine in the blood

Fig. 15.10 Structure of the thyroid gland and regulation of hormone scretion.

Box 15.2 Thyroid hormones and the control of metabolic rate (cont.)

As thyroxine has such wide-ranging and important effects, it is not surprising that the amount of it which is secreted into the blood must be carefully regulated. The cell bodies of neurones in the hypothalamus secrete a hormone called **thyrotropin releasing hormone** or **TRH**. This hormone passes along the axons of the neurones, and is released into blood vessels which take it directly to the **anterior pituitary gland** (Fig. 15.10). Here, the TRH stimulates the secretion of **thyrotropic hormone** (sometimes known as thyroid stimulating hormone), **TSH**, into the blood. TSH acts on the thyroid gland, stimulating the secretion of thyroxine. The levels of thyroxine in the blood are monitored by both the hypothalamus and the pituitary gland. There is negative feedback, so that if thyroxine levels rise too high, the secretion of TRH and TSH is reduced. In many mammals, the secretion of TSH increases after exposure to cold, but it is not certain if this happens in humans.

Q3 (a) Outline the functions of thyroxine in human growth. (2)

The control of thyroxine release involves the interaction between several endocrine glands and the hormones they produce.

(b) Describe how the concentration of thyroxine in the blood is regulated. (4)

UCLES (modified) 1996 (*Total 6 marks*)

Q4 (a) Give **one** reason why the core temperature of a healthy rabbit kept at an environmental temperature of 10 °C might increase. (1)

(b) Describe how a mammal such as a rabbit is able to detect changes in its core temperature. (2)

A rabbit was kept at an environmental temperature of 10 °C. The graph shows how the ear temperature of the rabbit varied with its core temperature.

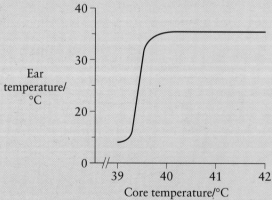

(c) Explain the immediate cause of the change in ear temperature which occurs when the core temperature increases from 39 °C to 40 °C. (2)

AEB 1995 (*Total 5 marks*)

STRUCTURE AND FUNCTION OF THE KIDNEYS

The kidneys have important roles to play in regulating the composition of body fluids. They remove various substances from the blood, and **excrete** them from the body in solution in water. Excretion is the removal of waste products of metabolism from the body. Many of these waste products are harmful or **toxic**, and would cause damage to cells if allowed to accumulate.

Before we consider the structure and functions of the kidneys, we will look at the source of one of the substances excreted by the kidneys – urea.

15.11   The formation of urea

Urea is a small organic molecule containing nitrogen. Its molecular formula is $CO(NH_2)_2$. Urea is made in the liver, from where it passes into the blood. Large concentrations of urea in the blood can damage cells, so it must be removed constantly. As the blood passes through the kidneys, urea is removed from it and excreted in urine.

Urea is produced in the liver from amino acids. The human body is unable to store proteins or amino acids, and so if more protein is eaten than is required by the body, the excess must be disposed of. However, amino acids contain useful energy and it would be wasteful to lose this entirely. The amino acids are therefore converted to carbohydrates or fats, which *can* be stored or used in respiration.

Amino acids, unlike carbohydrates or fats, contain nitrogen. This is in the form of an amino group, NH_2. Before amino acids are converted to carbohydrate or fat, the amino group is removed. This is called **deamination**. Deamination takes place in cells in the liver.

Fig. 15.11 shows how deamination takes place. The nitrogen is removed from the amino acid to produce **ammonia**. This is a very soluble and very toxic substance which would damage cells if allowed to accumulate. The ammonia is therefore converted to urea by combining it with carbon dioxide.

15.12   The structure of the kidneys

Fig. 15.13 shows the position and structure of the human kidneys. The kidneys are part of the **urinary** system, which also includes the **ureters**, **bladder** and **urethra**.

Each kidney is supplied with oxygenated blood via an artery which branches from the aorta, the **renal artery**. Deoxygenated blood returns from the kidneys in the **renal veins**. Urine produced in the kidneys flows down the

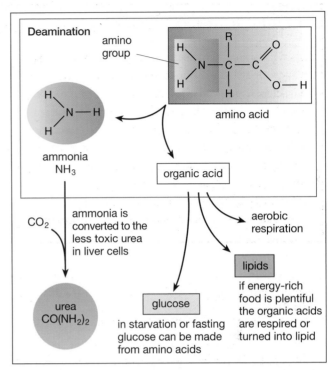

Fig. 15.11   Deamination.

Box 15.3   The ornithine cycle

Fig. 15.12 shows how urea is formed from amino acids, in more detail than is shown in Fig. 15.11. This process is known as the **ornithine cycle**, or the **urea cycle**.

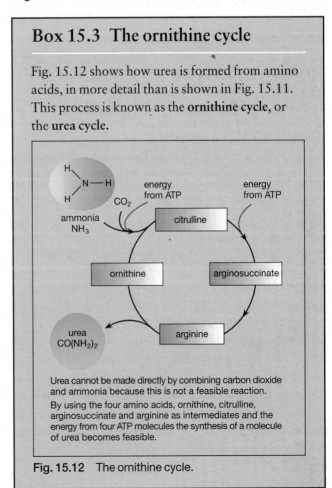

Urea cannot be made directly by combining carbon dioxide and ammonia because this is not a feasible reaction.

By using the four amino acids, ornithine, citrulline, arginosuccinate and arginine as intermediates and the energy from four ATP molecules the synthesis of a molecule of urea becomes feasible.

Fig. 15.12   The ornithine cycle.

Box 15.4 Nitrogenous excretory products

As you have seen in Section 15.11, the first nitrogen-containing product of deamination is **ammonia**. In mammals, ammonia is too soluble and too toxic to be allowed to remain in existence for long, and it is therefore rapidly converted to the less soluble, and much less toxic, substance **urea**. Mammals are said to be **ureotelic**.

However, if an animal has large quantities of water available in which ammonia can be dissolved and removed from the body, then there is no need to waste energy by converting it to urea. Many aquatic organisms, such as protozoa and bony fish, excrete excess nitrogen in the form of ammonia. They are said to be **ammonotelic**.

Birds and terrestrial insects produce a different nitrogenous excretory product. This is **uric acid**, which is virtually non-toxic and only slightly soluble in water. These organisms are said to be

uricotelic. (Aquatic insects, like most aquatic animals, are ammonotelic.) Uric acid is a purine, with a molecular structure very similar to that of adenine and guanine. The metabolic pathway by which uric acid is produced from ammonia is much longer and more complex than the pathway which produces urea, and uses quite large amounts of ATP. However, for birds and insects the energy cost appears to be more than balanced by the advantages of excreting their nitrogenous wastes in this form. Because uric acid is non-toxic and only slightly soluble, it can be excreted as a paste rather than in solution, thus conserving water. Moreover, for birds, which develop inside an egg with a shell, the excretion of urea would lead to a build-up of a highly concentrated solution around the developing embryo. This would draw water out of the embryo's cells by osmosis. The uric acid which the embryo excretes accumulates as a paste in a particular area inside the egg, where it causes no problems.

---

ureters to the bladder where it can be stored. The exit from the bladder is controlled by a **sphincter muscle**, which is under voluntary control. When the sphincter relaxes, urine flows from the bladder along the urethra, to the outside. The ureters, bladder and urethra all have very stretchy walls.

A kidney contains about 1.2 million tubules called **nephrons**. Each nephron begins as a hollow, cup-shaped **renal capsule** (sometimes known as a **Bowman's capsule**) in the outer part or **cortex** of the kidney. From here, the tubule runs towards the centre of the kidney. The part nearest the renal capsule is highly coiled, and is known as the **proximal convoluted tubule**. This leads into a straight section which turns upwards with a hairpin bend, called the **loop of Henle**. In human kidneys, some loops of Henle are quite short, while others are long and dip deeply into the **medulla**. The loop of Henle leads into the **distal convoluted tubule** and finally into a **collecting duct**. Several nephrons feed into the same collecting duct. The collecting ducts all eventually drain into the pelvis of the kidney, from where the urine flows into the ureter.

Each nephron has blood vessels closely associated with

it. An **afferent arteriole** brings blood towards each renal capsule, dividing to form a network of capillaries called a **glomerulus** in the hollow of the capsule. The blood leaves the capillaries in an **efferent arteriole**, which is narrower than the afferent arteriole. The efferent arteriole divides to form capillaries which run alongside and around the nephron, before joining together to form venules which carry blood into the renal vein.

15.13 Ultrafiltration

Kidneys produce urine in a two-stage process. Firstly, small molecules and ions are **filtered** out of the blood in the glomerulus into the renal capsule. Next, any of these molecules and ions which are required by the body are taken back from the nephron into the blood once more, in a process called **reabsorption**.

Fig. 15.14 shows how filtration occurs between the glomerulus and the cavity of the renal capsule. It is known as **ultrafiltration** because it filters out molecules which are much smaller than the particles that are separated by filters such as filter paper.

The actual 'filter' is the **basement membrane** of the lining, or **endothelium**, of the capillaries in the glomerulus.

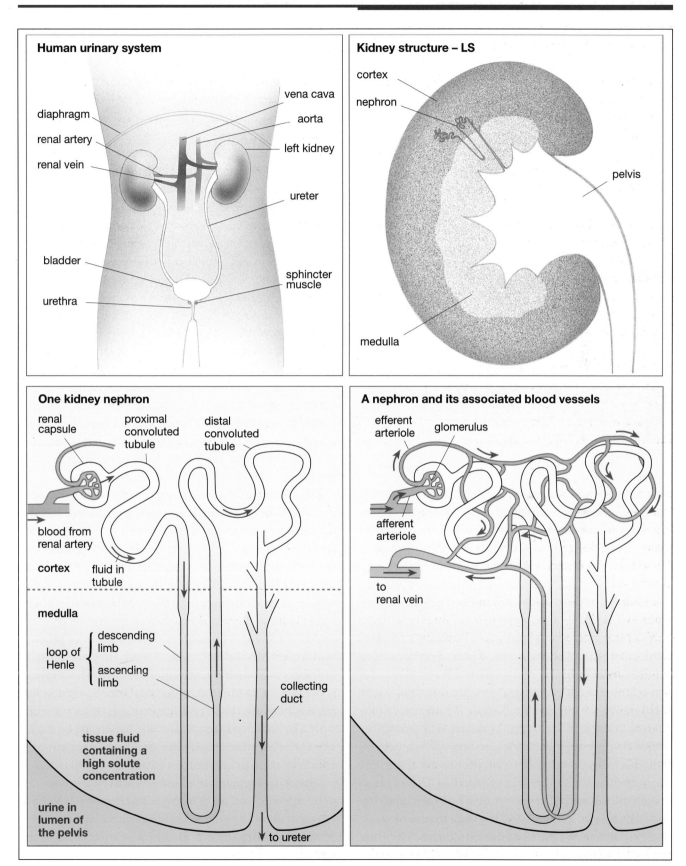

Fig. 15.13 The kidney

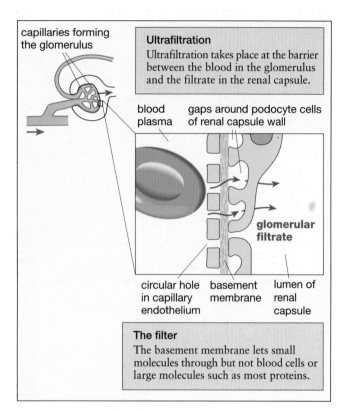

Ultrafiltration

Ultrafiltration takes place at the barrier between the blood in the glomerulus and the filtrate in the renal capsule.

blood plasma | gaps around podocyte cells of renal capsule wall

glomerular filtrate

circular hole in capillary endothelium | basement membrane | lumen of renal capsule

The filter

The basement membrane lets small molecules through but not blood cells or large molecules such as most proteins.

Fig. 15.14 Ultrafiltration.

This is made up a network of collagen and glycoproteins. These allow through molecules with a relative molecular mass of less than about 69 000, but prevent the passage of molecules which are larger than this. The endothelium of the blood capillary, and the **epithelium** of the renal capsule, are both very permeable and present almost no barrier to liquids passing through them. The endothelium of the blood capillary has gaps between its cells, and also holes *in* the cells. The epithelium of the renal capsule is made up of cells called **podocytes**, which again have many gaps between them.

A relatively high hydrostatic pressure is built up in the capillaries in the glomerulus, because the diameter of the efferent artery is less than that of the afferent artery. The hydrostatic pressure inside the renal capsule is much less than this. This pressure difference forces fluid through from the blood into the renal capsule. (Box 15.5 explains this in more detail.) Red and white blood cells, platelets and large protein molecules are too large to pass through. They remain in the blood in the capillaries. The fluid entering the renal capsule, which is called the **glomerular filtrate**, is almost identical to blood plasma, but without the proteins of large molecular mass.

15.14 Selective reabsorption in the proximal convoluted tubule

As the glomerular filtrate flows along the nephron various substances move out of it, across the cells making up the nephron wall, and into the blood in the capillaries running alongside the nephron. This process is called **selective reabsorption**.

Most reabsorption takes place as the fluid flows through the **proximal convoluted tubule**. The cells in the walls of this part of the nephron have microvilli (Fig. 15.16) which increase the surface area in contact with the fluid, and therefore increase the rate at which substances can be absorbed from it. The other side of the cells, furthest from the lumen of the nephron and nearest to the blood capillaries, also have folded surfaces. Near this side of the cells there are many mitochondria.

These mitochondria provide ATP for the active transport of sodium ions out of the cells. The sodium ions diffuse through the tissue fluid, across the endothelium of the capillaries and into the blood in the capillaries. The active transport of sodium ions out of the cells lining the nephron maintains a low concentration of sodium inside them, so sodium continually moves *into* these cells from the filtrate in the nephron, down its concentration gradient.

The sodium ions move into the cells through transporter proteins. These are **cotransporters**, which allow sodium ions and another substance to move in at the same time. (Fig. 3.32 shows how a cotransporter works.) There are several different cotransporters in the cell surface membranes of the cells lining the proximal convoluted tubule, including glucose–sodium cotransporters. The sodium ions are moving down their concentration gradient, and this provides enough energy to pull the glucose molecules into the cell, even though they are actually moving *against* their concentration gradient. The net result is the same as if glucose molecules were being actively transported into the cell – but, of course, this is not quite true! The active transport is actually happening on the far side of the cell, moving sodium ions out and so creating the concentration gradient for sodium ions. This kind of transport is sometimes called **indirect active transport**.

By this mechanism, a high proportion of the sodium ions and all of the glucose in the glomerular filtrate are reabsorbed into the blood. As these solutes leave the filtrate, they reduce its concentration. This raises its water potential above the water potential of the blood, so water moves from the filtrate and into the blood by osmosis. The

Box 15.5 Filtration pressure in the glomerulus

The rate at which fluid passes from the glomerulus into the renal capsule is determined by the differences in **water potential** between them. Fluid moves from a region of high water potential to a region of low water potential. Water potential is determined by the **hydrostatic pressure** of the liquid, and its **solute potential** (Section 3.26).

water potential = solute potential + hydrostatic pressure

The fluid inside a capillary of the glomerulus has a hydrostatic pressure of approximately 6 kPa, while the fluid inside the renal capsule has a hydrostatic pressure of approximately 1.5 kPa; the reason for this difference is explained in Section 15.13. This difference in hydrostatic pressure tends to raise the water potential of the fluid in the capillaries above the water potential of the fluid in the renal capsule.

The concentration of the blood inside the glomerulus is much greater than in other parts of the body. This is because a lot of water is lost from the blood as it filters through into the renal capsule. The proteins are left behind, producing a concentrated solution with a relatively *low* solute potential. However, the fluid inside the renal capsule is less concentrated than this, because it does not contain any proteins; it therefore has a relatively *high* solute potential. This difference in solute potential tends to lower the water potential of the fluid in the capillaries below the water potential of the fluid in the renal capsule.

The overall difference in water potential between the capillaries and the renal capsule therefore depends on the relative effects of hydrostatic

pressure and solute potential (Fig. 15.15). In fact, the difference in hydrostatic pressure outweighs the difference in solute potential. The water potential of the fluid in the capillaries is greater than the water potential of the fluid in the renal capsule. The overall difference is called the **net filtration pressure**, and it causes fluid to move from the capillaries into the renal capsule.

Filtration pressure
The filtration pressure determines the rate of filtration. The filtration pressure is the water potential difference across the basement membrane.

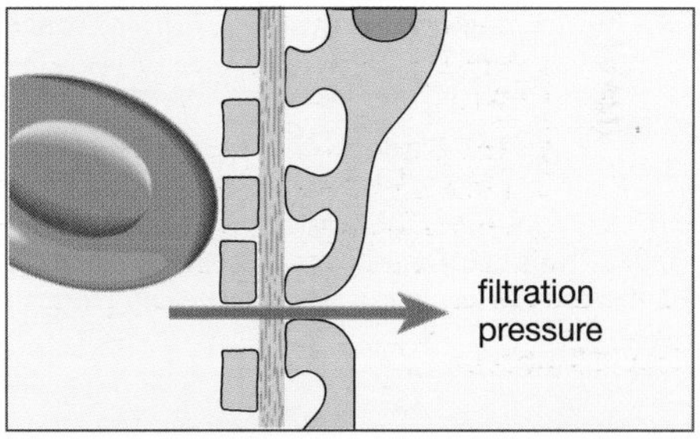

filtration pressure

The filtration pressure is the result of two opposing effects. The osmotic effect (solute potential difference) exerts a pressure which would cause an uptake of water into the capillaries, but this is more than cancelled by the higher hydrostatic pressure in the glomerulus.

hydrostatic pressure difference between capillary and renal capsule

solute potential difference between renal capsule and capillary

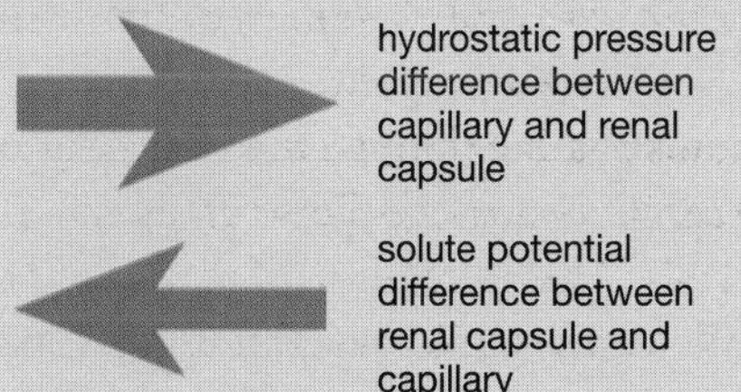

Fig. 15.15 Filtration pressure.

water 'follows' the sodium ions and glucose. About 65% of the water in the filtrate is reabsorbed in the proximal convoluted tubule. Amino acids, vitamins and chloride ions are also reabsorbed here.

Perhaps rather surprisingly (considering that one of the roles of the kidneys is to remove urea from the blood), almost half of the urea in the filtrate is also reabsorbed here. Urea simply diffuses from the filtrate into the blood down its concentration gradient. However, because so much water is also being reabsorbed from the filtrate, the concentration of urea in the filtrate actually *increases* as the filtrate flows down the tubule.

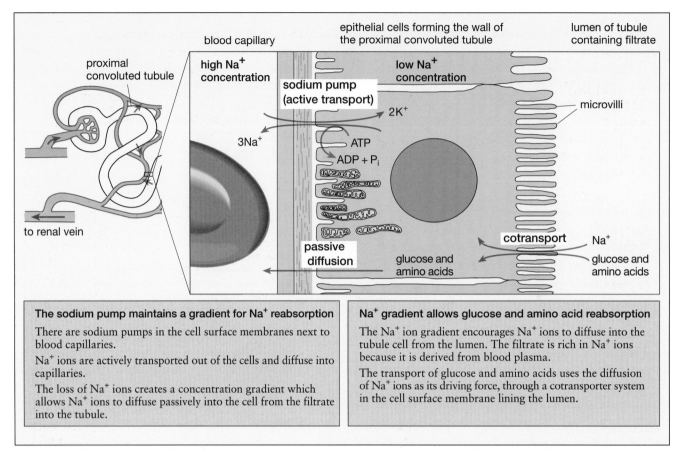

Fig. 15.16 Selective reabsorption of sodium ions, glucose and amino acids into the proximal convoluted tubule.

15.15 The loop of Henle

About one-third of the nephrons in a human kidney have very long loops of Henle, dipping far down into the medulla of the kidney before looping back up again. These long loops are important in water conservation. They make it possible for urine to be excreted which has a higher concentration than the blood. In mammals which live in deserts, such as jerboas, all the nephrons have long loops of Henle, and this enables these animals to excrete very small quantities of very concentrated urine.

The role of the long loops of Henle is to create a very high concentration of salts in the tissue fluid in the medulla of the kidney. They do this by a **countercurrent mechanism**.

Fig. 15.17 shows how this mechanism works. 'Countercurrent' means that fluids flow past each other in opposite directions. Fluid flows down one side of the loop – the **descending limb**, and up the other side – the **ascending limb**.

It is easiest to understand how the countercurrent mechanism builds up a high salt concentration by beginning with the *second* part of the loop, the ascending limb. The walls of the upper part of the ascending limb are impermeable to water. The cells here actively transport sodium and chloride ions out of the fluid in the tubule, into the tissue fluid outside. As the two limbs are so close to one another, this produces a high concentration of sodium and chloride ions around the descending limb.

The walls of the descending limb are permeable to water. As the fluid flows down this part of the loop, it is surrounded by tissue fluid with a high concentration of ions and therefore a low water potential. Water therefore moves out of the descending limb, by osmosis down the water potential gradient, into the tissue fluid. At the same time, sodium and chloride ions diffuse *into* the fluid in the tubule, down their concentration gradient. The outward movement of the water, and the inward movement of the sodium and chloride ions, increase the concentration of the fluid inside the tubule.

By the time the fluid reaches the bottom of the descending limb and begins to turn the hairpin, it has lost a lot of water and gained a lot of sodium and chloride ions. It is very concentrated. The longer the loop, the more concentrated it will become.

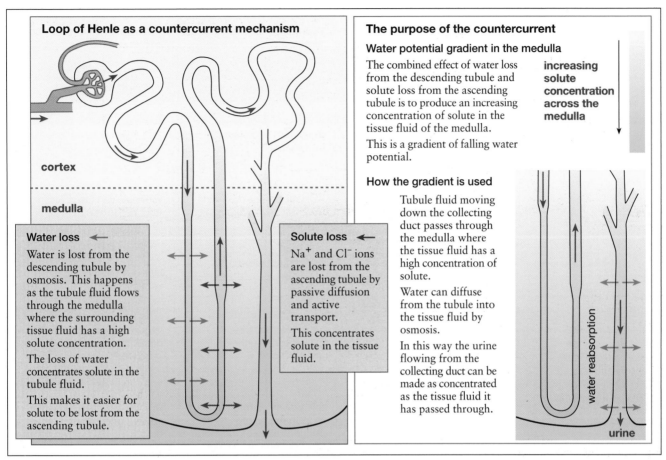

Loop of Henle as a countercurrent mechanism

cortex

medulla

Water loss ←

Water is lost from the descending tubule by osmosis. This happens as the tubule fluid flows through the medulla where the surrounding tissue fluid has a high solute concentration.

The loss of water concentrates solute in the tubule fluid.

This makes it easier for solute to be lost from the ascending tubule.

Solute loss ←

Na^+ and Cl^- ions are lost from the ascending tubule by passive diffusion and active transport.

This concentrates solute in the tissue fluid.

The purpose of the countercurrent

Water potential gradient in the medulla

The combined effect of water loss from the descending tubule and solute loss from the ascending tubule is to produce an increasing concentration of solute in the tissue fluid of the medulla.

This is a gradient of falling water potential.

increasing solute concentration across the medulla

How the gradient is used

Tubule fluid moving down the collecting duct passes through the medulla where the tissue fluid has a high concentration of solute.

Water can diffuse from the tubule into the tissue fluid by osmosis.

In this way the urine flowing from the collecting duct can be made as concentrated as the tissue fluid it has passed through.

water reabsorption

urine

Fig. 15.17   The countercurrent mechanism in the loop of Henle.

As the concentrated fluid flows round the hairpin and begins to flow up the ascending limb, sodium and chloride ions move out of it and into the tissue fluid. Because the tissue fluid is so concentrated, it is relatively easy for these ions to move out. This outward movement of these ions builds up a high concentration in the tissue fluid in this part of the kidney.

As the fluid continues up the ascending limb, it continues to lose sodium and chloride ions, and therefore becomes less concentrated. However, it is still relatively easy for these ions to be actively transported out because these regions are next to regions of the descending limb where the fluid is less concentrated. All the way along the loop, the concentrations in the two sides are never very different from each other. The concentration gradient against which active transport has to work is therefore never very great.

How does this mechanism help to conserve water? You have seen how the loop of Henle produces a high concentration of sodium and chloride ions in the tissue fluid in the medulla of the kidney. The final part of each

nephron, the **collecting duct**, also passes through this region. As the fluid flows through the collecting ducts, water can be drawn out of them, by osmosis, into the concentrated tissue fluid in the medulla. The more concentrated the tissue fluid, the more water can be drawn out, and the more concentrated the urine can be.

A complex network of blood capillaries runs alongside the loop of Henle. These capillaries supply oxygen and nutrients so that the cells in the walls of the loop can produce the large amounts of ATP they need for active transport. The capillaries also take away much of the salt and water from the tissue fluid in the medulla, helping to maintain the gradients built up by the loop.

15.16   Osmoregulation

The kidneys play a central role in the regulation of the water content of the body. This is called **osmoregulation**.

The water content of the blood is monitored by **osmoreceptor** cells in the **hypothalamus**. The cell bodies of these nerve cells produce **antidiuretic hormone, ADH,** which is a small polypeptide. ADH passes along the axons

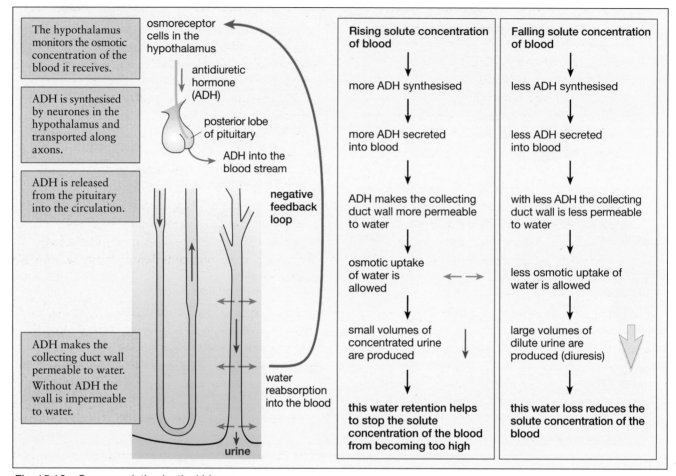

Fig. 15.18 Osmoregulation by the kidneys.

of the nerve cell, which lead into the **posterior pituitary gland** (Fig. 15.18).

When the water content of the blood is lower than normal, these nerve cells are stimulated and produce action potentials. When the action potential arrives at the ending of the axons, it causes ADH to be released – in just the same way that the arrival of an action potential causes neurotransmitter to be released at a synapse. However, in this case the ADH does not pass to receptors on a postsynaptic neurone, but is secreted into the blood. It is carried in the blood to all parts of the body, including its target organs – the kidneys.

ADH is taken up by receptors on the cell surface membranes of cells in the collecting ducts. This causes the membranes to become more permeable to water. As the fluid passes down the collecting duct, through the medulla with its high salt concentration in its tissue fluid, water can move out of the duct and into the tissue fluid by osmosis. The fluid in the collecting duct therefore becomes more concentrated. The person produces small volumes of highly concentrated urine.

If, on the other hand, the osmoreceptors detect a higher than normal content of water in the blood, then they do not produce action potentials and no ADH is released into the blood. The collecting duct cells become almost impermeable to water, so water is not reabsorbed from the fluid as it flows down the collecting duct. Large volumes of dilute urine are produced. The production of large volumes of dilute urine is called **diuresis**, so you can see how ADH acquired its name.

You can probably see that, while this mechanism can readily remove excess water from the body, it does not do anything to *add* water to the body when the blood is too concentrated. The best it can do is make sure that as little water as possible is lost in the urine. Water can only be added to the body by eating or drinking. At the same time that the osmoreceptors in the hypothalamus cause the release of ADH, they also stimulate **thirst centres** in the brain. This produces a sensation of thirst, causing the person to drink liquids.

Box 15.6 Osmoregulation in *Amoeba*

Amoeba is a genus of single-celled protoctists. There are many different species, some of which live in the sea, some in fresh water and some in the soil. Several species live as parasites in the digestive systems of animals, including humans. Amoebae are animal-like protoctists (Section 22.3) and do not have cell walls.

Freshwater amoebae, like many other animal-like freshwater protoctists, have to use energy to control their water content. The water in which they live has a higher water potential than their cytoplasm, and therefore water moves into the cell by osmosis, through the partially permeable cell surface membrane. If nothing were done about this, the cytoplasm would increase in volume to such an extent that the cell would burst (Fig. 3.30).

However, this excess water is removed from the cell by an organelle called a **contractile vacuole** (Fig. 15.19). Mitochondria produce ATP by aerobic respiration, and the hydrolysis of ATP is used to provide energy to fill the contractile vacuole with water. It is still not certain exactly how this is done, but it appears to involve the active transport of ions – possibly hydrogen ions – across the membranes of many small vesicles. These small vacuoles grow and fuse to form a large contractile vacuole. This continues to increase in size, eventually fusing with the cell surface membrane and emptying its contents outside the cell.

The contractile vacuole fills and empties at regular intervals, the interval depending largely on the water potential of the environment. Marine amoebae usually do not have contractile vacuoles at all.

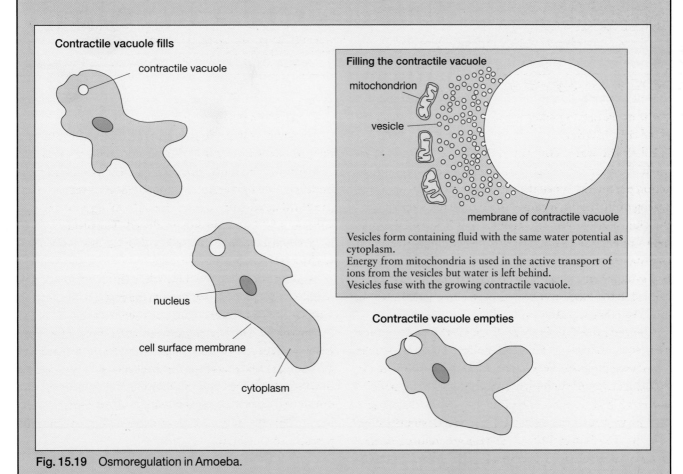

Fig. 15.19 Osmoregulation in Amoeba.

Box 15.7 Regulation of blood pH

The pH of the blood is maintained at around 7.40 in arterial blood, and 7.35 in venous blood. pH is a measure of the concentration of hydrogen ions. The more hydrogen ions, the lower the pH and the more acidic the blood. Venous blood has a slightly lower pH than arterial blood because it contains more carbon dioxide. Carbon dioxide reacts with water to produce carbonic acid:

$$CO_2 + H_2O \rightleftharpoons H_2CO_3$$
$$\text{carbonic acid}$$

Carbonic acid dissociates to produce hydrogen ions and hydrogencarbonate ions:

$$H_2CO_3 \rightleftharpoons H^+ + HCO_3^-$$

Carbonic acid is a weak acid, which means that it does not dissociate readily and therefore does not produce very high concentrations of hydrogen ions.

It is essential that blood pH is tightly controlled, because even small fluctuations can damage protein structure. Proteins such as receptors in cell surface membranes and enzymes are especially vulnerable. If blood pH drops below 6.8 or rises above 8.0, a person is unlikely to survive for more than a few hours.

There are three mechanisms by which pH is controlled in the human body. These are **buffers**, the **respiratory centre** in the brain and the **kidneys**.

Buffers

A buffer is a substance which absorbs hydrogen ions when their concentration is high, and releases them when their concentration is low. In doing this, buffers tend to keep the hydrogen ion concentration constant. Many proteins are buffers. Haemoglobin, for example, is a very important buffer in the blood. This is described in Section 10.13.

All weak acids act as buffers. Carbonic acid, for example, is an excellent buffer. In a solution with a high concentration of hydrogen ions, it has even less tendency than usual to dissociate. The balance of the equation:

$$H_2CO_3 \rightleftharpoons H^+ + HCO_3^-$$

shifts to the left, and fewer hydrogen ions are produced. In a solution with a low concentration of hydrogen ions, the balance of the equation shifts to the right; the carbonic acid has a greater tendency than usual to dissociate, releasing more hydrogen ions into solution and decreasing the pH.

The respiratory centre

The respiratory centre is part of the medulla oblongata in the brain. It contains receptors which are sensitive to the hydrogen ion concentration of the blood. A high hydrogen ion concentration usually indicates a build-up of carbon dioxide. The respiratory centre responds to this by increasing breathing rate, thus helping to speed up the removal of the carbon dioxide. This is described in Section 12.8.

The kidneys

The kidneys help to regulate pH by altering the rate at which they excrete hydrogen ions. When blood pH is too low, more hydrogen ions are excreted. When blood pH is too high, fewer hydrogen ions are excreted.

Hydrogen ions are continually secreted into the fluid as it passes along the nephron. This happens in all parts of the nephron. The rate at which they are secreted depends on the pH of the blood. If blood pH is low, then more hydrogen ions are secreted into the fluid in the nephron, and therefore more hydrogen ions are lost from the body in the urine. If blood pH is high, then fewer hydrogen ions are secreted into the nephron; they remain in the body rather than being passed out in the urine.

Box 15.8 Aldosterone

Aldosterone is a hormone secreted by the cortex (outer region) of the **adrenal glands.** (The central region of the adrenal glands, called the medulla, secretes adrenaline.) Aldosterone helps to maintain the correct blood pressure in the body. Blood pressure is related to the total volume of body fluids; the greater the fluid volume, the greater the blood pressure. The volume of body fluids is related to the concentration of sodium ions; high sodium ion concentrations tend to result in the retention of water in the body fluids. Thus the maintenance of correct blood pressure involves regulation of the concentration of sodium ions, Na^+, in the body.

Aldosterone is secreted in response to signals from the kidneys. If the sodium ion concentration is too low, cells in the walls of the afferent and efferent arterioles of the glomeruli in the kidneys secrete an enzyme called **renin.** These cells are part of the **juxtaglomerular apparatus.** Renin passes into the blood where it acts on its substrate, a protein called **angiotensinogen,** converting it to **angiotensin.** The arrival of angiotensin at the adrenal glands causes aldosterone to be secreted into the blood.

Aldosterone is, as its name suggests, a steroid hormone. It acts by switching on the transcription of various genes in cells lining the kidney tubules, resulting in the production of a number of proteins. About one or two hours after the aldosterone has been received by the tubule cells, the production of these proteins results in an increased rate of reabsorption of sodium ions from the glomerular filtrate in the tubules. Thus, fewer sodium ions are lost in the urine, and more are retained in the blood.

15.17 Dialysis

If the kidneys stop working, a condition called **renal failure**, the concentrations of many substances in the blood and tissue fluid quickly become higher or lower than they should be. The first signs of renal failure result from the retention of excessive amounts of salts (especially sodium) and water in the body. This produces high blood pressure, and also an increase in the amount of tissue fluid which causes swelling known as **oedema.** After a few days, urea and other substances accumulate to dangerous levels. Blood pH drops. Untreated renal failure is usually fatal within two weeks or less.

Renal failure can be treated with **dialysis** (Fig. 15.20). In this process, the person's blood is passed through many tiny tubes made of a partially permeable membrane known as dialysis tubing. The tubes lie in a liquid called dialysis fluid, which is carefully made up to have a similar concentration of glucose and other essential substances as normal blood, but no urea. As the blood passes through the dialysis tubing, small molecules such as urea are able to diffuse through it into the dialysis fluid. Both the blood and the dialysis fluid flow continuously past each other, so that diffusion gradients are maintained.

The blood is normally tapped from a vein in the patient's arm or leg, and moved by a special type of pump, which is very gentle and will not damage the red blood cells, before being passed into the dialysis tubing. The pump slightly increases the pressure of the blood, which helps to speed up the movement of substances out of it, through the membrane, just as the blood pressure in the glomerulus speeds up filtration in a functioning kidney. A substance called heparin is normally added to the blood, to stop it clotting before it returns to the person's body. After flowing through the tubing, the blood passes through a bubble trap to remove any air bubbles which might cause fatal blockages in the person's blood vessels.

Dialysis has to be done regularly, at least twice a week for several hours at a time, for as long as the person's kidneys are not working. If the kidneys are permanently damaged, then the ideal solution is a kidney transplant, but this is not always possible and not always successful. The reason for failure of a kidney transplant is almost always because the person's immune system (Section 21.15) treats the transplanted kidney as though it were an invading disease-causing organism, attacking it and destroying its cells. However, if the tissue-type of the donated kidney is carefully matched to that of the recipient, there is a better chance of success. Drugs which reduce the activity of the immune system, called immunosuppressants, are taken by recipients of any kind of transplant, including kidneys, to reduce the chance of rejection by their immune system.

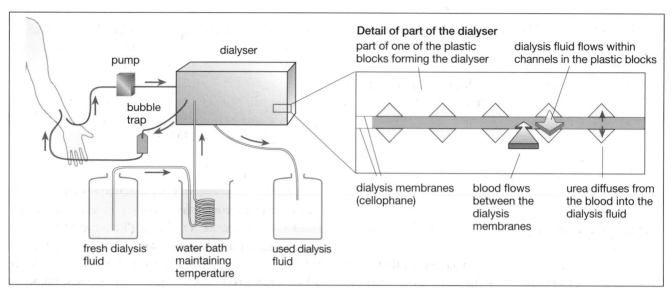

Fig. 15.20 Dialysis.

Q5 The kangaroo rat lives in hot deserts. The drawing shows the results of an investigation into the animal's water balance. The animal was given only dry seeds to eat and nothing to drink.

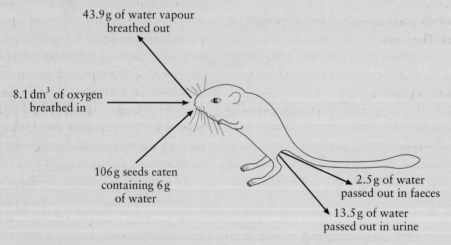

43.9 g of water vapour breathed out

8.1 dm^3 of oxygen breathed in

106 g seeds eaten containing 6 g of water

2.5 g of water passed out in faeces

13.5 g of water passed out in urine

The animal obtained only 6 g of water directly from its food. It obtained the rest of its water from the oxidation of carbohydrates present in the seeds.

(a) (i) Name the process in which carbohydrates are oxidised inside living cells. *(1)*

(ii) Assuming the water intake and output were balanced, calculate the mass of water the animal obtained by oxidation of carbohydrate during the investigation. Show your working. *(2)*

(b) The kangaroo rat uses much less water than humans to excrete urea. Further investigation showed that the blood of the kangaroo rat contained high amounts of the hormone ADH.

(i) Explain the role of the medulla of the kidney in the reabsorption of water from the fluid in the kidney tubule. *(6)*

(ii) Explain how a high level of ADH secretion helps the kangaroo rat to conserve water. *(3)*

NEAB 1995

(Total 12 marks)

REGULATORY MECHANISMS IN PLANTS

15.18 Growth substances in plants

Plants, like animals, use chemicals to carry information from one place to another. These chemicals are sometimes called hormones but, because they differ in some ways from animal hormones, they are more usually known as **growth substances**.

Plant growth substances are not produced in endocrine glands – indeed, they are not produced in glands of any kind. They are usually made by cells in quite widespread areas, but the amounts produced are so small that it is sometimes difficult to pinpoint exactly which groups of cells are making them.

Another difference from animal hormones is that many plant growth substances act on the same tissue as the one which made them – they are not always transported away from their site of manufacture to their target cells. But many do move. For example, **auxin** is made by cells in the tips of many shoots, but it has its effects on cells further down the shoot. Plant growth substances may move from one part of a plant to another by diffusion, active transport or by mass flow in solution in phloem sap, or in the xylem transpiration stream.

Most plant physiologists recognise five groups of plant growth substances. These are:

- **auxins**, which were the first plant growth substances to be discovered. They stimulate cell elongation in stems, amongst many other processes.
- **gibberellins**, which promote growth of stems and germination of seeds.
- **cytokinins**, which promote cell division.
- **abscisic acid**, which inhibits growth and seed germination.
- **ethene**, which is a gas that stimulates fruit ripening.

There is much that is still not known or understood about plant growth substances and their actions. One reason for this is that one type of growth substance may influence many different processes in a plant, and many different growth substances influence the same process. Two growth substances may act together to produce a larger, or quite different, effect from that which either of them would have on its own. This is known as **synergism**. Alternatively, the presence of two growth substances may reduce each other's effects. This is known as **antagonism**. In many instances, it appears that it is the balance between concentrations of different growth substances which actually determines the effect on the plant. Moreover,

these effects can differ in the same plant in different tissues or different stages of development, and in different species.

In the sections which follow, we will concentrate on just a small selection of the many and varied effects of each of the growth substances considered.

15.19 Auxins

There are several slightly different types of naturally occurring auxins, and also several which are manufactured commercially. The first auxin to be discovered was **indoleacetic acid** or **IAA**, by Frits Went in Holland in 1926. He was researching the process by which stems grow towards the light, a response known as phototropism.

● Auxins and phototropism

Plants, like animals, respond to stimuli from their environment. However, unlike animals, plants cannot move freely, and many of their responses are by means of growth. If the growth response is in a direction determined by the stimulus, it is known as a **tropism**. A prefix is added to this term to describe the type of stimulus to which the plant is responding. A growth response to light is **phototropism**, to gravity **geotropism** or **gravitropism**, and to touch **thigmotropism**. If the response of the plant is to grow towards the stimulus, it is described as **positive**, while if it grows away from the stimulus, the response is **negative**. Thus, when plant shoots grow towards light they are said to show **positive phototropism**.

Went's experiments were done with shoots of germinating oat grains. These shoots are simple to work with because they are covered with a sheath called a **coleoptile** and are relatively thick and sturdy. Went showed that if he cut the tip from a coleoptile, placed it on an agar block for a while, and then placed the agar block asymmetrically on a second decapitated coleoptile, the second coleoptile grew in a curved shape rather than straight upwards (Fig. 15.21). It curved away from the side on which the agar block was placed. Went concluded that a chemical made in the coleoptile tip diffused into the agar block, and then into the second decapitated coleoptile, where it stimulated growth. Because the agar block was placed asymmetrically, one side of the second coleoptile received more of this chemical than the other side, and so grew faster, resulting in curvature.

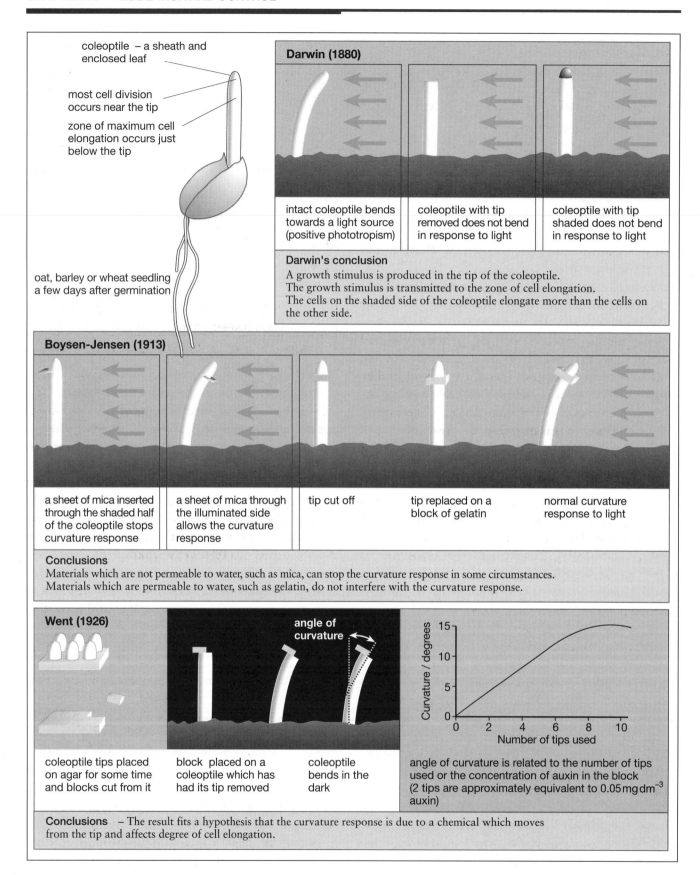

coleoptile – a sheath and
enclosed leaf

most cell division
occurs near the tip

zone of maximum cell
elongation occurs just
below the tip

oat, barley or wheat seedling
a few days after germination

Darwin (1880)

| intact coleoptile bends towards a light source (positive phototropism) | coleoptile with tip removed does not bend in response to light | coleoptile with tip shaded does not bend in response to light |

Darwin's conclusion
A growth stimulus is produced in the tip of the coleoptile.
The growth stimulus is transmitted to the zone of cell elongation.
The cells on the shaded side of the coleoptile elongate more than the cells on the other side.

Boysen-Jensen (1913)

| a sheet of mica inserted through the shaded half of the coleoptile stops curvature response | a sheet of mica through the illuminated side allows the curvature response | tip cut off | tip replaced on a block of gelatin | normal curvature response to light |

Conclusions
Materials which are not permeable to water, such as mica, can stop the curvature response in some circumstances.
Materials which are permeable to water, such as gelatin, do not interfere with the curvature response.

Went (1926)

angle of curvature

| coleoptile tips placed on agar for some time and blocks cut from it | block placed on a coleoptile which has had its tip removed | coleoptile bends in the dark | angle of curvature is related to the number of tips used or the concentration of auxin in the block (2 tips are approximately equivalent to 0.05 mg dm^{-3} auxin) |

Curvature / degrees

Number of tips used

Conclusions – The result fits a hypothesis that the curvature response is due to a chemical which moves from the tip and affects degree of cell elongation.

Fig. 15.21 Some early experiments on phototropism using oat coleoptiles.

It is now known that the chemical involved was IAA, and IAA has since been discovered in many other plants. IAA is synthesised in parts of the plant where cells are dividing rapidly, especially the dividing regions near the tips of stems – the **apical meristems**. IAA is transported within the plant in one of two ways. The first way is by an active process using ATP, in which the IAA is moved in a particular direction from cell to cell (for example from the tip of a shoot downwards). The second way is in the phloem sap, which simply carries the auxin in whichever direction the phloem sap is travelling.

In stems, auxin causes cells to elongate. The degree of elongation is proportional to the concentration of auxin, up to an optimum above which auxin actually inhibits growth (Fig. 15.22). This fact can be used to estimate the concentration of auxin in an unknown sample. The sample can be placed on one side of a decapitated coleoptile, and the degree of curvature measured and compared with the degree of curvature produced by samples of known concentration. This is called a **bioassay**.

How is auxin involved in phototropism? There is still no clear answer to this question, and research is still continuing to test several different hypotheses. One of these hypotheses suggests that light from one side somehow causes auxin to be transported from the bright side of a shoot to the shady side; this increases the rate of cell elongation on the shady side, and so produces curved growth. The evidence for this hypothesis in the shoots of cereal grains is strong, but it seems that other mechanisms may occur in other kinds of plants.

● **Other effects of auxins**

Auxin appears to have many effects in plants, besides stimulating cell elongation. For example, auxin is responsible for **apical dominance**. In the shoots of many plants, side shoots do not grow if the main shoot is growing. If the bud at the tip of the main shoot, called the **apical bud**, is removed, then buds lower down the shoot, called **lateral buds**, burst into life and produce side shoots. Gardeners make use of this fact to keep plants small and bushy; if the apical buds are pinched out, then many side shoots are produced. Experiments suggest that this effect is caused by auxin, which is made in the apical bud and travels down the stem to the lateral buds where it inhibits their growth. Removing the apical bud removes this inhibition. The effect also seems to involve the growth substances **cytokinin** and **abscisic acid**, but the details of the mechanism are still not understood.

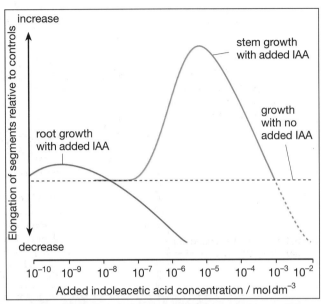

Fig. 15.22   The effect of adding IAA to stem and root segments.

Despite our lack of understanding of just what auxins can do and how they do it, much use is made of them in horticulture. Usually, synthetic auxins are used, because they are much less likely to be broken down by enzymes inside the plant than naturally occurring ones such as IAA. One very widely used synthetic auxin is called **2,4-D**. This is a herbicide (plant-killing substance) which kills broad-leaved plants but not cereals and grasses. It is therefore used as a **selective weedkiller** to kill weeds in cereal crops and on lawns.

Another commercial use of synthetic auxin is to stimulate cuttings to grow roots. It is sold as **rooting hormone**.

15.20 Gibberellins

Gibberellins are plant growth substances which promote stem elongation and seed germination. They are synthesised in seeds and probably in cells in most other parts of a plant, especially in young leaves.

If gibberellins are applied to genetically dwarf plants, or to plants at a stage of their growth where many leaves are produced close together on a stem (such as cabbages), the stems rapidly elongate. Some types of cabbages, for example, will grow up to 2 m tall when treated with gibberellins. It is thought that most plants produce gibberellins to regulate the elongation of their stems, but little is known about how gibberellins do this.

The role of gibberellin in the germination of at least

Box 15.9 What and where is the receptor in phototropism?

In any response by a living organism, there must be a receptor which receives information from the environment, and so detects changes in it to which the organism then responds. In phototropism, we would expect this receptor to be a molecule which is affected by light; a change in this molecule would then start off a chain of events resulting in the uneven distribution of auxin described in Section 15.19.

Early experiments on phototropism indicated that it is the tip of coleoptile which detects differences in light intensity. However, it is still not certain exactly what the photoreceptor is. One method of attempting to find out is to expose coleoptiles to light of different wavelengths, and to measure the degree of response to them. In this way, an **action spectrum** can be determined (Fig. 15.23). This action spectrum can then be compared with the **absorption spectrum** of any pigment which it is thought might be the photoreceptor molecule. A close match would support this idea.

The light-absorbing molecules carotene and riboflavin are found in many plant tissues, and both of these pigments have been suspected to be the receptor involved in phototropism. If you compare the action and absorption spectra in Fig. 15.23, you can see that there is a considerable similarity between all three curves. Carotene looks to be a likely candidate, as its absorption spectrum matches the action spectrum for phototropic response very closely in the 400 to 500 nm range. However, you can see that carotene does not absorb much light in the 350 to 400 nm range, yet there is a peak in the action spectrum at 370 nm. Riboflavin, on the other hand, does have a peak round about 370 nm, but does not show the same pattern as the action spectrum at longer wavelengths.

At the moment, it is thought most likely that riboflavin is the photoreceptor. It appears likely that the absorption spectrum in Fig. 15.23, which is obtained when riboflavin is in solution in water, is probably not the same as its absorption spectrum when it is in a plant cell. In life, riboflavin may be combined with a protein in the cell, or embedded in the cell surface membrane; it is thought likely that this could alter its absortion spectrum in such a way that it would match the action spectrum for phototropism very closely.

As yet, however, no-one understands how the absorption of light by a photoreceptor molecule in the coleoptile tip results in the redistribution of auxin in it, and hence in growth towards the light.

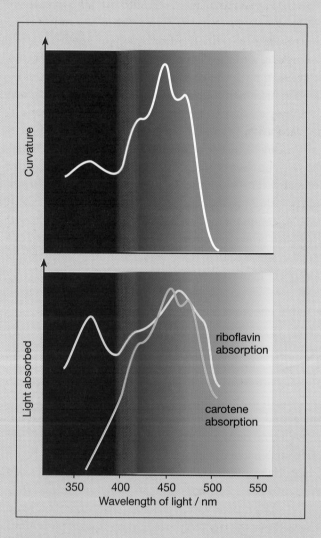

Fig. 15.23 Action spectrum for the phototropic response and absorption spectra for riboflavin and carotene.

Box 15.10 Geotropism

Most plant roots grow downwards, into the soil, where they can absorb water and mineral salts and stabilise the plant. They grow towards the direction from which gravity is acting, and so are said to be **positively geotropic.**

Plant roots perceive the direction from which gravity acts by means of **statoliths** (Fig. 15.24). A statolith is an amyloplast – that is a plastid containing starch grains. Unlike 'ordinary' amyloplasts, such as those that are found in storage tissues like potato tubers and which often contain a single large starch grain, statoliths usually contain several small starch grains. There are also several statoliths in a cell. A cell containing statoliths is called a **statocyte**. Statocytes are found in the root cap. (Many animals have a similar method of gravity detection, but as animals do not store starch they may use other dense materials such as calcium carbonate.)

It is thought that gravity pulls the statoliths to the 'bottom' of the statocytes, that is to the side from which gravity is acting. This somehow sets in motion a chain of events which culminates in the growth of the root towards gravity. If a root is lying on its side, the accumulation of statoliths on the lower surface causes this side to grow more slowly than the upper surface. The root therefore bends downwards (Fig. 15.24).

Very little is known for certain about exactly how this growth response is brought about. One hypothesis suggests that auxin is involved. The auxin in roots is brought down to them from the shoots, where it is made. Quite small concentrations of auxin inhibit the growth of roots (Fig. 15.22), and it is possible that auxin may accumulate on the lower surface of the root, inhibiting its growth compared to the rate of growth of the upper surface. However, this is by no means certain, and we still have a lot to learn about the mechanism by which roots respond to gravity.

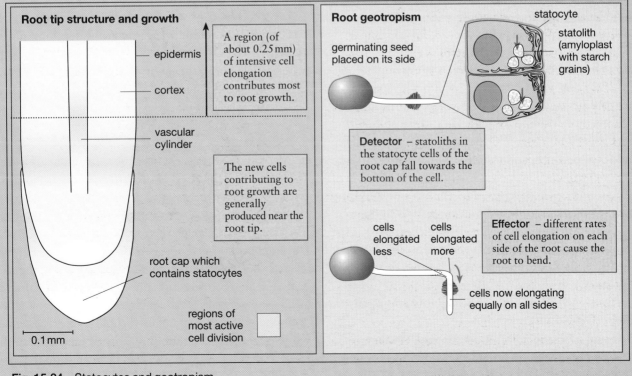

Fig. 15.24 Statocytes and geotropism.

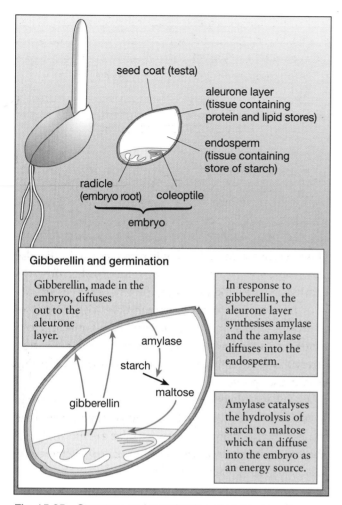

seed coat (testa)

aleurone layer
(tissue containing
protein and lipid stores)

endosperm
(tissue containing
store of starch)

radicle
(embryo root)   coleoptile

embryo

Gibberellin and germination

Gibberellin, made in the
embryo, diffuses
out to the
aleurone
layer.

In response to
gibberellin, the
aleurone layer
synthesises amylase
and the amylase
diffuses into the
endosperm.

amylase

starch

maltose

gibberellin

Amylase catalyses
the hydrolysis of
starch to maltose
which can diffuse
into the embryo as
an energy source.

Fig. 15.25 Structure and germination of a barley seed.

some types of seeds, such as barley, is better understood.
Fig. 15.25 shows the structure of a barley seed. The
embryo is surrounded by food stores, mostly in the form
of starch. Starch is a polysaccharide and is insoluble and
metabolically inactive. In order to be transported to the
cells of the embyro, and to be used by them, it must be
converted to maltose which is soluble. The conversion of
starch to maltose is catalysed by the enzyme **amylase**,
which is secreted by cells in the **aleurone layer** of the seed.
The amylase is produced when gibberellin arrives at the
aleurone layer, having been secreted by the embryo.
Gibberellin activates the gene which codes for amylase
production.

15.21   Cytokinins

Cytokinins have a chemical structure similar to that of the
base adenine. Cytokinins promote cell division. Normally,
most cells in an adult plant do not divide, but if such cells
are placed on nutrient agar jelly to which cytokinin has

been added, they may divide repeatedly to produce a
'lump' of cells called a **callus**. Cytokinin is therefore useful
in plant tissue culture.

In a normal plant, cytokinin levels are highest in young
growing organs, such as young fruits and young leaves,
and also in root tips. However, this does not necessarily
mean that this is where cytokinins are actually synthesised.
No-one is yet certain, but one hypothesis suggests that
cytokinins are synthesised in root tips and transported to
all parts of the plant in the xylem. They then tend to
accumulate in rapidly growing regions.

Cytokinins seem to be able to keep leaves 'young' and
stop them aging and dying – that is they delay
senescence. They appear to cause transport of nutrients
to the leaf, ensuring that the leaf is a 'sink' for phloem
transport.

15.22   Abscisic acid

Abscisic acid, or **ABA**, often acts as an inhibitory plant
growth substance. It appears to have several roles, of
which the best known are in seed development and
germination, and in reducing water loss from leaves.
Abscisic acid gets its name from its supposed role in leaf
abscission, the dropping of leaves from deciduous trees,
but it is now known that it influences this in only a very
few species.

A seed develops from a fertilised ovule. After
fertilisation, the zygote within the ovule develops into an
embryo by repeated divisions of its cells. At the same time
other cells around the embryo divide to produce food
stores. Eventually the seed becomes mature and ready to
be shed from the parent plant. The mature seed has a very
low water content and is metabolically inactive. It is said
to be **dormant**.

These various stages in the development of a seed
appear to be regulated by varying concentrations of
hormones. In the early stages, cytokinin levels are high as
the cells rapidly divide to form the embryo. Cytokinin
levels then decline, and levels of gibberellin and auxin rise.
During these stages there is no abscisic acid present, but
its levels begin to rise as the embryo matures and the seed
dries out and becomes dormant. The presence of abscisic
acid in some species is thought to prevent the germination
of the seeds, that is to maintain their dormancy. However,
while it is often true that applying abscisic acid to the
seeds of many species stops them from germinating, it is
much less clear what actually happens in normal intact
seeds. As in many other situations, it looks as though

interactions between many hormones may be involved, and that these interactions and their effects are not the same in every species of plant.

A quite different role of abscisic acid is in helping a plant to survive stress. If a plant is subjected to difficult conditions, such as drought or very low temperatures, the levels of abscisic acid in its tissues increase. One rapid response to these raised abscisic acid concentrations is stomatal closure. This is described in Section 12.18. Over a longer term, abscisic acid is involved in the process called 'cold-hardening', in which plants exposed to low temperatures become adapted to cold conditions and better able to withstand freezing. Exactly how it does this is not known, but it is possible that abscisic acid stimulates the production of proteins which somehow protect the plant cells from damage.

15.23 Ethene

Ethene is a very simple molecule, with the formula C_2H_4. It is a gas and can easily diffuse from one part of a plant to another, and also from one plant to another, through the air. Ethene shares some characteristics with abscisic acid – for example it is synthesised in plant tissues which are subjected to stress.

Ethene seems to affect almost every aspect of plant growth and development which has so far been investigated. Its best known effect is the stimulation of fruit ripening. Ripening fruits produce ethene, which stimulates the ripening of other fruits nearby. Bananas, which are picked and transported in an unripe state, can be stimulated to begin the ripening process just before they go on sale by exposing them to ethene.

15.24 Phytochrome

Phytochrome is a protein found in all green plants so far investigated. Many responses of plants to red and far-red light suggested that such a pigment should exist, but it was many years before it was actually isolated and purified, which was first achieved in 1964. It was difficult to do this because phytochrome is present in plant tissues in only very low concentrations.

Phytochrome is not a plant growth substance; it is a photoreceptor pigment. It is a small protein. It exists in two interconvertible forms. Phytochrome is made in a plant cell in a form called P_r. The letter 'r' stands for 'red', and this form of phytochrome absorbs mostly red light – that is light with a wavelength of about 666 nm. It is therefore a blue pigment. (However, its concentration in

tissues is much too small to make them look blue.) When P_r absorbs red light, it changes to a different blue-green form called P_{fr}. When P_{fr} absorbs far-red light, with a wavelength of about 730 nm, it changes back to P_r.

$$P_r \; \underset{\text{far-red light}}{\overset{\text{red light}}{\rightleftharpoons}} \; P_{fr}$$

White light, such as sunlight, contains both red and far-red light, but because of the balance between the rates at which P_r and P_{fr} are interconverted, a plant tissue irradiated with white light contains more P_{fr} than P_r. However, in the dark, P_{fr} slowly reconverts to P_r. P_{fr} also slowly disappears because it is gradually broken down by enzymes. In the dark, therefore, there is more P_r than P_{fr}.

P_{fr} is the 'active' form of phytochrome. The presence of P_{fr} in a tissue stimulates some events and inhibits others. It is not yet understood how P_{fr} does this, but it may be by affecting membrane permeability, and/or by affecting gene transcription.

We will look at two events in the life cycle of a plant in which phytochrome is involved, seed germination and the initiation of flowering. Both of these are examples of **photomorphogenesis,** which is the control of structural development in response to light.

● Seed germination

When seeds are released from the parent plant, they are often not ready to germinate. They are said to be **dormant**. Before a seed will germinate a number of conditions must be satisfied. Moisture and oxygen must be present, as well as a suitable temperature. Most seeds also require light. You may be rather surprised by this, as most of the seeds used in laboratory experiments do *not* need light for germination! However, these tend to be seeds from crop plants, and they are not typical of the vast majority of wild plants.

In light-sensitive seeds, such as lettuces, sunlight increases the amount of P_{fr} in the seed, and this stimulates germination. In most seeds, it appears that P_r cannot be converted to P_{fr} until there is plenty of water in the seed, so a dry seed will not germinate even if it is exposed to sunlight.

If a light-sensitive seed is provided with water and the appropriate temperature, and red light is shone onto it, it will germinate. If, however, it is given a flash of far-red light after illumination with red light, it will not germinate.

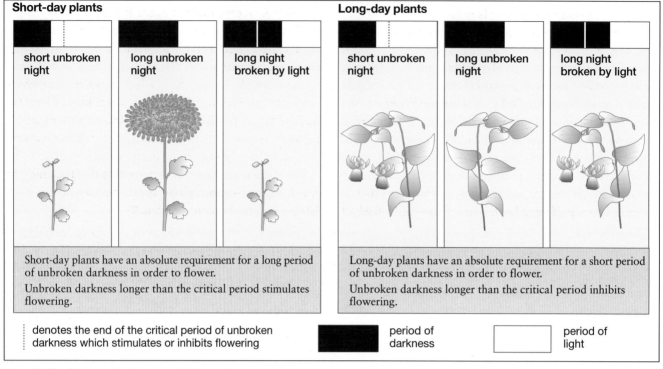

Short-day plants

short unbroken night	long unbroken night	long night broken by light

Short-day plants have an absolute requirement for a long period of unbroken darkness in order to flower.

Unbroken darkness longer than the critical period stimulates flowering.

Long-day plants

short unbroken night	long unbroken night	long night broken by light

Long-day plants have an absolute requirement for a short period of unbroken darkness in order to flower.

Unbroken darkness longer than the critical period inhibits flowering.

⋮ denotes the end of the critical period of unbroken darkness which stimulates or inhibits flowering

█ period of darkness

☐ period of light

Fig. 15.26 Photoperiodic control of flowering.

This is because the far-red light converts the P_{fr} back to P_r. Without P_{fr}, germination will not occur.

What advantages are there in seeds requiring light, especially red light, for germination?

- Light-sensitive seeds are usually small. It makes sense for them to require light before they will germinate as this indicates that they are very near to the surface of the soil. If they germinated while deep in the ground, they might not reach the surface and be able to photosynthesise before they had used up all their food reserves.
- The requirement for light may spread germination of a population of seeds over many years, rather than them all germinating at once. Each year, only a fraction of them may be disturbed and exposed to light. This helps to minimise competition between the plants, and also ensures that some plants survive even if there is a disastrous year in which the adult plants cannot set seed.
- Seeds lying on the ground in dense woodland will not germinate until a tree has fallen, or a fire has destroyed the vegetation above them. This is useful as the shade created by a dense canopy of leaves could prevent the plant from growing successfully. Leaves allow more far-red light than red light to pass through them. Therefore a seed lying on the ground beneath other

leaves will receive more far-red light than red light, which will favour the conversion of P_{fr} to P_r; this will not stimulate germination. When a tree falls, the white light converts P_r to P_{fr}, and the seed germinates.

● **Photoperiodic control of flowering**

Photoperiodism is a response by an organism to changes in day length. Animals may respond to day length by hibernating, growing different coats for summer and winter, or by their reproductive behaviour. Plants may respond to day length by their growth pattern, including flowering.

Many plants only flower at certain times of year. Flowering involves complex changes in the patterns of development at the tips of shoots to form flower buds. In some plants, called **long-day plants**, flower buds are only formed when the day length exceeds a certain value, called the **critical value**, within each 24-hour period. These plants tend to flower in spring and summer. In others, called **short-day plants**, flowering only occurs when the day length is less than a critical value. These plants tend to flower in autumn. The critical value varies from species to species. Examples of long-day plants include spring barley, wheat and spinach, while tobacco, soy beans and autumn-flowering chrysanthemums are short-day plants.

Experiments show that it is actually the length of uninterrupted darkness which determines whether or not a plant will flower. A short-day plant requires a long uninterrupted night (Fig. 15.26). For example, if a brief flash of red light is given to a short-day plant during a night which is long enough to induce flowering, the plant will not flower. If, however, the flash of red light is followed by a flash of far-red light, then the plant will flower.

This happens because P_{fr} inhibits flowering in short-day plants. The long dark nights required by short-day plants allow the concentration of P_{fr} to fall low enough for its inhibitory effect to be removed. However, a flash of red light during the night converts P_r to P_{fr}, so flowering is inhibited. A subsequent flash of far-red light reconverts the P_{fr} to P_r, so the inhibition is once more removed and flowering can take place.

The phytochrome pigments which produce these effects are in the leaves of the plant. It is still not known how the information is passed from these photoreceptor pigments in the leaves, to the growing points, where flower buds are produced in response to the disappearance of P_{fr}. Some experiments indicate that a growth substance may be involved, and – although it has not yet been detected – it has been given the name **florigen**. ■

Q6 In an investigation into photoperiodism, groups of plants of the same species were exposed to cycles made up of varying dark periods alternating with a light period of either 4 or 16 hours. The mean number of flowers produced by each group of plants is shown in the graph below.

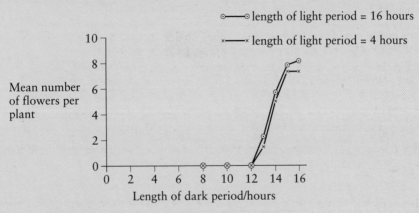

(a) (i) Which of the following terms best identifies this species? *(1)*
     short-day   long-day   day-neutral

    (ii) Give evidence from the graph to support your answer. *(2)*

(b) Describe how you would show that the flowering stimulus is detected by the leaves and not by the stem apex where the flowers are produced. *(3)*

AEB 1993   *(Total 6 marks)*

Q7 The soil in many tropical rain forests is very poor in nutrients such as nitrate and calcium ions. In some rain forests there are herbaceous plants which, as well as having roots in the soil, have some roots that grow upwards over the surface of tree trunks.

(a) Give **two** external features by which you could distinguish a stem of one of these plants from an upward-growing root. *(2)*

(b) (i) Give **two** stimuli to which these upward growing roots might be responding. *(1)*

    (ii) What type of behavioural response are these roots displaying? *(1)*

    (iii) Explain how this behavioural response might be an advantage to the plant in nutrient-poor soil. *(1)*

AEB 1993   *(Total 5 marks)*

Q8 The graph below shows the rate of glucose reabsorption in, and excretion from a mammalian kidney in relation to the glucose concentration in the plasma.

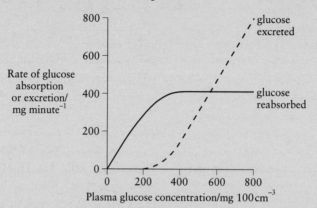

(a) In which part of the nephron is glucose reabsorbed? *(1)*

(b) Explain the shape of the glucose reabsorption curve when the plasma glucose concentration is:
   (i) between 0 and 200 mg 100 cm^{-3} *(1)*
   (ii) over 400 mg 100 cm^{-3} *(1)*

(c) Use the graph to explain why glucose may occur in the urine of diabetics. *(2)*

AEB 1995 *(Total 5 marks)*

Q9 The graph below shows the relation between metabolic rate and body mass in mammals.

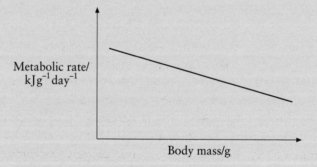

(a) What type of correlation exists between these two variables? *(1)*

(b) Explain why the metabolic rate per gram of body mass is higher in a small mammal such as a mouse than in a large mammal like a horse. *(2)*

(c) Explain the advantages to small mammals of having tissues with a larger number of mitochondria per gram of body mass than tissues of larger mammals. *(2)*

AEB 1993 *(Total 5 marks)*

16 Support and movement

Large organisms require support, especially if they live on land rather than in water. Supporting structures are known as skeletons. Movement in plants is limited, but many animals can move actively, using highly specialised cells which form muscles. Skeletons can provide firm anchors against which these muscles can act, and can transmit forces produced by the muscles from one part of the body to another.

16.1 Support and movement in different organisms

The body of any living organism must be supported in some way, so that it does not collapse and can remain in shape. Aquatic organisms are partially supported by the water in which they live, as water provides buoyancy, but terrestrial organisms must provide all their own supporting mechanisms. The majority of terrestrial organisms possess tissues which are specialised to provide such support.

In animals, supporting tissues are often organised into a structure called a **skeleton**. The skeleton often has another role to play, which is to provide a firm, resistant structure against which **muscles** can act, producing **movement**. Most animals are able to move their whole bodies from place to place, a process called **locomotion**. Movement also occurs within an animal's body. For example, muscles in the heart propel blood around the body, while muscles in the walls of the alimentary canal move food along it. Movement can also be produced by cilia (Section 3.13).

Plants do not undergo locomotion. They therefore do not possess such elaborate skeletons as are found in many types of animals. Plants do, however, make growth movements called **tropisms** (Section 15.19), in which the direction of the growth is related to the direction of the stimulus. Parts of a plant can also make movements called **nastic movements,** in which the direction of the movement has no relation to the direction of the stimulus. The opening and closing of stomata (Section 12.17) is an example of a nastic movement. Nastic movements usually rely on changes in turgidity (Fig. 3.31) of cells and, as you will see, turgor plays an important role in plant support.

SUPPORT IN PLANTS

16.2 Types of cells providing support

Parenchyma cells (Fig. 16.1) form the 'background' tissue in most parts of a plant, including the cortex of stems and roots and in the mesophyll of leaves. They are also found scattered amongst xylem vessels and phloem sieve tubes in the vascular bundles. Parenchyma cells usually have a relatively thin primary cellulose wall, with little if any extra secondary thickening. They carry out many activities; for example, those in the leaf are specialised for photosynthesis (palisade cells are parenchyma cells), while those in roots may be specialised for starch storage.

Parenchyma cells also play an important role in support. When the cytoplasm contains plenty of water, it pushes out on the cell wall. Such a cell is said to be **turgid**. (Turgor is described in relation to water potential in Fig. 3.31.) A group of turgid cells provides a firm supporting tissue. If, however, water is lost from the cytoplasm of the parenchyma cells, the cytoplasm stops pushing outwards on the cell wall and the cells become **flaccid**. The tissue loses its rigidity and the plant **wilts**.

Other cells are more specialised to provide support than parenchyma. **Collenchyma** cells are very like parenchyma cells, but their cellulose cell walls are thicker; often, the thickening is concentrated at the corners. These thickened cell walls provide mechanical support, yet remain slightly flexible and fully permeable to water and other substances. The cells are alive, and often possess chloroplasts and can photosynthesise. Collenchyma is found in the cortex of stems, in petioles (leaf stalks) and in leaves.

Sclerenchyma cells are different in that they have thickened secondary cell walls which contain **lignin**. These cells have no living contents. Sclerenchyma cells may be shaped like roughly regular polygons, or show various degrees of elongation. The less elongated ones are called **sclereids** or **stone cells**; long, narrow, hollow sclerenchyma cells are called **fibres**. Sclereids are fairly randomly distributed in a plant (you may have bitten into some in a pear fruit – they are very hard), and also make

Parenchyma

These cells provide support in the mesophyll of leaves and cortex of non-woody stems when they are well supplied with water and are turgid.

The cells tend not to be very elongated. They usually have a thin primary wall of cellulose and an active cytoplasm.
The cells can be loosely packed forming intercellular spaces.

thin primary cell wall made of cellulose

intercellular space

active cytoplasm

vacuole

Collenchyma

These cells provide support by having a thickened cellulose wall, which makes them strong. Cellulose walls have high tensile strength, resisting bending and stretching, but can 'give' slightly which helps to support areas where the cells are actively growing.

LS   TS

thick primary cell wall made of cellulose

These are cells which are specialised for support and are greatly elongated. They have a primary wall of cellulose which is thickened to a variable extent enclosing a living cytoplasm. The cells tend to be closely packed with few intercellular spaces.

Sclerenchyma and supporting cells in xylem

These cells provide support by having thick lignified walls, which are strong and slightly elastic. Sclerenchyma and xylem fibres, xylem vessels and tracheids resist forces of stretching and bending (tensile strength) and forces of compression.

Sclereids can form a tough protective layer, for example in a seed's coat (testa). They are also found singly or in small groups in other tissues.

In xylem vessels the secondary wall can be laid down in rings, spirals (quite elastic) or in nearly complete layers (less elastic).

Sclerenchyma

Fibre LS

Fibre TS

Sclereids

thick lignified secondary wall

Sclerenchyma cells are specialised for support and are often elongated. The less elongated cells are sclereids and more elongated ones are fibres. They have very thick walls with secondary layers of lignin and have no cytoplasm.

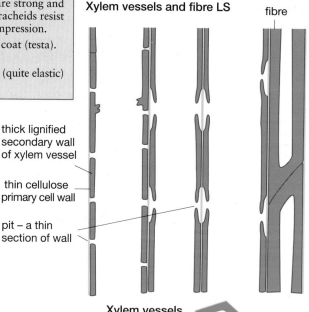

Xylem vessels and fibre LS

fibre

thick lignified secondary wall of xylem vessel

thin cellulose primary cell wall

pit – a thin section of wall

Xylem vessels have thick lignified walls and are specialised for transport and support. They are all greatly elongated and have no cytoplasm.

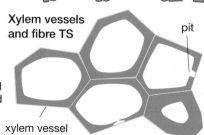

Xylem vessels and fibre TS

pit

xylem vessel

Fig. 16.1 Supporting tissues in plants.

up the hard testa of seeds such as peas and beans. Fibres are often associated with the vascular bundles in all parts of a plant. Linen threads are groups of sclerenchyma fibres.

Xylem vessels also provide considerable support because they have lignified secondary cell walls (Section 11.2 and Fig. 16.1).

16.3 Positions of supporting tissues in plant stems and roots

All parts of plants contain supporting tissues, but the greatest concentration of tissues providing the most support – the lignified sclerenchyma and xylem vessels – occurs in particular areas in the roots, stems and leaves.

Xylem and sclerenchyma are found in the centre of a root (Fig. 16.2). The forces which roots normally have to withstand result from grazing animals pulling on the shoots of the plant, or from wind acting against the shoots, buffeting them sideways. Both of these produce a 'pulling' force or **tension** on the roots. The central column of lignified tissues is able to withstand these forces very

effectively, without breaking. This arrangement also makes roots flexible.

In young stems of many herbaceous (non-woody) plants, the lignified tissues are arranged in a circle towards the outer edge (Fig. 16.2). This enables the stem to resist **bending** forces, such as are produced by wind.

Trees and shrubs develop large amounts of xylem in their trunk and roots. Each year, a new ring of xylem is added and serves for one or two years in water and ion transport. After that its only function is to provide support.

Leaves, like stems, are exposed to the wind, and they may also be battered by raindrops. The main function of most leaves is photosynthesis, and they have a broad, thin, flat shape which maximises the amount of sunlight they can intercept. The supporting tissues in leaves are mostly associated with the vascular bundles ('veins') which branch throughout the leaf. This branching network helps to hold the leaf out flat and also to resist breaking and tearing.

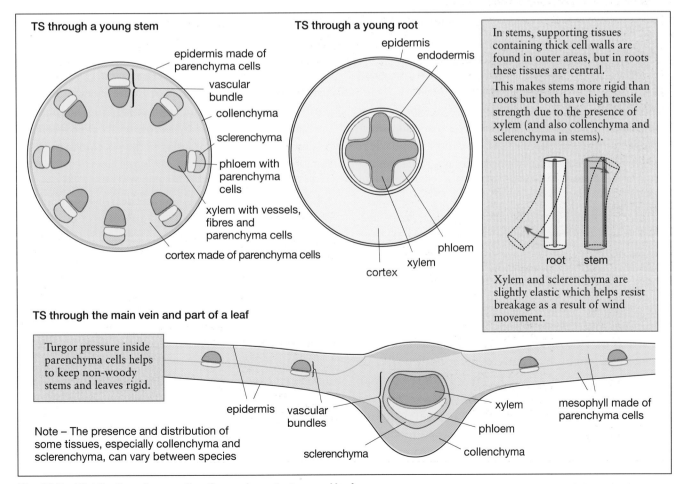

Fig. 16.2 Distribution of supporting tissues in root, stem and leaf.

SKELETONS IN ANIMALS

16.4   Types of skeletons

The word 'skeleton' probably conjures up a picture of human bones. But the term has a wider meaning than this. A skeleton can be defined as a structure which provides support and shape to an organism, and which allows forces to be transmitted from one part to another. Thus, plants as well as animals can be considered to have skeletons. In this section we will look only at animal skeletons.

An animal's skeleton may be an **endoskeleton** or an **exoskeleton**. An endoskeleton is inside the body, while an exoskeleton is on the outside forming an outer covering. The human skeleton is an endoskeleton, while that of an insect is an exoskeleton.

Endoskeletons may be composed of bone or cartilage or they may just consist of a fluid-filled compartment within the body. This is called a **hydrostatic skeleton**. Many nonvertebrates, such as sea anemones and earthworms, have hydrostatic skeletons. These do have one disadvantage compared to other types of skeleton – because they are not made of hard substances, they are not able to provide protection to vulnerable parts of the body which is an important role of many hard skeletons.

16.5   Muscles and skeletons

Muscles are tissues specialised to produce movement. They contain two proteins called **actin** and **myosin**, which can slide between each other and so cause the muscle to shorten or **contract**. Muscles can do this with considerable force, using energy from the hydrolysis of ATP (Section 16.11).

However, muscles are not able to lengthen themselves again; they have to be 'pulled' back to their original shape. For this reason, muscles are often (but by no means always) found in pairs, arranged so that the contraction of one produces a force which pulls on the other and causes it to lengthen. Such muscles are said to be **antagonistic**. The biceps and triceps muscles, attached to the bones in the arm (Fig. 16.5) are an antagonistic pair. So are the circular and longitudinal muscles in the body wall of an earthworm (Fig. 16.3) and in the wall of the human alimentary canal (Figs. 13.3 and 13.4).

Muscles must have some firm structure to act against if they are to produce movement. This structure must be able to transmit the forces generated by the muscles to other parts of the body. Solids are able to transmit forces, and so are liquids under compression. Thus, either a solid material such as bone or a pressurised liquid in a hydrostatic skeleton can serve as a skeleton against which muscles can act.

In the Sections 16.6 to 16.8 which follow, we will look at the way in which three different types of skeleton provide a means of transmitting forces generated by muscles. Sections 16.9 to 16.12 describe the detailed structure of muscles and explain how they produce movement.

16.6   The hydrostatic skeleton of an earthworm

Fig. 16.3 shows the internal structure of an earthworm. Earthworms belong to the phylum Annelida. They have a **coelom**, which is a fluid-filled cavity lying between two body layers called **mesoderm**. (You can read more about the general structure of annelids, and about mesoderm, in Sections 22.16 and 22.12.) The outer layer of mesoderm, in the body wall, contains muscles. **Circular muscles** have fibres running round the body, while **longitudinal muscles** are arranged in blocks with their fibres running along the length of the body. The circular muscles are nearer to the outside of the earthworm, and the longitudinal muscles lie inside them.

The skeleton of an earthworm is the fluid inside its coelom. Earthworms are **metamerically segmented** animals. This means that their bodies are made up of many similar, repeating segments. Each segment is separated from the next by a cross wall called a **septum** (plural **septa**). The septa divide the coelom into many compartments.

When the circular muscles around a group of segments contract, they shorten and therefore decrease the diameter of those segments. The fluid inside the coelom is incompressible, so it cannot be squeezed into a smaller volume. As the volume of the fluid in each segment remains the same, the segment must become longer. So, the incompressibility of the coelomic fluid causes it to transmit the force produced by the circular muscles to the other tissues around the coelom. Contraction of the circular muscles therefore makes the earthworm's body longer and thinner.

When the longitudinal muscles contract, they shorten the body. The incompressibility of the coelomic fluid causes the segments to widen, so the earthworm's body becomes shorter and fatter.

The circular and longitudinal muscles are antagonistic. Contraction of the circular muscles lengthens the segments, and the force they produce is transmitted by the

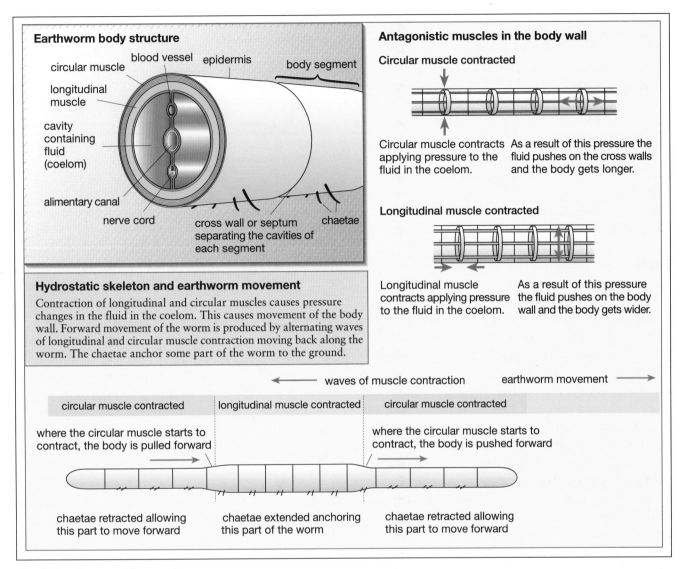

Earthworm body structure

circular muscle
blood vessel
epidermis
body segment
longitudinal muscle
cavity containing fluid (coelom)
alimentary canal
nerve cord
cross wall or septum separating the cavities of each segment
chaetae

Antagonistic muscles in the body wall

Circular muscle contracted

Circular muscle contracts applying pressure to the fluid in the coelom.

As a result of this pressure the fluid pushes on the cross walls and the body gets longer.

Longitudinal muscle contracted

Longitudinal muscle contracts applying pressure to the fluid in the coelom.

As a result of this pressure the fluid pushes on the body wall and the body gets wider.

Hydrostatic skeleton and earthworm movement

Contraction of longitudinal and circular muscles causes pressure changes in the fluid in the coelom. This causes movement of the body wall. Forward movement of the worm is produced by alternating waves of longitudinal and circular muscle contraction moving back along the worm. The chaetae anchor some part of the worm to the ground.

waves of muscle contraction ← earthworm movement →

circular muscle contracted | longitudinal muscle contracted | circular muscle contracted

where the circular muscle starts to contract, the body is pulled forward

where the circular muscle starts to contract, the body is pushed forward

chaetae retracted allowing this part to move forward

chaetae extended anchoring this part of the worm

chaetae retracted allowing this part to move forward

Fig. 16.3 Movement in an earthworm.

coelomic fluid so that a pulling force is exerted on the longitudinal muscles. Contraction of the longitudinal muscles similarly produces a pulling force on the circular muscles.

Fig. 16.3 shows how the earthworm uses alternate contractions of the circular and longitudinal muscles in different parts of its body, to produce movement. The contractions occur in waves along the body, beginning at the front and working backwards. If this were all that happened, the worm would just get wider and narrower on the spot. However, the worm also uses tiny stiff bristles, called **chaetae**, to anchor parts of its body to the ground. This allows other parts to be pulled towards, or pushed away from, these stationary areas.

16.7 The endoskeleton of a mammal

Mammals have skeletons made of two hard tissues, **bone** and **cartilage**.

Bone is a living tissue. It contains living cells called **osteocytes** surrounded by a **matrix** which they have secreted. This matrix makes up the major part of bone (Fig. 16.4). The matrix contains tiny crystals of an inorganic mineral similar to **hydroxyapatite** (a form of calcium phosphate which has the formula $Ca_5(PO_4)_3OH$) and fibres of the fibrous protein **collagen**. The osteocytes remain alive, and so require supplies of oxygen and nutrients which are brought to them by blood vessels. The calcium phosphate gives bone great strength to resist compressive forces, enabling it to provide support. Many bones have approximately four times the compressive strength of concrete. The collagen fibres provide elasticity.

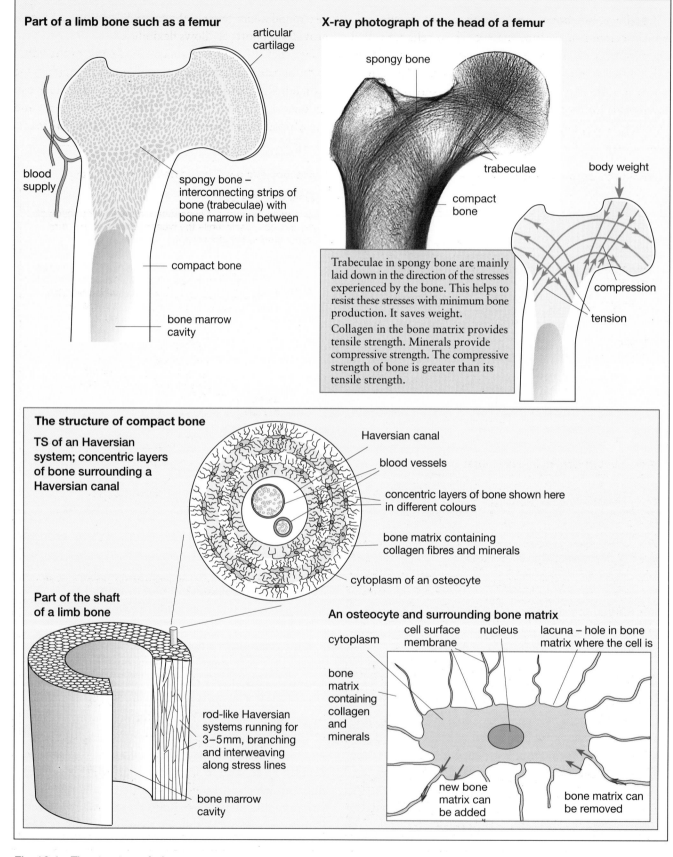

Part of a limb bone such as a femur

articular cartilage

blood supply

spongy bone – interconnecting strips of bone (trabeculae) with bone marrow in between

compact bone

bone marrow cavity

X-ray photograph of the head of a femur

spongy bone

trabeculae

compact bone

body weight

compression

tension

Trabeculae in spongy bone are mainly laid down in the direction of the stresses experienced by the bone. This helps to resist these stresses with minimum bone production. It saves weight.

Collagen in the bone matrix provides tensile strength. Minerals provide compressive strength. The compressive strength of bone is greater than its tensile strength.

The structure of compact bone

TS of an Haversian system; concentric layers of bone surrounding a Haversian canal

Haversian canal

blood vessels

concentric layers of bone shown here in different colours

bone matrix containing collagen fibres and minerals

cytoplasm of an osteocyte

Part of the shaft of a limb bone

rod-like Haversian systems running for 3–5 mm, branching and interweaving along stress lines

bone marrow cavity

An osteocyte and surrounding bone matrix

cytoplasm

cell surface membrane

nucleus

lacuna – hole in bone matrix where the cell is

bone matrix containing collagen and minerals

new bone matrix can be added

bone matrix can be removed

Fig. 16.4 The structure of a bone.

Cartilage, like bone, is a living tissue containing cells which secrete a supporting matrix. These cells are called **chondrocytes**. Cartilage does not usually contain calcium salts, and it is more flexible and elastic than bone. In an adult mammal, the ends of the bones at moveable (synovial) joints are covered with cartilage. Because cartilage is very slippery, it reduces friction. Cartilage is also found in the pinna of the ear and in the nose, where it provides support yet allows flexibility.

Fig. 16.5 shows the arrangement of some of the bones in the human arm. The arrangement not only supports the arm, but also provides attachment for muscles which can produce movement. The joint between the humerus and the ulna and radius at the elbow is a **synovial joint**.

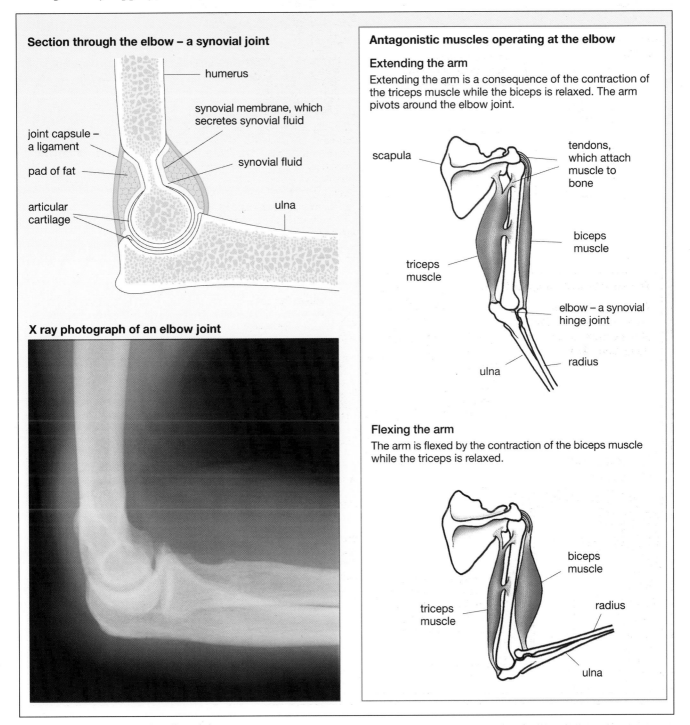

Section through the elbow – a synovial joint

- humerus
- synovial membrane, which secretes synovial fluid
- joint capsule – a ligament
- synovial fluid
- pad of fat
- articular cartilage
- ulna

X ray photograph of an elbow joint

Antagonistic muscles operating at the elbow

Extending the arm

Extending the arm is a consequence of the contraction of the triceps muscle while the biceps is relaxed. The arm pivots around the elbow joint.

- scapula
- tendons, which attach muscle to bone
- biceps muscle
- triceps muscle
- elbow – a synovial hinge joint
- ulna
- radius

Flexing the arm

The arm is flexed by the contraction of the biceps muscle while the triceps is relaxed.

- biceps muscle
- triceps muscle
- radius
- ulna

Fig. 16.5 Movement at the elbow joint.

Synovial joints allow movement between the bones. Friction is reduced by the cartilage on the ends of the bones and also by a very small amount of thick, viscous **synovial fluid** which acts as a lubricant. The bones are held in position by **ligaments**, which are made from the protein collagen. The collagen fibres in ligaments are arranged in layers, and they provide strength while allowing some elasticity.

Muscles are attached to the bones on either side of the joint by means of **tendons**. Tendons, like ligaments, are made of collagen, but in tendons the collagen fibres are arranged in parallel bundles like cables, and tendons are much less stretchy than ligaments. The two main muscles which produce movement at the elbow joint are named according to the number of tendons which attach their upper ends. They are the **biceps** and the **triceps**. Fig. 16.5 shows how this pair of antagonistic muscles produces movement at the joint.

16.8   The exoskeleton of an insect

Insects belong to the class Insecta within the phylum Arthropoda. Like all arthropods, they have a hard covering over their body containing **chitin**. This covering is an **exoskeleton**, and is sometimes known as a **cuticle**. The exoskeleton is secreted by the cells in the epidermis which lies beneath it, but the exoskeleton itself is not alive and cannot grow. All arthropods therefore have to shed their old exoskeleton periodically as they grow – a process known as ecdysis – and grow a new, larger one.

Arthropods, like annelids, have segmented bodies. Unlike annelids they have jointed legs, and most insects have two pairs of wings. Legs and wings are all attached to a part of the body known as the thorax which is made up of three segments. In order to allow free movement, the parts of the skeleton which occur at joints such as those in the legs are thinner and more flexible than elsewhere. Fig. 16.6 shows how the exoskeleton acts as an attachment for muscles, and how these muscles produce flight movements.

As well as providing support to the insect's body and a firm attachment for muscles, an insect's exoskeleton also gives some protection from small predators (although large ones have no difficulty in crunching through it). The exoskeleton is, however, extremely efficient in preventing loss of water from the insect's body surface as it is waterproof. This, together with other ways of reducing water loss, such as the exchange of gases through a tracheal system (Section 12.13) and the excretion of nitrogenous waste as uric acid (Box 15.4), have enabled many insects to be very successful terrestrial animals and able to live in habitats where water is in short supply.

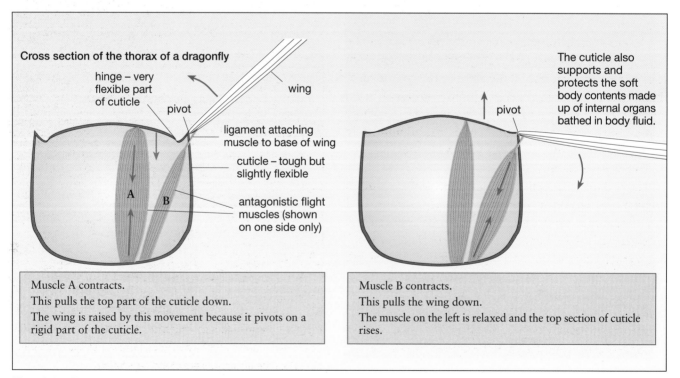

Fig. 16.6   Flight movements in an insect.

HOW MUSCLES PRODUCE MOVEMENT

16.9 The structure of a skeletal muscle cell

Figs. 16.7 and 16.8 show the structure of muscle. This is **skeletal** muscle, the type of muscle which is attached to the bones of the skeleton, and which you use for making voluntary movements such as walking. The biceps and triceps are skeletal muscles. The other types of muscle found in animals are **cardiac muscle** and **smooth muscle**, and these are described in Box 16.1.

Skeletal muscle looks stripey when seen with a light or electron microscope, and so is often known as **striated** (striped) muscle. The stripes are produced by a regular pattern of protein filaments which are lined up to form alternating light and dark bands. It is these proteins, **actin** and **myosin**, which are responsible for the contraction of the muscle.

The cells which make up skeletal muscles are called **muscle fibres**. Each cell, like any other cell, is covered by a cell surface membrane, which is sometimes given the special name **sarcolemma**. This membrane folds deeply into the interior of the cell in places, forming **transverse tubules** or **t-tubules**.

The contents of a muscle fibre are basically similar to the contents of any cell – there is cytoplasm, mitochondria, and endoplasmic reticulum. However, the internal organisation and structure of these components result in a type of cell which looks very different from other cells in the body.

Skeletal muscle fibres are very large cells. They can be up to 80 μm in diameter and many centimetres long. Each cell has many nuclei which lie close to the cell surface. Inside the cell there are several bundles of **myofibrils**, containing actin and myosin, which run along the whole length of the cell. Large numbers of **mitochondria** lie alongside the myofibrils, mostly between them and the cell surface membrane.

The **endoplasmic reticulum** of a muscle fibre is often known as **sarcoplasmic reticulum**. It is very extensive and forms cisternae (Section 3.9) running both around and along the cell. The membranes of some of these cisternae are very closely associated with the infoldings of the cell surface membrane (t-tubules) which, as you will see, are very important in allowing depolarisations to travel through the interior of the muscle fibre. The cisternae contain large amounts of calcium ions which are essential in triggering the contraction of the muscle fibre.

16.10 The structure of a myofibril

It is the myofibrils within a muscle fibre cell which make it look stripey under the microscope. The stripes on each myofibril within a cell are lined up with each other.

A myofibril contains two types of filament. **Thick filaments** are about 15 nm in diameter and are made of a protein called **myosin**. **Thin filaments** are about 7 nm in diameter and are made mostly of the protein **actin**.

One end of each actin filament is anchored to a structure called a **Z disc** (or Z line) which runs right across the myofibril (Fig. 16.8). The part of a myofibril between two Z discs is called a **sarcomere**. The myosin filaments lie in the central region of each sarcomere and are anchored to an **M disc** (or M line). For part of their lengths the actin and myosin filaments lie between each other, and this part of the sarcomere looks dark. The parts made up of actin filaments only, at each end of the sarcomere nearest to the Z discs, look light in colour, while the parts made up of myosin filaments only, at the centre of the sarcomere, are intermediate in colour. Each of these bands has its own name, as shown on Fig. 16.8. When seen end on, the myosin and actin filaments are arranged in a regular hexagonal pattern.

This description is of a myofibril in a resting muscle fibre. What happens when the muscle contracts?

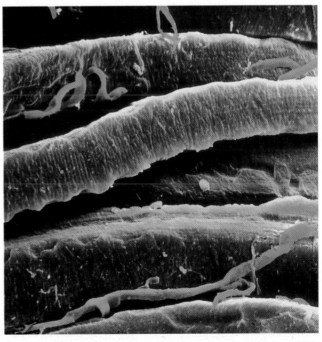

Fig. 16.7 False colour scanning electron micrograph (× 1500) of skeletal muscle fibres (red). Each fibre is a single long, thin cell. The blue structures are blood capillaries.

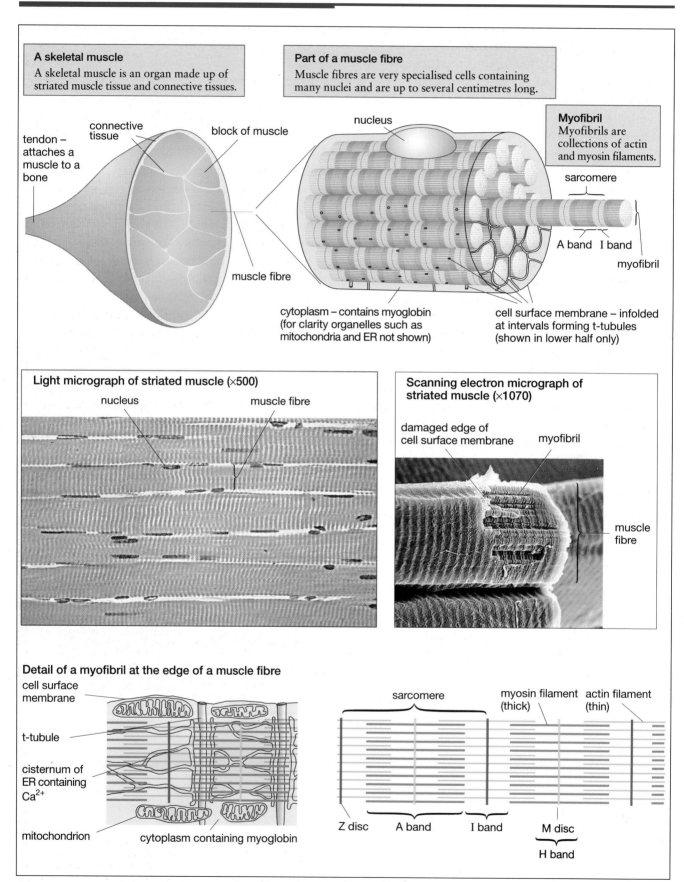

A skeletal muscle
A skeletal muscle is an organ made up of striated muscle tissue and connective tissues.

Part of a muscle fibre
Muscle fibres are very specialised cells containing many nuclei and are up to several centimetres long.

Myofibril
Myofibrils are collections of actin and myosin filaments.

tendon – attaches a muscle to a bone

connective tissue

block of muscle

muscle fibre

nucleus

sarcomere

A band   I band

myofibril

cytoplasm – contains myoglobin (for clarity organelles such as mitochondria and ER not shown)

cell surface membrane – infolded at intervals forming t-tubules (shown in lower half only)

Light micrograph of striated muscle (×500)

nucleus

muscle fibre

Scanning electron micrograph of striated muscle (×1070)

damaged edge of cell surface membrane

myofibril

muscle fibre

Detail of a myofibril at the edge of a muscle fibre

cell surface membrane

t-tubule

cisternum of ER containing Ca²⁺

mitochondrion

cytoplasm containing myoglobin

sarcomere

myosin filament (thick)

actin filament (thin)

Z disc   A band   I band   M disc

H band

Fig. 16.8   The structure of striated muscle.

Box 16.1 Cardiac and smooth muscle

These two types of muscle are responsible for internal movement in animals.

Cardiac muscle is found only in the heart. Like skeletal muscle it is striated, each cell containing fibrils made up of sarcomeres. The mechanism of contraction is very similar to that of skeletal muscle which is described in Sections 16.11 and 16.12.

However, cardiac muscle differs from skeletal muscle in several ways. The cells, or fibres, are smaller, each one being about 80 μm long and 15 μm in diameter. Each cell has one nucleus. These cells branch and form connections with adjacent cells. Thick structures which are continuous with the cell surface membranes (sarcolemmas), called **intercalated discs**, separate the end of each fibre from its neighbour (Fig. 16.9). These discs include specialised cell junctions called gap junctions. Tiny channels through these gap junctions connect the cells and allow the wave of depolarisation to sweep rapidly along through the wall of the heart (Section 10.5).

Cardiac muscle has more mitochondria than skeletal muscle. Most skeletal muscles do not have to contract for long periods of time and, in any case, they can if necessary respire anaerobically. Cardiac muscle must have a continuous supply of oxygen, and can only perform its repetitive, regular contractions if it respires aerobically.

Smooth muscle is rather different in structure from both skeletal and cardiac muscle. It does not look striped under the microscope, and so is sometimes called **non-striated** muscle. It is made up of individual cells each with their own nucleus. The cells are quite long and thin (about 400 μm long and 5 μm wide) and lie parallel to each other. Smooth muscle is found in many places in the body, including the walls of the alimentary canal, blood vessels and the uterus. It is not under voluntary control.

Smooth muscle cells contract more slowly and steadily than either skeletal or cardiac muscle. As in other types of muscle, the contraction is caused by the sliding of myosin and actin filaments, but these are not arranged to form myofibrils or sarcomeres. Contraction is initiated by action potentials arriving along neurones of the autonomic nervous system (Section 14.5), and may be affected by the action of hormones such as adrenaline and oxytocin.

Light micrograph of cardiac muscle (×500)

Cardiac muscle

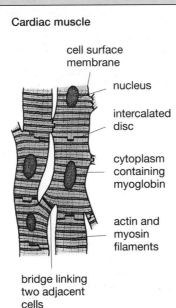

cell surface membrane

nucleus

intercalated disc

cytoplasm containing myoglobin

actin and myosin filaments

bridge linking two adjacent cells

Light micrograph of smooth muscle (×640)

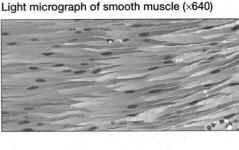

Smooth muscle

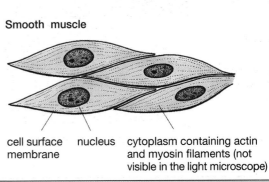

cell surface membrane

nucleus

cytoplasm containing actin and myosin filaments (not visible in the light microscope)

Fig. 16.9 Cardiac and smooth muscle.

16.11 Sliding filaments and muscle contraction

Muscles contract as the actin and myosin filaments slide between each other, shortening each sarcomere in a muscle fibre.

Figs. 16.10 and 16.11 show how this happens. In effect, the myosin molecules 'walk' along the actin filaments.

Each myosin filament is made up of many myosin molecules, each of which has a head which acts as an enzyme which can hydrolyse ATP – in other words **ATP synthase**. In a resting muscle, each myosin head has ADP and inorganic phosphate, P_i, bound to it. When an action potential arrives, the myosin head binds to the actin filament lying next to it, and then tilts by about 45°. As the myosin head tilts, it pushes the actin filament along by a distance of around 10 nm. The ADP and P_i leave the myosin heads while this is happening.

ATP then binds to the myosin heads while they are still attached to the actin filaments. The ATP synthase in the heads hydrolyses the ATP, converting it to ADP and P_i and releasing energy which is used to detach the heads from the actin filaments, and also to return them to their original angle. The ADP and P_i remain attached to the head, which is now ready to do the same thing all over again.

Although each myosin molecule can only produce a tiny force when its head tilts and pulls itself along an actin molecule, if there are millions of such actions going on inside a muscle fibre then the forces can add up to be very large indeed.

The cycle of the myosin heads attaching, tilting, detaching and straightening can be repeated about 5 times per second. Each time it happens the actin filaments are pulled about 10 nm towards the centre of the sarcomere, so the Z discs are brought closer together.

When action potentials stop arriving, the cycle stops. The myosin heads stay in their resting position, not attached to the actin filaments. The muscle will stay in its shortened state unless something pulls it out again. This could be done, for example, by the muscle's own weight, or by another muscle contracting. Myosin can only 'walk' one way along actin filaments, so muscles can only produce force when they shorten.

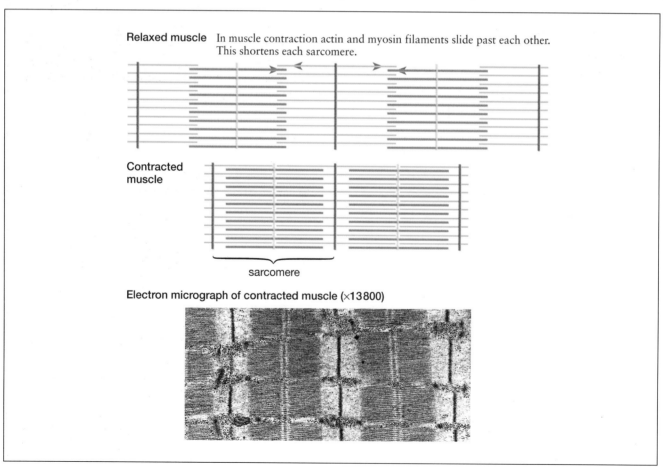

Relaxed muscle In muscle contraction actin and myosin filaments slide past each other. This shortens each sarcomere.

Contracted muscle

sarcomere

Electron micrograph of contracted muscle (×13800)

Fig. 16.10 The sliding filament mechanism of muscle contraction.

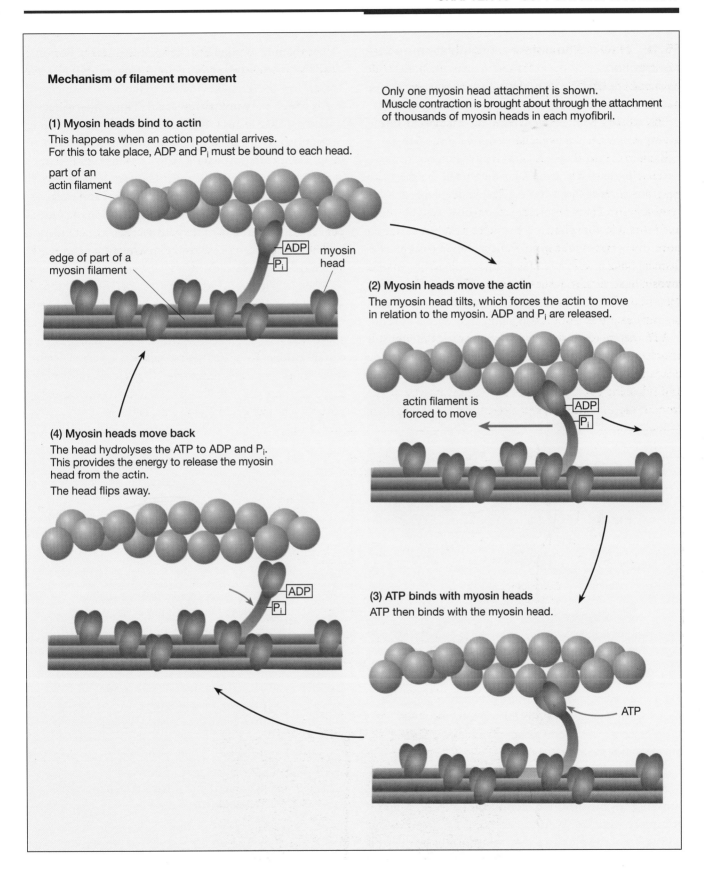

Mechanism of filament movement

Only one myosin head attachment is shown.
Muscle contraction is brought about through the attachment of thousands of myosin heads in each myofibril.

(1) Myosin heads bind to actin
This happens when an action potential arrives.
For this to take place, ADP and P_i must be bound to each head.

part of an
actin filament

edge of part of a
myosin filament

ADP
P_i

myosin
head

(2) Myosin heads move the actin
The myosin head tilts, which forces the actin to move in relation to the myosin. ADP and P_i are released.

actin filament is
forced to move

ADP
P_i

(4) Myosin heads move back
The head hydrolyses the ATP to ADP and P_i.
This provides the energy to release the myosin head from the actin.
The head flips away.

ADP
P_i

(3) ATP binds with myosin heads
ATP then binds with the myosin head.

ATP

Fig. 16.11   How filaments slide.

16.12   How action potentials stimulate muscle contraction

Skeletal muscles are stimulated to contract by action potentials arriving along motor neurones (Chapter 14).

The meeting point between the axon of a motor neurone and a muscle fibre is called a **motor end plate**, or a **neuromuscular junction** (Fig. 16.12). Whatever its name, it is really just a synapse (Section 14.10) in which the postsynaptic membrane is the cell surface membrane of a muscle fibre. The transmitter substance is acetylcholine. When an action potential arrives at the presynaptic membrane (the membrane of the motor neurone) acetylcholine is released. This diffuses across the synaptic cleft and slots into its receptors on the postsynaptic membrane, causing depolarisation across the membrane. An action potential is then generated which spreads rapidly along the cell surface membrane of the muscle fibre.

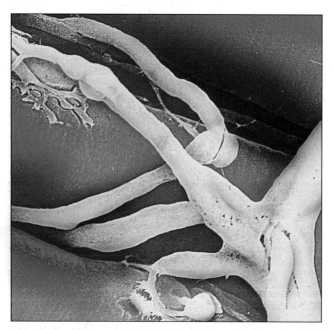

Fig. 16.12   False colour scanning electron micrograph of a neuromuscular junction. The motor neurone (yellow) has many branches which form synapses with the cell surface membranes of the muscle fibres (pink).

As this action potential spreads along the surface of the muscle cell, the infolded membranes which form the transverse tubules (Section 16.9) become depolarised. This affects the membranes of the closely associated sarcoplasmic reticulum, opening up calcium ion channels. Calcium ions flood out of the cisternae of the sarcoplasmic reticulum into the cytoplasm of the muscle cell.

The calcium ions bind to the actin filaments. (Box 16.2 describes this in a little more detail.) This makes it possible for the myosin filaments to bind to the actin filaments as well, which they immediately do. Thus, the release of calcium ions sets off the cycle of events described in Section 16.11.

When action potentials stop arriving, ATP-driven pumps in the sarcoplasmic reticulum membranes actively transport calcium ions out of the cytoplasm and back into the cisternae. A relatively high concentration of calcium ions is built up, ready to flow down their concentration gradient back into the cytoplasm when the next action potential arrives. ∎

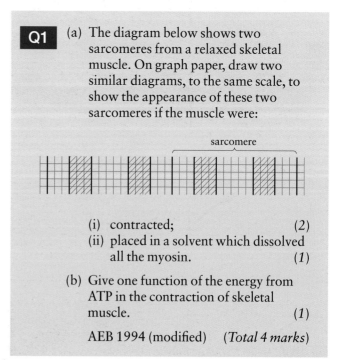

Q1   (a)   The diagram below shows two sarcomeres from a relaxed skeletal muscle. On graph paper, draw two similar diagrams, to the same scale, to show the appearance of these two sarcomeres if the muscle were:

(i)   contracted;   (2)
(ii)   placed in a solvent which dissolved all the myosin.   (1)

(b)   Give one function of the energy from ATP in the contraction of skeletal muscle.   (1)

AEB 1994 (modified)   (*Total 4 marks*)

Box 16.2 How calcium regulates muscle contraction

Fig. 16.13 shows the structure of an actin filament in skeletal muscle. The core of each filament is a polymer of many globular actin molecules which form a helix. A second protein, called **tropomyosin**, forms a 'coiled coil' around the actin helix. A third protein, **troponin**, binds to both the actin and tropomyosin part of the filament.

In a relaxed muscle, the Ca^{2+} ions are inside the cisternae of the sarcoplasmic reticulum and safely away from the actin filaments. The troponin and tropomyosin molecules cover the sites on the actin filaments to which the heads of myosin molecules would bind. When Ca^{2+} ions flood into the cytoplasm, they bind to troponin. This causes a shape change in the troponin molecules which moves the troponin and tropomyosin molecules away from the myosin binding site. Myosin heads can therefore bind with the actin molecules and the muscle begins to contract.

In resting muscle

In muscle that is not contracting troponin and tropomyosin cover the sites on the actin to which myosin heads can bind.

actin

troponin

tropomyosin

myosin

When an action potential arrives

When an action potential spreads along a muscle fibre, it is carried into the fibre along the t-tubule membrane. This causes the release of Ca^{2+} ions from the cisternae of endoplasmic reticulum into the cytoplasm.

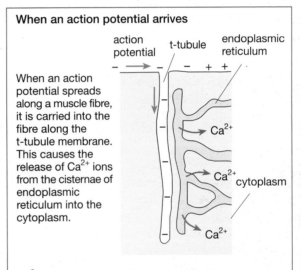

Ca^{2+} ions bind to troponin. The troponin changes shape. This causes the troponin and tropomyosin to move away from the myosin binding site. Myosin heads can now bind and the muscle fibre contracts.

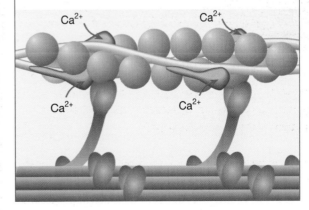

Fig. 16.13 How calcium regulates muscle contraction.

Box 16.3 Muscles and sport

A person's sporting ability may be greatly affected by the size, strength and endurance of their muscles. To understand this, we need to consider the different ways in which energy can be supplied to a contracting muscle. The immediate source of energy is ATP. A muscle usually contains enough ATP for around 3 seconds of activity, so more ATP must be constantly made while a muscle is active.

The fastest way of doing this is to use a substance called **creatine phosphate**. This substance, like ATP, can be hydrolysed to release energy, forming creatine and inorganic phosphate. The energy released can be used to convert ADP and P_i to ATP. There is enough creatine phosphate in a muscle to provide ATP to last for up to 10 seconds or so. This is almost enough for a high-class sprinter to run a 100 m race, and is certainly enough for a high jumper to complete a jump.

ATP can also be produced by **glycolysis** followed by **lactic fermentation** (anaerobic respiration). This can be done rapidly, using glucose as a fuel, and it does not require oxygen. However, the waste product lactic acid builds up after a short time (Section 9.5), so anaerobic respiration cannot be used for long periods of activity. In this case, **aerobic respiration** is used. Long and middle distance runners therefore rely largely on aerobic respiration. Runners of distances between 200 m and 400 m may rely heavily on anaerobic respiration, and build up a very large oxygen debt (Section 9.5). This is one of the reasons why 400 m has a reputation as being one of the toughest distances to run.

Skeletal muscle relies on glucose as the main fuel supply for both anaerobic and aerobic respiration. Muscles store glucose as glycogen. A high carbohydrate diet can greatly increase the amount of glycogen stored, which can be as high as $40\,g\,kg^{-1}$ of muscle tissue. A marathon runner who has been eating a high carbohydrate diet will probably have enough glycogen in their muscles to last for about 240 minutes, while a high fat diet would have built up stores of glycogen which would last for only about 90 minutes.

Training can help muscles to change their structure and physiology, so that they make better use of these systems of ATP generation. Regular exercise against a load stimulates muscle growth, mostly by increasing the diameters of individual muscle cells. Within these enlarged cells, more myofibrils, more mitochondria, more ATP, more creatine phosphate and more stored triglycerides (which can be used as a fuel) are found. Such exercise is therefore very useful to a sprinter, or to anyone performing a sport in which fast, powerful muscle contraction is required over a relatively short period of time.

Endurance training involves steadier work over longer periods of time. This particularly affects cardiac muscle. Endurance training can increase the mass of the muscle of the heart, and the volume of the chambers, by up to 40%. This increase allows more blood to be moved out of the heart at each beat, so people who have undergone such training tend to have a lower heart rate (Section 10.6).

Does this mean that any of us can, by training, make ourselves into the type of athlete we would most like to be? Unfortunately, there are important differences in people's muscles which are genetically determined and which cannot be altered by any amount of training. The fibres in muscles are of two types, called **fast twitch** and **slow twitch**. Fast twitch muscle fibres are adapted for very rapid, short-term work, while slow twitch fibres are adapted for endurance work. Fast twitch fibres are about twice the diameter of slow twitch fibres, and contain large stores of creatine phosphate. They rely largely on this, and anaerobic respiration, to supply ATP. Slow twitch fibres rely largely on aerobic respiration. They have more myoglobin (a pigment which stores oxygen, described in Box 10.3), and have more blood capillaries closely associated with them. The relative proportions of fast twitch and slow twitch fibres which people have in their muscles are determined by the genes they inherit and cannot be affected by training. If you have lots of slow twitch fibres, you may make an excellent marathon runner, but you will never be another Linford Christie.

Q2 The table below refers to three different plant cells found in stems. Copy and complete the table by writing the appropriate word or words in the empty boxes.

Cell type	*One* characteristic structural feature	*One* function
sieve tube element		
		transport of water and mineral ions
	walls thickened in the corners	support

ULEAC 1996 *(Total 5 marks)*

Q3 The figure below shows the skeleton of a front leg from an armadillo.

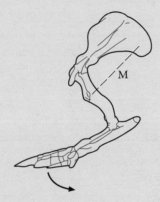

(a) Copy the figure and draw on a straight line to represent a muscle which would cause the lower leg to move in the direction shown by the arrow. *(1)*

(b) Suggest **two** features of the muscle **M** which would indicate that this mammal has powerful limbs suited to digging. *(2)*

The figure below shows a cross-section through a mammalian leg bone.

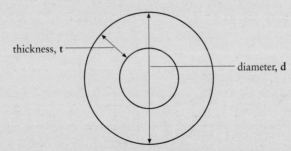

(c) In mammals the average value of the diameter to thickness ratio (D/t) is 4.4. In birds this value is 13.
   (i) Give **one** advantage of a high diameter to thickness ratio to a bird. *(1)*
   (ii) Give **one** way in which the structure of a bird bone provides sufficient strength to resist bending despite having a high diameter to thickness ratio. *(1)*

AEB 1995 *(Total 5 marks)*

Q4 The relationship between the force applied to a material and the resulting change in its length is called the modulus of elasticity. Rubber has a low modulus of elasticity because a fairly small force produces a considerable change in length; concrete has a high modulus because a very large force produces only a small change in length.

The table below shows the values of the modulus of elasticity for some biologically important materials.

Material	Modulus of elasticity/Pa
bone	1.2×10^{10}
cellulose	4.9×10^{9}
elastin	5.9×10^{5}

(a) Use the information in the table to explain why bone is particularly suitable as skeletal material.

(2)

(b) Suggest whether the modulus of elasticity for lignin would be most similar to that of bone, cellulose or elastin. Give a reason for your answer.

(1)

(c) Elastin is a protein. Suggest **one** feature of the structure of an elastin molecule which might explain its modulus of elasticity.

(2)

AEB 1995

(Total 5 marks)

Q5 Figure 1 below shows a sarcomere from a skeletal muscle. Figure 2 shows a cross-section through this sarcomere as it would appear when seen on an electron micrograph.

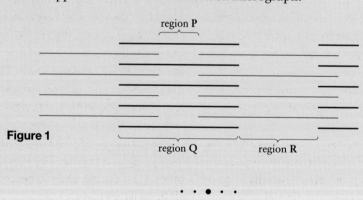

Figure 1

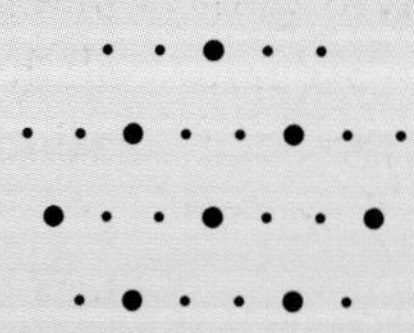

Figure 2

(a) Copy figure 1 and draw on a line to show from where the cross-section in figure 2 was taken. (1)

(b) Name the main protein found in region **P**. (1)

(c) When the muscle contracts, what happens to the length of:
   (i) region **Q**; (1)
   (ii) region **R**? (1)

(d) Explain why there is an increase in the rate of respiration of muscle when it contracts. (3)

NEAB 1995

(Total 7 marks)

17 Reproduction in animals

Animals use both asexual and sexual methods of reproduction. In sexual reproduction, which is the only way in which mammals such as humans can reproduce, haploid gametes are brought together to form a diploid zygote, which then develops into an embryo. In mammals, this happens inside the female's body, and the embryo develops within the mother's uterus, attached to a life support system called a placenta. Hormones regulate sexual development and activity in both male and female.

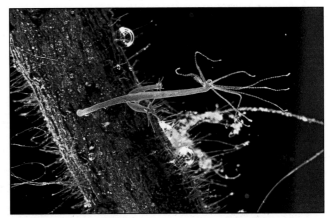

Fig. 17.1 *Hydra viridis* is a freshwater cnidarian (Section 22.13) about 5 mm long, which can reproduce both sexually and asexually. This one is reproducing asexually producing offspring by growing 'buds', each of which eventually separates from the parent.

ASEXUAL AND SEXUAL REPRODUCTION IN ANIMALS

17.1 Asexual reproduction

Asexual reproduction is the production of new individuals from a single parent, and involves cell division by **mitosis** (Section 4.2). The daughter cells formed by mitosis are genetically identical with the parent cell, so the daughter organisms produced by asexual reproduction are genetically identical with their parent and with each other. A group of genetically identical organisms is known as a **clone**.

Asexual reproduction is more common in plants (Section 18.1) than in animals, but many species of animals do use this form of reproduction, usually as part of a life cycle in which sexual reproduction also occurs. The tiny freshwater cnidarian (Section 22.13) *Hydra*, for example, produces offspring by growing buds from its body (Fig. 17.1).

17.2 Sexual reproduction

Sexual reproduction produces new organisms from one or two parents. Within the parent or parents, diploid cells divide by **meiosis** (Sections 4.3 and 4.4) to produce specialised haploid sex cells called **gametes**. Because meiosis involves crossing over and independent assortment of chromosomes, the gametes are genetically different from the parent's cells, and also from each other.

Usually, gametes are of two different types. One type is

relatively small and moves, and this is the **male** gamete. The other type is larger and does not move actively, and this is the **female** gamete. In many animal species, an individual produces only one type of gamete and is therefore either male or female. However, in some species each individual produces both types of gamete and is said to be **hermaphrodite**. Earthworms and garden snails are examples of hermaphrodites.

In a process called **fertilisation**, two gametes fuse to form a diploid **zygote**. The zygote divides repeatedly by mitosis, producing a new multicellular organism in which all the cells are genetically identical to each other but have a different makeup from the cells of other organisms. This is true even if the two gametes came from the same hermaphrodite parent, because the gametes will contain different combinations of alleles and so will produce a zygote with a different combination of alleles from the parent. However, self-fertilisation is rare.

Thus, while asexual reproduction produces clones of genetically identical individuals, sexual reproduction produces groups of genetically different individuals.

In this chapter, we will concentrate on sexual reproduction in humans. Reproduction in plants is described in Chapter 18.

REPRODUCTION IN HUMANS

17.3 The male and female reproductive systems

Fig. 17.2 shows the reproductive organs of a man and a woman.

A male gamete is called a **spermatozoon** (plural **spermatozoa**) or simply sperm. Sperm are made in the **testes**, inside hundreds of tiny **seminiferous tubules**, after which the sperm pass into a coiled tube called the **epididymis** and then into the **vas deferens**. Sperm are stored in both the epididymis and vas deferens, and can remain there for about a month before beginning to lose their fertility.

The two vasa deferentia lead upwards and eventually join the **urethra**, which also carries urine from the bladder. The urethra passes through the **penis** to the outside. Just before the two vasa deferentia join the urethra, a duct from the **seminal vesicles** enters each one. Ducts from the **prostate gland** also enter the urethra. The seminal vesicles and prostate gland secrete fluids which mix with the sperms to form **semen**.

The female gametes, called eggs, are made in the **ovaries**. Once a month, an egg is ejected from one of the ovaries and passes into the opening of an oviduct or **Fallopian tube**. The oviducts lead into the **uterus**, where an embryo will develop if an egg is fertilised. The uterus has a strong, muscular outer wall or **myometrium**, and a softer inner wall with a well developed blood supply, called the **endometrium**. At the base of the uterus is a narrow opening guarded by a ring of muscles, called the **cervix**. The **vagina** connects the uterus to the outside.

17.4 Spermatogenesis

Spermatogenesis is the production of sperm. It happens in the testes, beginning when a boy is between about 11 and 15 years old, and continuing throughout the rest of life. About 100 to 200 million sperm are made each day.

Fig. 17.3 shows how spermatogenesis takes place. Each seminiferous tubule is surrounded by a layer of epithelium on which sit **spermatogonia**. These are diploid cells, and they divide by mitosis to produce more diploid cells. Some of these stay near the edge of the tubule and form more spermatogonia, but some move towards the middle of the tubule and grow larger, forming cells called **primary spermatocytes**.

Each primary spermatocyte then begins to divide by meiosis. The first meiotic division (Section 4.4) forms two **secondary spermatocytes** from each primary spermatocyte. The secondary spermatocytes are haploid. Two or three days later, each secondary spermatocyte undergoes the second meiotic division, producing two haploid **spermatids**. Over the next few weeks, each spermatid gradually develops into a **spermatozoon**. The whole process, from epithelial cell to sperm, takes around 64 days.

As these stages take place, the cells get closer and closer to the lumen in the middle of the tubule. They are nourished by very large, non-dividing cells called **Sertoli cells**, or 'nurse cells'. These are so much bigger than the developing sperm cells that one Sertoli cell reaches all the way from the epithelium to the centre of the tubule. The cytoplasm of the Sertoli cells surrounds the developing sperm cells.

A fully formed sperm looks very different from any other type of cell found in the human body. The nucleus is contained within the head, and there is only a thin layer of cytoplasm between the nucleus and the cell surface membrane. Right at the tip of the head is the **acrosome**, which is a membrane-bound compartment formed from the Golgi apparatus that contains hydrolytic enzymes.

The tail of a sperm contains microtubules running along its entire length, arranged in the 9 + 2 pattern which is found in cilia (Fig. 3.15). These microtubules are responsible for the swimming movements of the sperm. They obtain ATP for this activity from many mitochondria which are packed closely in a region called the middle piece just behind the head of the sperm.

Fully formed sperm move from the lumen of the seminiferous tubules to the epididymis, carried in fluid secreted by the Sertoli cells. At this stage, they do not swim, but they gradually become able to do so after a day or so in the epididymis. However, they do not make use of their swimming ability until they are ejaculated; it seems that proteins secreted by cells in the epididymis inhibit their activity. Once released, a healthy sperm can swim at up to 4 mm per minute.

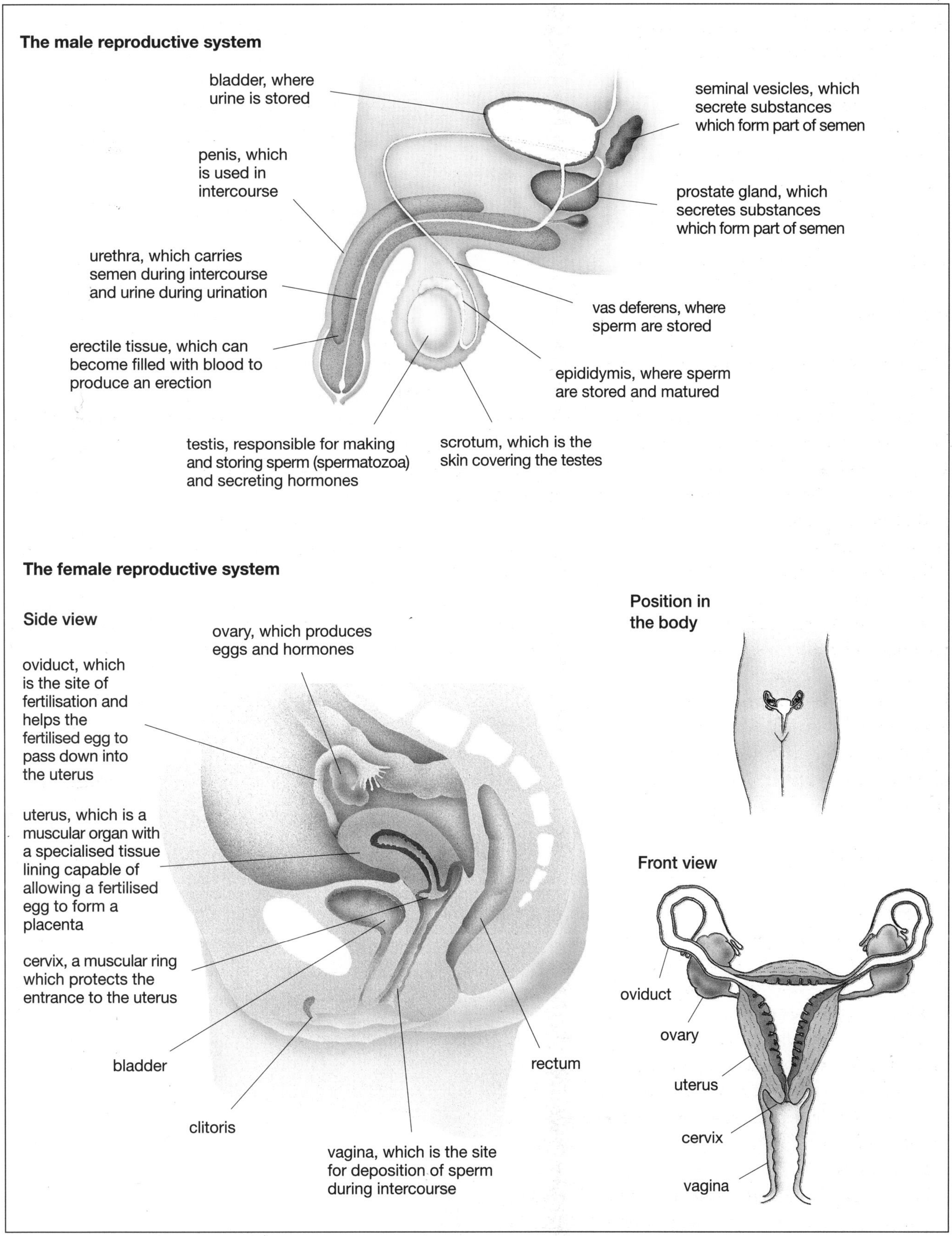

The male reproductive system

bladder, where urine is stored

penis, which is used in intercourse

urethra, which carries semen during intercourse and urine during urination

erectile tissue, which can become filled with blood to produce an erection

seminal vesicles, which secrete substances which form part of semen

prostate gland, which secretes substances which form part of semen

vas deferens, where sperm are stored

epididymis, where sperm are stored and matured

testis, responsible for making and storing sperm (spermatozoa) and secreting hormones

scrotum, which is the skin covering the testes

The female reproductive system

Side view

ovary, which produces eggs and hormones

oviduct, which is the site of fertilisation and helps the fertilised egg to pass down into the uterus

uterus, which is a muscular organ with a specialised tissue lining capable of allowing a fertilised egg to form a placenta

cervix, a muscular ring which protects the entrance to the uterus

bladder

clitoris

rectum

vagina, which is the site for deposition of sperm during intercourse

Position in the body

Front view

oviduct

ovary

uterus

cervix

vagina

Fig. 17.2 The structure of human male and female reproductive systems.

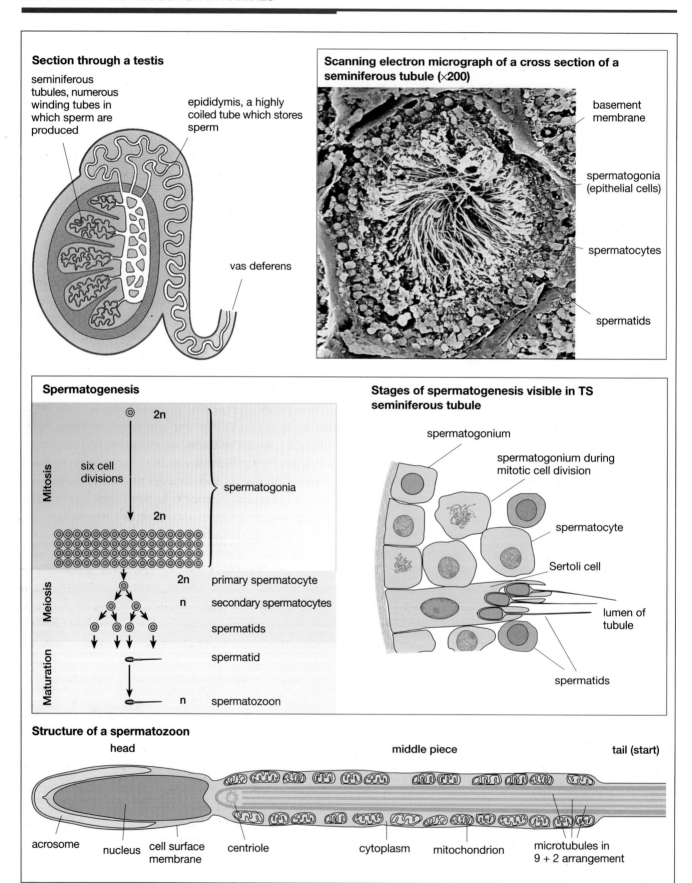

Section through a testis

seminiferous tubules, numerous winding tubes in which sperm are produced

epididymis, a highly coiled tube which stores sperm

vas deferens

Scanning electron micrograph of a cross section of a seminiferous tubule (×200)

basement membrane

spermatogonia (epithelial cells)

spermatocytes

spermatids

Spermatogenesis

2n

Mitosis — six cell divisions

2n

spermatogonia

Meiosis

2n — primary spermatocyte

n — secondary spermatocytes

spermatids

Maturation

spermatid

n — spermatozoon

Stages of spermatogenesis visible in TS seminiferous tubule

spermatogonium

spermatogonium during mitotic cell division

spermatocyte

Sertoli cell

lumen of tubule

spermatids

Structure of a spermatozoon

head

middle piece

tail (start)

acrosome

nucleus

cell surface membrane

centriole

cytoplasm

mitochondrion

microtubules in 9 + 2 arrangement

Fig. 17.3 Structure of the testis and spermatogenesis.

17.5 Oogenesis

Fig. 17.4 shows the structure of a human ovary. Each ovary in an adult woman weighs about 15 g, and contains many potential eggs in various stages of development.

Unlike the production of sperm in a male, the process of oogenesis begins extremely early in a girl's life, when she is an embryo. At only about 5 to 6 weeks after a zygote has been formed, some of the cells in the tiny embryo's developing ovaries divide by mitosis to produce diploid **oogonia**. By the time the embryo is 24 weeks old, she already has many millions of oogonia in her ovaries.

During these early weeks, continuing until about 6 months after birth, the oogonia begin the first division of meiosis. Cells in this stage of their development are called **primary oocytes**. They do not complete this division, remaining in prophase I for many years. Many of the primary oocytes disappear, so that by the time a girl reaches puberty, she has about 400 000 of them in her ovaries. These remaining primary oocytes are each about 20 µm in diameter.

As the primary oocyte begins to enter prophase I of meiosis, some of the surrounding cells in the ovary form a layer around it, producing a **primordial follicle**. Over time, while the oocyte remains in prophase I, some of the follicles develop into **primary follicles**, in which there are several layers of surrounding cells called **granulosa cells**. Other cells from the ovary form yet more layers around the outside of each follicle, forming a **theca**. The granulosa cells secrete a protective layer of glycoproteins which forms the **zona pellucida** around the oocyte.

The primary follicles remain like this until the girl reaches puberty. At puberty, hormones are produced which stimulate the primary follicles to develop into **secondary follicles**. A fluid-filled cavity develops in the follicle and the oocyte gets larger. One of these secondary follicles begins to grow more rapidly to form a fully developed **ovarian follicle** (sometimes called a Graafian follicle or pre-ovulatory follicle) which is about 1.0 to 1.5 cm in diameter. While this is happening, the primary oocyte inside it at last completes the first meiotic division begun so many years ago. The division of the cell is unequal, producing one relatively large cell and one tiny cell, called a **polar body**. The new, large, haploid cell which is produced is called a **secondary oocyte**. It continues straight on into the second division of meiosis, but again it stops before it has finished, this time remaining in metaphase II.

The follicle then ruptures, shedding the secondary oocyte which is still surrounded by granulosa cells from the ovary. Cilia at the mouth of the oviduct create a movement of fluids, drawing the oocyte into the oviduct. Cilia and gentle peristaltic movements of the walls of the oviduct slowly move the oocyte towards the uterus. This may be the end of the story, because if it is not fertilised it simply dies. If, however, it is fertilised by a sperm, then it finally completes the second division of meiosis, once again producing a tiny polar body and one large cell containing both the sperm nucleus and the egg nucleus.

17.6 Fertilisation

The eggs of humans, like all mammals, are fertilised inside the female's body. Internal fertilisation is used by most terrestrial animals and terrestrial plants, as it is the surest method of getting a male gamete to a female gamete without either of them being exposed to the drying effects of air. (Box 18.2 in the next chapter discusses the different types of fertilisation used by organisms living in different environments.)

In the male, stimulation of various parts of the body, especially the head of the penis, or simply thinking sexual thoughts, results in impulses being sent from the brain along parasympathetic nerves to the arteries in the penis. These impulses cause the arteries to dilate, filling spaces within the erectile tissue of the penis with blood under high pressure. This makes the penis become hard and erect. If the sexual stimuli become more intense, then impulses pass along sympathetic nerves to the vasa deferentia. These contract and push the sperm within them into the urethra. The muscles around the prostate gland and then the seminal vesicles also contract, forcing out fluid which mixes with the sperm. The fluid from the prostate gland is alkaline and contains citrate and calcium ions, while the fluid from the seminal vesicles contains fructose. The mixture of sperm and these two fluids is called **semen**. It has a pH of about 7.5.

Rhythmic contractions of muscles then produce waves of pressure within the urethra, which ejaculate semen from the penis. One ejaculation may release about 3 to 4 cm³ of semen, containing approximately 200 million to 400 million sperm. When they are first ejaculated, these sperm can swim only weakly and are not able to fertilise an egg. Changes take place over the next one to ten hours which make them able to swim much more actively, and also change the membrane around the acrosome so that it will be able to release its enzymes if it comes into contact with an egg. These changes are called **capacitation**.

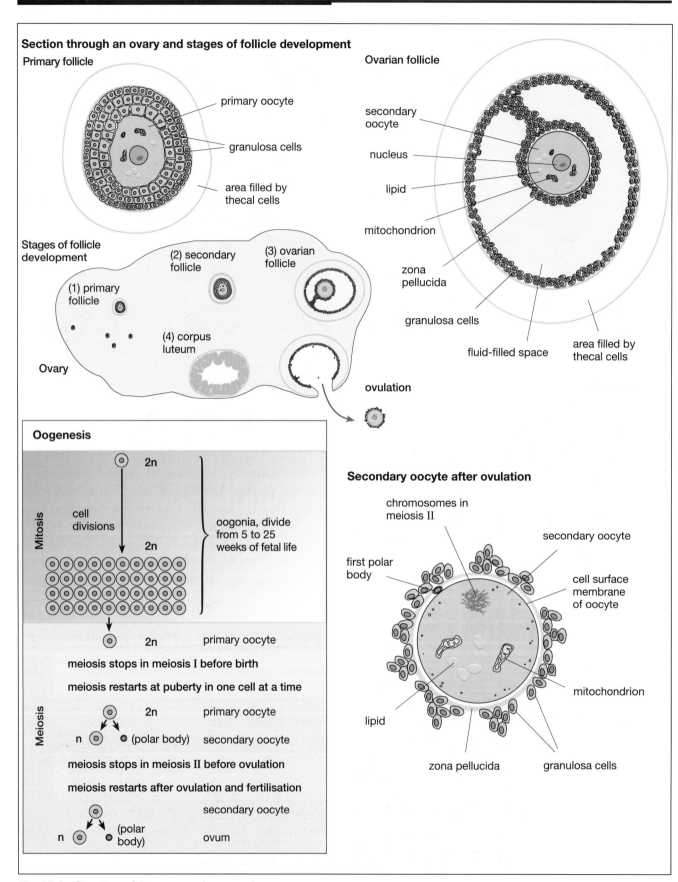

Section through an ovary and stages of follicle development

Primary follicle

- primary oocyte
- granulosa cells
- area filled by thecal cells

Ovarian follicle

- secondary oocyte
- nucleus
- lipid
- mitochondrion
- zona pellucida
- granulosa cells
- fluid-filled space
- area filled by thecal cells

Stages of follicle development

(1) primary follicle
(2) secondary follicle
(3) ovarian follicle
(4) corpus luteum

Ovary

ovulation

Oogenesis

2n

Mitosis

cell divisions

2n

oogonia, divide from 5 to 25 weeks of fetal life

2n   primary oocyte

meiosis stops in meiosis I before birth

meiosis restarts at puberty in one cell at a time

Meiosis

2n   primary oocyte

n   (polar body)   secondary oocyte

meiosis stops in meiosis II before ovulation

meiosis restarts after ovulation and fertilisation

secondary oocyte

n   (polar body)   ovum

Secondary oocyte after ovulation

- chromosomes in meiosis II
- secondary oocyte
- first polar body
- cell surface membrane of oocyte
- mitochondrion
- lipid
- zona pellucida
- granulosa cells

Fig. 17.4   Structure of the ovary and oogenesis.

Secondary oocyte before fertilisation

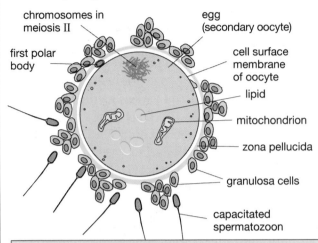

chromosomes in meiosis II

egg (secondary oocyte)

first polar body

cell surface membrane of oocyte

lipid

mitochondrion

zona pellucida

granulosa cells

capacitated spermatozoon

A capacitated spermatozoon swims vigorously towards an oocyte. It is also capable of releasing enzymes from its acrosome to digest a way through the layer of granulosa cells still attached to the oocyte.

Events leading to fertilisation (1) one sperm attaches

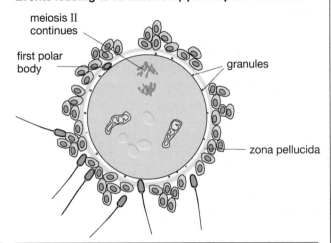

meiosis II continues

first polar body

granules

zona pellucida

The first spermatozoon to digest a way through the zona pellucida, using enzymes from its acrosome, fuses with the membrane of the egg. Granules are released from the egg which prevents another spermatozoon from binding to the zona pellucida. Meiosis restarts.

Events leading to fertilisation (2) the sperm enters

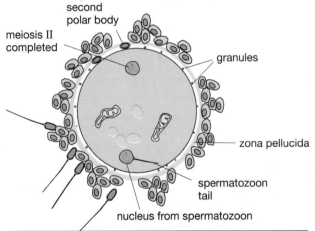

second polar body

meiosis II completed

granules

zona pellucida

spermatozoon tail

nucleus from spermatozoon

The spermatozoon enters the egg. Meiosis II is completed and a second polar body is expelled.

Fertilisation

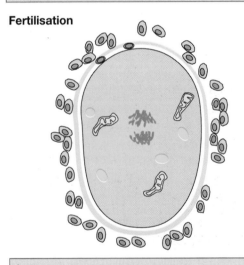

After 18 to 20 hours the two nuclei combine and the zygote immediately starts to divide by mitosis.

Scanning electron micrograph of a zygote just after fertilisation (×720)

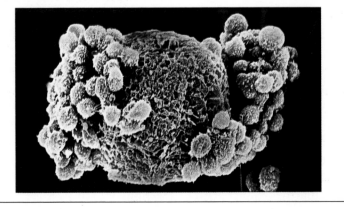

Fertilisation of this oocyte took place 24 hours before. Spermatozoa, shown yellow, can still be seen on the surface. Granulosa cells occur on the left and right of the oocyte.

Fig. 17.5 Fertilisation.

Within the female, stimulation of parts of the body and thinking sexual thoughts can cause parasympathetic signals to pass to some of the sexual organs. The clitoris erects in a similar way to the penis of the male, and fluid containing mucus is secreted inside the vagina. The mucus is important in lubrication, allowing the male's erect penis to move easily in the vagina. This movement, and stimulation of the clitoris, may cause a similar series of rhythmical muscular contractions of the vagina and uterus.

If ejaculation takes place while the penis is in the vagina, semen is deposited close to the cervix. The pH inside the vagina is low, about 3.5 to 4.0, and this would kill the sperm if they were not surrounded by the alkaline fluid from the prostate gland which partially neutralises the vaginal fluids. The sperm pass into the cervix where they stay for several hours, trickling into the uterus where they become capacitated. They swim up through the uterus, towards the oviducts. Only a very small number of them, perhaps one in 100 000, will manage to make the full journey. It takes several hours for them to do so.

Sperm do not seem to be attracted to an egg in the oviduct, but find it by chance. The sperm's acrosome releases enzymes which digest a pathway through the granulosa cells which still surround the egg (Fig. 17.5). When the sperm head reaches the zona pellucida, receptors on its membrane bind to a receptor protein in the zona pellucida, and this stimulates the acrosome to release all the rest of its enzymes. These digest the zona pellucida and allow the head of the sperm to pass through, and then to fuse with the membrane of the egg. As this happens, the egg releases granules, by exocytosis, into the space around it. The granules move into the zona pellucida and change the receptors in it so that sperm can no longer bind with them. This stops more than one sperm fertilising the egg.

As the sperm fuses with it, the egg is stimulated to complete the second division of meiosis (Section 17.5), and the second polar body is released. The sperm chromosomes enter the egg. Fertilisation has now taken place. The cell which has been formed is called a zygote, and it contains 46 chromosomes – 23 from the egg and 23 from the sperm.

17.7 Implantation and the placenta

The zygote slowly moves down the oviduct towards the uterus, propelled by cilia which line the oviduct. This takes about 3 or 4 days, and while it is happening the zygote divides several times by mitosis. By the time it reaches the uterus, it is a ball of about 100 cells with a central fluid-filled cavity and is called a **blastocyst**.

On arrival in the uterus, the blastocyst normally remains there for another 2 or 3 days. Then it **implants** in the lining, or endometrium, of the uterus. Implantation depends on special cells on the surface of the blastocyst, called **trophoblasts,** which secrete enzymes which partially digest cells in the endometrium. The tiny blastocyst 'burrows' into the endometrium, eventually becoming completely surrounded by it (Fig. 17.6). While this is happening, other cells of the blastocyst are dividing to form the **embryo**. The embryo receives its nourishment at this time from the products of digestion of the endometrium by the trophoblasts.

The trophoblast cells continue to divide, producing many tiny projections called **villi** which project into the endometrium. Within the villi, blood capillaries form. At the same time, the endometrium also develops, forming spaces around the villi called **sinuses** which are filled with the mother's blood. The whole structure, made up partly of the mother's tissues from the endometrium and partly of tissues produced from the trophoblasts, is called the **placenta.**

Fig. 17.6 shows the structure of a fully formed placenta. By this stage, the embryo has developed most of its organs and is now called a **fetus**. Oxygenated blood is brought to the sinuses through the mother's arteries, and taken back to her heart in veins. On the fetus's side, deoxygenated blood flows from the fetus along two **umbilical arteries** to capillaries in the villi. Here, the fetus's blood is brought very close to the mother's blood in the sinuses, although there is no direct contact between them. Oxygen is released from the mother's haemoglobin, diffuses across the thin barriers separating it from the fetus's blood, and combines with the fetus's haemoglobin in its red blood cells. (The reason that this happens is explained in Box 10.3.) Oxygenated blood then flows back to the fetus in the **umbilical vein.**

The large surface area provided by the villi enables this exchange of oxygen between the mother and the fetus to take place rapidly. Carbon dioxide is exchanged in the opposite direction, also by diffusion. Many other substances can pass between the mother's and the fetus's blood, across the cells which separate them, and these substances move by a variety of transport methods (Sections 3.23 to 3.28). For example, glucose moves by facilitated diffusion (and probably other methods as well)

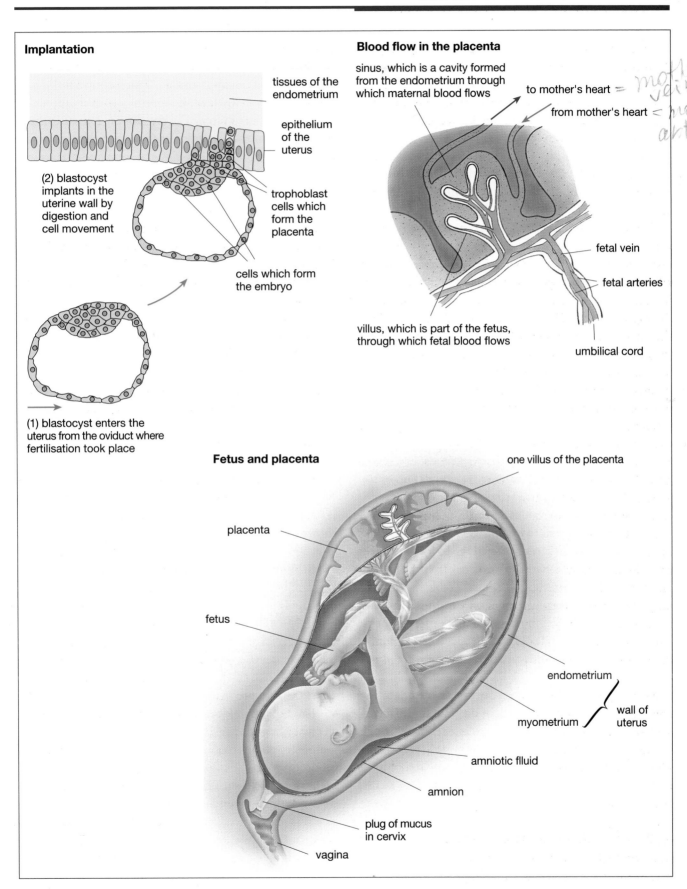

Implantation

tissues of the endometrium

epithelium of the uterus

(2) blastocyst implants in the uterine wall by digestion and cell movement

trophoblast cells which form the placenta

cells which form the embryo

(1) blastocyst enters the uterus from the oviduct where fertilisation took place

Blood flow in the placenta

sinus, which is a cavity formed from the endometrium through which maternal blood flows

to mother's heart

from mother's heart

mothers vein

mothers artery

fetal vein

fetal arteries

umbilical cord

villus, which is part of the fetus, through which fetal blood flows

Fetus and placenta

one villus of the placenta

placenta

fetus

endometrium

myometrium

wall of uterus

amniotic flluid

amnion

plug of mucus in cervix

vagina

Fig. 17.6   Implantation and the placenta.

and amino acids by active transport. Antibodies, of the IgG class (Section 21.9), inorganic ions, vitamins and water also cross the placenta from mother to fetus, while urea diffuses from the fetus to the mother. Most drugs, such as nicotine and alcohol, also freely cross from the mother's blood to the fetus's blood.

As well as providing a site where substances can be exchanged between the mother and the fetus, the placenta functions as an endocrine gland throughout pregnancy. This role is described in Section 17.12.

17.8 Birth

In humans, the fetus develops inside the uterus for approximately nine months. During this time it is supplied with all its requirements via the placenta, which grows as the fetus grows. The fetus is surrounded by a sac called the **amnion** which contains amniotic fluid. This helps to support the fetus and also protects it from mechanical shocks.

Towards the end of pregnancy, changes begin to take place in the activity of the uterus wall. It is not certain exactly what causes the process of birth to begin, but it appears to be a combination of hormones produced by the mother and the fetus (described in Section 17.12) and also the stretching of the walls of the uterus and of the cervix as the fetus's head enters it.

When birth begins, the muscles in the uterus wall begin to contract strongly and rhythmically. These contractions stretch the cervix, widening it until the baby's head can pass through. The cervix softens in late pregnancy, making it possible for this to happen. To begin with, the contractions may take place about once every 30 minutes, but they gradually become stronger and more frequent. Once the cervix has widened completely, contractions of the uterus and also of the muscles in the wall of the abdomen push down on the baby, until it passes through the cervix and vagina and into the outside world.

Within 45 minutes of the birth of the baby, the placenta is shed from the mother's uterus and passes out through the cervix and vagina as the 'afterbirth'. When this happens, some blood is lost from the mother's blood vessels which previously supplied the placenta. However, these vessels constrict quite rapidly, ensuring that blood loss is not too great nor lasts for too long. The umbilical cord is cut and clamped and will eventually form the baby's navel.

From now on, the baby's body must carry out all physiological processes on its own, with no help from the placenta. Breathing begins, and for the first time oxygen diffuses across the alveolar walls and into the baby's blood capillaries in its lungs. The kidneys will have already begun to work while the fetus was in the uterus, as will the digestive system; the developing fetus swallows quite large amounts of amniotic fluid during the last two or three months of its life in the uterus, and this passes through the alimentary canal in the normal way.

17.9 Lactation

Mammals such as humans are unique in possessing **mammary glands**. During pregnancy, the mother's glands within the breasts grow and become able to produce milk. The production and secretion of milk is called **lactation**. Changes in the hormones in the mother's body which occur just before and at birth (described in Section 17.12) cause small amounts of a substance called **colostrum** to be produced at first, and then milk.

Colostrum contains high concentrations of a kind of antibody called **immunoglobulin A** or IgA (Section 21.9) which, together with the IgG which the baby received across the placenta while it was in the uterus, helps to protect the newborn baby from infectious diseases. In other respects, colostrum is very similar in composition to milk.

Milk is about 88% water. Tiny globules of **fat** float in it, which makes it an opaque rather than a transparent liquid. The fats are mostly triglycerides (Section 1.18) which provide a source of energy for the baby. The kinds of fatty acids in these triglycerides vary according to what the mother eats, and there is evidence that a good range of fatty acids is important for the development of the baby's brain. Milk also contains the disaccharide **lactose** which, like fats, provides energy. Lactose is also used within the baby's body to make the monosaccharide galactose, which is essential for the formation of myelin (Section 14.2). Several **proteins** are found in milk. There are also various minerals, especially **calcium**.

The sucking of the baby on a nipple stimulates the mammary glands to produce more milk, and they can go on doing so for several years if the child continues to breast feed for this length of time. However, if the mother does not breast feed her baby, the breasts usually stop producing milk after about a week.

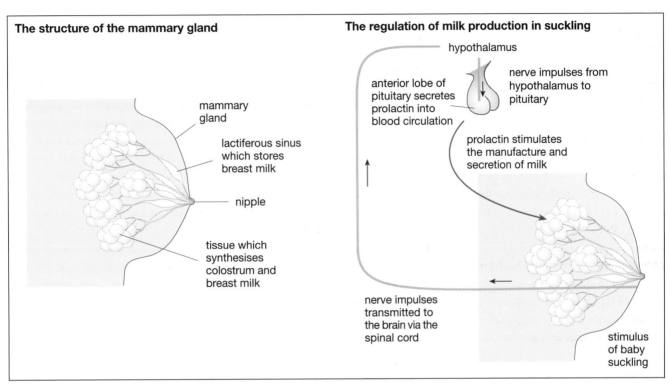

Fig. 17.7 Lactation.

Q1

(a) Describe the structure of the placenta and explain how important materials are able to pass between mother and fetus. (12)

(b) With reference to **named** examples, discuss the problems that may arise when toxic materials pass from mother to fetus across the placenta. (6)

UCLES 1995 *(Total 18 marks)*

HORMONAL CONTROL OF REPRODUCTION

17.10 Male sex hormones

Male sex hormones are known as **androgens**. The most important of these is **testosterone**. Testosterone is a steroid hormone (Fig. 15.3) which is produced by the testes. The cells which make testosterone are in between the seminiferous tubules and are called **interstitial cells** or **Leydig cells**.

Testosterone begins to be made by these cells while the baby is developing in the uterus, and this causes the embryo to develop male characteristics including a penis, scrotum, prostate gland and seminal vesicles. In girl babies, only very small amounts of testosterone are secreted. This results in the absence of these male characteristics and in the development of a uterus and vagina.

During childhood, almost all the Leydig cells in the testes disappear and only a very little testosterone is produced. At puberty, Leydig cells reappear and testosterone secretion begins again, causing enlargement of the penis and also the development of **secondary sexual characteristics**, such as the growth of body hair and the enlargement of the larynx, which makes the voice deeper. Testosterone also increases the activity of sebaceous glands in the skin which can cause acne.

Testosterone increases the rate of production of many proteins, especially in muscles. This is an **anabolic** effect, and so testosterone is an anabolic steroid hormone. It causes muscular development and also increased bone growth. Because of these effects, testosterone has been illegally used by athletes to try to improve their performance, but there are many dangers associated with its prolonged use, especially liver damage.

The secretion of testosterone by the Leydig cells is under the control of another hormone called **luteinising hormone, LH**. This hormone is secreted from the anterior pituitary gland. A negative feedback loop regulates the amounts of hormones secreted; high levels of testosterone inhibit the secretion of LH, thus reducing the production of more testosterone. Testosterone production therefore continues at a fairly steady day-to-day rate. However, the amount secreted does vary throughout life, peaking at around 20 years old and then slowly declining.

17.11 The female sexual cycle

In contrast to the relatively steady secretion of testosterone in a man, the secretion of reproductive hormones in a woman follows a cycle which repeats itself approximately every month. This cycle is known as the **menstrual cycle**.

There are two female sex hormones secreted by the ovaries – **oestrogen** and **progesterone**. Oestrogen and progesterone, like testosterone, are steroid hormones. The secretion of these hormones is under the control of two glycoprotein hormones secreted by the anterior pituitary gland. These are **luteinising hormone, LH** and **follicle stimulating hormone, FSH**.

Oestrogen begins to be secreted by a girl's ovaries when she reaches puberty. It causes an increase in size of the reproductive organs, and also the development of secondary sexual characteristics such as growth of the breasts. Like testosterone, oestrogen causes bone growth, but this is less marked than in boys and it stops earlier. When a woman reaches her mid-forties or fifties, the secretion of oestrogen by her ovaries drops, and in some women this can cause the bones to become weak, a condition known as osteoporosis.

The main role of progesterone is to prepare the lining of the uterus for pregnancy. As you will see in Section 17.12, progesterone is secreted in especially large quantities throughout pregnancy.

Fig. 17.8 shows the changes in the rates of secretion of oestrogen, progesterone, FSH and LH during a woman's menstrual cycle. The cycle shown is 28 days long, but it is quite common for women to have cycles as short as 20 days or as long as 34 days. The first day of menstruation is taken as being day 1 of the cycle.

During the first few days of the cycle, the secretion of FSH and LH from the anterior pituitary gland increases slightly. This stimulates the growth of a few primary follicles in the ovaries, although eventually only one of these in one ovary normally develops much further. The granulosa cells (Section 17.5) in the developing follicle secrete oestrogen, and you can see on the graph that the level of oestrogen rises sharply at this time. The rise in oestrogen inhibits the secretion of FSH and LH, and their levels therefore drop. The oestrogen causes the endometrium of the uterus to thicken – by day 12 it has become about 3 to 4 mm thick.

At about day 12 of the cycle, the secretion of LH suddenly rises sharply. The rise in LH causes the granulosa cells to slow down their secretion of oestrogen and switch over to secreting progesterone (you can see this on the

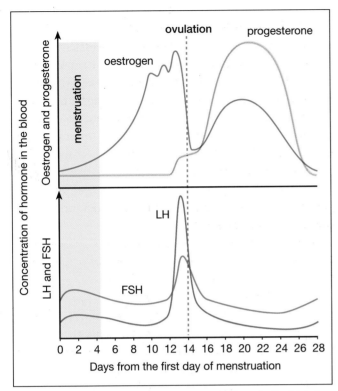

Fig. 17.8 Changes in hormone concentrations in the blood during the menstrual cycle.

graph in Fig. 17.8). It also causes ovulation. Ovulation normally occurs half-way through the cycle – that is on day 14 if the cycle is a 28-day one.

When the egg has left the follicle, the remaining granulosa cells, stimulated by the high levels of LH, rapidly enlarge and fill up with a yellow substance. The mass of cells is called a yellow body or **corpus luteum**. The cells secrete a lot of progesterone and smaller amounts of oestrogen, and you can see the progesterone and oestrogen levels rising on the graph at this time. The progesterone causes continued development of the endometrium, including an increase in its blood supply and the amount of nutrients such as glycogen and lipids in its cells. Its thickness grows to about 5 to 6 mm. The endometrium is therefore prepared to receive and nourish a blastocyst (Section 17.7) if the egg which has just been released from the ovary is fertilised.

If the egg is not fertilised, the oestrogen and progesterone secreted by the corpus luteum inhibit the secretion of FSH and LH from the anterior pituitary. Their levels fall, so the corpus luteum is no longer stimulated by LH and degenerates. All four hormones therefore drop to low concentrations at this last stage of the cycle. Once oestrogen and progesterone levels drop far

enough, their inhibitory effect on the anterior pituitary gland ceases and FSH and LH begin to be secreted again. The cycle has begun once more. The drop in oestrogen and progesterone at the end of the cycle removes the stimulation for the endometrium to develop and it begins to break down. It is lost through the vagina over the first 4 to 7 days of the next cycle in the process of menstruation.

17.12 Hormones during pregnancy and after birth

If the egg which is released from the ovary at day 14 is fertilised, then a different sequence of events takes place.

The trophoblast cells (Section 17.7) of the blastocyst secrete a hormone called human **chorionic gonadotrophin, HCG** (Fig. 17.9). This hormone has a molecular structure very like LH and it has very similar effects. It stimulates the corpus luteum in the ovary to increase its output of oestrogen and progesterone, which stimulates further development of the endometrium. The presence of HCG therefore keeps the corpus luteum active and the endometrium intact, rather than breaking down as they would in a normal menstrual cycle.

Over the next few weeks, the placenta develops. It secretes oestrogen and progesterone. By about 5 to 6 weeks after fertilisation, it is secreting enough of these hormones to maintain the endometrium. The corpus luteum is no longer required and slowly disintegrates, disappearing by about 12 weeks after fertilisation. The amounts of these two hormones, especially progesterone, increase throughout pregnancy (Fig. 17.9). They cause enlargement of the uterus and breasts and maintain the endometrium. Progesterone inhibits the ability of the muscles in the uterus to contract, so minimising the chance that labour might begin too early.

Towards the end of pregnancy, the level of oestrogen rises with respect to the level of progesterone, and it is thought that this may help to increase the ability of the uterine muscles to contract. A hormone called **oxytocin** is also secreted at this time, both by the mother's posterior pituitary gland and by the fetus. This hormone causes contraction of the muscles in the uterus. Stretching of the cervix by the baby's head increases the secretion of oxytocin. As a result of a combination of these factors, birth takes place.

During pregnancy, another hormone, **prolactin**, is secreted from the mother's anterior pituitary gland. This hormone promotes the production of milk, but its effect is prevented when levels of oestrogen and progesterone are high. When the baby has been born and the placenta (which was secreting the oestrogen and progesterone) has been lost from the mother's body, the prolactin is able to cause an effect and the breasts begin to produce milk. The 'base' level of prolactin drops immediately after birth, but it rises temporarily every time the baby suckles. The supply of milk therefore matches the demands of the baby. Oxytocin is also important in ensuring that the milk in the breast is allowed to flow to the nipple. Some mothers have difficulty in breast feeding their baby, and this is often caused by a lack of secretion of oxytocin which can be affected by her emotional state. ■

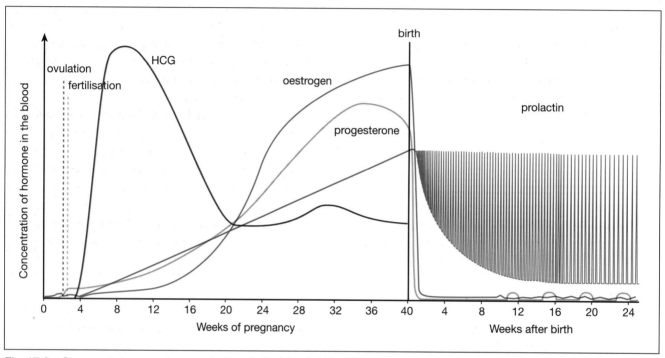

Fig. 17.9 Changes in hormonal concentrations in the blood during and after pregnancy.

Q2 The table below refers to the hormones involved in human reproduction. Copy and complete the table by writing the appropriate words in the empty boxes.

Hormone	Role
	repair of endometrium
prolactin	
	stimulates ovulation
progesterone	
follicle stimulating hormone	

ULEAC 1995

(Total 5 marks)

Box 17.1 Oestrous cycles

All female mammals have reproductive cycles that are controlled by hormones. In most mammals the female's behaviour changes when she is about to ovulate, and this stage is called **oestrus**. A cycle in which oestrus occurs is called an **oestrous cycle**. In women, there is no evidence for any behavioural change around the time of ovulation, and so the human cycle is not an oestrous cycle. Indeed, the name 'menstrual cycle' is not really very accurate either because it means 'monthly', and many women's cycles are significantly longer or shorter than this. Perhaps the term 'ovarian cycle' would be better!

Oestrous behaviour in animals indicates that ovulation is about to occur. The female becomes ready to mate, and willing to accept a male; this is clearly the time at which fertilisation is likely to be most successful. Farmers can use the signs of oestrus in farm animals to know when to artificially inseminate a female or when to allow a male to mate with her.

For example, male pigs (boars) secrete chemicals called **pheromones** in their saliva. A pheromone is a hormone-like substance, but it is usually volatile and passes into the atmosphere around the animal where it can be smelt by other animals. Female pigs (sows) only respond to the boar's pheromones when they are in oestrus. The sow becomes immobile when she smells them, and will allow a person to push down on her back. To find out whether a sow is in oestrus and ready to mate, a farmer can buy aerosol cans of boar pheromones which he can spray near to the female and note her behaviour. Interestingly, the underground fungi, truffles, produce chemicals which are very like the pheromones released by boars, which is perhaps why sows can often be trained to hunt out truffles.

Q3 The graph below shows changes in the mean diameters of follicles and corpora lutea in the ovary of a pig over a period of 40 days.

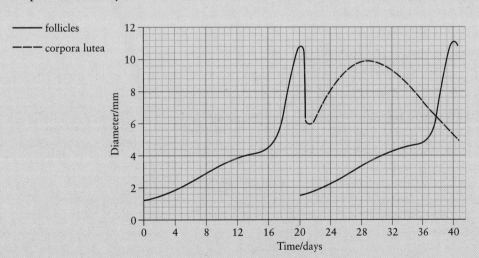

(a) Between which days is fertilisation most likely to occur? Explain your answer. (3)

(b) In the cycle represented in the graph, fertilisation did not occur. Give two pieces of evidence from the graph to support this. (2)

(c) Describe the part played by hormones in controlling the changes in size of the follicles. (3)

AEB 1997 (specimen) (*Total 8 marks*)

Box 17.2 Using hormones to control human fertility

Reproductive hormones can be used both to increase and decrease fertility in humans.

Increasing fertility using IVF

There are many reasons why couples are unable to have children. For example, gametogenesis may not occur efficiently in either the man or woman; there may be blockages in the vasa deferentia or oviducts; or the woman's endometrium may not become prepared for implantation. In some cases, a technique called **in vitro fertilisation**, or **IVF**, may allow the woman to become pregnant.

The first success for human IVF came in 1978, and since then the technique has been used quite widely. However, success rates are not high, and the chances of a couple having a baby as a result of IVF range from about 20% if the woman is in the 25–34 age group to 7% in the 40–44 age group.

Usually, the woman's own pituitary gland activity is first suppressed. She is then given LH and FSH which stimulate the development of several follicles in her ovaries. The woman's oestrogen and LH levels are then monitored and the follicles are observed using ultrasound scans. When the follicles are ready, LH is given to stimulate their maturation. About 30 hours after this, just before ovulation would take place, the eggs are removed from her ovaries.

The collected eggs are checked to make sure that they look healthy and are at the correct state of development. For example, the presence of a polar body shows that the egg has completed the first meiotic division.

Semen is then collected, either from the woman's partner or from an anonymous donor if her partner is infertile. The semen may be fresh, or frozen; frozen semen can be stored for many years. The semen is washed in a suitable medium which allows the sperm to undergo capacitation, and then is added to the eggs. The temperature is kept at around 37 °C. The next day, the eggs are inspected to see if fertilisation has occurred. If so, then they are usually left to develop to the two-cell stage.

Any two-cell embryos resulting from this process can either be frozen for later use, or implanted into the woman. She must, of course, be at the correct stage of her menstrual cycle with the endometrium in a state ready to accept them. Usually, the embryos are placed in the uterus through the vagina and cervix. Up to three embryos are used, because not all of them are likely to implant successfully.

If implantation is successful, then the pregnancy and birth are likely to proceed normally. If necessary, the woman can be given hormones, such as progesterone, to help to maintain her pregnancy.

Using hormones for contraception

There are many possible ways in which reproductive hormones can theoretically prevent conception, but at the moment only three methods are used as methods of birth control in humans. These are the badly named 'morning after' pill, hormones which inhibit ovulation and hormones which prevent sperm transport from the cervix to the oviduct. All of these are used by women. At the moment, there is no hormonal contraceptive method for use by men, but research has now indicated some possible methods of inhibiting sperm production without unwanted side effects.

The 'morning after' pill acquired this popular name beause it is taken after sexual intercourse. One version contains a mixture of oestrogen and progesterone, which disturbs the transport of egg, sperm and blastocyst. Another method is to use an antiprogestogen (progestogen is a name for the group of hormones similar to progesterone) called Ru486. Ru486 works by binding to progesterone receptors in the cell surface membranes of progesterone's target cells. This stops progesterone having its normal effects, and so prevents the development of the endometrium and successful implantation. Ru486 can also terminate a pregnancy which is already established, and is 80% successful in achieving this up to 42 days after fertilisation.

Box 17.2 Using hormones to control human fertility (cont.)

Hormones which inhibit ovulation may be taken orally, by injections, or by slow-release skin patches or implants. The hormones may consist of progestogens only, or a combination of progestogens and oestrogen. In recent years, the proportion of oestrogen has been decreased because it is associated with side effects such as an increased risk of thrombosis (the development of blood clots inside veins). These hormones work by inhibiting the release of FSH and LH from the pituitary, which stops ovulation occurring. However, progestogen-only pills may still allow ovulation to occur; they appear to work by preventing the next stages leading to fertilisation and implantation taking place normally, for example by making the mucus in the cervix impenetrable to sperm, or by preventing the capacitation of sperm in the female's body.

The great advantage of this method over other methods of contraception is that, if the hormones are taken regularly, it is extremely effective at preventing conception. However, great care has to be taken not to miss even a single dose, as this can allow fertilisation to take place. Another advantage is that when the contraceptive is no longer taken, the effects are quickly reversed, and the woman does not usually have to wait too long before she is fertile again.

Q4 The diagram below shows the production of follicles, ovulation and the formation of a corpus luteum in a human ovary. The stages in the cycle are shown clockwise round the ovary from **A** to **G**.

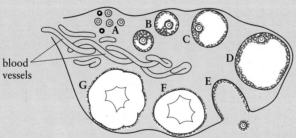

(a) Which of the lettered structures would you expect to produce the largest quantity of progesterone? *(1)*

(b) The 'combined' pill is an oral contraceptive containing both oestrogen and progesterone. How would you expect the stages in the ovary to differ from those shown in the diagram in a woman who had been taking the combined pill for the previous year? Explain your answer. *(3)*

(c) The graph below shows the changes which took place in the diameter of a follicle during part of a menstrual cycle.

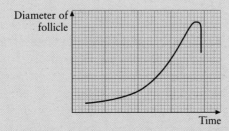

Copy the graph and mark with an arrow the time when ovulation occurred. *(1)*

AEB 1994 *(Total 5 marks)*

Q5 Records of human fertility for the period 1930 to 1990 have shown changes in the sperm counts of normal men.

The table below summarises the changing percentages of men with high or low sperm counts over the period of sixty years.

High sperm count >100×10^6 sperm cm^{-3}
Low sperm count <20×10^6 sperm cm^{-3}

Time period	Men with high sperm counts/%	Men with low sperm counts/%
1930–1950	50	5
1951–1960	45	4
1961–1970	28	14
1971–1980	21	11
1981–1990	15	18

(a) (i) Comment on the changes in the percentage of men with high sperm counts during the period 1930 to 1990. (3)

(ii) Compare the figure for men with low sperm counts with those with high sperm counts over the same period. (3)

(b) Explain why it is necessary for large numbers of sperms to be produced when only one sperm is required to bring about fertilisation. (2)

(c) Exposure of pregnant women to high levels of certain oestrogens during early pregnancy can result in reproductive disorders in their male offspring.

It appears that a number of compounds in the environment can mimic the action of oestrogens when ingested. Such compounds, termed oestrogenic chemicals, are found in pesticides, such as DDT and PCBs, and also in the breakdown products of certain detergents. They accumulate in the fatty tissue and have the same effect as oestrogens, which play a major role in the menstrual cycle.
(i) Describe the normal role of oestrogens in the menstrual cycle. (3)
(ii) Suggest how the oestrogenic chemicals pass from the mother to the developing fetus. (3)

ULEAC 1996   *(Total 14 marks)*

Q6 Read through the following account of the hormonal control of the menstrual cycle and copy and complete it using the most appropriate word or words to complete the account.

The release of .... from the anterior pituitary gland induces the development

of primary follicles. Another hormone from the anterior pituitary gland stimulates the thecal cells to

produce ...., which controls the repair of the ....

after menstruation. At ovulation, a .... is released from the mature follicle.

The remaining follicular cells form the .... which begins to secrete

.... , inhibiting the release of the hormones from the anterior pituitary gland.

ULEAC 1996   *(Total 6 marks)*

Q7 In humans, the female breast contains structures called alveoli, which are responsible for producing the secretions that make up the milk released after the birth of a baby. The alveoli are collections of cells that surround a central space or lumen. Secretions from the cells pass into the lumen and from there move into milk ducts, which deliver milk to the nipple.

The figure below shows the arrangement and structure of the alveolar cells.

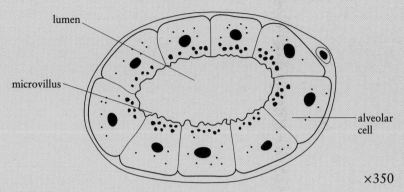

×350

One important material in the milk is the protein casein.

(a) (i) State **precisely** where in the alveolar cell the synthesis of casein would take place. (1)

    (ii) Outline the mechanism by which casein will be secreted into the lumen. (2)

    (iii) Suggest **two** other nutritional materials that are found in milk. (2)

The graph below shows the changes in hormone levels in a woman before and after giving birth.

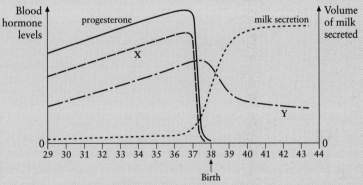

(b) (i) Identify the hormones **X** and **Y**. (2)

    (ii) Explain how lactation is stimulated at birth. (3)

    (iii) Describe how breast feeding may prolong milk production after birth. (2)

UCLES 1995   (*Total 12 marks*)

Q8 The figure below shows the structure of part of a sperm cell, drawn from an electron micrograph.

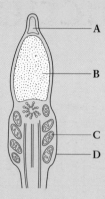

(a) Name structures **A** to **D**. (2)

(b) (i) What type of organelle is structure **A**? (1)
    (ii) Outline the role of structure **A** in the process of fertilisation. (3)

(c) Describe how a mature sperm cell is produced from a primary spermatocyte. (3)

Human semen contains very large numbers of spermatozoa, with the sperm count of a fertile man as high as 150×10^6 per cm^3. If the sperm count drops below 20×10^6 per cm^3 the man will have significantly lowered fertility. It is not clear why such high counts of sperm are necessary for successful fertilisation. A recent study has analysed sperm counts of human males taken between 1930 and 1990. The results are shown in the graph below.

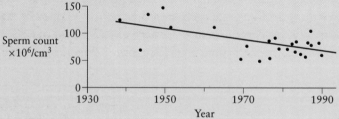

© Adapted by permission from *BMJ*, 1992

Some scientists have attributed the changes in sperm counts to the effects of oestrogens in the environment, which can bind to oestrogen receptors in the body. The pesticide DDT is one of many chemicals which have been shown to act in this way. Other chemicals can act as anti-oestrogens and block the activity of oestrogen receptors.

Others have questioned the link between environmental oestrogens and sperm counts. Instead, they attribute the changes in sperm count to increases in sexually transmitted disease, or question whether the sperm count data are accurate.

(d) Suggest **one** reason why two sperm counts taken at different times, from the same man, might vary. (1)

(e) Using the information in the graph, describe the changes in sperm count between 1930 and 1990. (2)

(f) Suggest **two** reasons why large numbers of sperm may be necessary for successful fertilisation. (2)

(g) (i) Suggest **three** sites where oestrogen receptors may be found in the body. (3)
    (ii) State **two** roles of oestrogen in the body. (2)

(h) Suggest **one** reason for the rise in the concentration of oestrogens in the environment. (1)

UCLES 1995 *(Total 20 marks)*

18 Reproduction in plants

Many plants are able to reproduce both asexually and sexually. Sexually reproducing plants have alternating haploid and diploid stages in their life cycles, and this alternation of generations is clearly visible in the life cycle of a liverwort or a fern. In flowering plants, the haploid stage of the life cycle is much reduced. The flowers of flowering plants are organs specialised for sexual reproduction on land, where mechanisms are needed which allow the transfer of male to female gametes without any danger of them drying out.

ASEXUAL REPRODUCTION IN PLANTS

18.1 Vegetative reproduction

Asexual reproduction (Section 17.1) is much more common in plants than in animals. Many species of plants are able to reproduce both sexually and asexually. Growth in a plant which does not involve the development of structures involved in sexual reproduction is sometimes known as **vegetative growth**. So the growth of new individuals by asexual reproduction is known as **vegetative reproduction**.

Fig. 18.1 shows asexual reproduction in a strawberry plant. Here, stems called **runners** grow horizontally from the parent plant, and put out roots at a node (a place on the stem from which a leaf stalk grows, and where there is a bud). The roots grow downwards into the soil, while the bud grows upwards and forms a young plant. Eventually, the connection between the original parent plant and the daughter plant withers. By this time, the daughter plant will probably have begun to grow runners of its own.

Virtually every part of one plant or another can be involved in asexual reproduction. You may like to try to think of some examples of plants which grow new individuals from their roots or from their leaves.

The cells in the new individuals produced by asexual reproduction are formed by mitosis and so, of course, are genetically identical to each other and to their parent. They form a **clone**. Horticulturists often wish to produce

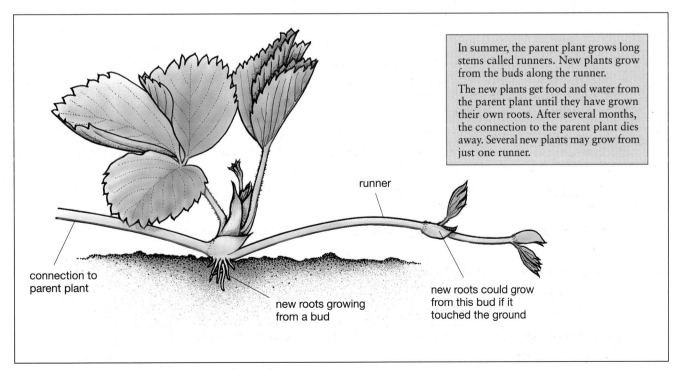

In summer, the parent plant grows long stems called runners. New plants grow from the buds along the runner.

The new plants get food and water from the parent plant until they have grown their own roots. After several months, the connection to the parent plant dies away. Several new plants may grow from just one runner.

runner

connection to parent plant

new roots growing from a bud

new roots could grow from this bud if it touched the ground

Fig. 18.1   Asexual reproduction in a strawberry plant.

large quantities of genetically identical plants, as these will all grow in a similar way and produce a similar crop. This makes them easier to tend, harvest and market. Such methods as grafting and taking cuttings have been used for hundreds of years, and still are used very widely. However, in recent years the technique of **tissue culture** has been developed which allows very large numbers of genetically identical new plants to be produced from a very small number of original cells taken from a parent. It involves taking a small piece of tissue from the parent plant, and placing it on sterile agar containing nutrients and plant growth substances (Section 15.18) which stimulate the cells to divide by mitosis. They are kept in controlled conditions of light and temperature, and quickly grow into complete little plants which can later be removed from the agar and planted into soil.

Asexual reproduction can be advantageous to plants growing in natural conditions, as it can enable rapid coverage of the ground in a suitable environment. However, the genetic uniformity of the offspring can be a problem, for example if a parasite or other pest is able to infect these plants. If one plant has no defence against the pest, then this is true of all of them and the whole population may be killed. This is also a problem for plant breeders, as genetically uniform crop plants can become vulnerable to pests and diseases which may sweep through an entire crop. Genetic variation can help to lessen the probability that such widespread infection will occur, as at least some of the plants may have a gene which confers resistance to the pest. In the wild, almost all species of plants are able to reproduce sexually, so ensuring genetic variation in their offspring. In horticulture and agriculture, plant breeders maintain stocks of many different varieties of crop plants which can be used in breeding programmes to introduce new genes into commercially available varieties (Section 7.13).

REPRODUCTION IN LIVERWORTS AND FERNS

Almost all plants, like animals, reproduce sexually – that is, they produce haploid gametes which fuse to form a diploid zygote which then grows to form an adult plant. Most of this chapter concentrates on reproduction in flowering plants, but firstly we will look at sexual reproduction in two less familiar types of plant – liverworts and ferns.

18.2 The life cycle of a liverwort

Liverworts belong to the phylum **Bryophyta** (Section 22.7). They are not very big plants, and you may never have noticed a liverwort growing. However, once you know what to look for, they are easy to find. Liverworts grow in damp places, often where it is shady. You may find them on the banks of streams, on bricks or stones at the base of damp walls, or on the soil on top of flowerpots.

Fig. 18.2 shows the structure of a common liverwort in Britain called *Pellia epiphylla*. The plant which you see growing is **haploid** – that is, each cell contains a single set of chromosomes rather than the two complete sets which are present in the diploid cells of almost all adult animals and flowering plants. The structure of this haploid plant is very simple. Liverworts have no true roots or stems, just a simple flat body called a **thallus**. The thallus lies close to the ground, to which it is attached by single-celled structures called **rhizoids**. The rhizoids do take up water and mineral salts from the soil, but the whole thallus can also absorb these substances when raindrops splash onto it. Most of the cells in the thallus contain chloroplasts and photosynthesise. Unlike the leaf of a flowering plant the thallus has no waxy cuticle covering its surface, and so it easily loses water. This is one reason why liverworts usually grow in damp places. There are no xylem vessels or phloem tubes, so water cannot easily be transported to different parts of the plant, and the only support is given by cellulose cell walls and turgor (Section 16.2). This, combined with the problems of water loss, prevents liverworts from growing very big.

The thallus reproduces by producing haploid gametes, and so it is called a **gametophyte** ('gamete-producing plant'). On the upper surface of the thallus, male gametes develop in small depressions called **antheridia**. As the cells of the thallus are already haploid, these gametes are produced by mitosis. The male gametes are long, thin cells with two very long flagella. They are called **antherozoids**, or **sperm**. At the edges of the thallus, the female gametes,

The liverwort *Pellia epiphylla*

Ecology

Pellia epiphylla occurs on the banks of ditches and streams throughout Britain. It also grows on wet peat surfaces in moorland and mountains and is more common on acid soils.

The haploid thallus carries out photosynthesis and absorbs mineral nutrients from water which splashes onto it.

Liverwort

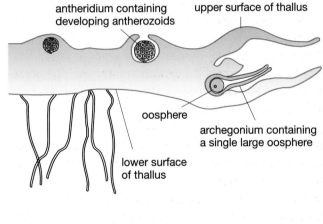

haploid spores released

sporogonium (diploid), containing ripening haploid spores

thallus

antheridia

archegonium at thallus tip

rhizoids

Thallus TS

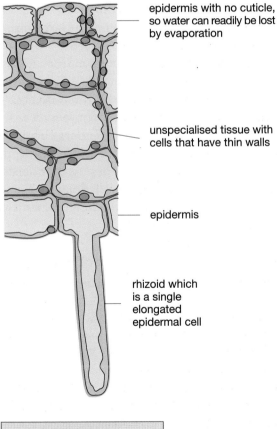

epidermis with no cuticle, so water can readily be lost by evaporation

unspecialised tissue with cells that have thin walls

epidermis

rhizoid which is a single elongated epidermal cell

The rhizoids (haploid) can absorb water but their main function is to anchor the thallus to the ground.

Thallus TS – showing the position of antheridia and archegonia

antheridium containing developing antherozoids

upper surface of thallus

oosphere

archegonium containing a single large oosphere

lower surface of thallus

Fertilisation

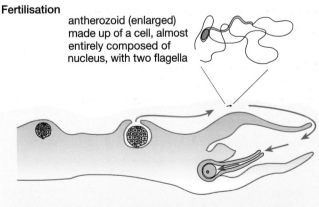

antherozoid (enlarged) made up of a cell, almost entirely composed of nucleus, with two flagella

Mature antherozoids swim from the antheridia to an archegonium when the thallus has a water film over it.

An antherozoid that swims down the narrow neck of the archegonium can fertilise the oosphere, which then grows into a sporogonium.

Fig. 18.2 Reproduction in a liverwort.

called **oospheres** or **eggs**, are formed by mitosis inside **archegonia**. Whereas large numbers of sperm are made in each antheridium, only one egg is made in each archegonium.

Fertilisation happens when the sperm swim to the egg while it is still in the archegonium. They can only do this when there is a film of water on the surface of the thallus, so that they have something to swim through and so that they do not dry out. Fertilisation therefore happens in wet weather. Splashing of raindrops may also be important in transferring the sperm to the eggs, especially from one thallus to another. The sperm are attracted to the egg by chemicals, especially sugars, which it secretes.

Fertilisation takes place inside the archegonium, producing a diploid zygote. The zygote divides by mitosis, eventually producing a diploid structure called a **sporogonium**. This stays attached to the thallus which provides it with food. At the tip of the sporogonium a spherical structure called a **spore capsule** develops. Inside this some of the diploid cells, called **spore mother cells**, divide by meiosis to produce haploid **spores**. (A spore is one or more cells, often surrounded by a protective waterproof covering, which can be dispersed from where it was made and grow into a new organism.) Because the sporogonium produces spores, it is called a **sporophyte**.

After a while, the spore capsule bursts, flinging out the spores. If a spore lands in a suitable moist place, it germinates. Mitosis takes place, forming a new haploid thallus.

So you can see that there are two alternating stages or 'generations' in the life cycle of a liverwort – a haploid gametophyte which produces gametes by mitosis and a diploid sporophyte which produces spores by meiosis. This kind of life cycle is said to show **alternation of generations**. The life cycle of *Pellia* is shown in Fig. 18.3.

18.3 The life cycle of a fern

Ferns belong to the phylum **Filicinophyta** (Section 22.8). Fig. 18.4 shows the structure of the male fern, *Dryopteris filix-mas*. This fern is very common, and you can find it growing in woodland and other shady places all over Britain.

Ferns, like liverworts, have a clearly marked alternation of generations in their life cycle. The large fern plant which you see growing is the diploid sporophyte. It is much larger, and structurally much more complex, than either the thallus or the sporogonium of a liverwort. Ferns have true **roots** which can penetrate quite deeply into the soil. The roots absorb water and minerals as well as anchor the plant. The male fern has large leaves, called **fronds**, with a large surface area for the absorption of sunlight and carbon dioxide for photosynthesis. The fronds are divided into 'leaflets' called **pinnae**. The surface of the fronds is covered with a waterproof **cuticle**, and

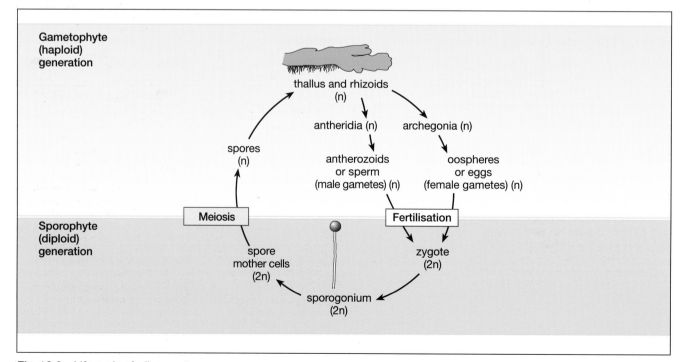

Fig. 18.3 Life cycle of a liverwort.

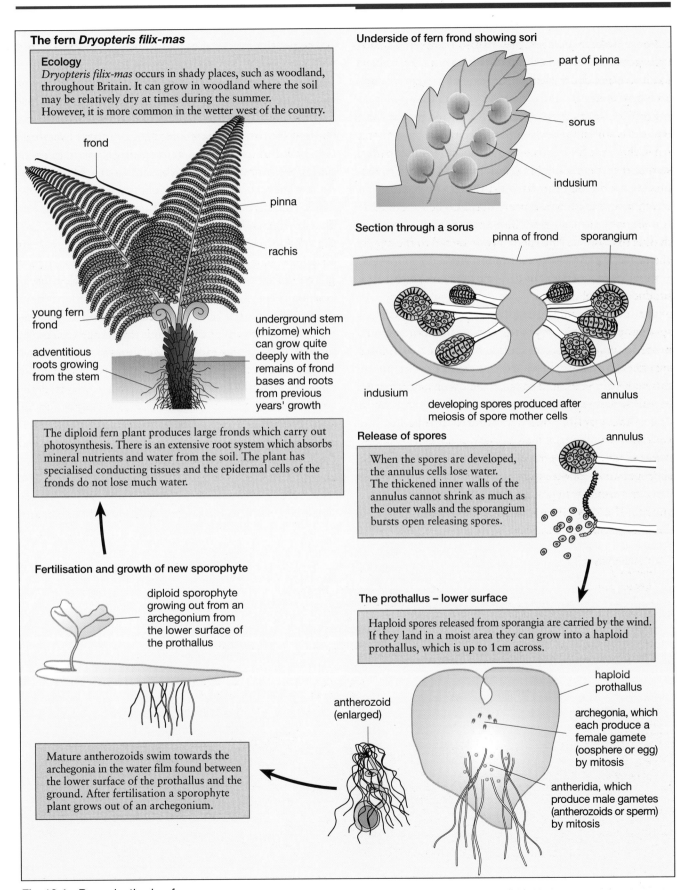

The fern *Dryopteris filix-mas*

Ecology
Dryopteris filix-mas occurs in shady places, such as woodland, throughout Britain. It can grow in woodland where the soil may be relatively dry at times during the summer.
However, it is more common in the wetter west of the country.

frond

pinna

rachis

young fern frond

adventitious roots growing from the stem

underground stem (rhizome) which can grow quite deeply with the remains of frond bases and roots from previous years' growth

The diploid fern plant produces large fronds which carry out photosynthesis. There is an extensive root system which absorbs mineral nutrients and water from the soil. The plant has specialised conducting tissues and the epidermal cells of the fronds do not lose much water.

Underside of fern frond showing sori

part of pinna

sorus

indusium

Section through a sorus

pinna of frond

sporangium

indusium

annulus

developing spores produced after meiosis of spore mother cells

Release of spores

annulus

When the spores are developed, the annulus cells lose water. The thickened inner walls of the annulus cannot shrink as much as the outer walls and the sporangium bursts open releasing spores.

Fertilisation and growth of new sporophyte

diploid sporophyte growing out from an archegonium from the lower surface of the prothallus

Mature antherozoids swim towards the archegonia in the water film found between the lower surface of the prothallus and the ground. After fertilisation a sporophyte plant grows out of an archegonium.

The prothallus – lower surface

Haploid spores released from sporangia are carried by the wind. If they land in a moist area they can grow into a haploid prothallus, which is up to 1 cm across.

antherozoid (enlarged)

haploid prothallus

archegonia, which each produce a female gamete (oosphere or egg) by mitosis

antheridia, which produce male gametes (antherozoids or sperm) by mitosis

Fig. 18.4 Reproduction in a fern.

there are stomata on the upper and lower epidermis which can be closed by guard cells to conserve water. Ferns have xylem vessels and phloem tubes; the xylem vessels transport water to all parts of the plant and also help to support it. Thus, ferns can grow in drier places than liverworts, and they can grow larger.

The spores are produced on the undersides of the fronds, in structures called **sporangia**. (This name is very similar to, but not the same as, the 'sporogonium' in which spores are formed in a liverwort – make sure that you do not confuse them!) The sporangia are found in clusters called **sori**, and each sorus is covered by a protective 'hood' called an **indusium**. Inside the sporangia, diploid spore mother cells divide by meiosis to produce haploid spores.

The spores are released in dry conditions as a strip of cells called the **annulus**, in the wall of the sporangium, curls back and ruptures the sporangium. Fig. 18.4 explains how this happens. The spores are carried away on air currents. They germinate in moist conditions, dividing by mitosis to form a haploid structure which is quite similar to the thallus of a liverwort; it is called a **prothallus**. It is about one centimetre across and very thin, so it is unlikely that you will ever have noticed one. The prothallus has no cuticle and no supportive or specialised conducting tissue, so it can only grow in moist conditions.

The prothallus is the gametophyte generation in the fern's life cycle. Male gametes and female gametes are produced by mitosis inside antheridia and archegonia respectively, both on the underside of the prothallus. Fertilisation takes place in a very similar way to liverworts (Section 18.2) to form a diploid zygote. As in the liverwort, this remains inside the archegonium as it divides repeatedly by mitosis. It develops into a new sporophyte. At first, the embryo sporophyte obtains its nutrients from the prothallus, but once it has formed its first leaves it can photosynthesise for itself. The gametophyte then dies, and the sporophyte continues to grow to form a new fern plant.

You can see that the life cycle of *Dryopteris* (Fig. 18.5) is in many ways similar to that of *Pellia*. Both of them show alternation of generations, with a haploid gamete-forming gametophyte alternating with a diploid spore-forming sporophyte. However, whereas in the liverwort the gametophyte is the 'dominant' stage, in the fern this role is taken by the sporophyte.

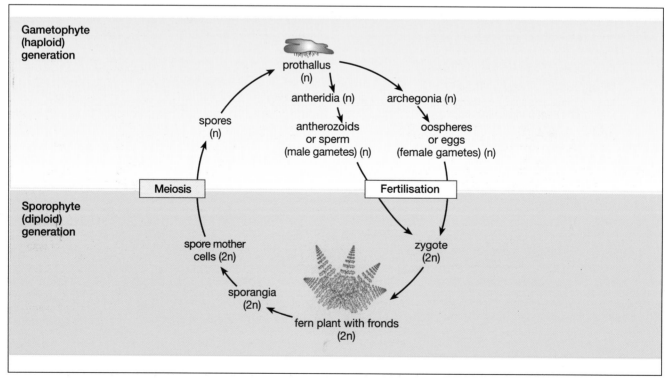

Fig. 18.5 Life cycle of a fern.

SEXUAL REPRODUCTION IN FLOWERING PLANTS

18.4   The structure of a flower

Flowering plants belong to the phylum **Angiospermophyta** (Section 22.10). They differ from all other kinds of plants in having true flowers.

Fig. 18.6 shows the structure of a generalised flower and also a flower belonging to the Papilionaceae. The different parts of the flower are arranged in rings, sometimes called whorls, attached to the top of the flower stalk or **receptacle**. These parts are always arranged in the same order, as shown in Fig. 18.6.

The outer whorl is called the **calyx** and is made up of **sepals**. In many flowers these are dull in colour, and their main function is to protect all the other parts of the flower while it is still a bud. The next whorl is the **corolla**, made up of **petals**. In insect-pollinated flowers the petals are often brightly coloured and scented, as their function is to attract insects to the flower. The petals advertise the presence of the flower from a distance, and the colour and scent of the petals may determine the kind of insect or other animal which is attracted (Fig. 18.7). In tropical countries, for example, many flowers are pollinated by birds and these often have bright red flowers. The dark reddish-brown, strangely marked flowers of *Stapelia*

smell like rotten meat, and attract flies. In many flowers, **nectaries** secrete a sugar-rich fluid called nectar, again in order to attract insects for pollination.

The next whorl is made up of the male parts of the flower and is called the **androecium**. It contains several – often very many – **stamens**, each of which has a stalk called a **filament** supporting an **anther**. Inside the anthers, the male gametes are formed inside **pollen grains**. This is described in Sections 18.5 and 18.8.

Finally, in the centre of the flower, the female parts or **carpels** are found. These make up the **gynaecium**. There are one or more **ovaries**, each containing one or more **ovules**, inside which the female gametes develop inside an **embryo sac**. At the top of each ovary is a **style** which supports a **stigma**. The stigma has the function of capturing pollen grains, one of the first stages in the series of events which will bring the male gametes to the female gametes.

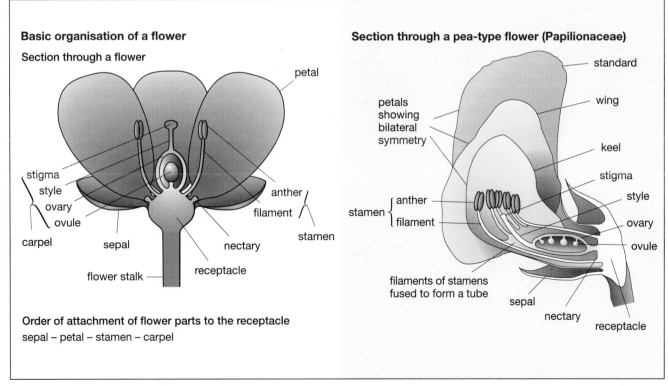

Fig. 18.6   The structure of a flower.

Fig. 18.7 (top) Many insects are not sensitive to red light, but many birds are. Flowers adapted for pollination by birds are often red. Nectar provides a reward for pollination. (bottom) The flowers of *Stapelia* smell like rotting meat, and this attracts bluebottle flies which inadvertently act as pollinators.

18.5 Formation of pollen grains

Male gametes are produced inside pollen grains. Pollen grains are formed inside the anthers (Fig. 18.8). Each anther contains four compartments called **pollen sacs**. The wall of each pollen sac contains several layers of cells. One of the outer layers is made up of cells with thickened walls and is called the **fibrous layer**; this helps to liberate the pollen grains when they are ripe. The innermost layer

is called the **tapetum**. The cells in this layer help to provide nutrients to the developing pollen grains.

In the centre of each pollen sac, diploid **pollen mother cells** divide by meiosis, each producing four haploid cells. In some species, these stay together in a group of four called a **tetrad**, but in others they separate. Each of the haploid cells develops a tough protective wall around itself, becoming a **pollen grain**. The wall is made up of two layers, an outer very tough, waterproof **exine** and an inner **intine**. In places, the exine is absent, leaving a thin area in the wall called a **pit**. The form and structure of the exine varies from species to species, and it is possible to identify a plant just by looking at its pollen grains. They often have spikes or knobs to help them to stick to the bodies of insects.

The haploid nucleus inside each pollen grain divides by mitosis, forming two haploid cells separated by a very thin cell wall. One of these haploid nuclei is called the **generative nucleus**, and the other is the **tube nucleus**.

When the pollen grains are fully formed, the anthers split open in a process called **dehiscence**. They split along a line between the two pollen sacs on either side (Fig. 18.8), exposing the pollen grains on the surface. Before following the pollen grains further, we will look at how the female gamete-forming structures develop to a similar stage.

18.6 Formation of the embryo sac

The female gametes are produced inside structures called embryo sacs which develop inside the ovules (Fig. 18.9).

Ovules are found inside ovaries. Each ovule is connected to the ovary by a stalk called the **funicle**. The ovule has an outer covering, or **integuments**, surrounding a tissue made up of relatively undifferentiated cells called the **nucellus**. At one end of the ovule, the integuments do not quite meet, leaving an opening called the **micropyle**. The other end of the ovule, furthest from the micropyle and nearest to the funicle, is called the **chalaza**.

Inside each ovule, a large, diploid, **spore mother cell** develops. This cell divides by meiosis to produce four haploid cells. All but one of these degenerates, and the one surviving haploid cell then develops into an **embryo sac**.

The embryo sac absorbs nutrients from the nucellus and grows larger. Its nucleus divides by mitosis three times, forming eight haploid nuclei. Two of these nuclei are found near the centre of the embryo sac, with no cell membranes around them. The other six arrange themselves at the ends of the embryo sac, three at one end

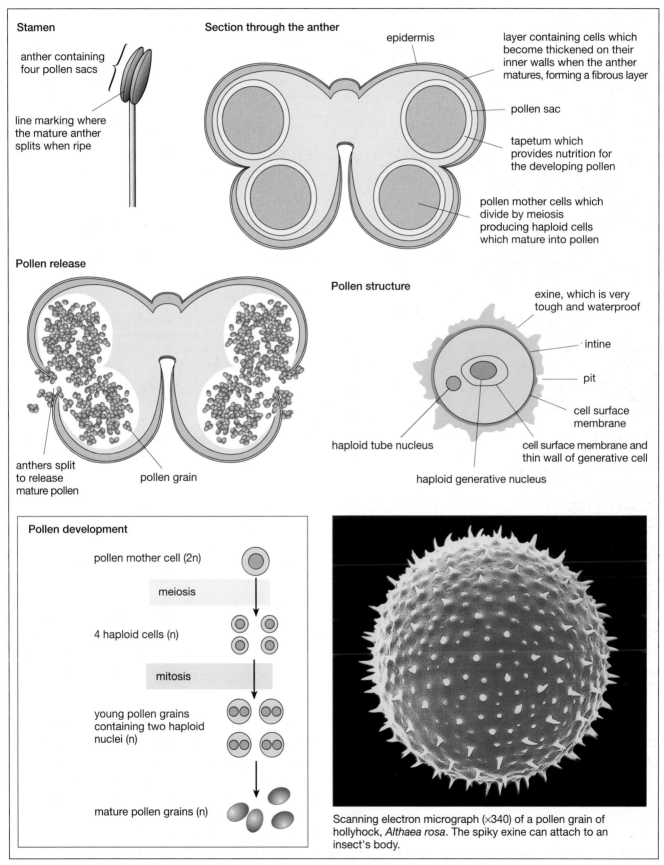

Stamen

anther containing four pollen sacs

line marking where the mature anther splits when ripe

Section through the anther

epidermis

layer containing cells which become thickened on their inner walls when the anther matures, forming a fibrous layer

pollen sac

tapetum which provides nutrition for the developing pollen

pollen mother cells which divide by meiosis producing haploid cells which mature into pollen

Pollen release

anthers split to release mature pollen

pollen grain

Pollen structure

exine, which is very tough and waterproof

intine

pit

cell surface membrane

cell surface membrane and thin wall of generative cell

haploid tube nucleus

haploid generative nucleus

Pollen development

pollen mother cell (2n)

meiosis

4 haploid cells (n)

mitosis

young pollen grains containing two haploid nuclei (n)

mature pollen grains (n)

Scanning electron micrograph (×340) of a pollen grain of hollyhock, *Althaea rosa*. The spiky exine can attach to an insect's body.

Fig. 18.8 The production of pollen in an anther.

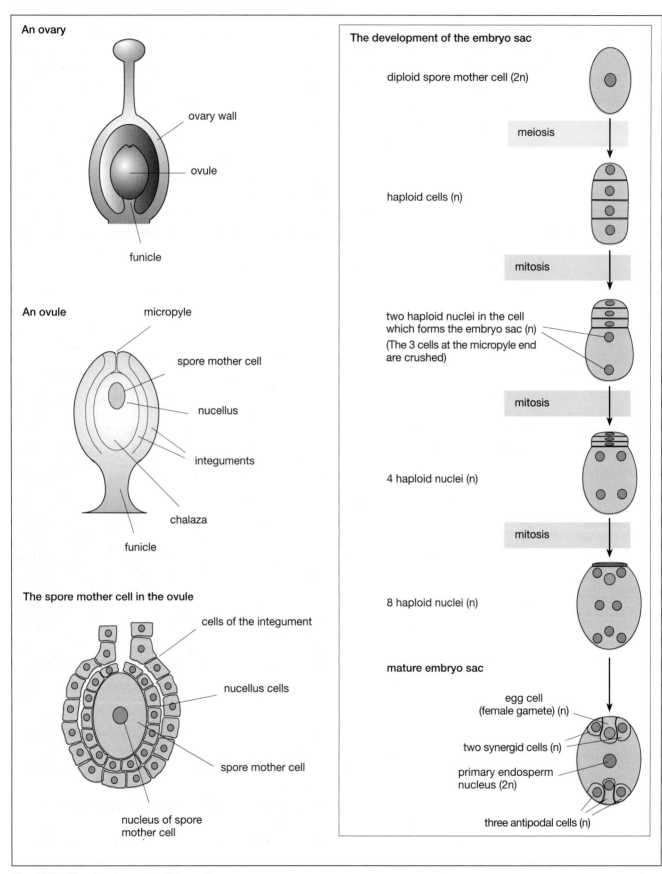

An ovary

ovary wall

ovule

funicle

An ovule

micropyle

spore mother cell

nucellus

integuments

chalaza

funicle

The spore mother cell in the ovule

cells of the integument

nucellus cells

spore mother cell

nucleus of spore mother cell

The development of the embryo sac

diploid spore mother cell (2n)

meiosis

haploid cells (n)

mitosis

two haploid nuclei in the cell which forms the embryo sac (n) (The 3 cells at the micropyle end are crushed)

mitosis

4 haploid nuclei (n)

mitosis

8 haploid nuclei (n)

mature embryo sac

egg cell (female gamete) (n)

two synergid cells (n)

primary endosperm nucleus (2n)

three antipodal cells (n)

Fig. 18.9 The development of the embryo sac.

and three at the other, and usually develop cell membranes. The three haploid cells at the end nearest the chalaza are called **antipodal cells**. One of the haploid cells at the end nearest to the micropyle is a little larger than the other two. This is the **female gamete**, the **egg cell**. The other two cells at this end are called **synergids**. The two nuclei in the middle may fuse together to form a single diploid nucleus called the **primary endosperm nucleus**. Thus, a mature embryo sac usually contains six haploid nuclei and one diploid nucleus.

18.7 Pollination

Pollination is the transfer of pollen from the anther, where it was made, to a stigma. Many species of plants have mechanisms which ensure that the pollen is transferred to a different individual of the same species; this is called **cross pollination**. (Box 18.1 describes some of these mechanisms.) In other species, such as the garden pea, it is usual for pollen to be transferred to the stigma of the same flower; this is called **self pollination**.

As neither plants nor pollen grains can move actively from place to place, other agents are used to transfer the pollen grains. These include **animals**, such as insects, birds, bats and other small mammals such as mice, and the **wind**. A few aquatic plants make use of **water currents** to transfer pollen. We will look at how pollination happens in an insect-pollinated flower and a wind-pollinated flower.

Insect-pollinated flowers attract insects by providing a 'reward' for them when they visit the flower. This reward is often either carbohydrate-rich nectar or protein-rich pollen, or sometimes both. The flower advertises the presence of these foods with brightly coloured petals and/or a scent. The petals are frequently arranged to provide a landing platform for insects. When the insect arrives at the flower, it brushes against the anthers as it collects its 'reward'. Some of the pollen grains stick to its body. The insect flies away, and will often go straight to another similar flower. Here, some of the pollen grains may brush off its body onto the stigma.

It is clear that both the plant and the insect benefit from this arrangement. Insects and flowers have evolved together over millions of years, and this has resulted in some very elaborate pollination mechanisms. Some flowers, such as orchids, have such complex pollination mechanisms that they can only be pollinated by one species of insect (Fig. 18.10).

Wind-pollinated flowers have no need to attract insects,

so they do not waste resources in producing large, brightly coloured petals or nectar. They are usually relatively small flowers, and are often held on long stalks so that they can easily catch the wind. Fig. 18.11 shows the structure of a typical grass flower. The filaments are long and dangle freely out of the flower; they are very flexible, and move easily in the wind, shaking the pollen free from the anthers. Huge quantities of tiny, light pollen grains are produced, and you can often see clouds of this pollen floating up from flowering grasses if you brush against them. (Grass pollen is one of the main culprits causing hay fever.) The stigmas are long and feathery, and protrude from the flower. Their large exposed surface increases their chance of catching pollen grains floating on the wind.

Fig. 18.10 (top) Plants belonging to the Papilionaceae have flowers whose petals provide a landing platform for bees. As the bee thrusts its head inside the flower in search of nectar, pollen is either deposited onto its back from the anthers, or removed from it by the stigma.

(bottom) Many orchids have evolved very complex pollinating mechanisms which rely on a single species of insect. This bucket orchid from Costa Rica provides a tunnel through which a *Coryanthes* bee pushes its way, emerging with pollen-containing structures attached to its thorax.

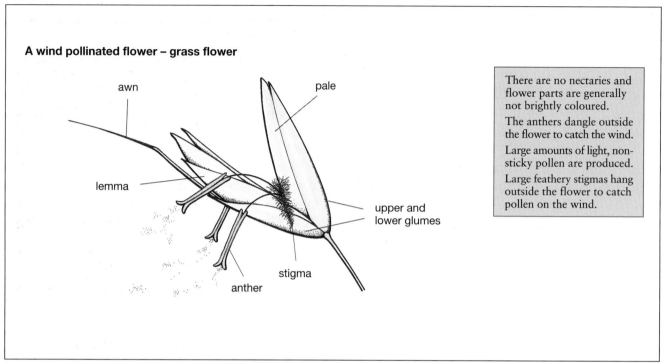

A wind pollinated flower – grass flower

awn

pale

lemma

upper and
lower glumes

stigma

anther

There are no nectaries and
flower parts are generally
not brightly coloured.

The anthers dangle outside
the flower to catch the wind.

Large amounts of light, non-
sticky pollen are produced.

Large feathery stigmas hang
outside the flower to catch
pollen on the wind.

Fig. 18.11 Structure of a wind-pollinated flower.

18.8 Fertilisation

Pollination results in the arrival of pollen grains on to the stigma. The pollen grains stick to the surface of the stigma, absorb water and begin to germinate. This normally only happens if the pollen grain is on the stigma of the same species of flower, and – in some species – if it is on the stigma of a different flower of the same species. (You can read more about this in Box 18.1.)

The contents of the pollen grain push out through one of the pits in the wall, forming a **pollen tube** (Fig. 18.12). The tube grows down through the style towards an ovule. The tube nucleus (Section 18.5) remains close to the tip of the tube as it makes its way through the style. Digestive enzymes are secreted from the tip of the tube, which is probably directed towards the ovule by chemicals which the ovule secretes. As the tube grows, the generative nucleus divides by mitosis, forming two haploid **male gametes**.

In most plants, the pollen tube enters the ovule through the micropyle, although in a few species it may digest its way in through the chalaza. Once the tube has penetrated the ovule, the tube nucleus degenerates as its role is completed. Behind it, the two male gametes make their way into the embryo sac.

As you would expect, one of the male gametes fuses with the egg cell, forming a **diploid zygote**. But, in plants, a double fertilisation takes place inside the embryo sac. The other male gamete fuses with the diploid nucleus in the centre of the embryo sac, forming a **triploid** nucleus (that is, possessing three sets of chromosomes). This triploid nucleus is called the **endosperm** nucleus.

Q1 Give an account of the adaptations of flowers to insect and wind pollination as illustrated by the flowers of the Papilionaceae and a grass.

ULEAC 1996 *(Total 10 marks)*

(1) Pollen germination

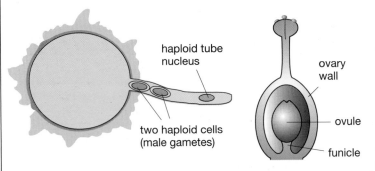

haploid tube nucleus

two haploid cells (male gametes)

ovary wall

ovule

funicle

Scanning electron micrograph of germinating pollen on a stigma (×540)

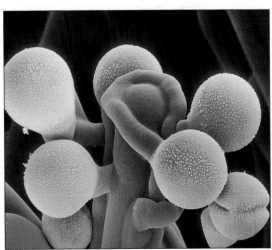

The haploid generative cell divides by mitosis. The pollen tube grows through the pollen wall. Pollen germination is often stimulated by the presence of sugar solutions.

The pollen tube penetrates the stigma and style.
It grows between the walls of the tissues.

(2) The pollen tube enters the ovule

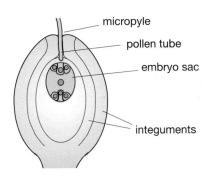

micropyle

pollen tube

embryo sac

integuments

The pollen tube grows into the ovule at the micropyle, where there is a gap in the integuments covering the ovule.

(3) Fertilisation – (only embryo sac and pollen tube shown)

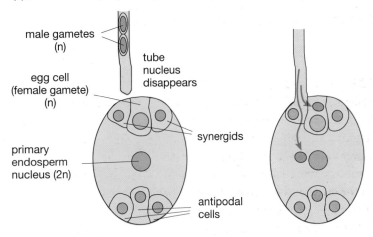

male gametes (n)

tube nucleus disappears

egg cell (female gamete) (n)

synergids

primary endosperm nucleus (2n)

antipodal cells

The pollen tube penetrates the embryo sac by growing into one of the synergids.

The nucleus of one male gamete penetrates the egg cell and fertilises it, forming a diploid zygote.

The other male nucleus combines with the primary endosperm nucleus to form a triploid endosperm nucleus.

(4) Products of fertilisation

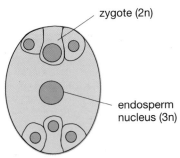

zygote (2n)

endosperm nucleus (3n)

Fig. 18.12   Fertilisation.

Box 18.1 Outbreeding mechanisms

Many species of plants have mechanisms which make it almost impossible for self-fertilisation to take place. Fertilisation can only occur between different plants of the same species, and sometimes only between unrelated plants of the same species. This is called **outbreeding**. In some plant species self-fertilisation or breeding between closely related individuals is possible. This is called **inbreeding**.

Outbreeding increases the amount of genetic variation in the population. Unrelated individuals are more likely to possess different alleles of genes than closely related individuals, so outbreeding maintains a relatively large number of different alleles in the population. Inbreeding over several generations, on the other hand, can result in almost every individual in the population possessing the same alleles. Many reasons have been put forward as to why genetic variation is 'desirable' within a population. One widely held view is that this makes it more likely that at least some individuals will have resistance against any particular parasite or pathogen.

There are many different mechanisms which have evolved to ensure outbreeding. We can only look at some of them here.

Mechanisms preventing self-pollination

In hollies, each individual plant bears either male or female flowers, but never both. The plants are said to be **dioecious**, and clearly self-pollination is impossible.

Many species of plants have flowers in which the pollen is ripe and ready to be shed well before the stigma is ripe on the same flower. This is called **protandry**, and it is very common. It occurs, for example, in the rose-bay willow-herb (Fig. 18.13). More rarely, the stigma may ripen before the anthers, a condition called **protogyny**. Figwort and bluebell are protogynous plants.

Self-pollination prevented by protandry
e.g. rose-bay willow-herb (*Epilobium angustifolium*)

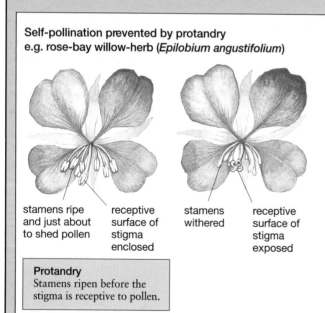

stamens ripe and just about to shed pollen | receptive surface of stigma enclosed

stamens withered | receptive surface of stigma exposed

Protandry
Stamens ripen before the stigma is receptive to pollen.

Self-pollination reduced by the special design of the primrose flower (*Primula vulgaris*)

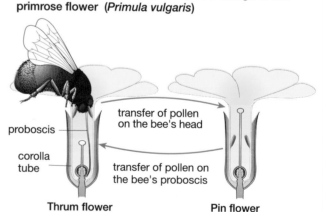

proboscis

corolla tube

transfer of pollen on the bee's head

transfer of pollen on the bee's proboscis

Thrum flower   **Pin flower**

The bee visits the flower to obtain nectar. Nectar is produced at the base of the petals and is held there because the petals are fused here forming a tube. The bee has to thrust its head into the long corolla tube so that the proboscis can reach the nectar. Any pollen attached to the proboscis after a visit to a pin flower can pollinate the thrum flower's stigma. Pollen is deposited on the bee's head by the thrum flower which can pollinate the stigma of a pin flower.

Fig. 18.13 Outbreeding mechanisms.

Box 18.1 Outbreeding mechanisms (cont.)

The flowers of primroses (Fig. 18.13) are of two types, called 'pin' and 'thrum'. Pin flowers have a long style, holding the stigma well above the anthers. Thrum flowers have a short style, so that the stigma is below the anthers. This makes it awkward for pollen to be transferred from anther to stigma on a pin flower, but there are also other mechanisms which prevent fertilisation from happening if self-pollination should occur.

Mechanisms preventing self-fertilisation
Even if pollen from a closely related plant, or even the same plant, does land on a stigma, it may not develop a pollen tube. In many species, including grasses, tomatoes and tobacco plants, the compatibility of pollen and stigma is determined by a gene called **S**, which has many different alleles. This gene codes for a protein which is involved in cell recognition, and pollen grains and stigmas with different alleles of this gene produce different varieties of the protein. If a pollen grain lands on a stigma with the same alleles of this gene as its own, it either will not germinate at all, or the pollen tube will not grow all the way through the style.

18.9   Development of a seed

Once fertilisation has taken place, the ovule is called a **seed**. It remains attached to the parent plant and continues to receive nutrients from it as it develops. Fig. 18.14 shows how a seed develops.

The diploid zygote divides by mitosis to form an **embryo plant**, attached to the wall of the ovule by a large **basal cell** and a little column of cells called the **suspensor**. The embryo develops a **radicle** or embryo root, a **plumule** or embryo shoot, and two **cotyledons**. In some species, the cotyledons will become the first leaves, the 'seed leaves', of the young plant when the seed germinates, while in others the plumule is the first part to reach the light and photosynthesise. In many species, the cells of the cotyledons build up large stores of food within the seed, such as starch, which will be used by the embryo in the early stages of germination.

The triploid endosperm nucleus also divides by mitosis, forming a tissue called the **endosperm** which surrounds the developing embryo. The function of the endosperm is to provide nourishment for the embryo. In some seeds, the endosperm has completed its function within a few days of fertilisation and disappears. In others, such as cereal grains (Fig. 15.24) it remains as the main storage tissue to provide nutrients during germination.

While all this is happening, the integuments of the ovule are developing into the **testa** of the seed. This involves thickening and toughening, as waterproof substances such as lignin are laid down in the cell walls. The small gap in the integuments, the **micropyle**, remains as a tiny hole in the testa.

The wall of the ovary also undergoes changes after fertilisation. The ovary becomes a **fruit**, and its wall becomes the **pericarp** of the fruit. The seeds are, of course, contained within the fruit, and the fruit is often adapted to disperse the seeds away from the parent plant. The pericarp may become fleshy and sweet-tasting to attract animals, or it may develop hooks and spines to stick to their hair. Wind-catching projections may form, or the fruit may become dry and hard, later splitting forcefully and throwing the seeds in all directions. In many species, other parts of the flower are involved in these developments; in dandelions, for example, the calyx becomes the 'parachute' of the fruit. In general, however, the various parts of the flower have completed their role by now, and they wither and fall off as the seeds develop inside the fruits.

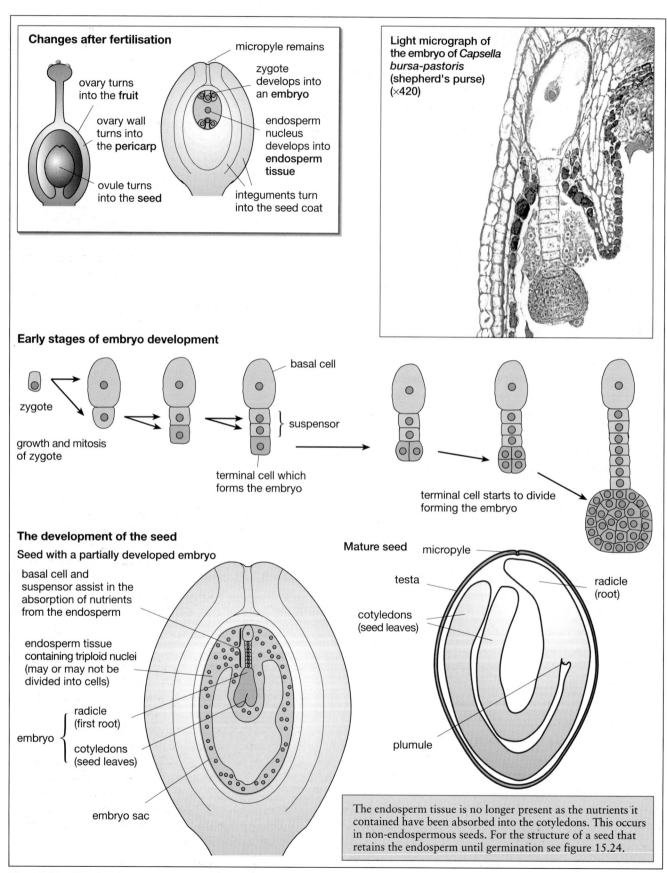

Changes after fertilisation

ovary turns into the **fruit**

ovary wall turns into the **pericarp**

ovule turns into the **seed**

micropyle remains

zygote develops into an **embryo**

endosperm nucleus develops into **endosperm tissue**

integuments turn into the seed coat

Light micrograph of the embryo of *Capsella bursa-pastoris* (shepherd's purse) (×420)

Early stages of embryo development

zygote

growth and mitosis of zygote

basal cell

suspensor

terminal cell which forms the embryo

terminal cell starts to divide forming the embryo

The development of the seed

Seed with a partially developed embryo

basal cell and suspensor assist in the absorption of nutrients from the endosperm

endosperm tissue containing triploid nuclei (may or may not be divided into cells)

embryo { radicle (first root)

cotyledons (seed leaves)

embryo sac

Mature seed   micropyle

testa

cotyledons (seed leaves)

radicle (root)

plumule

The endosperm tissue is no longer present as the nutrients it contained have been absorbed into the cotyledons. This occurs in non-endospermous seeds. For the structure of a seed that retains the endosperm until germination see figure 15.24.

Fig. 18.14   The development of the seed.

18.10 Seed dormancy and germination

In some species of plants, such as the common garden weed groundsel, the seeds are ready to germinate as soon as they leave the parent plant. More commonly, the seeds are in a state of suspended growth, called **dormancy**, when they are shed. Towards the end of their development, while still attached to the parent plant, water is withdrawn from them until their water content is as little as 5% of that of other plant tissues. This dryness helps seeds to survive for many years in very hostile conditions, such as drought, or extreme heat or cold. The relative concentrations of hormones, such as ABA, gibberellin and cytokinin (Sections 15.20 and 15.22), are also thought to keep the seed in a state of dormancy.

The exact conditions required for a seed to break dormancy and begin to germinate differ from species to species. Some require particular types of light (Section 15.24); almost all require exposure to a particular range of temperature, an adequate supply of oxygen, and water. As germination begins, water is absorbed into the seed and hydrolytic enzymes, such as amylases, break down the food stores into smaller soluble molecules (Fig. 15.24). These are transported to the developing embryo in which the nutrients are used to supply materials and energy to allow the cells to divide and lengthen.

First the radicle and then the plumule – or the cotyledons followed by the plumule – emerge from the seed. The radicle is positively geotropic (Section 15.19) and grows downwards. It can then absorb more water from the soil, as well as inorganic ions, allowing the rest of the seedling to grow even more rapidly. The plumule is negatively geotropic and positively phototropic, and grows up above the soil.

Up until this point, all of the growth of the seedling depended on the use of nutrients such as starch and protein which were stored in either the cotyledons or endosperm. Some of these nutrients are used to form new molecules and structures such as cellulose in cell walls. Some of them are respired, at first anaerobically (because oxygen cannot easily penetrate the seed) and then aerobically, so that some of the carbon atoms from them are released as carbon dioxide. The dry mass of a germinating seedling therefore drops during these early stages of germination. Once the plumule gets above ground, however, photosynthesis can begin. Now carbon atoms from carbon dioxide in the air are fixed and become incorporated into new molecules in the plant, so its dry mass begins to increase (Fig. 18.15). ■

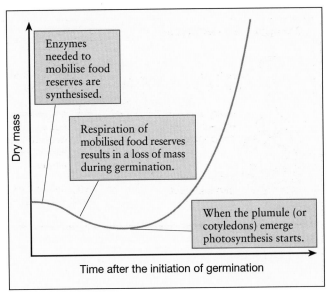

Fig. 18.15 Changes in dry mass during germination of a seed.

Within the graph:
- Enzymes needed to mobilise food reserves are synthesised.
- Respiration of mobilised food reserves results in a loss of mass during germination.
- When the plumule (or cotyledons) emerge photosynthesis starts.

Axis labels: Dry mass (y-axis); Time after the initiation of germination (x-axis).

Q2 Read through the following passage on flowering plant reproduction then copy it, filling in the blanks with the most appropriate word or words to complete the account.

The transfer of pollen grains from the .... of a flower on one plant to the .... of a flower on another plant of the same species is known as .... pollination. The pollen grains may be carried from one plant to another by .... or .... This type of pollination favours .... and flowers may have special features to encourage it. Species in which there are separate male and female plants are called .... Where male and female reproductive structures are found in the same flower, they may mature at different times. In the condition known as .... , the male reproductive structures ripen before the female.

ULEAC 1995   (*Total 8 marks*)

Box 18.2 Gamete transfer in water and on land

Life first evolved in water. No-one is quite sure when or how this happened, but the earliest fossils so far discovered are about 3500 million years old, so it is thought that the earliest forms of life may have appeared about 4000 million years ago. For millions of years, life was confined to water. The earliest fossils of land plants and land-living arthropods are 420 million years old, and the first land-living vertebrates do not appear until about 350 million years ago.

The transition from aquatic life to terrestrial life involved overcoming many difficulties. Water loss from body surfaces would rapidly dry out an unprotected body, and all terrestrial organisms have some method of reducing this (see, for example, Section 12.2). Support is also a difficulty (Section 16.1). Yet another problem to be solved is getting male and female gametes together, in sexual reproduction.

In most aquatic organisms, male gametes swim through the water to the female gametes. Fertilisation takes place outside the body of the parents – this is called **external fertilisation**. The chances of successful fertilisation greatly increase if the release of male and female gametes is synchronised, but even when this happens there is great wastage. Organisms using this method of fertilisation normally produce very large quantities of gametes, to make up for the wastage.

As plants and animals moved on to the land, external fertilisation clearly became much more difficult to achieve. Nevertheless, many terrestrial organisms do still depend on it. Liverworts and ferns still require a film of water, or splashing raindrops, to transfer their male gametes to the female gametes. Most amphibians such as frogs and toads still have to return to water, where eggs and sperm are released into the water so that fertilisation can take place. All of these organisms are therefore still tied to wet conditions at some stage in their life cycle.

Both plants and animals, however, have evolved other methods of gamete transfer which make them much more independent of external supplies of water. Flowering plants have male gametes encased in waterproof coverings, in the form of pollen grains, which can survive long periods of time in dry air. The male gamete completes its journey to the female gamete safely protected inside the style of the flower, never coming into direct contact with the air. This is a form of **internal fertilisation**. Many non-vertebrates and all reptiles, birds and mammals use internal fertilisation. The male introduces sperm – often in a fluid such as semen, or in a protective sac – into the female, and fertilisation takes place inside the female's body.

As well as protecting gametes from drying out, internal fertilisation has another benefit – it increases the chances of a male gamete successfully meeting a female one, and so reduces wastage. This is especially true in animals, where the male gametes can be directly delivered to the female by the male; it is less true in flowering plants, where the delivery of pollen is a less certain process. Internal fertilisation has therefore also developed in many aquatic organisms, such as dogfish and barnacles, the advantage being that fewer gametes need to be produced to ensure successful reproduction than if external fertilisation were used.

Box 18.3 Alternation of generations in a flowering plant

The life cycle of a flowering plant follows the same essential sequence as that of a liverwort or fern. Two different generations are involved – a haploid gamete-producing gametophyte and a diploid spore-producing sporophyte (Fig. 18.16).

The adult plant is the **diploid sporophyte** generation. Like all sporophytes, it produces **haploid spores** by meiosis. Unlike the male fern, these spores are of two different kinds, so flowering plants are said to be **heterosporous**.

One kind of spore is the **pollen grain**. Pollen grains are very small, and so they are called **microspores**. The other type of spore is the **embryo sac**; this is larger than the pollen grains and is known as a **megaspore**.

As in liverworts and ferns, the haploid spores divide by mitosis to produce a **haploid gametophyte** generation. The microspores produce a male gametophyte made up of just a few haploid cells, the contents of the pollen grain. The megaspores produce the female gametophyte – a few haploid cells, the contents of the embryo sac. Thus, the gametophyte generation in a flowering plant is extremely reduced compared with that of a liverwort or a fern. Both male and female gametophytes remain inside their 'spore cases' (the wall of the pollen grain and the wall of the embryo sac), never developing into an independent stage.

Gametophytes produce gametes by mitosis, and this is what happens inside the pollen grains and embryo sac. Two male gametes are formed inside each pollen grain, which fuse with two haploid nuclei inside the embryo sac. The diploid zygote formed by one of these fusions divides by mitosis to form a new plant – a new diploid sporophyte.

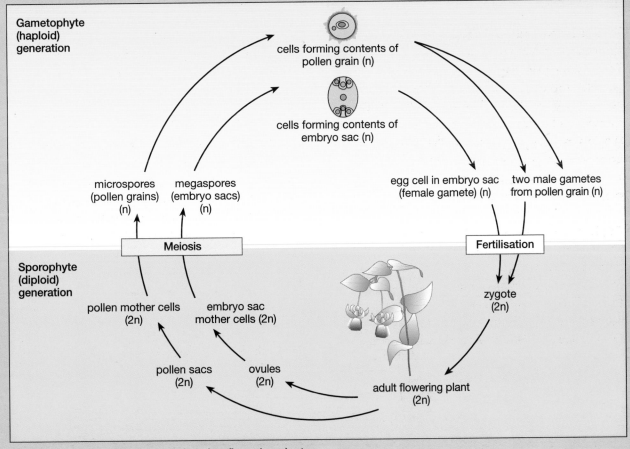

Fig. 18.16 Alternation of generations in a flowering plant.

Q3 (a) Describe the external features of a fern sporophyte. (7)

(b) Describe where mitosis and meiosis occur in the life cycle of a fern, and explain the significance of each process within the life cycle. (8)

(c) Suggest reasons for the preference of most ferns for moist habitats. (3)

UCLES 1995 (*Total 18 marks*)

Q4 The figure below shows a section through a seed containing a developing embryo.

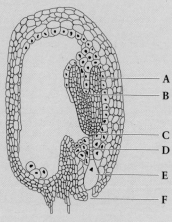

(a) Name the structures **A–F**. (3)

Developing seeds may contain cotyledons and/or endosperm.

(b) (i) Describe **one similarity** in the role of these two structures. (1)
   (ii) State **one difference** in the genetic make up of these structures. (1)

(c) State **one** function of each of the following structures.
   testa
   micropyle (2)

(d) Describe the structural changes that occur after fertilisation when
   (i)   an ovule develops into a seed; (3)
   (ii) an ovary develops into a fruit. (2)

UCLES 1995 (*Total 12 marks*)

Q5 Pollen from many species of plants will germinate on artificial media. Germination on water is generally poor, and any pollen tubes formed usually burst.

The figure below shows the effect of sucrose concentration on pollen tube growth, with or without the addition of a very small amount of borate. (Borate is a salt containing the element boron.) The pollen tubes were measured at a fixed time after germination had occurred.

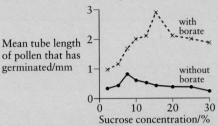

Two different hypotheses were put forward to explain the role of **sucrose** in pollen tube growth.
(1) It is used to provide the pollen tube with energy.
(2) It prevents the bursting of the pollen tube by osmosis.

(a) Describe a simple experiment you might carry out to eliminate one of these hypotheses.   (3)

(b) Borate was used in these experiments at extremely low concentration. Suggest **one** possible explanation for its effect on pollen tube growth.   (2)

Suspensions of different densities of pollen grains were made up in solutions containing 10% sucrose with added borate and allowed to germinate under standardised conditions. The figure below shows the percentage germination of pollen at different densities for two series of suspensions. One series was made up with water ('control'). A second series was made up with water that had been shaken with a large amount of pollen and then filtered ('plus extract of pollen').

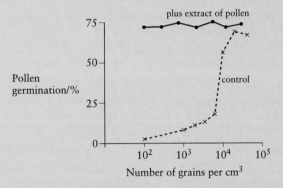

(c) Suggest an explanation for the results shown in the figure above.   (2)

Pollen from one species of plant was scattered on the surface of dishes containing sucrose agar medium. In two **separate** experiments, slices of stigmas of two different plant species, P and Q, were placed on individual dishes of the medium treated with pollen. The growth of the pollen tubes at different distances from the stigma slices is shown in the figure below.

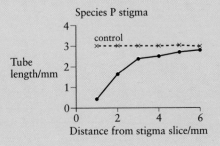
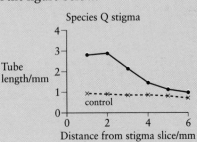

(d) (i) Explain what the 'controls' represent in the last figure.
   (ii) What evidence is there from the graphs to indicate that the two experiments were carried out
        for different periods of time? (2)

(e) Suggest an explanation for the results shown in the last figure. (2)

NEAB 1995 (*Total 11 marks*)

Q6 The graph below shows changes in the mean length of stamen filaments in a flower before the anthers
shed their pollen.

It also shows the effect of immersion in a solution containing 10^{-5} mol dm^{-3} of the plant growth
substance IAA on filaments of the same species of plant removed before they had elongated.

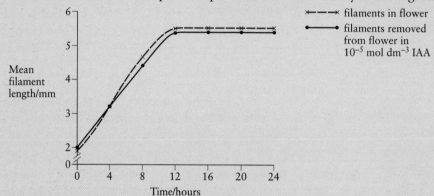

(a) (i) Give evidence from the graph which suggests that filament elongation in the intact flower
        may be controlled by a plant growth substance. (1)
   (ii) What control would you set up to ensure that elongation of the removed filaments was
        caused by IAA and not by any other substance in the filament itself? Explain your answer. (2)

You are required to design an experiment to test whether a chemical in pollen grains influences
filament elongation.

(b) List the main steps in your procedure. (3)

(c) Describe **two** features that it would be necessary to keep constant. Give a reason for your answer
    in each case. (2)

(d) Explain why it might be better to express the results as percentage change in length rather than
    mean filament length. (2)

AEB 1994 (*Total 10 marks*)

19 Ecology

Ecology is the study of organisms within their environment, including the way in which organisms interact with each other and with the non-living parts of the environment. Energy enters most ecosystems as light, is transferred from one organism to another as chemical energy, and returns to the environment as heat. Atoms such as carbon and nitrogen circulate between the living and non-living components of ecosystems. Interactions between living organisms and their environment affect the distribution of species and also the sizes of their populations.

ENERGY FLOW THROUGH ECOSYSTEMS
19.1 Energy transfer between organisms
Living cells require energy for many purposes which are outlined in Section 8.1. The immediate source of energy is almost always ATP which is produced by respiration (Section 9.1). Respiration transfers energy from other organic molecules, such as glucose, to ATP molecules.

The energy in these organic molecules can be thought of as **chemical energy**. The original source of almost all of the chemical energy in living organisms is **light energy**, which is captured by green plants and other photosynthetic organisms and transferred to organic compounds, such as carbohydrates, during photosynthesis. Photosynthetic organisms (green plants, algae and photosynthetic bacteria) therefore supply almost all the chemical energy used by living organisms. They are said to be **producers.**

Animals and fungi obtain their supplies of chemical energy by feeding on other organisms. They are **consumers.** Herbivorous animals, which feed on plants, are **primary consumers**. Carnivorous animals, which feed on herbivores, are **secondary consumers**. Carnivores which feed on secondary consumers are **tertiary consumers,** and so on. Most fungi, some animals and some bacteria feed on dead organisms or waste material from them, and these organisms are called **decomposers.**

The level at which an organism feeds in this sequence of energy transfer is called a **trophic level.** Producers are at the first trophic level, primary consumers at the second, and so on.

A simple diagram showing how energy passes from one organism to another is called a **food chain** (Fig. 19.1). The arrows in a food chain indicate the direction of energy transfer from one organism to another. However, most organisms feed on more than one other kind of organism, and more details of their feeding relationships can be shown in a **food web**.

Looking at the food web in Fig. 19.1, you can see that many individual organisms do not always feed at the same trophic level. For example, dragonfly larvae feed as secondary consumers and as tertiary consumers. Organisms such as the water flea *Daphnia*, which regularly feed as primary consumers and higher order consumers, are called **omnivores**.

19.2   Energy losses in food webs
As energy is transferred from one organism to another in a food web, a large proportion of it is lost to the surrounding environment. In a pond, for example, a certain amount of sunlight energy falls on to the water surface, and a proportion of this energy is converted to chemical energy by the producers. The producers use some of this energy themselves, for example for fuelling active transport, and this energy is lost from the producers as heat energy. Some of the energy is stored by the producers in chemicals which make up their bodies, and this energy is available to the herbivores.

However, the herbivores will not be able to use all of the chemical energy stored in the producers. Not all of the parts of plants may be edible, or it may not be possible for the herbivores to digest and absorb all of the plant material they eat. On average, in a terrestrial (land-based) food web, only about 10% of the energy in the producers will be transferred into the herbivores. This percentage is larger in an aquatic food web. The herbivores will use some of this energy, for processes such as moving and active transport, and once again a high proportion of the energy will be lost to the environment as heat. Only a small proportion of the energy transferred to the herbivores is available to be transferred to the carnivores. This pattern continues along the food chain, with approximately 90% of the energy being lost at each transfer between trophic levels.

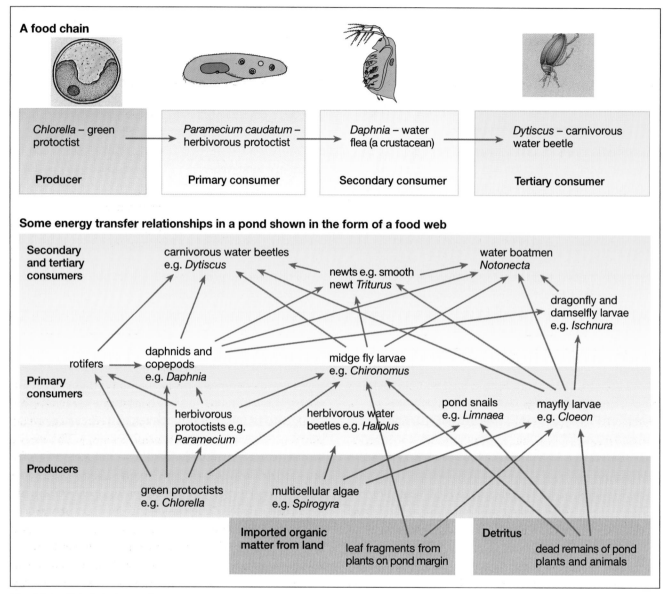

A food chain

Chlorella – green protoctist	*Paramecium caudatum* – herbivorous protoctist	*Daphnia* – water flea (a crustacean)	*Dytiscus* – carnivorous water beetle
Producer	Primary consumer	Secondary consumer	Tertiary consumer

Some energy transfer relationships in a pond shown in the form of a food web

Secondary and tertiary consumers: carnivorous water beetles e.g. *Dytiscus*; newts e.g. smooth newt *Triturus*; water boatmen *Notonecta*; dragonfly and damselfly larvae e.g. *Ischnura*

Primary consumers: rotifers; daphnids and copepods e.g. *Daphnia*; herbivorous protoctists e.g. *Paramecium*; midge fly larvae e.g. *Chironomus*; herbivorous water beetles e.g. *Haliplus*; pond snails e.g. *Limnaea*; mayfly larvae e.g. *Cloeon*

Producers: green protoctists e.g. *Chlorella*; multicellular algae e.g. *Spirogyra*

Imported organic matter from land: leaf fragments from plants on pond margin

Detritus: dead remains of pond plants and animals

Fig. 19.1 Food chain and food web for a freshwater pond.

19.3 Pyramids of numbers, biomass and energy

Ecologists are interested in measuring these energy transfers and losses because they affect the numbers of organisms which can exist at different trophic levels. For example, in the pond in which the food web shown in Fig. 19.1 operates you would almost certainly find that the herbivorous animals would considerably outnumber the carnivorous animals. This happens because there is more energy available to the herbivores in the pond than to the carnivores. The amount of tissue which can be kept alive is dependent on the amount of energy available to it.

Pyramids can be drawn to represent the proportions of energy which are lost in a food web. Fig. 19.2 shows a pyramid for the food web in the pond shown in Fig. 19.1. The producers are shown at the bottom of the pyramid, with the higher trophic levels stacked on top in sequence. The area of each box in the pyramid represents the quantity of whatever is being measured. This can be **numbers, biomass** or **energy**. In the pond food web, the shape of all three kinds of pyramids is very similar, so only one is shown. However, this is not always so, and in some food webs the relative sizes of the boxes in different kinds of pyramids can be very different.

In a **pyramid of numbers**, each box represents the numbers of all the organisms feeding at a particular trophic level in the pond. The data for drawing this kind of pyramid is – in theory – relatively easy to obtain; all you

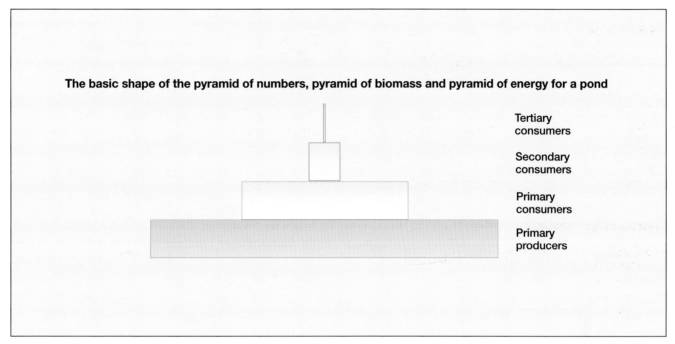

The basic shape of the pyramid of numbers, pyramid of biomass and pyramid of energy for a pond

Tertiary consumers

Secondary consumers

Primary consumers

Primary producers

Fig. 19.2 Pyramids of number, biomass and energy.

have to do is to catch everything in the pond, decide what trophic level each organism feeds at and count them. In practice, however, even this is extremely time-consuming. It makes it easier if just a small area of the pond is sampled, but it still takes many person-hours to gather all this information.

Pyramids of numbers do not always tell the full story about what is happening as energy passes along food webs. Just counting numbers of organisms gives no information about 'how much organism' there is. Organisms clearly vary greatly in size, and it is not really very informative if you equate the numbers of tiny organisms such as *Daphnia* with the numbers of larger organisms such as smooth newts. A better picture of the relative amounts of living tissues which are present at each trophic level is given by a **pyramid of biomass**. To obtain this information, the **dry mass** of all the organisms at each trophic level is measured. This is done by heating the organisms in an oven to a temperature of about 80 °C to drive off all the water. After a while they are weighed, and then put back into the oven for a little longer, then reweighed. This continues until two consecutive weighings give the same reading, indicating that all the water has been driven off. This method is obviously not a very pleasant one to carry out on animals, and so researchers will normally just measure the 'wet mass' of animals such as newts, and perhaps refer to previously published figures to estimate what their dry mass would be.

But even a pyramid of biomass does not give the best information about energy availability at each trophic level, because different tissues in different organisms contain different amounts of chemical energy. This can be determined by burning the organism and measuring the amount of heat released per gram. This is done in a **calorimeter** (Fig. 9.1), where the energy released from the organism's tissues heats water. If the mass of water is known, and the amount by which its temperature rises is measured, then the amount of heat released can be calculated. If this is carried out for all the organisms in each trophic level in the pond, then a **pyramid of energy** can be drawn. Pyramids of energy give much the best picture of what is happening to the energy in a food web. You can imagine, though, how awkward and time-consuming it is to obtain this amount of information, so ecologists often make do with pyramids of numbers or biomass instead.

19.4 Productivity

In the previous section, we have been considering the situation at one moment in time in the pond. It is often more useful to know how much energy is passing through a trophic level over a period of time. This is called **productivity**. Productivity is a measure of the amount of energy incorporated into the organisms in a trophic level, in a given area, over a certain period of time. The area used is normally one square metre, and the time is normally one year, so productivity is measured in units of kilojoules per square metre per year, that is $\mathbf{kJ\,m^{-2}\,year^{-1}}$.

The rate at which producers convert light energy into chemical energy is called **primary productivity**. **Gross primary productivity**, GPP, is the total amount of chemical energy incorporated into the producers. The producers, as explained in Section 19.2, use some of this energy themselves. They convert organic compounds to ATP in respiration and then use the ATP to supply energy for their needs. This energy is finally lost as heat to the environment. The remaining energy is available to the herbivores, and this is known as **net primary productivity**, NPP.

$$NPP = GPP - \text{energy used in respiration}$$

Primary productivity varies greatly in different environments. The rate at which plants can convert light energy to chemical energy is affected by many factors, such as the amount of sunlight falling onto them, the amount of water available, the temperature, and the amount of nutrients such as nitrates and phosphates (Fig. 19.3). In natural ecosystems, primary productivity tends to be higher in tropical regions than in high latitudes (areas closer to the Poles), because plants get more light and higher temperatures in the tropics. However, the most productive areas of the oceans are often in cold regions, because here upwelling of colder water to the surface brings up plant nutrients (Box 19.3); in deep tropical waters, even though there is ample light and warm water, productivity may be limited because plant nutrients are in short supply.

NUTRIENT CYCLES

19.5 Materials required by living organisms

Living organisms require more than a supply of energy – they require materials from which to build their bodies. Living organisms are built from a relatively small number of different kinds of atoms. Of these, **carbon**, **hydrogen** and **oxygen** are the most common, with **nitrogen** following closely behind. Smaller amounts of several other kinds of atoms are also required, such as phosphorus, calcium, iron, magnesium, sodium, potassium and chlorine.

Animals obtain most of the atoms from which they will build their bodies in the form of organic molecules. You cannot use oxygen, carbon dioxide or nitrogen from the air to supply any of the oxygen, carbon or nitrogen atoms which you need to build the protein, carbohydrate and fat molecules from which your body is made. You get all these atoms from organic molecules, such as proteins, carbohydrates and fats which you eat.

Once again, as for supplies of energy, animals depend on plants to supply them with their requirements. Unlike animals, plants *are* able to make use of inorganic sources of these atoms. Plants use carbon dioxide from the air and water from the soil to provide carbon, oxygen and hydrogen atoms to make carbohydrates and fats. They use nitrate and ammonium ions to supply nitrogen atoms to make proteins.

These atoms are passed from organism to organism, being reused time and time again as part of different molecules in different organisms. They can be passed back out into the environment, and then taken in by plants once more before being passed on to animals. The atoms **cycle** between living organisms and the environment.

Fig. 19.3 Crop productivity depends partly on the type of crop grown and partly on environmental factors. Sugar cane (left) can have a very high productivity, but requires warm temperatures, high light intensities and plentiful supplies of water. Maize is also potentially highly productive, but the productivity of the crop which will be planted in this ground (right) will be limited by an inadequate water supply.

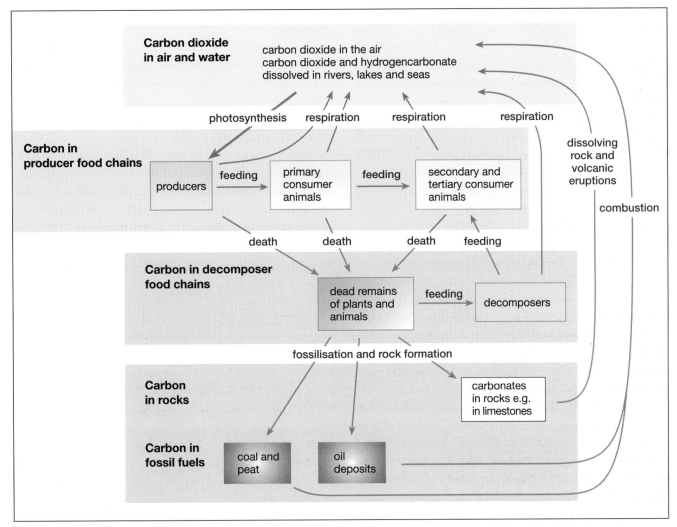

Fig. 19.4 The carbon cycle.

19.6   The carbon cycle

Figs. 19.4 and 19.5 show how carbon atoms are passed around from one organism to another, and between the organisms and their environment.

The atmosphere contains carbon dioxide. This is present in only very small proportions; carbon dioxide makes up less than 0.04% of the air. Nevertheless, this is the initial source of all the carbon atoms in the bodies of living organisms.

Plants, algae and blue-greens (cyanobacteria) take carbon dioxide from the air and incorporate the carbon atoms into carbohydrates, and later other organic compounds, in the process of photosynthesis. Large quantities of carbon are locked up inside the tissues of trees and other plants. In Britain, the plants in one hectare of mature woodland may contain as much as 200 tonnes of carbon. Some of these carbon-containing compounds are respired by the plant, and returned to the atmosphere

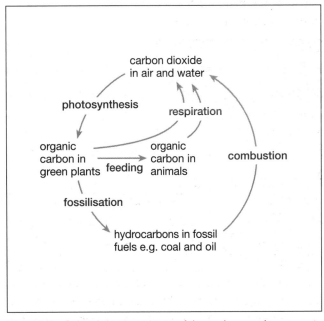

Fig. 19.5   Some important parts of the carbon cycle.

as carbon dioxide once more. In a growing plant, more carbon atoms are taken in than are given out, but in a mature forest tree the amounts of carbon dioxide absorbed for photosynthesis and given out as a result of respiration may be almost equal.

Animals obtain their supply of carbon by eating plants or by eating other animals. Carbohydrates, fats and proteins are digested and absorbed and used to build other carbohydrates, fats and proteins in their bodies. As in plants, respiration of some of these molecules results in the release of carbon dioxide to the air.

Not all plants or animals are eaten by other animals, however. Waste materials and dead bodies are used as food sources by decomposers, such as fungi and bacteria. These organisms digest the organic substances in their food source, and incorporate some of the carbon atoms into their own bodies. Some of the carbon-containing molecules will be used as substrates in respiration, and once again returned to the atmosphere as carbon dioxide.

In conditions where dead plant material cannot rapidly be broken down by decomposers, such as where soils are waterlogged and oxygen is in short supply, decay may only be partial and plant remains will accumulate in large quantities. This is how peat is formed. In Britain, peat soils hold huge amounts of carbon which was once part of living plants; a deep peat soil may contain about 1000 tonnes of carbon per hectare. 300 million years ago, in the Carboniferous period, huge areas of swamps covered many parts of the world, and vast quantities of semi-decayed plant material accumulated, eventually forming coal. Coal is a fossil fuel; oil and natural gas formed in a similar way, from the remains of microorganisms. Large quantities of carbon are locked up in fossil fuels.

Combustion of any of these carbon-containing materials – trees or other plants, peat or fossil fuels – releases carbon dioxide into the air. There is concern that an increase in these processes in recent years is adding more carbon dioxide to the atmosphere than is being removed from it, and the possible consequences of this are discussed in Section 20.2.

In the sea, there is another major pathway a carbon atom can follow. Many marine organisms make shells containing calcium carbonate; the carbonate ions in this substance contain carbon. When these organisms die, their shells fall to the sea bed. Huge deposits of such shells, built up over thousands of years, form limestone rocks. Earth movements may carry these rocks deep into the Earth, from where the carbon atoms may be returned

to the atmosphere by volcanic eruptions which release carbon dioxide. Alternatively, the rocks may be lifted above sea level, where they become exposed to the air. Rain, which is slightly acidic, reacts with the carbonates in limestone rocks and releases carbon dioxide.

19.7 The nitrogen cycle

Living organisms need nitrogen atoms to make proteins and nucleic acids (DNA and RNA). The atmosphere contains very large amounts of nitrogen – about 79% of the air is nitrogen gas – but only very few organisms are able to make use of this source. Even green plants cannot use gaseous nitrogen. Figs. 19.6 and 19.7 show how nitrogen atoms circulate between organisms and the environment.

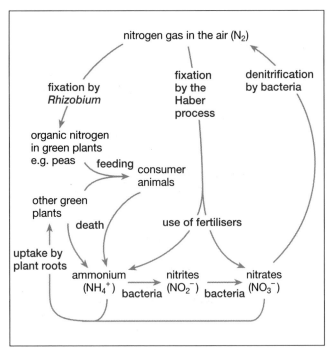

Fig. 19.6   Some important parts of the nitrogen cycle.

● Nitrogen fixation

Nitrogen gas is composed of molecules in which two nitrogen atoms are bonded together by three covalent bonds. This arrangement is very stable, and so nitrogen molecules are very unreactive. Before nitrogen can be used by most living organisms, it has to be combined with other atoms to produce molecules or ions such as nitrate, NO_3^- and ammonium, NH_4^+, which are more reactive and can take part in metabolic reactions.

The conversion of nitrogen gas to these more reactive substances is called **nitrogen fixation**.

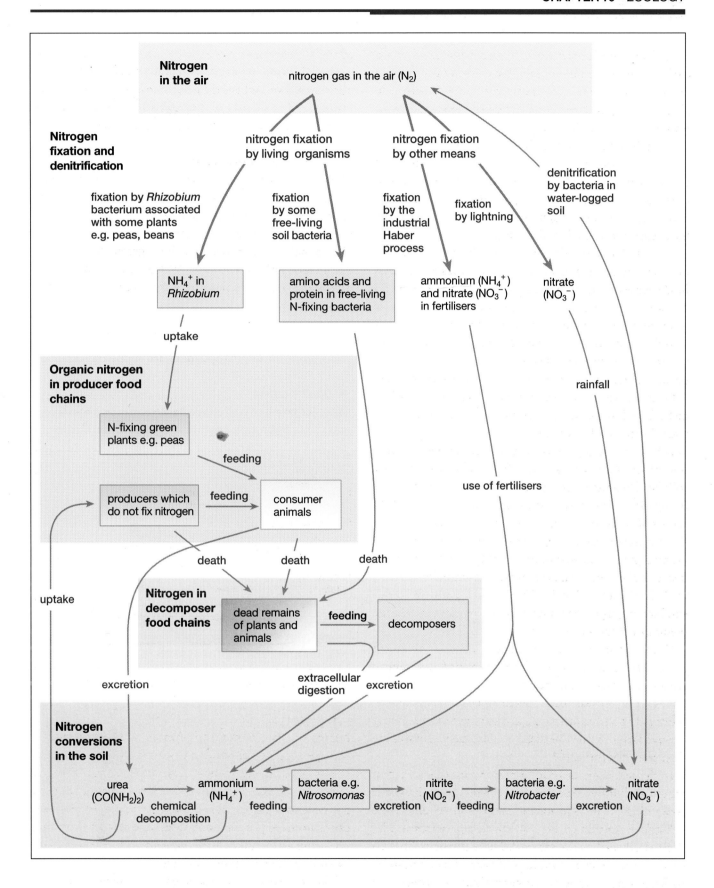

Fig. 19.7   The nitrogen cycle.

Nitrogen fixation occurs whenever lightning flashes through the air. The huge amounts of energy in a lightning flash can break nitrogen molecules apart, and allow nitrogen atoms to react with oxygen in the air to form nitrogen oxides. These dissolve in raindrops, and fall to the ground, where they form nitrites (NO_2^-) and nitrates.

Very large quantities of nitrogen are fixed industrially, in the Haber process, to produce nitrogen-containing fertilisers. Nitrogen and hydrogen gas are reacted together under high pressure to produce ammonia, NH_3. Some of the ammonia is then used to make nitric acid, which in turn can be used to make nitrates. Ammonium nitrate (NH_4NO_3) is the most widely used fertiliser in the world.

Some prokaryotic organisms are also able to fix nitrogen. Some bacteria, including blue-greens, possess an enzyme called **nitrogenase**. This enzyme can catalyse the reduction of nitrogen gas to ammonium ions. This reaction can only take place in conditions where no oxygen is present, and it requires a considerable input of energy. For this reason, most nitrogen fixation takes place when the nitrogen-fixing organism is living in close association with a plant. The bacterium *Rhizobium*, for example, lives freely in the soil and also in root nodules of plants belonging to the pea family, but it only fixes nitrogen when it is in a root nodule. This is described in Box 13.5.

● Nitrogen in primary producer food chains

Nitrates formed by lightning, or applied to the soil in fertilisers, can be absorbed by plant roots. (Ammonium ions can also be absorbed by plants, but there are rarely many ammonium ions available in the soil for reasons explained below.) Inside the plant cells, nitrate ions are reduced to ammonium ions, which can then be used to make amino acids (Section 8.6). The ammonium ions produced by nitrogen-fixing bacteria are used in the same way. The plant can then use the amino acids to make proteins.

Animals obtain their nitrogen in the form of proteins, when they eat plants or other animals.

● Nitrogen in decomposer food chains

Many decomposers which feed on dead bodies and waste materials – such as faeces and urine – from living organisms digest proteins extracellularly. They secrete proteases which break down the proteins into amino acids. The decomposers may then absorb these amino acids and incorporate them into their own bodies.

● Ammonification

Some of the amino acids are deaminated (Section 15.11) by decomposers, producing ammonium ions which pass into the soil. Urea, present in animal urine, is also converted to ammonium in the soil. This process is called **ammonification**.

● Nitrification

Ammonium ions in the soil are quickly acted upon by **nitrifying bacteria**, for example *Nitrosomonas*, which convert the ammonium ions to nitrite ions. Other types of nitrifying bacteria, for example *Nitrobacter*, further oxidise nitrite ions to nitrate ions. These bacteria are chemoautotrophs, obtaining their energy from these oxidation reactions (Box 8.1). As nitrification requires a supply of oxygen, it happens most rapidly in well-aerated soils. The nitrate ions produced as a result of nitrification can then be taken up by plants to use in protein formation.

● Denitrification

Another group of bacteria reduces nitrate ions to nitrogen gas. This reduction requires anaerobic conditions, so these bacteria are most active in poorly aerated, waterlogged soils.

Q1 (a) Describe the role of microorganisms in
　　　　(i) the carbon cycle, and　　　*(4)*
　　　　(ii) the nitrogen cycle.　　　　*(4)*

　　(b) Discuss why only a small proportion of the energy in sunlight reaching the surface of the Earth reaches the top carnivores in food chains.　　*(10)*

UCLES 1995　　　　*(Total 18 marks)*

STUDYING ECOSYSTEMS

19.8 Some terms used in ecology

The term 'ecology' was first introduced in 1867, and ecologists still argue about exactly what ecology is. One working definition is that it is the study of the interactions between organisms and their environment which determine the distribution of organisms and their abundance. As you can imagine, this is a very broad area of study, and it is easy to get confused if you do not define what you are studying very clearly. To help to 'pin down' ecological studies and their interpretation, a number of terms have developed and been defined. Ecologists still disagree over exact definitions of some of them, but the descriptions which follow are widely accepted. Fig. 19.8 illustrates how some of these terms can be applied to a pond and the organisms which live in it.

A **habitat** is a place where organisms live. In Fig. 19.8, the pond is the habitat of many different organisms. Within this habitat, some organisms have their own

specialised habitat; for example, *Tubifex* worms live in sediment on the bottom, in conditions where oxygen concentrations are low. The term 'habitat' is often used to mean the kind of place in which a particular species of organism can live, such as the range of pH of the water and the range of dissolved oxygen concentration in which it is found.

Many different species of organisms live within a habitat. All of the organisms of one species that live in the same place at the same time make up a **population** of that species. A population is a breeding group, and includes all the individuals of that species which can interbreed with each other. All of the *Notonecta* (water boatmen) in the pond make up a population. However, at certain times of year they leave the water and fly to other ponds, so their population could be considered to include all the water boatmen in nearby ponds as well.

All the populations in the area make up the **community**. A community is made up of all the different species of

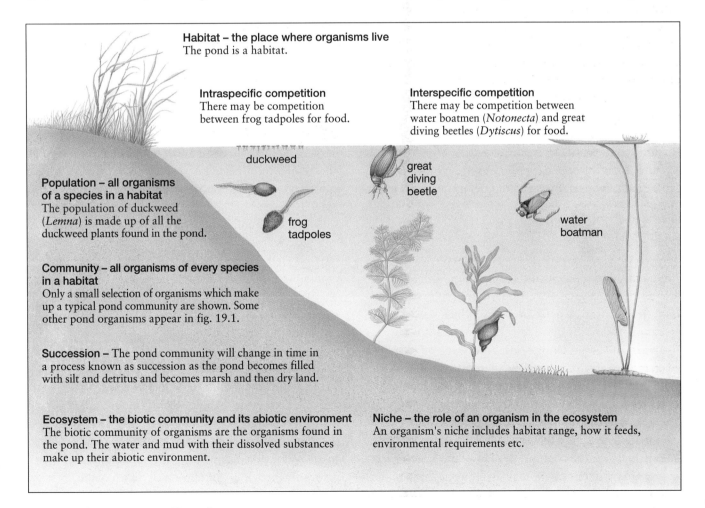

Habitat – the place where organisms live
The pond is a habitat.

Intraspecific competition
There may be competition between frog tadpoles for food.

Interspecific competition
There may be competition between water boatmen (*Notonecta*) and great diving beetles (*Dytiscus*) for food.

duckweed

great diving beetle

water boatman

frog tadpoles

Population – all organisms of a species in a habitat
The population of duckweed (*Lemna*) is made up of all the duckweed plants found in the pond.

Community – all organisms of every species in a habitat
Only a small selection of organisms which make up a typical pond community are shown. Some other pond organisms appear in fig. 19.1.

Succession – The pond community will change in time in a process known as succession as the pond becomes filled with silt and detritus and becomes marsh and then dry land.

Ecosystem – the biotic community and its abiotic environment
The biotic community of organisms are the organisms found in the pond. The water and mud with their dissolved substances make up their abiotic environment.

Niche – the role of an organism in the ecosystem
An organism's niche includes habitat range, how it feeds, environmental requirements etc.

Fig. 19.8   Some terms used in ecology.

organisms that live in the same place at the same time and interact with each other. Communities may remain fairly stable over a period of time, or they may be in a process of gradual change. This gradual change is called **succession**. Eventually, succession may result in the formation of a stable community which is called a **climax community**. Succession is described in Sections 19.17 and 19.18.

The pond contains both living (the organisms) and non-living components (the water, dissolved gases, stones and soil). The living components are called **biotic** components, and the non-living components are **abiotic** components. These interact with each other in many ways. The biotic community and its abiotic environment are known as an **ecosystem**. The pond, with its living organisms and all the abiotic components, can be considered to be an ecosystem.

In order to study features such as energy flow between organisms, it is often convenient to consider an ecosystem as a self-contained unit; if you do not do this you end up trying to measure energy flow through all the living organisms in the world! However, it is important to remember that no ecosystem is ever completely isolated from other ecosystems, and that energy does flow between one ecosystem and another. Ecosystems do not have sharply defined boundaries.

Within an ecosystem, each species of organism plays a particular role. The term **niche** is used to describe this role. An organism's niche has very many aspects, and it is virtually impossible to describe a niche completely. It includes what the organism eats, how it captures its food, what eats it, the excretory materials it produces and so on. Within a community, each species has a niche which differs in at least some ways from the niches of all the other species in the same community.

Nevertheless, niches of different species do overlap, and this can lead to **interspecific competition**. 'Interspecific' means 'between species'. Competition results when two or more organisms require a resource which is insufficient to supply the needs of all of them. For example, water boatmen and great diving beetles both feed on tadpoles, so if tadpoles are in short supply, there may be competition for food between these two species. Experiments suggest that if two species have extremely similar niches, then one species will probably die out when this kind of competition occurs, so that both species will not be able to coexist in the same community. However, species with overlapping niches can coexist, so long as these niches also have non-overlapping areas. For example, water boatmen and great diving beetles each have other food

sources, and they feed in different ways. Water boatmen take much of their prey near to or on the surface of the water, whereas great diving beetles tend to spend more time hunting amongst weeds deeper in the water.

Competition also exists within a species, and this is called **intraspecific competition**. This is an important factor in determining population size, and is discussed in Section 19.15.

19.9 Sampling

When you are studying an ecosystem or a habitat, the information you want to know usually includes:

- what lives there, and

- the abundance of each species which lives there.

You may also want to know whether the different species are distributed evenly in the area you are studying, or whether there is a pattern to their distribution.

It is usually impossible to make an exhaustive, complete survey, counting and mapping every individual organism. You will therefore need to **sample** just part of the area. If this is done carefully, then you can assume that your sample provides a fair picture of the overall species distribution in the area.

The techniques you will use for sampling, what you will measure and how you will measure it, depend very much on the kind of habitat you are investigating (for example, whether it is terrestrial or aquatic, woodland or moorland and so on) and what you want to know. In Sections 19.10 to 19.13, some of the basic methods of sampling are described. You will almost certainly use some of these in your practical work – but you will almost certainly meet others as well. There is such a wide range of these that it is impossible to describe them all here, and you will need to refer to other sources, such as practical guides, for information about more specialist sampling and measuring techniques.

19.10 Using quadrats

Fig. 19.9 shows sampling techniques you might use when studying a terrestrial habitat, such as moorland, grassland or a rocky shore.

In this situation, you would probably decide to use a square frame called a **quadrat**. (Do not confuse this with a quadrant which is a quarter of a circle.) A quadrat marks off an area of ground within which you can make a thorough survey of which species are present, and how many of each of them there are. If the quadrat is too big, it is very difficult to do this accurately. If the quadrat is too small, it does not give you a very good sample of the habitat as a whole. In practice, it is found that a quadrat with sides of 0.5 m, that is with an area of 0.25 m², is the best size in many terrestrial situations (Fig. 19.9).

Having placed the quadrat on the ground, you first have to identify each species within it, probably using a key. You then estimate the abundance of each species. You could:

- use an abundance scale, such as the **ACFOR** scale. ACFOR stands for Abundant, Common, Frequent, Occasional or Rare, and you simply make an estimate of which of these best describes the abundance of each species within your quadrat.

- count the actual **number of individuals** of each species. This is possible with sedentary animals on a rocky shore, but very difficult with plants as it is often impossible to decide when you are looking at one individual plant and when you are looking at many individuals growing next to each other.

- estimate the **percentage cover** of each species – that is, the proportion of the area within the quadrat which it occupies. To help with this, you could use a quadrat with wires running across it at 10 cm intervals in each direction, dividing the quadrat into 25 'mini-quadrats'.

You might also use a **point quadrat**. This is a frame with holes in it at regular intervals. You place the frame on the ground, and then lower a long pin through each hole in turn, recording the species of plant which you hit with the pin. More than one plant may be hit, as leaves of one plant often lie above the leaves of another; in this case, both species are recorded (Fig. 19.9).

19.11 Where do you sample?

You will need to record what is present in many quadrats in order to obtain a reasonable sample of the area you are studying. How do you decide where to place your quadrats?

● Random sampling

If the area looks reasonably uniform, or if it looks as though the species distribution is 'patchy' with no clear pattern, then it is probably best to sample the whole area randomly. This means that you use chance to determine where your quadrats should be placed, rather than making a conscious decision about where to put them. Random sampling is important if the results are to be statistically analysed.

A very basic way of doing this is to stand within the area, and just throw the quadrat over your shoulder. However, although this a very simple technique to use, it is not truly random. You are still quite likely to make sure (even subconsciously!) that your quadrat does not fall into the bit of the habitat covered with a dense thicket of brambles and nettles.

A better way is to use a calculator to generate **random numbers**, and then to use these as coordinates to determine the placing of each quadrat. First, you define the area you are going to study and use two sides of this area as axes. Standing at the 'origin', you generate two random numbers. The first is the x coordinate, and you either walk this number of strides along the x axis or measure this number of metres (or other units, depending on the total size of the area you are studying). The second number is the y coordinate, and this determines the spot at which you place the quadrat.

● Systematic sampling

In some situations, you may have particular reasons for wanting to sample more systematically. For example, you may want to investigate how vegetation changes as a dry meadow grades into a wet, marshy area. In this case, you could sample along a **transect**.

A transect is a line. You can choose where the line runs, and then lay down a tape or string to mark it out. You then sample the organisms present along this line. You can do this:

- by recording each organism which is touching the line at suitable, regular intervals. This is called a **line transect**.

- by placing a quadrat against the line, recording its contents as described in Section 19.10, and then placing the next quadrat immediately touching the first one; you repeat this all along the transect. This technique samples a 0.5 m wide 'belt' along the transect, and so is called a **belt transect**.

- by placing quadrats at regular intervals along the transect, say at every 10 m. This is called an **interrupted belt transect**.

Frame quadrats – choice of size

Optimum size depends on the habitat. In meadowland it may be 25 cm but to sample trees in woodland it may need to be many metres.

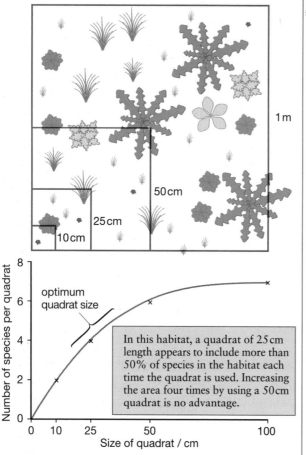

In this habitat, a quadrat of 25 cm length appears to include more than 50% of species in the habitat each time the quadrat is used. Increasing the area four times by using a 50 cm quadrat is no advantage.

Frame quadrats – estimation of abundance

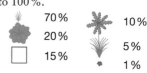

(1) Number

Counting organisms is impossible and inappropriate here.

(2) Percentage cover

This is a rough estimate to the nearest 5 or 10% and need not add up to 100%.

70%
20%
15%
10%
5%
1%

(3) Arbitrary abundance scale e.g. ACFOR

The scale can be made to approximate to percentage cover.
A – abundant (80 to 100%), C – common (60 to 80%),
F – frequent (40 to 60%), O – occasional (20 to 40%),
R – rare (0 to 20%)

Point quadrats

Using point quadrats gives a more accurate and consistent estimate of percentage cover.

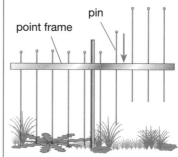

The higher the percentage cover, the more likely a pin will touch a leaf as it is lowered.

The number of touches is proportional to % cover.

If one leaf is found over another the pin may touch both. Both are counted.

This method is less susceptible to error than some other estimates of abundance.

Line transect – a line across one or more habitats

The organisms found at regular points along a line are noted. Transects are used to detect changes in community composition along a line across one or more habitats.

Belt transect and interrupted belt transect

The abundance of organisms within quadrats placed at regular points along a line is noted.

belt transect   interrupted belt transect

Fig. 19.9   Sampling plant and static animal communities to determine distribution and abundance.

19.12 What do your samples tell you?

You can use the results from the sampling techniques described in Sections 19.10 and 19.11 to determine various aspects of the distribution of the species within the sampled area.

● Species frequency (or percentage frequency)

The species frequency, or percentage frequency, is a measure of the chance of a particular species being found within any one quadrat. It is very easy to measure; you just record whether the species was present or absent in each quadrat you analyse. For example, if you placed your quadrat 50 times, and found daisies in 22 of these placings, then the species frequency for daisies is $22/50 \times 100 = 44\%$.

● Species density

This tells you how many individuals of the species there are per m^2. Clearly, you can only calculate this if you were able to count individuals within the quadrat; you cannot use it if you recorded your results using the ACFOR scale or percentage cover (Section 19.10).

To work this out, you take your results from each quadrat and average them out. For example, you might have the following results for a species of sea anemone on a rocky shore, using a quadrat with an area of $0.25\,m^2$.

Quadrat number	1	2	3	4	5	6	7	8	9	10
Number of individuals of this species	0	3	0	1	0	0	5	2	0	1

Ten quadrats were placed, so a total area of $10 \times 0.25\,m^2$, which equals $2.5\,m^2$, was sampled. The total number of sea anemones found in this area was 12. Therefore the mean species density for this species is $12/2.5 = 4$ per m^2.

● Species cover

This tells you the percentage of the area which is occupied by a particular species. You work it out just like species density, but using figures for the percentage of ground covered in each of the quadrats rather than numbers of individuals in each quadrat.

19.13 Estimating populations of mobile organisms

Quadrats are excellent for sampling organisms which sit still in one place for at least most of the time. However, they are of little use with mobile organisms such as insects or small mammals.

Fig. 19.10 shows some techniques which can be used to capture mobile organisms, and estimate their population numbers. Small mammals, such as mice and voles, can be caught in a **Longworth trap**. Insects and other non-vertebrates, such as spiders, can be captured by **sweep netting**. Nets can also be used for capturing aquatic organisms; the techniques for this vary according to the size of the body of water, and whether it is still or moving.

A widely used method of estimating the population size of mobile organisms is the **mark, release, recapture** technique. First, as many individuals as possible are caught. Each individual is marked, in a way which will not affect its future chance of survival. For example, a patch of fur can be clipped from a vole, or a small spot of waterproof paint put onto a water boatman. The marked individuals are counted, returned to their habitat, and left to mix in with all the rest of the population. The reasoning behind this method assumes that this mixing is complete and random – if it is not, then the subsequent calculation is meaningless. Another assumption is that there is no significant immigration or emigration, nor a significant change in the population size, during the period of sampling.

When enough time has elapsed for mixing to take place, another large sample is captured. The number of marked individuals is counted, and also the number of unmarked individuals. The proportion of marked to unmarked can then be used to calculate the total number of individuals in the population. For example, if you find that one-tenth of the second sample were marked, then you assume that you originally caught one-tenth of the total population in your first sample. The equation is:

$$\text{number in population} = \frac{\substack{\text{number caught} \\ \text{in 1st sample}} \times \substack{\text{number caught} \\ \text{in 2nd sample}}}{\substack{\text{number of marked individuals} \\ \text{in 2nd sample}}}$$

Setting a Longworth trap to catch small mammals. The traps are checked at least once a day and the captured animals identified and marked before being released.

Using a vacuum pump to capture nonvertebrates within a quadrat. The animals from each quadrat are collected into the apparatus for later identification and counting.

Sweep netting for insects in vegetation. A standard method of moving the net is used in each area to be sampled.

Kick sampling in flowing water. The person disturbs the stream bed with her feet, so that organisms are swept downstream into the net. The organisms in the net are tipped into containers for identification and counting.

Mark–release–recapture method of estimating population size

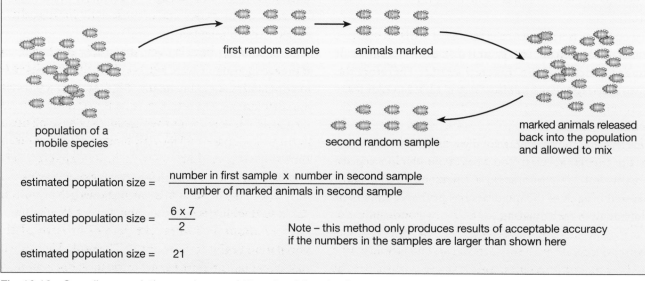

population of a mobile species

first random sample

animals marked

marked animals released back into the population and allowed to mix

second random sample

$$\text{estimated population size} = \frac{\text{number in first sample} \times \text{number in second sample}}{\text{number of marked animals in second sample}}$$

$$\text{estimated population size} = \frac{6 \times 7}{2}$$

Note – this method only produces results of acceptable accuracy if the numbers in the samples are larger than shown here

estimated population size =   21

Fig. 19.10   Sampling populations and communities of mobile animals.

POPULATIONS

19.14 The sigmoid growth curve

People have long been interested in the way in which animal populations fluctuate. Before agriculture was developed, sizes of populations of animals which were hunted for food must have been important to their hunters. Agriculture all over the world is affected by fluctuations in the size of populations of pests which damage crops. And the current increase in the human population is a cause for concern about what may happen in the future.

The study of what controls and determines the sizes of populations is therefore an important one, and knowledge is steadily increasing about the factors which affect population size in many different species. However, despite much work over many years, biologists still do not understand exactly what causes populations to increase and decrease in the way that they sometimes do. In the next section, we will look at some ideas about what determines and controls populations in the wild. First, however, we will consider a simpler situation – the growth of a bacterial population in the laboratory.

Escherichia coli is a bacterium which commonly lives in the human alimentary canal. It respires aerobically if oxygen is present, but can also respire anaerobically for long periods of time if oxygen is in short supply. *E. coli* can be grown in a liquid containing a variety of organic nutrients, such as glucose, amino acids and vitamins, called nutrient broth. The bacteria reproduce asexually, the cells splitting into two in a process called binary fission. The size of the population can be measured by counting the number of cells in a certain volume of the broth.

Fig. 19.11 is a graph of the results of measurements of the growth of an *E. coli* population in a conical flask, made over two days. A small number of cells was introduced to the flask at time 0, and then samples taken at intervals after that. You can see that, at first, the number of bacterial cells was too small to detect in the samples, and that it is not until 8 hours after the beginning of the experiment that the population begins to grow significantly. This early stage, before growth is detected, is called the **lag phase**. During the early part of the lag phase, the bacteria are adjusting to their new conditions. For example, they have a wide variety of enzymes they can synthesise to allow the absorption and metabolism of a wide range of nutrients, and it takes a while for the appropriate genes to be switched on to make the enzymes

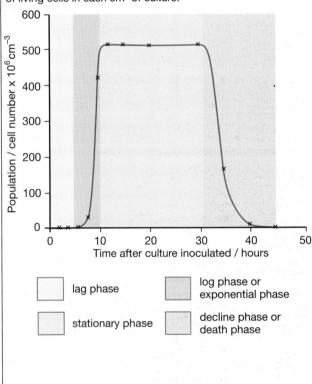

A nutrient broth was inoculated with *E.coli* at time 0. The culture was sampled at intervals and the living cell concentration for the culture was determined at these sampling times.

The graph shows a line of best fit between the sampling points. The bacterial population is expressed as millions of living cells in each cm^3 of culture.

lag phase

log phase or exponential phase

stationary phase

decline phase or death phase

Fig. 19.11 Growth curve of a culture of *E. coli*.

required for the particular kind of nutrients available. Even when the bacteria begin to divide, it takes a while before their numbers increase sufficiently for the cells to be detected in the samples.

Once the lag phase is over, the numbers of bacteria increase rapidly. This stage is called the **log phase** or **exponential phase**. During the log phase, bacterial cells are dividing and reproducing at their maximum rate for the particular conditions they are in; they have plenty of nutrients and space, and the only limitation to their rate of reproduction is their own in-built capacity. The population growth during this phase is exponential – that is, it repeatedly doubles in a particular length of time. In this case, doubling is occurring about every 25 minutes.

After about 10 hours, the rate of growth of the population begins to slow down. The probable cause of this is that one or more of the nutrients are beginning to run out. By 12 hours, the population has stopped growing;

the number of new cells being produced is matched by the number of cells dying. This is called the **stationary phase**. Eventually, nutrient levels become so low that more reproduction cannot take place. There may also be cumulative changes in the broth caused by waste products from the bacteria which prevent further reproduction. Now death rate is greater than 'birth rate', and the population begins to decline. This is called the **decline** or **death phase**.

The populations of many organisms follow this pattern, if they are kept in a limited space with limited supplies of whatever resources they need. The curve is known as a **sigmoid growth curve**; the word 'sigmoid' means 'S-shaped'. (This description really refers to the first three stages of the curve and does not include the death phase.) But do populations in more natural conditions behave like this?

19.15   Factors affecting population size

It is possible for a wild population to have a pattern of population growth similar to that shown in Fig. 19.11. For example, you could imagine that two or three rabbits were introduced to an island on which there were no other large herbivores, but there was plenty of grass. The rabbits would probably take a while to settle down and begin to breed (lag phase), but would then breed rapidly (log phase). Once the population got to a certain level, the supply of grass or the amount of space available for making burrows and breeding might begin to be in short supply. Competition would take place between the rabbits for these limited resources, reducing their rate of reproduction and increasing their death rate. The rate of growth of the population would begin to slow, so the curve would level off (stationary phase). However, unlike the bacterial population imprisoned in their flask with a finite supply of nutrients, the rabbits would be unlikely to all die. The grass would eventually regrow, so the rabbits would be able to continue to survive on the island.

The resources in short supply – food for the bacteria in the flask, food and breeding space for the rabbits on the island – are **limiting factors**, preventing unlimited growth of the population. Each of these examples is a **density-dependent factor**. The greater the size (density) of the population, the more strongly this factor acts. As the rabbit population grows, these factors increase in their effect, slowing the rate of growth. As the rabbit population decreases, these density-dependent factors ease, allowing the population to increase again. Once the initial rapid growth phase is over, density-dependent factors act to keep the population fairly steady over a long period of time.

Populations are also influenced by **density-independent factors**. These are environmental factors which act just as strongly no matter what the size of the population. For example, a very cold winter might kill a certain percentage of all the wrens in Great Britain no matter what their population size. So long as the population is not reduced to such a low level that it cannot recover, and so long as the climate does not change permanently, the wrens will probably eventually return to their original numbers.

Factors which influence and regulate the populations of wild organisms are very difficult to identify and measure. In practice, several different factors probably affect the population sizes of most organisms. It is not always even possible to draw a sharp dividing line between density-dependent and density-independent factors. Box 19.2 discusses examples of the factors which may be involved in regulating the sizes of some predator and prey populations.

19.16   Carrying capacity

Density-dependent factors help to maintain a population at a fairly stable size. This population size represents the maximum density of organisms which can be supported permanently in that area and is known as the **carrying capacity** of that area for that species. The carrying capacity may be determined by one particular factor – such as breeding space – or it may be a result of the interaction of two or more factors.

If one of these factors changes, then the carrying capacity also changes. Arable farmers are very aware of this. If a field is planted with beans, then the food supply for bean aphids is greatly increased, increasing the carrying capacity of that area for bean aphids. The bean aphid population therefore rises rapidly. Use will probably then be made of a density-independent factor – toxic chemicals – to reduce the aphid population by spraying the field with insecticide.

Box 19.1 Growth curves and growth rate curves

The graph in Fig. 19.11 is a simple **growth curve**. In a growth curve for a population, the number of individuals in the population is plotted against time. You can also plot growth curves for individual organisms, in which some measurement of the size of the organism – for example dry mass – is plotted against time.

Another method of showing this type of information graphically, either for population growth or an individual's growth, is to draw a **growth rate curve**. In this case, the *rate* of growth is calculated over each successive time interval, and then plotted against time. Fig. 19.12 shows how this is done.

The data used to construct the simple growth curve shown in Fig.19.11 are shown below

Time / hours	0	2	4	6	8	10	12	15	20	30	35	40	45
Population / cell number x 10^6 cm^{-3}	0	0	0	1	30	420	512	513	511	513	164	9	1

How to construct a growth rate graph from growth data

Calculate the increase in population between each sampling time.

Increase between samples / cell number x 10^6 cm^{-3}		0	0	1	29	390	92	1	−2	2	−349	−155	−8

Calculate the growth rate between the sampling times.
This is done by dividing the increment between two samples by the time between the two samples.

Growth rate / increase in cell number x 10^6 cm^{-3} hr^{-1}		0	0	0.5	14.5	180	46	−0.3	−0.4	0.2	−69.8	−31	−1.6

Plot a graph of growth rate against time.

Growth rate graph

Comparison of growth rate graph and simple growth curve

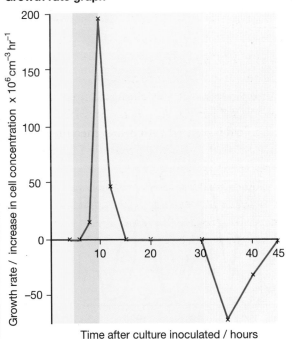

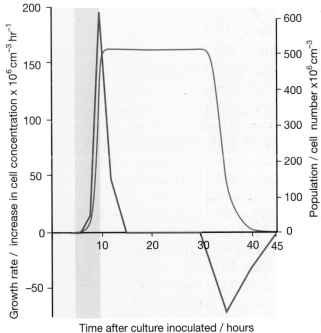

Fig. 19.12   Growth rate curve of a culture of *E. coli*.

Box 19.2 Cycles in predator–prey populations

Some populations of mammals, particularly in areas with very cold winters, show regular cycles in their population numbers. For example, lemming populations in Scandinavia show three-year cycles; lynx and snowshoe hares in northern Canada show ten-year cycles. Many theories have been put forward to explain these cycles, and computer programs have been used to try to model and predict them.

The snowshoe hare–lynx data (Fig. 19.13) were collected from fur trapping records, which were kept for almost 200 years. Their populations rise and fall with a periodicity of around 10 years. Snowshoe hares are the main prey of lynx, and lynx are the main predators of snowshoe hares. An early suggestion to explain the oscillations in their population numbers was that a rise in the snowshoe hare population was followed by a rise in the lynx population as their food supply increased. The increased population of lynx then reduced the

snowshoe hare population, which in turn reduced the lynx population, and so on.

This explanation is still thought to be partly true, but it does not explain the 'blips' in the pattern, nor why some peaks and troughs are so much lower than others. Ecologists have therefore suggested that the picture is more complicated than a simple predator–prey relationship, involving other factors. For example, when the snowshoe hare population becomes very high, then competition for food in winter becomes more intense. The more the plants are grazed, the more they respond by secreting defence chemicals called terpenes, which make it more difficult for the hares to digest the food they eat. The snowshoe hare population therefore drops, causing the lynx population to drop also.

Yet another possibility is that parasites might be involved in some of these cycles. Increasing density of a population, and increasing weakness caused by

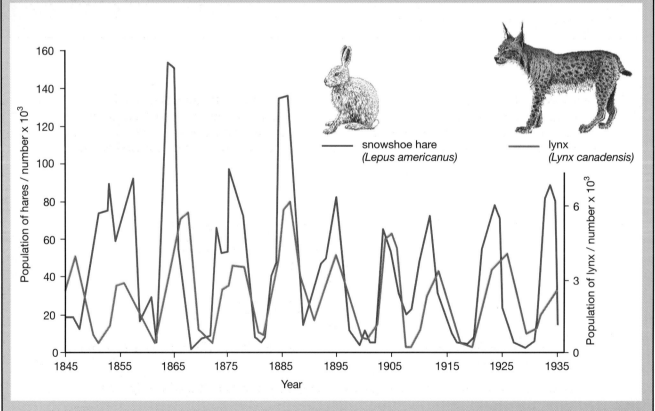

Fig. 19.13 Fluctuations in snowshoe hare and lynx populations.

Box 19.2 Cycles in predator–prey populations (cont.)

greater competition for food, can make individuals more susceptible to infection by parasites. This in turn could increase the death rate and bring a population down to lower levels. As the population size reduces, so the infection rate from the parasites reduces, and allows the population to increase once more. It has also been suggested that organisms might evolve resistance to parasites, so allowing their populations to grow; and then the parasite would evolve to overcome this resistance, so causing the population to drop again. However, there is as yet no firm evidence for this theory.

Chaos theory may help to explain the phenomenon of fluctuating animal populations. Chaos theory states that, in certain relationships, very small, virtually unmeasurable changes can have very large effects. There is strong circumstantial evidence that this does happen. For example, mathematicians have used data about oscillations in weasel and vole (predator and prey) populations in Finland to write equations relating the two populations to each other. They incorporated all the data they could

measure – amounts of food required by individuals of each species, changes in requirements at different times of year, maximum carrying capacities, reproductive rates and so on – into their equations, and then ran a computer simulation of what the populations should do over a period of time. The simulated results were very similar to what actually happens in these populations. There was a three- to five-year cycle, with the weasels lagging about a year behind the voles.

In both the real and simulated cycles, however, there were 'blips'. The mathematicians knew that these blips in their simulated results could not be caused by any other factor such as climate, because they had only fed certain factors into their equations and nothing else could possibly be affecting the outcome. The blips are purely the result of chaos. Perhaps, after all, the original ideas about predator–prey relationships, plus a small helping of chaos theory, may be enough to explain the striking oscillations in the populations of these animals.

Q2 Mites are small arthropods with a variety of feeding habits. The relationship between the populations of two species of mite, species **A** and species **B**, was investigated in a laboratory experiment. One of these species was a herbivore and the other was a predator which fed on the herbivorous species. The graph below shows the numbers of both species over a period of time.

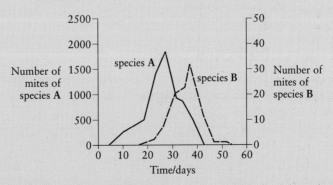

(a) Identify and explain **two** reasons why species **A** was most likely to have been the prey and species **B** the predator. (4)

(b) Describe how **one** abiotic factor might have influenced the results of this investigation. (1)

AEB 1995 (*Total 5 marks*)

Box 19.3 Seasonal changes in plankton numbers in the sea

Fig. 19.14 shows how the numbers of phytoplankton and zooplankton fluctuate over one year in the surface water of the North Atlantic Ocean. The explanations for these patterns show how biotic factors – food supply and predation – can interact with abiotic ones – temperature, wind, light and supplies of inorganic plant nutrients – to affect population sizes.

Plankton are small organisms which float in the sea and lakes; although some of them make active swimming movements, they are too small to be able to determine where they go, so they are carried around by water currents. **Phytoplankton** are photosynthetic plankton, while **zooplankton** are

animals which feed on phytoplankton and on each other. The phytoplankton are therefore the producers in this ecosystem. They have to remain close to the surface in order to obtain sunlight for photosynthesis. The zooplankton which feed on them often only do so at night, when they are relatively safe from predators. During the day, the zooplankton migrate vertically downwards.

In winter, low light levels and low temperatures limit the rate of photosynthesis. The productivity (Section 19.4) of the phytoplankton is therefore relatively low, and they can only support a relatively small number of consumers. Thus the numbers of both phytoplankton and zooplankton are low at this time of year.

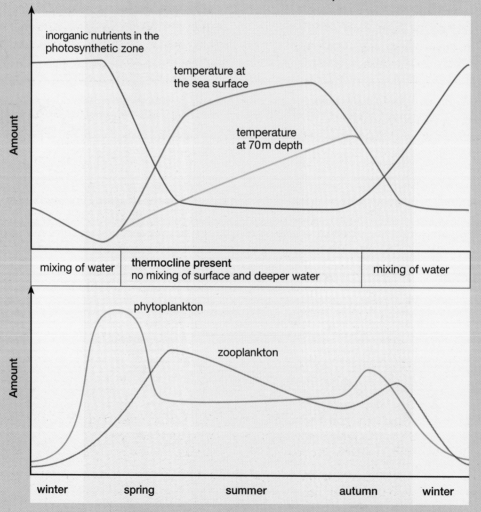

Fig. 19.14 Variations in the North Atlantic Ocean.

Box 19.3 Seasonal changes in plankton numbers in the sea (cont.)

As the days lengthen and temperature rises in spring, the productivity of the phytoplankton increases. Their number rises, and this is followed by a rise in the number of zooplankton which feed on them. However, the large number of phytoplankton rapidly use up nutrients, such as nitrates and phosphates, in the upper levels of the water. This limits the number of phytoplankton and by late spring the number begins to fall, then remains relatively steady throughout the summer.

In summer, the water near to the surface is warmed by the sun, and has a higher temperature than the deeper layers. Warm water is less dense than cold water, so the warm layer lies on top of the cold, and there is little mixing between them. There is often a fairly sharp boundary between the warm upper layers and the colder lower layers, called a **thermocline**. The thermocline remains present all through the summer. In autumn and winter,

however, the temperature of the upper layers of water falls. Now the difference in density between the upper and lower layers is less. Also, there are often strong winds at this time, and this results in mixing of the upper and lower layers of water. A fresh supply of nutrients (in the cold water) is therefore brought up to the surface. If this happens in autumn, when there is still enough light, and if temperatures are not too low, the phytoplankton can make use of these nutrients, and their number rises again. However, as temperature and light levels continue to drop as winter sets in, they are unable to make use of the nutrients and their number drops. Another factor causing this drop is that the winds mix the water so vigorously that many of the phytoplankton are carried deep under water where they have no light and die. The nutrients remain in the upper layers of the sea all winter, until the phytoplankton begin to use them once more in the spring.

Q3 The graph shows the changes in the numbers of microscopic floating organisms and physical factors in the surface waters of the North Sea during the course of a year.

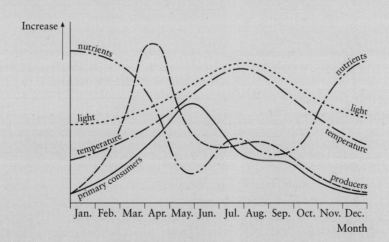

(a) Use information from the graph to suggest **two** explanations for **each** of the following,
   (i)   the rise in the number of producers during February and March;   (2)
   (ii) the decrease in the numbers of producers during May.   (2)

(b) Explain how **one** abiotic factor may bring about the increase in nutrient levels of the surface waters from October to December.   (2)

NEAB 1995   (*Total 6 marks*)

SUCCESSION
19.17   Community changes on glacial moraines

In the Northern hemisphere glaciers have been slowly retreating over the last 200 years. Glaciers are rivers of ice; they flow slowly towards the sea, carrying bits of broken rock and other debris with them. As they retreat, they leave this rock debris behind, forming a **moraine**. When it is first uncovered, there are no living things on the moraine.

For the last 80 years, ecologists have been studying how living organisms gradually colonise the newly uncovered moraines in Glacier Bay, Alaska. In fact, it is possible to look further back in time than this. Because the glaciers are retreating steadily, you can find areas of moraine which were first uncovered at different times, up to 200 years ago (Fig. 19.15).

The first living organisms to grow on the moraines are mosses, willow-herbs (called 'fireweed' in North America), mountain avens, and little prostrate willows. Because they are the first to colonise a new area, they are called **pioneer plants**. They grow sparsely in the poor soil; they are very short of nitrate ions, and often look yellow and stay small. However, mountain avens has a mutualistic relationship with nitrogen-fixing bacteria (Box 13.5) which helps it to survive in these conditions, and it rapidly forms a carpet over large areas of the moraine.

About 50 years after the moraine is first uncovered, alder trees have colonised the moraine, eventually forming dense thickets up to 9 m tall. These, too, have nitrogen-fixing bacteria in their root nodules. The nitrate content of the soil begins to increase (Fig. 19.16). The alders also affect the pH of the soil. The newly exposed moraine

(a) A retreating glacier leaves behind rock debris known as moraine.

(b) Pioneer plants such as mountain avens (*Dryas octopetala*) are the first to colonise the moraine.

(c) Over time, the pioneer plants alter the soil so that shrubs can grow.

(d) Eventually, poorly drained areas become covered with sphagnum bog, and drier areas with conifer forest.

Fig. 19.15   Succession in Glacier Bay, Alaska.

contains carbonates, and these produce an alkaline pH of around 8. Alder leaves, however, are slightly acidic, and when they fall and decay they release acids into the soil. Once alder thicket is established, the soil pH rapidly falls to about 5. The pioneer plants cannot compete successfully for light with the much taller alder and they disappear.

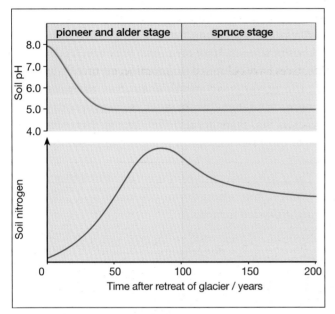

Fig. 19.16 Changes in soil pH and nitrogen content in Glacier Bay moraines.

Hemlock and sitka spruce begin to grow amongst the alders. They grow taller and more strongly than the alders, and eventually crowd them out. By around 170 years after the moraine was first exposed, the ground is covered by spruce forest. Spruce trees are not nitrogen-fixers, and they depend on the nitrate left in the soil by the alders.

What happens next depends largely on the drainage of the soil. In areas of good drainage, the spruce forest remains. In areas of poor drainage, *Sphagnum* mosses invade. These mosses hold water, making the ground even more waterlogged. This lowers the pH, and also lowers oxygen availability. The trees die, and the area ends up as a sphagnum bog.

19.18 The predictability of succession

The gradual change in the plant communities on the moraines in Glacier Bay is an example of **succession**. Succession is a directional change in a community over time. If the original area had no soil and no living organisms present, the change is known as **primary succession**. The example described in Section 19.17 is a primary succession. If the area was just disturbed, and there was soil present, then the change is a **secondary succession**. You could get secondary succession, for example, if an area of woodland was felled, or if an area of agricultural land was abandoned and then colonised by wild plants.

In a succession, the different communities are called **seral stages**. The final community is the **climax community**. In the Glacier Bay example, the alder thicket is a seral stage, and the spruce forest or sphagnum bog are climax communities. Climax communities are relatively stable, and they remain relatively unchanged unless there is some change in the environment, such as a forest fire or a change in climate.

Succession often follows a predictable course. One community alters the environment in such a way that it becomes possible for a different community to take over. This is what happens on the Glacier Bay moraines. First, pioneer species come in. These are plants which have good dispersal mechanisms, so they are likely to arrive early. Mountain avens and willow-herbs, for example, produce large amounts of fluffy seeds which can be carried long distances by the wind. Pioneer species must be adapted to be able to grow and reproduce in poor soils and exposed conditions. However, they are unlikely to be adapted to compete well with taller, stronger growing species on good soils.

The presence of the pioneer species changes the soil, and other aspects of the environment. For example, mountain avens adds nitrate to the soil. The plants also provide shelter, and their dead leaves produce humus. This allows alder to colonise, and the presence of the alder makes it impossible for the pioneer species to survive. The alder further increases the nitrate content of the soil and lowers its pH, providing suitable conditions for the establishment of spruce forests. A similar pattern is seen on almost every exposed moraine in the area of Glacier Bay.

In the early stages of succession, abiotic factors tend to be much more important than biotic ones in determining what can survive, and in what quantities. The availability of nutrients in the soil, wind exposure, water availability and temperature are likely to be far more influential than competition or grazing. Later, as more and more species colonise the area, biotic factors – especially competition – become more important.

Successions are not always so predictable as the one described above. Chance may play a part in determining the first species to arrive. If one species arrives first, in large numbers, then it may grow in very large numbers in the early stages of succession, even if it is not well adapted to the conditions. If it is the only plant there and does not have to compete, then it may manage to survive. Later, seeds of a different species better adapted to be a pioneer plant might arrive; it could then colonise the area and out-compete the first species. In this case, the change in the community has not taken place because of changes produced by the first arrivals, but really more by chance.

Some ecologists have suggested that succession should always result in the same climax community in any particular area, determined largely by the climate in that area. This final community is called **climatic climax**. For example, in Glacier Bay, the climatic climax community is spruce forest; in lowland England it is mixed woodland.

Fig. 19.17 In many parts of Britain, the climatic climax community is oak woodland.

However, the picture is rarely so straightforward because other factors also influence the type of climax community which will develop. You have seen, for example, how the degree of drainage of the soil influences the climax community in Glacier Bay. In the Scottish Highlands, climax communities include pine and birch forests (where there is little grazing by sheep and few fires), heather moorland (where there is some grazing and some fires) and grassland (where grazing is heavy and fires frequent). Throughout Great Britain, the activities of humans over thousands of years have had considerable effects on the types of climax community which have developed, so that the true climatic climax is seldom realised. This type of climax community is sometimes called a **plagioclimax**, and the succession which leads to it **deflected succession**.

Many of the landscapes which we enjoy and see as 'natural', such as chalk downlands or upland heather moors, are in fact created by humans. If we want to retain these 'artificial climax communities' then we have to continue with whatever activities determined their development in the first place. You can read more about this type of conservation in Chapter 20.

19.19 Diversity and stability

Species diversity is a measure of the variety of different species in an area. If an area has a *high* species diversity, this means that there is a large number of species, and that a good proportion of these species are present in reasonably large numbers. A *low* species diversity indicates that there are relatively few species, often with two or three species present in much higher numbers than the rest.

There are many different ways of calculating species diversity, but one commonly used and relatively straightforward formula is:

$$\text{diversity} = \frac{N(N-1)}{\Sigma n(n-1)}$$

where N is the total number of organisms, of all species, found in the area and n is the number of organisms of a particular species.

During succession the species diversity often increases with time. In the early stages, few species will be adapted to survive in what is often a harsh environment. Later, the conditions become less harsh and many more species are able to survive.

It has been suggested that a community with high species diversity tends to be more stable than one with low diversity. This means that the community is more likely to be able to 'bounce back' if it is disturbed in some way. However, experiments both in the laboratory and in the field have failed to find any support for this suggestion, and it appears unlikely that there is any correlation between diversity and stability.

On the other hand, there may be a connection between the stability of the environment, and the diversity of the climax community which develops within it. Tropical rainforests have a very high species diversity. They occupy about 6% of the land surface, yet they are thought to contain over 50% of all the species on Earth. It is not at all certain why this high diversity exists, but it may be partly due to the relatively large amounts of light energy entering rainforest ecosystems, and partly due to their relatively stable climate. This stability occurs not only over the relatively short time scale of a year (there are no distinct seasons as there are in temperate regions), but has also remained unchanging over thousands of years. In a temperate climate, each species must be adapted to survive within a wide temperature range, as cold winters alternate with warmer summers. This adaptation allows a particular species to live in a wide range of environments, and often across large geographical areas. However, species in a tropical forest do not become adapted to change; they become specialists at competing well within a narrow range of factors such as temperature and humidity. Each species tends to have a very narrow range of requirements, which leaves more 'room' for other species with slightly different requirements. ■

Q4 In a study of an oak tree the following numbers of organisms were obtained at each trophic level.

Trophic level	Number of organisms
producer	1
primary consumer	260 000
secondary consumer	40
tertiary consumer	3

(a) Sketch a pyramid of biomass to represent this food chain. (1)

(b) Suggest **two** reasons why there is such a large difference in the numbers of primary and secondary consumers. (2)

(c) The Venus flytrap is a green plant that catches and digests insects. It lives in wet, boggy places where mineral ions are scarce because they are washed out of the soil.
　(i) At which trophic level or levels would you put the Venus flytrap? Give a reason for your answer. (1)
　(ii) Describe the difference between the way in which the Venus flytrap obtains its nitrogen and the way in which other plants normally obtain this element. (2)

NEAB 1995　　　　　　　　　　　　　　　　　　　　　　　　　　　　　　(*Total 6 marks*)

Q5 Distinguish between

(a) *producer* and *consumer*; (2)

(b) *food chain* and *food web*; (2)

(c) *population* and *community*; (2)

(d) *niche* and *habitat*. (2)

UCLES 1995　　　　　　　　　　　　　　　　　　　　　　　　　　　　　　(*Total 8 marks*)

Q6   (a)   The diagram below shows some of the processes in the nitrogen cycle.

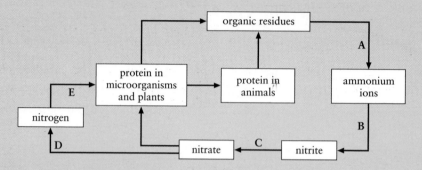

Microorganisms are involved in the stages labelled **A–E**.

Give the letter of **one** stage which involves:
- (i) nitrifying bacteria,
- (ii) denitrifying bacteria,
- (iii) nitrogen-fixing bacteria,
- (iv) saprophytic fungi.   *(4)*

(b)   The graph below shows the nitrate content at different depths in two similar fields. One field was mown and the grass removed; the other was grazed by sheep. Otherwise the two fields were treated identically.

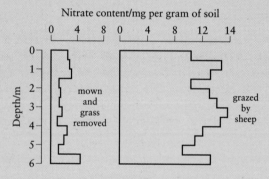

Suggest an explanation for the different nitrate 'profiles' in the two fields.   *(2)*

NEAB 1995   *(Total 6 marks)*

Q7   In an investigation to measure the size of a grasshopper population in a field, 30 grasshoppers were captured and marked with a small dot of paint before being released. The next day, 24 grasshoppers were captured using the same technique and of these, 6 were found to be marked with the paint dot.

(a)   Suggest a suitable technique for capturing grasshoppers.   *(1)*

(b)   Estimate the size of the grasshopper population in the field. Show your working.   *(2)*

(c)   Give **three** assumptions which must be made when estimating population size using the capture and recapture method.   *(3)*

NEAB 1995   *(Total 6 marks)*

Q8 A student planned an investigation to compare food chains in the leaf litter of a deciduous oakwood in the winter (cold season) and the summer (warm season).

In each season she collected ten comparable samples of leaf litter from the wood and extracted invertebrates from the samples using the apparatus shown in the diagram below.

The heat from the lamp dries out the litter from above, driving the invertebrates through the sieve at the bottom. Animals falling through the sieve are killed and preserved by the alcohol in the container. They can be identified and sorted into groups according to their trophic levels.

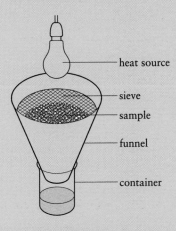

(a) Describe how the student could use the apparatus in a standard way to make a valid comparison of the litter from the winter and summer samples. *(3)*

(b) The student wished to construct pyramids of dry biomass to compare the food chain in winter and summer. The data obtained are shown in the table below.

Organism	Winter dry biomass / mg m^{-3}	Summer dry biomass / mg m^{-3}
leaf litter (plant material)	1200	900
herbivores (insects, millipedes)	100	300
primary carnivores (spiders)	40	120
secondary carnivores (centipedes)	10	40

(i) Suggest how the dry biomass of the leaf material could be determined. *(3)*
(ii) Give an advantage of using dry biomass for the pyramids rather than fresh biomass. *(1)*

ULEAC 1995 *(Total 7 marks)*

Q9 (a) With the aid of diagrams, describe what is meant by *pyramids of biomass* and *pyramids of energy*. *(8)*

(b) Discuss the efficiency of energy transfer between trophic levels. *(10)*

UCLES 1995 *(Total 18 marks)*

Q10 Clover is a leguminous plant. It can spread by producing creeping horizontal stems. The map shows the distribution of these horizontal clover stems in two neighbouring areas of soil, one dominated by grass and high in nitrate and the other with very little grass and low in nitrate.

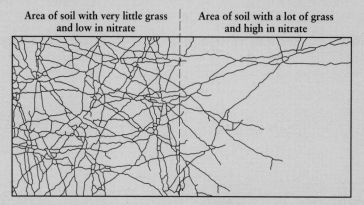

Area of soil with very little grass and low in nitrate   Area of soil with a lot of grass and high in nitrate

(a) (i) What name is given to the type of competition between grass and clover? (1)

    (ii) Explain why there is less clover and more grass growing in the area with high nitrate content. (2)

(b) Describe **two** differences between the growth patterns of the horizontal clover stems in the two areas. (1)

(c) Suggest **one** advantage of the growth pattern of these horizontal stems to clover plants growing in:

    (i) the low nitrate area: (1)

    (ii) the high nitrate area. (1)

AEB 1995   *(Total 6 marks)*

Q11 During succession there is a change in species composition of a community. There are also changes in species diversity, stability of the ecosystem, and in gross and net production until a climax community is reached.

(a) Explain what is meant by a climax community. (1)

(b) Explain **each** of the following changes which occur during succession.

    (i) Species diversity increases. (1)

    (ii) Gross production increases. (1)

    (iii) Stability of the ecosystem increases. (2)

(c) Give **two** reasons why farmland in the UK does **not** reach a climax community. (2)

NEAB 1995   *(Total 7 marks)*

20 Human effects on the environment

The growth of human populations, and increased use of resources, are having large effects on the Earth. Pollution of air, water and soil, and the destruction of habitats, tend to reduce biodiversity. Conservation attempts to maintain or increase biodiversity, but there are often conflicts between this and the interests of local people.

20.1   Human impacts on ecosystems

Humans first appeared on Earth around 2 million years ago, and since then we have coexisted with millions of other species on Earth. We form part of ecosystems, just as other organisms do. However, as human culture has developed, the impact we make on these ecosystems has become greater and greater. For example:

- as new tools and weapons were developed, hunting and harvesting of wild animals and plants became easier and more devastating, causing extinction of species such as the dodo.
- the development of agriculture continues to lead to the removal of natural vegetation over huge areas to make room for the growth of crops and farming of livestock. Also, in this century, the use of pesticides, herbicides and fertilisers has affected natural communities as well as organisms on farmland.
- the industrial revolution led to an upsurge in the demand for energy and other resources, which increased the amount of land disturbed by the extraction of materials such as fossil fuels, metal ores and gravel. More fossil fuels were burnt, releasing large amounts of gases such as carbon dioxide, sulphur dioxide and nitrogen oxides into the atmosphere.
- the growing human population, and the expectation of better living conditions and easier transport, has led to the building of larger cities and more roads. Pollution of water, land and air by human wastes and exhaust gases from vehicles has increased.

Within recent years people have begun to rediscover that we cannot exist in isolation from the living world around us. The quality of people's lives is likely to decrease if we do too much damage to the air, water and soil on which we depend. Conservation is taking a more important position in decisions made by governments and individuals.

However, the balance between the long-term widespread gains which might be achieved by conservation and the short-term, more focused gains to be made by local development projects frequently does not fall in favour of conservation. Governments are under great pressure to allow economic growth and expansion of industry and transport networks, as this can bring people immediate improvements in job prospects and living conditions. For example, new roads continue to be built in Britain because industries and many individuals want it to be possible to travel from one place to another more quickly, even though there is often strong opposition from groups of people who are concerned about the damage which may be done to the environment. Pressures to allow development at the expense of the natural environment are even greater in developing countries, where the conditions in which most people live may be well below those in industrialised countries. It is extremely difficult for a poor country to put conservation high on its list of priorities when people do not have enough to eat or comfortable homes to live in.

In this chapter, we will look at some of the more important ways in which humans have harmed the air, water and soil, and we will consider how conservation measures can help to limit or even reverse the damage. These are enormous topics, and we can do no more here than look very briefly at just some of the major issues. Another difficulty is that it is not always easy to categorise the kind of damage that is being done to a particular environment – many different factors are often involved.

AIR POLLUTION

20.2 The enhanced greenhouse effect and global warming

The Earth is warm because we receive radiation from the Sun. Much of this radiation reaches the atmosphere as short-wave radiation which passes through the atmosphere and reaches the ground (Fig. 20.1). Some of the radiation is absorbed by the ground and re-emitted as long-wave radiation which warms the atmosphere.

Within the atmosphere there are several gases which absorb this long-wave radiation, preventing much of it from passing out and away from the Earth. These gases include **carbon dioxide, methane** and **water vapour.** They form a 'blanket' around the Earth, keeping in the long-wave radiation and therefore keeping the air and the ground warmer than it would otherwise be. This effect is very similar to the way in which the glass in a greenhouse keeps the air and soil inside it warm, and so it has become known as the **greenhouse effect**. The gases which cause it are sometimes known as **greenhouse gases**.

The greenhouse effect is very important to life on Earth. Without it, temperatures would be so cold that it is unlikely that life would have evolved at all. However, there is concern that human activities are currently increasing the amount of carbon dioxide (and also methane) in the atmosphere, which would increase the greenhouse effect and perhaps lead to a rise in global temperatures. This is called the **enhanced greenhouse effect**, and the rise in temperature is called **global warming.**

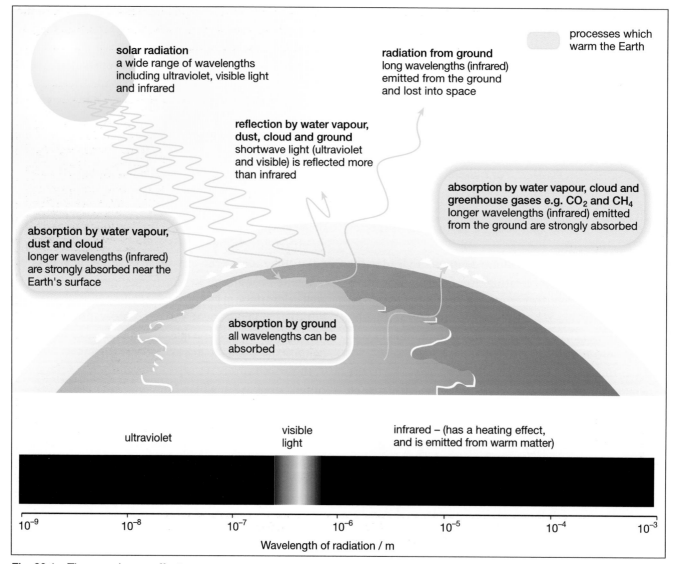

Fig. 20.1 The greenhouse effect.

There is much disagreement amongst scientists about exactly what is happening to the Earth's temperature, what is causing these effects, and what might be the result. All agree that carbon dioxide concentrations are rising, but what is causing this rise? How will this affect average global temperature, and temperatures in any particular country? How will any change in temperature affect natural ecosystems and agriculture? There are no clear answers to these questions, and it seems probable that we shall not be able to predict them – we shall not know what the effects will be until they have taken place. We will look at each question in turn.

● What is causing the rise in atmospheric carbon dioxide concentration?

Fig. 20.2 shows carbon dioxide concentrations over the last 160 000 years. These measurements were made from the bubbles of gas trapped in a 2083 m long core of ice taken at Vostok in Antarctica. You can see how the carbon dioxide levels have fluctuated over this time. No-one is sure what caused these fluctuations. If you look back at the diagram of the carbon cycle (Fig. 19.4) you will see that there are many processes which release carbon dioxide into the air, such as volcanic eruptions and weathering of limestones. Perhaps an increase in one or more of these processes produced the peak in carbon dioxide levels which occurred 140 000 years ago.

However, the current rise in carbon dioxide levels is worrying, because current carbon dioxide levels are already very high. Before the industrial revolution, there were about 270 ppm (parts per million) of carbon dioxide in the atmosphere. Now there are about 350 ppm. It is possible that this increase has nothing to do with human activities, and has entirely natural causes. But many scientists think that it could be at least partly due to the increased burning of fossil fuels. Some scientists suggest

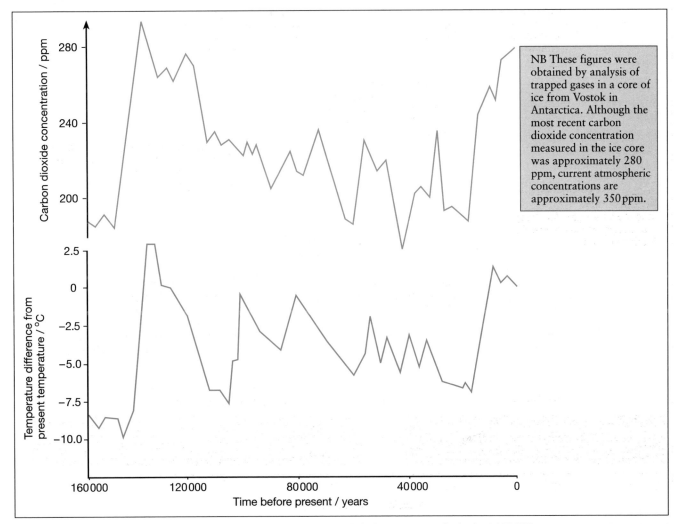

NB These figures were obtained by analysis of trapped gases in a core of ice from Vostok in Antarctica. Although the most recent carbon dioxide concentration measured in the ice core was approximately 280 ppm, current atmospheric concentrations are approximately 350 ppm.

Fig. 20.2 Changes in carbon dioxide concentrations and mean global temperature in the last 160 000 years.

that, if fossil fuel burning continues to increase at current rates, carbon dioxide levels could rise to 500 ppm by the year 2050.

Another suggested cause of the rise is deforestation. Photosynthesis removes carbon dioxide from the atmosphere, and locks up the carbon as organic molecules in plants. However, a mature tree which is not growing takes in only about as much carbon dioxide as it gives out (as a waste product of respiration), so just cutting down trees does not affect the atmospheric carbon dioxide levels. It is not until these trees are burnt, or decay, that the carbon they contain is released into the atmosphere. But even then, the land on which the trees are growing is usually rapidly recolonised by plants or planted with crops, which grow and photosynthesise, probably taking in as much or even more carbon dioxide than the trees were doing. Moreover, recent measurements of the rate of deforestation in many areas of the world suggest that its extent was previously overestimated. (Even if deforestation is not to blame for the rise in carbon dioxide levels, it is undoubtedly damaging to the environment in many other ways – you can read about this in Section 20.10.) It is also important to realise that the land is not the only place where photosynthesis takes place. Seas cover much more of the Earth's surface than land does, and there is much photosynthetic activity by marine phytoplankton.

● Will the rise in carbon dioxide levels cause global warming?

The Vostok ice core was also used to estimate the temperatures on Earth at the time the air bubbles were trapped. The bubbles were analysed to measure the ratio of two isotopes of oxygen, ^{18}O and ^{16}O, which varies with global temperature. The estimates of the temperatures over the last 160 000 years are shown in Fig. 20.2.

You can see how the temperature fluctuations closely match the carbon dioxide fluctuations. Does this mean that carbon dioxide concentrations directly affect temperatures? There is no direct proof that this is so – it could equally well mean that temperature affects carbon dioxide concentrations, or that there is some other factor which is affecting both of them. Other factors which may be relevant include sunspot activity and the variation in the distance of the Earth from the Sun. But, because we do know that carbon dioxide acts as a greenhouse gas, most scientists currently accept the hypothesis that carbon dioxide levels do affect global temperatures.

The exact effect that the current rise in carbon dioxide levels might have on global temperatures is impossible to predict. No-one knows how much the Earth's average temperature is likely to rise by. Nor is it known how such changes would affect particular parts of the Earth. For example, Britain is kept warmer than it would otherwise be by a current of warm water, the Gulf Stream, which flows north-eastward across the Atlantic Ocean. Ocean currents are produced by uneven heating of the Earth's atmosphere and surface, which produce wind and water movements. Just a small change in global temperatures could cause a current suddenly to change its direction. If the Gulf Sream no longer flowed past Britain, then our climate would become noticeably colder while other parts of the world would become warmer.

We also need to be aware of the 'natural' cycles of temperature change which have been taking place on Earth. In the last 850 000 years there have been about nine periods when ice has advanced from the poles and covered much of North America and western Europe. These periods are called Ice Ages, and they have alternated with warmer interglacials. At the moment, we are in an interglacial which started about 14 000 years ago. Perhaps we are due to move to another Ice Age? Perhaps global warming will slow this process?

● What effects might global warming have?

No-one knows how global warming would affect the Earth. Many convincing arguments have been put forward suggesting various effects we could expect, but there are so many variables to be taken into account that it is impossible to predict just what might happen.

One suggestion is that a rise in temperature could cause melting of the icecaps, which could cause a rise in sea level. This could have devastating consequences for low-lying countries such as Bangladesh. It could also be disastrous for many other countries as most capital cities lie close to sea level. A rise in sea level sounds a straightforward and reasonable suggestion, but even this is controversial; some scientists have argued for exactly the opposite effect! With warmer temperatures more water vapour evaporates from the sea; this produces more water vapour in the atmosphere which may increase snowfall over the poles. More ice would build up in the Antarctic and Arctic, while the amount of water in the oceans might be reduced.

Temperature changes and an increase in carbon dioxide levels could also affect the rate of plant growth. Several long-term experiments (Fig. 20.3) are being conducted to investigate the effect of raised carbon dioxide levels on plants, and these are producing mixed results. In increased carbon dioxide levels some species of plants grow faster, some initially grow faster and then slow down, while others actually grow more slowly. These responses vary when temperatures are raised, and they are also affected by the amounts of nutrients in the soil. These early results suggest that, as different species of plants are likely to respond differently, then the balance of different species within plant communities is likely to change if carbon dioxide levels continue to increase, and if global warming takes place. It is currently impossible to predict these effects.

Fig. 20.3 Trees are being grown in open-topped chambers in which the concentrations of gases can be varied, to investigate the effects on plant growth.

● Can we reduce the rate of increase in carbon dioxide levels?

Most people believe that we should attempt to reduce the rate at which carbon dioxide levels are rising. An international summit at Rio de Janeiro in 1992 brought agreement between many countries to try to do this. Measures which can be taken include:

- reducing the amount of fossil fuels which are burnt; this can be done by using other sources of energy to generate electricity (such as nuclear fuels, wind and water), by making our use of fossil fuels more efficient (such as by using 'lean-burn' engines in cars), and by reducing demand for energy by industry and individuals (such as by installing insulation in homes, and building more energy-efficient houses and offices).
- reducing the rate of deforestation, and planting more trees where possible.
- conserving soils, especially peat, which contain large amounts of carbon.

Some success has already been achieved, but – as always – a balance has to be reached between what environmentalists think is needed, and what economists and industrialists think is needed. Governments would like to please everyone, and it has so far not proved politically possible to introduce *really* tough measures to reduce carbon dioxide output in any country. The United Kingdom's target is to reduce emissions to 1990 levels by the year 2000.

20.3   Ozone in the stratosphere

Ozone is a gas which occurs naturally in the Earth's atmosphere. It has the formula O_3. Much of the ozone in the atmosphere is found very high above the ground, mostly between 20 and 35 km above the ground, in the stratosphere (Fig. 20.4). More ozone is found over the polar regions than over the equator, because high-level air currents carry it from the equator, where much of it is formed, towards the poles.

In the stratosphere, ozone molecules are constantly being formed as ultraviolet light from the Sun causes oxygen molecules to break apart:

$$O_2 \rightarrow O + O$$
$$O_2 + O \rightarrow O_3$$

Ozone also breaks down in this region of the atmosphere, again quite naturally:

$$O_3 \rightarrow O_2 + O$$
$$O_3 + O \rightarrow 2O_2$$

Until recently, these reactions resulted in the rates of formation and breakdown of ozone being about equal, so that the amount of ozone in the high atmosphere remained roughly constant. This high-level ozone is important to us and other living things, because it absorbs much of the ultraviolet light from the Sun, preventing it penetrating to the ground. Ultraviolet light can damage living cells, causing mutations which may lead to skin cancer and other problems. It can also cause cataracts, a disease in which the lens in the eye becomes opaque. Larger amounts of ultraviolet light reaching the Earth could reduce productivity in the oceans, or reduce yields from food crops.

Satellite measurements of the amount of ozone in the stratosphere began in the 1970s (Fig. 20.5). Ozone concentration is measured in Dobson units; one Dobson unit represents an ozone concentration of about one part per billion. In 1985, people first began to realise that these measurements showed that the ozone concentration over

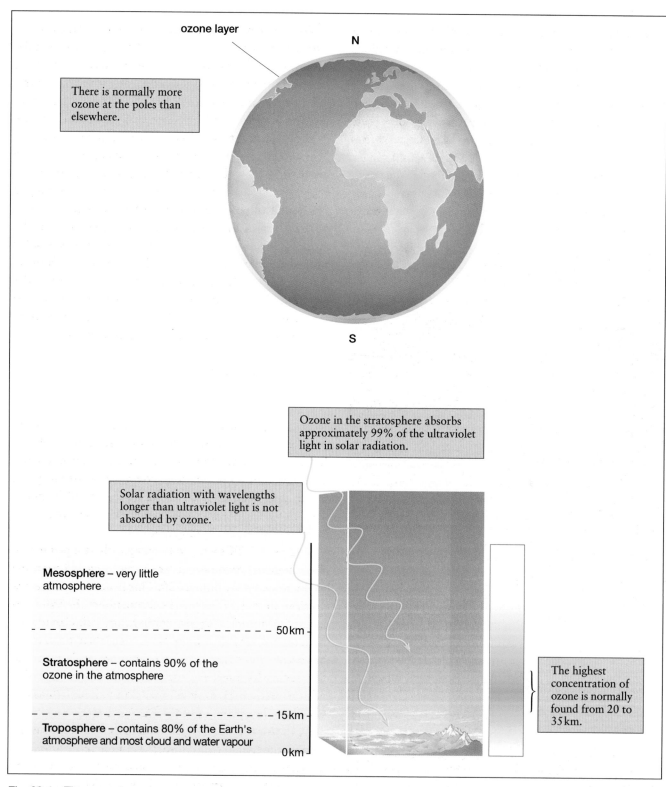

Fig. 20.4   The ozone layer.

the Antarctic was dropping considerably, especially in spring. For example, in the early 1970s the concentrations in October (Antarctic spring) were about 300 Dobson units, but in 1993 they were only 90 Dobson units. This reduction in ozone in the stratosphere has acquired the popular name 'the hole in the ozone layer', but it is not really a hole – there is still ozone there. More recently, ozone concentrations over the Arctic have also begun to fall, and the Arctic ozone 'hole' can spread as far south as Britain. On March 5th 1996, the concentration of ozone over Britain reached a record low of 195 Dobson units, compared to an average for that time of year of 365 Dobson units.

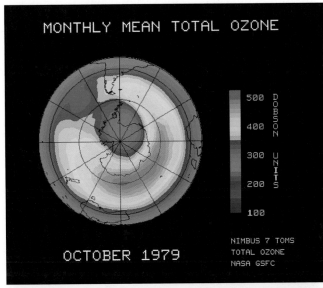

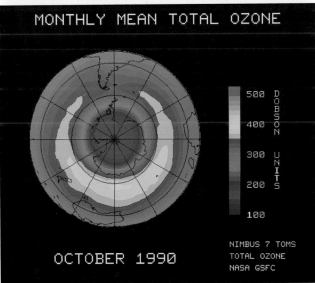

Fig. 20.5 Maps of the ozone concentrations over Antarctica, made by using data collected by the Nimbus-7 weather satellite.

The main cause of ozone depletion is **chlorofluorocarbons,** or **CFCs.** These are highly stable, unreactive chemicals which were widely used as propellants in aerosols and coolants in refrigerators. Their unreactivity made it difficult for people to believe at first that they could be causing problems in the atmosphere, but it has now been proved that this is so.

In fact, it is this unreactivity which allows CFCs to reach the stratosphere and affect the ozone layer. When they are released into the air, they can remain unchanged for over 100 years, giving plenty of time for them to spread gradually upwards. Once they reach the stratosphere, they are affected by the high levels of solar radiation there. This can cause highly reactive chlorine atoms in the CFCs to be split away from the rest of the molecule. The chlorine atoms react with ozone molecules to form chlorine monoxide, which then reacts with oxygen atoms to reform chlorine atoms once more.

$$Cl + O_3 \rightarrow ClO + O_2$$
$$ClO + O \rightarrow Cl + O_2$$

This can go on and on; the chlorine atoms keep reappearing and reacting with more ozone molecules. It has been estimated that one chlorine atom can destroy 100 000 molecules of ozone over a period of one year. Eventually, the chlorine atoms are removed from the atmosphere as they take part in other chemical reactions, but this can take a very long time.

If all use of CFCs were to be completely stopped today, the amount of ozone in the stratosphere would continue to decrease until about 2020. This is because there are already so many CFCs in the atmosphere. In 1987, 24 countries signed an agreement in Montreal, Canada, to reduce emissions of CFCs by 50%. Since then, however, it has been realised that the problem was worse than anyone realised at that time, and that stricter measures than this will be needed. Most developed countries, such as the USA and the countries of the EU, have made very good progress in stopping the production of CFCs. However, some large users of CFCs, such as India and China, did not sign the agreement and are still using CFCs. Chemists are developing alternative chemicals which can be used as substitutes, but several of these have proved to cause environmental problems of their own. So some progress has been made in protecting the ozone layer, but we are far from completely solving the problem.

20.4   Acid rain

When fossil fuels are burnt, some of the elements within their molecules combine with oxygen and form oxides. The oxide produced in the largest quantity is carbon dioxide; you have already seen some of the problems this may cause (Section 20.2). However, some fossil fuels, especially coal, also contain significant amounts of sulphur, and the combustion of these fuels releases **sulphur dioxide** into the atmosphere. Most sulphur dioxide is produced by the combustion of fossil fuels by industry, and in the generation of electricity (Fig. 20.6). Nitrogen oxides are produced as nitrogen and oxygen combine in internal combustion engines and are released in vehicle exhaust gases.

Carbon dioxide, sulphur dioxide and nitrogen oxides all form acidic solutions when they dissolve in water. Even in unpolluted air there is some carbon dioxide present, and this dissolves in rain drops to produce rain with a pH of about 5.6. Rain is, therefore, usually slightly acidic. But when sulphur dioxide and nitrogen oxides are present in any quantity, they can make the rain much more acidic. Examples of rain with a pH as low as 1.5 have been recorded in several different areas of the world.

Sulphur dioxide is an unpleasant gas, and regulations ensure that industries which burn fossil fuels and release waste gases must do so through very tall chimneys. This keeps the gases away from the local environment, but it then causes problems further afield. The gases enter the atmosphere high above the ground, and so are more likely to be carried away by the wind. As they travel, they undergo complex oxidation reactions; for example, sulphur dioxide, SO_2, oxidises and reacts with water to form sulphuric acid, H_2SO_4. They can be carried hundreds of miles before they eventually fall to the ground as acid snow or rain. This has created international problems, as pollution from one country (for example France or Britain) may produce acid rain in another (for example Sweden).

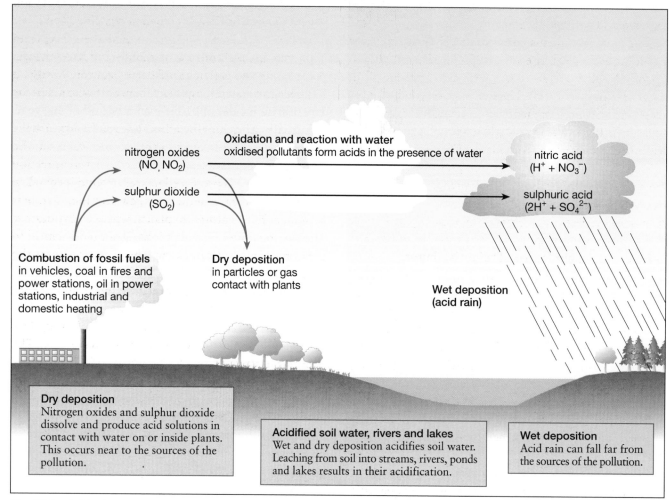

Fig. 20.6   Acid rain.

The effects of acid rain depend very much on the geology of the area on which it falls. Lime (calcium carbonate) reacts with acids and neutralises them, so acid rain falling on a limestone area, where the soil or water contains lime, does little harm. However, other kinds of soil are more sensitive. The acid rain may leach out minerals from the soil, so that it loses its fertility. If the soil pH drops too low, then some species of plants are unable to grow.

There is now little doubt that acid rain does adversely affect trees and other plants, although the precise effects are not yet fully understood. There are many problems in researching the effects of acid rain on natural vegetation; for example, it is not easy to separate the effects of acid rain from those of other pollutants (such as low-level ozone, described in Section 20.5). Laboratory experiments need to run for long periods of time before the results are valid. Evidence is growing, however, to suggest that acid rain does weaken trees. It may not directly kill them, but it may lower their ability to withstand other stresses, such as extreme cold weather or droughts.

Acid rain also harms aquatic life. As the rain water percolates through the soil, its low pH enables it to dissolve positively charged ions such as aluminium, lead, mercury and calcium. These ions are washed into waterways. Aluminium ions can damage the functioning of fish gills, especially in young fish. Heavy metals such as lead and mercury are toxic to many living organisms.

The only solution to the acid rain problem is to reduce emissions of sulphur dioxide and nitrogen oxides. This can be done by:

- burning less fossil fuels. This has the advantage that it cuts down carbon dioxide emissions as well (Section 20.2).
- removing sulphur from coal before it is burnt.
- burning coal in the form of a suspension of small particles mixed with finely ground limestone; the sulphur oxides combine with the calcium to form solid calcium sulphates. This is an advantage because calcium sulphate is a useful material; when it is combined with water it forms gypsum, which is used in the manufacture of some types of building materials.
- passing the waste gases through a 'scrubber', or flue gas desulphurisation system, in which they flow through a spray of lime and water which removes the sulphur.
- passing exhaust gases from vehicle engines through a catalytic converter which converts nitrogen oxides to nitrogen gas. (Vehicle engines emit only tiny quantities of sulphur dioxide.)

These methods all cost money, and the cost must finally be met by the consumers. If electricity generation, for example, is to release less sulphur dioxide, then electricity becomes more expensive. However, it is generally accepted that acid rain is a pollution problem which can and must be solved, and great strides have been taken in reducing its incidence.

20.5 Other atmospheric pollutants

The three examples of air pollution discussed in Sections 20.2 to 20.4 all involve pollutants travelling over large distances and having global effects. There are also many air pollutants which act more locally. Some of these are described below.

- Burning almost anything releases tiny particles of carbon and other substances, called **particulates**. Poorly maintained diesel engines can release large amounts of particulates in exhaust fumes. Large amounts of dust particles can also be sent up into the air by building projects or road construction. Particles from these and other sources may be breathed in by people and other animals, or fall on to plants covering their leaves and preventing the absorption of sunlight and gas exchange. It is now realised that particulates can cause breathing problems in people, especially in people who are prone to asthma (Box 12.2).

- **Ozone** is also a problem at low levels of the atmosphere. (Remember, however, that ozone *high* in the atmosphere is very useful to us as described in Section 20.3.) Ozone is produced nearer ground level when sunlight interacts with nitrogen dioxide. Ozone is thought to be harmful to plants, where it may destroy leaves or kill the whole plant. It is also harmful to animals in large quantities, because it affects the respiratory system.

- Nitrogen oxides, ozone and gaseous hydrocarbons released from vehicle exhausts may interact when sunlight is strong, to form **photochemical smog**. This can form a thick brownish blanket over a city. The problem is worst when there is little wind, and when the city lies in a valley, so that the air is trapped (Fig. 20.7).

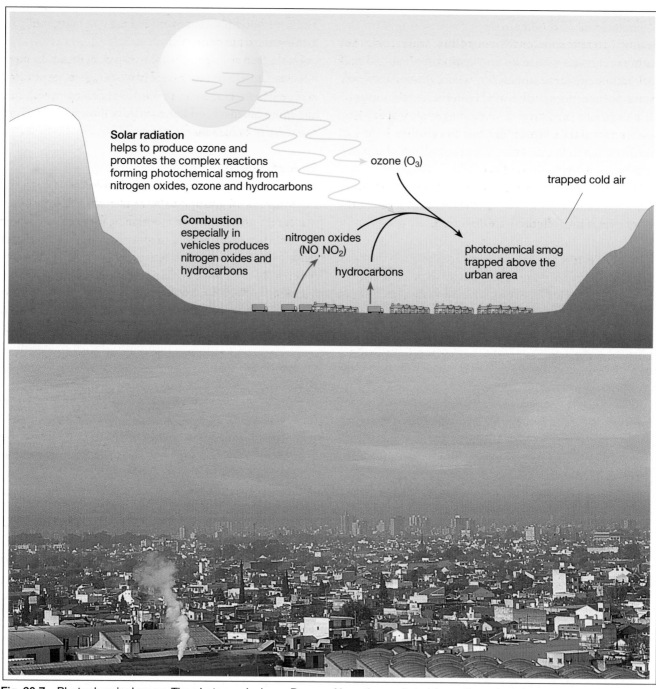

Fig. 20.7 Photochemical smog. The photograph shows Buenos Aires, the capital of Argentina, where in some weather conditions a layer of photochemical smog hangs over the city. The problem is caused by exhaust gases from the city's slow-moving traffic.

Q1

(a) With the aid of a diagram, describe how carbon is cycled within terrestrial (land-based) and within aquatic ecosystems.   (9)

(b) Discuss the ways in which human activities may affect the balance of the carbon cycle, and so affect the environment.   (9)

UCLES 1995   *(Total 18 marks)*

WATER POLLUTION

Many different substances can pollute water, and they come from many different sources (Fig. 20.8). Water pollutants may harm aquatic life in rivers, lakes or the sea. Some pollutants can be harmful to humans if they get into drinking water, and most countries have national drinking water standards which set out maximum levels of contaminants, such as metals, pesticides and nitrate, which can safely be allowed in drinking water.

In the sections which follow, some of the more important sources of water pollution, and some of the more important pollutants are discussed.

20.6 Sewage

Sewage is liquid waste produced from homes (faeces and urine, waste water from baths and washing machines), industry and run-off from streets. It contains a very wide range of potentially harmful substances, ranging from pathogens to heavy metals.

Untreated sewage is known as **raw sewage**. In most developed countries the majority of sewage is now treated before it is discharged, so that it has little, if any, effect on the environment. But if raw sewage is allowed to flow into rivers it can cause a number of problems.

● Eutrophication

Lakes, ponds and rivers with very low levels of nutrients are said to be **oligotrophic** ('few nutrients'). Oligotrophic waters are often found on moorlands, for example, where the soils are naturally poor in nutrients; they are very clear and clean-looking, with few plants growing in them. Bodies of water with higher quantities of nutrients are **eutrophic** ('true nutrients'). Naturally eutrophic ponds and lakes often occur in lowland areas where soils contain

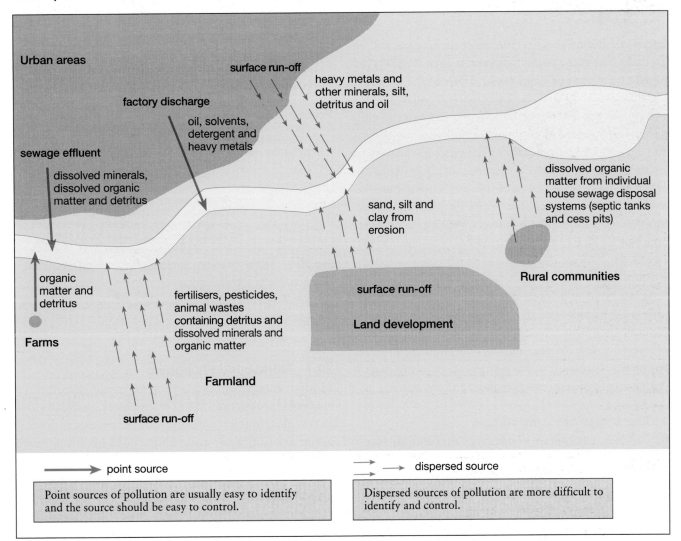

Fig. 20.8   Some sources of water pollution.

more nutrients; they have many plants growing in them.

A heavily polluted body of water, with large amounts of extra nutrients added from an external source such as raw sewage, is said to be **hypertrophic** ('excess nutrients'). However, the term **eutrophication** has become widely used to describe the processes described above, in which water becomes hypertrophic. Eutrophication usually results in a decrease in biodiversity (Section 20.14).

Raw sewage contains many organic substances (for example from human faeces or waste from food-processing industries) which can act as nutrients for bacteria and fungi. Where the raw sewage flows into a river, populations of these microorganisms may become very large (Fig. 20.9). Most of them are aerobic, and they take large quantities of oxygen from the water as they respire. This reduces the amount of oxygen available for other organisms which may die or escape from the area by moving up- or downstream.

The greater the amount of organic matter, the more bacteria there will be, and the faster the oxygen will be used up. The rate at which oxygen is used is called the **biochemical oxygen demand**, or **BOD**, of the water. If water has a high BOD, it indicates that it is polluted.

Raw sewage often contains large quantities of tiny particles suspended in water so that it looks grey-brown and cloudy. These particles stop light getting through to plants growing in the river, so they cannot photosynthesise and they die. The lack of photosynthesis contributes to the lack of oxygen in the water. As the plants die, they form yet more nutrients for bacteria, making the problem even worse.

● **Pathogens**

Raw sewage is very likely to contain human pathogens (disease-causing organisms). People swimming in water contaminated with raw sewage, or drinking it, are at risk of infection with diseases such as poliomyelitis. In some countries, this kind of pollution can result in major epidemics of diseases such as typhoid and cholera.

● **Other substances in raw sewage**

Raw sewage may contain a wide range of chemicals which are poisonous, or **toxic**, to living organisms. These include heavy metals and organic chemicals from industry. Some of their effects are described in Section 20.9. Other potentially harmful substances include **detergents** and ions such as **phosphate** (which have a similar effect to nitrates, described in Section 20.7).

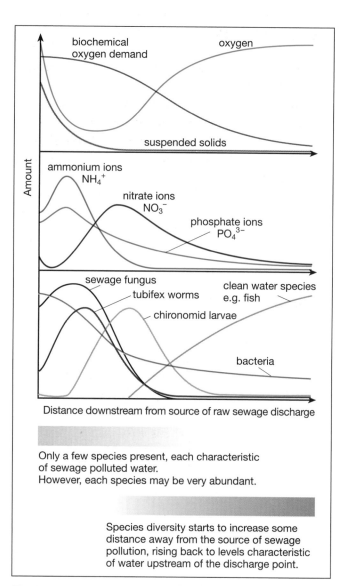

Fig. 20.9 Trends in some physical, chemical and biological components of a freshwater stream affected by raw sewage discharge. NB The curves show trends only, and not absolute values.

20.7 Nitrate and phosphate

Modern agriculture uses a wide variety of chemicals to maximise production. Without fertilisers, pesticides and herbicides, much less food could be produced from a given area of land, and food would be much more expensive than it is today. However, many of the chemicals used are potentially dangerous to living organisms, including humans, and they must be used with care. Pollution problems can also arise from the intensive rearing of livestock, and poor soil management.

Fertilisers are used to increase yields of crops. So-called

Box 20.1 Indicator species

The degree of pollution in an area affects the species of organisms which can live there. For example, in fresh water, certain species can only live in unpolluted water with high oxygen concentrations, while others can survive in very polluted water (Fig. 20.10). The presence or absence of these species can be used to indicate how polluted the water is, so they are known as **indicator species**. It is often quicker and easier to assess pollution by looking for indicator species rather than by making a chemical analysis of the water. However, as some of the species are found in water with quite a wide range of pollution, what you really need to look at is the *community* present, rather than just one or two species. Just three species in each type of community are shown here, although in reality many more would be looked for.

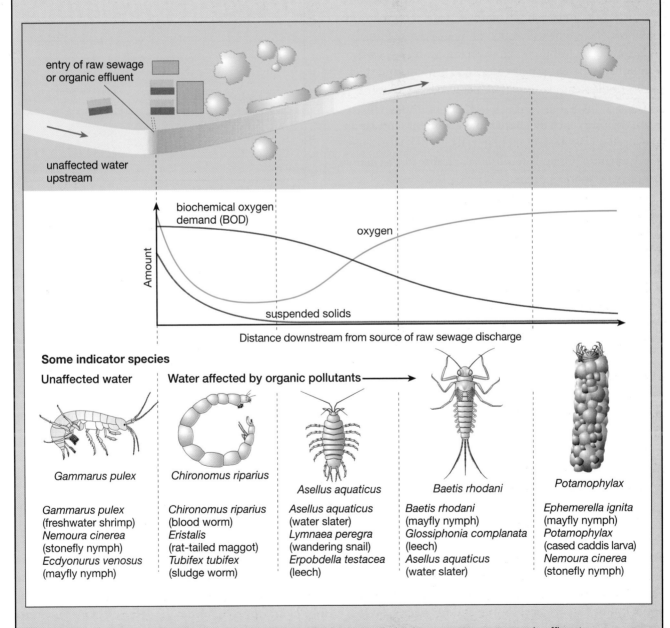

Fig. 20.10   Indicator species for eutrophication as a result of water pollution by raw sewage or organic effluent.

'organic' fertilisers include manure and slurry, while inorganic fertilisers include chemicals such as ammonium nitrate and phosphate. All of these can cause pollution if they are not applied to the land with care, often resulting in eutrophication (Section 20.6).

Nitrate ions tend to cause more problems as pollutants than phosphate ions. This is partly because they are more soluble in water than phosphate ions, and therefore leach more easily from the soil, and partly because the growth of aquatic plants is often limited more by shortage of nitrate than by shortage of phosphate. However, phosphate ions can cause problems of their own, because if they *do* wash into watercourses they can accumulate in sediment, increasing its fertility for long periods of time.

Nitrate from fertilisers can wash into waterways when rain falls. It increases plant and algal growth, and thick layers of filamentous algae (blanket weed) may cover the surface of the water. These block out light from other plants below, which die. Bacterial populations increase as they feed on the dead plant materials, so BOD increases (Section 20.6). Organic fertilisers can cause just as many problems as inorganic ones.

Most soils contain significant amounts of nitrate ions, which are formed by natural nitrification processes (Fig. 19.6). Nitrate fertilisers only need to be applied when the rate of use of nitrate by a growing crop outstrips the natural rate of production of nitrate in the soil (Fig. 20.11). There are very thorough guidelines and controls for farmers on the use of nitrogen-containing fertilisers, and these are strictly adhered to by most farmers. It is, after all, very much in their interest to keep the fertilisers on their land, where they can be used by crops, rather than letting them run off into rivers and be wasted. Measures include:

● calculating the optimum amount of fertiliser to apply, so that the plants will quickly absorb all of the nutrient ions.

● applying fertilisers when plants are growing, rather than when the land is empty or the crops are dormant; in Britain, this means avoiding applying fertilisers in autumn and winter where possible.

● not applying fertilisers when rain is forecast.

● not ploughing land or applying fertilisers close to water courses; a 'buffer zone' of a few metres is recommended.

Nitrate ions are also thought to be harmful to humans if large quantities are present in drinking water. At the moment, EU regulations stipulate that drinking water should contain no more than 50 ppm of nitrate ions.

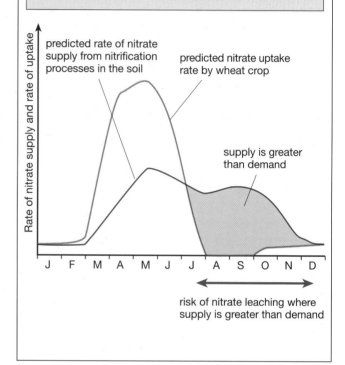

Predicting possible nitrate leaching from a wheatfield

Computers can simulate the likely rates of nitrate supply and demand in a field of wheat. In the absence of fertiliser use the demand of the crop for nitrate can be compared with the supply of nitrate. It is then possible to see when supply is greater than demand, which might lead to nitrate leaching into water.

Under normal conditions about 90% of soil nitrate comes from nitrification rather than fertiliser use.

Fig. 20.11 Computer simulation of nitrate leaching potential in a wheat field.

However, the evidence for this low value is quite slender, and there is no firm proof that levels above this would really cause any health problems. There have been a very few cases of an illness called 'blue baby syndrome', in which young babies were fed on milk made up using water containing very high concentrations of nitrate. Bacteria in the stomach reduce nitrate to nitrite, and the nitrite affects haemoglobin, preventing it from carrying oxygen efficiently. It is also thought that there may be a causal link between nitrite and stomach cancer, but the evidence for this is very tenuous, and the incidence of stomach cancer in Britain has been falling steadily.

Nevertheless, no-one wants their drinking water to contain unnecessary substances such as nitrates, and water companies have a duty to supply water containing less than 50 ppm of nitrate. It is very difficult to remove nitrate from water, so clearly it is important to take measures to make sure that it does not get into water in

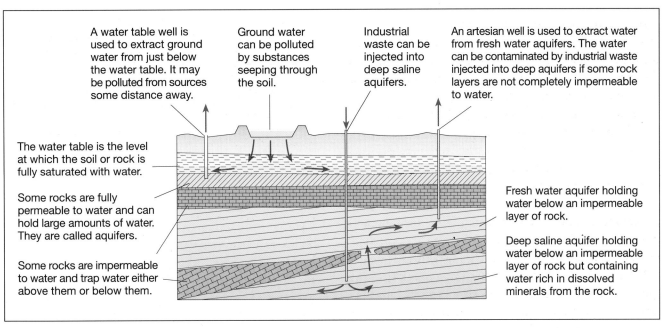

A water table well is used to extract ground water from just below the water table. It may be polluted from sources some distance away.

Ground water can be polluted by substances seeping through the soil.

Industrial waste can be injected into deep saline aquifers.

An artesian well is used to extract water from fresh water aquifers. The water can be contaminated by industrial waste injected into deep aquifers if some rock layers are not completely impermeable to water.

The water table is the level at which the soil or rock is fully saturated with water.

Some rocks are fully permeable to water and can hold large amounts of water. They are called aquifers.

Some rocks are impermeable to water and trap water either above them or below them.

Fresh water aquifer holding water below an impermeable layer of rock.

Deep saline aquifer holding water below an impermeable layer of rock but containing water rich in dissolved minerals from the rock.

Fig. 20.12 Pollution of ground water.

the first place. Even with new controls on fertiliser use, this will take many years because there is already a lot of nitrate in ground water (Fig. 20.12) which will take a long time to disappear.

20.8 Oil

Oil is a very visible form of water pollution. When large oil spills occur, such as when an oil tanker is damaged (Fig. 20.13), the resultant oil slicks can spread over large areas of the sea. They also wash up onto beaches where their appearance and smell make them very obvious. Many people are therefore more aware of the problems caused by oil pollution than those caused by less visible pollutants such as nitrate, which may be a more serious problem over a long timescale.

Oil harms living organisms in many ways. It sticks to the feathers of birds, preventing them flying. As they try to clean their feathers, they swallow the oil, which can kill them. Body surfaces of other animals can also be harmed. Oil can block the filter-feeding mechanisms of animals. The oil spill from the *Exxon Valdez* in Alaska in 1989 is estimated to have killed at least 250 000 birds, thousands of marine mammals and countless non-vertebrates.

On the shore, oil coats the surfaces of rocks, sand, animals and plants, while in open water it covers the surface with a dark film. This stops light penetrating, so plants cannot photosynthesise and food chains may be disrupted.

Fig. 20.13 High pressure, hot water hoses were used to clean oil from rocks after the *Exxon Valdez* oil spill.

There is no clear agreement on the best way to deal with an oil spill. Left alone, oil is gradually broken down by bacteria; this happens faster if the oil slick is broken up by rough water and high winds. Most of the harmful effects of an oil spill happen very quickly, and the environment will recover naturally on its own. However, people often cannot wait for the oil to disappear naturally, and want to speed up its dispersal. Detergents may be sprayed onto the slick, to emulsify the oil (Section 13.9). Hot water may be sprayed onto shorelines, in an attempt to wash the oil into the sea. But detergents themselves can kill living organisms, and the hot water sprayed at high pressure can kill small organisms which had survived the initial oil spill.

20.9 Pollutants from manufacturing industry

Heavy metals, such as mercury and cadmium, may enter watercourses in waste from industries. They are **persistent** chemicals – metals cannot be metabolised by living organisms – and many of them are very toxic.

Mercury is used in many industries, for example in making switches and batteries and as a catalyst in the plastics industry, and it is a waste product from the paper industry. One example where large quantities of mercury have polluted rivers is in the Madeira River Basin in Brazil, where it is used in gold mining. Some microorganisms convert metallic mercury to **methyl mercury**. This compound accumulates along food chains, and has become a major problem in some aquatic ecosystems where the fish contain so much of it that people may die if they eat them.

Cadmium is used in the manufacture of red and yellow pigments used as paints, nickel–cadmium batteries and in electroplating. It is very toxic to plants and animals. In Japan, cadmium from a zinc-smelting industry got into water which was used for irrigating rice plants. The plants took up cadmium and were later eaten by people. Many people, especially elderly women, became very ill with weakened and deformed bones. Cadmium and other heavy metals have also entered European rivers such as the Rhine (Fig. 20.14) in increasing amounts as industries have developed during the twentieth century.

Polychlorinated biphenyls, or **PCBs**, are another group of substances which accumulate along food chains. They have a very wide range of uses in industry, and for many years they were unregulated because they were thought to be inert and harmless. It was not until the 1970s that their use was restricted, and by then many soils and sediments in rivers and lakes had become contaminated with them. PCBs cause a range of problems in animals, such as reproductive failure. In humans, high concentrations cause a distressing skin disease known as chloracne, and may also increase the risk of some types of cancer.

Many industries use water to cool machinery. Electricity generating plants use large amounts of water in this way. The water becomes warm during this process, and may be returned to the river or sea from which it was extracted at a relatively high temperature. This causes **thermal pollution**.

Warm water can hold less dissolved oxygen than cold water. Thermal pollution of water therefore tends to lower oxygen concentration, and this may mean that there is not enough oxygen to support some species of organisms.

Many aquatic species can only survive or reproduce in a fairly narrow temperature range. For example, trout cannot survive if the water temperature rises above 25 °C, and they will not reproduce if it is above 14 °C. Carp and pike, on the other hand, live and reproduce successfully up to temperatures as high as 35 °C. Thus, some species may move away from the warm-water area, while others may move in. Changes in temperature can also affect the availability of the organisms on which fish feed.

In many cases, good use is now being made of the warm water, rather than just letting it flow back into a river. It may be used to help to warm buildings, or to grow warm-water organisms for food. If no commercially viable use can be found for it, then it can be stored in ponds for a time, until it has cooled sufficiently to be allowed back into the river.

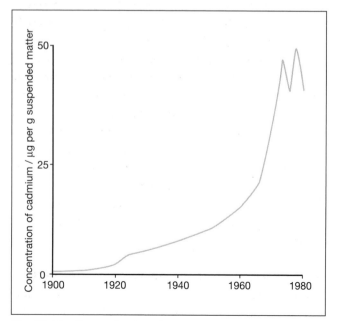

Fig. 20.14 Contamination of the Rhine by the heavy metal cadmium.

> **Q2** Give an account of the ways in which human activities lead to the pollution of water.
>
> ULEAC 1996 *(Total 10 marks)*

DAMAGE TO TERRESTRIAL ECOSYSTEMS
20.10   Deforestation

Much of the Earth's surface was once covered by forest. Forest is the climax vegetation (Section 19.18) over large areas of land, but not where the climate is very cold or very dry.

In Europe, large areas of forest were cleared many centuries ago; forests were seen as frightening places containing dangerous animals, which needed to be tamed and made safe. The cutting down of forests also provided wood for fuel and building, and land for agriculture. In developed countries, the perception of forests has now changed and they are seen as desirable features. So, the extent of forests in regions such as Europe and North America is currently increasing.

In developing countries, however, governments do not usually see forests as desirable in themselves. Forests are still primarily sources of products such as timber, as well as potential agricultural land. In some areas of the world, forests are being destroyed at a very worrying rate (Fig. 20.15). During the last 50 years or so, the rate of deforestation in Brazil, for example, has been very similar to the rate of deforestation which took place in the United States during the nineteenth century.

Fig. 20.15   A satellite photograph showing deforestation in a small part of the Amazon Basin in Brazil. Although much of the forest remains in this area, it is very fragmented and so less valuable as a habitat.

As developed countries are mostly in temperate regions, and developing countries in warmer regions, these differences in perception mean that the area of temperate forests is now slightly increasing, while the area of tropical forests is decreasing.

Precise figures for current rates of deforestation are difficult to come by. Satellite surveys are not as accurate as they were once thought to be, and it is very difficult to make surveys on the ground. It is now believed that earlier estimates of 20 or 30 hectares of forest being lost each minute are much too high. The differences between current estimates from different sources are so great that we really cannot pretend to know just how fast our forests are being destoyed, but a rough working figure is that about 1% of tropical forests is lost each year.

● Why does deforestation occur?

High rates of deforestation are often – but not always – associated with high rates of population growth. As human population grows, more land is needed for **growing crops**, so more land is cleared. Deforestation can also happen, however, when populations are stable, if crops are to be grown for sale to other countries. This has probably been an important factor in Brazil, for example, where deforestation has provided land for farming cattle for beef for export.

The building of new **roads** may require the removal of forests. Often, if a new road passes through a previously uninhabited forested area, large patches of forest may be cut down along the road for the building of houses and to produce cleared land for agriculture.

Commercial logging is also a prime cause of deforestation. Unmanaged logging operations cut down trees without replacing them. Even though only some forest trees may be required by the loggers, their cutting and removal can damage large areas of the forest.

Demand for **fuelwood** is a cause of deforestation in some parts of the world, especially in developing countries. In rural areas, people collect their own fuelwood locally, but in cities large quantities of fuelwood may be brought from quite distant forests and sold commercially.

● How does deforestation damage the environment?

Deforestation may contribute to the increase in carbon dioxide levels in the atmosphere, although this effect may not be as great as was once thought. This is explained in Section 20.2.

One very worrying result of deforestation is **habitat destruction**. Tropical rainforests are the most species-rich environments on Earth, and many of the species which live in them have very small ranges. The removal or disturbance of large areas of forest can easily result in the extinction of many plant and animal species.

There is some evidence that large-scale deforestation can also affect **climate** (Fig. 20.16). Trees release large quantities of water vapour into the atmosphere in the process of transpiration. If trees are removed, then water is more likely to run off the soil and into water courses rather than being taken up by vegetation and returned to the air. This can result in the atmosphere becoming drier, so that less rain falls.

The removal of trees can allow **soil erosion** to occur. Plant roots help to hold soil in place. Leaves absorb the impact of rain drops. When plant cover is lost, rain hits the soil directly, loosening soil particles and allowing them to be washed away by run-off or blown away by wind. This is particularly important on slopes. The eroded soil may silt up water courses, which cannot then cope with carrying away large quantities of water and flooding may result. The loss of the soil from the land means that it becomes less fertile.

● **How can deforestation and its effects be reduced?**

Current concerns about the loss of tropical forests have resulted in some financial help being given to developing countries by industrialised countries. If money is available, then **conservation areas** can be established. However, it is important that this is done with the involvement not only of local governments but also of local people or it is unlikely to be successful. Frequently, local people are very happy to be able to save their forests so long as they have access to alternative sources of income (Box 20.2).

Where forests are to be used for timber production, then sustainable **forest management systems** should be employed. This means that trees are cut down selectively and, as far as possible, without damaging other unwanted vegetation. The forest is then either left to regenerate naturally or replanted. Consumers of timber products should ensure that they only buy products which have come from forests managed in this way.

Where removal of trees for fuelwood is a problem, it is sometimes possible to use **other sources of energy**, such as solar power. A project in Kenya, for example, is showing people how to build very simple solar-heated ovens which could greatly reduce the use of fuelwood (Fig. 20.17).

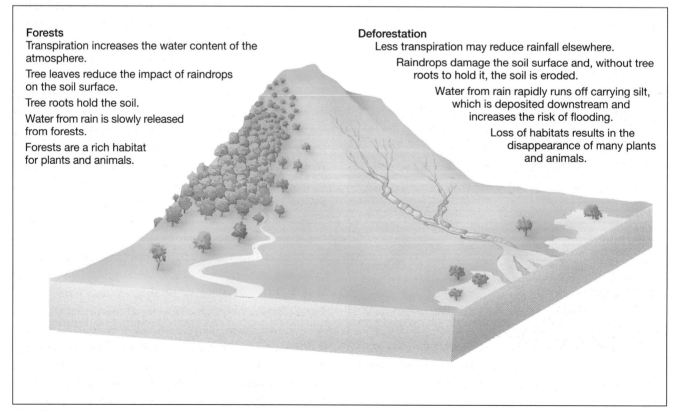

Forests
Transpiration increases the water content of the atmosphere.

Tree leaves reduce the impact of raindrops on the soil surface.

Tree roots hold the soil.

Water from rain is slowly released from forests.

Forests are a rich habitat for plants and animals.

Deforestation
Less transpiration may reduce rainfall elsewhere.

Raindrops damage the soil surface and, without tree roots to hold it, the soil is eroded.

Water from rain rapidly runs off carrying silt, which is deposited downstream and increases the risk of flooding.

Loss of habitats results in the disappearance of many plants and animals.

Fig. 20.16 Deforestation.

Fig. 20.17 A workshop supported by volunteers from the charity Earthwatch helped this Kenyan headmistress build a solar oven. Getting it home was rather more difficult.

20.11 Desertification and soil erosion

Deserts occur naturally wherever the climate is too dry to support substantial plant growth. Some ecologists define a desert as a region where annual rainfall is less than 500 mm per year. Deserts can be hot or cold – it is lack of availability of water which helps to make an area a desert,

Fig. 20.18 Overgrazing by goats in this dry area of Botswana is leaving the soil exposed to wind and rain, resulting in erosion.

not its temperature. Desert soils are often rich in inorganic nutrients, but lack humus. They are therefore light and easily eroded by wind or rain.

In some parts of the world, human activities are causing land which has been used for agriculture to become desert. These areas are **marginal lands**, where rainfall is low but just enough to sustain the vegetation needed for grazing a few animals or growing a few crops. If anything is done which reduces the ability of the soil to retain water after rainfall, then the land may become a true desert. Desertification is a serious problem in some parts of the world (Fig. 20.18).

Overgrazing can cause desertification. If grazing animals destroy the vegetation by preventing new seedlings from germinating, eating too much of the vegetation or trampling it, then the soil becomes exposed to rain and wind and is more easily eroded (Section 20.10). Marginal lands can survive grazing if there are not too many animals, and if the animals are moved from place to place. Problems occur when more animals are grazed than the land can support, or if they stay in one area too long. This can happen when formerly nomadic people settle down in one area, perhaps because a deep well has been dug to provide a permanent source of water.

Deforestation or over-collection of wood to use for fuel can also remove plant cover and lead to desertification. This is described in Section 20.10.

Cultivation of marginal land for **arable crops** may expose vulnerable soils to erosion, causing loss of soil cover and loss of fertility. This can be made worse if attempts are made at **irrigation**. If the irrigation water is taken from ground water, then the water table may be lowered, making it even more difficult for plants to obtain the water they need. Moreover, when the irrigation water evaporates from the soil surface, it leaves salts behind. Over a period of years, the land may become so salty that it can no longer grow either the crops or the natural vegetation.

Soil erosion usually follows when desertification happens, but soil erosion is not just a problem in desert regions or marginal lands. Huge quantities of soil are lost from high-quality agricultural land each year, even in developed countries such as Britain. A good, nutrient- and humus-rich soil takes many hundreds of years to develop, and it cannot be replaced quickly if it is lost. Good farming practices can greatly reduce the amounts of soil lost by erosion; some of these are shown in Fig. 20.19.

(a) Farmers in Burkina Faso, West Africa, are shown how they can use lines of stones to reduce soil erosion. The lines are built along contours, holding water and preventing it from running rapidly downhill. Soil that has been picked up by the water will settle in the pools behind the lines of stones. They can apply techniques learnt in this small-scale demonstration to larger-scale projects.

(b) In Mauretania, on the western edge of the Sahara desert, wind-blown sand is a major problem. Plants which would otherwise survive may be killed just because sand covers them faster than they can grow. Simple fences made from local materials can help to prevent the sand blowing away.

(c) Trees planted in this barren area in Nepal should help to hold the thin soil in place, reducing erosion by water and wind. In many different parts of the world, rural communities have learnt to plant at least two trees for every one they cut down to use for fuel or building.

(d) On steep hillsides, terraces allow cultivation without soil erosion. Here, rice is being grown in Bali. The terraces, and the ridges along their outer edges, hold the water when the rice paddies are flooded.

Fig. 20.19　Methods of reducing soil erosion.

Box 20.2 A community forest project in Ecuador

Can individuals do anything to help to arrest the rate of loss of tropical forests? Four people – a lawyer, an accountant, an anthropologist and an ecologist – believed that they could. In 1994, they founded a charity which they named People Allied for Nature, PAN. Their goal is to help local communities in tropical nations to protect and learn more about their forests. They chose to work in an area called Loma Alta, in western Ecuador.

Ecuador is situated on the northwest coast of South America (Fig. 20.20); its capital, Quito, lies almost on the equator. The Andes mountains run on a roughly north–south line through the country, dropping steeply towards the Pacific where a smaller range of mountains borders the shore. These coastal ranges are capped with cloud forests and are surrounded by drier areas. Such isolation has resulted in many endemic species (species which are found nowhere else). Land along the coast is owned by small communities of people.

In 1936, there were only a few houses in Loma Alta, and they were surrounded by forest. By 1970, much of the forest had gone, except on the more remote hill tops. It had been cut down by local people to provide land for growing crops such as bananas, papaya, coffee and citrus trees. At that time the Ecuadorian government encouraged this use of forested land, although this has now changed. Timber companies cut down trees to provide wood to build expanding towns.

The forest on the higher slopes is 'cloud forest', blanketed by fog between June and November. The forest holds and protects the soil, captures the moisture from the clouds, and provides wildlife habitats. The loss of the forest resulted in the soil becoming drier, and in a reduction of water in lowland streams, making the area less suitable for farming. Even more worrying is that the climate has become drier in the last 50 years. Is this related to the loss of the forest? It is impossible to be sure.

In 1986, the people of Loma Alta asked for help from the national government because a cattle rancher from outside their area had begun to cut down a large area of the forest to make grazing land. The government responded by establishing a Bosque Protector, or 'protected forest' covering 4000 acres. The Loma Alta community has property rights in the Bosque Protector. However, until recently they have taken little interest in it. The people make money by growing a crop called paja toquilla, a palm-like fibre used for making Panama hats, and this crop grows best in the cool moist

(a) Loma Alta is on the west coast of Ecuador.

(b) Unspoilt cloud forest on the high slopes.

Fig. 20.20 Ecuador forest project.

Box 20.2 A community forest project in Ecuador (cont.)

climate around 300 m up the slopes, just where the cloud forest grows. They clear small areas of forest to grow this crop. But clearing the forest dries the soil – so just how much forest can be cut down without losing the conditions needed to grow paja toquilla? Above 300 m, the forest is relatively undamaged. It has been used mainly for providing timber, but the people only take out large mature trees, and are selective about which trees they use. Here the forest is still luxuriant, with thick vegetation beneath the trees.

The people of Loma Alta do value their forest, they do have rights over it, and there is an elected local council and many committees which act on local issues. Yet little was being done to conserve the Bosque Protector. The problem is partly that much of the forest belongs to everyone, rather than anyone in particular, and these areas have suffered much more than the areas allocated to specific families. People have to work very hard to make a living, and don't have spare time, energy or money to spend on forest conservation. They don't derive much income from the forest, and have seen it as something to be cut down so that they can grow paja toquilla. They have not recognised the forest's value as a cloud harvester.

PAN's aim is to work *with* the people who live in Loma Alta, to help them to understand the importance of their remaining forest, and to help them to plan for the future. PAN began by talking to everyone in the community about their forest and finding out what people think about it, and how they use it. As a result of these discussions, the local people asked PAN to carry out a study of their forest, to see how well they are doing at conserving it. The study of the forest is being carried out by trained biologists from America and Ecuador, with the help of local people and volunteers from many different countries, including some from charities such as Earthwatch. Throughout the project, the aim is to involve fully the people who live in Loma Alta, and never to impose on them decisions from

outside. PAN are making recommendations to the people about what they can do to ensure that their remaining forest is not destroyed. The local people can then decide which of these suggestions they can take on board.

Many different people and organisations, with many different skills and strengths, need to work together to bring about changes. PAN's project is strongly supported by INEFAN, the government agency responsible for forest and wildlife management in Ecuador. Non-government organisations such as Fundacion Natura are also working with people in the same region, helping them to replant forests and to appreciate their natural resources. PAN's work in Loma Alta uses methods developed by IFRI, the International Forest Resources and Institution programme, based at Indiana University in the USA. IFRI is collecting information about people and forests in many different parts of the world, to see if some common principles can be found to help people to manage their forests sustainably. No amount of international conventions and agreements can succeed in reducing rates of deforestation in developing countries, unless the people who live in and use the forests are consulted and involved in making the decisions about them.

Fig. 20.20 **(c)** This family derives income from growing paja toquilla, which is hanging up to dry behind them.

CONTROLLING PESTS

Agriculture produces large populations of a single species of animal or crop plant living in one area. This provides a large food supply for some organisms, such as insects, allowing their populations to become much larger than they would otherwise be (Section 19.15). These organisms rapidly become **pests**.

20.12 Pesticides and herbicides

Pesticides are used in agriculture to reduce wastage of crops from damage by insects and fungi, and also to kill pests which harm animals, such as the mite which causes sheep scab. Herbicides are used to kill weeds, reducing competition with crop plants and so increasing yields. Like fertilisers (Section 20.7), pesticides and herbicides can wash off land on which they are used and enter water courses, causing problems there as well as on land.

Many plants produce their own chemicals to ward off attack by insects, and extracts from these plants have long been used as natural insecticides. One of these, **pyrethrum**, used to be obtained from the dried flower heads of a species of chrysanthemum. Now, similar substances called **pyrethroids** are synthesised industrially. Pyrethroids harm insects, but not mammals, and they also break down rapidly. They therefore cause few pollution problems. However, many insects are resistant to them, so other insecticides also have to be used.

In 1939, a substance called **dichloro-diphenyl trichloroethane** was discovered. It is commonly known as DDT. DDT is one of several organochlorine substances which are highly toxic to insects but not very toxic to mammals. It is relatively easy and cheap to make, and it has been very widely used all over the world. It has probably saved millions of people's lives, because it has been used to control the mosquitoes which spread malaria.

However, it was soon discovered that DDT was causing large-scale problems in the environment. DDT is a **broad spectrum** insecticide, which means that it kills all insects, not just the ones you want it to kill. Some of these may be natural predators of the pest. Resistant strains of the pest insect often evolve (Section 7.9), and – if their predators have been killed – their populations can become even larger than before the insecticide was applied.

Another problem with DDT is that it is **persistent**. It is chemically very stable, and does not readily break down. It is fat-soluble and accumulates in fatty tissues in animals. An insect-eating bird such as the thrush might eat hundreds of insects, each containing a small amount of DDT, and most of that DDT would remain in the thrush's body. A predatory bird might eat many thrushes, so that its body would end up with an even higher concentration of DDT than the concentration in a thrush. This process, in which a substance accumulates in larger and larger concentrations as it is passed along a food chain, is called **bioaccumulation** (Fig. 20.21). The large concentrations of DDT which built up in some predators, such as peregrine falcons, in the 1950s and 1960s caused their populations to fall drastically (Fig. 20.22).

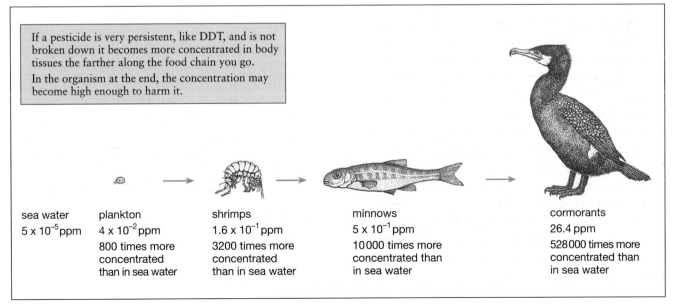

If a pesticide is very persistent, like DDT, and is not broken down it becomes more concentrated in body tissues the farther along the food chain you go.

In the organism at the end, the concentration may become high enough to harm it.

sea water	plankton	shrimps	minnows	cormorants
5×10^{-5} ppm	4×10^{-2} ppm	1.6×10^{-1} ppm	5×10^{-1} ppm	26.4 ppm
	800 times more concentrated than in sea water	3200 times more concentrated than in sea water	10 000 times more concentrated than in sea water	528 000 times more concentrated than in sea water

Fig. 20.21 Bioaccumulation of a persistent pesticide like DDT in a food chain in the 1970s.

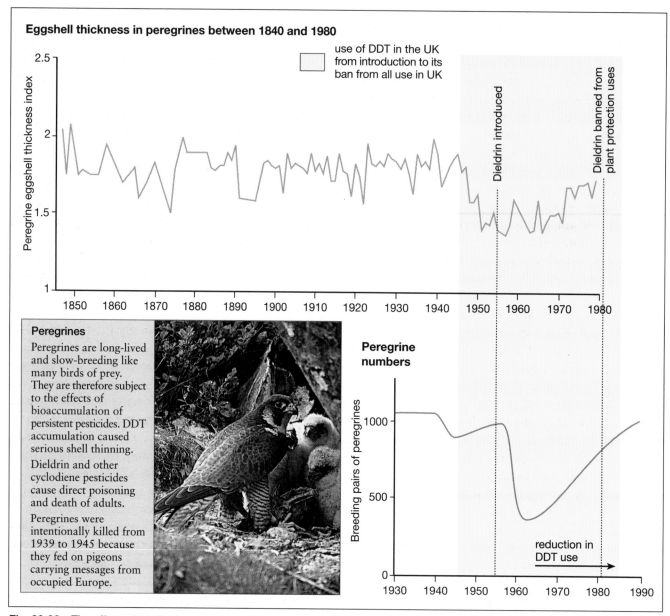

Fig. 20.22   The effect of pesticide use on peregrines.

Q3

(a) Is there any evidence in the graphs in Fig. 20.22 that DDT use has had a damaging effect on peregrine populations?

(b) Comparing the two graphs, why might the reduction in shell thickness not be expected to have an immediate effect on peregrine numbers?

(c) Could the use of dieldrin help to explain the drop in peregrine numbers or the fall in shell thickness?

The use of DDT is now banned in developed countries, but it is still widely used in many developing countries where the harm it does to the environment is seen to be outweighed by the good it does in controlling insects which carry disease and harm crops. Another argument in favour of its continued use in tropical and semi-tropical countries is that it does break down more rapidly in higher temperatures. However, most biologists would very much like to see DDT replaced by less harmful pesticides as soon as possible.

Most pesticides which are now in use are more **specific** than DDT, and also **non-persistent**. However, even these are causing some unforeseen problems. For example, **organophosphates** are now suspected of causing nerve damage in humans. There is concern that traces of pesticides which remain on food intended for human consumption, known as **pesticide residues**, may cause health problems. Chemists continue to search for the ideal pesticides – cheap and easy to manufacture, entirely specific for the insect pest, and entirely non-persistent.

20.13 Alternatives to pesticides

No-one wants to use pesticides if they do not have to. Pesticides are expensive, difficult to handle safely, dangerous to non-pest organisms, and pests often develop resistance to them. Many agricultural systems now use **integrated pest management systems, IPMs,** in which pesticides are just part of the control measures taken against pests.

Many IPMs involve the use of natural predators or parasites of the pest to keep their numbers down to an acceptable level. This is called **biological control.** For example, a bacterium called *Bacillus thuringiensis* can be bought as a spray which is applied to cabbage plants infested with caterpillars. The bacterium infects and kills the caterpillars without harming other insects.

Biological control methods have many advantages over pesticides. They are much more specific than most pesticides, the pest does not normally develop resistance to the control organism, and the control organism usually needs to be applied much less frequently than a pesticide. However, they do have their problems. For example:

- it is not always possible to find a suitable predator or parasite to control a particular pest, which can live in the conditions under which the pest is thriving.
- great care has to be taken if a predator or parasite is brought in from another place, because it is not possible to predict the effects it may have in its new environment.

Cane toads, for example, imported into Australia to control beetles which were eating sugar cane crops, turned out to have a liking for many of Australia's rare and endangered small marsupials. The cane toad has spread rapidly and is now a pest itself.

- the predator or parasite will probably not entirely destroy the pest, but will maintain its population at a low level. Farmers must be prepared to accept this.

Besides introducing predators or parasites from outside, natural ones can be encouraged by providing them with places to breed close to fields in which crops are being grown. Hedges, wide unploughed field margins, or even strips of grass left across a cultivated field can act as refuges for predators such as ladybirds, which can have a significant effect on the population size of pests such as aphids.

Insect pest populations can sometimes be reduced by releasing large numbers of **sterile males.** Large numbers of insects are bred in a laboratory; the females are destroyed, and the males made sterile, usually by radiation or chemicals. The sterile males are then released into an area where the pest is a problem. If there are enough of them, then the chances that a 'wild' female will mate with a sterile male is greater than the chance that she will mate with a 'wild' fertile male, so fewer eggs hatch and the population drops. This has been done very successfully in the southern United States and in northern Africa to control a fly which lays eggs in open wounds of humans and farm animals; the eggs hatch into maggots called screw-worms and often kill the infected animal.

Other ingredients of an IPM plan may include **crop rotation**, where different crops are grown on a particular piece of land each year. If the same crop is grown over and over again, then pest populations can build up to very high levels. If its food plant is missing for a year or more, however, the pest population will drop or even disappear. Crop rotation also helps to maintain soil fertility, because each kind of crop takes a different balance of nutrient ions from the soil.

Pesticide use can also be reduced by growing varieties of crops which have **natural resistance** to pests and diseases. These may be produced by conventional selective breeding (Section 7.12) or by genetic engineering (Section 5.14). It often takes longer for pests to develop their own counter-resistance to these plants' defences than it would for resistance to develop against pesticides.

CONSERVATION

20.14   What is conservation?

Conservation, in the biological sense, can have a wide range of meanings and can involve many processes. These processes range from setting up protected and undisturbed areas where wildlife can continue to exist with minimum interference from humans, to the establishment of complex management techniques designed to maintain an ecosystem in the form that humans decide they would like it to be.

Most people involved in conservation would now agree that their aim is to ensure the continuing existence of species, their habitats and biological communities. Conservation aims to maintain **biological diversity**. Biological diversity, sometimes known as biodiversity, is not an easy term to define. It includes species diversity (Section 19.19), but goes further than that. It involves not only the maintenance of a wide range of species, but also high genetic diversity within each species and within its populations, and the existence of a wide range of habitats and ecosystems within any particular area. In 1992, 152 nations signed a Convention on Biological Diversity at which it was defined as 'the variability among living organisms from all sources including ... terrestrial, marine and other aquatic ecosystems, and the ecological complexes of which they are part; this includes diversity within species, between species and of ecosystems'.

Many human activities can reduce biodiversity. Changes in land use (for example in agriculture, road building and building of homes) which destroy or fragment habitats, tourism, commercial uses of particular species and pollution can all reduce biodiversity. As human populations increase, these effects increase. The 1992 Convention was an important landmark, because it was the first international recognition of the importance of biodiversity, and the first international attempt to try to reduce its loss.

Why should we maintain diversity? For many ecologists, there is no need to answer this question at all – it is simply obvious that the variety of habitats and living organisms on Earth is not only a delight but also a responsibility, and that we have a moral obligation to care for them. But there are also more practical arguments for maintaining biodiversity. For example, there is evidence that a reduction in biodiversity may reduce climatic stability. Loss of diversity in ecosystems may result in drought or flooding in particular areas (Section 20.10). Loss of genetic diversity in populations may result in their

extinction (Section 7.13). Species which we do not yet know very much about may prove to be useful to humans.

20.15   Applying conservation measures

The application of measures to try to maintain or increase biodiversity in a particular area often involves conflicts. People put values not only on wildlife and habitats, but also on jobs, local economy and freedom of human activities. It is important that these different views should be recognised and appreciated, and that a balance should be achieved between them. Extremists on either side of the argument can frequently do more harm for their cause than good. Conservation measures are unlikely to be successful unless the local community is fully supportive of them (Box 20.2).

Conservation requires an interdisciplinary approach. It is not just something for ecologists to do, but also requires input from experts in taxonomy, genetics, economics, law, politics and education. It is not always easy to make the necessary bridges; ecologists may not have a very good understanding of politics for example, while economists may not understand the biological issues.

Conservation almost always requires a source of funding. Governments may provide funds for particular projects in their own country, or as development aid in other countries. International conservation organisations such as the World Wide Fund for Nature raise large sums of money from individuals and industry. Local conservation organisations, such as local Wildlife Trusts (Box 20.3) work on a smaller scale, once again raising money from membership fees, various fund-raising events and local sponsorship by businesses. People who actively support conservation may spend more time organising fund-raising events than working directly in conservation!

There are many different approaches to conservation. It may include the establishment of protected areas, in which living organisms and their habitat are given priority over the activities of humans. It may involve the removal of introduced species which do not naturally belong in an ecosystem, and perhaps the reintroduction of species which have been lost from it. It usually involves particular management techniques, which will have been developed after a thorough study of the habitats and species interactions in a particular area. No two conservation projects are ever quite the same. Box 20.3 describes one small conservation success story, as an example of the issues involved in preserving an important wildlife habitat for the future. ■

Box 20.3 Asham Meads – a small conservation success story

In 1986, a small team of scientists working for BBONT, the Wildlife Trust for Berkshire, Buckinghamshire and Oxfordshire, discovered an exciting site in Oxfordshire, now known as Asham Meads. The site is only small – just under 23 hectares in area – but contains a great diversity of habitats, including hedges, oak woodland, withy (willow) beds, scrub and a pond, each with their own communities. But perhaps the most interesting part is the meadows. A traditional meadow is an area of grassland which is harvested for hay, and most meadows in England have at some time been 'improved' by the addition of fertiliser and sowing with seeds from more productive types of grasses than occur naturally. The addition of fertiliser increases the fertility of the soil, which almost irreversibly reduces species diversity. The meadows at Asham Meads are unusual in that there appears to be a very long history of management without reseeding or application of fertiliser. They have a low fertility, and contain 20 plant species which are indicators of an ancient, unimproved meadow.

The BBONT team sent a report to the government organisation with responsibility for conservation, the Nature Conservancy Council. (This organisation has now become English Nature.) The information provided by BBONT indicated that Asham Meads contained many nationally declining species, including green-winged orchids and black hairstreak butterflies, indicating that the site should be considered of national importance as an excellent example of a now very rare unimproved grassland community. The Nature Conservancy Council responded quickly, and notified the area as an official Site of Special Scientific Interest, an SSSI.

In order to protect sites such as Asham Meads, positive action has to be taken. Any number of activities could easily change the habitat so that rare species are lost. For example, the meadows could be ploughed or reseeded, or sprayed with herbicides. BBONT decided that the best way to protect the site was to buy it, which they did in 1987, using money raised locally and also extensive grant aid from the local District Council.

At this stage, the meadows were being cut for hay in summer, left for a month or two for the meadow to begin to regrow, then grazed by a small number of cattle, well below the stocking densities which are now common on farmland. BBONT decided to continue this practice. This management regime keeps the fertility of the soil low, as the cut grass is removed from the land rather than being allowed to rot and return nutrients into the soil. Extra fertility promotes grass growth, which then out-competes and shades other flowering plants. Mowing therefore helps to maintain species diversity, because less competitive and more stress-tolerant species such as green-winged orchids can exist. Grazing also helps to do this. Grazing could be done

Fig. 20.23   A black hairstreak butterfly.

Fig. 20.24   Green-winged orchids.

Box 20.3 Asham Meads - a small conservation success story (cont.)

either by cattle or sheep, and it was decided to graze with sheep. The mowing and grazing arrest succession; without this, the meadows would gradually turn into scrub.

The hedges and thickets also require careful management. They contain blackthorn, which is a food plant for the caterpillars of the nationally rare black hairstreak butterfly. The caterpillars feed on young shoots growing on mature plants, so BBONT try to coppice 5% of the hedge each year, in autumn or winter. Coppicing involves cutting old stems back to ground level, after which the plant produces new, strong growth. This not only provides an ideal habitat for the black hairstreaks, but also denser cover for breeding birds and mammals.

How is such conservation funded? BBONT is one of many Wildlife Trusts in Britain. All of them are charities, and their income comes from membership subscriptions, grants from local or national government, and sponsorship from industry. They have to keep their costs down. They have a small number of staff with expertise in particular areas, but much of the conservation work, such as the coppicing at Asham Meads, and monitoring of the numbers and distribution of species such as the green-winged orchids and black hairstreak butterflies, is done by volunteers. BBONT do not have their own mowing machinery or livestock, so they allow a local farmer to harvest the meadows for hay and graze his sheep on them.

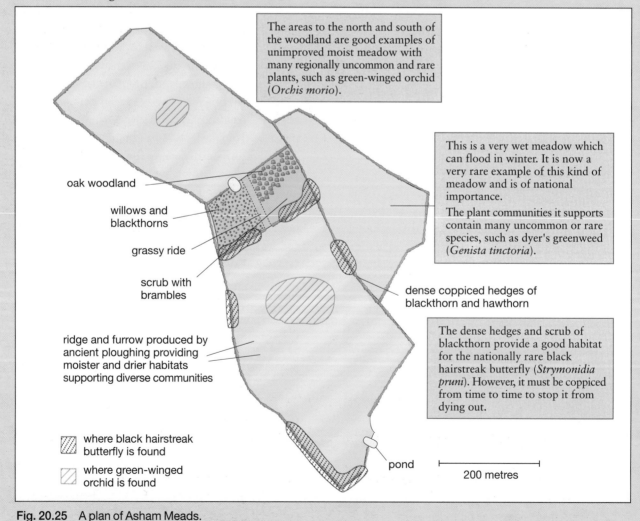

The areas to the north and south of the woodland are good examples of unimproved moist meadow with many regionally uncommon and rare plants, such as green-winged orchid (*Orchis morio*).

This is a very wet meadow which can flood in winter. It is now a very rare example of this kind of meadow and is of national importance.

The plant communities it supports contain many uncommon or rare species, such as dyer's greenweed (*Genista tinctoria*).

The dense hedges and scrub of blackthorn provide a good habitat for the nationally rare black hairstreak butterfly (*Strymonidia pruni*). However, it must be coppiced from time to time to stop it from dying out.

oak woodland

willows and blackthorns

grassy ride

scrub with brambles

ridge and furrow produced by ancient ploughing providing moister and drier habitats supporting diverse communities

dense coppiced hedges of blackthorn and hawthorn

pond

200 metres

where black hairstreak butterfly is found

where green-winged orchid is found

Fig. 20.25 A plan of Asham Meads.

Q4 The diagram below shows some of the processes involved in the cycling of nitrogen in an ecosystem.

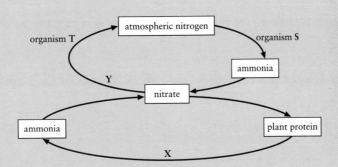

(a) (i) State the genus of **one** organism represented by the letter **S** and **one** organism represented by the letter **T** in the diagram. (2)

    (ii) Name the processes represented by the arrows **X** and **Y**. (2)

(b) Explain how excessive use of nitrate fertilisers might lead to eutrophication of a lake. (3)

ULEAC 1996   *(Total 7 marks)*

Q5 Spider mites are important pests of cucumbers. The graphs below show the results of an experiment using a chemical pesticide and biological control on two plots of cucumber plants infested with mites.

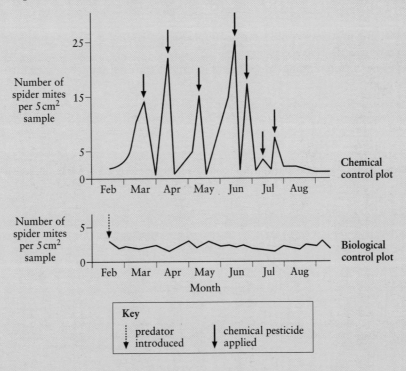

(a) Using evidence from the graphs, give **two** possible advantages of biological control over chemical control. (2)

(b) Describe **two** features of a predator that are essential if it is to be a successful biological control agent. (2)

AEB 1995   *(Total 4 marks)*

Q6 (a) Explain the dangers that the use of chlorofluorocarbons and DDT has posed to living organisms and to the environment. *(16)*

(b) What steps are now being taken to minimise further damage to the environment by these chemicals? *(7)*

UCLES 1992 *(Total 23 marks)*

Q7 The table below shows data referring to productivity in two ecosystems, rain forest and a field of a herbaceous annual crop plant. All figures are in MJ m⁻² year⁻¹.

	Rain forest	Crop
gross primary production	188	102
respiration by autotrophs	134	38
net primary production	54	64
respiration by heterotrophs	54	3

Use the information in the table and your own knowledge to answer the following questions.

(a) (i) Explain what is meant by gross primary production. *(1)*

(ii) Suggest **one** reason for the difference in the gross primary production between the forest and the crop plants. *(1)*

(b) Explain:
(i) how farming practices could have resulted in the different values for respiration by heterotrophs in the two ecosystems; *(2)*
(ii) how deforestation might cause an increase in the amount of carbon dioxide in the atmosphere. *(1)*

AEB 1995 *(Total 5 marks)*

Q8 Coppicing is a technique of woodland management in which trees are cut down regularly. Open spaces or areas of reduced tree canopy are thus produced.

(a) The diagram below shows the food web in part of a coppiced woodland.

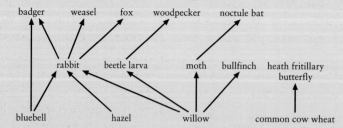

(i) State how many trophic levels are shown. *(1)*
(ii) State why there are usually not more than **four** trophic levels in a food web. *(1)*

(b) (i) Suggest how coppicing may change the ground flora of a woodland. *(1)*
(ii) Suggest a reason why this change may occur. *(1)*

ULEAC 1995 *(Total 4 marks)*

21 Infectious disease and immunity

Infectious diseases are caused by pathogens. The human body has many natural defences which help to prevent pathogens from entering and reproducing inside it. If they do succeed in entering, the immune system comes into play to attack and destroy them.

ORGANISMS WHICH CAUSE DISEASE

An infectious disease is one which can be passed on from one organism to another. Most infectious diseases are caused by organisms which invade the body and reproduce in it, causing damage to living cells. Organisms which do this are called **pathogens**. There are also a few infectious diseases which are not caused by other living organisms, but by proteins called prions. The cattle disease BSE and the human disease CJD are two such diseases, and they are described in Box 21.1.

Five types of pathogens are important in causing human diseases. Table 21.1 lists some examples of diseases caused by each type.

21.1 Viruses

Fig. 21.1 shows the structure of two different types of viruses. Viruses are extremely small, ranging in size from about 10 nm to 300 nm in diameter. They were first seen in the 1940s, when electron microscopes had been developed.

All viruses have a **protein** coat, called a **capsid**, surrounding a **nucleic acid**. The nucleic acid may be either **RNA or DNA**.

Some viruses also have an **envelope** surrounding them, which is made of lipid, protein and glycoprotein. Some contain **enzymes** which help the virus to reproduce.

When a virus is outside a living cell, it is inert. It demonstrates none of the characteristics of living things. Viruses are only able to reproduce inside living cells, using the cell's energy-generating machinery and some of the cell's molecules to build new virus particles. Thus viruses

Type of pathogen	Examples of diseases they cause
viruses	influenza measles poliomyelitis AIDS
bacteria	gonorrhoea syphilis bacterial meningitis tuberculosis
protoctists	malaria some forms of dysentery sleeping sickness
fungi	ringworm athlete's foot thrush
worms	bilharzia

Table 21.1 Pathogenic organisms.

are **obligate parasites**. The virus's RNA or DNA contains the codes for making the proteins in its capsid, and the host cell follows these instructions to make new viruses. The virus turns the host cell into a virus factory.

Fig. 21.3 shows how viruses can reproduce. The virus first recognises a suitable cell, by interactions between a protein or glycoprotein on its surface and a receptor molecule in the host cell's cell surface membrane. The virus can only enter the cell if this interaction occurs, so viruses are quite specific for cells in a particular species of organism, or even a particular type of cell within an organism. Different viruses may use different mechanisms to enter the host cell. Once inside the host cell, the virus's nucleic acid (RNA or DNA) is released. The host cell then

Adenovirus – a naked capsid virus with DNA (×27 000 000)

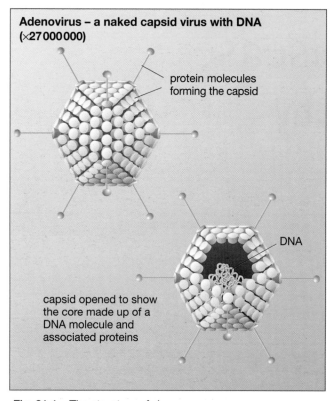

protein molecules forming the capsid

DNA

capsid opened to show the core made up of a DNA molecule and associated proteins

HIV – an enveloped virus with RNA (×27 000 000)

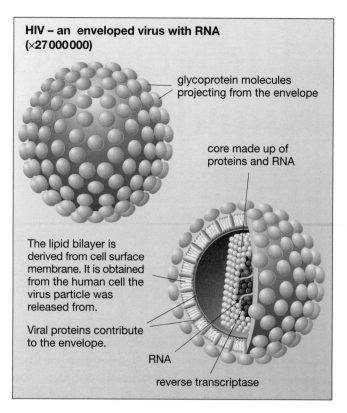

glycoprotein molecules projecting from the envelope

core made up of proteins and RNA

The lipid bilayer is derived from cell surface membrane. It is obtained from the human cell the virus particle was released from.

Viral proteins contribute to the envelope.

RNA

reverse transcriptase

Fig. 21.1 The structure of viruses.

follows the code on the nucleic acid to make new viral proteins, and the nucleic acid replicates to produce new copies of itself. Eventually, the new copies of viral proteins and nucleic acid assemble themselves to form complete new viruses. They may be released gradually, or they may burst out of the cell ready to infect other cells.

21.2 Bacteria

Bacteria are prokaryotic organisms (Section 3.22); the structure of a bacterial cell is shown in Fig. 3.24. They are much larger than viruses (Fig. 21.2) but much smaller than human cells. Unlike viruses, most bacteria do not reproduce inside other living cells. Fig. 21.4 shows some examples of pathogenic bacteria.

Most bacteria do not cause disease. Most are free-living, feeding by photosynthesis, chemosynthesis (Box 8.1) or saprotrophically. We have many bacteria living within our bodies which usually do us no harm at all, and a few may even be helpful.

A few types of bacteria, however, can invade the human body where they multiply and cause disease. They often release poisonous substances called **toxins** which make

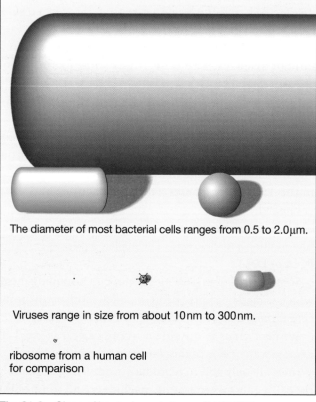

The diameter of most bacterial cells ranges from 0.5 to 2.0 μm.

Viruses range in size from about 10 nm to 300 nm.

ribosome from a human cell for comparison

Fig. 21.2 Sizes of bacteria and viruses (×22 500).

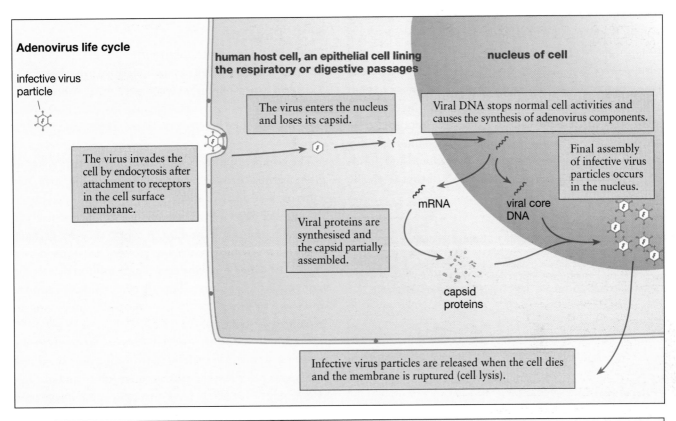

Adenovirus life cycle

infective virus particle

human host cell, an epithelial cell lining the respiratory or digestive passages

nucleus of cell

The virus enters the nucleus and loses its capsid.

Viral DNA stops normal cell activities and causes the synthesis of adenovirus components.

The virus invades the cell by endocytosis after attachment to receptors in the cell surface membrane.

Final assembly of infective virus particles occurs in the nucleus.

mRNA

viral core DNA

Viral proteins are synthesised and the capsid partially assembled.

capsid proteins

Infective virus particles are released when the cell dies and the membrane is ruptured (cell lysis).

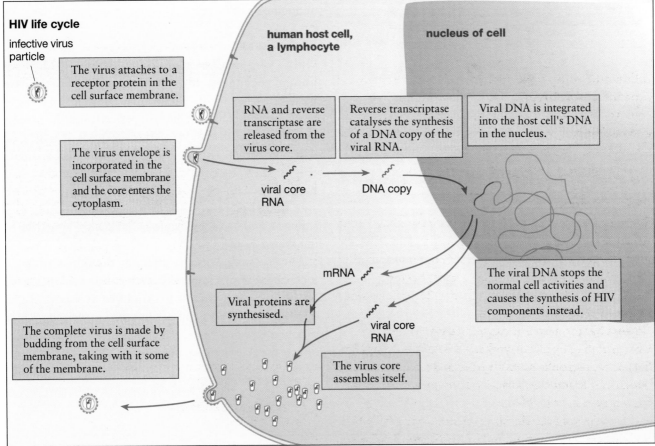

HIV life cycle

infective virus particle

human host cell, a lymphocyte

nucleus of cell

The virus attaches to a receptor protein in the cell surface membrane.

RNA and reverse transcriptase are released from the virus core.

Reverse transcriptase catalyses the synthesis of a DNA copy of the viral RNA.

Viral DNA is integrated into the host cell's DNA in the nucleus.

The virus envelope is incorporated in the cell surface membrane and the core enters the cytoplasm.

viral core RNA

DNA copy

The viral DNA stops the normal cell activities and causes the synthesis of HIV components instead.

mRNA

Viral proteins are synthesised.

viral core RNA

The complete virus is made by budding from the cell surface membrane, taking with it some of the membrane.

The virus core assembles itself.

Fig. 21.3 Life cycles of adenovirus and human immunodeficiency virus (HIV).

you ill. For example, *Clostridium tetani*, which is found in soil, produces a toxin that affects the nervous system and results in tetanus (Section 21.14). In other cases, some of the symptoms of the illness are caused by damage to your cells. The bacterium *Shigella*, for example, breeds in the alimentary canal and invades the mucosa (Section 13.5) of the colon, damaging the cells and causing pain. It is easily transmitted from person to person if unwashed hands contaminated by faeces come into contact with the mouth.

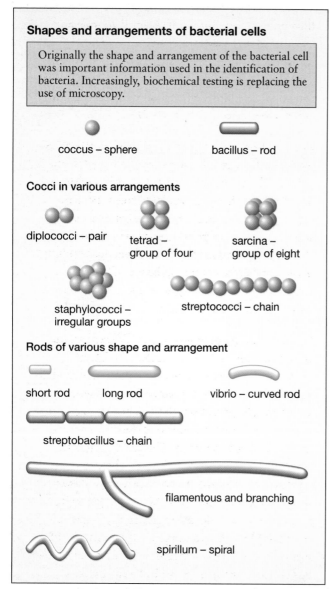

Shapes and arrangements of bacterial cells

Originally the shape and arrangement of the bacterial cell was important information used in the identification of bacteria. Increasingly, biochemical testing is replacing the use of microscopy.

coccus – sphere   bacillus – rod

Cocci in various arrangements

diplococci – pair   tetrad –   sarcina –
                      group of four   group of eight

staphylococci –   streptococci – chain
irregular groups

Rods of various shape and arrangement

short rod   long rod   vibrio – curved rod

streptobacillus – chain

filamentous and branching

spirillum – spiral

Fig. 21.4 Shapes of bacteria.

21.3 Protoctists

Protoctists are simple eukaryotic organisms; many of them are single-celled. They are described in Section 22.3. The term 'parasite', rather than 'pathogen', is often used to describe protoctists which cause disease. There is no clear dividing line between these two terms, and either is correct.

The number of diseases caused by protoctists is not as great as those caused by either viruses or bacteria, but some of these diseases are extremely important in terms of the number of people infected with them, particularly in tropical regions, and the damage which they do. Perhaps the most well-known is malaria, which is caused by a protoctist called *Plasmodium*. Three million people die from malaria each year. The life cycle of this organism and the way in which it is transmitted from person to person are described in Fig. 13.15.

Several kinds of protoctists cause infection in the alimentary canal. Travellers to tropical countries where hygiene is poor run the risk of infection from *Giardia*, which may be present in food or water contaminated with human faeces. It causes diarrhoea, general weakness and abdominal pain.

21.4 Fungi

Only a very small number of fungi (Section 22.5) are human pathogens. Many of these are **opportunistic** pathogens; they are often found living on mucosal surfaces (such as the mouth or vagina) of perfectly healthy people, and only cause disease when this surface is damaged, or when the person's immune system is weakened for some reason. The yeast *Candida* is an example. Around 80% of people have *Candida* living on mucosal surfaces, with no sign of disease. But sometimes it causes itching and soreness, and becomes visible as small white spots, when it is known as thrush.

Another fungal disease affecting the skin is athlete's foot, caused by the fungus *Tinea*. It is estimated that up to half of people living in Brtain have at least a slight infection from this fungus at some time in their life. *Tinea* produces enzymes which can digest keratin, and it usually infects the skin between the toes, causing it to crack and flake.

Box 21.1 Scrapie, BSE and CJD

Scrapie, BSE or 'mad cow disease' and CJD are all examples of **spongiform encephalopathies**. They are diseases of the brain where 'holes' appear in the brain tissue as cells die. Coordination is lost, other symptoms of derangement may appear, and death almost always results.

Encephalopathies have been known for many years, affecting many different species of animals, but until recently no-one knew what caused them. The human form, **Creutzfeldt–Jacob disease**, or CJD, occurs worldwide and affects about one person in a million, usually over 60 years of age. A similar disease affecting humans is **kuru**, but this is known only in certain tribes in Papua New Guinea where dead people used to be honoured by eating their brains; this practice has now stopped, and there are now very few cases of kuru. **Scrapie** affects sheep and goats, and gets its name because one symptom which often occurs is itching of the skin, causing the animal to scrape its body against trees and fences. **Bovine spongiform encephalopathy** (BSE) affects cattle.

Until recently, it was believed that all agents which could cause infectious diseases must contain nucleic acids, but no-one was able to find such an agent which caused encephalopathies. In 1980, it was suggested that something quite different was responsible for these diseases – a protein, called a **prion**. Scientists found this very difficult to accept at first, but it is now widely believed to be so.

The prion protein, **PrP**, is present in normal cells, where its role is not yet known. Molecules of the normal form of PrP are globular, consisting largely of α helices. But there is another form which this molecule can take, in which the tightly coiled α helices switch to β strands. These can interact to form β sheets (Section 1.13). It is this second form which causes the damage; somehow, its presence kills cells, leaving 'holes' in the brain. The presence of a PrP molecule in the β strand form can induce other, normal, PrP molecules to flip to this shape. So, if a few molecules of β-stranded PrP molecules get into an animal's brain, they can gradually cause normal PrP molecules to adopt this shape. The result is encephalopathy.

Diseases such as CJD do occur spontaneously; perhaps, as people age, some of their PrP molecules just change shape for no reason. They can also be transferred from one animal to another. CJD has been transferred to people through corneal transplants or in human growth hormone extracted from human brains. Scrapie is known to be transferred from an infected sheep to another, although the ways in which this happens are not fully understood. But, until recently, no-one had considered that there might be a danger in encephalopathy from one species transferring to another. We have lived with scrapie-infected sheep for a very long time, and studies have never found any link between scrapie and CJD.

But in 1986 a new form of the disease in cattle, BSE, was identified, and this has spread amongst cattle in Britain. The evidence suggests that this disease may have 'crossed the species barrier' from sheep to cattle, probably when cattle were fed on food supplements made from sheep meat and bones. A change in the preparation of this food had occurred in the late 1970s, involving the use of lower temperatures, which may have allowed prions to remain unaltered in the food.

Different species of animals have different amino acid sequences in their PrP molecules. There is evidence that one PrP molecule is most likely to be able to affect another if their amino acid sequences are similar. So, the closer the sequence is in two species, the more likely it is that the disease could be transmitted between them. Sheep PrP differs from cow PrP in only 7 amino acids; it is therefore not impossible for the disease to have 'jumped' from sheep to cattle. Human PrP, however, differs from cow PrP in more than 30 amino acids, so it would seem less likely that this prion disease can spread from cattle to humans than from sheep to cattle. But it is not completely impossible, because it is probable that some parts of the PrP molecule are more important than others in determining whether the β-stranded form can cause normal forms to 'flip' to the β-stranded state.

21.5 Worms

Several different phyla (Section 22.1) contain long thin organisms which are called 'worms'. The worms which cause illness belong to the phyla Nematoda (roundworms) and Platyhelminthes (flatworms). In Britain, disease caused by worms is rare, but worms are important pathogens in some developing countries.

The roundworm *Toxocara* is a parasite of cats and dogs, where it lives in the alimentary canal. The eggs pass out of the body in the faeces. If a person accidentally eats some of these eggs, they may hatch into larvae which penetrate the wall of the person's alimentary canal and invade tissues in various parts of the body, such as the liver and eyes. The illness is called toxocariosis, and usually results when a child has been playing in a grassy area contaminated with dog faeces.

The tapeworm *Taenia* is a platyhelminth. Its life cycle is described in Fig. 13.14. Tapeworm infection in humans is now very rare in Britain. However, the disease bilharzia or schistosomiasis, which is also caused by a platyhelminth, is common in some countries. The platyhelminth which causes bilharzia is called *Schistosoma*, and it lives in the blood of humans, causing a general feeling of illness, weight loss, fever and abdominal pain. If left untreated, it can be fatal. Like *Taenia*, *Schistosoma* has a complex life cycle involving a secondary host, in this case water snails. People are at most risk from infection with *Schistosoma* if they paddle or swim in water containing the parasite; the tiny larvae in the water will burrow through the person's skin.

BARRIERS AGAINST INFECTION
21.6 Preventing the entry of pathogens

The most effective way for the human body to avoid infection by pathogens is to prevent them gaining access.

Skin is a very effective barrier to the entry of pathogens. Only a few pathogens – mostly viruses – are known to be able to penetrate undamaged skin. We have our own 'flora' of harmless bacteria which live on healthy skin, but most pathogenic bacteria cannot survive there, partly because lactic acid and fatty acids secreted from sweat glands and sebaceous glands provide a pH which is too low for them. However, the common bacterium *Staphylococcus aureus* can thrive even on undamaged skin, and it often infects hair follicles and sebaceous glands. In some circumstances, *S. aureus* can invade the body and cause illness, which is sometimes fatal.

The normal bacterial 'flora' living on our body surfaces can help to prevent infection by other microorganisms. For example, the bacteria which normally live in the vagina keep the pH low by secreting lactic acid. If a person takes antibiotics, these bacteria may be killed. Then the pH of the vagina rises, and this may allow other microorganisms, such as *Candida*, to multiply to much greater population densities than usual, causing a thrush infection.

If skin is damaged, for example by cuts or extensive burns, then the way is open for bacteria to get into the underlying tissues. **Blood clotting** helps to seal wounds rapidly, until a more permanent repair is produced by mitosis of the cells surrounding the wound. A blood clot forms when the soluble, globular, blood protein fibrinogen is converted to the insoluble fibrous protein fibrin. This forms a mesh of strands across the wound in which platelets stick and red blood cells get trapped. This process is explained in Fig. 21.5.

Moist body surfaces, such as the surface of the eyes and mouth, are bathed with fluids which have some **bactericidal** action. An enzyme called **lysozyme** is present in saliva and tears, and this enzyme can damage and destroy many bacteria. Semen contains a bactericide called spermine; milk contains a bactericidal enzyme called lactoperoxidase. The **hydrochloric acid** secreted into the stomach is very effective in destroying bacteria ingested in food.

Mucus helps to protect the digestive and respiratory tracts from infection. It acts as a barrier so that bacteria cannot make contact with the epithelial cells lining the walls of the tubes. In the trachea and bronchi, the mucus is swept upwards to the back of the throat by cilia and then swallowed. Coughing and sneezing help to expel mucus containing microorganisms from the trachea and bronchi. Once the mucus is swallowed, the acid and enzymes in the stomach destroy any bacteria trapped in it.

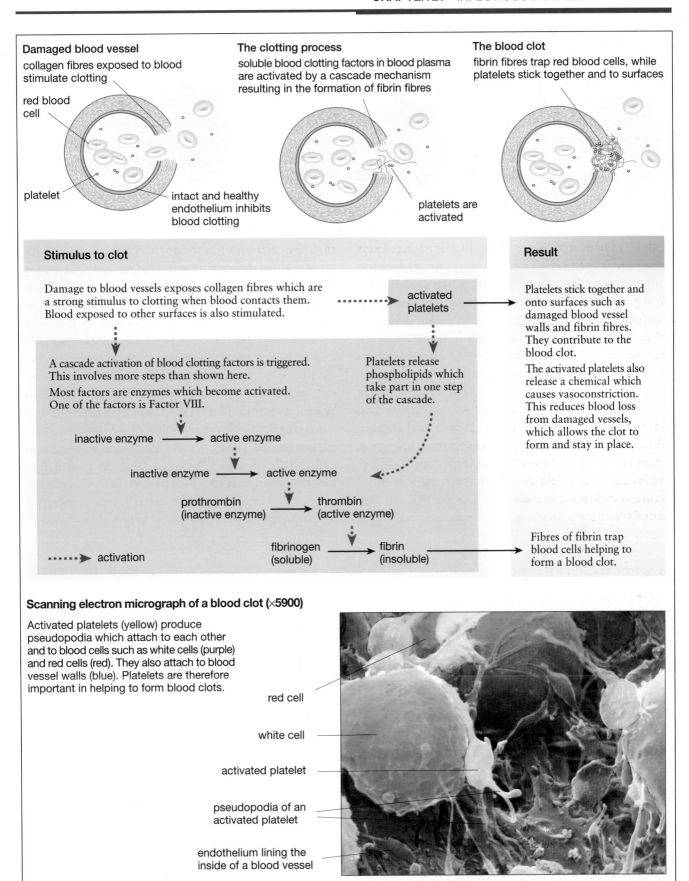

Damaged blood vessel

collagen fibres exposed to blood stimulate clotting

red blood cell

platelet

intact and healthy endothelium inhibits blood clotting

The clotting process

soluble blood clotting factors in blood plasma are activated by a cascade mechanism resulting in the formation of fibrin fibres

platelets are activated

The blood clot

fibrin fibres trap red blood cells, while platelets stick together and to surfaces

---

Stimulus to clot

Damage to blood vessels exposes collagen fibres which are a strong stimulus to clotting when blood contacts them. Blood exposed to other surfaces is also stimulated.

A cascade activation of blood clotting factors is triggered. This involves more steps than shown here.

Most factors are enzymes which become activated. One of the factors is Factor VIII.

inactive enzyme ⟶ active enzyme

inactive enzyme ⟶ active enzyme

prothrombin (inactive enzyme) ⟶ thrombin (active enzyme)

╌╌╌╌▶ activation

fibrinogen (soluble) ⟶ fibrin (insoluble)

activated platelets

Platelets release phospholipids which take part in one step of the cascade.

Result

Platelets stick together and onto surfaces such as damaged blood vessel walls and fibrin fibres. They contribute to the blood clot.

The activated platelets also release a chemical which causes vasoconstriction. This reduces blood loss from damaged vessels, which allows the clot to form and stay in place.

Fibres of fibrin trap blood cells helping to form a blood clot.

Scanning electron micrograph of a blood clot (×5900)

Activated platelets (yellow) produce pseudopodia which attach to each other and to blood cells such as white cells (purple) and red cells (red). They also attach to blood vessel walls (blue). Platelets are therefore important in helping to form blood clots.

red cell

white cell

activated platelet

pseudopodia of an activated platelet

endothelium lining the inside of a blood vessel

Fig. 21.5 Blood clotting.

THE IMMUNE SYSTEM

21.7 Self and non-self

Despite the lines of defence described in Section 21.6, potentially dangerous organisms do get into the human body. Many methods of attacking these invaders have evolved in mammals, and they are collectively known as the **immune response**.

It is clearly important that the human body should be able to recognise invading microorganisms. The features used to distinguish cells are chemicals on their surfaces, usually **proteins, carbohydrates, glycoproteins** (molecules made up of both protein and carbohydrate) or **glycolipids** (made up of lipid and carbohydrate). The cells within your own body have their own particular sets of these surface chemicals, and your immune system usually recognises these as being **self**. Cells with different chemicals on their surfaces are usually recognised as being **non-self** or 'foreign', and are attacked. A chemical which triggers such an attack is called an **antigen**. The exact mechanism by which your immune system distinguishes self from non-self is still not fully understood.

The ways in which non-self cells are attacked are very complex, and we still have much to learn about it. Indeed, the system *has* to be complex; if it were simple, then it would be relatively easy for pathogens to evolve defences against it. In the sections which follow, we will describe

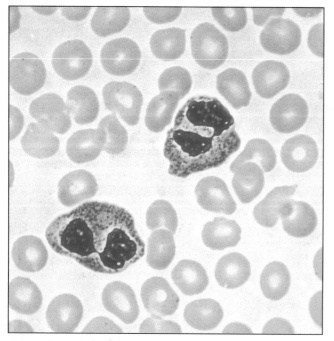

Fig. 21.6 Granulocytes in human blood. These are neutrophils, the commonest type of granulocyte. All granulocytes are phagocytic.

just some of the many ways in which the immune system fights off invaders.

21.8 Phagocytosis

Phagocytosis literally means 'cell eating' (Section 3.28 and Fig. 3.12). Two types of white blood cells are involved in destroying invading microorganisms by phagocytosis (Fig. 21.6).

Granulocytes (sometimes known as polymorphs) are the commonest white cells in the blood; they can squeeze out of blood capillaries and into tissues. You can recognise them by their multi-lobed nucleus, and the fact that in most of them their granular cytoplasm stains light pink with the specialist stains that are used for making blood films for microscopy (Fig. 21.6). They are relatively short-lived cells, often surviving only for hours or days, and they do not divide. They usually die when they have taken up and destroyed microorganisms by phagocytosis, so they have to be constantly replaced by new cells produced in the bone marrow. You make about 80 million granulocytes per minute in your bone marrow.

Macrophages, on the other hand, are found mostly in the connective tissues, around the basement membranes of small blood vessels, and patrolling the alveoli in the lungs. Macrophages are also present in the liver, where they are known as **Kupffer cells**. Large numbers of macrophages line the passages in lymph nodes in the spleen, where they can destroy bacteria in the lymph as it flows through.

Like granulocytes, macrophages begin their life in the bone marrow. They then enter the bloodstream where they are known as monocytes (Fig. 10.14). Some of them then migrate from the blood into the tissues and become macrophages. Macrophages are larger than granulocytes, and they can crawl around actively. Unlike granulocytes, they usually survive after phagocytosing microorganisms, and are therefore much longer lived.

For phagocytosis to take place, the microorganisms must first adhere to the cell surface membrane of the phagocyte. This process is helped by chemicals called **complement** (Box 21.2) which are always present in the blood plasma, and also by chemicals called **cytokines** (Box 21.3) which are produced by other white blood cells in response to the presence of particular antigens. Cytokines also make phagocytes more efficient at killing any microorganisms which they have taken into the cell.

Box 21.2 Complement

Complement is a collection of proteins which are always present in the blood plasma. It was first discovered in 1895, and was given the name 'complement' because it complements the activity of antibodies. Complement appears to be particularly important in fighting bacterial infections, and people who have a hereditary deficiency in one of the complement proteins are particularly susceptible to infection by some kinds of bacteria.

Many of the proteins which make up complement are enzymes. They are mostly present in an inactive state, and pieces of their molecules must be removed before they become active. Once one of them has been activated in this way, it acts as a catalyst for the activation of another in a cascade process (Fig. 21.7).

The cascade can be activated in one of two ways. Firstly, if an antibody binds to an antigen, then one of the complement proteins can bind to the antibody. The shape of the complement protein is changed by this process, and this sets off the cascade. The second way is by direct contact of a different complement protein with a 'non-self' surface, such as a bacterial cell membrane; once again, this causes a shape change in the complement protein and activates the cascade.

The result of the cascade is the production of proteins which can help to destroy invading microorganisms. There are three ways in which they do this.

Opsonisation – Some of the proteins produced when the complement cascade is activated bind to the surface of bacteria, coating them with a layer of protein called **opsonin**. Phagocytic cells have receptors which bind to opsonin, and this stimulates them to destroy the coated bacterium.

By attracting macrophages and other cells to the site of infection – Some of the newly produced complement proteins drift away from the place where they formed, into the tissue fluid and blood. Their presence attracts phagocytes and other white blood cells, which move towards the site by chemotaxis. This is important in the inflammatory response (Section 21.13).

By directly destroying the target which stimulated their production – A third kind of complement protein directly destroys the cells which stimulated its production, by making holes in their cell surface membranes.

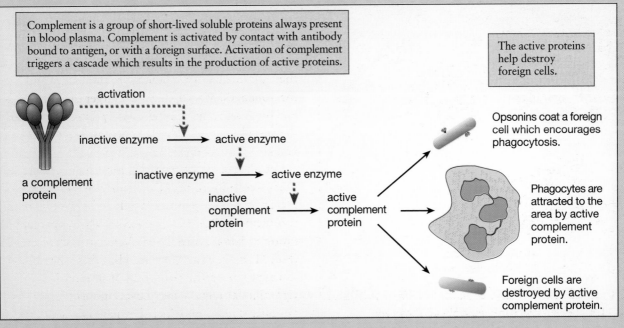

Complement is a group of short-lived soluble proteins always present in blood plasma. Complement is activated by contact with antibody bound to antigen, or with a foreign surface. Activation of complement triggers a cascade which results in the production of active proteins.

The active proteins help destroy foreign cells.

activation

inactive enzyme → active enzyme

inactive enzyme → active enzyme

a complement protein

inactive complement protein → active complement protein

Opsonins coat a foreign cell which encourages phagocytosis.

Phagocytes are attracted to the area by active complement protein.

Foreign cells are destroyed by active complement protein.

Fig. 21.7 Complement.

Box 21.3 Cytokines

Cytokines are small protein molecules which act as messengers between cells. At least 20 different cytokines are known, and more are still being discovered. They can have effects when present in only very tiny concentrations, which has made it difficult to find out exactly what they do, especially as they interact with each other. Many cytokines are secreted by T lymphocytes, but other cells also secrete them. Most cytokines act on cells very near to the ones which secrete them, and their effects are very short-lived.

One cytokine which has been known for many years is **interferon**. This protein is secreted by cells when they are infected by viruses. The interferon binds to specific receptors on uninfected cells nearby, triggering these cells to make certain enzymes. This reduces the translation of mRNA in the cell, and activates an endonuclease (Section 5.11). This stops mRNA derived from any viruses which subsequently infect the cell being used to synthesise viral proteins. It also, of course, stops the cell's own proteins being synthesised – but this is a price which has to be paid.

Another cytokine in which there is currently great interest is **tumour necrosis factor**, TNF. TNF is secreted by macrophages and T lymphocytes. It was given its name when it was discovered that it could cause some tumours to shrink, by reducing the blood supply to them. But TNF has many other effects, including the activation of phagocytic cells and the development of inflammation at the site of infection (Section 21.13). If large amounts of TNF are secreted, this reaction can be so great that too much fluid is lost from the blood system, producing a very dangerous condition known as vascular shock.

Q1 (a) Describe **two** ways in which the activity of viruses can give rise to disease symptoms.   (2)

Disease-causing microorganisms gain access to the body via one of its interfaces with the environment. These are shown in the diagram below.

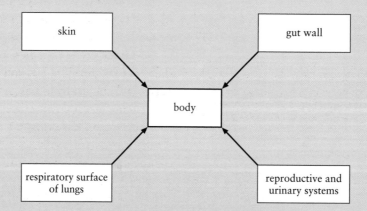

(b) Through which of these interfaces do the following gain access to the body:
   (i) an influenza virus?   (1)
   (ii) a *Salmonella* bacterium?   (1)

(c) How does the human body normally limit the access of microorganisms to the respiratory surface of the lungs?   (2)

NEAB 1995   *(Total 6 marks)*

21.9 Antibodies

The human body is able to produce chemicals which specifically react with particular antigens, helping to destroy them. These chemicals are known as **antibodies**. Antibodies are made by white blood cells called **lymphocytes**.

Fig. 21.8 shows the general structure of an antibody molecule. Antibodies are globular proteins, and – as they are part of the immune system – they are often known as **immunoglobulins**.

There are several different types of immunoglobulins, known by names such as immunoglobulin G, immunoglobulin M and so on. These names are usually shortened to IgG and IgM.

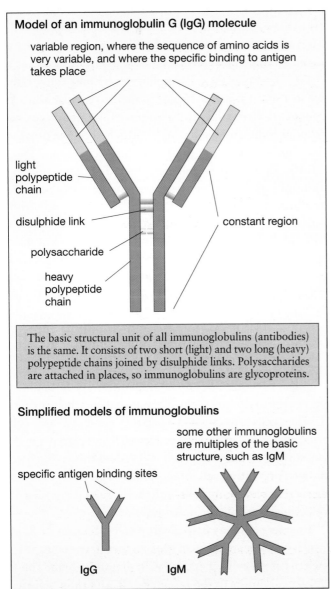

Model of an immunoglobulin G (IgG) molecule

variable region, where the sequence of amino acids is very variable, and where the specific binding to antigen takes place

light polypeptide chain

disulphide link

polysaccharide

heavy polypeptide chain

constant region

The basic structural unit of all immunoglobulins (antibodies) is the same. It consists of two short (light) and two long (heavy) polypeptide chains joined by disulphide links. Polysaccharides are attached in places, so immunoglobulins are glycoproteins.

Simplified models of immunoglobulins

some other immunoglobulins are multiples of the basic structure, such as IgM

specific antigen binding sites

IgG   IgM

Fig. 21.8 The structure of immunoglobulins (Ig).

All immunoglobulins within a particular type have a similar structure for part of their molecule, known as the 'constant region' (Fig. 21.8). But at one end of the molecule is a highly variable region. This part of the molecule can interact with antigens. It is believed that the human body is capable of making over a million different kinds of antibody molecules. Your immune system can probably provide an antibody molecule which will interact with almost any antigen which gets into your body.

There are several ways in which the binding of an antibody to an antigen can help to destroy it. Sometimes, the antibody may directly neutralise the antigen, for example if the antigen is a bacterial toxin. Usually, however, the binding of antibody to antigen activates other events which destroy the microorganism on which the antigen is present. This often involves the **complement** system (Box 21.2).

With so many possible antibodies, it would clearly be very wasteful for your lymphocytes to produce all of them in large quantities all of the time. Instead, particular antibodies are made in response to the presence of the particular antigen with which they can interact. This process is described in Section 21.11.

21.10 Lymphocytes

Lymphocytes are relatively small white blood cells, with a nucleus which readily takes up the stains used to make blood films, and with only a small amount of cytoplasm. Like all of the cells of the immune system, they are formed from cells in the bone marrow, called **stem cells**.

Lymphocytes are classified into two types according to the way they develop, but you cannot tell the difference between them just by looking at them. One type develops in the bone marrow, and these cells are **B lymphocytes**. The other type develops in the thymus gland (a gland which is present in the neck in children, but begins to disappear at puberty), and these are known as **T lymphocytes**.

B lymphocytes and T lymphocytes have different roles in the immune response. B lymphocytes secrete antibodies into body fluids, and this is sometimes known as the **humoral response**. 'Humour' is an old name for a body fluid, so this term refers to the fact that the antigens are destroyed by antibodies dissolved in 'fluids'. T cells do not secrete antibodies. The T cell itself helps to destroy antigens inside body cells, and so their role in the immune response is sometimes known as the **cell-mediated**

response. But it is now known that the two types of cell interact in quite complex ways (some of which are described in the next two sections) and so these two terms have only a limited use.

21.11 How B lymphocytes respond to antigen

Each B lymphocyte is able to make just one kind of antibody. There are thought to be around a million variants, each able to make a specific antibody. The B lymphocyte makes about 100 000 molecules of this antibody, which lie in its cell surface membrane with their variable regions projecting outwards. The B lymphocyte may spend its entire life like this, never doing anything very active at all. But if an antigen binds with its antibody molecules, then it is triggered into action (Fig. 21.9).

A B lymphocyte to which antigen molecules bind is stimulated to divide repeatedly by mitosis, so that within days there is a large population of identical B lymphocytes able to secrete this particular antibody. As the B lymphocytes are all genetically identical, they are known as a **clone**, and the process of their production is called **clonal proliferation**.

Many of the cells in the clone become **plasma cells**. Each plasma cell quickly develops extra endoplasmic reticulum and ribosomes, enabling it to synthesise and secrete large amounts of its particular antibody. A plasma cell can release up to 2000 antibody molecules per second; not suprisingly, these cells do not live for very long.

It takes a few days for enough B lymphocytes to be produced to make enough antibody to be detectable in the blood. During this time, the microorganism carrying the antigen which set off this response may have been able to form a large enough population to make you ill. Eventually, however, the antibodies may get the upper hand, destroying the microorganisms and allowing the symptoms of illness to subside.

The response described above, in which the B lymphocytes meet an antigen for the first time, is called the **primary response**. However, if the same antigen invades your body on a second occasion, a much faster response occurs which produces much larger quantities of the appropriate antibody, and this is called a **secondary response** (Fig. 21. 9). It happens because when the B lymphocytes divided during the primary response, some of them stopped dividing and secreting antibody and became **memory cells**. Quite large numbers of these cells – each capable of secreting the antibody specific for that particular antigen – remain in the body for a long time

after the first infection. They are capable of responding very quickly if the same antigen appears again. The response is often so fast and so effective that you are quite unaware that the microorganism ever entered your body. You have become **immune** to that particular disease.

21.12 How T lymphocytes respond to antigen

The antibodies produced by B lymphocytes are secreted into the body fluids, where they can bind to and help to destroy organisms which are *outside* your own cells. T lymphocytes, on the other hand, are involved in attacking microorganisms which are *inside* your cells.

T lymphocytes, like B lymphocytes, are each capable of making just one kind of molecule which can interact with just one kind of antigen. These molecules are not called antibodies, because they are never released from the cell. They remain attached to the T cell's membrane, and are called **T cell surface receptors**.

Like B lymphocytes, T lymphocytes become active only when a specific antigen binds to their particular surface receptor. However, the antigen alone produces no response; the antigen has to be attached to one of your own body cells before the T lymphocytes respond (Fig. 21.10). Body cells which are infected with a virus, for example, place molecules from the virus in their cell surface membranes, and this acts as a signal to T lymphocytes that their help is required.

Some T lymphocytes respond to the discovery of their 'own' antigen on another body cell by attaching to the antigen (and therefore to the cell) and destroying the cell. They are called **T killer cells**. They kill the infected cell by making holes in its cell surface membrane. If the infected cell can be killed before the virus has time to replicate, this can then greatly reduce the chances of other body cells becoming infected by it.

Other T lymphocytes do not kill infected cells, but help other cells to destroy them. They are called **T helper cells**. T helper cells are activated when they contact a body cell which has taken in antigen, processed it and placed it in its cell surface membrane. A cell which does this is called an **antigen presenting cell**. Macrophages and B cells can act as antigen presenting cells, and there are other groups of cells which specialise in doing just this.

T helper cells may help macrophages (Section 21.8) in which bacteria are thriving because they have managed to switch off the cell's machinery for digesting them. The T helper cell binds to the infected cell, and then secretes chemicals called **cytokines** (Box 21.3) which stimulate the

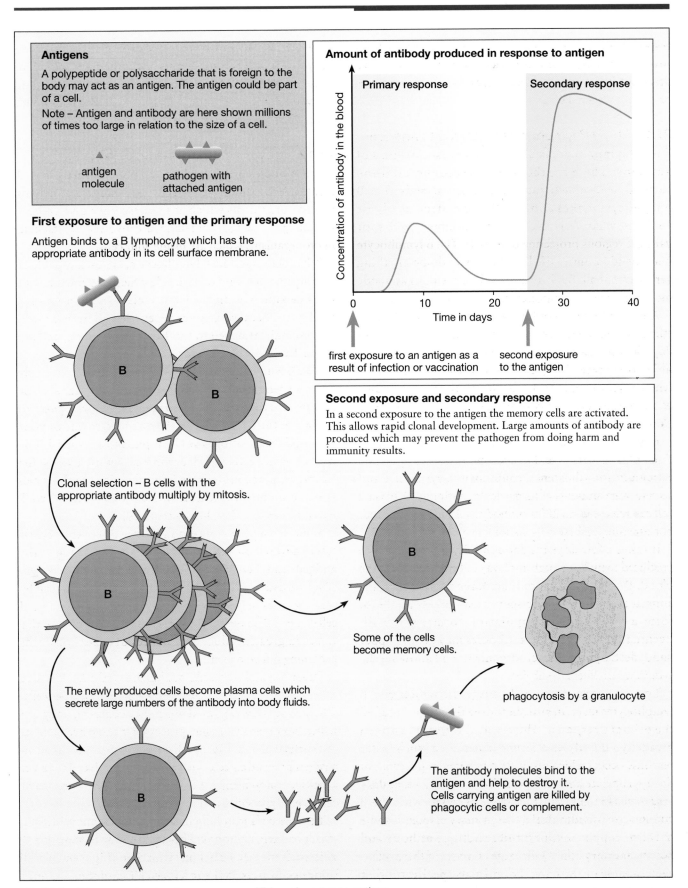

Antigens

A polypeptide or polysaccharide that is foreign to the body may act as an antigen. The antigen could be part of a cell.

Note – Antigen and antibody are here shown millions of times too large in relation to the size of a cell.

antigen molecule

pathogen with attached antigen

Amount of antibody produced in response to antigen

Primary response   Secondary response

Concentration of antibody in the blood

Time in days

first exposure to an antigen as a result of infection or vaccination

second exposure to the antigen

First exposure to antigen and the primary response

Antigen binds to a B lymphocyte which has the appropriate antibody in its cell surface membrane.

Second exposure and secondary response

In a second exposure to the antigen the memory cells are activated. This allows rapid clonal development. Large amounts of antibody are produced which may prevent the pathogen from doing harm and immunity results.

Clonal selection – B cells with the appropriate antibody multiply by mitosis.

Some of the cells become memory cells.

phagocytosis by a granulocyte

The newly produced cells become plasma cells which secrete large numbers of the antibody into body fluids.

The antibody molecules bind to the antigen and help to destroy it. Cells carrying antigen are killed by phagocytic cells or complement.

Fig. 21.9   Primary and secondary response of B lymphocytes to antigen.

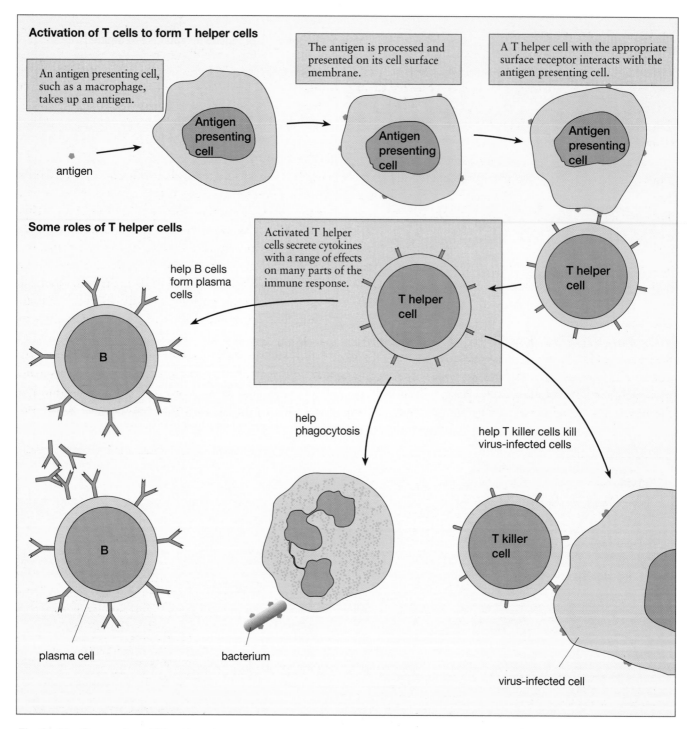

Fig. 21.10   Some roles of T lymphocytes.

macrophage to destroy the microorganisms within it. T helper cells also stimulate B cells to respond to antigens. A T helper cell with the particular surface receptor which fits that antigen binds with it, and then secretes cytokines which stimulate the B lymphocyte to react as described in Section 21.11.

Like B lymphocytes, T lymphocytes divide to form clones when they meet their own particular antigen. They, too, produce memory cells, which can help the body to respond more quickly and effectively if that particular antigen enters the body on a second occasion.

21.13 Inflammation

If a pathogen gets into a particular area of your body and begins to multiply, it is no use having your phagocytes and lymphocytes spread all over your body – you need them concentrated in the danger area. The process which brings this about is called the **inflammatory response**, and it results in inflammation (Fig. 21.11).

Imagine, for example, that a thorn has penetrated deep under your skin. Bacteria on the thorn begin to multiply. The presence of antigens on the bacteria, and your own damaged tissues, activate the complement system (Box 21.2). Chemicals are released which increase the blood supply to the area and make the capillaries more permeable. This brings more phagocytes and lymphocytes to the infected tissues. Phagocytes are attracted to the area by the chemicals, and they crawl out of the blood vessels into the infected area.

The extra blood supply makes the area look red, and the leakage of fluid from the blood makes it swollen. If all goes well, your body will win the battle against the pathogens, and the swelling and redness will subside as the infection is brought under control. Sometimes, a thick white mixture of dead bacteria, lymphocytes and phagocytes builds up, known as **pus**.

In some people, the presence of quite small amounts of antigens which don't pose any real danger to the body can bring about a completely 'over-the-top' inflammatory response. This is described in Box 21.4.

21.14 Vaccination

The first time an antigen enters your body, it takes time for your immune system to respond to it and destroy it; the response is a primary response (Section 21.11). This response includes the production of clones of B and T cells which specifically attack this antigen. This means that the next encounter with this antigen elicits a secondary response which is faster and greater than the primary response, so that the invading pathogen probably has no chance to multiply and make you ill. You are immune to the disease.

Vaccination aims to achieve this effect without you having to suffer illness. Antigens from a potential pathogen are modified in some way, so that they stimulate the same response from your immune system that the

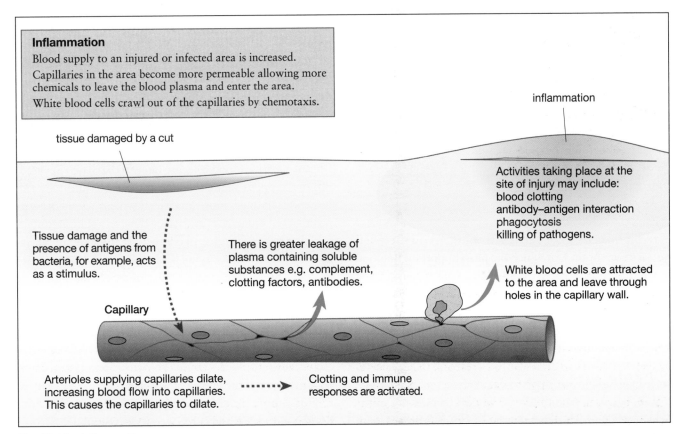

Inflammation
Blood supply to an injured or infected area is increased.
Capillaries in the area become more permeable allowing more chemicals to leave the blood plasma and enter the area.
White blood cells crawl out of the capillaries by chemotaxis.

tissue damaged by a cut

inflammation

Activities taking place at the site of injury may include:
blood clotting
antibody–antigen interaction
phagocytosis
killing of pathogens.

Tissue damage and the presence of antigens from bacteria, for example, acts as a stimulus.

There is greater leakage of plasma containing soluble substances e.g. complement, clotting factors, antibodies.

White blood cells are attracted to the area and leave through holes in the capillary wall.

Capillary

Arterioles supplying capillaries dilate, increasing blood flow into capillaries. This causes the capillaries to dilate.

Clotting and immune responses are activated.

Fig. 21.11   Inflammation.

'normal' antigen would, but don't make you ill. For example, a virus may be modified so that it still carries the same antigen as the disease-causing form, but does not cause disease itself. This has been done with measles, poliomyelitis and rubella viruses. The antigen for tetanus, which is caused by a bacterium, is given as an inactivated form of the toxin which is produced by the bacterium.

Producing effective vaccines is not an easy matter because getting the right balance between something which causes a vigorous primary response by your immune system, yet does not make you ill, is extremely difficult. In the ideal situation, the vaccine stimulates your immune system to mount a primary response, leaving a population of memory cells which will allow a strong secondary response if the antigen enters your body on another occasion. The smallpox vaccine was so successful in this respect, and was so widely administered to people all over the world, that this virus is now extinct – there were not enough susceptible human bodies left in which it could reproduce. The polio, measles, mumps and rubella vaccines are also very successful, and it is thought that it might even be possible to completely eradicate these diseases early in the 21st century. Other vaccines are less effective. Sometimes this is because the pathogen they target is variable, so that a vaccine against one form of it is useless against other forms.

21.15 Blood transfusions and transplants

The body's immune system reacts to any invasion from non-self organisms or chemicals. Usually, this is very beneficial. But there are times when medical treatments involve deliberately introducing non-self material into the body, and we do not want the immune system to attack and destroy it.

● Blood transfusions

Red blood cells have particular antigens on their cell surface membranes, of which the most important in blood transfusions are the A, B and Rhesus antigens. Each person has a particular combination of these antigens; if you have both the A and B antigen your blood group is AB, if you have A or B only your group is A or B respectively, and if you have neither your blood group is O. If you have the Rhesus antigen, you are Rh positive, and if you do not you are Rh negative.

People also have antibody in their blood plasma against whichever A or B antigen they lack. This is different from the 'usual' situation, where you do not produce antibody until you have come into contact with the relevant antigen. Fig. 21.12 shows the antibodies present in the blood of people with the four different ABO blood groups.

If blood containing an A or B antigen which you do not have on your own cells is transfused into your body, your antibodies bind to the red blood cells on the 'foreign' blood and make them clump together or **agglutinate**. The clumps can block blood vessels, which is very painful and can be fatal. In order to avoid this, care has to be taken to give a person blood which does not contain antigens against which they have an antibody. Group O blood is especially useful for donation in small amounts, because there are no A or B antigens on the red blood cells so, no matter what antibodies the recipient has, the cells will not be attacked.

The presence of antiA or antiB antibodies in the *donor's* blood usually does not cause any problems, no matter what antigens are present in the recipient's blood. This is because the antibodies are diluted by the recipient's blood plasma, so no significant agglutination occurs. However, if large amounts of blood need to be donated, then this dilution effect will not happen. So it is essential to match blood type in these cases.

The situation for the Rhesus antigen is different, because people who do not have this antigen on their red blood cells (Rh negative people) do not normally possess an antibody against it. However, if Rhesus positive blood does come into contact with the blood of a Rhesus negative person, then this person will make antibodies against it, just as would occur if any antigen invaded. On the first occasion, this is not likely to cause any problems, because by the time much antibody has been made the Rhesus positive blood cells are likely to have disappeared. But if it happens again, then the anti-Rhesus antibody will be produced much more quickly; it will attack the Rhesus positive red blood cells and cause them to agglutinate.

This problem is most likely to arise if a woman who is Rhesus negative is carrying a Rhesus positive baby in her uterus. Although the baby's red blood cells should not be able to get into her bloodstream through the placenta, this does sometimes happen during the later stages of pregnancy. She will make antibodies against the Rhesus antigen. If she subsequently has another Rhesus positive child, these antibodies could cross the placenta and cause agglutination of the baby's blood cells.

This is now prevented by testing the woman for the Rhesus antigen. If she is Rhesus negative and her partner is Rhesus positive, then there is a high chance that any

ABO blood group antigens and antibodies

Blood group	AB antigens on red cells	Antibodies in blood plasma to AB antigens
A	A	antiB
B	B	antiA
AB	A and B	none
O	neither A nor B	antiA and antiB

Rhesus blood group antigens and antibodies

Blood group	Rhesus antigens on red cells	Antibodies in blood plasma to Rhesus antigens
Rhesus +	present	none
Rhesus −	not present	none unless sensitised by contact with Rhesus antigen

ABO blood group compatibility in transfusion

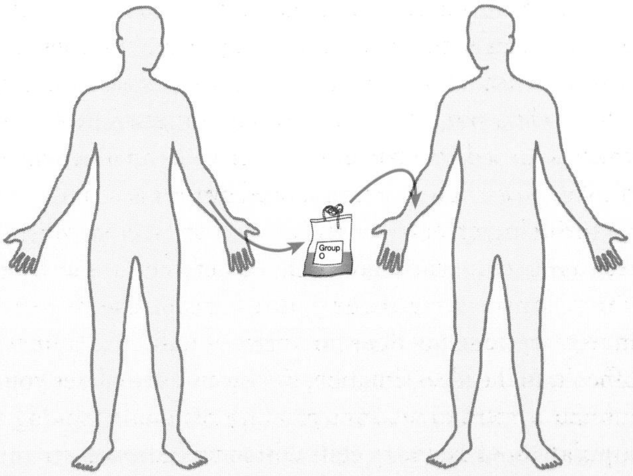

Donor	Recipient(s)
A	A and AB
B	B and AB
AB	AB
O	A, B, AB and O

Fig. 21.12   ABO and Rhesus blood group compatibilities.

child will be Rhesus positive. As soon as the woman has given birth to her first baby, she is given an injection of anti-Rhesus antibodies. These attach themselves to any Rhesus antigens that have got into her blood from her baby, and destroy the antigens before she makes antibodies against them herself.

● **Transplant rejection**

The surgical techniques of transplanting organs such as a kidney or a heart from a donor into a recipient are now well-established in many hospitals throughout the world. But however good the transplant surgeon, the transplant may later be rejected by the recipient's body.

We all carry a set of glycoproteins called **histocompatibility antigens** on our cell surface membranes. There are more than 30 different ones, and each of these 30 comes in several different varieties. The chance of any two unrelated people having an identical set of histocompatibility antigens on their cells is extremely small.

If an organ from a donor with a different set of histocompatibility antigens is transplanted into a recipient's body, the recipient's T helper cells recognise them as foreign and bind to them. This activates the T helper cells to secrete cytokines (Box 21.3). The cytokines activate T killer cells and phagocytes, which attack and destroy the cells of the transplanted organ. The cytokines also activate B lymphocytes, which secrete antibodies against the transplant. The cells in the transplant are destroyed, a process known as **rejection**.

In order to try to prevent rejection of transplants, attempts are made to find a donor whose histocompatibility antigens are as similar as possible to those of the recipient. The ideal situation is if the recipient has an identical twin. The histocompatibility antigens are coded for by genes and, as an identical twin has identical genes, the histocompatibility antigens will also be identical. Failing this, then the histocompatibility antigens of a potential donor can be matched against those of the recipient to try to find a donor with identical or very similar histocompatibility antigens. The closer the match, the less likely it is that the transplanted organ will be rejected.

The recipient is usually treated with drugs which reduce or prevent the response of their immune system to the antigens on the cells of the transplant. These drugs are called **immunosuppressants**. One immunosuppressant which is commonly used is **cyclosporin**. It works by interfering with the expression of the genes in the T helper cells which code for cytokine production. If the T helper cells do not secrete cytokines, then the T killer cells, B cells and phagocytes do not attack the cells in the transplant. But treatment with immunosuppressants leaves the patient vulnerable to infections, and there are sometimes other adverse side-effects as well.

21.16 Monoclonal antibodies

In Sections 21.9 and 21.11, you saw that there is a huge number of different antibodies which can be made by human B lymphocytes, and that each lymphocyte can make only one kind. In the 1970s, researchers wanted to be able to obtain large amounts of one particular antibody at a time, so that they could study it without interference

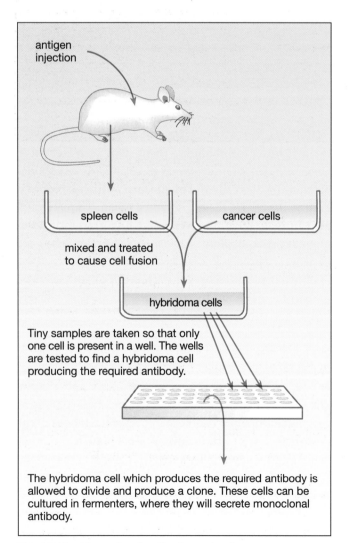

Tiny samples are taken so that only one cell is present in a well. The wells are tested to find a hybridoma cell producing the required antibody.

The hybridoma cell which produces the required antibody is allowed to divide and produce a clone. These cells can be cultured in fermenters, where they will secrete monoclonal antibody.

Fig. 21.13 Monoclonal antibody production.

from all the other antibodies which are usually present in a mammal's blood. Their aim was to produce a large clone of a particular type of B plasma cell, all secreting identical antibodies, known as **monoclonal antibodies**.

There is one problem in achieving this – B lymphocytes which divide to form clones do not secrete antibodies, and B lymphocytes which secrete antibodies do not divide. In 1975, a technique was developed to get around this problem (Fig. 21.13). B lymphocytes were fused with cancer cells, which, unlike other body cells, go on dividing indefinitely. The product of this fusion is called a **hybridoma**. The hybridoma divides to form a clone of cells which secrete monoclonal antibodies.

When this technique was first invented, no-one really knew what uses might be made of it. Since then, many applications have been found for monoclonal antibodies, both in research and in applications such as medical diagnosis and treatment. Their uses derive from the fact that any particular monoclonal antibody binds very specifically to a particular molecule.

For example, monoclonal antibodies can be used to locate places where blood clots have formed in the body of a person suspected of suffering from deep-vein thrombosis. First, a mouse is injected with human fibrin. Human fibrin acts as an antigen in the mouse. Mouse B lymphocytes with the antibody for human fibrin proliferate, especially in the spleen. After a month or so, the spleen contains large quantities of these lymphocytes. The mouse spleen cells are then mixed with cancer cells to form hybridomas which are checked to see which antibody they secrete. Hybridomas secreting the anti-fibrin antibody are then cultured in a fermenter, so that large amounts of this antibody are made. The antibody can be 'labelled' with a radioactive chemical which produces gamma radiation.

The labelled antibodies are then introduced into the patient's blood. As they are carried around the body in the bloodstream, they will bind to fibrin molecules. A gamma camera can be used to detect the position of the antibodies, and therefore of any blood clots, in the patient's body. ■

21.4 Allergies and auto-immune diseases

The activities of the immune system are sometimes misdirected and inappropriate, causing unpleasant and sometimes dangerous illnesses.

Allergies are a result of an over-reaction of the immune system to contact with antigens such as chemicals on pollen grains or dust mite faeces. Hay fever and asthma are examples of such illnesses.

Antigens which can produce this kind of response are called **allergens**. In a person with an allergy, contact with the antigen causes the production of large amounts of a kind of antibody called IgE. These antibodies act on cells called **mast cells**, which are found in all tissues, close to the walls of blood vessels. The mast cells release a chemical called **histamine** and also several cytokines (Box 21.3). These chemicals cause an acute inflammatory reaction (Fig. 21.11), in which blood vessels dilate, smooth muscle in airways contracts (Box 12.2), rashes appear on the skin, and tissues swell as fluid accumulates in them. Usually, none of this happens on the *first* contact with the allergen, but only on subsequent contacts when the person is said to have become 'sensitised'.

Several diseases are a result of a misdirected attack of the immune system on a person's own tissues, and these are known as **auto-immune diseases**. For some reason, the self-recognition system seriously breaks down. There seems to be some genetic component to this, because auto-immune diseases can run in families; but there is also an environmental component, and the development of an auto-immune disease may follow infection with a virus. There are many different auto-immune diseases, including rheumatoid arthritis (in which the cartilage at joints is attacked) and pernicious anaemia. In pernicious anaemia, B lymphocytes secreting the antibody to intrinsic factor (Section 13.7) divide to form plasma cells, which then secrete this antibody into the stomach. Here the antibody binds with intrinsic factor, so that it cannot bind to vitamin B_{12} and allow it to be absorbed in the small intestine.

Q2 Read the following passage on immune responses. Then copy it and fill in the spaces with the most appropriate word or words to complete the passage.

In humans, part of the defence against pathogens involves the white blood cells known as lymphocytes. These cells are produced in the .... Some of them, after production, go to the thymus gland and develop into .... Other cells go directly to the lymphoid tissue after production. These cells are known as .... and release free .... in response to antigens.

ULEAC 1996 *(Total 4 marks)*

Q3 A diseased kidney may be replaced with a healthy one transplanted from another person.

(a) Explain how the action of T lymphocytes would normally result in rejection of the transplanted kidney. (2)

(b) Describe **two** ways in which the chance of rejection may be reduced. (2)

(c) Explain why a kidney may be transplanted from one identical twin to another without risk of rejection. (2)

(d) Suggest why some illnesses, normally rare, occur more frequently in both AIDS patients and in those who have received transplants. (2)

NEAB 1995 *(Total 8 marks)*

Q4 The diagram below illustrates the process of producing monoclonal antibodies.

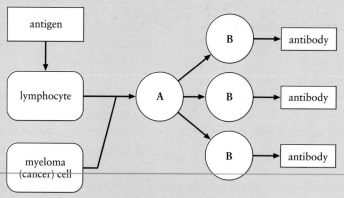

(a) (i) Name the type of cell labelled **A** in the diagram. (1)
   (ii) State the process by which the cells labelled **B** are produced. (1)

(b) Monoclonal antibodies can be used to locate specific molecules. Describe **one** use of monoclonal antibodies. (3)

ULEAC 1996 (*Total 5 marks*)

Q5 The graph shows the responses to **two** identical doses of the same antigen.

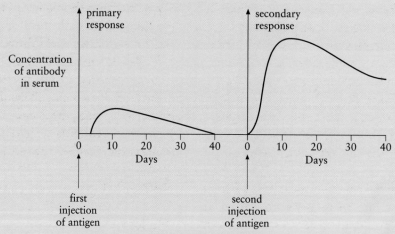

(a) (i) Identify **two** differences between the responses shown. (1)
   (ii) Briefly explain the mechanism which accounts for these differences. (3)

(b) How many days after the first injection should the second injection be given? Explain your answer. (1)

AEB 1997 (specimen) (*Total 5 marks*)

22 Classification

22.1 The principles of biological classification

Biological classification attempts to group living organisms according to how closely related we believe them to be. This is called **phylogenetic classification**. This kind of classification was first attempted in a scientific way by the Swedish naturalist Carl Linnaeus in 1735.

Linnaeus lived and worked a hundred years before Darwin was putting forward his ideas about evolution, so Linnaeus did not understand *why* some living organisms appear to be built on similar plans to others while others have quite different body plans. We now believe that basic structural similarities, such as the skeleton in a bird's wing and a human arm, indicate that these structures have each evolved from a single type of structure which was present in a common ancestor to both groups, perhaps many millions of years ago. Structures like this are called **homologous structures**. We can also use similarities and differences in the biochemistry of organisms, especially DNA and proteins, as clues to how closely related they are.

Often, whole sets of homologous structures are used in classifying organisms. For example, all chordates possess many homologous features, including a post-anal tail, gill slits and notochord (Section 22.18) at some point in their lives, and it is assumed that all organisms with this set of features have evolved from a common ancestor. Any organism possessing this set of features is classified as a chordate.

Even though Linnaeus did not understand how different kinds of organisms came to possess homologous structures, he used homologous structures to work out probable relationships between organisms. Each organism was classified into a particular species; Linnaeus named about 12 000 different species. We now attempt to define exactly how similar organisms have to be before they are classified in the same species, although there are many difficulties in deciding just where to draw the line. Possible definitions of the term 'species', and the problems associated with it, are discussed in Section 7.15.

Similar species are grouped together into a **genus** (plural genera). The name of an organism's genus and its species are used to give it a two-word Latin name, called a **binomial**. The binomial is written in italics. The name of the genus comes first and is given a capital letter; the name

of the species has small letters. Thus, for example, the binomial for a human is *Homo sapiens*, and the binomial for a primrose is *Primula vulgaris*. After writing the full binomial once, it is usual to write just the first letter of the genus each time it occurs, for example *P. vulgaris*.

Similar genera are grouped into **families**, families into **orders**, orders into **classes**, classes into **phyla** and phyla into **kingdoms**. This kind of multi-level grouping arrangement is called a **hierarchy**.

There is no definition about exactly what any of these groupings mean, so not surprisingly biologists do not always agree about them. For example, most biologists classify reptiles and birds as two different classes, but others think that they are so similar to one another that they should all be put into the same class. Similarly, many biologists are quite happy to classify all prokaryotes into the same kingdom, while others who study them in detail believe that they should be split into at least two, if not more, kingdoms.

In this book, we will follow a classification system which is widely used by biologists all over the world. (But do not be surprised if you sometimes come across different systems!) In this system, all living organisms are grouped into five kingdoms, the **Prokaryotae**, **Protoctista**, **Fungi**, **Plants** and **Animals**. Viruses do not fit into this classification. Their features are described in Section 21.1.

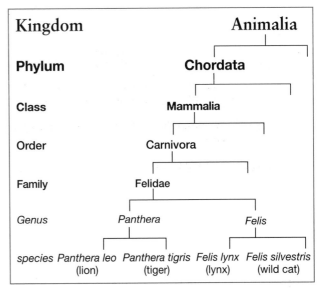

Fig. 22.1   The hierarchical system of classification.

KINGDOM PROKARYOTAE

22.2 Prokaryotes

This kingdom contains all the organisms whose cells have no nucleus and no membrane-bound organelles. They all exist either as single cells or as clusters of cells. They include all types of **bacteria,** including **blue-greens** (Fig. 22.2). Blue-greens are sometimes known as cyanobacteria ('cyano' means 'blue-green').

Microbiologists are not all in agreement about how closely related the different kinds of prokaryotes are. In particular, there is one group of prokaryotes, called the Archaea, which have very different kinds of molecules in their cells from those found in other prokaryotes. These differences are so great that the Archaea are considered to be no more closely related to other prokaryotes than they are to eukaryotes.

Prokaryotes have existed for longer on the Earth than any other kind of living organism. Some of the oldest fossils so far discovered, dating back 3.5 billion years, are **stromatolites.** These are mats made up of layers of prokaryotic organisms, with sediment trapped in between them. When these prokaryotes were alive, there was very little oxygen in the atmosphere. They were probably similar to purple and green bacteria which still live on Earth today. These bacteria use light energy to synthesise carbohydrates from carbon dioxide, but they do not produce oxygen.

Prokaryotes are extremely successful and have evolved into an enormous number of different forms that live in almost every possible habitat. A huge diversity of prokaryotes had already evolved well before the first eukaryotic organisms existed. Rocks dating back to 2 billion years ago contain fossils of many kinds of prokaryotes, including blue-greens. These bacteria photosynthesise in a similar way to modern green plants, and they would have released large amounts of oxygen into the atmosphere. This changed the Earth forever, as organisms which use oxygen – aerobic organisms – now evolved.

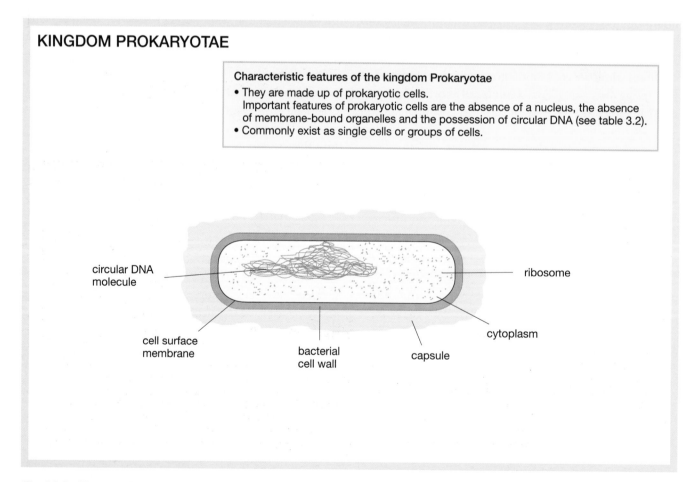

KINGDOM PROKARYOTAE

Characteristic features of the kingdom Prokaryotae
- They are made up of prokaryotic cells.
  Important features of prokaryotic cells are the absence of a nucleus, the absence of membrane-bound organelles and the possession of circular DNA (see table 3.2).
- Commonly exist as single cells or groups of cells.

circular DNA molecule

ribosome

cell surface membrane

bacterial cell wall

capsule

cytoplasm

Fig. 22.2 Kingdom Prokaryotae.

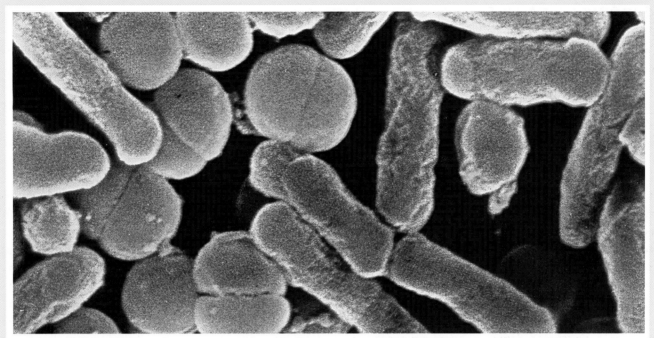

Bacteria from the human gut. The rod-shaped ones are *Escherichia coli*, and the spherical ones are *Streptococcus*. Both of these types of bacteria are found in normal healthy people, but they can occasionally cause illness. (×26 000)

Bacterial cells and groups of cells

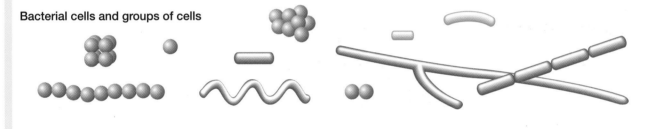

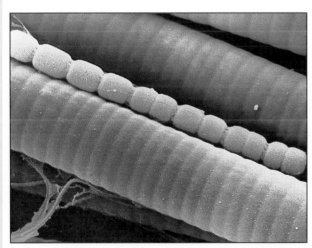

Two species of blue-green bacteria. The larger, cylindrical species is *Microcleus*, and the smaller one made up of a string of bead-like cells is *Anabaena*. All blue-green bacteria are photosynthetic, and *Anabaena* also fixes nitrogen. (×2600)

Three-and-a-half billion years ago, stromatolites were common, but now they are found in only a very few parts of the world. These are off the northwest coast of Australia, in a bay where the water is too salty for molluscs and other organisms which would graze on them. These stromatolites are made by blue-green bacteria which secrete lime, forming stony 'cushions'.

Fig. 22.2 *cont.*

KINGDOM PROTOCTISTA

The protoctists are a diverse group of organisms. They have eukaryotic cells. Many protoctists are single-celled, but some are multicellular. The protoctists include single-celled animal-like organisms, the **protozoa**, and also plant-like organisms, the **algae**. Many live in water.

22.3   Protozoa

The term 'protozoa' is used as a convenient name for all of the single-celled, motile (moving), animal-like protoctists (Fig. 22.4). There are many different kinds of protozoa, and they are often grouped into different phyla according to their methods of moving and feeding. Some move using pseudopodia, while others use cilia or flagella.

The cell of a protozoan has the basic structure of an animal cell. There is a cell surface membrane but no cell wall. Some protozoa, for example the ciliate *Paramecium*, have an especially well-developed cytoskeleton (Section 3.14) just beneath the cell surface membrane, called the **pellicle**, which helps to support the cell and hold it in shape. Some protozoa have tiny shells. Shells of amoebae that were made from calcium carbonate have accumulated on the sea bed in enormous quantities in the past, forming limestone rocks.

Protozoa which live in fresh water usually have a **contractile vacuole**, an organelle which removes excess water from the cell (Box 15.6).

Protozoa are heterotrophic organisms. Many of them live in the sea or fresh water where they feed on smaller protoctists and bacteria. Some, however, are parasitic, for example the malarial parasite *Plasmodium* (Box 13.6).

Others are mutualistic, such as the flagellated protozoa which live in the guts of termites and help the termites to digest the wood which they eat.

22.4   Algae

Algae (Fig. 22.5) are protoctists with cell walls and chorophyll. They feed by photosynthesis. Some of them have flagella and are motile. Most algae live in water, but some live on moist surfaces such as soil, stones or tree trunks.

Some algae are single-celled, but some are made up of aggregations of many cells. Single-celled algae include *Chlamydomonas*, which lives in freshwater ponds and swims actively using its flagella. Some multicellular algae are made up of many similar cells joined end to end, and these are known as filamentous algae. An example is *Spirogyra* which sometimes forms green mats of 'blanket weed' on the surface of ponds. Some, such as *Volvox*, form little spherical colonies of cells. Other multicellular algae are made up of sheets of cells which can become very large. Seaweeds are algae, and some of the largest of them can grow up to 30 m long. However, algae never have true roots, stems or leaves.

Algae are usually grouped according to the kinds of photosynthetic pigments they possess. The green algae have the same kind of pigments as green plants, including chlorophyll *a* and chlorophyll *b*. You may also have seen brown algae (for example the bladderwrack, *Fucus*) and red algae on the seashore. These do possess chlorophyll, but they also have other pigments which mask the green colour of the chlorophyll.

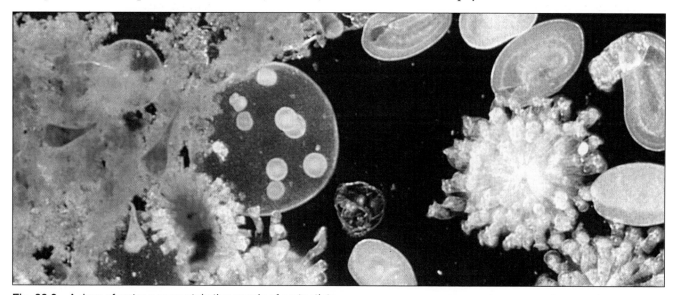

Fig. 22.3   A drop of water may contain thousands of protoctists.

KINGDOM PROTOCTISTA

> **Characteristic features of the kingdom Protoctista**
> • They are made up of eukaryotic cells.
> • Many organisms are single-celled and a few are multicellular.

Protozoa

Amoeba (×500)

- food vacuole containing an algal cell
- contractile vacuole
- nucleus
- cell surface membrane
- cytoplasm
- pseudopodium
- pseudopodia are used in movement

> **Characteristic features of protozoa**
> • These are animal-like protoctists having a cell surface membrane but no cell wall.
> • They are motile and phagocytic.

Amoeba proteus (×530)

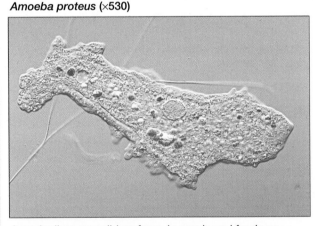

Amoeba lives on solid surfaces in ponds and feeds on prokaryotes and protoctists.

Radiolarian shells (×530)

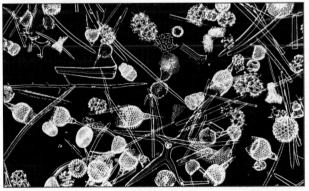

Radiolarians are closely related to *Amoeba*, but they have shells made of calcium carbonate. The Sphinx in Egypt is made from rock formed from radiolarian shells.

Trichonympha (×1500)

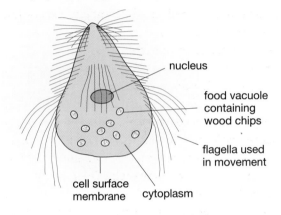

- nucleus
- food vacuole containing wood chips
- flagella used in movement
- cell surface membrane
- cytoplasm

Trichonympha lives in the gut of termites and feeds on wood chips ingested by the termite. This is a symbiotic relationship benefitting both the protoctist and the termite. The termite obtains nutrients from dead *Trichonympha*.

Paramecium (×2000)

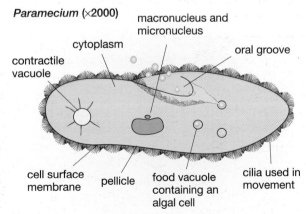

- macronucleus and micronucleus
- cytoplasm
- oral groove
- contractile vacuole
- cell surface membrane
- pellicle
- food vacuole containing an algal cell
- cilia used in movement

Paramecium lives in ponds and feeds on small protoctists and prokaryotes.

Fig. 22.4   Kingdom Protoctista: Protozoa.

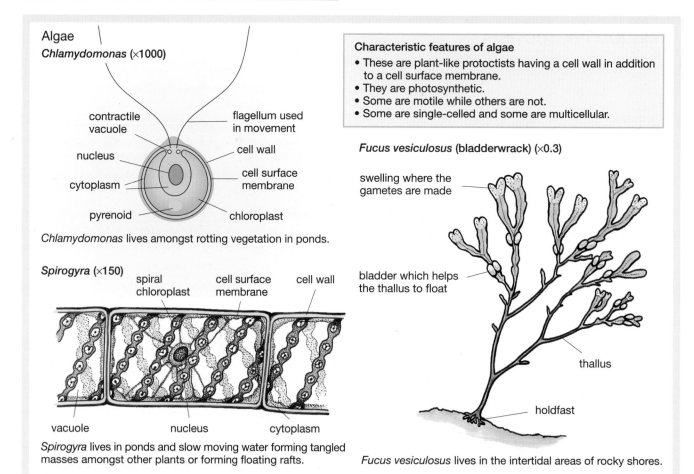

Algae
Chlamydomonas (×1000)

contractile vacuole

flagellum used in movement

nucleus

cell wall

cytoplasm

cell surface membrane

pyrenoid

chloroplast

Chlamydomonas lives amongst rotting vegetation in ponds.

Characteristic features of algae
- These are plant-like protoctists having a cell wall in addition to a cell surface membrane.
- They are photosynthetic.
- Some are motile while others are not.
- Some are single-celled and some are multicellular.

Fucus vesiculosus (bladderwrack) (×0.3)

swelling where the gametes are made

bladder which helps the thallus to float

thallus

holdfast

Fucus vesiculosus lives in the intertidal areas of rocky shores.

Spirogyra (×150)

spiral chloroplast

cell surface membrane

cell wall

vacuole

nucleus

cytoplasm

Spirogyra lives in ponds and slow moving water forming tangled masses amongst other plants or forming floating rafts.

Red, green and brown seaweeds growing on rocks on a sheltered shore in southern England. Their colours differ because they contain different proportions of a variety of photosynthetic pigments. At low tide when the seaweed is dry, very little photosynthesis occurs. When the tide comes in, the thalluses float in the water and their surfaces are more exposed to sunlight. Red and brown seaweeds can photosynthesise in deeper water than green ones, because they are able to absorb some of the blue light which penetrates deeper in the water than other wavelengths.

Fig. 22.5 Kingdom Protoctista: Algae.

KINGDOM FUNGI
22.5 Fungi

The fungi include mushrooms, yeasts and moulds. Fungi are eukaryotic organisms.

Fungal cells always have cell walls. As in plant cells, these walls are made mostly from polysaccharides. Many different polysaccharides, including cellulose and chitin, are found in fungal cell walls, and the biochemical composition of their walls is used in classifying fungi.

All fungi are heterotrophic and never contain chloroplasts. They feed saprotrophically, absorbing soluble organic substances, as well as inorganic ones, from their surroundings. Many fungi feed on dead and decaying organic matter, such as animal faeces, or human foods such as bread. Others feed as parasites on living organisms. There are many commercially important diseases of crop plants caused by parasitic fungi, such as potato blight and yellow rust disease of cereals, and a few are parasites of humans and other animals (Section 21.4). You can read more about how fungi feed in Section 13.13 and Box 13.4.

The main 'body' of most fungi is made up of long, thin threads called **hyphae**. Each hypha is one cell thick. In some fungi, the hyphae are divided up by cross walls, while in others there are no cross walls, so the hypha is just a tube of cytoplasm with many nuclei dotted about in it. This kind of structure is said to be **coenocytic**. A mass of hyphae, such as you may have seen growing over the surface of mouldy food, is called a **mycelium**. Yeasts are unusual fungi, in that they do not usually have hyphae but consist of single cells.

Fungi reproduce by producing **spores**, sometimes by asexual processes and sometimes by sexual ones. Mushrooms are spore-producing structures which develop from a fungal mycelium growing underground or on rotting wood. The spores form in the gills beneath the mushroom cap, and are carried away by the wind. You may also have seen much smaller spore-forming structures on filamentous fungi growing on decaying food; they look like little black or coloured specks amongst the furry threads of the mycelium.

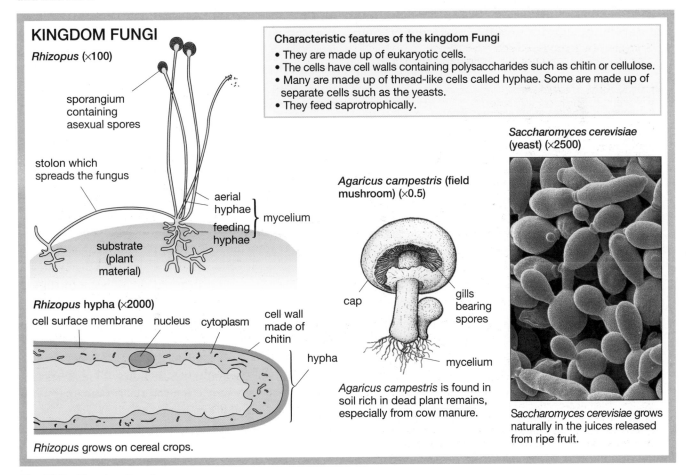

KINGDOM FUNGI

Rhizopus (×100)

sporangium containing asexual spores

stolon which spreads the fungus

aerial hyphae

feeding hyphae

} mycelium

substrate (plant material)

Characteristic features of the kingdom Fungi
- They are made up of eukaryotic cells.
- The cells have cell walls containing polysaccharides such as chitin or cellulose.
- Many are made up of thread-like cells called hyphae. Some are made up of separate cells such as the yeasts.
- They feed saprotrophically.

Rhizopus hypha (×2000)

cell surface membrane   nucleus   cytoplasm   cell wall made of chitin

hypha

Rhizopus grows on cereal crops.

Agaricus campestris (field mushroom) (×0.5)

cap

gills bearing spores

mycelium

Agaricus campestris is found in soil rich in dead plant remains, especially from cow manure.

Saccharomyces cerevisiae (yeast) (×2500)

Saccharomyces cerevisiae grows naturally in the juices released from ripe fruit.

Fig. 22.6 Kingdom Fungi.

KINGDOM PLANTAE
22.6   Characteristics of plants

The plant kingdom includes mosses, liverworts, horsetails, ferns, conifers and flowering plants. They are multicellular eukaryotes whose cells have cell walls made of cellulose. Almost all plants (with just a very few exceptions which live as parasites) are photosynthetic, and at least some of the cells in a plant contain chloroplasts.

The structure of plant cells is basically the same as the structure of the cells of some green algae (Section 22.4). They photosynthesise using the same pigments and the same biochemical pathways. But, while most green algae are aquatic organisms (such as the green seaweeds), plants are essentially adapted for living on land. It is thought that the land plants may have evolved from a marine green alga, which became adapted to live in wet places on land. The earliest fossils of upright land plants, *Cooksonia*, date back to 420 million years ago. They are small, with simple branched stems with no leaves or roots. These plants are now extinct, but they or other unknown early plants gradually evolved features which allowed them to live successfully on land, giving rise to modern terrestrial plants. Some of these features are discussed in Section 12.2, Section 16.1 and Box 18.2.

KINGDOM PLANTAE

Characteristic features of the kingdom Plantae
- The organisms are made up of eukaryotic cells.
- The body of the organism is multicellular.
- The cells have cell walls made of cellulose, in addition to a cell surface membrane.
- Some cells, at least, contain chloroplasts (except in some parasites) and the organisms feed by photosynthesis.

22.7   Phylum Bryophyta

The bryophytes include the mosses and liverworts. Of all the land plants, they are least well adapted for terrestrial conditions and are still reliant on water for sexual reproduction. Most of them are less than 15 cm tall and many are less than 2 cm tall; they are unable to grow much larger because they do not have any hard lignified tissues such as xylem to support them, nor do they have a vascular system to transport materials rapidly from one part of their body to another. Some mosses do, however, have some cells which are specialised for support and for transporting substances over short distances.

Bryophytes do not have true roots, and they are anchored to the ground by tiny filaments called **rhizoids**. In liverworts, these are often unicellular, while mosses tend to have multicellular rhizoids. Although rhizoids may absorb water and nutrients from the soil, this is not their main function, and other parts of the plant may carry out these processess as well.

Bryophytes have flat, green leafy structures for photosynthesis. If this is just a simple flat structure, it is called a **thallus**. But in many mosses and liverworts, there is a stem with many small **leaves** attached to it. These leaves don't have the same structure as the leaves of other plant phyla, and so it is often said that bryophytes do not have 'true' leaves. In many bryophytes, there is no protective waxy cuticle over the thallus or leaves, so they lose water easily in dry air, but others do have a cuticle. Many bryophytes have **stomata**, which can be closed to cut down water loss. Even if they do dry out, some of them are able to survive in a dry dormant state for many years, until it rains on them again. When moss cells lose water the thin cell wall collapses with the shrinking cell contents, unlike other plants in which the cell membrane tears away from the wall as they plasmolyse. This helps to explain why the cells can survive drying. When water is present they quickly swell up and almost instantly start to photosynthesise.

The main body of a bryophyte is a **haploid gametophyte**. It reproduces by producing gametes by mitosis which fuse to form a zygote. This then develops into a **diploid sporophyte** which produces spores by meiosis. The spores are dispersed and germinate to form gametophytes. This life cycle is described in Section 18.2.

Fig. 22.7   A wide range of plants grow in a temperate rainforest. Mosses, ferns, conifers and angiosperms are visible.

Phylum Bryophyta

> **Characteristic features of the phylum Bryophyta**
> - These are small plants with no true roots and with no transport tissues or any lignified cells. Mineral nutrients are absorbed directly into cells from the environment.
> - The body of the organism is simple and is sometimes not differentiated into stems and leaves.
> - The most noticeable and long-lived plant is the haploid gametophyte stage of the life cycle.
> - The sporophyte stage produces spores in spore cases.

Pellia epiphylla (a liverwort) (×1)

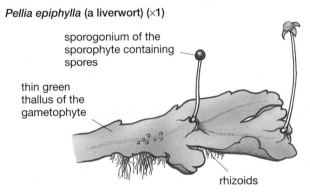

sporogonium of the sporophyte containing spores

thin green thallus of the gametophyte

rhizoids

Pellia is found on moist, shady stream banks and ditches.

Grimmia pulvinata (a moss) (×6)

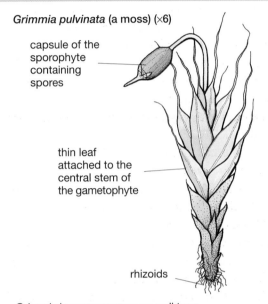

capsule of the sporophyte containing spores

thin leaf attached to the central stem of the gametophyte

rhizoids

Grimmia is very common on wall tops.

Pellia epiphylla with spore capsules.

Mosses growing in a woodland.

Fig. 22.8 Phylum Bryophyta.

22.8 Phylum Filicinophyta

This phylum includes the ferns. Ferns first appear in the fossil record about 380 million years ago. By the Carboniferous period, about 290 million years ago, low-lying swamps covered much of the land, in which forests of ferns and their close relatives, the club mosses and horsetails, grew. Some of these ferns were very tall. Ferns do grow up to 20 m in some parts of the world today; they are known as tree ferns, and most of them live in moist tropical forests. But the majority of modern ferns are much smaller plants than this, many of them growing in shady places beneath trees in forests or as epiphytes on the trees themselves. (An epiphyte is a plant which grows on another one, using it as support but not as a food source.)

Ferns are larger plants than bryophytes, and they have several adaptations for a terrestrial life-style which are not found in bryophytes. Ferns have true **roots**, which both anchor the plant in the soil and absorb water and inorganic ions. They have **leaves** called **fronds**, which are often **pinnate** (feather-like). The fronds look like coiled springs when they are young, and gradually unroll as they grow. The roots, stems and leaves contain **phloem** tissue, and the ferns have **lignified** tissues including **xylem**.

The lignified tissues provide support to ferns, allowing them to grow much larger than bryophytes. The vascular tissues (phloem and xylem) provide an efficient transport system which also enables ferns to grow to a large size. Most ferns have fronds with a protective waxy cuticle and stomata which cut down water loss. Thus ferns are able to grow in drier places than bryophytes. However, they still depend on water for part of their life cycle (Section 18.3), and this restricts the distribution of many species to moist habitats. Unlike bryophytes, the main stage in the fern life cycle is the **diploid sporophyte** generation, and you can often see **spores** developing on the underside of the fronds.

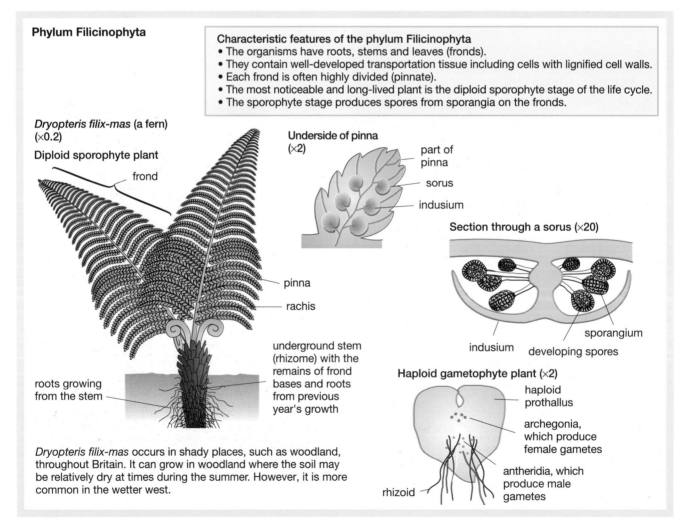

Phylum Filicinophyta

Characteristic features of the phylum Filicinophyta
- The organisms have roots, stems and leaves (fronds).
- They contain well-developed transportation tissue including cells with lignified cell walls.
- Each frond is often highly divided (pinnate).
- The most noticeable and long-lived plant is the diploid sporophyte stage of the life cycle.
- The sporophyte stage produces spores from sporangia on the fronds.

Dryopteris filix-mas (a fern) (×0.2)
Diploid sporophyte plant
frond

Underside of pinna (×2)
part of pinna
sorus
indusium

Section through a sorus (×20)
indusium
developing spores
sporangium

pinna
rachis

roots growing from the stem
underground stem (rhizome) with the remains of frond bases and roots from previous year's growth

Haploid gametophyte plant (×2)
haploid prothallus
archegonia, which produce female gametes
antheridia, which produce male gametes
rhizoid

Dryopteris filix-mas occurs in shady places, such as woodland, throughout Britain. It can grow in woodland where the soil may be relatively dry at times during the summer. However, it is more common in the wetter west.

Fig. 22.9 Phylum Filicinophyta.

22.9   Phylum Coniferophyta

This phylum includes the conifers. (They used to be classified as Class Gymnospermae, and you may still see this name in some books.) Both of these names describe important features of this group of plants. 'Coniferophyta' means 'cone-bearing'. 'Gymnospermae' means 'naked seeds', and refers to the fact that the conifers reproduce by producing seeds which are not protected within an ovary as they are in the other group of seed-bearing plants, the angiosperms (Section 22.10).

The conifers have evolved several features, especially in their methods of reproduction, which make them able to live successfully in a wider range of habitats than bryophytes or ferns. Whereas the male gametes of bryophytes and ferns must swim through a layer of moisture to reach the egg, the male gametes of conifers are protected inside a pollen grain, while the female gametes are protected inside ovules. The pollen grains and ovules are formed in male and female **cones**, each of which is made up of layers of scales. Pollen is carried to ovules by the wind. Once an ovule has been fertilised, it develops into a **seed**, still on the surface of one of the scales in a cone. The outer tissues of the ovule harden to form a protective seed coat. Thus conifers do not need moist conditions for reproduction, and can live in much drier habitats than bryophytes or ferns.

Conifers first appeared on Earth in the late Carboniferous period, about 280 million years ago, and they and their close relatives dominated the land for the next hundred million years or so. Today, conifers form huge forests in colder parts of the world, although some do grow in the tropics. Many modern conifers are tall trees with narrow leaves called needles, but some have broader leaves. The giant redwood of California, *Sequoiadendron giganteum*, which can grow to over 100 m tall, is a conifer.

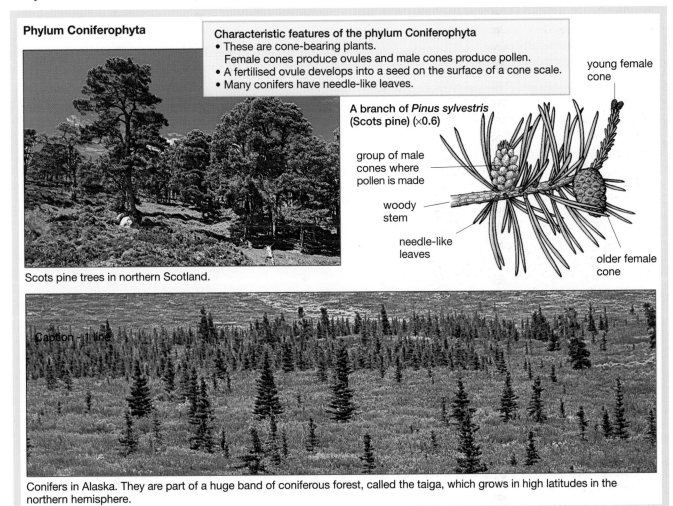

Phylum Coniferophyta

Characteristic features of the phylum Coniferophyta
- These are cone-bearing plants.
  Female cones produce ovules and male cones produce pollen.
- A fertilised ovule develops into a seed on the surface of a cone scale.
- Many conifers have needle-like leaves.

Scots pine trees in northern Scotland.

A branch of *Pinus sylvestris* (Scots pine) (×0.6)

young female cone

group of male cones where pollen is made

woody stem

needle-like leaves

older female cone

Conifers in Alaska. They are part of a huge band of coniferous forest, called the taiga, which grows in high latitudes in the northern hemisphere.

Fig. 22.10   Phylum Coniferophyta.

22.10 Phylum Angiospermophyta

These are the flowering plants. Like conifers, they form seeds, but these seeds develop inside an ovary which becomes a fruit. The word 'angiosperm' means 'container seeds'. You can read about the life cycle of an angiosperm and how it relates to the life cycle of other plant phyla in Box 18.3.

The most obvious feature of angiosperms, which immediately distinguishes them from all other plant phyla, is that they have **flowers**. A flower is formed from concentric circles of modified leaves; the inner ones surround the ovule to form the ovary, while the outer ones form petals and sepals. Although some angiosperms, like conifers, rely on wind pollination, many flowers are adapted to bring insects to the reproductive structures to help with pollination. The first angiosperms appeared on Earth about 200 million years ago, and since then many angiosperms and flying insects have evolved close relationships (Fig. 18.7).

Angiosperms are divided into two classes, the **Monocotyledoneae** and the **Dicotyledoneae**. These names refer to the number of cotyledons in their seeds – monocots have one cotyledon, while dicots have two. There are also other differences between them. The monocots, which include grasses, daffodils and lilies, often have strap-shaped leaves with parallel veins, while the dicots often have broader leaves with branching veins. Most monocots have their flower parts in multiples of three, while most dicots have theirs in multiples of four or five.

Today, angiosperms are the dominant plants in many habitats on Earth. About 300 000 species have been described and named, but there are certainly many new species to be discovered. Like conifers, they can grow to a very large size – over 90 m tall – while others are tiny, such as the duckweed you may have seen on the surface of a garden pond. Angiosperms are found in almost every possible habitat. Most commercially important crop plants are angiosperms.

Phylum Angiospermophyta

Characteristic features of the phylum Angiospermophyta
• These are flowering plants.
• A fertilised ovule develops into a seed inside the ovary, which becomes a fruit.

Characteristic features of the class Monocotyledoneae (Monocots)
• The seeds contain embryos with only one cotyledon.
• The leaves are often narrow with parallel veins.
• The flower parts are often in multiples of three.

Characteristic features of the class Dicotyledoneae (Dicots)
• The seeds contain embryos with two cotyledons.
• The leaves are often broad with branching veins.
• The flower parts are often in multiples of four or five.

This type of vegetation is found in many parts of the Mediterranean, where soil is thin and summers are hot and dry. It is called garrigue. The olive tree and euphorbias (the hummocky plants with yellow flowers) are dicots, and the tall yellow asphodels are monocots.

Fig. 22.11 Phylum Angiospermophyta.

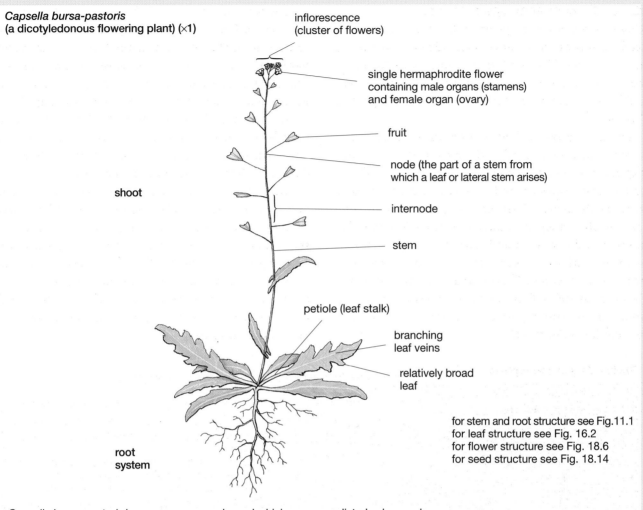

Capsella bursa-pastoris
(a dicotyledonous flowering plant) (×1)

inflorescence
(cluster of flowers)

single hermaphrodite flower
containing male organs (stamens)
and female organ (ovary)

fruit

node (the part of a stem from
which a leaf or lateral stem arises)

shoot

internode

stem

petiole (leaf stalk)

branching
leaf veins

relatively broad
leaf

for stem and root structure see Fig.11.1
for leaf structure see Fig. 16.2
for flower structure see Fig. 18.6
for seed structure see Fig. 18.14

root
system

Capsella bursa-pastoris is a common annual weed which grows on disturbed ground.

Cereal crops, such as millet (*Sorghum bicolor*) are monocots grown for their seeds which are good sources of starch and protein.
Millet is a staple food in many tropical and subtropical countries. Here it is growing on terraced hillsides in Nepal.

Fig. 22.11 *cont.*

KINGDOM ANIMALIA

22.11   Characteristics of animals

The animal kingdom contains all the organisms which are multicellular eukaryotes and whose cells do not have cell walls. Animals are heterotrophic organisms and never possess chloroplasts.

Most animals are **motile** – that is they can move their whole body from place to place. However, many kinds of animals spend most of their lives fixed to one spot. They are said to be **sessile**. A few very small animals, including the larval stages of some species, move by using cilia, but the great majority move using **muscle cells**. Apart from the sponges (Fig. 22.13) all animals have **nerve cells**, which have evolved alongside muscle tissue and help coordinate the contraction of the muscle cells. No other kingdom possesses either muscle cells or nerve cells.

22.12   Animal body plans

The first animals were probably simply colonies of protozoa in which all the cells were very similar. Over time, some of the cells within the organisms became specialised to carry out particular functions. This differentiation of cells allows **divison of labour**, in which each type of cell is adapted to carry out a particular set of functions, and the different types each make their own contribution to the overall functioning of the organism. The different kinds of cells are usually grouped together to form **tissues**, each tissue carrying out a particular function within the organism.

The sponges, which belong to the phylum **Porifera**, have a body plan which in many ways is rather like a simple colony of protozoa. Sponges are sessile filter-feeders. There are different kinds of cells in a sponge's body (Fig. 22.13), arranged into tissues, but each cell retains quite a high degree of independence. For example, if a sponge is squeezed through a silk mesh, so that all the individual cells are separated from each other, the cells can reassemble themselves to form a sponge once more. Sponges do not have nerve cells, although they do have cells which can contract in a similar way to the muscle cells of other animal phyla. Other types of specialised cells found in sponges include choanocytes, that have a flagellum which helps to draw water through the sponge's body, and porocytes, that are large ring-shaped cells through which water is drawn into the sponge.

One of the oldest phyla of animals in evolutionary terms, the cnidarians (jellyfish and sea anemones), has a body plan in which there are just two layers of tissues. These animals are said to be **diploblastic** (Fig. 22.15). The outer layer of tissues is called the **ectoderm**, and the inner layer is the **endoderm**. These two layers are separated by a jelly-like layer, not made of cells, called the **mesogloea**. The endoderm surrounds a gut cavity or **enteron**.

All of the other animal phyla have three layers of tissues, and they are said to be **triploblastic**. In these animals, a third layer of tissues called the **mesoderm** lies in between the ectoderm and endoderm. In many phyla of animals, a cavity forms within the mesoderm, called a **coelom**. Such animals are described as **coelomate**.

KINGDOM ANIMALIA

Characteristic features of the kingdom Animalia
- The organisms are made up of eukaryotic cells.
- The body of the organism is multicellular.
- The cells do not have cell walls, only a cell surface membrane.
- They do not photosynthesise but feed heterotrophically.

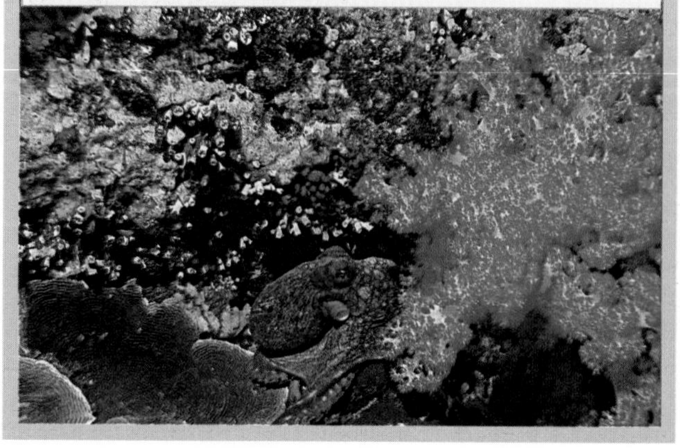

Fig. 22.12   Animals on a coral reef.

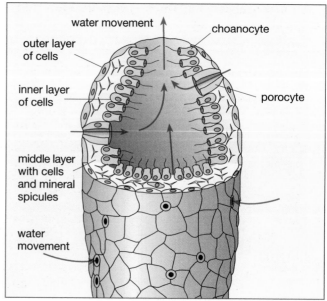

Fig. 22.13   Body structure of a sponge.

Diploblastic animals are **radially symmetrical**, while triploblastic animals are **bilaterally symmetrical** (Fig. 22.14). In a bilaterally symmetrical animal, the upper and lower (**dorsal** and **ventral**) surfaces are different, as are the front and back (**anterior** and **posterior**) ends of the body.

It is thought that the evolution of bilateral symmetry is related to the way that animals move. In general, radially symmetrical animals tend to be sessile or move in directions determined by ocean currents, while bilaterally symmetrical animals tend to be motile. If an animal always moves with one part of its body next to the surface over which it is moving, then this becomes its ventral surface. Desirable features for ventral surfaces are likely to be different from those for dorsal surfaces, so they have evolved differently. Moreover, if one end is always 'leading the way' as the animal moves, then this end is likely to meet new environmental features first. So it makes sense for this end to contain a greater number of receptors than the other end, and also a greater concentration of nervous tissue to analyse whatever information the receptors collect. We call this part of an animal's body its head, and the possession of a head is called **cephalisation**.

Unlike plants, where the different phyla appear at different times in the fossil record, fossils of almost all of the present-day animal phyla appear at the same time, around 600 million years ago. We therefore cannot use a *sequence* of fossils to help us to work out relationships between the different animal phyla. All we have to go on is the evidence we can see today, such as their body plans, their biochemistry and the way they develop from a fertilised egg to an adult.

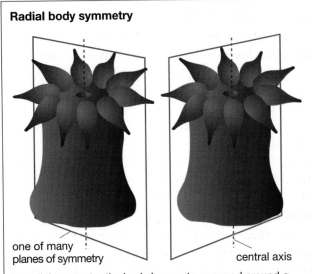

Radial body symmetry

one of many planes of symmetry   central axis

In radial symmetry the body has parts arranged around a central axis. There are many planes of sectioning around this axis which will produce equal body halves. The body is based on a cylindrical shape.

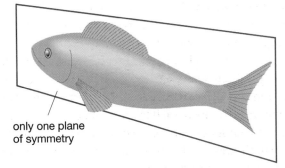

Bilateral body symmetry

only one plane of symmetry

In bilateral symmetry there is only one plane of sectioning which will produce equal body halves.

Fig. 22.14   Body symmetry in animals.

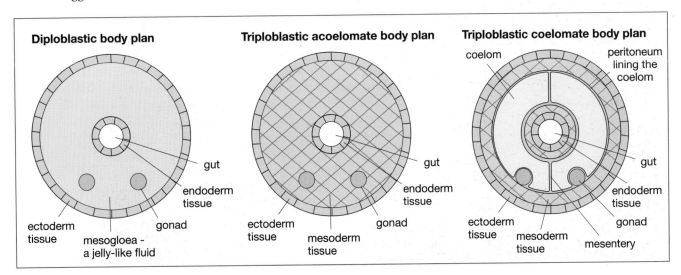

Fig. 22.15   Animal body plans.

22.13 Phylum Cnidaria

The cnidarians used to be called coelenterates, and you may still come across this older name in some books. This phylum includes the jellyfish, sea anemones and corals. They are radially symmetrical, diploblastic animals. They have a gut cavity with a single opening; food goes in (**ingestion**) and waste material goes out (**egestion**) through this same opening, called a mouth. The mouth is surrounded by a ring of tentacles.

There are two basic forms of cnidarians. One form is called a **polyp** which is a sessile animal that attaches the base of its body to a surface, with its mouth and tentacles facing upwards. The other form is called a **medusa**, and this swims freely in the water with its mouth and tentacles facing downwards. Sea anemones are polyps, while jellyfish are medusae. Some cnidarians have both of these forms in their life cycles.

All cnidarians live in water, most of them in the sea. Many of them are colonial, living in large groups of individual animals in which the tissues of one animal sometimes link directly with the tissues of others. Some of them make hard skeletons, often containing calcium carbonate, around their bodies. Coral reefs are formed by cnidarians. Almost all types of coral polyps, and some other cnidarians, contain algae inside their epidermal cells. The algae and the coral polyp have a mutualistic relationship (Section 13.14) in which the algae probably obtain nitrogen-containing substances from the feeding activities of the coral, while the coral receives substances such as glucose and glycerol from the photosynthetic activities of the algae. As the algae must have light for photosynthesis, coral reefs usually form only in shallow water.

Cnidarians are all carnivores, and they have special stinging cells called **nematocysts** in the epidermis of their tentacles. Each nematocyst contains a coiled tubular structure, which often has barbs on it (Fig. 22.17). When a prey organism brushes against a nematocyst, the coiled tube suddenly shoots out and embeds itself in the prey. A protein toxin may be contained in the tube, which paralyses the prey. This discharge process takes about 3 milliseconds. The prey is then pushed into the mouth by the tentacles.

A few cnidarians, especially jellyfish, have such powerful toxins in their nematocysts that they can cause extremely painful stings to humans. Some organisms, however, appear immune to the effects of nematocysts. Sea slugs (small marine molluscs), for example, feed on jellyfish and sea anemones with no ill effects. Some sea slugs even make use of the nematocysts themselves. Their digestive system is adapted to separate out the nematocysts they eat from the rest of their food, and the nematocysts are transported through the sea slug's body to its outer body surface. The nematocysts help to defend the sea slug from attack by predators.

Cnidarians have a very simple nervous system, in which the neurones are arranged in an irregular network throughout the body, called a **nerve net**. There is no 'brain'. They can move using muscle cells in their epidermis. Medusae swim actively, with pulsing movements of these muscles, while most polyps are less active.

Cnidarians do not have a transport system. Gas exchange takes place by diffusion through the body surface, and the gases move by diffusion to and from the body cells.

Fig. 22.16 A coral reef.

Phylum Cnidaria

> **Characteristic features of the phylum Cnidaria**
> • They are animals with a diploblastic body plan.
> • Their bodies are radially symmetrical.
> • They have a gut with a single opening surrounded by a ring of tentacles.

Longitudinal section through a cnidarian

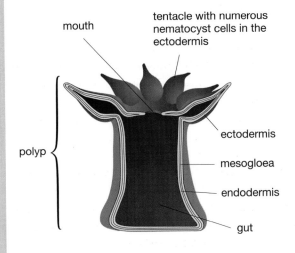

mouth

tentacle with numerous nematocyst cells in the ectodermis

polyp

ectodermis

mesogloea

endodermis

gut

Nematocysts

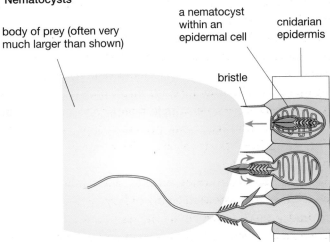

body of prey (often very much larger than shown)

a nematocyst within an epidermal cell

cnidarian epidermis

bristle

If the bristle is stimulated the nematocyst discharges. Spines pierce the body wall of the prey and a thread which releases toxin penetrates the body and paralyses it.

Hydra viridissima (green hydra) (×4)

asexual reproduction occurs by budding

Hydra viridissima is common in still, unpolluted water in ditches and ponds, where it feeds on freshwater plankton.

Aurelia aurita (a jellyfish) (×0.3)

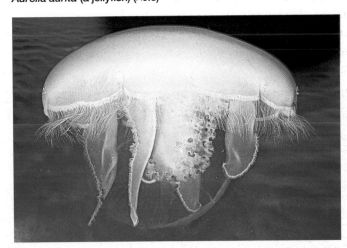

Aurelia is found near the sea surface. It feeds on marine plankton.

Fig. 22.17 Phylum Cnidaria.

22.14 Phylum Platyhelminthes

The platyhelminths are flatworms. They are triploblastic acoelomates. Most are no more than a few centimetres long, and many are less than a millimetre in size. Their name describes their body shape, which is usually dorsoventrally (top to bottom) flattened and very thin.

Flatworms all live in moist places. Some are free-living in sea water, fresh water or moist soil, but most are parasites which live inside other organisms. Some are important parasites of humans and other mammals; you can read about the life cycle of *Taenia* in Section 13.15.

Free-living flatworms are mostly carnivorous, but some feed on dead bodies of animals, while others feed on small algae. They have a gut with a single opening, so that the mouth is used for both ingestion and egestion. Parasitic flatworms may have a gut like this, or they may have no gut at all (e.g. *Taenia*).

Flatworms do not have circulatory systems. Oxygen is absorbed through the body wall, and their thin, flat body shape means that diffusion distances are short. In larger flatworms, the gut may have branches spreading into the tissues, so that digested food can easily diffuse to each cell which requires it.

Flatworms which can actively move do so using either the cilia which cover their body surface, or muscles, or both. They have a simple nervous system made up of a very simple brain near the anterior end, from which a net-like system of nerves spreads to all parts of the body. Free-living flatworms have simple eyes which can detect light but not form images.

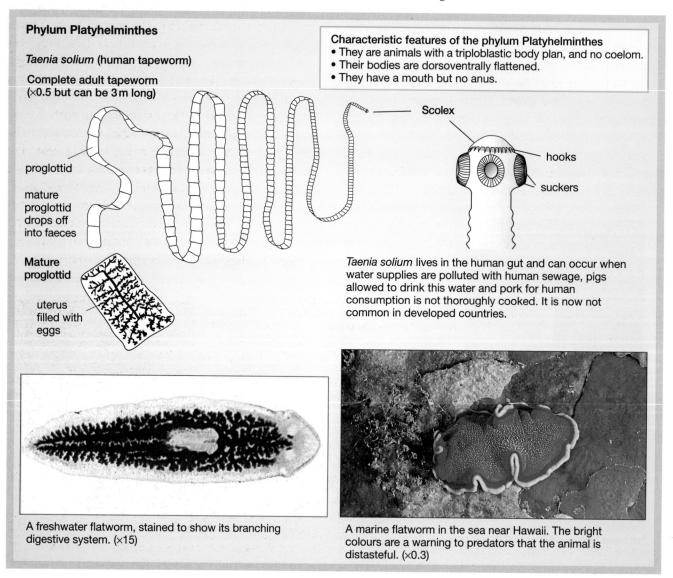

Phylum Platyhelminthes

Taenia solium (human tapeworm)

Complete adult tapeworm
(×0.5 but can be 3 m long)

Characteristic features of the phylum Platyhelminthes
• They are animals with a triploblastic body plan, and no coelom.
• Their bodies are dorsoventrally flattened.
• They have a mouth but no anus.

Scolex

hooks

suckers

proglottid

mature proglottid drops off into faeces

Mature proglottid

uterus filled with eggs

Taenia solium lives in the human gut and can occur when water supplies are polluted with human sewage, pigs allowed to drink this water and pork for human consumption is not thoroughly cooked. It is now not common in developed countries.

A freshwater flatworm, stained to show its branching digestive system. (×15)

A marine flatworm in the sea near Hawaii. The bright colours are a warning to predators that the animal is distasteful. (×0.3)

Fig. 22.18 Phylum Platyhelminthes.

22.15 Phylum Mollusca

The molluscs include slugs, snails, limpets, mussels and octopuses. Most are aquatic, living in the sea and in fresh water, though a relatively small number live on land.

There are several classes of molluscs of which the **gastropods**, **bivalves** and **cephalopods** are the most familiar. Gastropods include the terrestrial slugs and snails, as well as many of the shelled organisms you may find on the seashore, such as dog whelks and periwinkles. Bivalves include oysters and mussels. The cephalopods include octopuses, cuttlefish and squids.

Molluscs are triploblastic coelomates. They have soft bodies, with a flattened muscular **foot** on their ventral surface. Their body is often covered by a **shell**, which protects the internal organs. These are often known as the **visceral mass**. The shell is secreted by a layer of epidermal tissue called the **mantle**. There is usually a space between the shell and the visceral mass at the posterior end of the body, and this is called the **mantle cavity**.

Unlike cnidarians and platyhelminths, molluscs have a well-developed **blood system**. This is necessary because of their body shape; diffusion distances between their environment and the cells deep inside the visceral mass are much too great (Section 10.1). They also have surfaces specialised for gas exchange, called **gills**. The gills lie in the mantle cavity and water is moved over them by cilia.

Molluscs have evolved a wide range of lifestyles. Many of the gastropods are herbivores. They feed using a 'tongue' covered with hard teeth, called a **radula**, with which they scrape algae from surfaces such as rocks, or bite off larger pieces of seaweeds or the leaves of plants. Other gastropods, such as dog whelks, are carnivores. Dog whelks use their radula plus acidic secretions to drill holes in the shells of limpets or barnacles, before inserting their radula and eating the soft tissues inside.

Many bivalves are filter feeders. Box 13.3 describes how the mussel, *Mytilus edulis*, feeds. Filter-feeding bivalves are usually sessile, remaining in one spot for most of their lives. Others burrow into sand and mud. They draw the sand or mud into their bodies using tentacles covered with cilia, and then sort out what is edible before rejecting the rest. They are said to be deposit feeders.

Cephalopods are fast-moving carnivores. They are jet-propelled, squirting water from the mantle cavity to push themselves forwards through the water. They have tentacles at the front of their body, with which they capture prey. The largest known non-vertebrate animal, the giant squid, can grow to more than 16 m long, but most cephalopods are between about 5 cm and 1 m long.

Cephalopods have very highly developed nervous systems, with brains which are much larger and more complex in relation to their size than any other non-vertebrates. They behave in ways which we consider to be 'intelligent', in that they can learn quickly and remember what they have learned. They have eyes which are very like vertebrate eyes, a striking example of 'parallel evolution' in which similar structures have evolved independently of one another. They communicate with each other by changing colour patterns on their bodies, using pigment-containing cells which can be expanded or contracted.

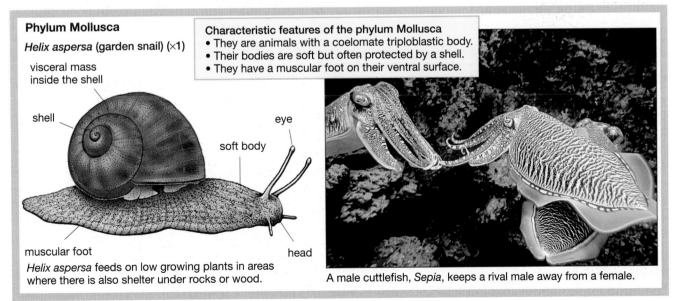

Phylum Mollusca

Helix aspersa (garden snail) (×1)

visceral mass inside the shell

shell

eye

soft body

muscular foot

head

Helix aspersa feeds on low growing plants in areas where there is also shelter under rocks or wood.

Characteristic features of the phylum Mollusca
- They are animals with a coelomate triploblastic body.
- Their bodies are soft but often protected by a shell.
- They have a muscular foot on their ventral surface.

A male cuttlefish, *Sepia*, keeps a rival male away from a female.

Fig. 22.19 Phylum Mollusca.

22.16   Phylum Annelida

'Annelid' means 'ringed', and the annelids are worms with bodies which look as though they are made up of a series of rings. They include the earthworms, ragworms and leeches.

Annelids are triploblastic coleomates. They are **metamerically segmented**, which means that their body is made up of a series of similar 'units' or segments. Each segment contains a similar pattern of organs such as nerves, blood vessels, muscles and excretory structures.

Annelids have soft bodies without a rigid skeleton. They are supported by the pressure of the fluid inside their coelom (Section 16.6). This provides enough support to allow some annelids to live in moist places on land, but most are aquatic. They have no waterproof covering over their body surface so they rapidly lose water in dry air. Gas exchange takes place through the general body surface, and they have a well-developed blood system to transport gases and other substances within their bodies. Most annelids are quite small animals, but giant earthworms in Australia can grow up to 3 m long.

Annelids have a nervous system made up of **cerebral ganglia** at the anterior end (a ganglion is a collection of nerve cells which forms a simple brain) and a **ventral nerve cord** which runs along the whole length of the body. Nerves branch off from this nerve cord into each segment, and they coordinate the actions of the muscles involved in movement. Movement is aided by tiny, stiff bristles called **chaetae**, which protrude from each segment.

There are three classes of annelids. The **Polychaeta** are marine annelids. 'Polychaete' means 'many bristles', and these annelids characteristically have several chaetae on each segment, attached to flaps called **parapodia**. Many polychaetes are active carnivores, hunting prey by swimming or crawling towards it and then killing and eating it using horny jaws. These polychaetes tend to have very well-developed heads, with many tentacles and sense organs which help in detecting potential prey. Other polychaetes live in burrows or tubes which they build from sand particles. They have many long tentacles which they fan out into the water and use for filter-feeding.

Earthworms belong to the class **Oligochaeta**. 'Oligochaete' means 'few bristles'. Oligochaetes do not have parapodia. Many oligochaetes are burrowers, either on land or in bottom sediments in fresh water or the sea. They are nearly all scavengers, feeding on dead plant material. They do not have such well-developed heads as the active, carnivorous polychaetes, and a quick glance is not always enough to tell which end of an oligochaete is which.

The third class of annelids is the **Hirudinea**, or leeches. Many leeches are ectoparasites, attaching themselves to the body surface of another animal and feeding on their blood and tissues. Leeches are less worm-like in shape than the other two groups of annelids, being more dorso-ventrally flattened and rather shorter and fatter. Another difference is that they do not have chaetae. All leeches have suckers which they use for movement, and also for fixing themselves to their host if they are parasites. Most leeches live in fresh water, or in moist places on land. A walk through vegetation in a humid tropical forest may provide you with a number of leeches attached to your legs.

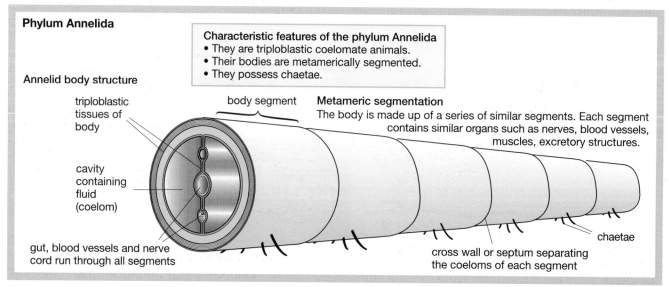

Fig. 22.20   Phylum Annelida.

Nereis virens (ragworm, a polychaete) (×1)

segmented body

mouth with
chitinous jaw

parapodia

Ragworms belong to the class Polychaeta. *Nereis virens* is found in sand and mud of sea shores. The flaps along the sides of the body are parapodia. There are eyes and tentacles on the head. This worm is an active carnivore.

Sabella (fan worm, a polychaete) (×1)

tentacles

tube made of sand grains cemented together

Sabella is found in intertidal sand on sea shores. It is a filter feeder. Small animals and plants floating in the water are trapped by mucus on the tentacles and carried down into the mouth. The worms make tubes out of sand particles, into which they retreat when the tide is out.

Hirudo medicinalis (medicinal leech) (×1)

Hirudo medicinalis is now uncommon in western Europe because of collection for medicinal use and because it is restricted to extensive marshland. It feeds on the blood of mammals.

Lumbricus terrestris (earthworm) (×1)

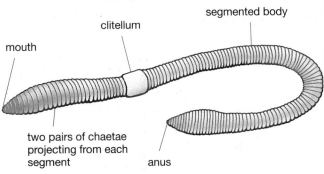

clitellum

segmented body

mouth

two pairs of chaetae projecting from each segment

anus

Lumbricus terrestris is common in moist humus-rich soil.

Fig. 22.20   Phylum Annelida *cont*.

22.17 Phylum Arthropoda

'Arthropod' means 'jointed leg'. It is easy to distinguish an arthropod from any other kind of non-vertebrate animal, because they are the only animals with jointed appendages (legs and antennae, for example).

Arthropods are triploblastic coelomates, though their coelom is much smaller than that of annelids. Like annelids, they are metamerically segmented, but in arthropods the individual segments are less similar to each other than is the case in annelids. Unlike annelids, arthropods possess a hard external skeleton and jointed limbs. Another difference between these two phyla is that whereas annelids have a blood system made up of vessels (rather like that of humans), the blood of arthropods fills their body cavity and bathes the organs directly. The nervous system of arthropods is based on the same plan as that of annelids, with a simple brain at the anterior end and a ventral nerve cord running along the length of the body. Despite the differences between them, the annelid and arthropod body designs are so similar that these two phyla are considered to be closely related.

In terms of numbers, both of individuals and of species, the arthropods outclass any other animal phylum. They live in almost every possible habitat on Earth, in the sea, fresh water and on land. Their jointed appendages have evolved into many different forms which are used not only for movement, but also for feeding, gas exchange and as sense organs. Their strong waterproof exoskeleton has enabled them to live in dry terrestrial environments. However, this skeleton cannot grow and has to be shed at intervals and replaced with a new, larger one. This, and the mechanical problems posed by supporting the body with an external skeleton rather than an internal one, appear to place an upper limit on the size which arthropods can attain.

There are several groups of arthropods, and we will consider just the four most familiar ones.

Spider, mites, scorpions and ticks belong to the Class **Arachnida**. (In some classification systems, the arachnids are classified with a few other groups of arthropods in the Class Chelicerata.) Most arachnids are terrestrial. They have a cuticle with an especially high lipid content, making it very waterproof and enabling some arachnids to live in very dry environments such as deserts. The easiest way to tell an arachnid from other arthropods is to count its legs – all arachnids have four pairs of legs. Their body appears to be divided into an anterior part called a cephalothorax, and a posterior part called the abdomen.

Almost all arachnids are carnivores, and some of them produce toxic venoms which help to kill or immobilise their prey.

Several classes of arthropods, including the lobsters, crabs, woodlice and water fleas, are grouped together into the subphylum **Crustacea**. There is a great variety of body plans amongst the crustaceans, but you can use the number of antennae to help you to identify them – all crustaceans have two pairs, while other kinds of arthropods have only one pair (for example chilopods and insects) or none at all (arachnids). Most crustaceans have a very hard exoskeleton, containing calcium carbonate. The great majority of them are aquatic, and those which do live on land, such as woodlice, tend to be confined to moist habitats.

Centipedes belong to the Class **Chilopoda**. They are active carnivores which can be found in soil and leaf litter in most parts of the world, where they hunt prey such as other smaller arthropods and earthworms. As you would expect in a predator, they have well-developed heads with strong jaws. Specialised appendages on either side of the mouth contain poison glands, and these are used to kill or immobilise their prey; a few kinds of tropical centipedes can give a person a painful bite. They have many legs, as suggested by their common name, and many centipedes are adapted for running.

Millipedes belong to the Class **Diplopoda**. Like centipedes, they have many legs, but they are herbivores rather than predators, and their heads do not have the well-developed killing appendages of the centipedes. They move relatively slowly, creeping through leaf litter and soil. For protection, many millipedes can curl up into a tight ball on which it is very difficult for a predator to get a grip. Some have glands which secrete foul-tasting liquids to deter other animals from eating them.

Perhaps the most familiar class of arthropods is the Class **Insecta**. More than 750 000 species of insects have been named and described, and there are thought to be several times this number again which have not yet been discovered. One feature which has contributed to this adaptive radiation is their ability to fly. Most insects have two pairs of wings, and this has enabled them to disperse rapidly to new areas, to escape from predators and to find sources of food which are not available to other animals. You can read about some other features of insects in Sections 12.13 to 12.15 and 16.8.

Insects are easy to distinguish from other arthropods. Their body is usually clearly divided into a head, a thorax and an abdomen. Three pairs of legs are attached to the thorax, as are the two pairs of wings. A few insects, however, do not have wings and in others there may appear to be only one pair. Houseflies, for example, look as though they have only one pair of wings, but if you look closely you can see that the hind pair is present as a pair of little knobs on stalks. These act like gyroscopes, helping the fly to keep its position in the air. In beetles, the first pair of wings has become a pair of tough covers, underneath which the more delicate hind wings are stored when the beetle is not flying.

The sheer numbers of insects on Earth, and also their lifestyles, make them of great importance to humans. Most flowering plants, including many food crops, need insects for pollination (Section 18.7). Insects may be important pests of crops, while others are important predators of these pests. Some insects are vectors of serious diseases, both of humans and animals (Box 13.6).

Phylum Arthropoda

> **Characteristic features of the phylum Arthropoda**
> • They are triploblastic coelomate animals.
> • Their bodies are segmented.
> • They have a hard exoskeleton.
> • They have jointed appendages (limbs).

Class Arachnida

> **Characteristic features of the class Arachnida**
> • They have no antennae.
> • They have four pairs of legs.
> • Their bodies are apparently divided into cephalothorax and abdomen.

Centruroides exilicauda (scorpion) (×0.6)

Most scorpions live in hot dry environments, and are well adapted to reduce water loss. They are predators, and the first pair of legs have evolved to become strong pincer-like claws. The poison gland in the tail is used for killing prey or in defence.

Areneus diadema (garden spider) (×4)

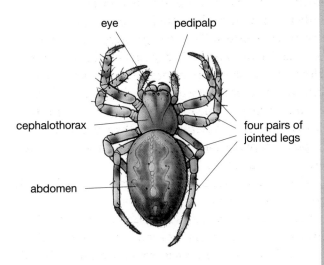

Areneus diadema is common in gardens, where it spins orb webs which catch flying insects.

Fig. 22.21　Phylum Arthropoda: Arachnida.

Subphylum Crustacea

Characteristic features of the subphylum Crustacea
- They have two pairs of antennae.
- Their exoskeleton usually contains calcium salts.

Spiny lobster (×0.4)

two pairs of antennae

Spiny lobsters are marine animals which feed as scavengers on the sea bed. Notice the two pairs of antennae, typical of crustaceans.

Class Chilopoda

Characteristic features of the class Chilopoda
- They have one pair of antennae.
- They have many legs, often long and adapted to running.
- Their bodies have a well-developed head and jaws.

Lithobius forficatus (centipede) (×2)

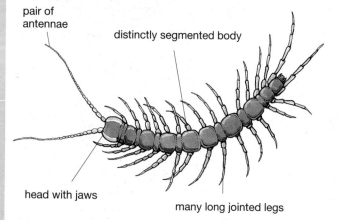

pair of antennae

distinctly segmented body

head with jaws

many long jointed legs

Lithobius forficatus is an active carnivore.

Armadillidium vulgare (woodlouse) (×4)

Most crustaceans are marine, but woodlice live in moist habitats on land. This species is able to reduce water loss by curling up into a ball, so that only surfaces protected by the exoskeleton are exposed to the air.

Daphnia pulex (water flea) (×12)

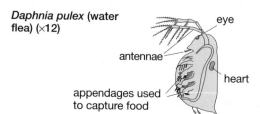

eye

antennae

heart

appendages used to capture food

Daphnia pulex live in organically rich still water. They feed on microscopic algae in the water.

Class Diplopoda

Characteristic features of the class Diplopoda
- They have one pair of antennae.
- They have many legs.
- Many body segments have two pairs of legs.

Millipede (×0.5)

segmented body

many jointed legs

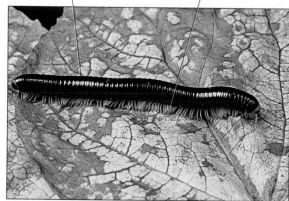

This large millipede is from Kenya. The red 'fringe' is its many jointed legs; there are two legs on most of the body segments.

Fig. 22.22 Phylum Arthropoda: Crustacea, Chilopoda, Diplopoda.

Class Insecta

> **Characteristic features of the class Insecta**
> • They have one pair of antennae.
> • Their bodies are divided into head, thorax and abdomen.
> • They have three pairs of legs, one attached to each thoracic segment.
> • They usually have two pairs of wings attached to the thorax.

Locusta migratoria (desert locust) (×1.5)

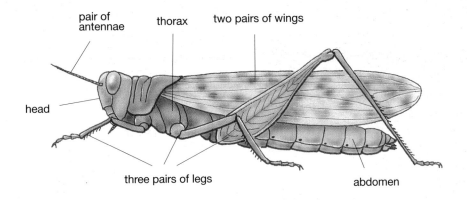

Locusta migratoria is a herbivore.

Head of *Tabernus* (horsefly) (×20)

Insects have compound eyes, made up of many facets each with its own lens. Between the two compound eyes, two small, black simple eyes can be seen. Compound eyes can focus light to produce images, and are especially good at detecting movement. Simple eyes sense light and darkness. Notice how some of the typical arthropod jointed appendages have evolved to become mouthparts – in this case adapted for biting and sucking blood from other animals. The antennae are very short.

Rhetus (butterfly) (×1)

This butterfly is from Ecuador. The single pair of antennae, typical of all insects, the division of the body into head, thorax and abdomen, and the two pairs of wings can all be clearly seen.

Fig. 22.23 Phylum Arthropoda: Insecta.

22.18 Phylum Chordata

The chordates include the familiar vertebrate groups – fish, amphibians, reptiles, birds and mammals – as well as some less well-known groups such as the tunicates (sea squirts) and cephalochordates.

Chordates are triploblastic coelomates. All chordates possess a **notochord** at some stage of their development, and it is this feature which gives them their name. The notochord is a stiff rod running along the body, close to the dorsal surface. It is made of cells containing large fluid-filled vacuoles, and it helps to provide support. Lying just above the notochord is the **nerve cord** (notice that one has an h and the other does not). This differs from the ventral, solid nerve cord of annelids and arthropods because it is dorsal and hollow.

Another characteristic feature of chordates is that they all have **pharyngeal slits** at some stage in their life. These are openings between the pharynx (the part of the alimentary canal between the mouth and the oesophagus) and the outside. Chordates also have a tail which extends beyond the anus, and is therefore said to be a **post-anal tail**. (In organisms such as annelids, the anus opens right at the end of the animal.)

The little animal *Branchiostoma* shows all of these features very clearly. It belongs to the subphylum Cephalochordata. *Branchiostoma* lives in sand in shallow seas in many parts of the world. It has muscle blocks along each side of its body, which contract in waves and make its body undulate from side to side. The flexible notochord provides firm support, yet can bend enough to allow this movement. *Branchiostoma* has fins to help to stabilise it when it swims. It feeds by drawing water into its pharynx, using cilia, and then filtering out food material as the water flows out through the pharyngeal slits.

The more familiar chordates belong to the subphylum **Vertebrata**, and are known as vertebrates. In many of these animals, most of the characteristic chordate features are seen only in the early stages of development, and are not visible in the adult. In the vertebrates, bones called vertebrae develop around the notochord and nerve cord. In most adult vertebrates, the notochord disappears as the vertebrae grow, leaving the nerve cord lying inside a protective tube formed by the vertebrae.

The group which we call 'fish' contains, according to most classification systems, five separate classes. They are all aquatic organisms, although a few species are able to spend some time on land. The most well-known are the cartilaginous fish, such as sharks, which belong to the class **Chondrichthyes**, and the bony fish, of the class **Osteichthyes**. Their names describe the material from which their skeletons are made. In the Chondrichthyes, the skeleton is made of cartilage all through their life, while in the Osteichthyes it begins as a cartilaginous skeleton, but much of the cartilage is later replaced by bone. The pharyngeal clefts in both groups are still visible when they are adults, as are their gill slits. In the cartilaginous fish, these are especially easy to see, but in the bony fish they are covered by a bony flap called the operculum. Both groups have fins on their bodies, and their body surfaces are covered with scales. In Chondrichthyes, the fins are fleshy, but in Osteichthyes the fins contain bony fin rays.

Frogs, toads, newts and salamanders belong to the class **Amphibia**. The amphibians evolved from fish, and they are partly adapted to live on land. However, most amphibians still have to return to water to lay their eggs. The eggs hatch into tadpoles which live in water and use gills for gas exchange. The tadpoles then change into adults in a process called metamorphosis. The adults have lungs which help with gas exchange, although they also use their skin for this. The skin is smooth with no covering of scales. Unlike fish, adult amphibians have four limbs, which they can use for swimming or for moving on land.

Animals belonging to the class **Reptilia** are much less dependent on water than the amphibians, and some reptiles can live in harsh terrestrial environments such as hot deserts. They lay eggs with waterproof shells, so they do not need to return to water to breed. Their skin is covered with protective horny scales and it is waterproof. Nevertheless, some reptiles, such as turtles, spend almost all of their lives in water. Like amphibians, reptiles have four limbs, although the snakes and a few lizards have lost their limbs in the process of evolution. Reptiles use lungs for gas exchange.

The birds, which belong to the class **Aves**, evolved from the reptiles, and there are so many close similarities between them that there is a strong argument for merging the two classes into one. However, birds are easy to distinguish from reptiles because their bodies are covered with feathers, and because the front pair of limbs is modified to form wings. All modern birds are endothermic (Section 15.6), whereas reptiles are ectothermic, but many biologists think that there is evidence that some extinct reptiles, such as some of the dinosaurs, may have been endothermic. Like reptiles, birds lay eggs with shells and have lungs for gas exchange.

The class to which humans belong, class **Mammalia**, also evolved from reptiles. Mammals, like birds, are endothermic. They have a body covered with hair. Two strange mammals, the platypus and the spiny anteater (echidna) lay eggs, but in all other mammals the young develop inside the mother's body, obtaining nutrients and other substances through a placenta (Section 17.7). The marsupial mammals, which include kangaroos, have a different type of placenta to the eutherian mammals (rabbits, humans and so on), and their young are born at a very early stage of development. All female mammals are able to secrete milk on which their young feed. In marsupials, the milk is secreted by nipples inside a pouch, and the tiny newly born young fixes itself firmly to a nipple soon after birth, completing its development inside the pouch. In eutherian mammals, the young are born at a much later stage of development, and in some species the young are active and able to fend for themselves very soon after birth. ■

Phylum Chordata
Clavelina picta (sea squirts) (×1)

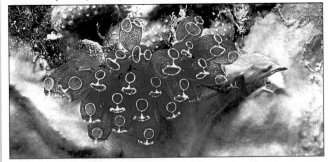

> **Characteristic features of the phylum Chordata**
> • They are animals that possess a notochord.
> • Their bodies have pharyngeal slits (gill slits).
> • They have a post-anal tail.
> • They have a dorsal hollow nerve cord.

Sea squirts belong to the group Tunicata. Although the adults do not look much like chordates, the larvae – which look like little tadpoles – go through a stage where they have a notochord. The adults are filter feeders, drawing water in through one opening and out through another.

Subphylum Cephalochordata
Branchiostoma (Amphioxus) (×2)

Branchiostoma lives in sandy and muddy sediments on the sea bed where it filter feeds. Its body structure is lacking many of the features of vertebrates – it has a very simple head, no heart and no cartilage or bones. However, it does have a notochord running the whole length of its body, and so it is a chordate.

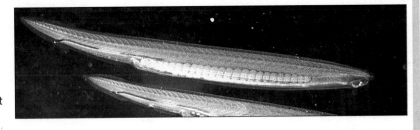

Subphylum Vertebrata
Class Chondrichythes

> **Characteristic features of the class Chondrichythes**
> • They have cartilaginous skeletons.
> • Their gill slits are visible.
> • They have fleshy fins.

Class Osteichthyes

> **Characteristic features of the class Osteichthyes**
> • They have bony skeletons.
> • Their gill slits are covered by an operculum.
> • They have fins with bony rays.

Carcharhinus amblyrhynchos (grey reef shark) (×0.03)

fleshy fin   gill slits

Clupea harengus (herring) (×0.25)

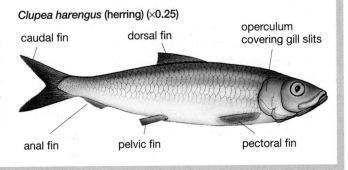

caudal fin   dorsal fin   operculum covering gill slits

anal fin   pelvic fin   pectoral fin

Fig. 22.24   Phylum Chordata.

Class Amphibia

Characteristic features of the class Amphibia
- They have smooth skin.
- They have four limbs.
- They have lungs.
- They lay unshelled eggs in water.
- They have a stage of the life cycle (tadpole) which has gills.

Triturus cristatus (crested newt) (×0.5)

Newts breed in still or slow-flowing fresh water, but can live in moist places on land outside the breeding season. They are carnivorous, feeding on small nonvertebrate animals.

Class Aves

Erithacus rubecula (robin) (×0.8)

Characteristic features of the class Aves
- They have feathers and scales covering their bodies.
- One pair of limbs is modified to form wings.
- They are endothermic.
- They lay shelled eggs.

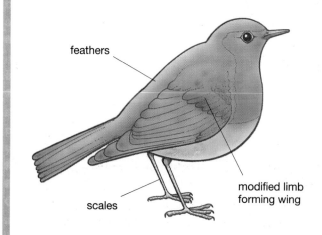

feathers

scales

modified limb forming wing

Class Reptilia

Characteristic features of the class Reptilia
- They have scaly skin.
- They have four limbs.
- They have lungs.
- They lay shelled eggs.

Natrix natrix (grass snake) (×0.6)

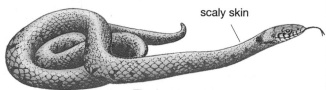

scaly skin

The four limbs are usually reduced in snakes to bones inside the body.

Grass snakes live in grassland or shady places, often near to water in which they sometimes swim. Eggs are laid in rotting vegetation and they generally feed on amphibians.

Class Mammalia

Characteristic features of the class Mammalia
- They have hair covering their bodies.
- They have four limbs.
- Their young usually develop inside the uterus and are connected with the mother by a placenta.
- They secrete milk to feed their young.

Tachyglossus aculeatus (echidna) (×0.13)

Echidnas only live in Australia. They belong to a group of mammals called monotremes which, unlike all other mammals, lay eggs.

Gazella thomsoni (Thomson's gazelle) (×0.035)

Thomson's gazelle is common in many African countries. It is a herbivore.

Fig. 22.24 *cont.*

Q1 A cladogram is a simple branching diagram which shows relationships between different groups of organisms. The cladogram below suggests, for example, that Fungi and Plantae are more closely related to each other than they are to Animalia.

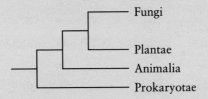

Fungi
Plantae
Animalia
Prokaryotae

Give:

(a) **one** feature shared by Fungi and Plantae which suggests that they are more closely related to each other than they are to Animalia; *(1)*

(b) **two** features which suggest that this view is not correct and Fungi are more closely related to Animalia than they are to Plantae; *(2)*

(c) **two** features of Prokaryotae which suggest that they are not closely related to any of the other three kingdoms. *(2)*

AEB 1994 *(Total 5 marks)*

Q2 The figure below shows the structure of an arthropod. It has the chitinous exoskeleton which is characteristic of all arthropods.

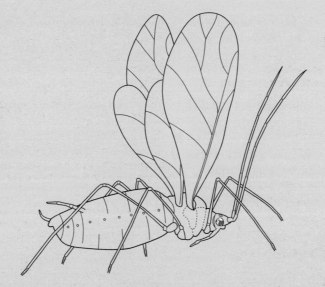

(a) State **two** other features, **visible in the figure,** which are characteristic of arthropods. *(2)*

(b) State the class of arthropod to which the example shown in the figure belongs, with **three** diagnostic features of the class that are **visible in the figure.** *(3)*

(c) (i) State the name of **one** structure, **visible in the figure,** that is used for gaseous exchange. *(1)*

   (ii) State the names of **two** structures, **visible in the figure,** that are used for sensing of external stimuli. *(2)*

UCLES 1995 *(Total 8 marks)*

Q3 (a) What is the difference between a natural classification and an artificial classification? *(1)*

(b) The following key distinguishes between five different kingdoms.

1	No membrane-bound organelles	kingdom **A**
	Membrane-bound organelles present	2
2	Hyphal mycelium present	kingdom **B**
	Hyphal mycelium absent	3
3	Multicellular or unicellular	kingdom **C**
	Multicellular only	4
4	Nutrition heterotrophic	kingdom **D**
	Nutrition autotrophic	kingdom **E**

Identify:
(i) kingdom **A**: *(1)*
(ii) kingdom **C**: *(1)*
(iii) kingdom **E**: *(1)*

AEB 1995 *(Total 4 marks)*

Q4 The table below refers to descriptions of some major groups of organisms. Copy the table and state the name of each group described in the spaces provided.

Features	Group
Heterotrophic organisms with rigid cell wall, body structure normally a mass of hyphae	
Photosynthetic organisms, with no flowers and no roots or stems or leaves, usually aquatic	
Photosynthetic non-flowering plants, with roots, stems and leaves	
Photosynthetic flowering plants, seeds enclosed in a fruit	
Heterotrophic, radially symmetrical, multicellular animals with nematocysts	
Heterotrophic, multicellular animals possessing a post-anal tail and pharyngeal clefts at some stage of their life	

ULEAC 1995 *(Total 6 marks)*

Q5 As with all members of its class, *Talpa europaea* has skin covered with hair. It is a typical member of the Insectivora being small and carnivorous.
Copy the table below and use this information to complete the table showing how *Talpa europaea* is classified. (4)

Phylum	
	Insectivora
Family	Talpidae
Genus	
Species	

AEB 1994

(Total 4 marks)

Q6 Copy and complete the table below with a tick if the statement is true or a cross if it is not true.

	Bryophyta (moss)	Filicinophyta (fern)	Angiospermophyta (flowering plant)
gametophyte is the dominant generation			
meiosis results in spore formation			
male gametes are motile			

AEB 1994

(Total 3 marks)

Q7 Copy the table below, and if a feature is present, place a tick (✓) in the appropriate box and if the feature is absent, place a cross (✗) in the appropriate box.

Feature	Chordates	Arthropods	Annelids
post-anal tail			
exoskeleton			
compound eyes			
chaetae			
visible external segmentation			

ULEAC 1996

(Total 5 marks)

Appendix 1
Some basic chemistry

If you are not very confident about any of the chemistry which you meet during your biology course, you may find this appendix helpful. It provides simple basic explanations of the chemical facts and concepts which you need to use and understand while studying biology at this level.

ATOMS AND MOLECULES
A1.1   Atoms and molecules

All substances, including the bodies of living organisms, are made of unimaginably small particles called **atoms**. There are about 90 naturally occurring kinds of atoms. Of these, only a few are important constituents of organisms. They are listed in Table A1.1.

Atoms differ from each other in size (Fig. A1.1). The smallest atoms are hydrogen atoms. Carbon atoms, which are one of the most important kinds of atom in building an organism's body, are twelve times more massive than hydrogen atoms. The mass of atoms is so small that we cannot use standard units, such as grams. Instead, we state the mass of an atom relative to the mass of a carbon atom, which is given a **relative atomic mass**, or A_r, of 12. Thus hydrogen has an A_r of 1. Oxygen atoms, which are larger than carbon atoms, have an A_r of 16.

In living organisms, atoms of hydrogen, carbon, oxygen and nitrogen do not exist on their own. They join together in groups of atoms, called **molecules**. A molecule may contain two or more atoms of the same kind joined together. An oxygen molecule, for example, contains two oxygen atoms (Fig. A1.2). We can show this in the **molecular formula** for oxygen, which is written O_2. This is the form in which oxygen is found in the air, and in which we breathe it in. Other molecules contain two or more different kinds of atoms joined together. A water molecule contains two hydrogen atoms and one oxygen atom. Its molecular formula is therefore H_2O.

A substance such as oxygen, which contains only one

Element	Symbol	Percentage of atoms in the body
hydrogen	H	59.4
oxygen	O	25.9
carbon	C	11.0
nitrogen	N	2.39
calcium	Ca	0.22
phosphorus	P	0.13
sulphur	S	0.13
potassium	K	0.04
chlorine	Cl	0.03
sodium	Na	0.03
magnesium	Mg	0.01
iodine	I	<0.01
iron	Fe	<0.01
zinc	Zn	<0.01
copper	Cu	<0.01

The percentages in the table are those in the body of a human. Percentages in the bodies of other animals, and even of plants, are very similar for the first four elements but vary rather more for the remaining eleven.

Table A1.1 The most important elements in living organisms.

chemical kind of atom, is called an **element**. Obviously, there are as many kinds of element as there are chemical kinds of atoms. A substance such as water, which contains molecules made of more than one kind of atom, is called a **compound**. Most substances from which living organisms are made are compounds.

Many of these compounds, such as polysaccharides, fats, proteins and nucleic acids, have enormous molecules, made of hundreds or thousands of atoms joined together. Part of a cellulose molecule, which is a polysaccharide, is shown in Fig. A1.2. These huge molecules are called **macromolecules**.

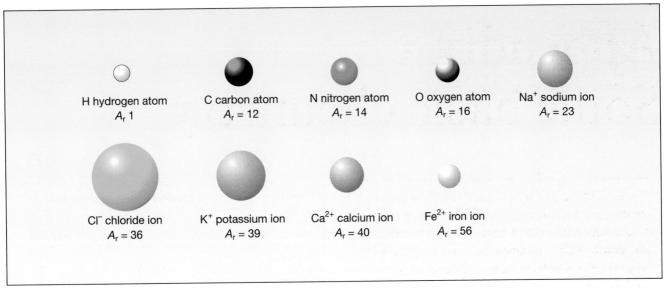

Fig. A1.1 Some atoms and ions important to living organisms.

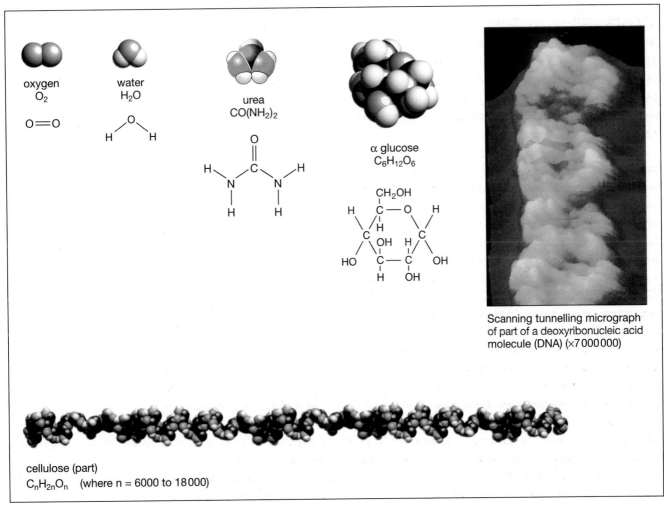

Scanning tunnelling micrograph of part of a deoxyribonucleic acid molecule (DNA) (×7 000 000)

Fig. A1.2 Some molecules important to living organisms.

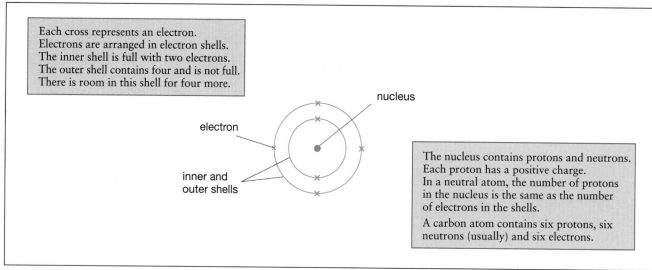

Fig. A1.3   An atom of carbon.

Each cross represents an electron.
Electrons are arranged in electron shells.
The inner shell is full with two electrons.
The outer shell contains four and is not full.
There is room in this shell for four more.

nucleus

electron

inner and
outer shells

The nucleus contains protons and neutrons.
Each proton has a positive charge.
In a neutral atom, the number of protons
in the nucleus is the same as the number
of electrons in the shells.

A carbon atom contains six protons, six
neutrons (usually) and six electrons.

A1.2   How atoms form molecules

An atom is made up of three kinds of smaller particles, called **neutrons**, **protons**, and **electrons**. Protons and neutrons each have the same mass, but electrons have almost no mass. Fig. A1.3 shows where these three particles are in an atom. The neutrons and protons are found in the centre, or **nucleus**, of an atom. (Do not confuse the nucleus of an atom with the nucleus of a cell. A cell nucleus actually *contains* millions upon millions of atoms.) The electrons orbit around the nucleus, arranged in **shells**. Between the electrons and the nucleus is complete nothingness – most of an atom is empty space.

Protons have a positive electrical charge and electrons have a negative electrical charge. Neutrons, as their name suggests, have no charge at all. In an atom, the number of protons is exactly equal to the number of electrons. The positive charge of the protons is exactly cancelled out by the negative charge of the electrons. An atom is therefore **neutral** – it has no overall electrical charge.

Atoms are most stable when their outer shell of electrons is complete. The inner shell is complete when it contains two electrons, and each of the next two shells are complete when they contain eight electrons.

In Section A1.1, you saw that atoms often group together to form molecules. Why do they do this?

Atoms join together because this is a way of filling their outer shells of electrons. In most of the substances from which living organisms are made, atoms tend to bond together by **sharing** some of their outer electrons. This kind of bonding is called **covalent bonding**. The covalently bonded atoms form a **molecule**.

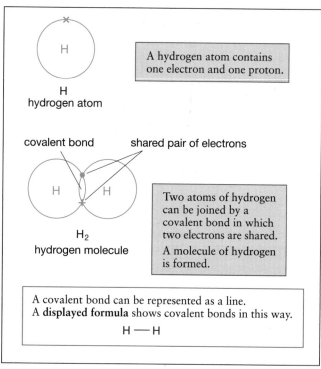

Fig. A1.4   Covalent bonding in hydrogen.

H
hydrogen atom

A hydrogen atom contains
one electron and one proton.

covalent bond

shared pair of electrons

H₂
hydrogen molecule

Two atoms of hydrogen
can be joined by a
covalent bond in which
two electrons are shared.
A molecule of hydrogen
is formed.

A covalent bond can be represented as a line.
A **displayed formula** shows covalent bonds in this way.

H — H

Fig. A1.4 shows how two hydrogen atoms share their outer electrons, to become a hydrogen molecule. By doing this, they each end up with a full outer shell of two electrons. *One* pair of electrons is shared between them, and we therefore say that there is a **single bond** between them.

Fig. A1.5 shows two other biologically important molecules, both of which have single covalent bonds between their atoms.

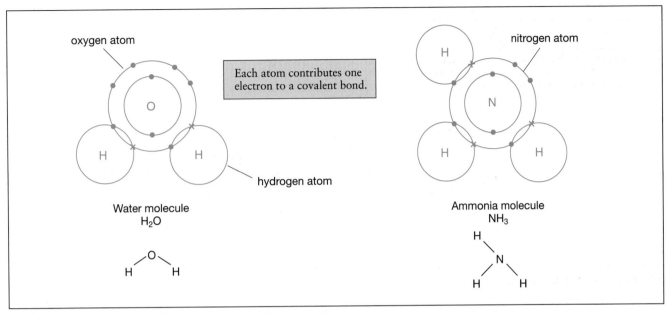

Fig. A1.5 Covalent bonding in water and ammonia.

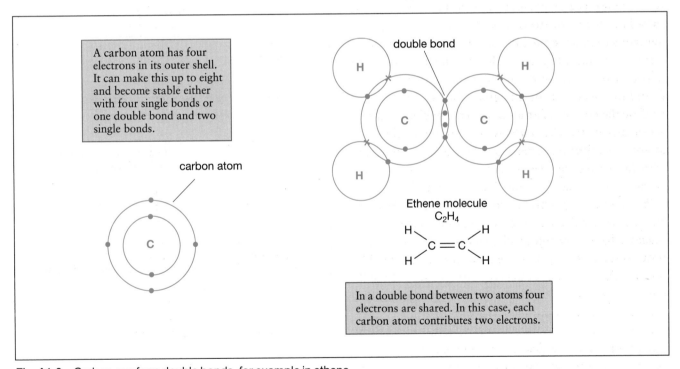

Fig. A1.6 Carbon can form double bonds, for example in ethene.

Sometimes, more than one pair of electrons is shared between the atoms in a covalently bonded molecule. If *two* pairs are shared, then a **double bond** is formed. This frequently happens between two carbon atoms, or between a carbon atom and oxygen atom. Fig. A1.6 shows the structure of a molecule of **ethene** (which used to be known as ethylene), which is a gas produced by many fruits when they are ripening. Ethene molecules have a

double bond between their two carbon atoms. Notice how the double bond is shown in the displayed formula.

Atoms which are sharing electrons, and have full outer shells, are usually very stable. Therefore the atoms in covalently bonded molecules will not separate from each other very readily. We say that covalent bonds are *strong* bonds.

Box A1.1 How many bonds?

In Section A1.3, you have seen that a covalent bond is formed when two atoms share one pair of electrons. It is useful for you to know and remember *how many* bonds four of the most important atoms in living organisms can form.

A **hydrogen** atom has only one electron. It can form one covalent bond by sharing this electron with another atom. Hydrogen atoms can only form **one** bond.

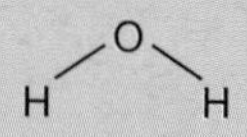

Oxygen atoms have six electrons in their outer shell. They have space for two more electrons in this shell. They can therefore share two pairs of electrons with other atoms, as in a water molecule. Oxygen atoms can form **two** bonds.

Nitrogen atoms have five electrons in their outer shell. They have space for three more electrons in this shell. They can therefore form **three** bonds.

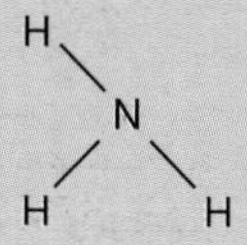

Carbon atoms have four electrons in their outer shell, so they have space for four more. They can therefore form **four** bonds.

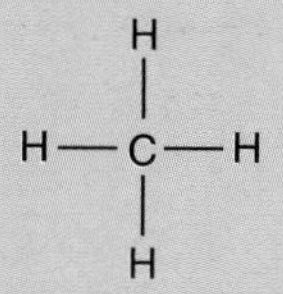

All you have to remember is **HONC 1234!** You will find this useful in checking if you have drawn a correct displayed formula for a particular compound. Count the bonds on each atom – if they don't match, then you are wrong. (You could still be wrong, of course, even if you have got the right number of bonds – but still…). For example, a molecule of the amino acid glycine has the formula:

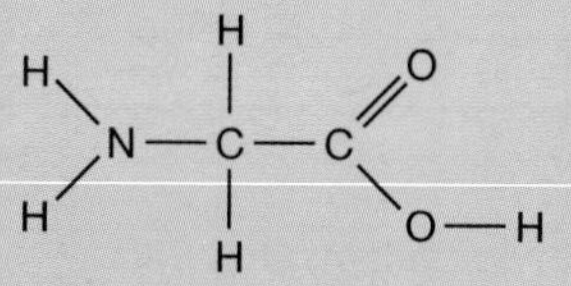

Count up the bonds on each atom – there should be one on each H, two on each O, three on the N and four on each C. Remember that a double bond counts as two.

A1.3 Ions

Many atoms have a tendency to gain or shed electrons from their outer shells, to make it complete. When this happens, their number of protons and electrons no longer balances, so they end up with an overall electrical charge. An atom in this state is called an **ion**.

Sodium ions are important in living organisms. The structure of a sodium atom, whose symbol is **Na**, is shown in Fig. A1.7. You can see that it has just one electron in its outer shell. The easiest way for it to have a full outer shell is to *lose* this lone electron. When it does this, it ends up with one more proton than electrons. It therefore has an overall electrical charge of +1. We show this by writing **Na$^+$**. Atoms of all metals tend to lose electrons and become positively charged ions. Some other positively charged ions which are important to living organisms are listed in Table A1.2.

Atoms of non-metals can more easily fill their outer shells by *gaining* electrons, thus becoming negatively charged. Fig. A1.8 shows how a chlorine atom becomes a negatively charged chloride ion, Cl$^-$. Table A1.3 lists some other negatively charged ions found in living organisms.

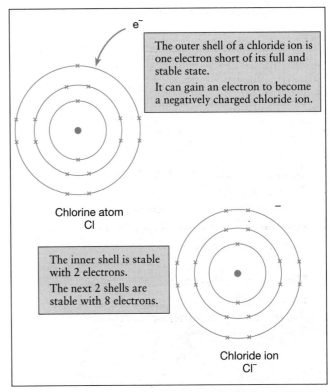

The outer shell of a chloride ion is one electron short of its full and stable state.

It can gain an electron to become a negatively charged chloride ion.

Chlorine atom
Cl

The inner shell is stable with 2 electrons.
The next 2 shells are stable with 8 electrons.

Chloride ion
Cl$^-$

Fig. A1.8   A chlorine atom becomes a chloride ion by gaining an electron.

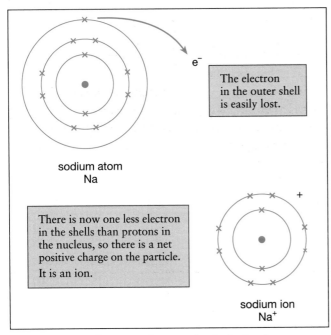

The electron in the outer shell is easily lost.

There is now one less electron in the shells than protons in the nucleus, so there is a net positive charge on the particle. It is an ion.

sodium atom
Na

sodium ion
Na$^+$

Fig. A1.7   A sodium atom forms an ion by losing the outermost electron.

Ion	Symbol
hydrogen	H$^+$
sodium	Na$^+$
potassium	K$^+$
calcium	Ca^{2+}

Table A1.2 Some important positive ions in living organisms.

Ion	Symbol
chloride	Cl$^-$
carbonate	CO$_3^{2-}$
hydrogencarbonate	HCO$_3^-$
phosphate	PO$_4^{3-}$

Table A1.3 Some important negative ions in living organisms.

What happens if a negatively charged chloride ion, and a positively charged sodium ion, find themselves close to each other? As you can imagine, their opposite charges cause them to be strongly attracted to each other. We say that the positive and negative ions are held together by an **ionic bond**. An ionic compound, **sodium chloride**, is formed. In a crystal of sodium chloride, many sodium ions and chloride ions arrange themselves in a regular pattern called a **lattice** (Fig. A1.9).

Solid ionic compounds such as sodium chloride are not commonly found in living organisms. This is because living organisms contain large amounts of water, and many ionic compounds are soluble in water. Section 1.5 explains how sodium chloride, for example, dissolves in water. The sodium and chloride ions are kept separate from one another by the water molecules. There are some exceptions, however. Bone contains an ionic compound made up of positively charged calcium ions, which form a lattice with negatively charged phosphate ions. About 70% by weight of bone is made up of this compound.

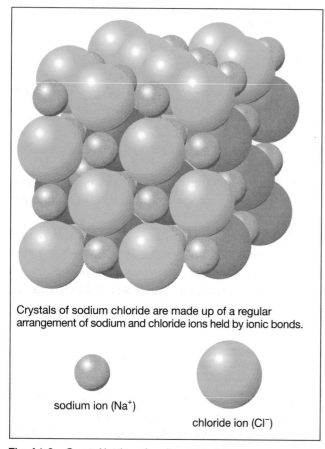

Crystals of sodium chloride are made up of a regular arrangement of sodium and chloride ions held by ionic bonds.

sodium ion (Na$^+$)

chloride ion (Cl$^-$)

Fig. A1.9 Crystal lattice of sodium chloride.

A1.4   Other types of bond

You now know about two types of bond – covalent bonds and ionic bonds. There are other types of bond which hold atoms together in organic substances. (Organic substances are ones which contain carbon; almost all substances which make up living organisms are organic.)

Two of these bond types – hydrogen bonds and van der Waals forces – are very important in living organisms, and are described in Box 1.3.

CHEMICAL EQUATIONS
A1.5   Molecular formulae

You may remember that there are about 90 different chemical kinds of atoms, and therefore 90 different elements. Each of these is given a symbol, made up of one or two letters. The ones which are most important in living things are listed in Table A1.1. If you do not already know these symbols, it is well worth learning them. Most are easy to remember because they are simply the first letter of the name – C for carbon, N for nitrogen and so on. A few are more awkward. Do make sure that you remember that Na stands for sodium, and K for potassium, or you will get in a muddle when you try to learn about how nerve impulses are transmitted, for example.

When we write the molecular formula of a compound, we use subscripts (numbers written just below the line) to show **how many** of each kind of atom are present in one molecule of that compound. A glucose molecule, for example, contains 6 carbon atoms, 12 hydrogen atoms and 6 oxygen atoms. The molecular formula tells us this in shorthand: $C_6H_{12}O_6$.

Sometimes, you may need to show that there are *two* glucose molecules. You do this by writing a normal-sized 2 in front of the formula: $2C_6H_{12}O_6$.

A1.6   Equations

A chemical equation shows you what happens when a chemical reaction takes place. In a chemical reaction, one or more substances called **reactants** rearrange their atoms to form one or more new substances called **products**.

One reaction which takes place in living cells, and which you may have seen happening in a test tube, is the breakdown of hydrogen peroxide to water and oxygen. (Hydrogen peroxide is a by-product of some other reactions in living organisms and is extremely toxic. So every cell has enzymes which rapidly cause its breakdown.) A **word equation** for this reaction is:

hydrogen peroxide → water + oxygen

A hydrogen peroxide molecule is made of two hydrogen atoms and two oxygen atoms. It therefore has the formula

H_2O_2. As you know, the formula for water is H_2O, while the formula for an oxygen molecule is O_2.

In this reaction, one of the oxygen atoms leaves each hydrogen peroxide molecule (Fig. A1.10). This converts each hydrogen peroxide molecule into a water molecule. The oxygen atom will instantly join with another oxygen atom to form an oxygen molecule. You can see, for this to happen, you need *two* hydrogen peroxide molecules for every *one* oxygen molecule which is formed. We show this in the **balanced equation** for the reaction:

$$2H_2O_2 \rightarrow 2H_2O + O_2$$

To check if your balanced equation is correct, count up the atoms of each kind on each side of the equation. You should end up with the same numbers that you started with – you cannot lose or create atoms! Here, there are four hydrogen atoms on each side, and four oxygen atoms.

ACIDS AND BASES

A1.7 Acids

You will meet acids – and sometimes bases – quite frequently in your practical work in biology, and also in many areas of theory. It is important that you know what they are, and what **pH** is.

An **acid** is a substance which produces **hydrogen ions**, H^+, when it is in solution. (Hydrogen atoms contain one proton and one electron, so a hydrogen ion is just a proton on its own.) An acid which does this very readily, producing a lot of hydrogen ions, is called a **strong acid**. Hydrochloric acid, which is secreted by the walls of the stomach, is a strong acid:

$$HCl \rightarrow H^+ + Cl^-$$

Ethanoic acid (it used to be called acetic acid), which is found in vinegar, does not readily produce hydrogen ions, and is a **weak** acid:

$$CH_3COOH \rightleftharpoons CH_3COO^- + H^+$$

Notice the arrow going both ways in this equation. This shows that the reaction is reversible – it goes both ways.

A1.8 Bases

A base is a substance which removes hydrogen ions from solution. Bases neutralise acids. Bases which are soluble in water are called alkalis.

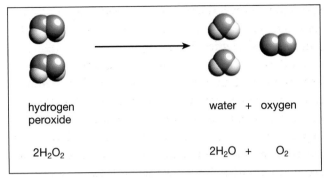

Fig. A1.10 Two molecules of hydrogen peroxide break down into two molecules of water and one molecule of oxygen.

Like acids, bases can be strong or weak. **Sodium hydroxide** is a strong base. In water, it forms sodium ions and hydroxide ions, OH^-:

$$NaOH \rightarrow Na^+ + OH^-$$

The hydroxide ions combine with hydrogen ions in an acidic solution, to form water molecules:

$$OH^- + H^+ \rightarrow H_2O$$

This removes hydrogen ions from the solution, so the solution is no longer an acid. The sodium hydroxide has neutralised the acid.

Sodium hydrogencarbonate, $NaHCO_3$, is a weak base which is secreted by the pancreas. It passes into the duodenum as part of the pancreatic juice, and neutralises the hydrochloric acid in the partly digested food entering the duodenum from the stomach.

A1.9 pH

The pH scale is used to indicate how acidic or basic (alkaline) a solution is. It is a measurement of the concentration of hydrogen ions in the solution. However, because of the way in which this is measured, it turns out that a solution with a lot of hydrogen ions has a low pH, while one with only a few has a high pH.

Fig. A1.11 shows the pH scale. A pH of 7 is neutral, anything below 7 is acidic, and anything above 7 is basic (alkaline).

If you need to measure the pH of a solution, you may be able to use a **pH meter**. This is an electrode which you place in the solution and gives you a readout on a digital display. If you do not have a pH meter, or if you do not need an accurate figure, then you can use an **indicator**. This is a liquid which changes colour according to the pH. You are almost sure to use one called Universal Indicator at some time. The colours of this indicator at different pHs are shown in Fig. A1.11. It is useful because it changes colour across the whole pH range. Other indicators, such as **hydrogencarbonate indicator**, change colour across a narrow range of pH, which may be very useful in particular experiments.

pH is very important to living organisms. pH affects the shape and therefore the functions of proteins, especially enzymes. This is described in Box 1.2 and Section 2.7. Because of this, we have mechanisms in our bodies to keep the pH of blood and other fluids almost constant, at just over 7. These mechanisms are described in Box 15.7. If pH strays much above or below normal, then a person becomes very ill. A blood pH of less than 6.8 is likely to result in coma, and then death. A blood pH of more than 8.0 may cause convulsions, again resulting in death.

ENERGY IN CHEMICAL REACTIONS
A1.10 Exothermic and endothermic reactions

Molecules and ionic compounds can be thought of as containing energy, which we can call 'chemical energy'. When a reaction occurs in which one kind of molecule changes into another, energy changes take place.

In some chemical reactions, the total chemical energy of the products is less than the total chemical energy of the reactants. Energy cannot be created or destroyed during a chemical reaction, so the 'left over' energy appears as heat energy. The surroundings get hotter when the reaction occurs. This kind of reaction is called an **exothermic reaction** (Fig. A1.12).

In other chemical reactions, the total chemical energy of the products is more than the total chemical energy of the reactants. For this kind of reaction to take place, energy has to be provided from elsewhere. Sometimes, the energy can be provided as heat energy. The heat energy comes from the environment – for example, you may provide energy by heating the reactants in a test tube. This kind of reaction is called an **endothermic reaction** (Fig. A1.12).

In many chemical reactions, no matter whether they are exothermic or endothermic, the reactants have to pass through a stage in which the molecules temporarily contain even more energy than either the reactants or the products. For the reaction to happen, this extra energy must be provided from somewhere. The extra energy is called **activation energy** (Fig. A1.12). Enzymes are such

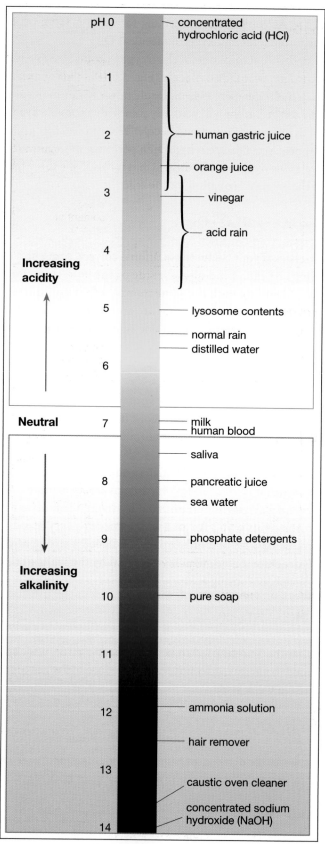

Fig. A1.11 The pH scale shown in the colours of Universal Indicator solution.

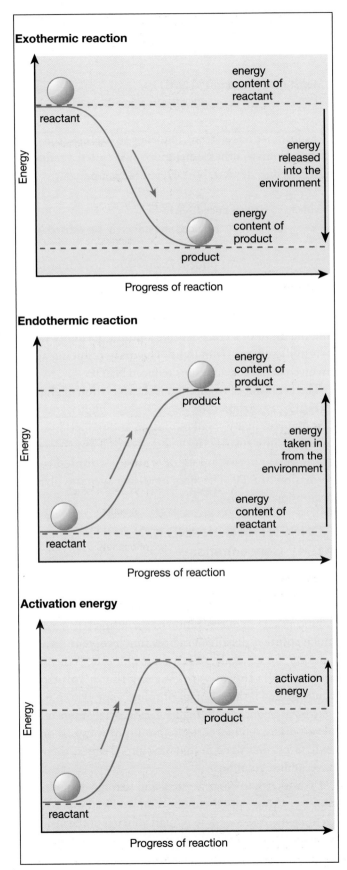

Exothermic reaction

energy content of reactant

reactant

Energy

energy released into the environment

energy content of product

product

Progress of reaction

Endothermic reaction

energy content of product

product

Energy

energy taken in from the environment

energy content of reactant

reactant

Progress of reaction

Activation energy

activation energy

product

Energy

reactant

Progress of reaction

Fig. A1.12   Energy changes in reactions.

effective catalysts because they provide ways for the reactants to change into products without having to pass through such a high energy stage. They lower the activation energy required by a reaction.

On the whole, the chemical reactions which take place in living organisms have evolved so that very large energy changes are avoided. Often, a series of reactions which each involve a relatively small energy change takes place, rather than one single one involving a large energy change. For example, in a laboratory, glucose can be converted to carbon dioxide and water by burning it in oxygen. This is an exothermic reaction which releases a very large amount of heat energy if it takes place in one step. In a living cell, the same result is achieved through a series of many smaller reactions, each of which involves relatively small energy changes (Figs. 9.2, 9.4 and 9.5).

A1.11   Coupled reactions

If all the chemical reactions which took place in living organisms either required heat energy to be put in, or released heat energy, then very great temperature changes might take place within living cells. Metabolic reactions have evolved so that this does not usually happen. Instead, the energy is transferred into or from the reaction from *another* reaction which takes place at the same time. The energy released from an exothermic reaction, for example, can be used to provide energy to an endothermic reaction. When this happens, the two reactions are said to be **coupled**.

One of the endothermic reactions which is most frequently used to provide energy in this way is the hydrolysis of ATP:

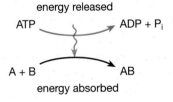

energy released

ATP → ADP + P_i

A + B → AB

energy absorbed

The conversion of substance A and substance B to substance AB requires energy; it is an endothermic reaction. The hydrolysis of ATP to form ADP and inorganic phosphate is an exothermic reaction. The energy released from this can be used to provide the energy required for A and B to be converted to AB.

ATP is used by every living cell in very large amounts (Box 1.4). Much of the chemical activity of a cell is therefore concerned with regenerating ATP, providing energy to fuel the recombination of inorganic phosphate with ADP. Respiration (Chapter 9) is the main process by which this is done.

OXIDATION AND REDUCTION

A1.12   Redox reactions

Oxidation is defined as the loss of electrons from a substance. **Reduction** is the gain of electrons by a substance.

Many chemical reactions involve the oxidation of one substance and the reduction of another. Oxidation and reduction always take place simultaneously, and a reaction in which they occur is called a **redox reaction**. Electrons are lost by one substance and taken up by another.

For example, during the light-dependent reaction of photosynthesis, chlorophyll molecules lose electrons. They are oxidised. The electrons are taken up by an electron carrier, which is therefore reduced. The carrier passes the electrons to another carrier, becoming oxidised. The electrons are passed on from carrier to carrier, eventually being taken up by oxidised NADP, which is therefore reduced. (The structures of NADP, and the similar compound NAD, are shown in Box 1.2.)

In biological redox reactions, hydrogen atoms are often involved. A hydrogen atom is, in effect, a hydrogen ion and an electron. Gaining a hydrogen atom means gaining a hydrogen ion and an electron, so this is an example of reduction. During some of the stages of respiration (Chapter 9) the coenzyme NAD accepts hydrogen ions and electrons and becomes reduced:

$$NAD^+ \qquad + H^+ + 2e^- \; \rightarrow \; NADH$$
(oxidised NAD) (reduced NAD)

Reduced NAD can be oxidised to oxidised NAD by releasing hydrogen ions and electrons:

$$NADH \qquad \rightarrow \; NAD^+ \qquad + H^+ + 2e^-$$
(reduced NAD) (oxidised NAD)

A1.13   Oxidising and reducing agents

If a substance has a strong tendency to take electrons from other substances, it is called an **oxidising agent**. Oxidised NAD, NAD^+, is an example of an oxidising agent. It readily accepts electrons from other substances, as shown in the equation in Section A1.12. NAD^+ acts as an oxidising agent during respiration. Oxidising agents become reduced as they oxidise other substances.

$$\text{substance X + oxidised NAD} \rightarrow$$
$$\text{oxidised substance X + reduced NAD}$$

If a substance has a strong tendency to lose electrons and donate them to other substances, it is called a **reducing agent**. Reduced NAD, NADH, is a reducing agent:

$$\text{substance Y + reduced NAD} \rightarrow$$
$$\text{reduced substance Y + oxidised NAD}$$

The net result of photosynthesis is the reduction of carbon dioxide, CO_2, to carbohydrate, $(CH_2O)_n$. In effect, hydrogen is added to the carbon dioxide. This involves many small oxidation and reduction steps along the way, and the input of a considerable amount of energy which originally comes from light. The main reducing agent involved in photosynthesis is reduced NADP.

The net result of respiration is the oxidation of glucose, $C_6H_{12}O_6$, to carbon dioxide, CO_2. Like photosynthesis, this involves many small oxidation and reduction steps, but this time results in the release of a considerable amount of energy, much of which is coupled to the formation of ATP. The main oxidising agent involved in respiration is oxidised NAD.

CONCENTRATION AND MOLARITY

A1.14   Concentration

When you are working with solutions, for example when doing osmosis investigations or working with enzymes, you often need to know how concentrated a particular solution is. The concentration of a solution tells you how much **solute** is dissolved in how much **solvent**. In a salt solution, for example, salt (sodium chloride) is the solute and water is the solvent. We say that a solution is **concentrated** if there is a lot of solute – for example, you may have a concentrated salt solution where there is a lot of salt dissolved in a certain amount of water. If only a little salt is dissolved in that amount of water, then you have a **dilute** solution.

Do notice that 'concentrated' and 'strong' do not mean the same thing – nor do 'dilute' and 'weak'. Look back at sections A1.7 and A1.8 to remind yourself of the meaning of 'strong' and 'weak'.

In biology, there are two common methods of measuring concentration.

1 Percentage

You may be given a solution which says it is, for example, '10% sucrose solution'. This usually means that 10 g of sucrose have been dissolved in 100 g of water. As 1 cm^3 of water has a mass of 1 g, in practice this solution would be made up by dissolving 10 g of sucrose in 100 cm^3 of water.

2 Moles per cubic decimetre

This is written as **mol dm^{-3}**. It is a measure of how many particles of the solute are present in one cubic decimetre of the solution. (One cubic decimetre is the same as one litre.)

Fig. 1.3 shows what happens when a molecular substance such as glucose, and an ionic substance such as sodium chloride, dissolve in water. You can see that when the solute is a molecular substance, then the particles in the solution are molecules. If the solute is an ionic substance, then the particles are ions.

'Moles per cubic decimetre' is a particularly useful way of describing concentration because you can directly compare the numbers of molecules in different solutions. For example, one litre (1 dm^3) of a glucose solution with a concentration of 1 mol dm^{-3} and one litre (1 dm^3) of a glycerol solution with a concentration of 1 mol dm^{-3} both contain the same number of glucose and glycerol molecules respectively. (Just out of interest, this number is enormous – 6×10^{23} molecules!) Each of them contains half as many solute molecules as does the same volume of a sucrose solution with a concentration of 2 mol dm^{-3}.

However, when sodium chloride dissolves in water, the sodium ions and chloride ions separate. One cubic decimetre of a 1 mol dm^{-3} solution of sodium chloride contains 6×10^{23} sodium ions *and* 6×10^{23} chloride ions. The total number of particles in a 1 mol dm^{-3} solution of sodium chloride is twice as many as in a 1 mol dm^{-3} solution of a molecular substance such as glucose.

This is probably all you will need to know about concentration of solutions. However, if you find that you are expected to be able to make up solutions for yourself, then look at Box A1.2.

Box A1.2 Making up solutions

To make up a solution with a particular concentration in mol dm^{-3}, you need to know the **molar mass** of the solute. 'Molar mass' means the relative molar mass of one molecule of the substance in question, expressed in grams.

A 1 mol dm^{-3} solution contains one molar mass of solute dissolved in 1 dm^3 of solution. A 2 mol dm^{-3} solution contains two molar masses of solute dissolved in 1 dm^3 of solution.

Let us see how you would go about making 1 dm^3 of a 2 mol dm^{-3} glucose solution.

1 Write down the formula for glucose, which is $C_6H_{12}O_6$.

2 Look up the A_r of each of the kinds of atom in the molecule. (You will find these in Fig. 1.1). These are: C 12 H 1 O 16

3 Now find the relative molar mass, M_r of glucose. You do this by adding up all of the A_rs of the atoms in the molecule. Multiply the number of each sort of atom by its A_r, and add them all up. The calculation is:

$$(6 \times 12) + (12 \times 1) + (6 \times 16) = 72 + 12 + 96 = 180.$$

180 is the relative molecular mass of glucose.

4 You are making a **2 mol dm^{-3}** glucose solution, so you need **two** lots of 180 g – that is 360 g of glucose – dissolved in 1 dm^3 of solution. So you weigh out 360 g of glucose, and place it in a container such as a volumetric flask. Add distilled water, mixing and swirling all the time to help the glucose to dissolve. Add enough distilled water to make exactly 1 dm^3 of solution.

Appendix 2 Units

A2.1 SI units

'SI' stands for 'Système International d'Unités', which means International System of Units. SI units are used in most parts of the world.

There are seven 'base' SI units. The ones you are most likely to use in Biology are:

metre, for measurements of length	symbol **m**
kilogram, for measurements of mass	symbol **kg**
second, for measurements of time	symbol **s**
ampere, for measurements of electric current	symbol **A**
kelvin, for measurements of temperature difference	symbol **K**
mole, for measurements of amount of substance	symbol **mol**

Notice that all of the full names of the units begin with a small letter. Most of the symbols also begin with a small letter, but where they were named after a person (Kelvin and Ampere) the abbreviated form has a capital letter. Notice also that you do not put a full stop after the abbreviation (unless, of course, it comes at the end of a sentence).

Each of these base SI units is defined in a precise way. For example, the metre is defined as the distance travelled by light in a vacuum in $\frac{1}{229\,792\,458}$ seconds. This definition is so strange because, of course, metres were being used as a unit of measurement long before anyone knew anything about the speed of light. If we could start again, we would probably use a much more sensible number!

There are also some other units which you will use. These are derived from the seven base units by multiplying or dividing them by one another, and so they are called 'derived units'. Each derived unit is defined in terms of the base units, but you do not need to know what these definitions are. The most commonly used derived units in Biology are:

newton, for measurements of force	symbol **N**
pascal, for measurements of pressure	symbol **Pa**
joule, for measurements of energy	symbol **J**

Often, it is helpful to use multiples or sub-multiples of these units. This is done by putting a prefix in front of the unit. Table A2.1 shows all of these prefixes, but you are only likely to come across a few of them. For biologists, the sub-multiples of the metre are perhaps the most frequently encountered, and you should make certain that you know exactly what a micrometre and a nanometre are.

Prefix	Multiple of unit	Symbol
exa	$\times 10^{18}$	E
peta	$\times 10^{15}$	P
tera	$\times 10^{12}$	T
giga	$\times 10^{9}$	G
mega	$\times 10^{6}$	M
kilo	$\times 1000$ or 10^{3}	k
hecto	$\times 100$	H
deca	$\times 10$	da
deci	$\times 1/10$	d
centi	$\times 1/100$	c
milli	$\times 1/1000$ or 10^{-3}	m
micro	$\times 10^{-6}$	μ
nano	$\times 10^{-9}$	n
pico	$\times 10^{-12}$	p
femto	$\times 10^{-15}$	f
atto	$\times 10^{-18}$	a

All of the prefixes are shown here, but in practice you are most likely to use only the ones shown in blue.

Table A2.1 Prefixes for units.

A2.2 Dealing with units in calculations

When multiplying and dividing numbers in calculations, you do the same with the units as you do with the numbers. For example, you know that to find the area of a square with sides of 2 mm, you multiply 2×2 to determine that it has 4 units of area. To find what these units are, you also multiply the original units – that is, mm × mm to determine that the units are mm^2.

sporophyte
    of fern   400–2
    of flowering plant   415
    of liverwort   400
sporozoite   294, 295
stabilising selection   156, 157
Stahl   100
stains
    differential   222
    Gram   72
    in light microscopy   51
stamens   403
Staphylococcus aureus   482
starch   9
    digestion in mouth   278
    digestion in small intestine   281
    hydrolysis in germination   353
    structure   11
stationary phase   433, 434
statocyte   353
statolith   353
stele   235, 236
stem cells   487
stem structure   235–6
    supporting tissues   361
steroids   324, 325
sticky ends   116
stigma   403
stomach   278–80
stomata
    and transpiration   238–9
    effect of abscisic acid   355
    in fern   402
    mechanism of closure   266, 268
stone cells   359, 360
Streptococcus   499
stress, in plants   355
stretch receptors
    and breathing rate   255
    and heart rate   212–13
striated muscle, structure   367–8
stroke volume   210
stroma   174–5
stromatolites   498–9
style   403
suberin   242
submucosa   277
substrate concentration, effect on
      enzymes   40–1
succession   440–2
    deflected   442
succulents   240
sucrase   281
sucrose
    structure and functions   10
    transport in phloem   245
sugars   6–10
    disaccharides   9–10
    monosaccharides   6–8
    non-reducing   8
    reducing   8
sulphanilamide   44
sulphur dioxide   454–5

support   359–66
    in animals   359, 362–6
    in plants   359–61
surface area
    and gas exchange   249–50
    and need for transport system   205
surfactant   252, 253
suspensor   411, 412
sweat glands   334
symbiosis   291
    between plants and fungi   243
    between plants and *Rhizobium*
      288–9
symmetry, in body plans   511
sympathetic nerves   302–3
    in temperature regulation   332, 334
    neurotransmitters   312
    to heart   212–13
symplast pathway   243, 244
synapse   308–10
    integration   311
    with muscle   372
synaptic cleft   308–10
synergids   406–7
synergism   349
synovial joint   365–6
systemic circulation   206, 218
systole   208–9

T helper cells   488, 490
T lymphocytes   487–8, 490
t-tubules   367–8
Taenia
    as parasite   291–2
    classification   514
tapetum   404–5
tapeworm   291–2, 514
taxis   320–1
telophase
    in meiosis   90–1
    in mitosis   84–5
temperature
    as limiting factor in photosynthesis
      188
    effect on enzyme activity   39–40
    effect on oxygen solubility   251
    regulation   331–4
temporal summation   311
tendons
    in arm   365–6
    in heart   207–9
test cross
    dihybrid   140
    monohybrid   129
testa   411–12
    structure   360
testes   378–80
    as endocrine gland   325
testosterone   325, 388
tetanus   480
tetrad   404, 405
thallus
    of algae   502

    of liverwort   398–400, 504–5
theca   381–2
thermal pollution   462
thermocline   439
thiamine   194
    in diet   274
thick filaments   367–8
thigmotropism   349
thin filaments   367–8
thirst centres   344
threshold potential   314
thrombin   482
    inhibition of   44
thrush   480, 482
thylakoid   174–5
    ATP synthesis in   180
    structure   69
thymine   28
thyroglobulin   335
thyroid gland   325, 333, 335–6
thyroid stimulating hormone, *see* TSH
thyrotropin releasing hormone   333,
    335–6
thyroxine   333, 335
    regulation of secretion   335
tidal volume   257
Tinea   480
tissue fluid   231–2, 233
tissues   50
TNF (tumour necrosis factor)   486
tonoplast   68
toxins
    action at synapses   312
    action on nerves   306
    from bacteria   478
Toxocara   482
trabeculae   364
trachea
    in humans   252–3
    in insects   264
tracheoles   264
training
    and muscles   374
    effect on heart rate   211
transamination   187
transcription   103
    effect of thyroxine   335
transect   429–30
transfer cell   245–6
transfer RNA, *see* tRNA
transferase   35
translation   105–6
    effect of interferon   486
translocation
    in phloem   245
    of chromosome   107
transpiration   238–9
transpiration pull   238
transplants   493–4
transport
    by blood   221
    in fish   206
    in mammals   205–33

in plants 235–46
of carbon dioxide 228–30
of oxygen 221–7
transporters
in cell surface membrane 78–9
in root hair cell 243
transverse tubules 367, 368
triceps 365–6
Trichonympha 501
triglycerides 23–4
triose 7
triose phosphate 193
in Calvin cycle 181–2
in glycolysis 192
uses in plants 181, 186
triplet, in DNA 98
triploblastic 510–11
tRNA (transfer RNA) 104–6
trophic level 419
trophoblasts 384–5, 389
tropisms 349–51
tropomyosin 373
troponin 373
trypsin 45
in small intestine 281
trypsinogen 281
TSH (thyroid stimulating hormone) 335–6
tube nucleus 404, 405
tubulin 61
tumour 87
tumour necrosis factor, *see* TNF
tunicates 523
turgor 78, 359

ultrafiltration 338, 340
ultraviolet light 451–3
umbilical cord 384–5
uracil 28
urea 337
ureotelic 338
urethra 378, 379
uric acid 338
uricotelic 338
uterus 378–9

vaccination 491–2
vacuoles 68
vagina 378, 379
vagus nerve 302
to heart 212
to stomach 284
valves
in heart 207–9
in lymphatics 231
in vein 218
van der Waals forces
in phospholipid bilayer 26
in proteins 19
variation
causes of 148–50
continuous 149
discontinuous 149

environmental 148
genetic 148
vas deferens 378–80
vascular bundle 235–6
vascular shock 486
vascular tissue in plants 235–7
vasoconstriction
in blood clotting 483
in temperature regulation 332
vasodilation
in allergy 495
in inflammation 491
in temperature regulation 334
vector 113, 116–17, 123
vegetative reproduction 397–8
veins 215–20
vena cava 208
ventilation
in fish 261–2
in humans 152, 254–5
in insects 264–5
ventilation rate 255
effect of exercise 256
ventral surface 511
ventral nerve cord 516
ventral root, of spinal nerve 299, 301
ventricles
in brain 302
in heart 207–8
venule 216–17
vertebrates, classification 522–4
vessels, xylem 235–7
villi 282–3
in placenta 384–5
in small intestine 280
viruses 477–9
visceral mass 515
vital capacity 257
vitamin A
absorption in small intestine 282–3
in diet 274
in rhodopsin formation 314
vitamin B_1 194
in diet 274
vitamin B_2 194
in diet 274
vitamin B_3 194
in diet 274
vitamin B_{12}
absorption 280, 283
in diet 274
vitamin C
absorption in small intestine 283
and iron absorption 283
in diet 274
vitamin D
absorption in small intestine 282–3
and calcium absorption 283
in diet 274
vitamin K 282–3
vitamins
in diet 274

in respiration 194
voltage-gated channels 303

water 1–5
water potential 75–7
water
absorption in small intestine 283
and stomatal opening 267
as a solvent 4–5
conservation by kidney 343
density 3
dipoles 1
hydrogen bonding in 1–2
in temperature regulation 334
latent heat of vaporisation 2–3
movement into roots 242
pollution of 457
potential 75–7
specific heat capacity 2
thermal properties 1
viscosity 4
Went 349–50
wheat
breeding 158–9
polyploidy in 166
willowherb 410
wilting 359
wood, digestion 290
woody stem 269

X chromosome 135
xerophytes 238, 240
xylem
position in stem and root 237
structure 235, 237
support 359–60

Y chromosome 135
yeast
classification 503
feeding 290
production of alcohol 199

Z disc 367–8
Z scheme 178
zona pellucida 381–4
zooplankton 438–9